ALLARD

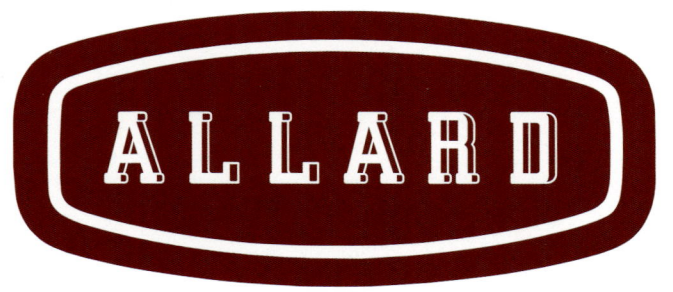

ALLARD MOTOR COMPANY
THE RECORDS AND BEYOND

VOLUME TWO

○ GAVIN ALLARD ○

ALLARD MOTOR COMPANY
THE RECORDS AND BEYOND

VOLUME TWO

GAVIN ALLARD

Published 2023
ISBN: 978-1-956309-06-5

Printed by Interpress Ltd., Hungary
for the publisher
Dalton Watson Fine Books
Glyn and Jean Morris
Deerfield, IL 60015 USA

www.daltonwatson.com

'It is better to burn out, than fade away'

Allard K2 owner Patrick Slevin to myself just as we pulled away, foot down, to drive through the town at the Watkins Glen 50th anniversary celebration in 1998.

Business man, father, motor engineer, inventor and racing driver, Sydney Allard was all of these — wearing a tie as a true gentleman in each role.

•CONTENTS•

ADLARDS MADE ALLARDS

Between 1936 and 1945, Adlards Motors built twelve specials, the first being for Sydney's personal use. His success in that car at motor trials would lead to successive orders from like-minded motor trialists, interspersed with construction of replacements to the original car CLK 5.

None of these cars are included within the factory records which are the core of this book, however without the existence of these twelve, there would not have been any of the subsequent production cars.

Note that these dates are construction completion dates as best as research can determine, Appendix 1: The 'Domesday' book has, in some cases, a differing registration date for these cars (page 679).

The cars were constructed in the following order:

#1	CLK 5	March 1936
#2	AUK 795	July 1937
#3	ELL 300	November 1937
#4	ELX 50	December 1937
#5	EXH 455	December 1937
#6	EYO 750	May 1938
#7	FGF 290	October 1938
#8	FGP 750	December 1938
#9	FLX 650	March 1939
#10	FXP 469	May 1939
#11	FXP 470	May 1939
#12	LMP 192	October 1945*

*completed after cessation of the war

CLK 5 at West Heath, Bagshot, Surrey. Jim Mac, who was Sydney's friend and noted mechanic, looks over the trapped car with Sydney's soon to be sister-in-law, Edna May looking on (she had been in the car and was carried to *'terra firma'*). The date is 13th February 1936 just one day before its first noted event, the Coventry Trial, and only 18 days after the donor car was purchased. This car, without competition number, is in its first design iteration, likely getting an off-road shake down test. CLK 5 was built by Sydney for himself and as such went through numerous developmental changes and repairs, often event by event. (COURTESY OF MARION PORTER)

CLK 5 shortly after the President's Trophy trial 1937 showing cups won so far.

Between 1932 and 1935, Sydney had modified three cars with varied success for motor trials and sprints, these being a three-wheeler Morgan he converted to four wheels, a Talbot and a lightened Ford TT. His first true Allard special is CLK 5, being widely understood to be formed from a crashed 1936 Ford 48 coupe, making the base vehicle virtually new. However, a letter to the soon-to-be-owner of the second Allard special shows that Adlards advised that the Ford 1934 Type 40 was a far better base for a trialist's car than a 1936, which he was considering, so this could have been the basis of CLK 5. As the car does not exist today, this remains an open question. PHOTOGRAPH DATED 1ST MARCH 1937 – (COURTESY OF MARION PORTER)

Sydney wins the Highland Challenge Trophy with the only clean sheet in the Highland Two-Day Trial, March 1937, with his wife Eleanor. Four more trials cars would follow this blueprint in 1937 alone.

AUK 795 was the first ever Allard built to order for a client, George E. Gilson, who was indecisive with what he wanted from Adlards, but his aim was a car as competitive as CLK 5. It was an expensive undertaking but as the drawing, letter and specifications show he did place an order and Sydney's future business was underway. The first of all Allard owners, Fred D. Gilson is generally cited as owner but the letters and specification are clearly marked G. E. Gilson, perhaps the vehicle was shared by the Gilsons.

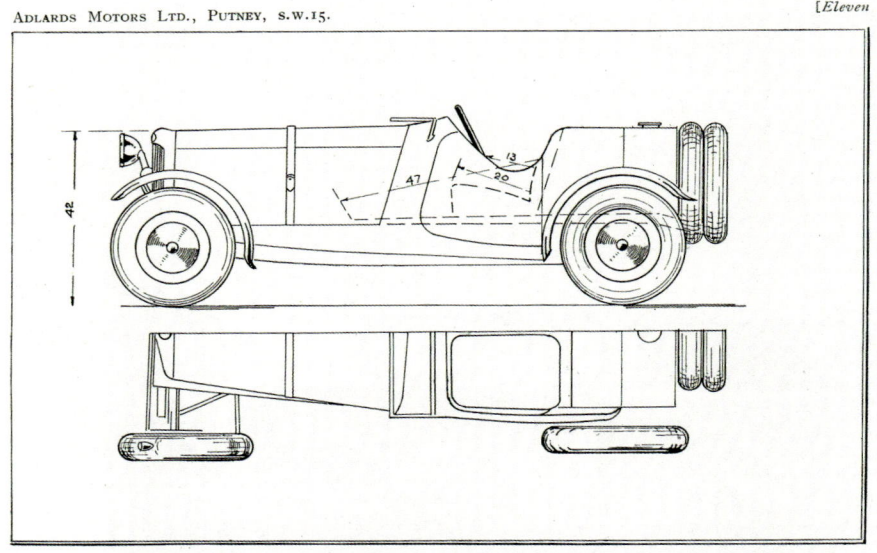

The drawing is extracted from the first proof of the Adlards' V8 brochure for the Allard Special and by Sydney's hand, he chose to exclude this page from the final version.

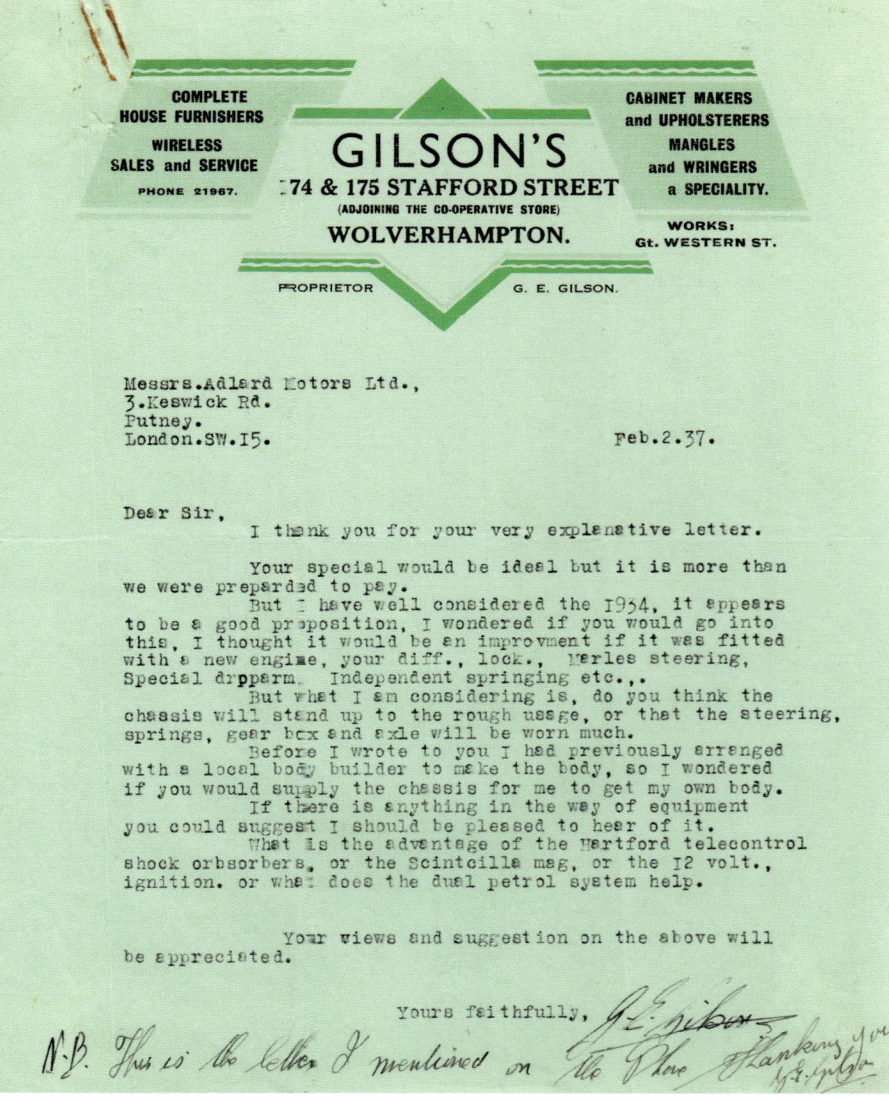

This letter from G. E. Gilson on 2nd February 1937 shows he was thinking of a 1934 Ford basis but eventually it was a ground up new car that was confirmed with Adlards' specification and Ranalah-supplied body.

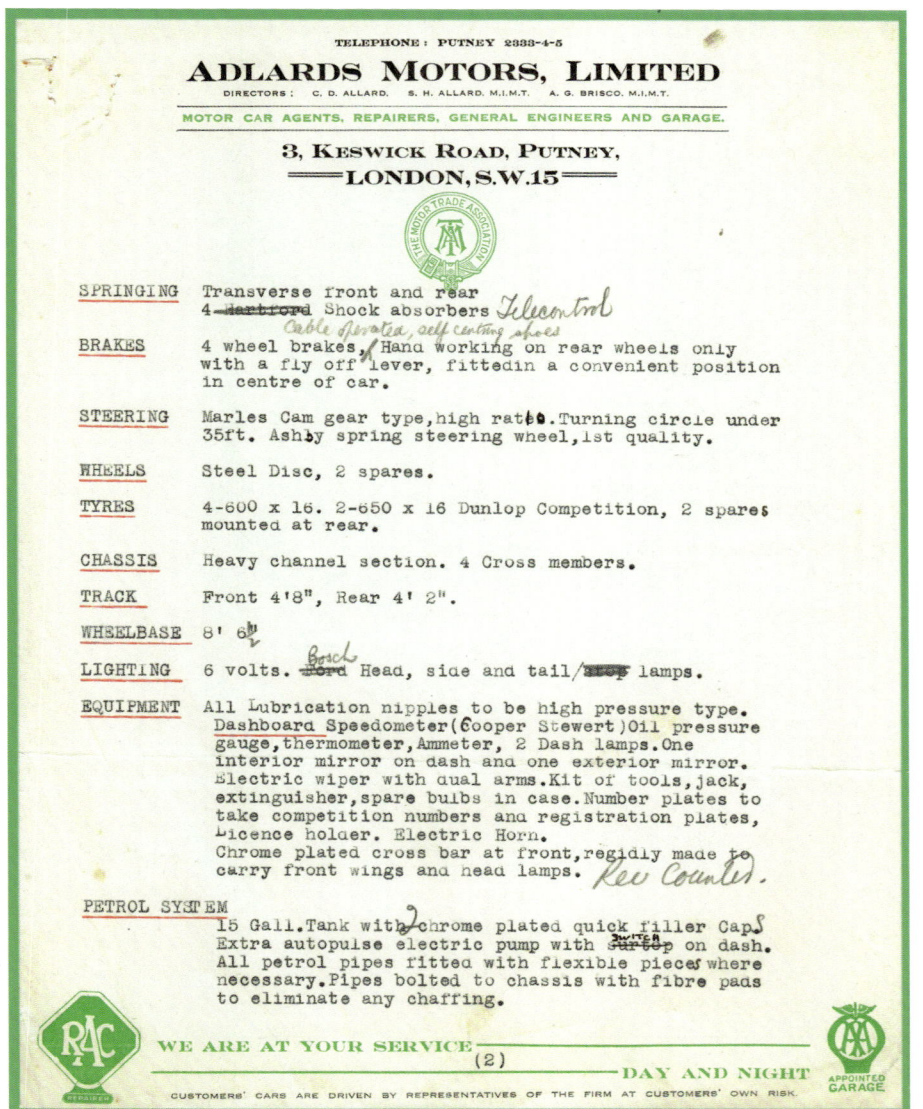

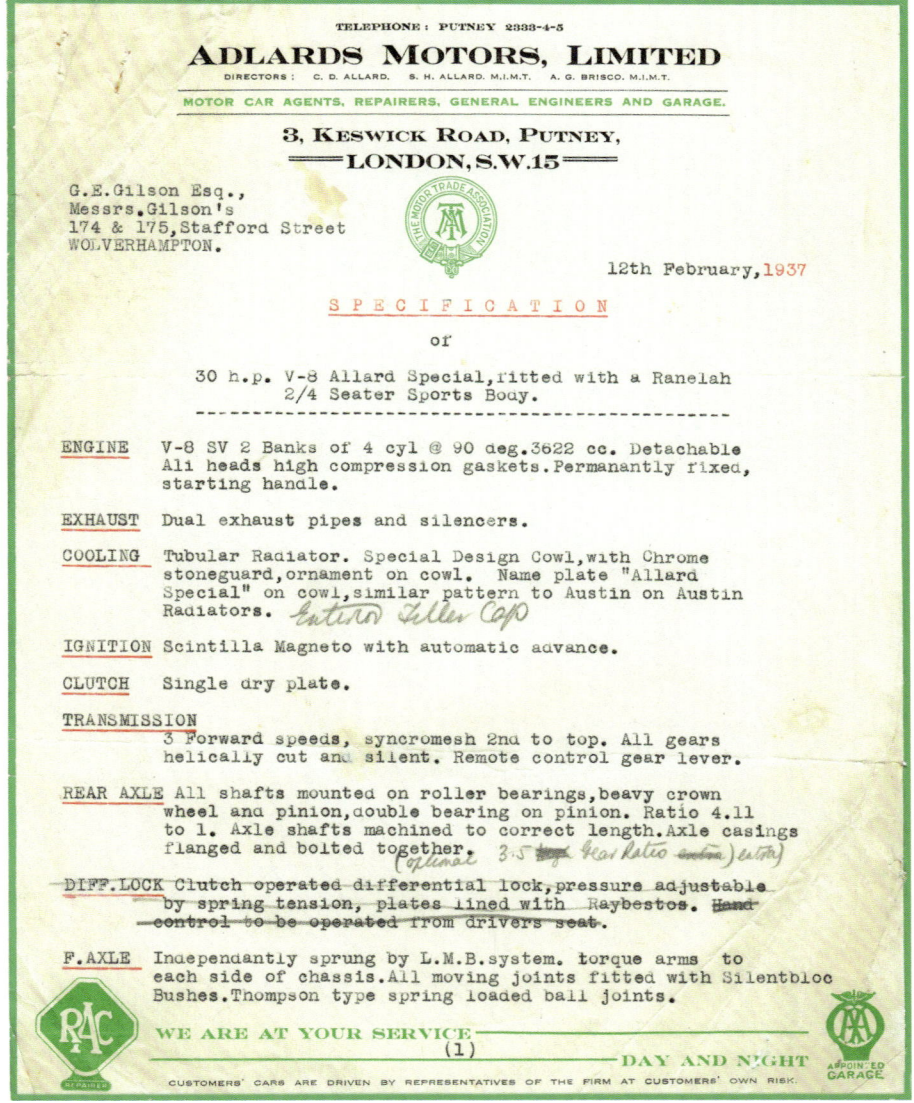

This detailed specification from Adlards for Gilson is clear in what is being delivered including Sydney's corrections.

The beautifully headed and framed paper reveals directors are S. H. Allard, his mother, Cecilia Allard, and Alf Brisco who was placed on the board by father Arthur to ensure Sydney remained on track financially and Adlards did so whilst offering such a wide variety of services.

ADLARDS MOTORS LTD., PUTNEY, S.W.15.   [*Three*

This chassis photograph of AUK 795 is extracted from the first proof of the Adlards' V8 brochure for the Allard Special (1937). Sydney chose to exclude this in favour of a bodied car with the amassed cups. Refer to photograph of CLK 5, page 404. The success of this particular car combined with the original CLK 5 would result in further orders until the outbreak of war.

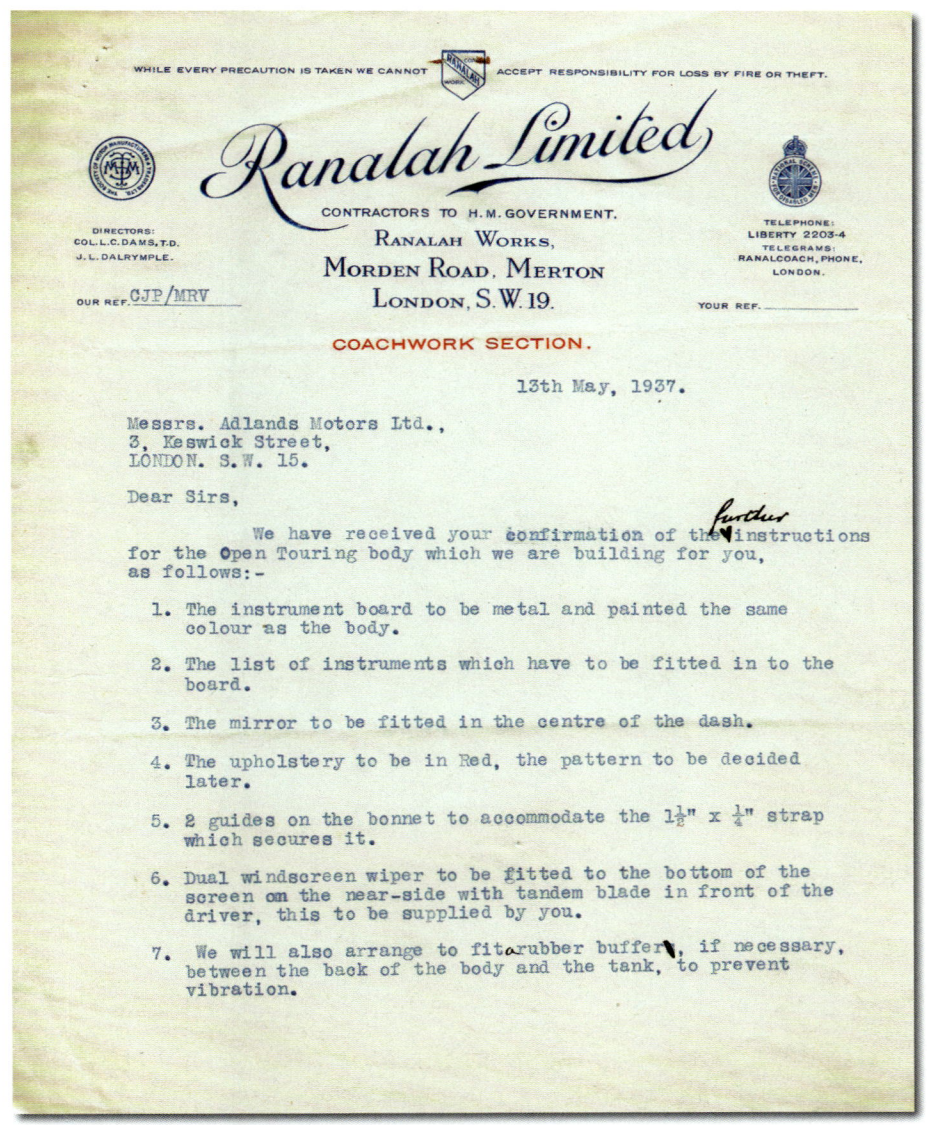

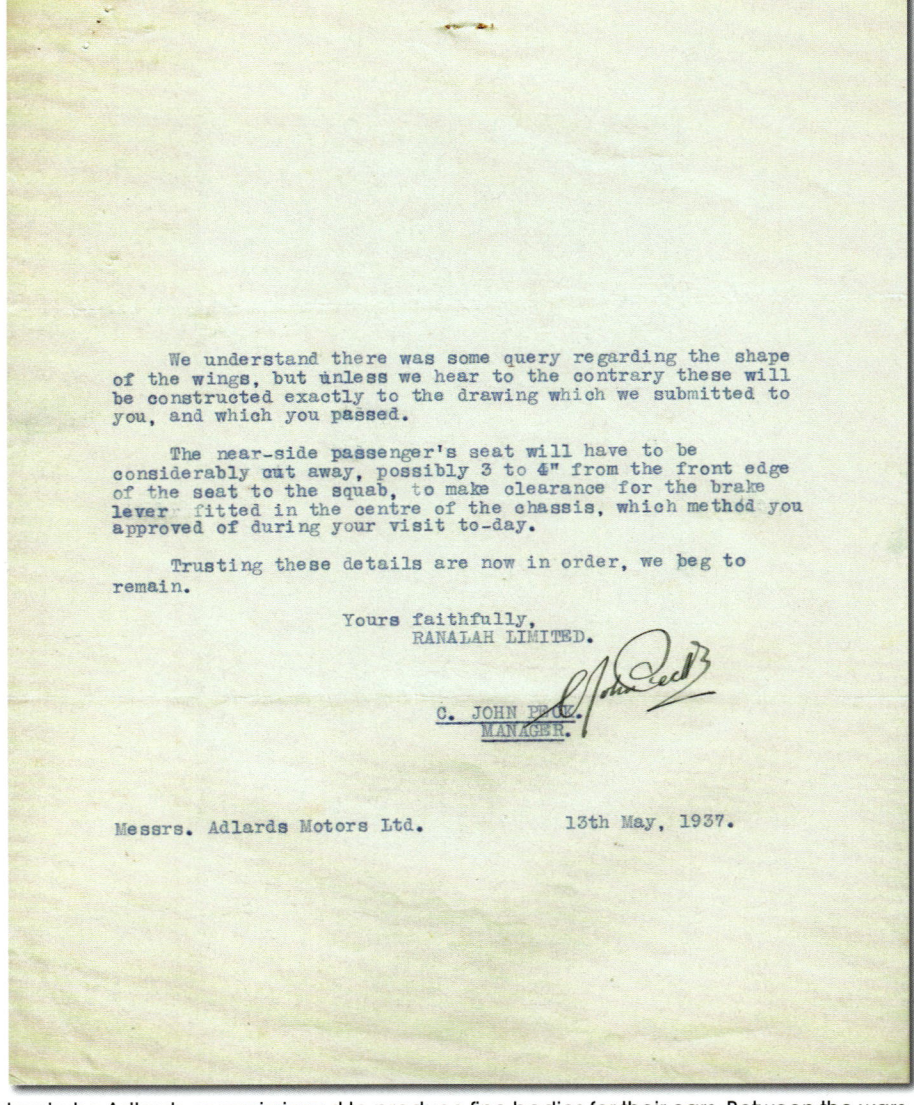

WHILE EVERY PRECAUTION IS TAKEN WE CANNOT ACCEPT RESPONSIBILITY FOR LOSS BY FIRE OR THEFT.

Ranalah Limited

CONTRACTORS TO H.M. GOVERNMENT.

DIRECTORS:
COL. L. C. DAMS, T.D.
J. L. DALRYMPLE.

RANALAH WORKS,
MORDEN ROAD, MERTON
LONDON, S.W. 19.

TELEPHONE:
LIBERTY 2203-4
TELEGRAMS:
RANALCOACH, PHONE,
LONDON.

OUR REF. CJP/MRV   YOUR REF. _____

COACHWORK SECTION.

13th May, 1937.

Messrs. Adlands Motors Ltd.,
3, Keswick Street,
LONDON. S.W. 15.

Dear Sirs,

We have received your confirmation of the *further* instructions for the Open Touring body which we are building for you, as follows:-

1. The instrument board to be metal and painted the same colour as the body.

2. The list of instruments which have to be fitted in to the board.

3. The mirror to be fitted in the centre of the dash.

4. The upholstery to be in Red, the pattern to be decided later.

5. 2 guides on the bonnet to accommodate the $1\frac{1}{2}$" x $\frac{1}{4}$" strap which secures it.

6. Dual windscreen wiper to be fitted to the bottom of the screen on the near-side with tandem blade in front of the driver, this to be supplied by you.

7. We will also arrange to fit rubber buffers, if necessary, between the back of the body and the tank, to prevent vibration.

We understand there was some query regarding the shape of the wings, but unless we hear to the contrary these will be constructed exactly to the drawing which we submitted to you, and which you passed.

The near-side passenger's seat will have to be considerably cut away, possibly 3 to 4" from the front edge of the seat to the squab, to make clearance for the brake lever fitted in the centre of the chassis, which method you approved of during your visit to-day.

Trusting these details are now in order, we beg to remain.

Yours faithfully,
RANALAH LIMITED.

C. JOHN PEUL.
MANAGER.

Messrs. Adlards Motors Ltd.   13th May, 1937.

Ranalah, located in South West London, were one of several London-based 'motor carriage makers' who Adlards commissioned to produce fine bodies for their cars. Between the wars, they also bodied Railtons. Car body production ceased by the start of WWII, their premises then being occupied post-war by notable Rolls-Royce dealer, Jack Barclay.

This photograph is extracted from the first proof of Adlards' V8 brochure for the Allard Special, AUK 795 (1937).

This photograph is extracted from the first proof of Adlards' V8 brochure for the Allard Special, AUK 795 (1937).

This photograph is extracted from the first proof of Adlards' V8 brochure for the Allard Special, AUK 795 (1937).

The Autocar
The Leading Motoring Journal

PROPRIETORS:
ILIFFE & SONS LTD.

Dorset House,
Stamford Street,
London, S.E.1.

December 17th, 1937.

S. H. Allard, Esq.,
Adlards Motors, Ltd.,
3, Keswick Road,
Putney, S.W.15.

Dear Mr. Allard,

I had a word with Mr. Canham over the telephone today, following our trip along the downland tracks with the Special, and feel that I would particularly like to let you have a word personally.

It did the job amazingly, to me, at any rate. I could scarcely have believed that a car could have gone through so much mud, even with knobbly tyres. Also I like very much indeed the way it handles on the ordinary road, and there is certainly something quite fascinating about the quiet sports car idea with plenty of power behind it. You seem to have got driving position and vision and the general feel just right, too. It has served our purpose admirably, and we hope will make an interesting story on the lines originally suggested.

We have had the car cleaned up this morning, which was very definitely necessary!

There is just one other point. I noticed yesterday that the near-side front hub plate is dented. I am not conscious of having touched anything, certainly not on the road in the ordinary way. It may have happened on our tracks, but even there I do not remember anything that could have caused it. Do you remember this having been done already?

Yours sincerely,

ELL 300 was built for Sydney as a replacement of CLK 5 having sold that car to noted trials driver and friend Guy Warburton. It was styled similarly to AUK 795. The letter and photograph are by *The Autocar* who were delighted with the vehicle in their charge. The related article appeared as '5000BC Motoring!' in *Autocar's* December 1937 issue. Mr Linfield (driver) and un-named colleague from *The Autocar* magazine are seen in the car. (*THE AUTOCAR*)

London to Bournemouth Trial 20th March 1938. Children dash to see ELL 300, in which Sydney won a 1st class award and a team award.

Allards were becoming extremely regular sights inside magazines, but now the they appeared on covers too – *Motorsport* repeated ELX 50 on their cover in 1944.

ELX 50 was the first V12-engined Allard. It was built for Ken Hutchison featuring a Lincoln engine and gearbox. Sydney borrowed this car for the Junior Car Club Rally at Brooklands in 1938.

Sydney is accompanied by his wife Eleanor in Hutchison's ELX 50 which he borrowed to compete in the Kentish Border Sporting Trial on Sunday, 27th November 1938. They went on to win the Team Trophy and Alexander Bronze.

Sydney, in a sporting jacket and hovering over the engine, is accompanied by long-time friend and Sales Manager Reg Canham (with white handkerchief standing directly to the right of Sydney) and with Ken Hutchison in light trousers looking on. ELX 50 has the Tailwagger 1 signwriting and the team is heading toward Prescott Hillclimb in 1939. (COURTESY OF FERRET FOTOGRAPHICS)

Ken Hutchison's ELX 50, Guy Warburton's CLK 5 and Sydney's ELL 300 line up at an unknown location in trials trim. They competed as a successful team called the 'Tailwaggers' often supported by their wives as navigators. My grandmother, Eleanor Allard, is to the right, with 'Kitty' Hutchison to her immediate right, and Mrs Warburton adjacent to ELX 50. Sydney's ELL 300 was suffering from rear axle or wheel issues here. (COURTESY OF KERRY HORAN)

2/4 SEATER SPORTS TOURER.

EXH 455 is the 4-Seater Sports Tourer that was built for Sydney's father and driven by a chauffeur. The car was retained within Adlards during the war years. This artist's impression is extracted from the first proof of the Adlards' V12 brochure for the Allard Special (1938). The model was also offered with a V12 option.

EXH 455 is a fine tourer, shown with hood up.

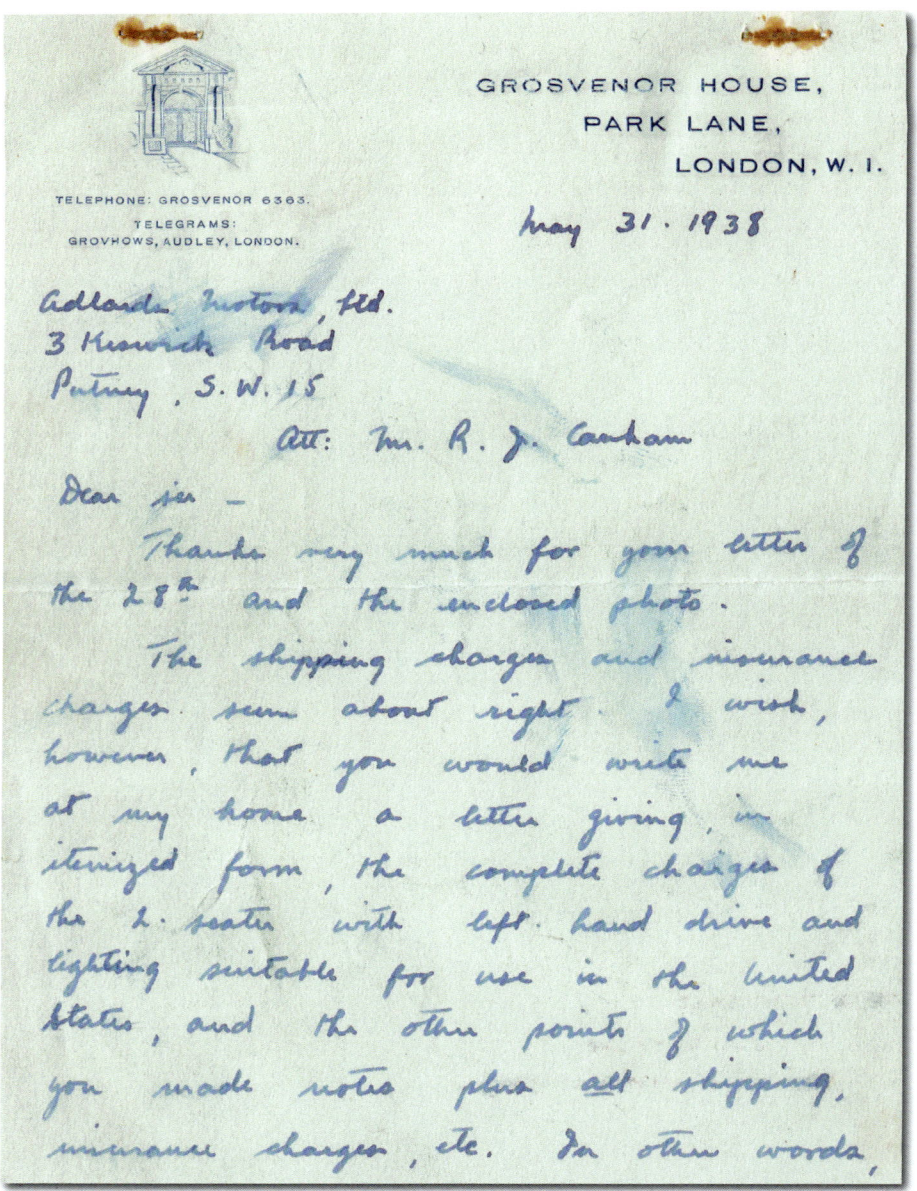

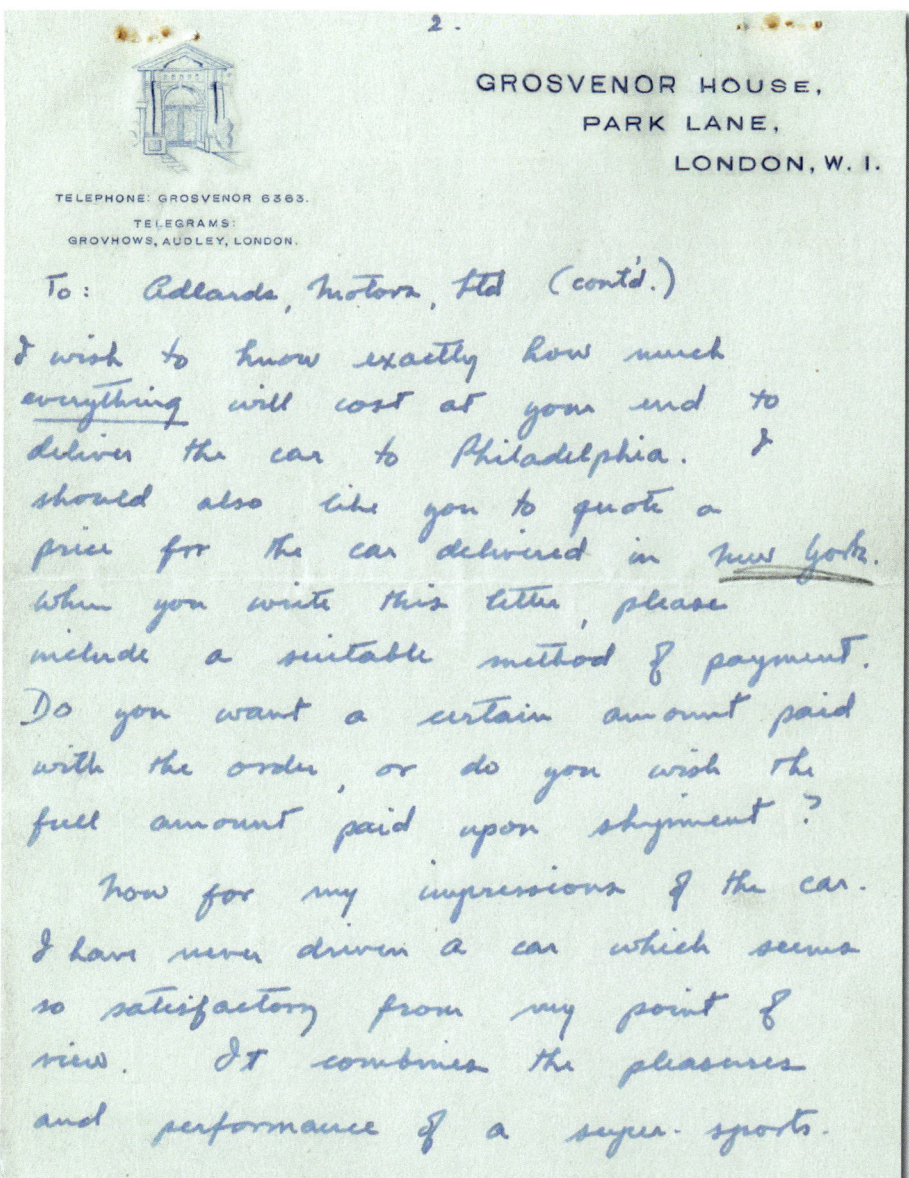

Att. Mr R.J. Canham

Dear Sir,

Thanks very much for your letter of the 28th and the enclosed photo.

The shipping charges and insurance charges seem about right. I wish, however, that you would write me at my home a letter giving, in itemised form, the complete charges of the 2-seater with left-hand drive and lighting suitable for use in the United States, and the other points of which you made notes plus all shipping, insurance charges, etc. In other words,

I wish to know exactly how much everything will cost at your end to deliver the car to Philadelphia. I should also like you to quote a price for the car delivered in New York. When you write this letter, please include a suitable method of payment. Do you want a certain amount paid with the order, or do you wish the full amount paid upon shipment?

Now for my impression of the car. I have never driven a car which seems so satisfactory from my point of view. It combines the pleasures and performance of a super sports

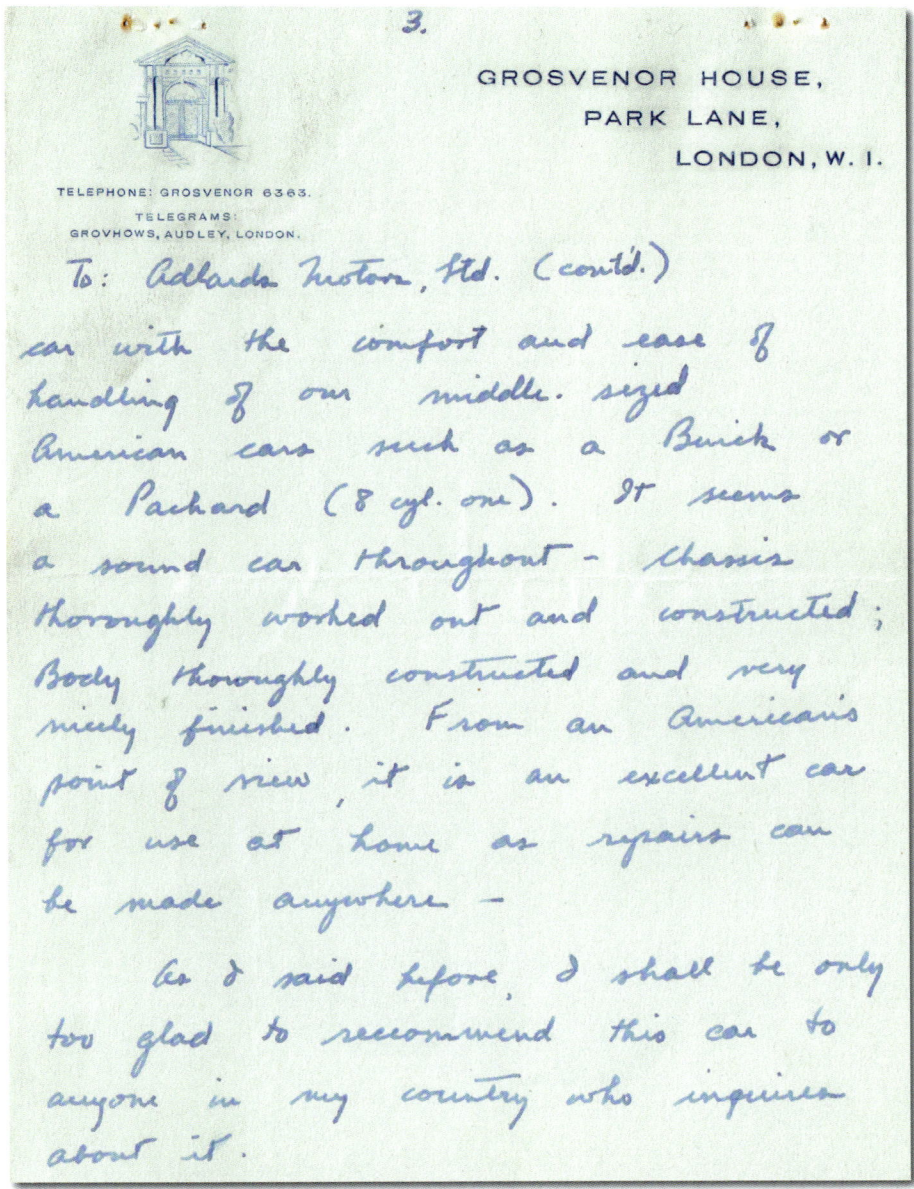

GROSVENOR HOUSE,
PARK LANE,
LONDON, W. I.

TELEPHONE: GROSVENOR 6363.
TELEGRAMS:
GROVHOWS, AUDLEY, LONDON.

To: Adlards Motors, Ltd. (cont'd.)

car with the comfort and ease of handling of our middle-sized American cars such as a Buick or a Packard (8 cyl. one). It seems a sound car throughout – chassis thoroughly worked out and constructed; Body thoroughly constructed and very nicely finished. From an American's point of view, it is an excellent car for use at home as repairs can be made anywhere –

As I said before, I shall be only too glad to recommend this car to anyone in my country who inquires about it.

GROSVENOR HOUSE,
PARK LANE,
LONDON, W. I.

TELEPHONE: GROSVENOR 6363.
TELEGRAMS:
GROVHOWS, AUDLEY, LONDON.

To: Adlards Motors, Ltd. (cont'd.)

I certainly hope, upon my return home, that I will find myself in a position to place an immediate order for the car.

In the meantime, any additional pictures, literature, etc. will be much appreciated. I trust to find a letter from you when I reach home.

Thanking you for your favors, I remain

Very truly yours,

Paul E. Wilson
Buena Vista
Wilmington
Delaware
U.S.A.

---

car with the comfort and ease of handling of our middle-sized American cars such as Buick or a Packard (8 cyl one). It seems a sound car throughout – chassis thoroughly worked out and constructed; Body thoroughly constructed and very nicely finished. From an American's point of view, it is an excellent car for use at home as repairs can be made anywhere –

As I said before, I shall be only too glad to recommend this car to anyone in my country who enquires about it.

I certainly hope, upon my return home, that I will find myself in a position to place an immediate order for the car. In the meantime, any additional pictures, literature, etc. will be much appreciated. I trust to find a letter from you when I reach home.

Thanking you for your favors, I remain

Very truly yours,

Paul E Wilson

This letter represents the first one from prospective American Allard owners and suggests that Allard was already making an impression over the pond after only a very short time in existence. Paul Wilson did not go on to buy an Allard.

Allard Special on Production Basis

Four-Seater Sports Tourer and Two-Seater Now Available

INCREASED facilities have been arranged for the Allard Special on a production basis, and a new four-seater sports tourer and a two-seater are offered by the firm concerned, Adlards Motors, Ltd., 3, Keswick Road, Putney, London, S.W.15.

The earlier form of Competition two-seater has made a name for itself by numerous successes in trials. The new types are more suitable for general work as regards accommodation, wing design, and so forth. The two-seater is priced at £460 with the 30 h.p. V8 engine, or £560 with the V twelve-cylinder engine, whilst the four-seater tourer is offered at £495. The four-seater body is by Coachcraft, the two-seater by Whittingham and Mitchel.

Equipment of the new Competition two-seater includes knock-off wire wheels, Bosch lighting, remote-control gear lever, and a fly-off hand brake, as well as a spring-spoked steering wheel. Equipment and detail specification can be considerably modified to suit individual requirements. The Competition model is also available at £480 and £570 respectively, according to the engine.

More Volkswagen Details

AS progress with Herr Hitler's plan for a mass-produced car for the German people continues more details become available.

Further to the description published in *The Autocar* of June 3rd, one of the most complete which has yet appeared, it is now learnt that the 1,200 c.c. four-cylinder, horizontally opposed engine will have overhead valves and a four-speed gear box in unit with the differential. The engine, which is air-cooled,

That successful trials special, the Allard, becomes more refined.

has a fan driven from the crankshaft and an oil cooler.

Wide use has been made throughout the chassis and body of synthetic materials, and it is even said that the body panels will be of plastic material and the upholstery of synthetic leather.

The building of the factory is well under way

D16

Little is known about the 2-seater (EYO 750) at the bottom of the advertisement. It was likely used as a demonstrator and is seen with the 4-seater EXH 455. It was used for at least one event, with Sydney also driving it occasionally. It remained at Adlards during the war years.

The first brochures for Allard are distinctive and evocative. The artwork of the V8 copy is certainly weaker than the V12, but the contents equally inspire the potential competitive motorist to think what they might achieve at the controls.

The foreword in the V12 brochure shows Sydney using a narrative that states competition success begats a fine car for the sporting driver on the public road.

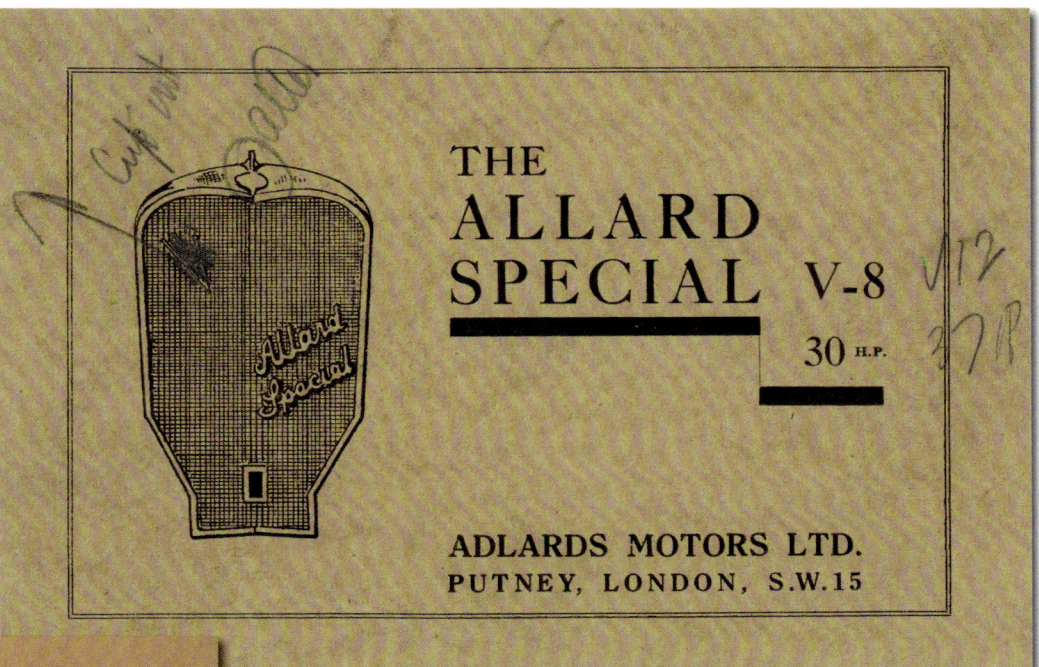

THE
ALLARD
SPECIAL V-8
30 H.P.

ADLARDS MOTORS LTD.
PUTNEY, LONDON, S.W.15

The ALLARD SPECIAL
V-8
V-12

By courtesy of "The Motor."

ADLARDS MOTORS LTD., PUTNEY, S.W.15.   [One

FOREWORD

THE ALLARD SPECIAL CARS have been designed to provide a reliable and fast car suitable both for road work and sporting events. The high power to weight ratio, coupled with correct weight distribution gives a performance only rivalled by a racing car, yet without any undue effort.

The results of these cars in sporting events are sufficient proof of their reliability, and road tests by various motoring correspondents in every case stress the fine performance, smooth riding, efficient braking and good road holding capabilities.

The Allard Special is the car for those who want speed with reliability.

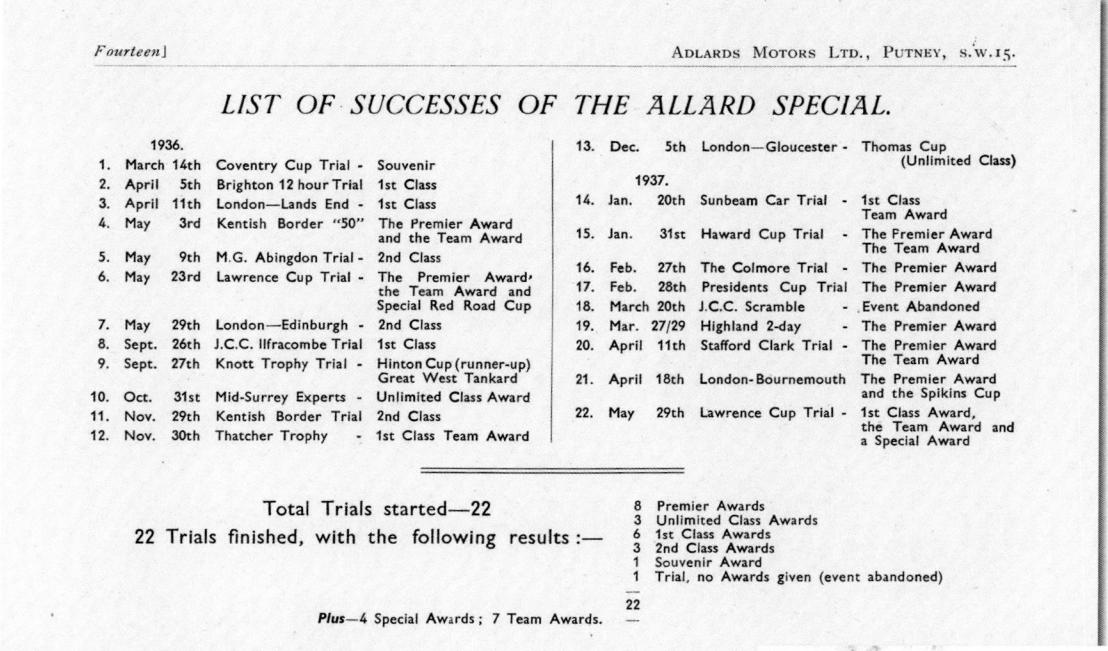

Fourteen]   ADLARDS MOTORS LTD., PUTNEY, S.W.15.

LIST OF SUCCESSES OF THE ALLARD SPECIAL.

1936.

1.	March 14th	Coventry Cup Trial -	Souvenir
2.	April 5th	Brighton 12 hour Trial	1st Class
3.	April 11th	London—Lands End -	1st Class
4.	May 3rd	Kentish Border "50"	The Premier Award and the Team Award
5.	May 9th	M.G. Abingdon Trial -	2nd Class
6.	May 23rd	Lawrence Cup Trial -	The Premier Award, the Team Award and Special Red Road Cup
7.	May 29th	London—Edinburgh -	2nd Class
8.	Sept. 26th	J.C.C. Ilfracombe Trial	1st Class
9.	Sept. 27th	Knott Trophy Trial -	Hinton Cup (runner-up) Great West Tankard
10.	Oct. 31st	Mid-Surrey Experts -	Unlimited Class Award
11.	Nov. 29th	Kentish Border Trial	2nd Class
12.	Nov. 30th	Thatcher Trophy -	1st Class Team Award
13.	Dec. 5th	London—Gloucester -	Thomas Cup (Unlimited Class)

1937.

14.	Jan. 20th	Sunbeam Car Trial -	1st Class Team Award
15.	Jan. 31st	Haward Cup Trial -	The Premier Award The Team Award
16.	Feb. 27th	The Colmore Trial -	The Premier Award
17.	Feb. 28th	Presidents Cup Trial	The Premier Award
18.	March 20th	J.C.C. Scramble -	Event Abandoned
19.	Mar. 27/29	Highland 2-day -	The Premier Award
20.	April 11th	Stafford Clark Trial -	The Premier Award The Team Award
21.	April 18th	London-Bournemouth	The Premier Award and the Spikins Cup
22.	May 29th	Lawrence Cup Trial -	1st Class Award, the Team Award and a Special Award

Total Trials started—22

22 Trials finished, with the following results :—

- 8 Premier Awards
- 3 Unlimited Class Awards
- 6 1st Class Awards
- 3 2nd Class Awards
- 1 Souvenir Award
- 1 Trial, no Awards given (event abandoned)

22

Plus—4 Special Awards ; 7 Team Awards.

Sixteen]   ADLARDS MOTORS LTD., PUTNEY, S.W.15.

Extracts from Motor Journals.

1. S. H. A. made one of the fastest climbs ever seen at Nailsworth. M.G. Trial
—*" The Motor,"* 12/5/6.

2. ——S. H. A. driving that wonderful yellow Ford V-8 with independent front suspension. Experts' Trial.—*" The Light Car,"* 6/11/6.

3. At Nailsworth it is worth recording that Allard again distinguished himself by taking his Ford V-8 Special up visibly faster than anyone else. London-Gloucester.
—*" The Sporting Life,"* 7/12/6.

4. Things that impressed us in 1936. S. H. A. climbing almost any hill in almost any trial.
—*" The Motor,"* 22/12/6.

5. Then S. H. A.'s primrose coloured, long snouted, ultra light, ultra lively Ford made it look easier still.——
——First was the timed climb of Ferriscourt, where S. H. A. clocked 28.75 secs., the only man to beat half a minute. London-Gloucester. —*" The Motor,"* 8/12/6.

6. Occasional efforts stood out :—S. Allard, in his " Allard Special " Ford V-8, sailed to the top in an effortless manner, and foreshadowed his performance on other hills.
——the notorious Red Roads, one of the most difficult hills known to Trials. Last Sunday it was in its very worst mood : of the 40 odd drivers only one—S. Allard—got to the top, a performance which well deserved the applause which greeted it. The Sunbeam Car Trial.
—*" Light Car,"* 29/1/7.

7. For five years in succession small cars have won the Colmore Trophy. This time the Trophy goes to S. H. Allard, driving his Allard Special, that very sporting cream coloured open two-seater.—*" The Autocar,"* 5/5/7.

8. But S. H. Allard, with his famous Allard Special, shot up spectacularly with no chance to pick a course. J.C.C. Scramble.
—*" The Autocar,"* 26/3/7.

9. The only competitor to finish the trial entirely without loss of marks was S. H. Allard, with his Allard Special—a very fine show indeed. The Highland 2-day Trial.
—*" The Motor,"* 30/3/7.

10. A new hill, even more difficult than Section 4 and Red Roads——only one of the 44 starters, S. H. Allard, climbed it. The Lawrence Cup Trial.
—*" The Motor,"* 1/6/37.

The list of successes speaks for itself, with 21 awards for 22 events (one event was abandoned). This was included in the brochure sleeve.

The comments are waxing lyrical about Sydney and his car; indeed he has added more from other sources in pencil on this proof.

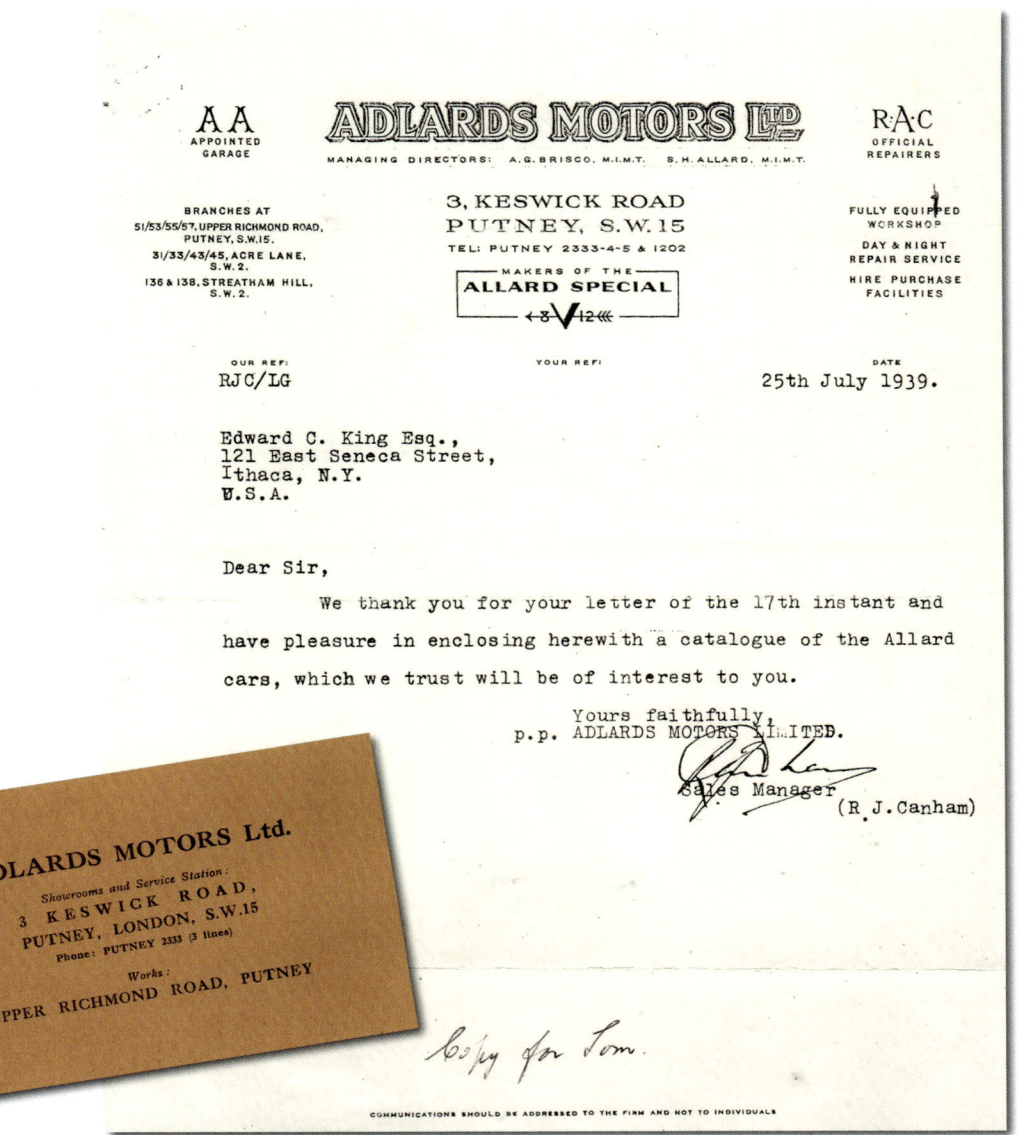

This is the second American enquiry recorded and is notable as much for that, as the change in the letterhead, compared with the headed paper for the first Allard specification. Sydney's mother was no longer a director, there is an additional telephone line and a list of associated addresses. Being both AA (Automobile Association) and RAC (Royal Automobile Club) appointed repairers suggests business was good in 1939.

This well-illustrated advertisement fits the period perfectly with frankly outlandish performance figures as many cars of the day would struggle to exceed 50 mph.

(*MOTOREVU* MAGAZINE DECEMBER 1939)

FGF 290 was Ken Hutchison's replacement to ELX 50, here seen in February 1939 at Thurnham Hall on the Bossom Trophy.

Ken Hutchison and Kitty Hutchison receive some marshal assistance during the Wye Cup Trial 1938.

FGP 750 is Sydney's third trials car with inset picture showing sprint car form but seemingly incomplete without mudguards. Location is unknown.

BELOW: Sydney at JCC (Junior Car Club) rally held at Brooklands, Surrey on 25th March 1939 where he won a first class award. The building with the tower survives to this day.

(INSET – COURTESY OF KERRY HORAN)

FGP 750 now in trials form where Sydney and Eleanor win a second class award and Team award at the Highland Two-Day Trial in April 1939. The car is signwritten 'Tailwagger II' noting its replacement of ELL 300.

Adlards Made Allards

Lewes Speed Trials 29th July 1939 was a keenly followed event; perhaps a surprising entrant behind in the Rolls-Royce suggests outright speed was necessary not turning ability.

Prescott Hillclimb July 1939, this venue was Sydney's most successful, but this was not his day. There is much to be said for the opinion that you cannot know your limit in a car until you exceed it.

FLX 650 was built for Commander D. G. Silcock and he competed in the car with some success then retained the car through the war having it recommissioned by Adlards in 1946.

FLX 650 perhaps looks ever better from the rear side. As with most of the pre-war cars it went through changes until its eventual demise down an alpine ravine in 1950.

FXP 469 is quite the mystery car, as records are non-existent. It may have been a works car to start with but unlikely as more photographs would have been evident. Regardless, this is an Allard in the more upright tradition. (COURTESY OF KERRY HORAN)

G. L. Hancock driving FXP 469 at the Lands End Trial in 1950. (COURTESY FERRET FOTOGRAPHICS)

FXP 470 is a particularly fine car, built for V. S. A. Biggs, and is notable for featuring spats. It was completed as war clouds grew on the horizon.

FXP 470 completely disappeared from history in 1946. An advertisement placed by Continental Cars was the last time this car appeared in a magazine.

LMG 192 is the last of twelve cars, possibly registered in 1941, but not completed until after the war in October 1945. It is shown in this year with Sydney and passenger, Reg Canham at Bagshot Heath, this being Sydney's fourth special.

Maurice Wick was an avid 'Allardist' and after purchasing LMG 192, he is seen here winning the Gloucester Cup at the London to Gloucester Trial with time to wave.

ALLARD – THE PRODUCTION CARS

The New Allard

The New Allard is a truly modern car. It incorporates every up-to-minute feature called for by the discriminating motorist. Yet, in spite of its modern design, every part of the car has been thoroughly proved. Since 1936 the Allard has won a reputation as Britain's premier competition car, and now in addition to the short chassis sports two-seaters there are offered the drop-head coupé and the four-seater tourer. The Allard cars have been designed to provide a reliable and fast car suitable both for roadwork and sporting events. The high power-weight ratio, coupled with correct weight distribution, gives a high performance without undue effort.

The results gained by these cars in sporting events since 1936 are sufficient proof of their reliability, and road tests by various motoring correspondents in every case stress the fine performance, smooth riding, efficient braking and good road-holding capabilities.

All models embody the same advanced engineering features which have won the Allard its outstanding reputation. Some of the outstanding Allard advantages :—

(1) New rigid box section chassis with independent front wheel suspension and correct weight distribution ensures exceptional road-holding and safety. (2) Large, smooth acting and powerful 4-wheel hydraulic brakes and racing type fly-off hand brake. (3) Engine, made by Ford Motor Co. Ltd. (4) Excellent ground clearance (9 inches). (5) The famous Marles steering, light but positive. (6) Excellent visibility due to the curved radiator front and low bonnet with perfect driving position. (7) Latest type, double-acting, self-recuperating shock absorbers. (8) Steering column adjusts for length and height, adjustable seats. (9) Low running costs in proportion to performance. (10) Service and parts readily available.

SPORTS TWO SEATER

FOUR SEATER TOURER

DROP HEAD COUPÉ

ALLARD

ALLARD MOTOR COMPANY LTD., 24-28 CLAPHAM HIGH STREET, LONDON, S.W.4

ALMOTCO, LONDON

MACAULAY 3201

The production cars, defined as any model for which more than two were built, constitute the vast majority of Allards and are included in the chassis records.

Many of the official Allard Motor Company photographs were taken by John Farthing, hired on a contract basis and paid as he produced work.
I was fortunate enough to meet him at the 'Allards and the Moving Image' gathering I created and hosted at Surrey in 1997.

The order of the models revealed in this chapter is chronological, being determined by first that is delivered. By this method, the first car is not the first listed chassis, but actually the sixth car constructed. This J1 (pages 443, 444, 445 and 628) built for close friend and customer, A. G. Imhof, made quite a scene in 1946, being taken on a continental tour that was serialised in *The Autocar* to great fanfare.

I have been honoured to have been contacted by Imhof's daughter, Chrissie, whilst creating this book. She generously donated a complete photographic collection that was assembled by her mother and father during his exploits with Allard pre-war specials and later, several J2 models. Imhof's company design office had influence in the design and look of the post-war cars during his constant association with Sydney and Allards in general.

The Allard was on the public stage and was to remain there in a recovering Britain into the 1950s.

LEFT: Literature dated 1948 shows the primary models on offer.

A. G. Imhof with his J1 – a startling example of motoring style taking British motoring out of the thirties. This car, HLP 5 (chassis 106), was the first J1, toured across three countries and was serialised in *The Autocar*. It also was one of three Allards in the 1946 RAC Cavalcade in London *(see page 628)*. (COURTESY OF CHRISSIE KONIG)

Mrs Imhof with the J1 at the Parc du Cinquantenaire, Brussels during their three-country tour. (COURTESY OF CHRISSIE KONIG)

Mrs Imhof with the J1 at the Palais du Centenaire, Brussels, with unknown passenger. Compelling architecture behind captures the eye nearly as much as the car. (COURTESY OF CHRISSIE KONIG)

Jim Appleton enjoying his J1 HXC 578 (chassis 110) so much he bought another, shown on the opposite page.

Jim Appleton and his second J1 seen here (JYH 413) with a huge array of awards. It was a car completed by his own engineer after taking delivery of a J1 chassis from Allard, this car gets the same designation of chassis 110 as his first J1 HXC 578. However the truth is likely it did not get a chassis designation and was perhaps a tax saving manoeuvre.

The K1 would prove to be the most prolific two-seater Allard. Seen here with the hood up (roof for USA) the sporting motorist would delight at the expanse of bonnet (hood for USA) before them from their small cockpit. The first K1 was chassis 104 and almost identical to the J1, but with a 6-inch longer wheelbase. The way to tell them apart is the J1 door was cut around the rear wing. The last K1 was made in 1950.

This photograph, touched up by an artist's pen and brush many decades ago, shows the car at, what I consider, its best with wheel spats, small bumpers and wheel cover.

A 1948 version of the K1 in open trim, a real treat for the British motorist. The photograph would be used in official advertising literature.

A quarter rear view of the K1, chassis 367, shows it had road presence at all angles. (COURTESY OF KERRY HORAN)

London Motor Show, Earls Court, circa 1948, shows the dashboard in detail.
(COURTESY OF THE ALLARD OWNERS CLUB)

Lucas electrics of worldwide fame clear to see in this engine bay image.
(COURTESY OF THE ALLARD OWNERS CLUB)

The L-type, and indeed this very car, HLB 424 (chassis 102), was to feature with two others (HLP 5, chassis 106 and FLX 650, pre-war) in the 1946 SMMT Jubilee Cavalcade in London in front of thousands of Londoners and the Royal family. The three can be seen at Adlards premises at 3 Keswick Road, page 628. The last car to be produced was chassis 1701, exported to the USA in April 1950. The keen-eyed amongst the readers will notice a grille with too many rungs, Allard dropped the number soon after, as it was one of the contributing factors to overheating of the side-valve V8. (COURTESY OF THE NATIONAL MOTOR MUSEUM)

Almost certainly taken at Clapham Common, London this early morning shot frames the 1948 L-type very well with the Silver Birch trees abundant in the area. Many Allard photographs were taken there being local to the works and readers will become familiar with the scenery throughout this book. The photograph would be used in official advertising literature.

An L-type shown in black from the rear side in closed trim displays the length of the car.

An M-type drophead coupe with wheel spats. The first experimental chassis was number 107, and number 208 was the first production car in April, 1947. A national body workers' strike stopped all body production until the next complete car, chassis 329 in November 1947. Number 1545 was the last production chassis in January 1950, but Sydney had a special with leaf springs and a smaller aluminium-panelled coupe body delivered in February 1950 (registration KLO 122).

This early morning shot captures a 1948 M-type in resplendent fashion. It is likely this car is JLK 957 (chassis 331) which was purchased by the British broadcaster Richard Dimbleby.

The photograph would be used in official advertising literature.

An M-type shown in black from the side in open trim.

This works M-type, JYM 272 (chassis 594C), would be driven in the 1949 Monte Carlo rally by Leonard Potter. (COURTESY ALLARD OWNERS CLUB)

There is artist's work on this image of the M-type.

Both split and continuous bumpers were available on this model. (COURTESY OF KERRY HORAN)

The punched hole Ford wheels reveal that this is an earlier M-type. (COURTESY ALLARD OWNERS CLUB)

The staff member clearly did not move quickly enough for the photographer outside the Park Hill works, Clapham. The M-type chassis is shown here complete with engine. (COURTESY ALLARD OWNERS CLUB)

Four-seater coupe, 9ft. 4ins. wheelbase

ALLARD

Since 1936 Britain's premier competition car, the new Allard, is now in production in four forms ; on the long chassis a four-seater coupe, sports four-seater coupe and saloon, and on the short chassis a new competition two-seater. All models embody the very advanced engineering features which have won the Allard its outstanding reputation—very high power/weight ratio, independent front suspension, powerful V-8 cylinder engine, new lower, lighter, stronger and more rigid chassis, together with absolute reliability and superb road holding.

A catalogue giving full details is available on request.

Overseas distributors are now being appointed and enquiries are invited from first-class firms.

Saloon, 9ft. 4ins. wheelbase.

Competition two-seater, 8ft. 10ins. wheelbase.

ALLARD MOTOR COMPANY LIMITED, 74, PARK HILL, CLAPHAM, LONDON, S.W.4.   BRIXTON 6431

An especially rare photograph of an Allard accessory, the simple car jack. (COURTESY ALLARD OWNERS CLUB)

The prototype J2, chassis 888 (KXC 170), the styling possibly largely derived from Sydney's special JGP 473, noticeable by exposed front suspension coils which would soon be enclosed in development. This was not the first delivered (chassis 1515) as it was built for Sydney's personal use. The last J2 was chassis 2179, exported to the USA in November 1951.

Eleanor Allard, here in chassis 888 (KXC 170) at its first event, 17th July 1949 at the Prescott Hillclimb, gaining third place overall and ladies FTD (fastest time of the day). Sydney would get FTD with Warburton in HLF 601 the first post-war special gaining second.

During my research I have discovered that at the Brighton Speed Trials in 1949 with KXC 170, Eleanor not only won the Ladies Cup with ease, but defeated Sydney's timed runs that day with both hers, indeed her combined time would have been the overall winner, defeating the victorious Delahaye that day if women had been able to enter the over 2000cc sports cars class.

Eleanor Allard, seen again at the same location and at the same time, with the photographer in the frame. Not surprisingly, the car garnered much attention. Zora Arkus-Duntov would soon receive his J2, chassis 1515, and the Allard story started in earnest!

J2 chassis 888's absolutely no-frills dashboard with the all-important rev gauge directly in-front of the driver. If you should wish to know your speed then eyes glance left but I respectfully suggest you are not driving hard enough if you choose to do that, let the passenger panic.

Eleanor and sister Edna look on as Sydney and right-hand man, Jim Mac, clean plugs in KXC 170, now a Cadillac-engined car, after an experimental engine has been allowed into Britain even with harsh import restrictions.

The location is the Rest-and-be-Thankful Hillclimb, Scotland in 1950 where they would see a second J2 in the same event. (COURTESY OF MARION PORTER)

Famous 1930's Brooklands racing driver, Kay Petre, samples the J2 LLP 798 (chassis 1735), declaring it a *'wonderful car'*. After her racing career she became a motoring journalist. One wonders if she ever met Sydney at his events at Brooklands.

J2 show chassis with the ARDUN O.H.V. engine which was partially successful in uplifting the 85hp single carburettor Ford side-valve engine to near 140hp.

The P-type, later to be called the P1, became the core of Allard production; the company's staple factory saloon (sedan in USA) would account for almost 30% of total sales. This is the prototype P1 (chassis 627) exhibited at the 1948 London Motor Show. Production started in September 1949 with chassis 1502, and not finishing until October 1952 with chassis 3107.

A well-prepared P1 would be driven by Sydney to overall victory in the 1952 Monte Carlo Rally, a huge achievement which lost some impact with the death of King George VI just a week later.

A white P1 viewed from the top perhaps hides the tall sides to the car which had always been an acquired taste. The car was a winner with doctors and professionals around the world.

With the column shifter prominent, the dashboard had a well organised layout, this example not showing the heater and H.M.V. radio accessories which were fitted to some cars.

Companion shelves and ash trays are notable in this image.

The 1950 Allard K2 set aside the well-known waterfall grille for a condensed J2 style, pictured at Clapham Common. Although the wheelbase remained the same as the K1, this was a more roomy car, having a luggage boot and a bigger driving cockpit. The much reduced grille and vents in the sides were a new move for Allard. The first chassis was number 1700 (reg USU 339) in May 1950, and the last was 3167 in January 1953, followed by 3133 in November 1952*.

(*Tom Lush notes the last was number 3167, but clearly records it as a K3 in a run of K3s, so the comment is questioned)

The same 1950 Allard K2 is directly outside the Park Hill works and shows a proportionally well-balanced car. It would see some sales success.

A 1950 Allard K2 with the dual bumpers that were more popular in the USA.

The owner of a 1950 Allard K2 would be delighted with an adjustable steering column.

The production version of the Allard M2X was effectively a drophead coupe top on a P1 body. It did however differ from the P1 in that it had forward radius rods that were the same as on the J2X model. There was a short production run from chassis 2295 in November 1951 ending with chassis 3124 in August 1952. (COURTESY ALLARD OWNERS CLUB)

The Allard M2X in open trim.
(COURTESY OF KERRY HORAN)

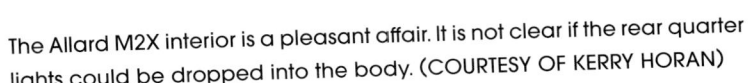

The Allard M2X interior is a pleasant affair. It is not clear if the rear quarter lights could be dropped into the body. (COURTESY OF KERRY HORAN)

The new J2X prototype being tested under the watchful eye of Zora Arkus-Duntov (father of the Corvette) during the period he worked as a consultant to Allard. This car is MGF 850 (chassis 2014) on a trade plate. Differences from the J2 were beneath in the form of forward-facing radius rods giving better steering geometry and thus allowing the engine to be moved forward with six inches more for the occupants. This model continued until November 1954 with chassis 3214. (COURTESY ALLARD OWNERS CLUB)

ALLARD   J.2.X. COMPETITION

LEFT: The J2X was really successful for Allard in the USA market, 'nervous drivers need not apply.'

BOTTOM (BOTH): Sydney Allard drives MGF 850 hard at Ibsley 1951 (right), the car was raced throughout its life (left).

Sydney Allard drives to victory at Ibsley in the new J2X ahead of Ken Watkins in an Allard (not seen in this photograph) and L. Wood in the Jaguar seen in the background. In a 7-lap race of under 13 minutes, he finished 50 seconds ahead of the Jaguar. This was a sure-fire advertisement for the car's abilities in the right hands.

Sydney Allard seals the victory at Ibsley by gaping Watkins to 10 seconds. The motoring press pick up the J2X story of the two cars and the model would become perhaps the most famous Allard ever produced.

LEFT: Here MGF 850 sporting an additional light used for Goodwood 9-hour events.

BOTTOM (BOTH): Works photographs showing the fine inner workings of the J2X for the reader's delight.

PANHARD ROD   BRAKE DRUMS.

DEAD AXLE TUBE.   DETACHABLE COVER
                 QUICK CHANGE DIFF. HOUSING.

PANHARD ROD.   BRAKE DRUMS.

DEAD AXLE TUBE   DETACHABLE COVER.
                 QUICK CHANGE DIFF. HOUSING.

A hopped-up Allard J2X, perhaps by Perry's Auto Shop, on display at Madison Square Gardens with model Barbara Vann. The white-walled cars have their appeal and, as such, appeared on motorsport covers. Having a hard top makes car this slightly more usable. (COURTESY KERRY HORAN)

The Allard Palm Beach (Mk.I) was a pretty car whose arrival was unfortunate in the fact it directly competed with Triumph's TR which it could not match for performance or price. Its limited success was sealed with the new Austin Healey 100 at £78 more. The Palm Beach was offered with the Ford Zephyr 6-cylinder engine and the much less used Consul 4-cylinder variant. The car was particularly popular in Scandinavian countries. A singular example with a Dodge 'red-ram' V8 engine was made (chassis 5151) in an effort to foster more of the type, but no more were made.

It was a move Allard felt they must make as the Ford side-valve V8 was an aging 1930's design. The photograph has a painted silhouette which was used to cut out the image for advertising literature, this being the factory original. (COURTESY ALLARD OWNERS CLUB)

Another well-proportioned car by Allard, the Palm Beach might just have been their saviour with a possible contract to supply in the USA for tens, perhaps hundreds, of cars, but Sydney could not close the New York deal in 1952. The first chassis was 5000 with bug eyes that were later dropped. Until recently, chassis 5157 (from August 1955) was thought to be the last, but others have appeared – numbers 5200 and 5201, both with little information. (COURTESY ALLARD OWNERS CLUB)

The chassis from the front (above) and rear (opposite page) with minimal seat setup to allow it to be driven to Hilton Brothers for bodywork. (COURTESY ALLARD OWNERS CLUB)

Rear ¾ view of the same car from page 486, with the cost-saving twin rail frame clear to see. (COURTESY ALLARD OWNERS CLUB)

One of the dashboard layouts with pockets to left and right.

Another dashboard layout. The model was offered with either bench seats or individual seats.

The works Palm Beach from the side.

The Le Mans development of the J2X model was in response to changes to the rules of Le Mans race entry. However, it can also be viewed as a natural progression of the car with the fully enveloped body. This particular car was a works entrant in the 1952 Le Mans and is MXF 969, chassis 3055. (COURTESY OF KERRY HORAN)

This car formed part of the Allard team at Shelsley Walsh International Hill Climb in August 1953 in the hands of Rupert de Larrinaga. Cyril Wick and Keith Darby comprised the rest. Allard engineer, Gil Jepson, stands to the left.

Rupert de Larrinaga takes OVT 983 up Prescott Hillclimb in 1954, Rupert was known to carry over the registration to each new competition car, in this case from J2 to J2X Le Mans.

The P2 Safari was a rather large estate car in the 'Woodie' style. The front end was very similar to the prototype M2s. Not a marketing success but it did appeal to a customer wishing to transport their sheep. This car (chassis 2058 as a prototype, then 4000) was one of two of consecutive registration plates for Sydney and his brother Dennis. The last chassis was 4510, but the last delivered was 4508 in May 1955. (COURTESY ALLARD OWNERS CLUB)

The P2 Safari MXA 555 has two vertical doors; the sister car had a dropping tailgate and lifting top glazed panel as per Dennis Allard's request. (COURTESY ALLARD OWNERS CLUB)

The same P2 Safari from the side. The photograph has a painted silhouette which was used to cut out the image for advertising literature, this being the factory original.

The P2 Safari chassis awaiting body, the twin rails evident as used with the Palm Beach, cheaper and quicker to produce than the earlier channels.

Allard – The Production Cars

The P2 Safari chassis awaiting body, here the view showing the bulkhead in more detail.

The P2 Safari chassis in another view.

The P2 Safari driver's side interior.

The P2 Safari and P2 Monte Carlo saloon chassis were the same. Here seen partially bodied.
(COURTESY ALLARD OWNERS CLUB)

The P2 Monte Carlo saloon was so named in celebration of Sydney's famous victory.

Matching the P2 Safari front it was never seen on British roads in any numbers. By 1953 Allard had a reducing budget and marketing then as today was critical. This model could not rely on just motor sport successes to raise the profile.

The P2 Monte Carlo saloon rear view. It is apparent that the dashboard matched the P2 Safari.

The Allard K3 is a fitting replacement to the K2, styled closely along the Palm Beach lines, and incredibly, even one of Allard's own advertising brochures has a Palm Beach mix up.

The photograph has a painted silhouette which was used to cut out the image for advertising literature, this being the factory original. This car, NGP 970 (chassis 3033), is the 1952 Show car, the first K3, and was sold to General Griswold of the USAF *(see page 614)* in November 1952.

The Allard K3 interior has a central instrument panel similar to the P2 series.

The Allard K3 interior with a different instrument panel to that on the prior page. (COURTESY OF KERRY HORAN)

The Allard K3 was another attractive model. The first production run car was chassis 3168 in December 1952 with all cars being exported until the last K3, chassis 3286, which remained in the UK for film producer, John Paddy Carstairs, in October 1954. (COURTESY OF KERRY HORAN)

The K3 with an American treatment; full white-walls, perhaps red wire wheels, chromed dual carburettor air filters and probably dual exhausts. This was an entirely new model for Allard with a shorter version of the tubular P2 saloon chassis having the De Dion rear axle and side gear change.

The JR was designed by engineer Dudley Hume as the competition car to challenge the Jaguar C-type at Le Mans and was capable of 160 mph on that circuit. Combined with Sydney's fearless driving ability, he led the first lap of the 1953 event ahead of Moss and Ascari.

Allard – The Production Cars

Seen here in the woods directly adjacent to the Le Mans circuit on the main straight after Tertre-Rouge corner, a replacement Cadillac engine is being installed courtesy of the logistical might of the USAF and General Curtis LeMay, (see page 614), a sports car exponent and keen on Allards. He and two other officers would have JRs, chassis 3402, 3403 and 3404 between them. Sydney's car would lead as they passed the stands for the first time; unfortunately it was also the last time, as brake failure occurred. This car is NLN 652, chassis 3402.

RIGHT: The JR with Sydney driving would feature in advertising, perhaps in some part due to the extraordinary angles he could achieve with the Ballamy front axle. With the exception of Sydney, almost everybody, including Sydney's Chief Engineer, Dudley Hume, felt the system had run its course, so it remained on this fast Allard – he was the Guv'nor after all.

BELOW LEFT: The Allard factory reveals Erwin Goldschmidt's JR, chassis 3401, the first JR, and perhaps the only one to be red with a painted radiator opening. These pictures are some of the many taken by Allard's in-house photographer, John Farthing.

Sydney Allard (top left, white shirt) works alongside Tom Lush (middle, with Vigzol motif on white overalls) to direct Jim Mac with a possible tyre change to JR (chassis 3403) during the 1953 Le Mans endurance race. Sydney had lead at the first lap of this event with his number 4 car (chassis 3402), abandoning with failed brake system soon after.

Testament must be given to those in my family and beyond who kept so much material for so long, including the preparation check lists for cars No. 4 and 5 for the 1953 Le Mans event. The programme also had the signatures of all the drivers, including Corvette's Zora Arkus-Duntov who commented 'to my good mechanic Sydney', it seems he was not one to give flowery praise and Sydney would have taken that comment with aplomb; a mechanic who lead the greatest sportscar race in the world.

The Palm Beach Mk.II was the last effort series by Allard, based at least partially on a design from USA-based employee, Mr Forsyth. The car was extremely attractive and offered with a Jaguar six-cylinder engine. It speaks of Sydney's lasting impact that Jaguar agreed for this model to be sold with Jaguar engines, not something they extended lightly.

A nicely fitted out dashboard with the established left and right pockets.

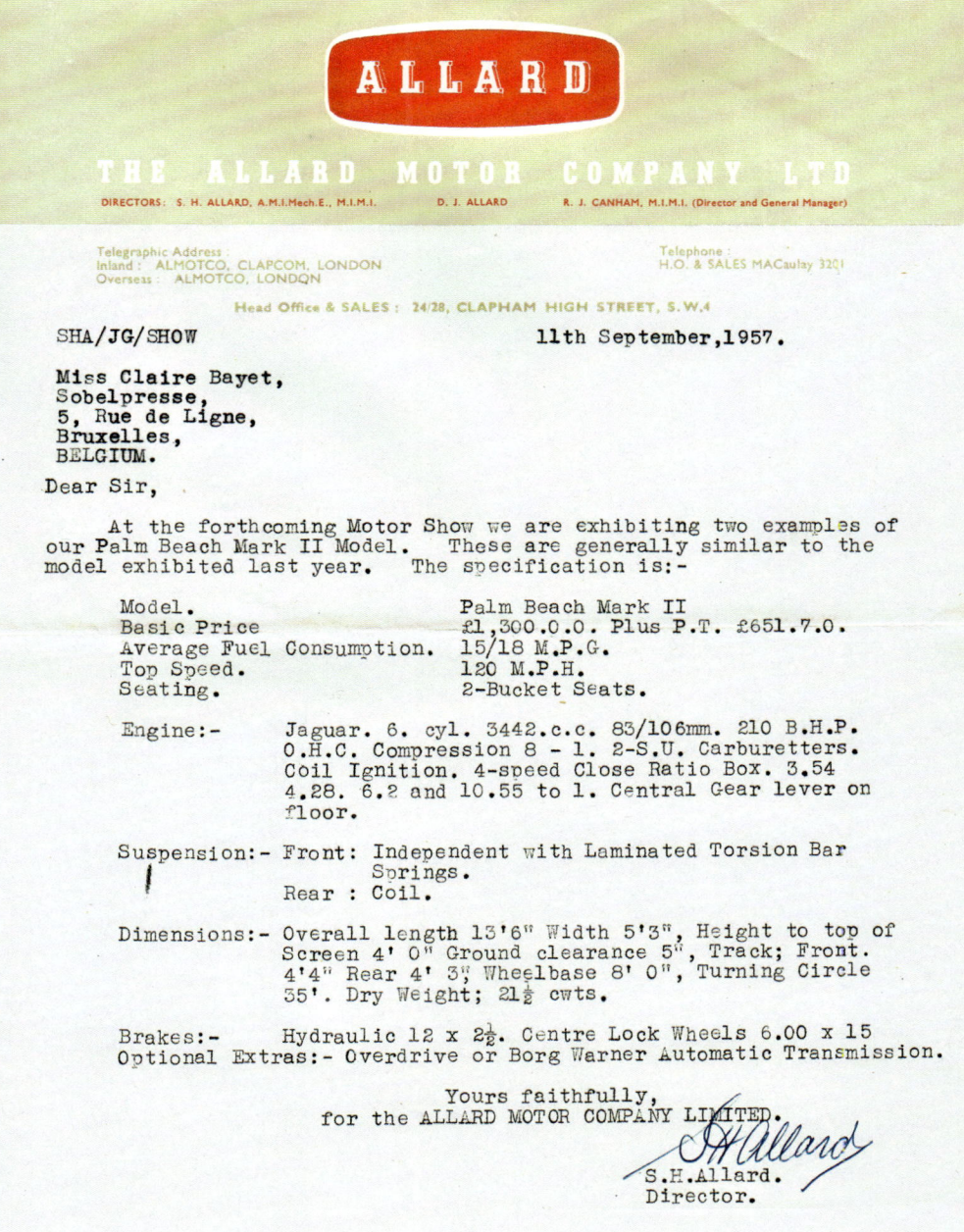

This letter personally signed by Sydney to an interested person in the Palm Beach would not slow the inevitable decline of the Allard business as sales never picked up.

There is no reduction in beauty with the closed trim.

The rear completes the confirmation of a well thought out car that had more potential than it achieved.

The Palm Beach GT in the only two iterations constructed, the left-hand with a Chrysler V8 (chassis 7105) and the right (UXB 793, chassis 7102) with a Jaguar six-cylinder, which was Sydney's personal car and was in my father's ownership in the 1980s.

The model sits well from the side, having seen both cars in real life they raise the question of the observer, what is it? Allard was widely considered to have ceased construction at this point.

The rear view is reminiscent of a later Triumph GT6, yet this proportion appears more resolved, a great achievement for a car that never fully stepped out of a prototype status.

The final photograph in the proof set shows an attractive car from all angles, a shame that it left the family, but a schoolboy could only dream.

The model was offered for test drives with the motoring press and was generally well received with a few reservations. Those were only held by serious competitive drivers and further development would have been necessary. I recall the windscreen was prone to cracking in the lower corner, a result of excessive chassis flex.

On a family day out, Sydney with his mother who is obviously proud of his huge achievements.

ALLARD – THE ONE-OFF CARS

The wonderful diversity of Allard is evident in this section with some limited production cars.

I have used author licence and some readers may observe that there were two M2X 'Whale' cars produced but as a model it never got beyond a prototype due to its unpopular appearance

Many one-offs occurred due to the national body workers strike in 1947, hence so many 'Woodies.' Cash had to flow within the business, as in any other, so creative juices flowed with small coachbuilder firms and some may even have been skilled homebuilds.

This is no way a complete list and I make no distinction between factory created vehicles and those completed after chassis delivery elsewhere as they are all of merit.

The only of Sydney's specials to have a chassis number (114), this was his first post-war special. This car was built at his S1 workshop, which is actually a hidden semi-lower floor area at the back of the left-hand side of the Clapham High Street address (S1's location can be seen on pages 551, 624 and 625 in the middle of the ornate stairs, and in the room on page 561 looking out to the backyard).

Sydney is seen here preparing for a run up the hill climb at Prescott, Gloucestershire early in 1946. I note his pre-war jacket and tie has also made it through the war years (see page 418).

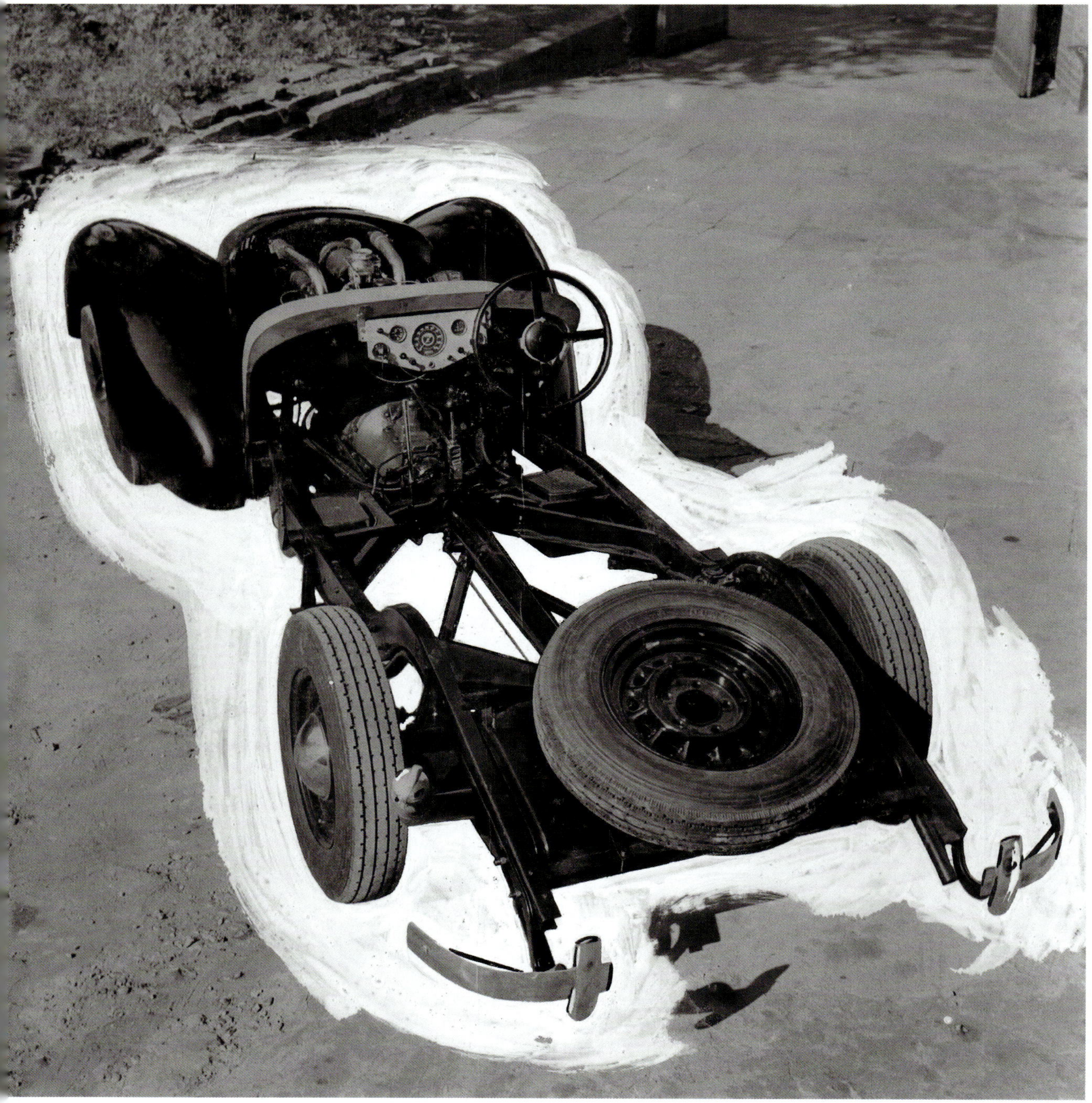

As noted on the title page, Allard Motor Company had to think quickly with the strike action and partially-bodied cars sold well. A study of the factory records from spring 1947 until end of 1947 will prove it; the term 'Chassis only' was a partially-bodied car. (COURTESY ALLARD OWNERS CLUB)

September 24, 1947. The Motor 5

IMMEDIATE DELIVERY OF ALLARD CHASSIS!

£670

Here is an exceptional opportunity. Immediate delivery can be given of a limited number of fully road-tested Allard chassis, either left- or right-hand drive. Chassis specification includes: independent front wheel suspension, Ford V8 engine, Lockheed brakes, Dunlop tyres, front wings, cowl, grille, bumpers, spare wheel, full Lucas electrical equipment including lamps, horns, indicators, wind-screen wiper, instrument panel with all instruments and Smith's Side Jacking system. Coupe chassis wheelbase 9' 4" — £670.-.-.

In addition to the above the two-seater 8' 10" chassis and open four-seater 9' 4" chassis at £670.-.- include bonnet, bonnet sides, and fittings, but not mounted. As the number of chassis available is limited immediate application is advised either to the Allard Motor Company or your local accredited Agent, listed at the bottom of this page.

ALLARD

ACCREDITED ALLARD AGENTS—Dagenham Motors Ltd., 8, Balderton St., W.1, A. E. Gould Ltd., 290-292, Regent St., W.1, F. English Ltd., Langley Rd., Branksome, Bournemouth, Hughes of Exeter, St. David's Hill, Exeter, Hartwells, Ltd., Banbury Rd., Oxford, Taylors (Glos) Ltd., 26, Worcester St., Gloucester, A. E. Harris, Ltd., 10-11, Castle St., Cardiff, Furrows Ltd., The Shrewsbury Garage, Coton Hill, Shrewsbury, Mann Egerton & Co., 31, King St., Norwich, Bristol Street Motors Ltd., 164-172, Bristol St., Birmingham 5, Universal Car Co. (Derby) Ltd., St. Helens St., Derby, H. E. Nunn & Co. Ltd., 282, Bury New Rd., Manchester, Tate of Leeds Ltd., New York Rd., Leeds 2, R. H. Patterson & Co., Ltd., Forth St. Works, Newcastle-upon-Tyne, George & Jobling, 140-160, Bothwell St., Glasgow, Alexanders of Edinburgh Ltd., Semple St., Edinburgh, Frew & Co. Ltd., 14, Princes St., Perth, R. E. Hamilton & Co., 32, Linenhall St., Belfast.

81

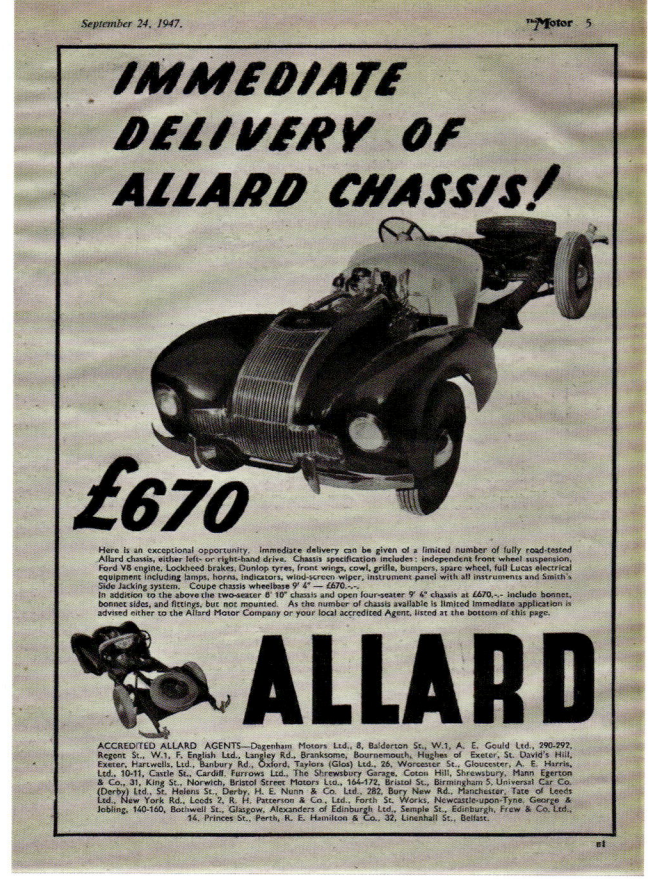

A photograph showing what was included for £670. (COURTESY OF KERRY HORAN)

Delivered to Tates in Leeds in May 1948, one wonders how long the rear end of chassis 533 survived unprotected. (COURTESY ALLARD OWNERS CLUB)

ABOVE: The bodywork on EAW 813 was created by the owner of Sentinel who made Steam Tractors/ Rollers and other machinery in Shrewsbury. (COURTESY SENTINEL DRIVERS CLUB)

LEFT: MVX 722 appears similar to the car on pages 534 and 535 in respect to both having a concealed roof assembly. (NATIONAL MOTOR MUSEUM)

LEFT: The K1 special body look is most successful.

BELOW: This could possibly be DFR 259, chassis 419, which is noted as a K1 but was not indicated as 'Chassis only' so may be incorrect. However, the car itself does appear thoroughly functional. (NATIONAL MOTOR MUSEUM)

Unidentified, yet a well-executed piece of work, if it were not for the final look being a bit upright 'rustic hearse-like' and suitable for those with tall hats. I make this comment, quite sure the car does not survive today.

·ALLARD·

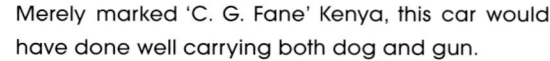

Merely marked 'C. G. Fane' Kenya, this car would have done well carrying both dog and gun.

Marked 'Mr Hall's Allard' with special body 21 May, 1948, this looks a fine example of coachbuilding, especially the sunroof. (NATIONAL MOTOR MUSEUM)

Allard – The One-off Cars

Registration W2479 suggests a Kenya-originated vehicle or neighbouring African country.

Sweeping lines of this M-type derivative clearly impressed Allard Motor Co., as it was glued in their album but without notation.

My favourite 'Woodie' is of high quality in finish and design, but again without identity.

Same car, but from a different source, this car pleases again. INSET: Perhaps a creation from the same coachbuilders. (COURTESY OF KERRY HORAN)

Col. John Dolphin was part of the early musterings of Britain's special forces called SOE (Special Operations Executive) during the war and was also a master inventor including a folding motorcycle for paratroopers, single-person submarine and even a preliminary design for the firing mechanism for an atomic weapon until he fell out with the weapons agency. There is a book in waiting for Col. Dolphin.

The registration here does not match his car in our listings as he brought it back numerous times. One visit was for a new chassis and there lies the issue, too much flex and too much weight.

Col. John Dolphin's car deserves a second picture. This car did feature in a newsreel too.

This was a factory creation (chassis 1740) that is difficult to believe, described as a tourer body (in principle) on a P-type chassis with an L-type rear, De Dion rear axle like a J2X and topped off with a K2 grill. This is the cream of one-offs and it is to the world's loss that this and all the other cars in a Swedish museum were completely destroyed in a fire in the 1990s. Its memory survives in this official photograph in the Allard Motor Company album.

PKJ 412 (chassis 2224) was a lengthened J2X chassis with a lightweight body built by a company experimenting with magnesium for sportscars as it is 2/3rds the weight compared to aluminium. A fine car was the result, but also an expensive one. (COURTESY OF MARION PORTER)

THESE TWO PAGES: Artistic touching up of the image as seen here did not help the M2, dubbed 'The Whale'. It was unpopular and even with the inventive self-lifting bonnet assembly, after two prototypes, it reverted to the production model M2X (pages 476 and 477), which was effectively a P1 with a droptop.

Hampton Court Palace, London in the background cannot uplift the M2's beauty, a noble venture that fell on stony ground.

An interesting study in automotive design, Goff Imhof's J2-based grand tourer LXN 5 (chassis 2011), sported a Mercury engine. The photographs reveal most of the frame. (COURTESY ALLARD OWNERS CLUB)

Goff Imhof had a design background and it is widely accepted he assisted Allard. A scale model was created and the resultant car looks quite successful, if only it was not so long in the bonnet. (COURTESY ALLARD OWNERS CLUB)

The fibreglass car does have its merits and is not unlike the TR series and the Austin Healey Sprite but the fibreglass concept went no further. INSET: The Allard factory prototype looks well from the side (chassis 5000) but the bug-eyed concept was dropped in favour of a far better looking car, which would be the Palm Beach.

This is a special-bodied JR made for Tommy Sopwith with a Sapphire engine. The car was named 'Sphinx', Allard supplied the chassis (number 3405) to Sopwith, who headed Armstrong-Siddeley Motors at the time. (COURTESY OF KERRY HORAN)

This saloon was coachbuilt by Abbotts of Farnham on a Palm Beach chassis with a Ford Zephyr engine (number 5110).

This Abbotts of Farnham saloon did not garner any copies, but is notable for the unusual headlamp positioning.

(COURTESY OF KERRY HORAN)

ALLARD – WITHOUT CHASSIS NUMBERS

These are specials and vehicles with a major Allard element but without a known chassis number.

The question of why these vehicle did not get chassis numbers is not easy to answer. I can venture a part answer in that with the Allard Clipper and the dragsters, separate companies were formed that would have limited any Allard Motor Company liability. As a minimal number of cars were produced by each company, chassis numbers were never assigned*.

The mechanised delights in the coming pages evoke the smells and sounds of their moment and set day to day business running to the back of the mind. Sydney Allard managed to juggle both with success for a good many years.

---

* Information gained from an auction of an Allard Clipper in October 2022 has revealed the vehicle does have an Allard chassis plate, although highly corroded. The record of the numbers issued has either been lost to history or was never recorded by Allard, therefore the cars remain within this chapter. It is also noted that the Anglia Allardette would have had a Ford chassis identification but was not noted in any Allard/Adlard records within the available archive. The Allardette is placed in this chapter for that reason.

JGP 473 was Sydney's second road-going, post-war Special and reminds many of the J2. It was based on a J frame with the same wheelbase and track. But perhaps this was just coincidental as Sydney certainly wanted to replace HLF 601 as he did not feel he was getting all he could from it; the engine did migrate from that car to this one. So in 1947, the untrimmed and unpainted car was out on the road in June and is seen here at Poole Speed Trial in September of that year.

JGP 473 seen here at Prescott in the paddock in May 1948 alongside Sydney's new single seater hill climb car known as the Steyr. An Allard M-type is in the background behind the admiring devotees.

An evocative image at Boness, Scotland where Sydney took fastest time of day (FTD) with the Steyr. Built from the seat outwards it was designed with lightness and grip at the forefront; what it looked like was secondary. Using an unlikely engine in the form of an air cooled, eight carburettors, eight-cylinder Austrian V8 designed for trucks and portable generators. Sydney saw an opportunity, gaining countless awards and FTDs, and took it to victory in the 1949 British Hillclimb Championship.

Sydney and Tom Lush inspecting the car. They were frequently changing the plugs and adjusting the eight carburettors.

The car was at its first event on the 11th May in 1947 and these trophies represent the awards from that year alone. The location is the Allard Sales room on Clapham High Street with the S1 'Special projects' workshop just under the stairs to the right of the photograph.

·ALLARD·

Definitely the smallest Allard, this speedway racer was called The Atom and in 1955 the 5'6" long car was seen as an opportunity on the speedway dirt tracks. British Speedway star Ronnie Moore is driving it but the car hit a rut and rolled, breaking his collarbone. It was fast with a 500cc JAP engine, supposedly on dope. Only two were ever constructed.

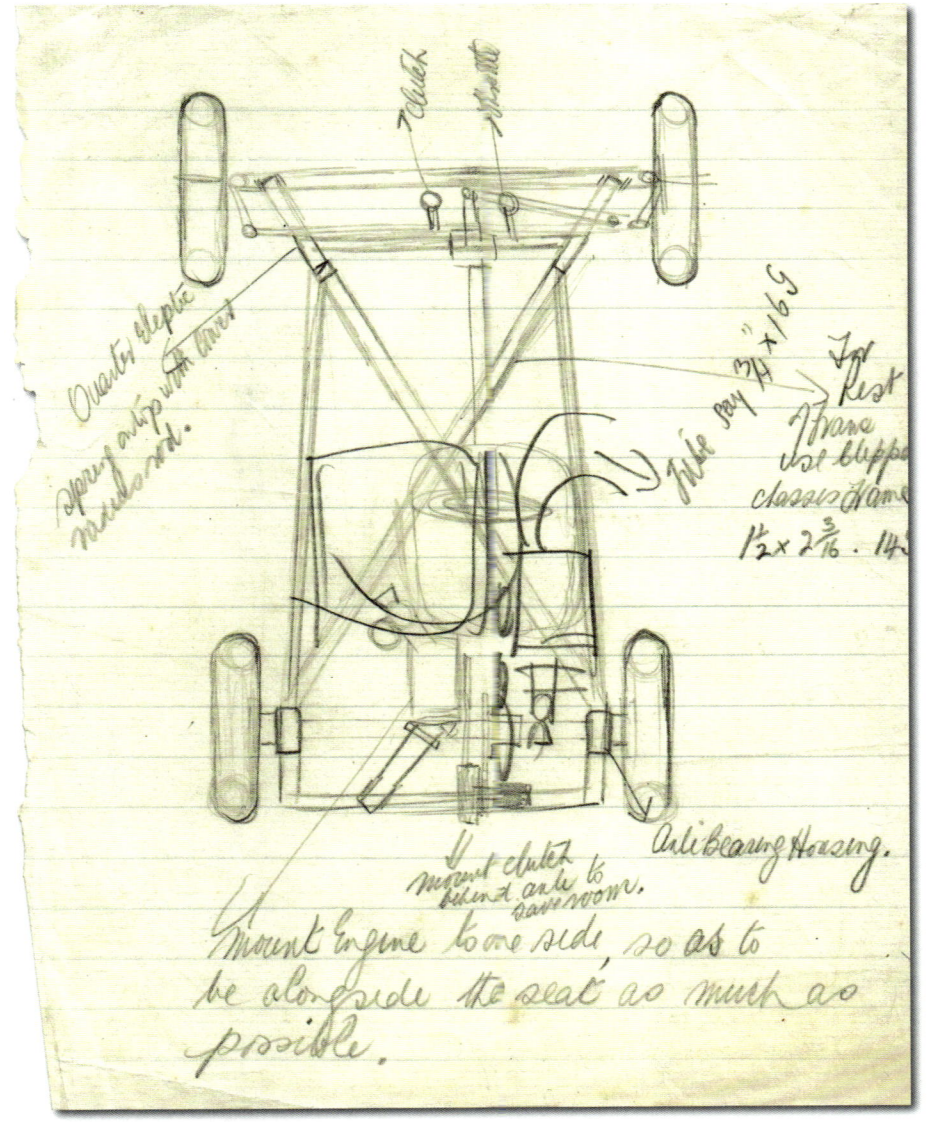

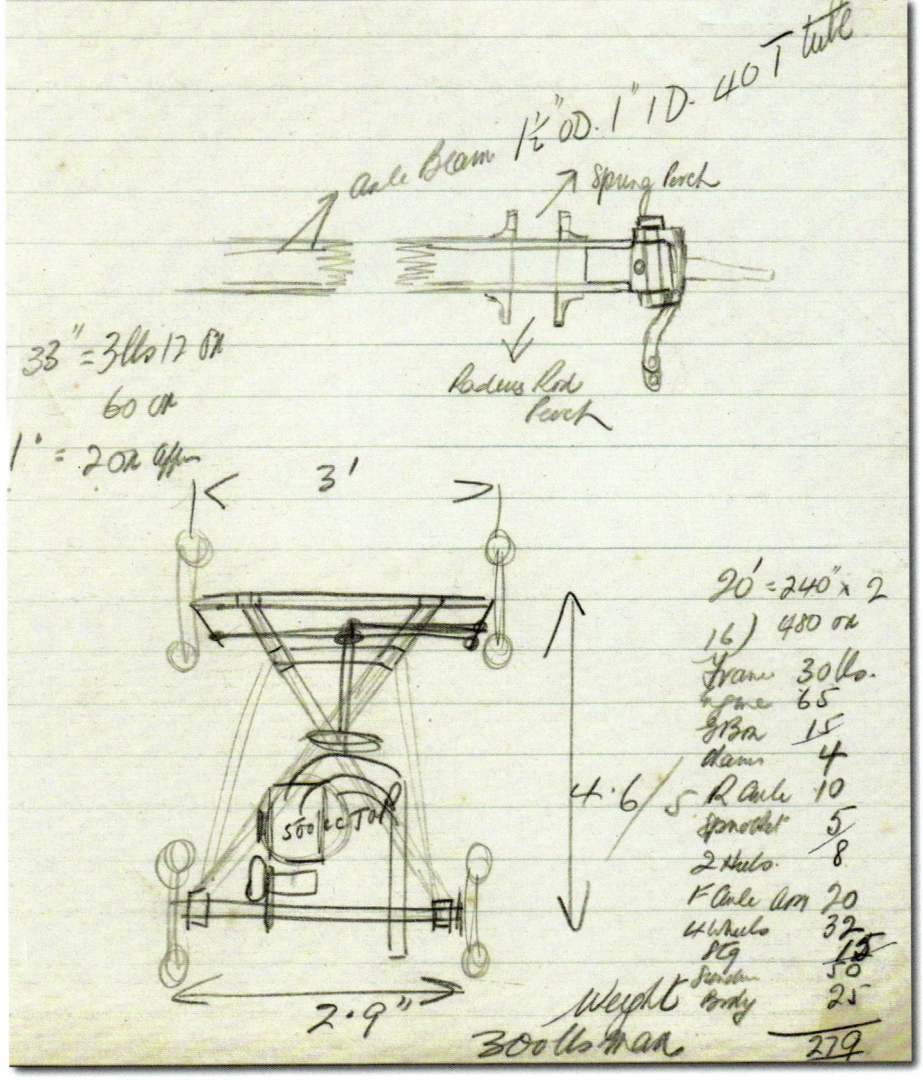

Ideas for the Atom in Sydney's hand.

JUC 5 was unique as it was the only time Allard allowed all their components and chassis to be supplied to another workshop for assembly. The client was close friend and business collaborator, Goff Imhof. Limited time was a factor in this agreement as Sydney was extremely busy. The resulting car was similar to the later J2 model and Imhof's influence drove some of that design impetus.

In the mid 1950s, a clever inventor, Herr Gottlieb caught Sydney's ear and attention. A project occurred as a separate sideline although it reeled in unwilling Allard employees like Gil Jepson. He told me the 346cc Villers engined 3-wheeler was awful and my father was the child tested out in the rear 'dickey' seat. It was a brave attempt with a movement which did gain traction, just not with Allard. Twenty Clippers were built, but few remain. (COURTESY OF KERRY HORAN)

In 1958 Sydney had not lost the concept 'lightness above all' and he reignited his relationship with the Austrian air cooled V8 in this new Steyr sports/sprint car. It was only mildly successful by his standards.

The Steyr at the Brighton Speed Trials in 1958 where Sydney would take on the ex-Imhof J2.

Sydney's S1 workshop was busy in 1958 with twin Steyr engines in a frame based on surplus Clipper rails with two gearboxes and of course 4-wheel drive which was something he had tried before with the Steyr single seater.

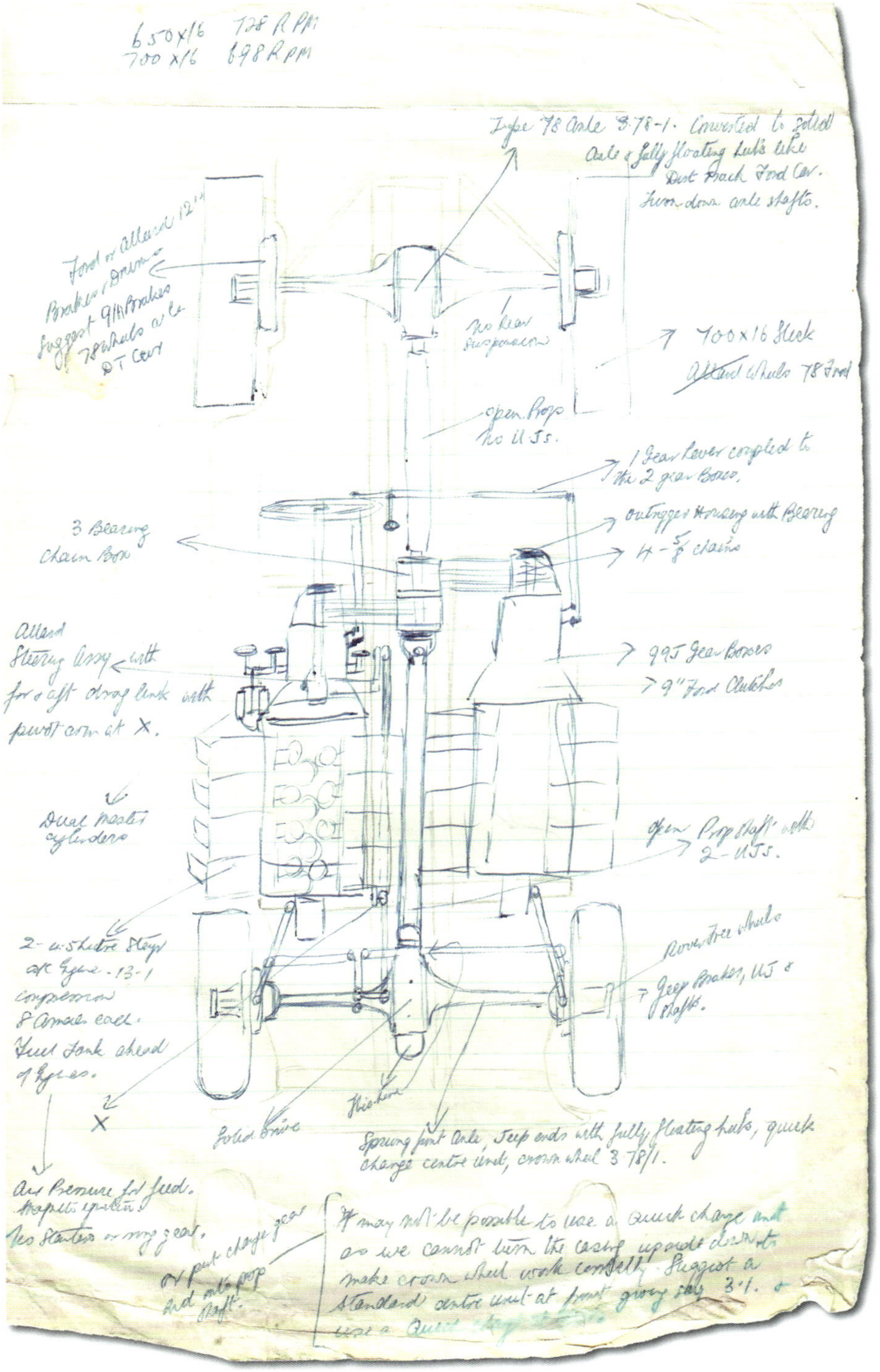

TOP: The twin Steyr is about to be push started on 7th September 1959 at the North Weald airfield.

ABOVE: The car in the S1 workshop showing just what an engineering project it was. It never fully ran.

RIGHT: One of Sydney's sketches of the car. (COURTESY OF KERRY HORAN)

·ALLARD·

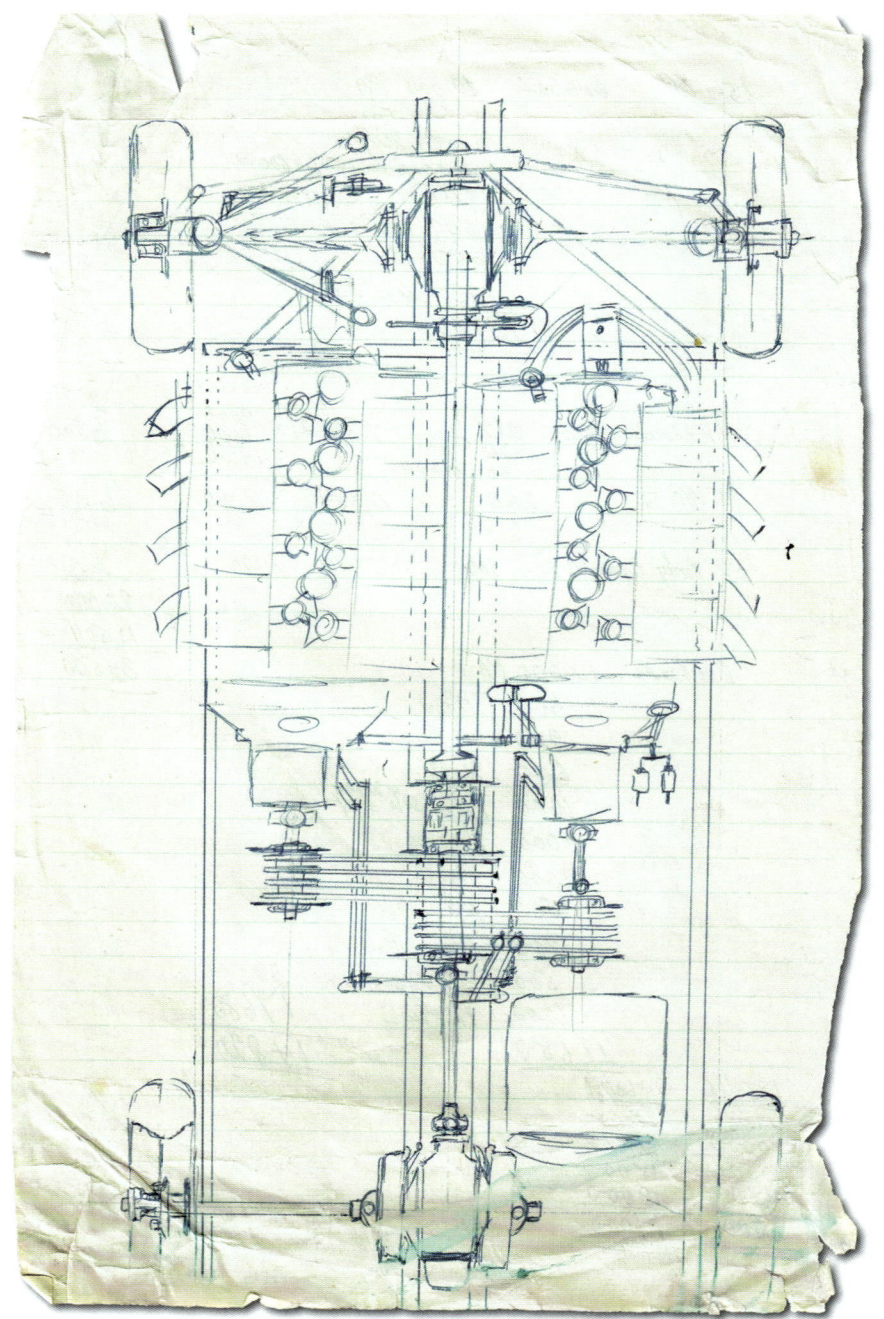

More sketches looking at drivetrain and suspension.

Within the S1 workshop in 1961, engineers John Hume (left) and David Hooper (middle) work with Sydney on their new sprint car that would be Britain's first dragster. The GMC front-blown Chrysler V8 creating some 500bhp or methanol made a big noise on the airfields of Britain.

With the creation of the car and the British Drag Association, Sydney had formed a motorsport which 1960's Britain relished. The car, now fully enveloped, was driven by my father Alan, which was a trial by fire. He recalls hitting two runway lights on one airfield which bounced him slightly into the wind and his helmet was torn straight off his face.

Parachute folding was now required in motorsport.

Possibly at the entrance to Silverstone, Alan Allard demonstrated the car around the circuit in 1963; his trusted rally navigator Rob Mackie looks on from the far right.

The 997cc Ford Anglia was transformed with a Shorrock C42B supercharger. Allard were specialists in this and eventually owners of Shorrock after a deal in 1959. Ford recognised a new model in the fully homologated 'Allardette' complete with anti-roll bars, front disc brakes and engine improvements beyond the supercharger.

The 997cc Ford Anglia has the Adlards dealership sticker in the rear window. Records have not been kept on how many were sold. A 1200cc and 1500cc variant was later offered with parts and accessories available at the Allard Performance Centre at 51 Upper Richmond Road, Putney.

The Dragon dragster was offered as a kit to buyers. A Ford Cortina 1500cc engine with a Shorrock supercharger running methanol was good enough for an impressive under 11 second quarter-mile in 1964 on road tyres. It was not a lucrative business proposal but created a huge buzz which was further whipped up with Allard's Drag Festivals in 1964 and 1965 where American competitors travelled from the USA. What a huge spectacle with my father Alan driving the only two British vehicles capable of taking on the Americans in any form.

The Dragon dragster seen from above with John Hume to the left and Alan Allard to the right.

The diminutive scale of the Dragon dragster is now clear with the Mini Clubman for comparison. My father managed to defeat the evenly matched American Doug Church in his naturally-aspirated, 2-litre Porsche-engined dragster in a race series at the festival.

John Hume bench tests the Dragon engine. Goggles, gloves and earphones were optional in 1964.

The Dragon kit and a whole range of performance accessories were available at Allard's stand at this motor racing show in 1964. The Decal Shop sign is a reminder that there was a close association with Dean Moon and his establishment in California with my father travelling there for a tour of dragster hot spots. Allard were the only British company to get their products into an American Drag performance company's catalogue, namely Moon. What actually sold will forever remain a mystery, but Allard returned the favour by offering Moon products in their catalogue. Enough interest was generated that 'The Beach Boys' visited the shop whilst recording in London in 1964.

The Dragoon (Drag Saloon) Anglia was displayed at the Racing Car show in 1966. It might have offered some distraction to my father as Sydney passed away quite young at 56 that April almost to the day that the Drag Strip Santa Pod in the UK opened. He had been instrumental in making that happen.

1967 and 1968 were busy ones as the original big Allard dragster was replaced with this more 'rail' like machine. The engine was taken from the old car and Alan is seen here attempting the quarter-mile world record which he took at 9.766 seconds running only 7 cylinders. The Americans would have easily beaten that at the time with Tony Nancy running under 8 seconds and Don Garlits even less but Americans did not wish to go through the FIA process in order to register their record.

A publicity shot for Castrol Oil during the quarter-mile world record event.

Another publicity shot for the quarter-mile world record event shows my father in suitable silver attire with my mother Lynda to his right and her father, Ted, to her right. George Brown's very fast Norton motorcycle can be seen to the left and partly out of shot on the right is friend and motoring journalist, Dennis 'Jenks' Jenkinson, who navigated for Stirling Moss in his incredible Mille Miglia win in 1955. My father was to beat Dennis in a light-hearted challenge with the two Dragon dragsters, the result of which meant Dennis shaved off his beard. Dad had quite a great skill at sprint events against capable adversaries.

THE PARTS WHICH MADE THE ALLARD

We are proud of this newcomer to our range, with its facilities for comfortable, fast and safe motoring under all types of weather conditions, and appreciate the confidence of our Distributors and Suppliers as evidenced by their association in the following pages

ALLARD MOTOR COMPANY LTD.,
24-28, CLAPHAM HIGH STREET, LONDON, S.W.4
Phone : Macaulay 3201   Cables : Almosco, London

The Allard truly is a car beyond the sum of its parts, but beyond the hundreds of repainted Ford parts, what does an Allard consist of?

The following pages record a cornucopia of elements from the humble hose clip to the mighty Marles steering gear.

PARAMOUNT
SHEET METAL
WORKS (LONDON) LTD.

Manufacturers of

WINGS.
RADIATOR GRILLES, etc. for
THE ALLARD MOTOR CO. LTD.

PANEL-BEATING, PROTOTYPE AND
ALL GENERAL SHEET METAL WORK

**22B HIGH STREET,
KINGSTON-ON-THAMES**

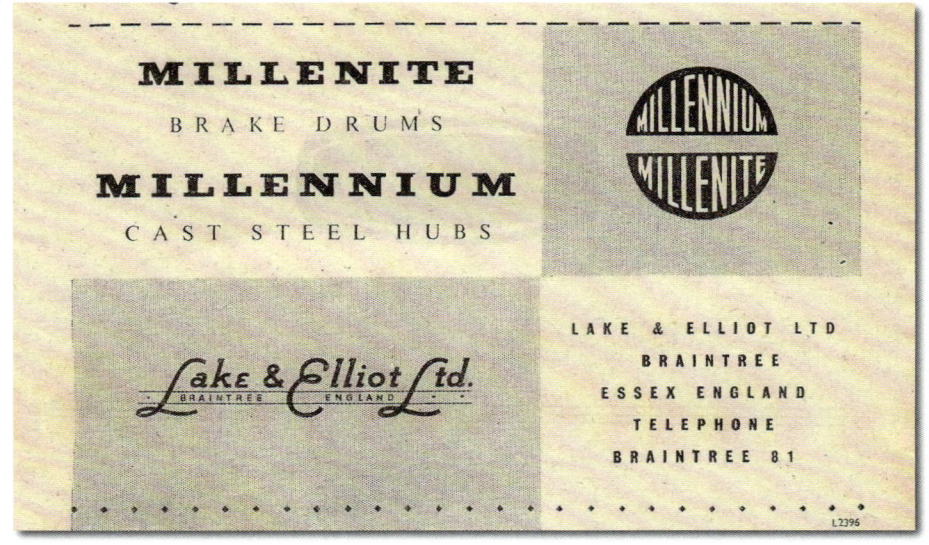

MILLENITE
BRAKE DRUMS

MILLENNIUM
CAST STEEL HUBS

MILLENNIUM
MILLENITE

Lake & Elliot Ltd.

LAKE & ELLIOT LTD
BRAINTREE
ESSEX ENGLAND
TELEPHONE
BRAINTREE 81

L2396

THE WINNING **ALLARD** SPORTS SALOON

MONTE CARLO RALLY, 1952

COACHWORK
BY
HILTON BROS. (COACHBUILDERS) **LTD.**
126 NEW KINGS RD., LONDON, S.W.6 Phone: Renown 1341

THE NEW ALLARD J2X TWO SEATER

is fitted with

AL-FIN

BONDED LIGHT ALLOY
BRAKE DRUMS

WELLWORTHY PISTON RINGS LTD. LYMINGTON, HANTS

AL-FIN BONDED BRAKE DRUMS MEAN BETTER BRAKING

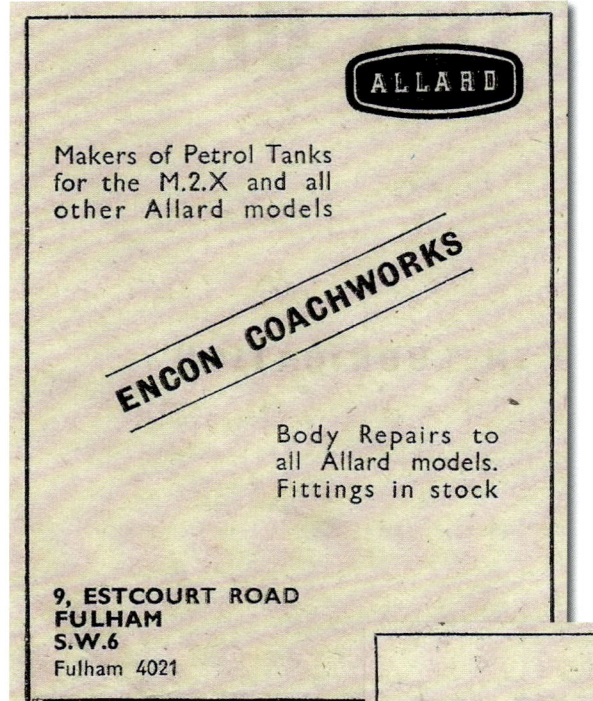

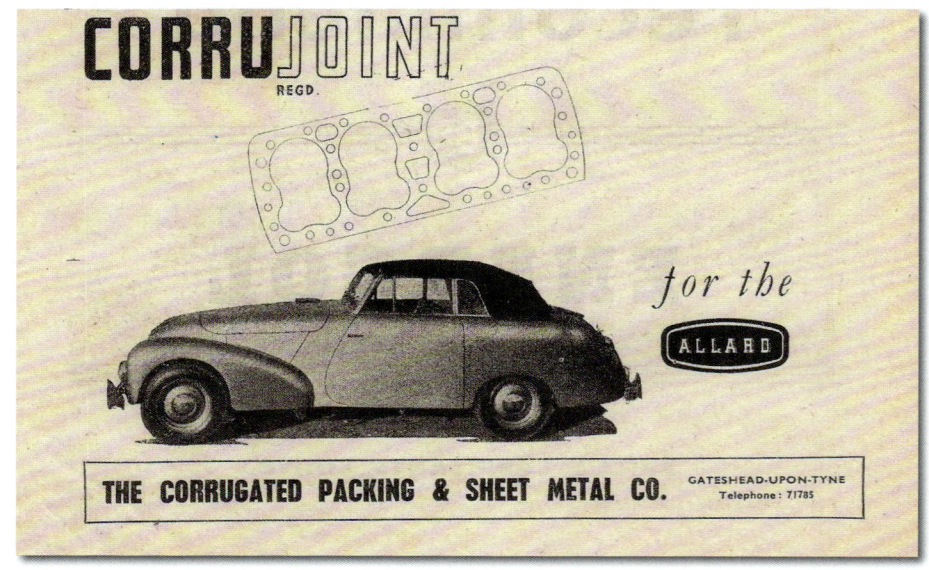

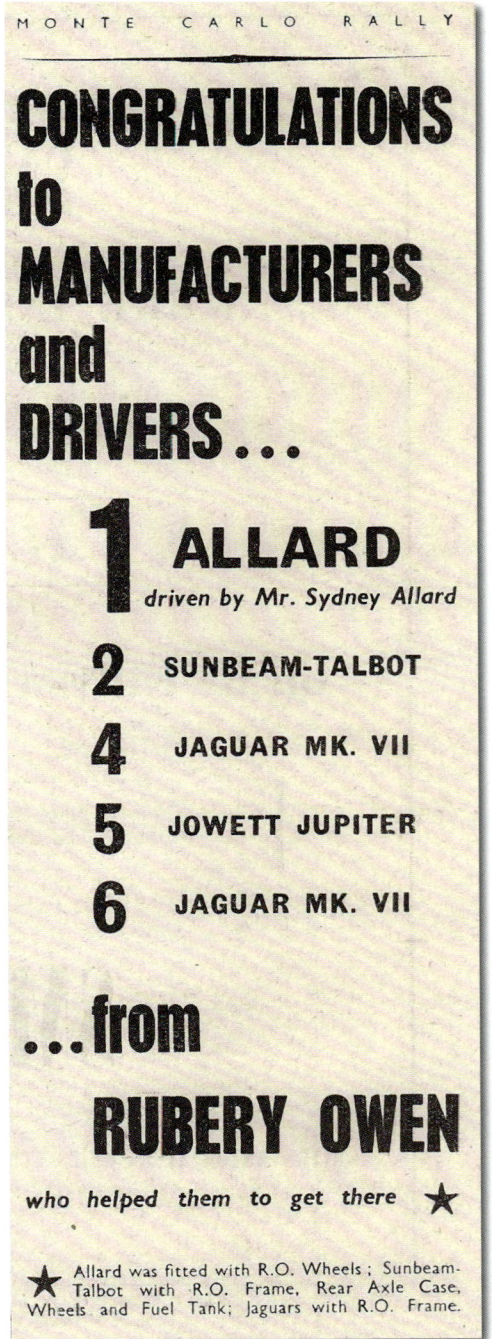

"To my mind," writes Mr. S. H. ALLARD, "the most valuable feature of VIGZOL is its fluidity at low and its maintenance of viscosity at high temperatures. I shall certainly continue to use this oil . . ."

VIGZOL

....THE RACE-PROVED OIL FOR ROAD & TRACK

The NEW ALLARD

M2X Drophead Coupe

THE VIGZOL OIL COMPANY LTD., VIGZOL HOUSE, GREENWICH, S.E.10

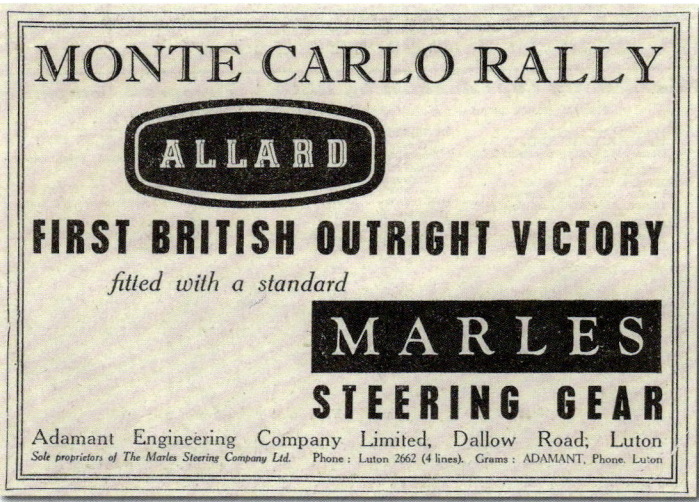

MONTE CARLO RALLY

ALLARD

FIRST BRITISH OUTRIGHT VICTORY

fitted with a standard

MARLES

STEERING GEAR

Adamant Engineering Company Limited, Dallow Road, Luton
Sole proprietors of The Marles Steering Company Ltd. Phone : Luton 2662 (4 lines). Grams : ADAMANT, Phone. Luton

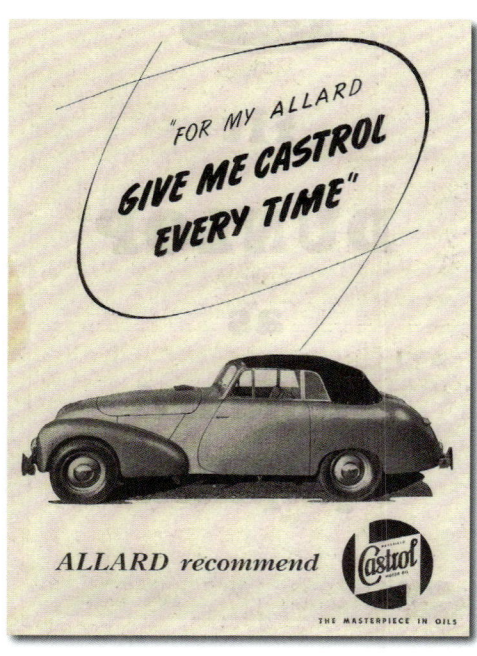

"FOR MY ALLARD
GIVE ME CASTROL
EVERY TIME"

ALLARD recommend Castrol

THE MASTERPIECE IN OILS

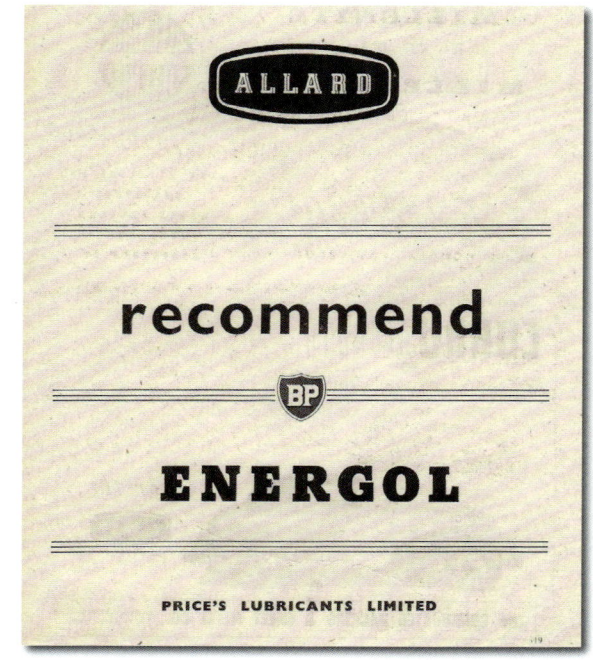

ALLARD

recommend

BP

ENERGOL

PRICE'S LUBRICANTS LIMITED

ALLARD

officially recommend

SHELL MOTOR OIL

SHELL LEADERSHIP IN LUBRICATION

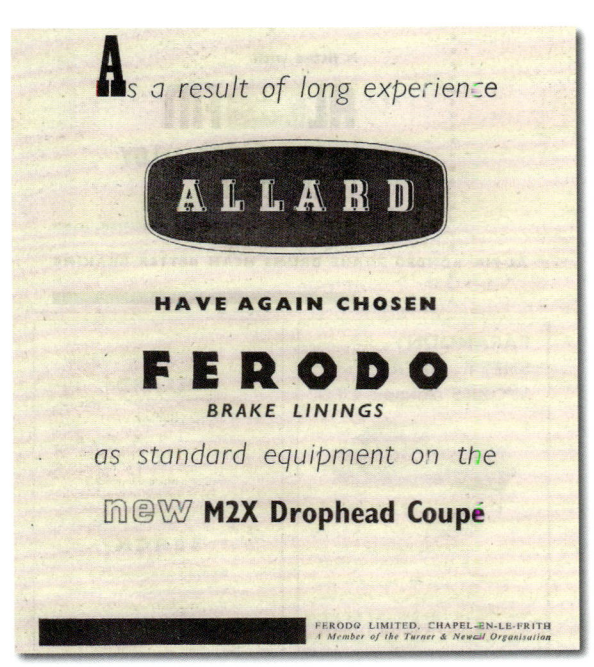

A s a result of long experience

ALLARD

HAVE AGAIN CHOSEN

FERODO
BRAKE LININGS

as standard equipment on the
new M2X Drophead Coupé

FERODO LIMITED, CHAPEL-EN-LE-FRITH
A Member of the Turner & Newall Organisation

Congratulations to
SYDNEY ALLARD

ON HIS MAGNIFICENT VICTORY
IN THE 1952 MONTE CARLO RALLY

ALLARD

fitted—of course—with

FERODO
BRAKE LININGS

FERODO LIMITED—CHAPEL-EN-LE-FRITH A Member of the Turner & Newall Organisation

Congratulations to Sydney Allard
on his outstanding British victory ★

★ British-built Allard wins outright
the Monte Carlo Rally using

LODGE
SPARKING PLUGS

This success is further proof that Lodge is the most
reliable plug for your engine.

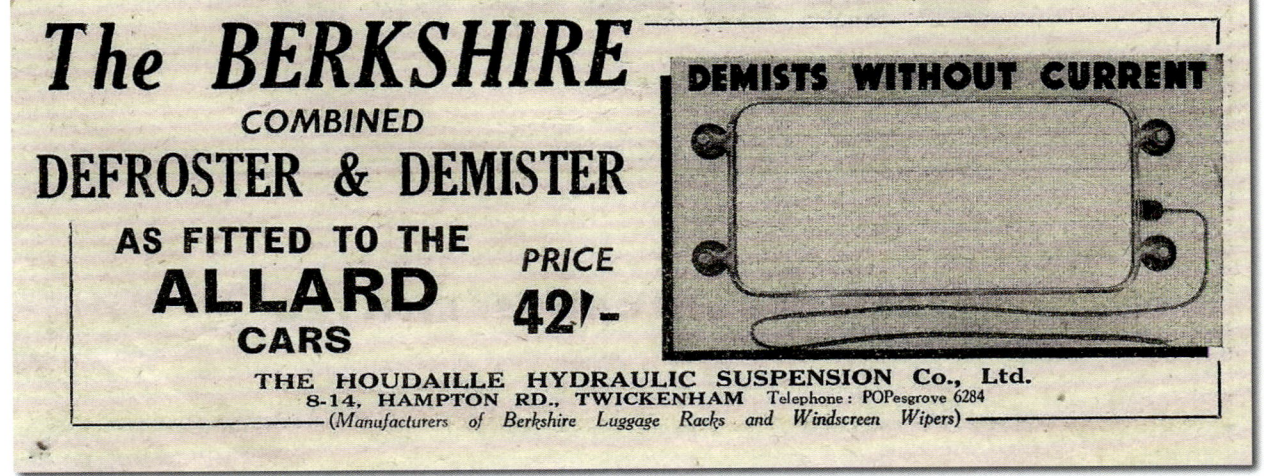

The BERKSHIRE
COMBINED
DEFROSTER & DEMISTER
AS FITTED TO THE
ALLARD PRICE
CARS **42/-**

DEMISTS WITHOUT CURRENT

THE HOUDAILLE HYDRAULIC SUSPENSION Co., Ltd.
8-14, HAMPTON RD., TWICKENHAM Telephone: POPesgrove 6284
(Manufacturers of Berkshire Luggage Racks and Windscreen Wipers)

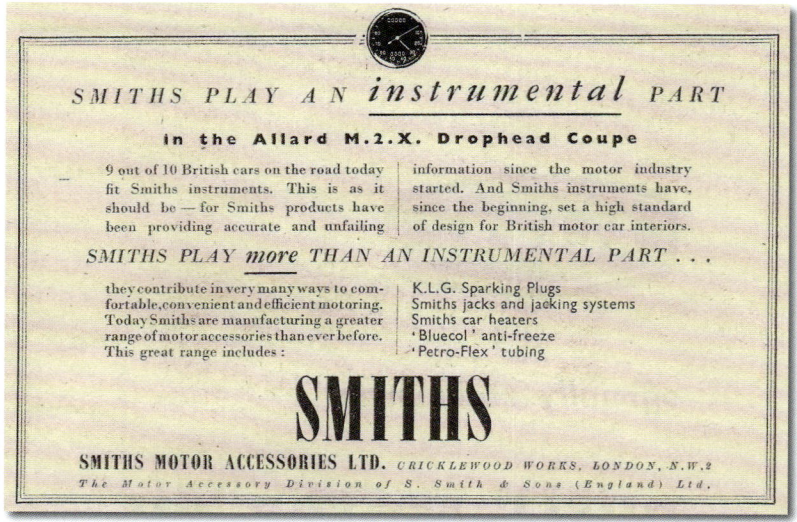

SMITHS PLAY AN *instrumental* PART

in the Allard M.2.X. Drophead Coupe

9 out of 10 British cars on the road today fit Smiths instruments. This is as it should be — for Smiths products have been providing accurate and unfailing information since the motor industry started. And Smiths instruments have, since the beginning, set a high standard of design for British motor car interiors.

SMITHS PLAY *more* THAN AN INSTRUMENTAL PART . . .

they contribute in very many ways to comfortable, convenient and efficient motoring. Today Smiths are manufacturing a greater range of motor accessories than ever before. This great range includes :

K.L.G. Sparking Plugs
Smiths jacks and jacking systems
Smiths car heaters
'Bluecol' anti-freeze
'Petro-Flex' tubing

SMITHS

SMITHS MOTOR ACCESSORIES LTD. *CRICKLEWOOD WORKS, LONDON, N.W.2*
The Motor Accessory Division of S. Smith & Sons (England) Ltd.

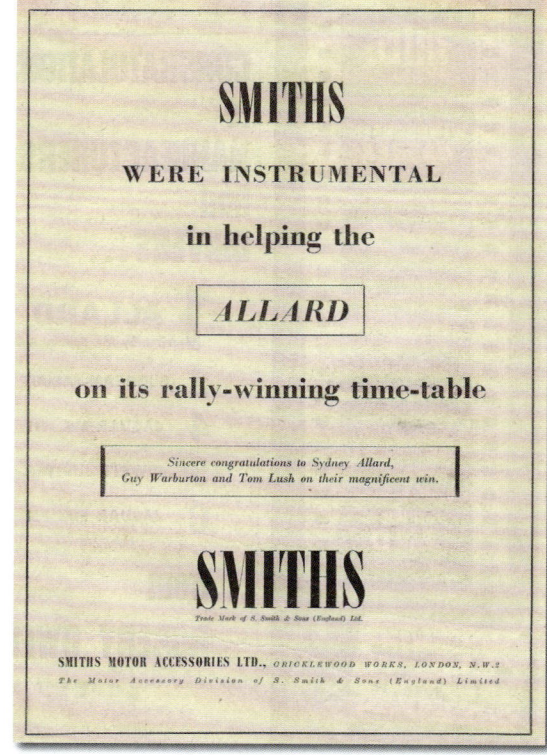

SMITHS

WERE INSTRUMENTAL

in helping the

ALLARD

on its rally-winning time-table

Sincere congratulations to Sydney Allard, Guy Warburton and Tom Lush on their magnificent win.

SMITHS

Trade Mark of S. Smith & Sons (England) Ltd.

SMITHS MOTOR ACCESSORIES LTD., CRICKLEWOOD WORKS, LONDON, N.W.2
The Motor Accessory Division of S. Smith & Sons (England) Limited

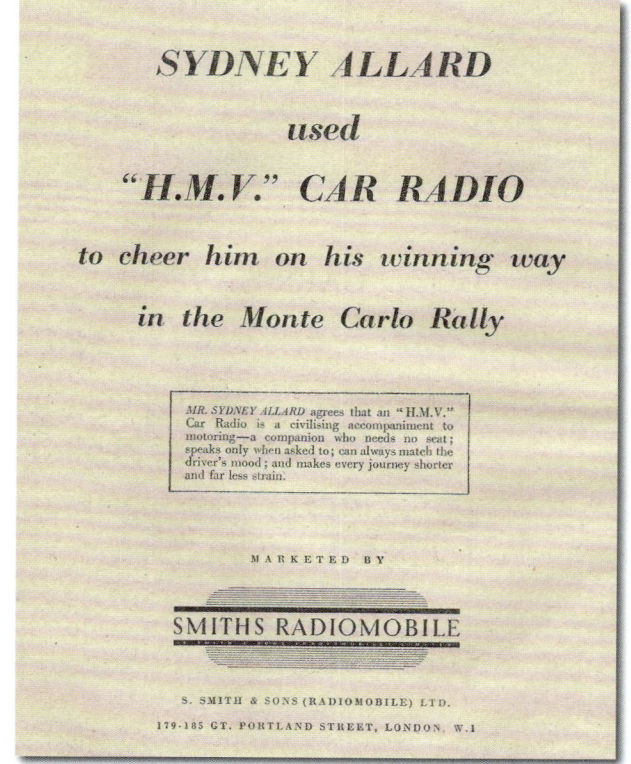

SYDNEY ALLARD

used

"H.M.V." CAR RADIO

to cheer him on his winning way

in the Monte Carlo Rally

MR. SYDNEY ALLARD agrees that an "H.M.V." Car Radio is a civilising accompaniment to motoring—a companion who needs no seat; speaks only when asked to; can always match the driver's mood; and makes every journey shorter and far less strain.

MARKETED BY

SMITHS RADIOMOBILE

S. SMITH & SONS (RADIOMOBILE) LTD.
179-185 GT. PORTLAND STREET, LONDON, W.1

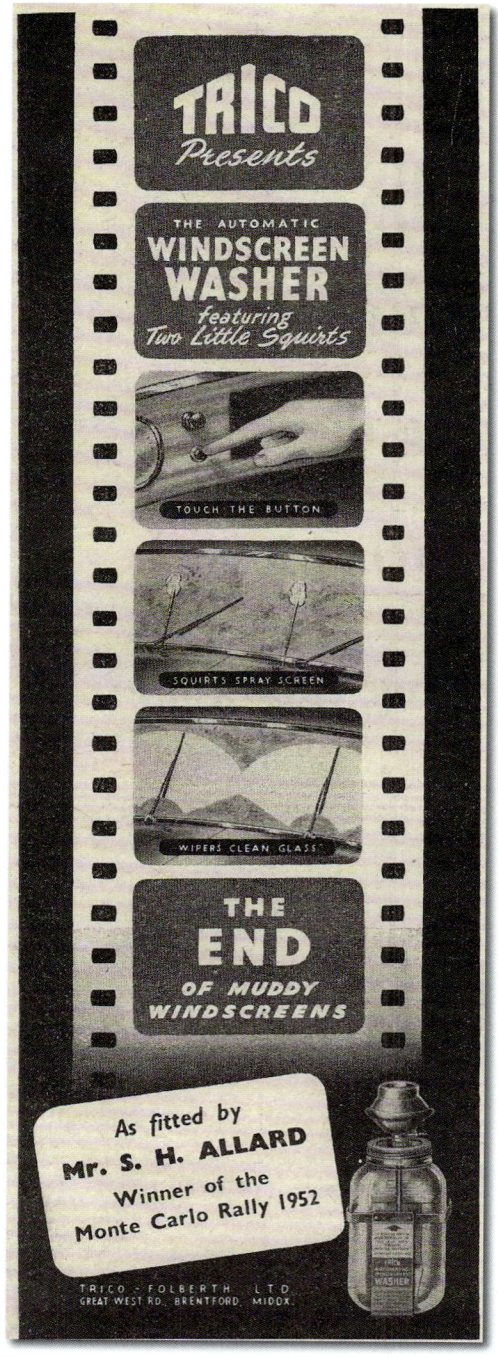

TRICO *Presents*

THE AUTOMATIC
WINDSCREEN WASHER
featuring
Two Little Squirts

TOUCH THE BUTTON

SQUIRTS SPRAY SCREEN

WIPERS CLEAN GLASS

THE END OF MUDDY WINDSCREENS

As fitted by
Mr. S. H. ALLARD
Winner of the
Monte Carlo Rally 1952

TRICO-FOLBERTH LTD.
GREAT WEST RD. BRENTFORD, MIDDX.

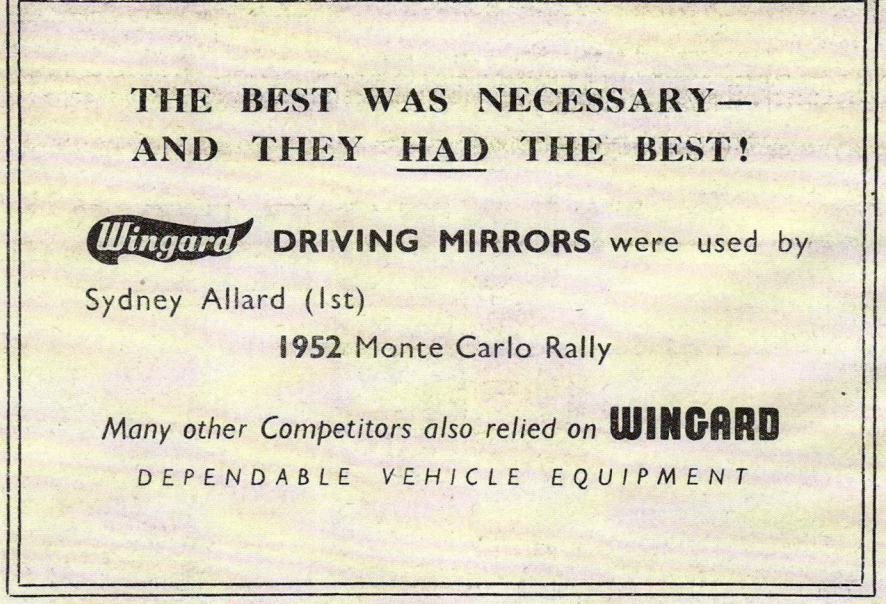

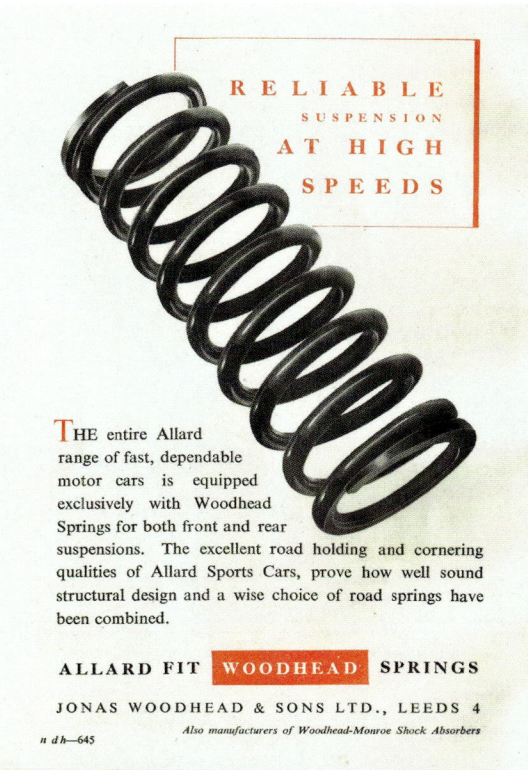
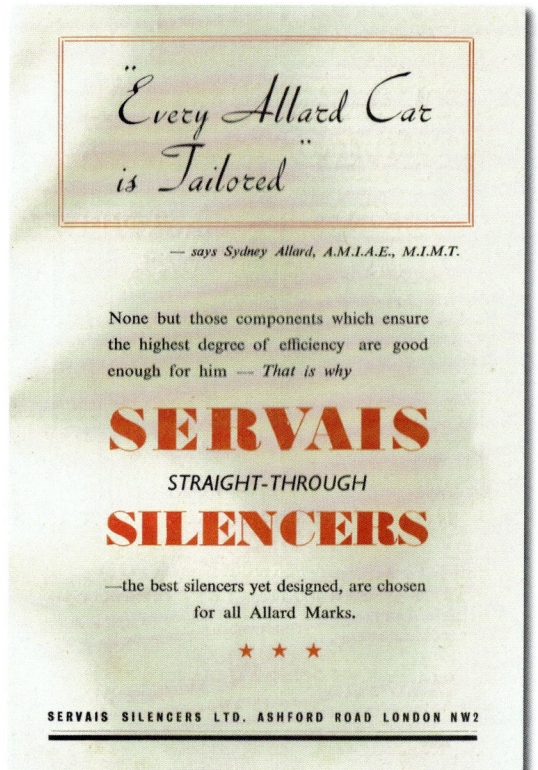
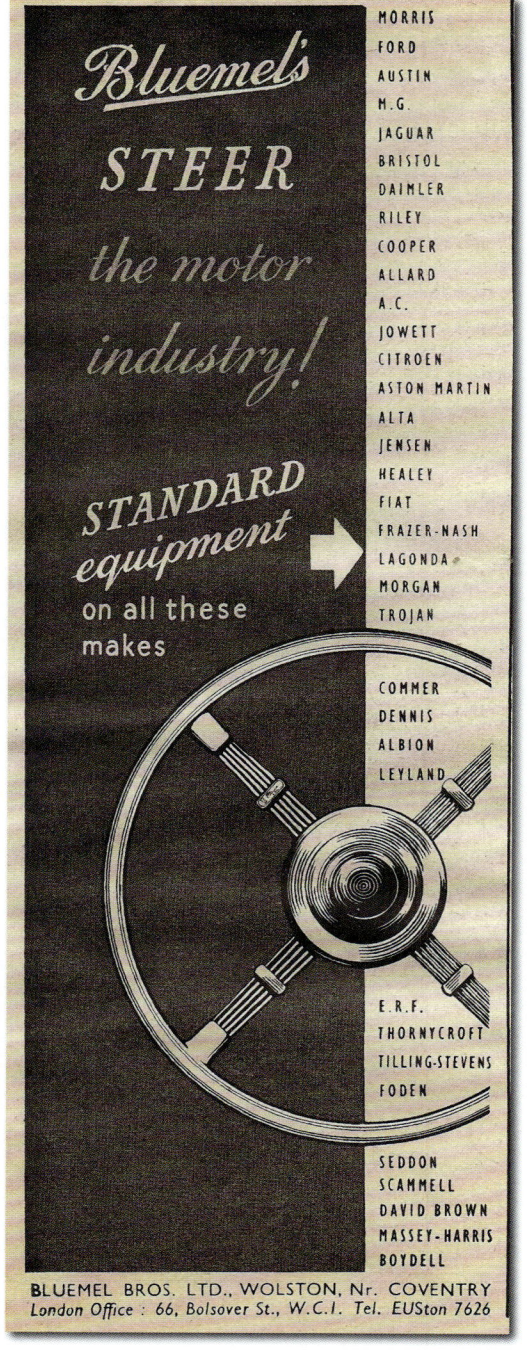

The Parts which Made the Allard

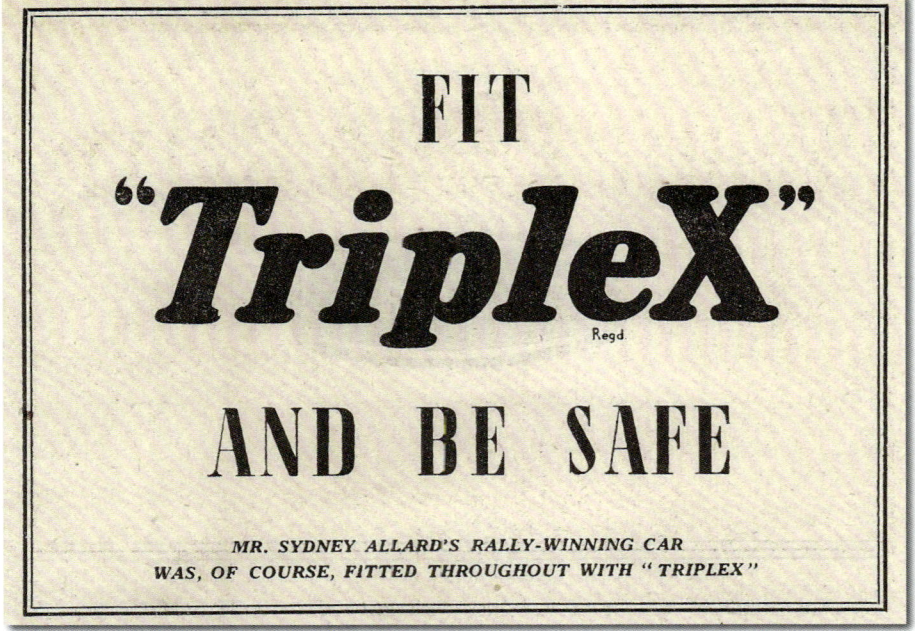

The Allard Motor Co. Ltd.

are proud to have contributed an important stimulus to the export trade of the British Motor Car Industry by providing both car and driver to obtain the

FIRST BRITISH
OUTRIGHT VICTORY
IN THE
MONTE CARLO RALLY
FOR 21 YEARS

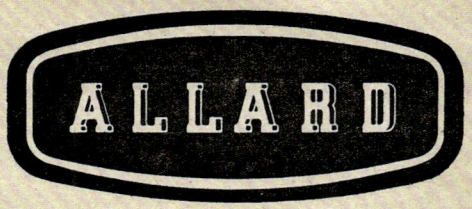

ALLARD MOTOR COMPANY LTD.
24-28, CLAPHAM HIGH STREET, LONDON, S.W.4
Phone: Macaulay 3201   Cables: Almotco, London

THE MEN WHO BUILT THE ALLARD

**ADLARDS MOTORS Ltd.,
LONDON
ADVERTISING
Ford**

Sydney Allard's motoring enterprise started from a healthy ember left by his father, Arthur, who had an existing firm on the Keswick Road, Putney and had expanded under the financial guidance of Alf Brisco to a healthy four premises by 1938.

Through photographs and extracts, many from the official Adlards Motors' album, it is clear that the Ford commercial and garage business intermixed with the Allard car enterprise in a heady, sometimes confusing mix.

Never a large firm, Adlards and Allard was scattered over numerous small premises in an area around Putney and Brixton then later post war in Clapham too.

With an emphasis on the social history, the photographs immerse the reader in the atmosphere which close knit small workshops created.

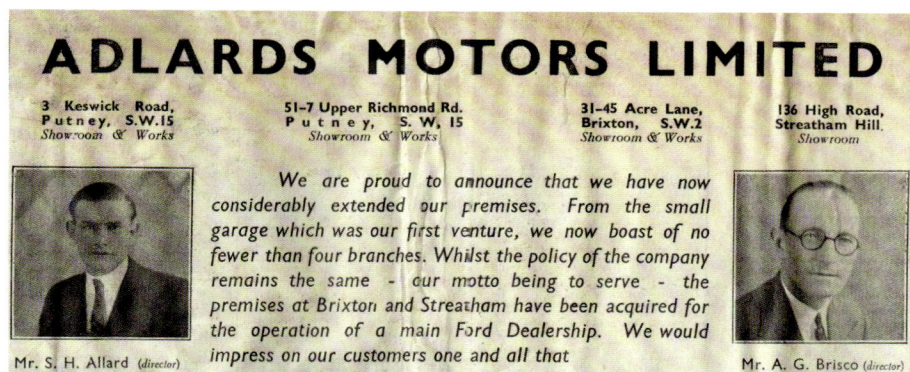

ADLARDS MOTORS LIMITED

3 Keswick Road, Putney, S.W.15
Showroom & Works

51–7 Upper Richmond Rd. Putney, S.W.15
Showroom & Works

31–45 Acre Lane, Brixton, S.W.2
Showroom & Works

136 High Road, Streatham Hill.
Showroom

We are proud to announce that we have now considerably extended our premises. From the small garage which was our first venture, we now boast of no fewer than four branches. Whilst the policy of the company remains the same - our motto being to serve - the premises at Brixton and Streatham have been acquired for the operation of a main Ford Dealership. We would impress on our customers one and all that

Mr. S. H. Allard *(director)* who controls the Brixton and Streatham Branches

Mr. A. G. Brisco *(director)* who controls the Putney Branches

"We grow bigger to serve you better"

The Boro' News 14.10.38.

Sydney Allard with Alf Brisco successfully expanded to four premises by 1938 and this was not down to Allard Special trials car production but to running a brisk cars sales, garage service and repair company as demonstrated by these advertisements.

Special tune up for Fords

HERE'S HOW WE DO IT!

1. We clean and adjust carburettor, fuel pump and sparking plugs.
2. We adjust fan belt, check water pumps, radiator and cooling system.
3. We check over entire ignition system and clean battery terminals and cables.

Genuine Ford Facilities cost less
ADLARDS
MOTORS LIMITED
31/33, 43/45 ACRE LANE, BRIXTON
Phone BRIXTON 6431-2-3-4   S.W.2

BRIX FREE PRESS   JULY 1948   L2953

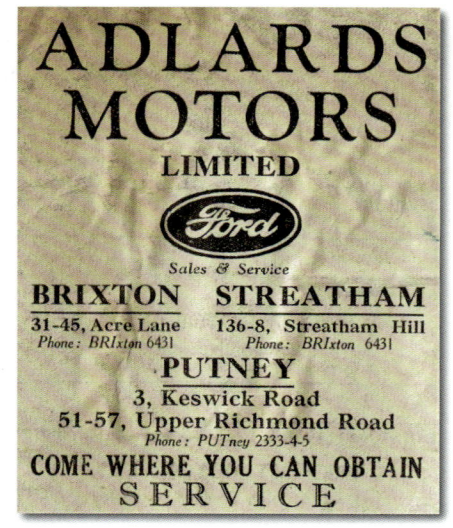

ADLARDS MOTORS LIMITED

Ford
Sales & Service

BRIXTON   **STREATHAM**
31–45, Acre Lane   136–8, Streatham Hill
Phone : BRIxton 6431   *Phone : BRIxton 6431*

PUTNEY
3, Keswick Road
51–57, Upper Richmond Road
Phone : PUTney 2333-4-5

COME WHERE YOU CAN OBTAIN
SERVICE

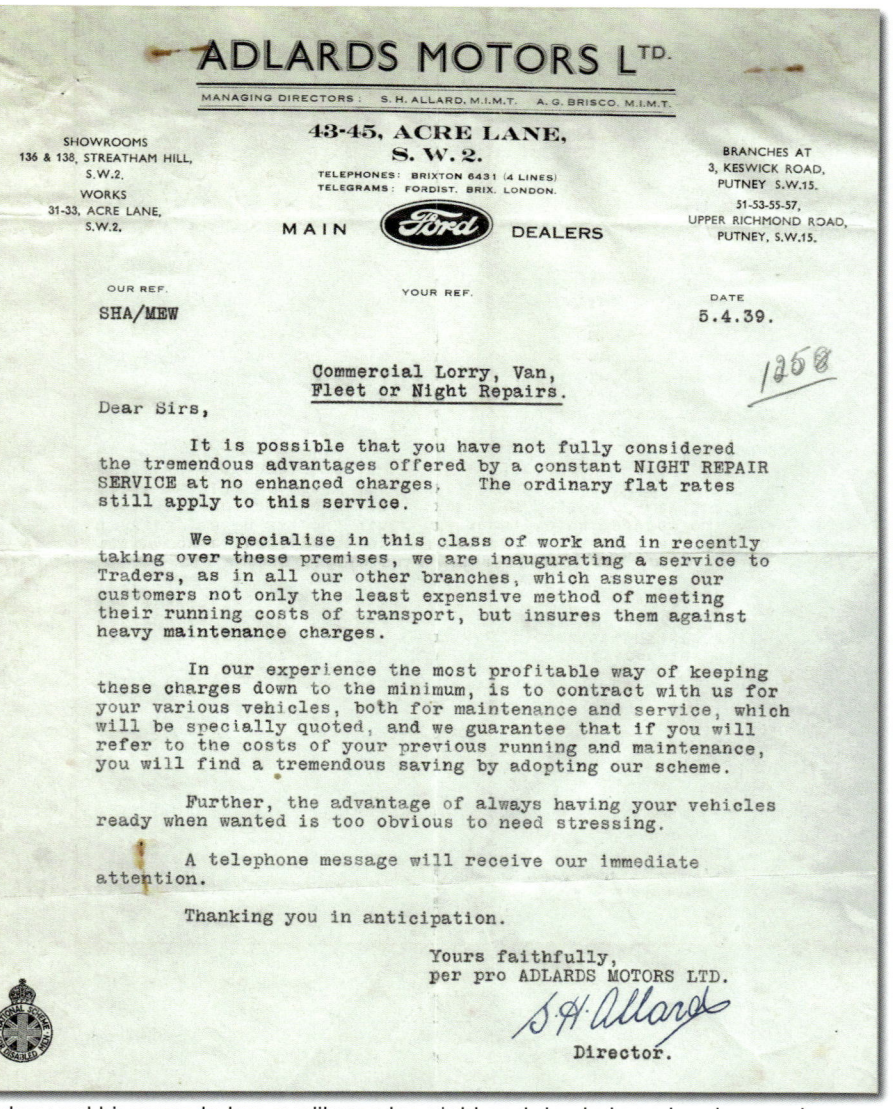

ADLARDS MOTORS LTD.

MANAGING DIRECTORS : S. H. ALLARD, M.I.M.T.   A. G. BRISCO, M.I.M.T.

SHOWROOMS
136 & 138, STREATHAM HILL, S.W.2.
WORKS
31-33, ACRE LANE, S.W.2.

43-45, ACRE LANE, S. W. 2.
TELEPHONES : BRIXTON 6431 (4 LINES)
TELEGRAMS : FORDIST. BRIX. LONDON.

MAIN *Ford* DEALERS

BRANCHES AT
3, KESWICK ROAD, PUTNEY S.W.15.
51-53-55-57, UPPER RICHMOND ROAD, PUTNEY, S.W.15.

OUR REF.
SHA/MEW

YOUR REF.

DATE
5.4.39.

1258

Commercial Lorry, Van, Fleet or Night Repairs.

Dear Sirs,

It is possible that you have not fully considered the tremendous advantages offered by a constant NIGHT REPAIR SERVICE at no enhanced charges. The ordinary flat rates still apply to this service.

We specialise in this class of work and in recently taking over these premises, we are inaugurating a service to Traders, as in all our other branches, which assures our customers not only the least expensive method of meeting their running costs of transport, but insures them against heavy maintenance charges.

In our experience the most profitable way of keeping these charges down to the minimum, is to contract with us for your various vehicles, both for maintenance and service, which will be specially quoted, and we guarantee that if you will refer to the costs of your previous running and maintenance, you will find a tremendous saving by adopting our scheme.

Further, the advantage of always having your vehicles ready when wanted is too obvious to need stressing.

A telephone message will receive our immediate attention.

Thanking you in anticipation.

Yours faithfully,
per pro ADLARDS MOTORS LTD.

S H Allard
Director.

Sydney put his name to top-quality service night and day to keep London moving.

Friend, customer and competitive driver, Ken Hutchison (right), is part of the 'Tailwagger' Trials car team looking at Sydney in the driving seat with the last of the trio, Guy Warburton, beside him, all outside the original salesroom/garage at 3 Keswick Road. Well-dressed customers within look on.

A more serious pose perhaps reflects the focused way Sydney (right) went about improving himself and others around him, Guy Warburton is stood left and Ken Hutchison is in the centre. The property behind included a block of flats above built by Sydney's father, a developer.

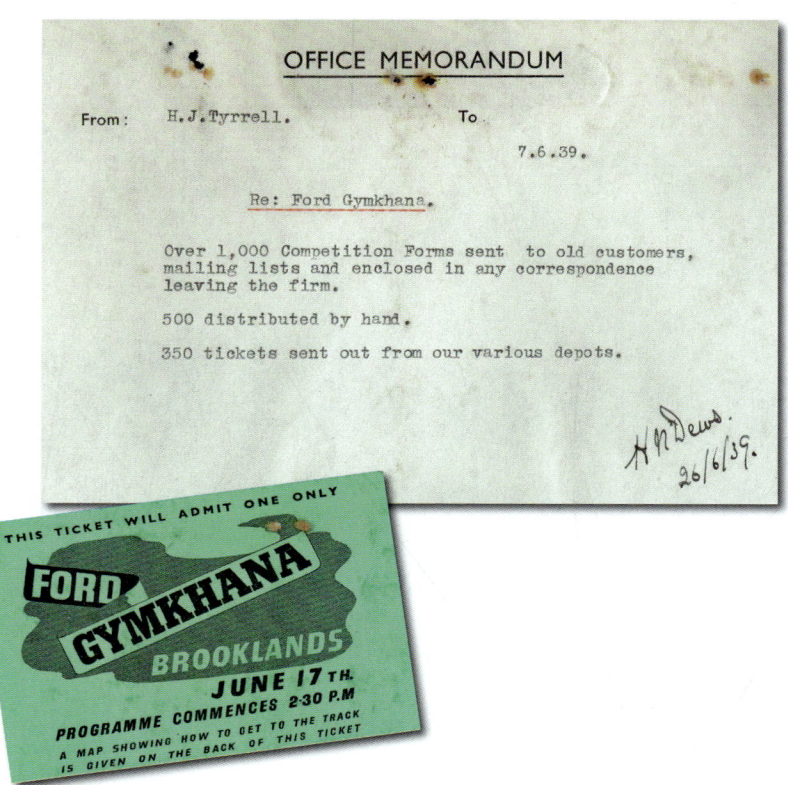

OFFICE MEMORANDUM

From: H.J.Tyrrell.   To
                                    7.6.39.

Re: Ford Gymkhana.

Over 1,000 Competition Forms sent to old customers,
mailing lists and enclosed in any correspondence
leaving the firm.

500 distributed by hand.

350 tickets sent out from our various depots.

H N Dews.
26/6/39.

FORD GYMKHANA BROOKLANDS JUNE 17TH.
THIS TICKET WILL ADMIT ONE ONLY
PROGRAMME COMMENCES 2·30 P.M
A MAP SHOWING HOW TO GET TO THE TRACK
IS GIVEN ON THE BACK OF THIS TICKET

EVENTS

BROOKLANDS JUNE 17TH

1. **MRS. GAMP LOSES HER BROOD**
   a humorous opening event.
2. **CAR FOOTBALL**
   shooting goals with the car bumpers.
3. **CAR SLALOM**
   bursting balloons while driving.
4. **DARE-DEVIL DRIVING**
   a series of alarming events.
5. **SAFETY FIRST**
   a driving skill test open to Ford owners.
6. **THE "SCOUT" SPEEDSTER FINALS**
   "race" for the championship.
7. **CONTINUATION OF SAFETY FIRST EVENT**
8. **WHEEL CHANGING CONTEST**
   open to Ford owners.
9. **HIGHLAND DANCING**
   a display by the Dagenham Girl Pipers.
10. **JUDGING THE CONCOURS D'ÉLÉGANCE**
11. **RAMP ROMPING**
    a team of drivers in a thrilling display.
12. **BOY SCOUTS' "SPEEDSTER" OBSTACLE RACE**
13. **CONCOURS PARADE**
14. **MORE DARE-DEVIL DRIVING**
    in still more alarming events.
15. **PRIZE PRESENTATION**
16. **BOY SCOUTS' CAMP FIRE**
    community singing.

COMMENTARY BY MR. T. H. WOODROOFFE, THE WELL-KNOWN COMMENTATOR.

FIVE HOURS OF INTENSE INTEREST
A MOTORING VARIETY SHOW.

Whatever meetings may have been staged at Brooklands in the past the Ford Gymkhana on June 17th bids fair to outstrip them all. It will be different in every way. Nothing quite like it has been seen before for variety, colour, comedy, thrills, novelties, and, given the weather of a typical summer day in June, we promise our visitors five hours of intense interest and amusement.

Take the squad of crazy thrill drivers. Their amazing exploits will hold you spellbound. They must be seen to be believed.
On the other end of this see-saw of motoring diversions come the Boy Scout Speedsters, hurtling along on a section of the Brooklands Track at six miles an hour or more on their home-made "racers" in a tussle for supremacy in the National Championship for 1939.
Then, sedate and dignified, the colourful splash of the famous Dagenham Girl Pipers in a flourish of pipes and Highland dancing—a display of merit comparable with professional Highland Dancers—but you must see them for yourself.
The "Clown" of the Show, with his inimitable bicycle manoeuvres, will make you roar with laughter between events and wherever opportunity presents itself.
For the "thrill of the track" you can have a demonstration ride round Brooklands in a Ford car, or if you wish to do so, you can enter one of the open competitions for Ford owners listed below. **And then** for the Scouts and for grown-ups too, there is the Scouts' Camp Fire and Community singing to wind up an afternoon of motoring entertainment and pleasure.

COME TO BROOKLANDS !
Sat., June 17th, 1939, 2.30—7.30 p.m.
Ask your Ford Dealer for Admission Tickets.

OPEN EVENTS

If you are a Ford owner . . .
SEND THIS BACK TO US NOW
(The address is given on the back of this folder.)

J

The competitions are so varied that there is something to interest every Ford owner. The Driving Skill contest will be a series of tests designed to find the best driver. It is divided into classes to give everyone a fair chance whether you own a Ford "Eight" or a V-8 "30." This contest is being run under the auspices of the B.A.R.C. If you do not fancy yourself as a "trials" driver, join in the car slalom—it should be great fun and no great skill is necessary.

If you are quick with your hands try your skill at the wheel changing contest. If you own a Ford ten years old or more, enter for the competition for the best-kept Ford car over that age or if you take a particular pride in your Ford, there is the Concours d'Elégance.

This is a FORD day. Don't hesitate to join in, the events are not difficult.

SPLENDID PRIZES FOR ALL WINNERS.

On receipt of this application addressed to Dept. J, Gymkhana, Ford Motor Company Limited, Dagenham, Essex, full information and entry forms will be sent.

1. Driving Skill Contests	
2. Competition for the Best Looking Ford Car	
3. The Best-kept Ford 10 Years Old or More (mileage will be considered)	
4. Car Slalom	
5. Wheel Changing Contest	
NAME	
ADDRESS	

YOU MAY ONLY ENTER ONE EVENT.
Place a X against the Competition you wish to enter.

As well as its use as a race track, Brooklands was available for the varied entertainment of customers, traders and employees. Later in 1939, the last ever race would take place there.

This photograph and the next two were provided by ex-Adlards employee, John Caluori, at the author's Allard film show event in 1997. After the event, he opened his Capri boot and displayed the records and memorabilia he had scooped from the Allard offices to ensure their survival.

This image shows the desk of the parts department at Acre Lane in the period from mid 1946 to 1950.

(COURTESY OF JOHN CALUORI)

Ford

MAIN DEALER

ADLARDS MOTORS LTD.

43-45 ACRE LANE, S.W.2

01-733 4150/1/2

J. E. CALUORI
Assistant Manager, Parts Division

The back of the parts department at Acre Lane. (COURTESY OF JOHN CALUORI)

The other half of the panorama of the parts department at Acre Lane including Serck radiators. Serck still trades today and made their first Allard radiator in some 70 years for Lloyd Allard with his continuation Allard JR chassis 3408 in 2019. (COURTESY OF JOHN CALUORI)

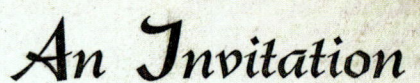

An Invitation

to DAGENHAM down

the RIVER THAMES

is extended to our " Stocking Dealers " to join us in a River Trip from Westminster Pier to visit The Ford Motor Co. Ltd. works on Tuesday the 20th, June, 1939.

This invitation is made with the kind co-operation of The Ford Motor Co. Ltd., and we look forward to what should be an enjoyable and interesting day.

In order that a similar invitation can be given to your Sales Staff and Works Manager, who possibly cannot leave business on the same day, we are arranging another trip to take place on Wednesday, 28th June, 1939.

Inside we give a few details of the proposed programme which we feel sure will appeal to you.

ADLARDS MOTORS, LTD.,
43/45 Acre Lane,
London, S.W.2.

To facilitate arrangements your reply by return will be esteemed that we may give definite catering instructions for lunch and tea.

ADLARDS MOTORS LTD
43/45 ACRE LANE
S.W.2
MAIN FORD DEALERS

June, 1939.

Dear Sir,

We herewith have pleasure in enclosing programme and booklet of tickets in connection with our visit to the Ford Factory at Dagenham.

We are indeed pleased to know you are honouring us with your company and trust the day will prove an interesting and successful one.

Yours faithfully,
Per pro ADLARDS MOTORS LTD.,
S. H. ALLARD,
Managing Director.

TIME SCHEDULE OF TRIP

11.0 a.m.   S.S. Queen Elizabeth leaves Westminster Pier. Luncheon served on board at latter part of trip.

1.45 p.m.   Party lands at Dagenham Jetty.

2.0 p.m.   Conducted tour round Ford Factory.

4.0 p.m.   Tea served at Factory.

5.0 p.m.   Boat leaves Dagenham Jetty and returns upstream.

6.30 p.m.   Boat arrives at Westminster Pier.

ADLARDS SPECIAL VISIT TO THE FORD FACTORY DAGENHAM

WEDNESDAY, 28th JUNE, 1939.

Please admit Bearer aboard **S.S. QUEEN ELIZABETH** without payment

Please sign this voucher below and hand in at Gangway.

Name

Firm

The Steam Ship departs from Westminster Pier at 11 a.m. sharp.

ADLARDS SPECIAL VISIT TO THE FORD FACTORY DAGENHAM

WEDNESDAY, 28th JUNE, 1939.

Please serve to Bearer **ONE LUNCHEON** without payment

Please give this voucher up to Table Steward.

All drinks apart from one supplied free with Lunch must be paid for on request.

ADLARDS
special visit to the
FORD FACTORY
Tuesday, June 20th

155

TICKET VOUCHERS ENCLOSED

Another Adlards trip is beautifully recorded in the Adlards Motors Ltd. official advertising album. Again traders and staff could choose from two dates to board a boat on the Thames and go to the Ford Dagenham plant. The firm understood the need to both foster trade and reward the staff.

Adlards Motors of Brixton organised two very enjoyable trips to the Works. The first, on June 20th, was for stockist Dealers and the second, on June 28th, for other motor traders in their trade territory. Altogether over 200 people accepted the invitation. Adlards feel that the visit has given them a lot of valuable local prestige, and their trade contact is more cordial than ever before.

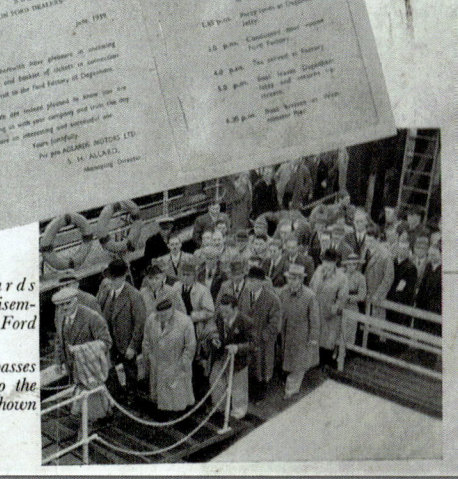

Some of Adlards Motors' Party disembarking at the Ford Jetty.
All tickets and passes were made up into the attractive wallet shown above.

A wonderful image taken by Ford of Dagenham. Within this group are the Allard and Adlards employees. A London tug in the background makes haste to escort its next ship out of the Thames estuary.

ABOVE: The elderly gent in the flat, an Allard craftsman, seems to be held with some esteem by his former colleagues.

BELOW: Tom Lush (top centre) and Allard General Manager, Reg Canham, speak to the captain before disembarking.

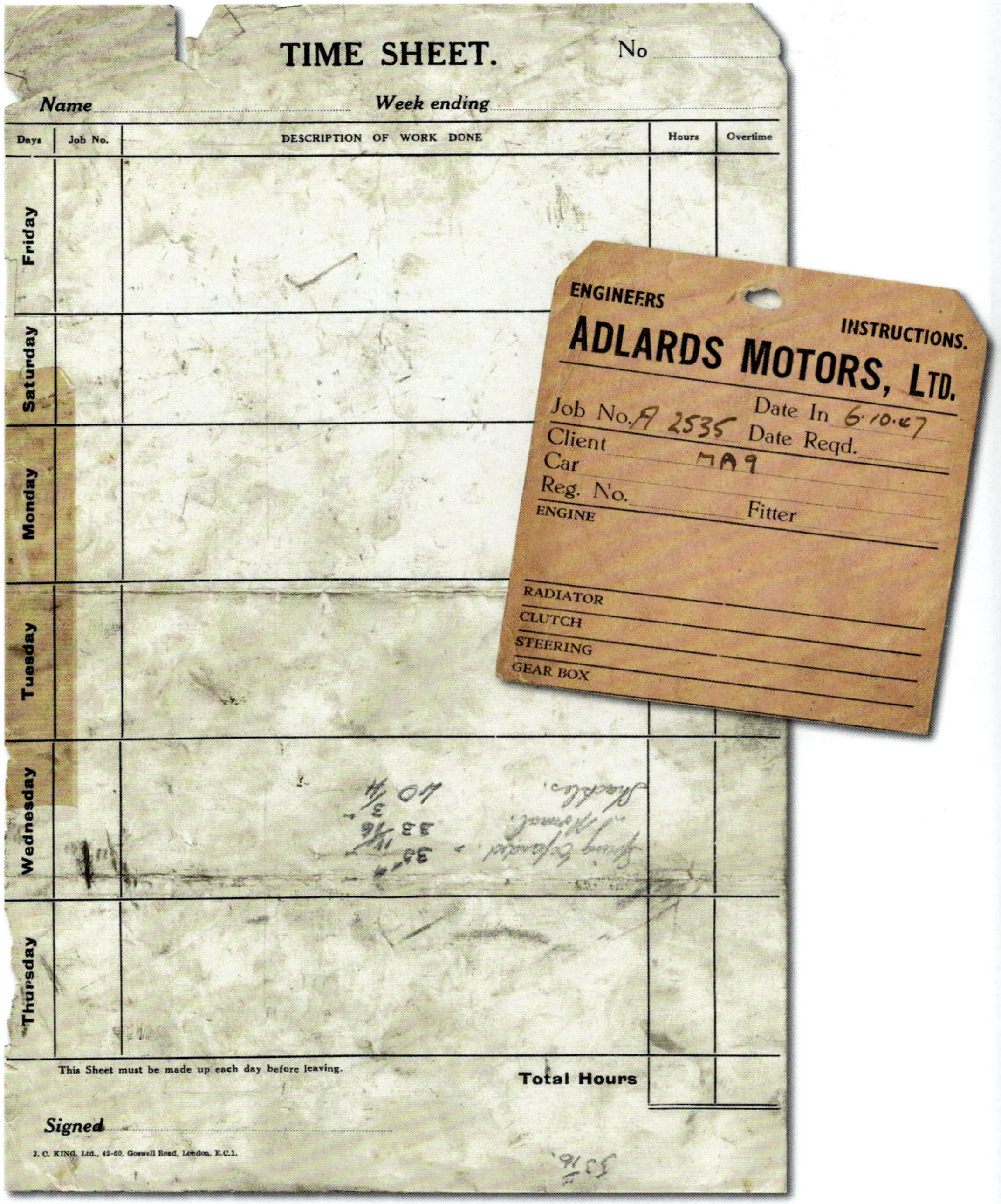

TIME SHEET.   No

Name ....   Week ending ....

Days	Job No.	DESCRIPTION OF WORK DONE	Hours	Overtime
Friday				
Saturday				
Monday				
Tuesday				
Wednesday				
Thursday				

This Sheet must be made up each day before leaving.   Total Hours

Signed ....

J. C. KING, Ltd., 42-60, Goswell Road, London, E.C.1.

ENGINEERS **INSTRUCTIONS.**

ADLARDS MOTORS, LTD.

Job No. A 2535   Date In 6·10·67
Client   Date Reqd.
Car   MA9
Reg. No.
ENGINE   Fitter

RADIATOR
CLUTCH
STEERING
GEAR BOX

An original blank timesheet and a partly complete Engineer's Instructions that would be hung on the frame of the cars.

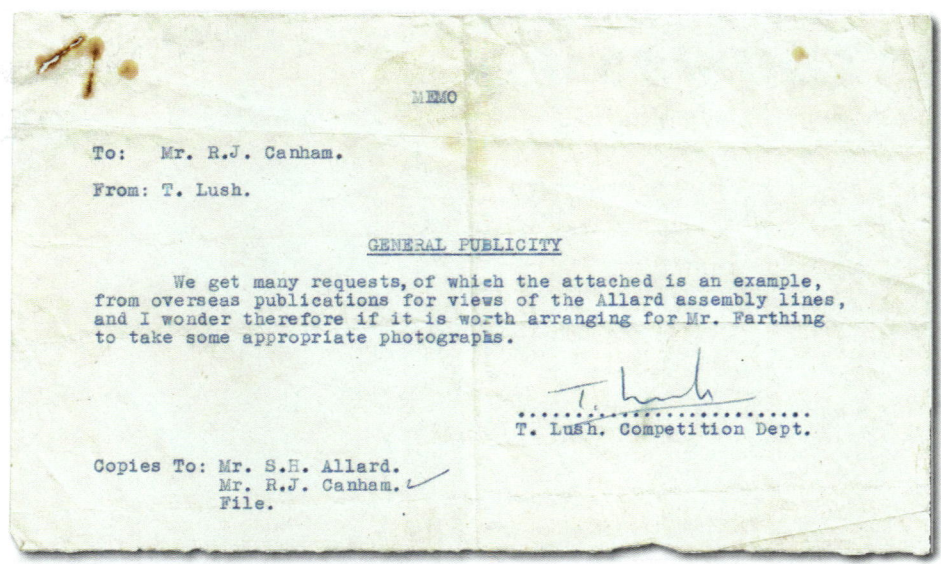

MEMO

To: Mr. R.J. Canham.

From: T. Lush.

GENERAL PUBLICITY

We get many requests, of which the attached is an example, from overseas publications for views of the Allard assembly lines, and I wonder therefore if it is worth arranging for Mr. Farthing to take some appropriate photographs.

T. Lush. Competition Dept.

Copies To: Mr. S.H. Allard.
Mr. R.J. Canham.
File.

This request resulted in photographs being taken in the factory or workshops although it was sometimes thought recording the back of house reality could put off customers of expensive vehicles. Photographic consultant, John Farthing, was called as and when required and the upper missive led to the set that follows.

On page 598, descriptions for the photographs of the build process were published in *The Motor* in March, 1948.

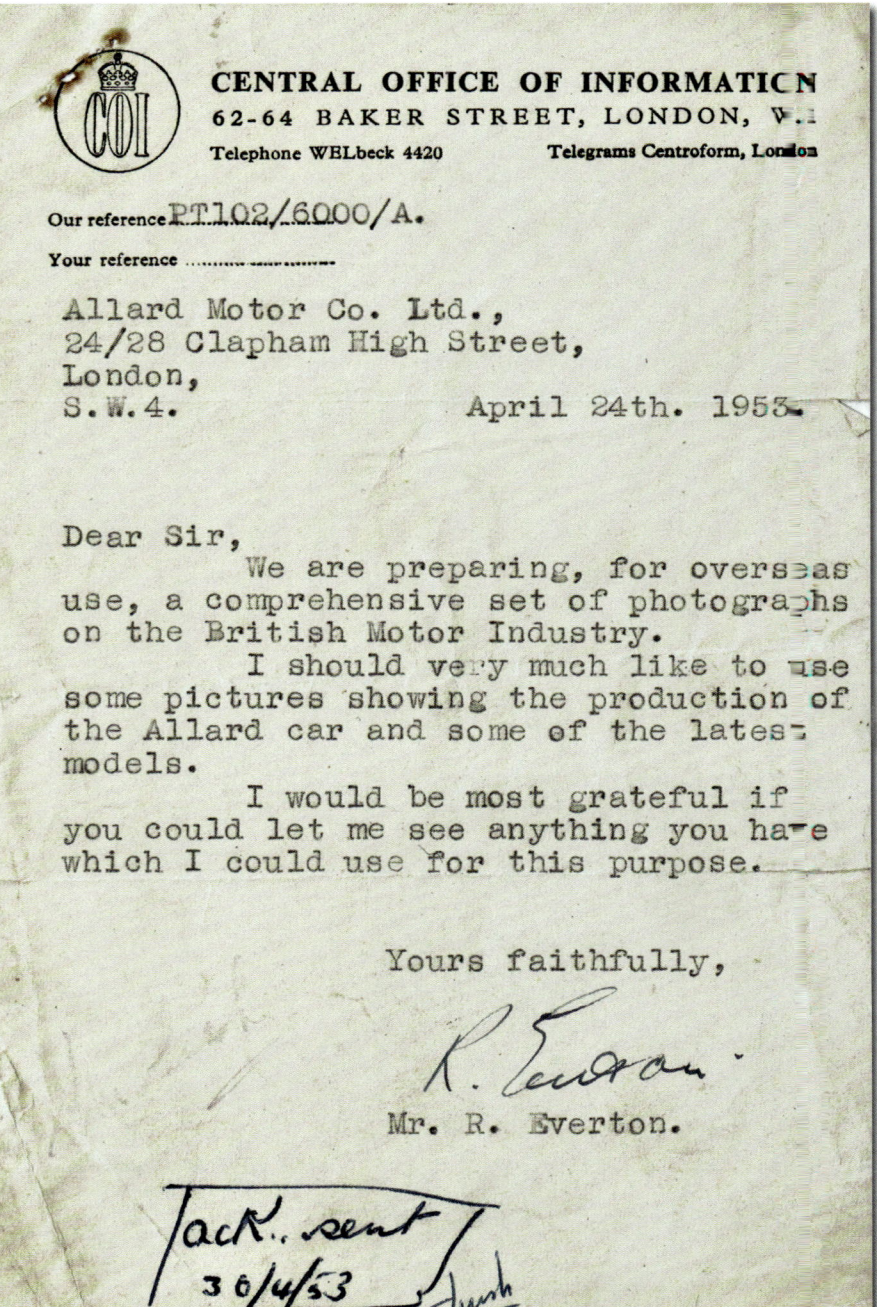

CENTRAL OFFICE OF INFORMATION
62-64 BAKER STREET, LONDON, W.1
Telephone WELbeck 4420   Telegrams Centroform, London

Our reference RT102/6000/A.

Your reference ....

Allard Motor Co. Ltd.,
24/28 Clapham High Street,
London,
S.W.4.   April 24th. 1953.

Dear Sir,

We are preparing, for overseas use, a comprehensive set of photographs on the British Motor Industry.

I should very much like to use some pictures showing the production of the Allard car and some of the latest models.

I would be most grateful if you could let me see anything you have which I could use for this purpose.

Yours faithfully,

Mr. R. Everton.

ack.. sent
30/4/53

OUTPUT from ENTHUSIASM

How a Company Directed by an Active Competitions Driver Builds High-performance Cars at a Reasonable Price

Reprinted from "The Motor," March 10, 1948

MANY readers will have watched with interest the evolution of the Allard car, from the pre-1939 era, when hardly two Allard Specials were ever made alike, to the present-day standardization of a few very closely related models which cater for quite a wide range of sporting tastes.

Sydney Allard's first Special was built out of Ford V8 components, with the idea that a high-performance car suitable for competitions could thereby be evolved cheaply and that spare parts also would be inexpensive. The Allard of to-day can no longer be described as a modified Ford V8, yet it retains the same advantages of using numerous components which are produced in large quantities and readily replaceable anywhere in the world.

In so far as a clear dividing line can be drawn it may be said that the major structural components of the Allard are, almost without exception, designed and made specially for the car. On the other hand, the majority of the moving parts, and those components which are subject to wear and may conceivably require eventual replacement, are either of Ford manufacture or are interchangeable with Ford components. Finally, the various open and convertible bodies which are available are, of course, all coachbuilt specially for the chassis.

Concentration of Effort

The Allard factory at Clapham is of considerable interest, and careful long-term planning having borne fruit, the present output of about 10 cars per week is steadily increasing. This production rate from a comparatively small works results from a well-conceived use of assembly jigs, and from a basic design which allows models of different characteristics to be produced without waste of effort.

The cross-braced, box-section chassis frame, to quote the example of the car's very foundation, is built up from pressings at Clapham, the same parts being used for all models. The wheelbase differs by 6 ins. as between two- and four-seater cars, however, and this difference is attained by varying the cross-bracing member location and shortening the front dumbirons as required.

The independent front suspension assembly is built up from special Allard forgings, and ribbed-drum Lockheed hydraulic brakes are employed, but such parts as hub bearings and steering ball joints are of Ford design. The rear axle assembly is basically Ford, but the narrower track of the open cars is obtained by cutting and rewelding the casing, then re-machining Ford-type axle shafts to suit. The torque tube is also shortened, and a Hardy-Spicer propeller shaft which eliminates the need for a centre steady bearing is installed.

Assembly processes can account for much of a car's cost, and the Allard Motor Company have evolved a flow production procedure which, without introducing an inflexibility of system unsuited to their individualistic product, does get work done with the minimum of costly delay. Cars progress systematically around the assembly shop, from the initial stage of a bare chassis frame until they are ready for the coachbuilders.

Favoured Practice

In accordance with a practice which is steadily growing in favour, the initial stages of assembly are carried out with the chassis frame upside down, in which attitude it is found easiest to install the independent front suspension system and the rear axle with its transverse spring. Once this stage has been passed, however, the car is set upon its own wheels, to pass on for engine installation and completion of assembly.

Three standard types of coachwork are available on the Allard—an open two-seater on the short chassis, an open four-seater on the long chassis, and a convertible coupé on a long chassis with a slightly increased rear track.

The various bodies are of advanced appearance, but use orthodox constructional methods, with steel mudguards and light-alloy body panels over a wooden frame. As with the chassis, however, production arrangements have been so planned as to give a fairly high output at the minimum cost consistent with the required quality standards.

All the bodies are built on jigs, so that sub-assemblies such as sections of framework or panelling are interchangeable and can be assembled into a car with the minimum of delay. The same standardization is extended to such components as hoods, the frames of which are built and covered before fitting to the car.

What sort of a car results from this scheme of mass-production in miniature, based on the policy of using standard components to the greatest possible extent, can best be judged from the Continental Road Test published in " The Motor " on March 10, 1948. What a visit to the factory reveals is how production in numbers has allowed a hand-built 3.6-litre sporting car, versatile enough to suit conditions almost anywhere in the world, to be marketed at a very competitive price.

Assembly begins with the building up of the chassis in this jig.

Rear axles are fitted with Lockheed brakes and Hardy Spicer propeller shafts.

Chassis frames are inverted for the installation of suspension systems, brake-operating gear and exhaust piping, then set upon their wheels and passed on for the mounting of engine, radiator and scuttle structure.

Finishing touches are given to a group of left-hand-drive models leaving the assembly line.

The jig-built coupe-body frames are panelled in aluminium.

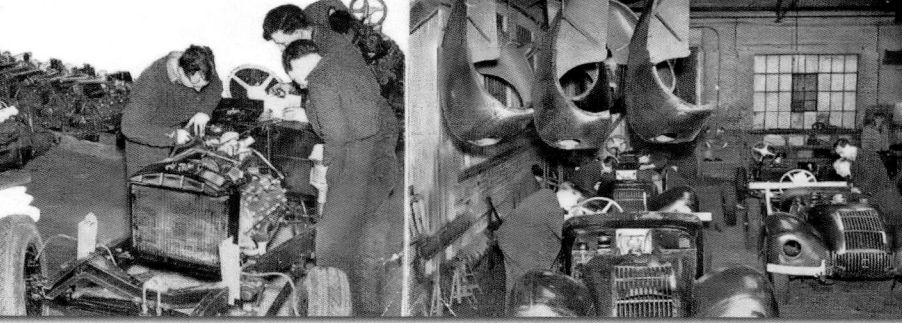

Cars are fitted with the steel wings and completed to a roadworthy stage at Clapham, while the bodies are built in an associated works at Fulham.

The Motor published the photographs and a description of their tour of the works in March 1948. The photographs on the following pages are the originals from the article.

The Men Who Built the Allard

The Men Who Built the Allard

The Men Who Built the Allard

The Men Who Built the Allard

The Men Who Built the Allard

The Men Who Built the Allard

This is the old gent with the flat cap that was on the river cruise (pages 595 and 596). He would have had to follow the Engineers Instructions for the camber angle on the front axle, as he was on axle assembly. As well as experienced craftsmen, Allard had junior apprentices and they were expected to move around all the separate disciplines and sections. Pages 615-617 offer further insight into these workers, with the reminiscences from a man who was on that shop floor.

These report cards for M-type chassis 834 reveal the extent of work that went into each vehicle and would have been used at the end of the production line to ensure a perfect car leaves for the customer.

From the left: Engineer Gil Jepson, Chief Engineer Dudley Hume and road tester, Jimmie Minnion, are about to take the P2 chassis out on a test run on public roads from outside the Allard works at Park Hill, Clapham.

Jimmie Minnion (left) and Gil Jepson (right) are the testers after Dudley gives his approval. It was all perfectly acceptable in 1950s London to move and test partially complete cars in this way, indeed cars without engines were known to be pushed between sites.

Commercial and industrial activity spilled into residential streets as here at Park Hill, Clapham. Today the area is gentrified and the old site is now an assisted living block of well-designed flats named 'Allard Gardens' built in the early 90s.

Here at Park Hill the J2X Le Mans MXF 974, chassis 3049, in 1952 sporting the No.49 for the Silverstone event of that year whilst Reg Canham (second from right) looked on. Other J2X chassis on wheels can be seen in the foreground. (COURTESY ALLARD OWNERS CLUB)

Again at Park Hill in the same workshop is the J2X Le Mans MXF 974 (chassis 3049). Zora Arkus-Duntov, seen here, would compete in this car in the 1952 Le Mans. This photograph is taken nearly during the same period of time as the one seen opposite, but different cars are present.

Whilst visiting the Allard Park Hill site in 1953, General Curtis LeMay (left) and General Griswold (second from right) both purchased Allard JRs, as did a third US serviceman, Col. Tilley. Reg Canham (second from left) joins the General for a smoke whilst Griswold exchanges a joke with Sales Manager Dave Davis (right). What looks like a K2 is in the foreground being worked on. INSET: LeMay and Canham moved around the K2 revealing more of the equipment and the factory. The hanging rear of a body can be seen on the rear wall. It appears Canham is making some notes with pencil and notepad, perhaps the particulars for the JR.

The memoirs of Ian Young, an Allard apprentice

The wonderful story from Ian Young, an apprentice at Allard in 1952-53 at the age of 16, his handwritten memories of those days were pushed through my brother's workshop letterbox. An almost impossible crossing of paths between himself and me in 2021 led to this.

It is a small world! Riding my electric bike in 2021 towards the redundant power station at Berkeley in Gloucestershire, I heard the unmistakable sound of a distant Allard car approaching. In a flash it brought back memories of my short but happy days as an apprentice at the Allard Factory in Putney. As the car came into sight I could not resist putting my hand up for the driver to stop[1] – quite what the driver thought I don't know! Perhaps he thought I was about to complain about the noise? I swiftly told him of the fact that I was an apprentice there. He naturally relaxed and warmed to me when I proceeded to recount the stories and facts about my cherished days at the works.

I had always shown a great interest in all aspects of cars while at school, reading all the books and car magazines that I could get my hands on. My father recognised my interest and decided that when I left school that I should embark on a five-year apprenticeship in mechanical engineering. This would be combined with attending a college to pass an engineering qualification to equip me finally to aspire to a respectable job. In those days the only apprenticeship being offered in the South was to spend five years at the Ford Motor Company at Dagenham. Leaving home at my tender years did not appeal to me. Somehow my father came to hear the Allard Motor Company were offering a so-called training scheme which was combined with an engineering course at the nearby Wandsworth Further Education College for one day per week.

Eventually the day came when together with my father we arrived at the factory to be greeted by the office manager who showed us around the noisy factory. I recall the sight of half completed cars being worked on by various people. The noise of machinery, lathes, drills, and presses filled the building with incessant noise and smells. Finally, we were ushered into an office and presented with a large legal document to sign. This was called an indentures document; it stated the employment terms and wages paid for the apprenticeship (in the first year £2.50 per week.) We duly parted leaving me with a feeling of excitement for this new world I was about to enter. I was told that as part of my learning process I would go through all of the departments associated with building an Allard car. Time would tell that this bunch of apprentices were really cheap labour as the earning aspect was small! However, the atmosphere in which we all worked was still enjoyable. I was ear-marked as a new recruit and as such was the victim of many jokes. I arrived one Monday feeling especially nervous, clutching my overalls and sandwiches. To get there involved a bus and train, arriving at 8am to clock in. Eventually when I had £30 I bought a BSA motorcycle to get to work.

Ian starting National Service after leaving Allard.
(COURTESY OF IAN YOUNG)

[1] Gavin Allard in a J2.

My first job was in the stores issuing Ford V8 parts to be painted and removing the Ford name so they could be sold as Allard spares![2] I almost froze when I saw Sydney Allard appear usually accompanied by a director called Reg Canham. Reg used to parade around the factory issuing instructions to the workers. Famous racing drivers used to appear namely John Heath, George Abecassis; also, famous film stars bought Allard cars, but I can't now recall names. My favourite model was the J2X. Most cars were bound for the USA with many sent without an engine. A company nearby, Encon Bros, (Allard owned) made bodies and wood frames. I recall the year when the JR model was built to race at Le Mans. I sat in it and steered (no motor) around to Encon Bros.

The factory was in a poor area of housing but 50 years later it became an exclusive residential house renowned for the unique Hurlingham Club for high society. One year 30 years ago I was asked to judge the cars there and came across a Safari Estate owned by the then managing director of Aston Martin. His son was in it and when I told him I had worked on it, he was speechless. After winning the Monte Carlo rally in the P model it put Allard on the map. The burly Sydney Allard was often seen at the factory and to me a humble 16-year-old, he was like God! Before the era of pop stars, the flamboyant models were bought by film stars who used to visit the factory. A guy who owned a large radio business on the Tottenham Court Road[3] was often at the factory with Sydney and I recall he was a well-known Allard winner at motor sports events. Great excitement surrounded the one-off J2 car being prepared for the Le Mans 24-hour race. Winning the Monte Carlo rally put Allard on the map for sales, but UK steel rationing put a restriction on sales.

I recall the new small Palm Beach model aimed at the US market (Ford engine) to compete with the TR2 Triumph and the Austin Healey, plus the unique Safari Estate car with wooden body. There was another Allard business at Brixton who were Ford dealers and perhaps were the start of Ford V8 Allard cars? I visited Encon Bros where cars were half built with wooden frames. Back at the factory, I was put in the so-called design department where a miserable man spent his days wielding a slide rule and saying nothing. Quite why I was with him I never knew! An expert panel beater called Stan made the wings for the lovely J2X model. One day Reg Canham stopped by his bench whilst he was hammering away and suggested an alternative way. Stan put down his hammer, took the fag out of his mouth and bravely replied, "Why don't you go and have a s**t and clear your head!" With the reply, Reg Canham slunk off.

Another Mr Young who also worked at Allard, this is the sort of letter a senior employee at Allard would have received as work subsided and faded away forever.

[2] This was a normal process and included cutting the front axle into two parts.

[3] HMV Radio – Goff Imhof

On one occasion was drilling with a pillar drill and my hair caught up as I was too close resulting in my hair being torn out. No health and safety regulations in those days! Lunch hours were spent playing football on the factory forecourt much to the disapproval of passing motorists! There was no canteen at the factory and pies, etc, came from a local shop. Adjoining the factory was an office where Sydney Allard's brother, Dennis Allard, worked. He arrived daily on a large Vincent Black Shadow motorcycle from Esher where the Allard family lived. The Fifties was the era of the small specialist car manufacturers. I could list twenty, but they all eventually faded away. Happy days! Locking back, I enjoyed working there but I was never taught anything useful. I recall helping putting engines and suspension units on to chassis. Most of the body and paint came with cars from Encon around the corner.

After approximately 18 months my pay packet included a note saying owing to adverse trading your employment is terminated. I was speechless and could not believe it. I wrongly assumed the factory was closing but not the case as it continued for a while with the Clipper 3-wheeler model. For me, I had to go into the army for National Service.

Ian Young today as he sets about writing his story.

I had never driven a J2 until April 2021, and it was just half a mile on the road around my brother's workshop so he could listen for any irksome noises. During my return, a lone senior man on an electric bike flagged me down, it was Ian Young, whose story is written on these pages.

It was extremely unlikely that an ex-Allard employee — 70 years later, and far from London — stops an Allard of the type he worked on, and that happened to be driven by an Allard family member.

THE DEALERSHIPS WHO SOLD THE ALLARD

By the late 1940s, the Allard Motor Company had built up a reputation, and gained a sizeable niche in the performance car market partially due to the running start Sydney gave himself by purchasing the spares leftover from the war effort and the business he had run in Hugon Road, Fulham (until 1946) servicing and repairing mainly Ford base vehicles from the front.

Motor businesses across the country, and within a short time, across the world, wanted to offer the Allard for sale and this needed a dealer network. By 1948, Sydney had built up a strong network across the nation as may be seen with this agents list on the right.

The map of the local area created by Allard at that time (see opposite page) shows just how close the Allard/Adlards network was to each other.

Look further and the national network is shown in advertisements and images extending to the USA and beyond.

For a brief number of years a small firm had a wide reach across the world.

ALLARD AGENTS

ALLARD SERVICE DEPT.
51 Upper Richmond Road, London SW15
Telephone Putney 2333

District	*Agent*
LONDON — SE & SW, Surrey, Kent, Sussex	Messrs Adlards Motors Ltd Acre Lane, Brixton SW2
London — W & NW, Middlesex, Hertfordshire, Bedfordshire	Messrs Dagenham Motors Ltd Balderton Street W1
London — WC, E & N, Essex	Messrs A. E. Gould Ltd 290-292 Regent Street W1
Hants, Wilts. and Dorset, Isle of Wight	Messrs F. English Ltd Langley Road, Branksome, Bournemouth
Somerset, Devon, Cornwall	Messrs Hughes of Exeter St. David's Hill, Exeter
Oxfordshire, Berkshire and Buckinghamshire	Messrs Hartwells Ltd Banbury Road, Oxford
Gloucestershire, Worcestershire, Herefordshire	Messrs Taylors (Gloucester) Ltd 26 Worcester Street, Gloucester
Glamorgan, Monmouth, Pembroke, Carmarthen, Brecknock, Radnor, Cardigan	Messrs A. E. Harris Ltd 10-11 Castle Street, Cardiff
Flint, Denbigh, Anglesey, Caernarvon, Merioneth, Montgomery, Shropshire	Messrs Furrows Ltd The Shrewsbury Garage, Cotton Hill Shrewsbury
Suffolk, Norfolk, Cambridge, Huntingdon	Messrs Mann Egerton & Co 31 King Street, Norwich
Warwickshire, Leicestershire, Northampton, Rutland	Bristol Street Motors Ltd 164-172 Bristol Street, Birmingham 5
Staffordshire, Derbyshire, Nottinghamshire, Lincolnshire	Universal Car Co (Derby) Ltd St. Helen's Street, Derby
Lancashire and Cheshire	Messrs H. E. Nunn & Co Ltd 282 Bury New Road, Manchester
Yorkshire	Messrs Tate of Leeds Ltd New York Road, Leeds 2
Cumberland, Westmorland, Durham, Northumberland	Messrs R. H. Patterson & Co Ltd Forth Street Works, Newcastle-on-Tyne
Wigtown, Kirkcudbright, Dumfries, Lanark, Ayr, Dumbarton, Renfrew, Stirling, Argyll, Bute, Arran	Messrs George & Jobling 140-160 Bothwell Street, Glasgow
Roxburgh, Berwick, Selkirk, Midlothian, East Lothian, West Lothian, Peebles	Messrs Alexanders of Edinburgh Ltd Semple Street, Edinburgh
Kincardine, Aberdeen, Inverness, Banff, Moray, Nairn, Perth, Ross, Cromarty, Sutherland, Hebrides, Skye, Angus, Fife, Caithness, Orkneys, Shetlands, Kinross, Clackmannan	Messrs Frew & Co Ltd 14 Princes Street, Perth
Northern Ireland	Messrs R. E. Hamilton & Co 32 Linenhall Street, Belfast

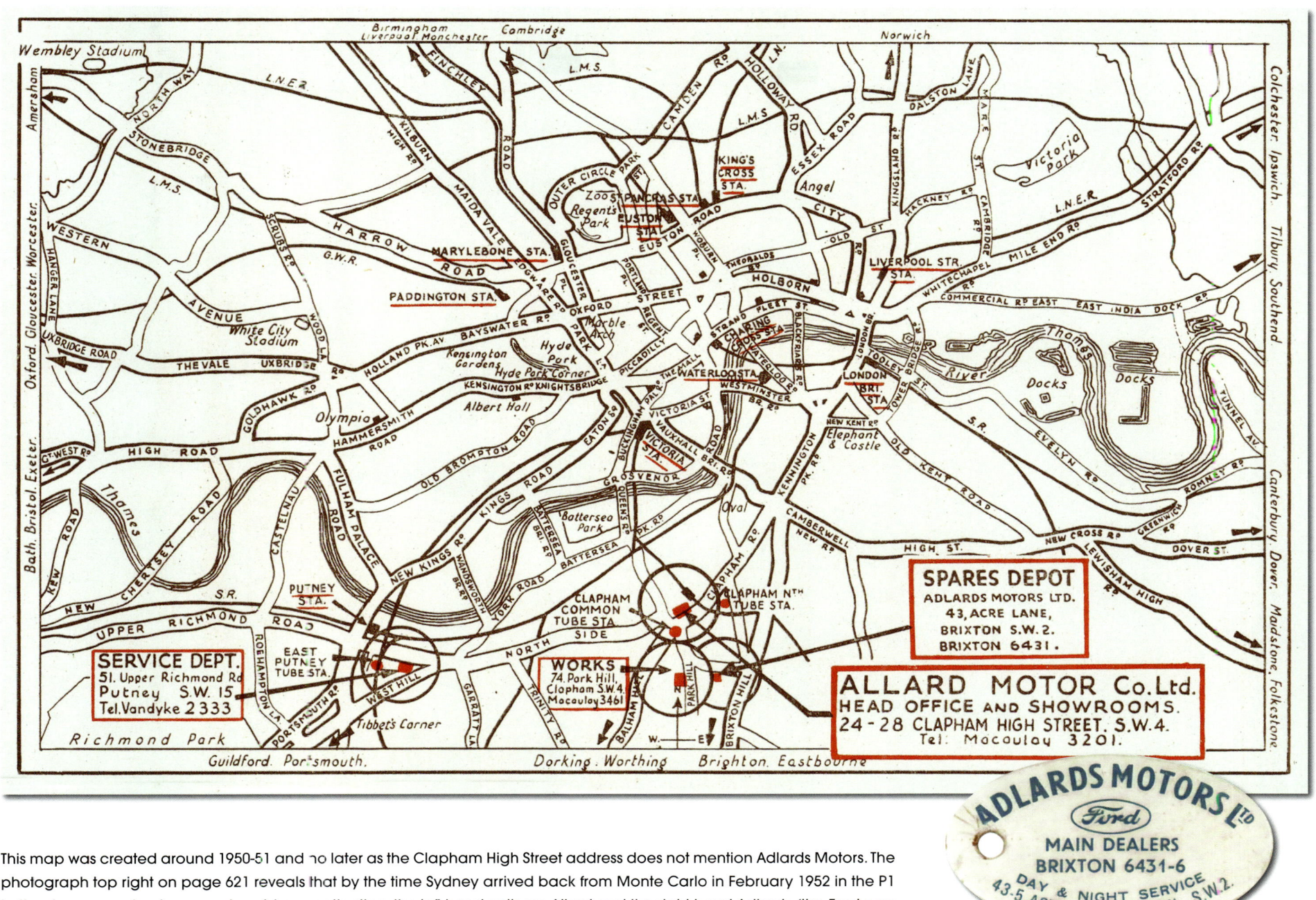

SERVICE DEPT.
51. Upper Richmond Rd
Putney S.W. 15
Tel. Vandyke 2333

WORKS
74. Park Hill,
Clapham S.W.4.
Macaulay 3461

SPARES DEPOT
ADLARDS MOTORS LTD.
43. ACRE LANE,
BRIXTON S.W. 2.
BRIXTON 6431.

ALLARD MOTOR Co. Ltd.
HEAD OFFICE AND SHOWROOMS.
24-28 CLAPHAM HIGH STREET. S.W.4.
Tel. Macaulay 3201.

ADLARDS MOTORS LTD
Ford
MAIN DEALERS
BRIXTON 6431-6
DAY & NIGHT SERVICE
43.5 ACRE LANE. LONDON, S.W.2.

This map was created around 1950-51 and no later as the Clapham High Street address does not mention Adlards Motors. The photograph top right on page 621 reveals that by the time Sydney arrived back from Monte Carlo in February 1952 in the P1 to the showrooms to cheers and world press attention, the left hand unit was Allard and the right hand Adlards (the Ford cars and commercial vehicles side) contrary to this map which does not note Adlards at all on the high street.

A mixture of items from the photograph with no Allards, a running board plaque and a motor magazine advert, how are these linked?

The fact the unmarked photograph was in the Allard family archive with a Rolls-Royce in the photo suggest that this is the Southern Motor Company location that was the same Park Hill works that Allard occupied from 1946. The businesses were closely linked by family. The May family owned the Southern Motor Company (Rolls-Royce, Bentley and other exclusive vehicle sales/refurbishment and coachbuilding), Alan May married Sydney's sister Mary and Sydney married Alan's sister Eleanor (in 1936). They had known each other from the Streatham and District Motorcycle Club. There is clearly wartime bomb damage so this could be anytime from May 1940 until 1944.

ABOVE/ABOVE LEFT: Clapham High Street in February 1952 after Sydney has returned from his Monte Carlo rally victory leaving the slightly battered P1 for onlookers to view.

LEFT: This was Sydney's monumental moment in his motoring career and it clearly was a big thing to staff and well-wishers.

The clearest photographs of the Clapham High Street showrooms are offered in the next set of four from the Adlards official album. This was the front of the Adlards' side. The Thames vans in some of the photographs date from 1952-1957, and the earlier models promoted the new vehicle range that became highly successful.

This is the second of the set showing the view into the shop and a small insight to the Allard side.

This shows the view into the shop from the Allard side with the ornate curved staircase to the rear that features on page 551 with the Steyr Allard. The area behind this concealed a room called the S1 workshop where Sydney would build some of his personal competition cars away from prying eyes.

The last in the set is right at the front viewing the whole room, the front doors not shown on this unlike the other side, probably because this side had advertising for Adlards Motors and Allard logos (pages 621 and 622).

Clapham High Street showrooms again, night time used to good effect with the wet road to show a super winter Monte Carlo scene with Sydney's 1959 Ford Zephyr rally car displayed in adjacent premises but around 1959 after Allard had ceased building cars. There has been a reface of the glazing for a more modern look. The Allard sign was gone, replaced with new backlit letters.

A closer picture shows arches have been formed joining the two premises and through one the ornate staircase survives. Several photographs exist of shop displays. This is one of the earliest and they are surprisingly accomplished in their arrangement. The addresses survive today with the long single storey shop and large Georgian style buildings at the rear that once housed Sydney's office.

This is the Keswick Road site immediately adjacent (to the right) to the sales room shown on pages 588 and 589. The three Allards used in the cavalcade age the scene to 1945 the pre-war FLX 650, the first L-type Allard HLB 424, chassis 102, and Goff Imhof's J1 HLP 5, chassis 106. Tom Lush stands to the far right with General Manager Reg Canham left of him.

(COURTESY OF CHRISSIE KONIG)

The Dealerships who Sold the Allard

An image of the same location, circa 1960.

Another view of Keswick Road here, the Allard Service sign clearly visible, customers would require spares and assistance for some years, laid testament to by the volume of letters I hold in the archive (refer to page 632). I should note that this site was by the junction with Upper Richmond road and only several hundred metres down the road was 51 Upper Richmond Road service department. This was the last item glued into the back page of the Adlards official album.

The Parts department at 51 Upper Richmond Road, Putney in approximately 1963 to 1965. The parts sold are performance related with the most impressive of those being supercharger systems of which Alan Allard (far left in doorway) became a notable expert. Later, he formed a career around this specialism. Allard bought the business from Chris Shorrock in 1959 and strongly promoted the products.

Dr. Johnston wrote a plea on a postcard of his M-type stranded on the street, albeit a high class street. Bill Tylee was stores manager and it is quite disconcerting to accept that Johnston knew Tylee so well. Perhaps the reader has better luck reading the registration to identify the car.

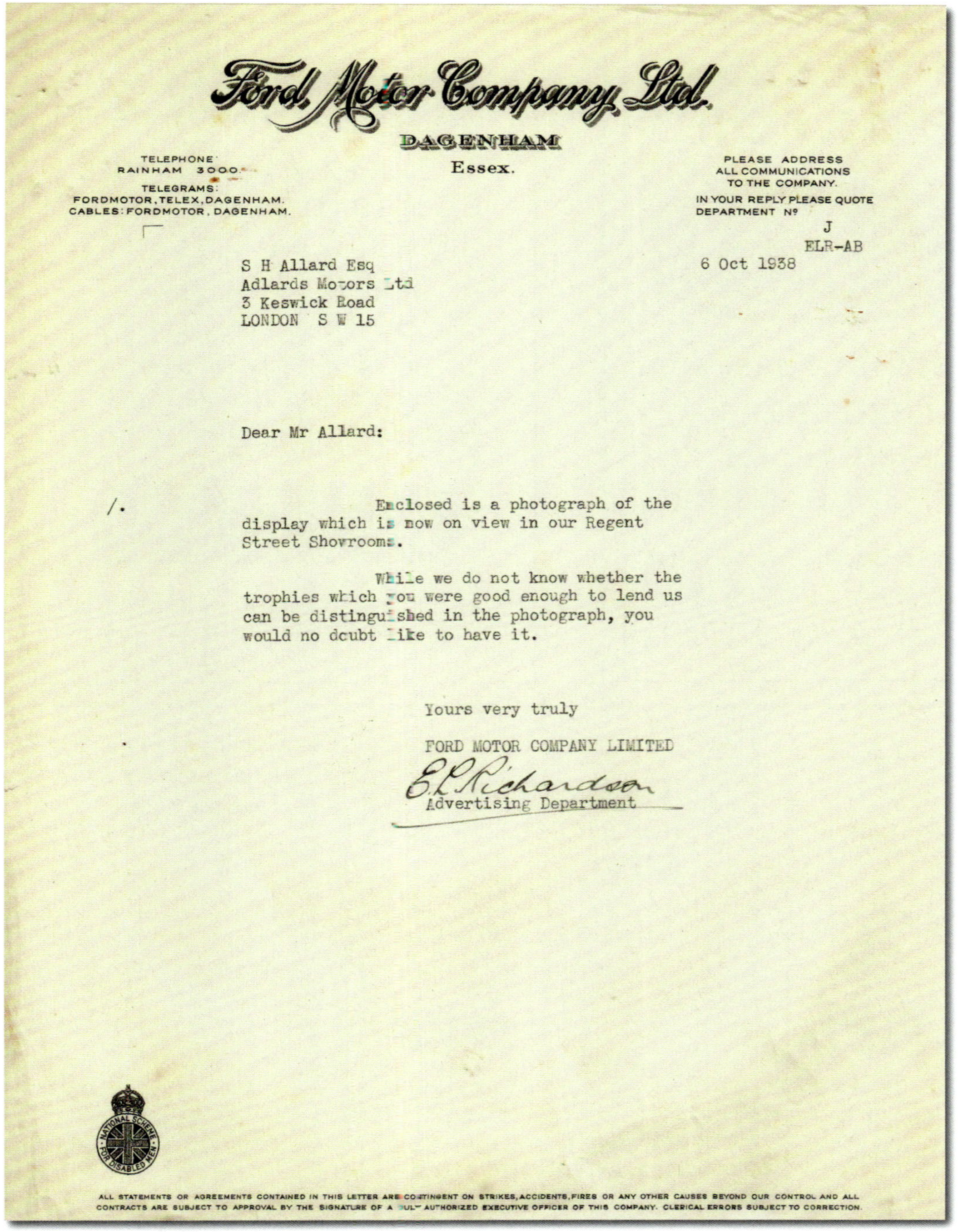

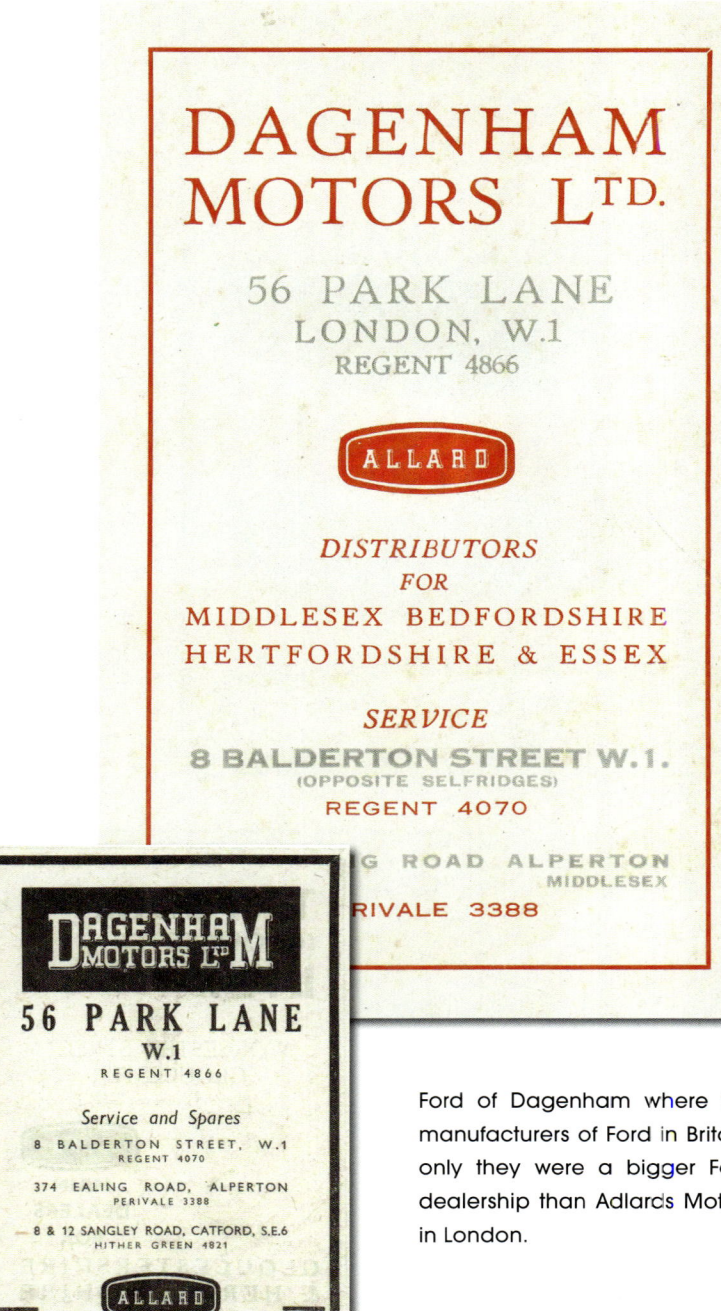

Ford Motor Company Ltd.
DAGENHAM
Essex.

TELEPHONE
RAINHAM 3000
TELEGRAMS:
FORDMOTOR, TELEX, DAGENHAM.
CABLES: FORDMOTOR, DAGENHAM.

PLEASE ADDRESS
ALL COMMUNICATIONS
TO THE COMPANY.
IN YOUR REPLY PLEASE QUOTE
DEPARTMENT Nº
J
ELR-AB

S H Allard Esq
Adlards Motors Ltd
3 Keswick Road
LONDON S W 15

6 Oct 1938

Dear Mr Allard:

/. Enclosed is a photograph of the display which is now on view in our Regent Street Showrooms.

While we do not know whether the trophies which you were good enough to lend us can be distinguished in the photograph, you would no doubt like to have it.

Yours very truly

FORD MOTOR COMPANY LIMITED

E L Richardson
Advertising Department

NATIONAL SCHEME FOR DISABLED MEN

ALL STATEMENTS OR AGREEMENTS CONTAINED IN THIS LETTER ARE CONTINGENT ON STRIKES, ACCIDENTS, FIRES OR ANY OTHER CAUSES BEYOND OUR CONTROL AND ALL CONTRACTS ARE SUBJECT TO APPROVAL BY THE SIGNATURE OF A DULY AUTHORIZED EXECUTIVE OFFICER OF THIS COMPANY. CLERICAL ERRORS SUBJECT TO CORRECTION.

Ford of Dagenham where the manufacturers of Ford in Britain, only they were a bigger Ford dealership than Adlards Motors in London.

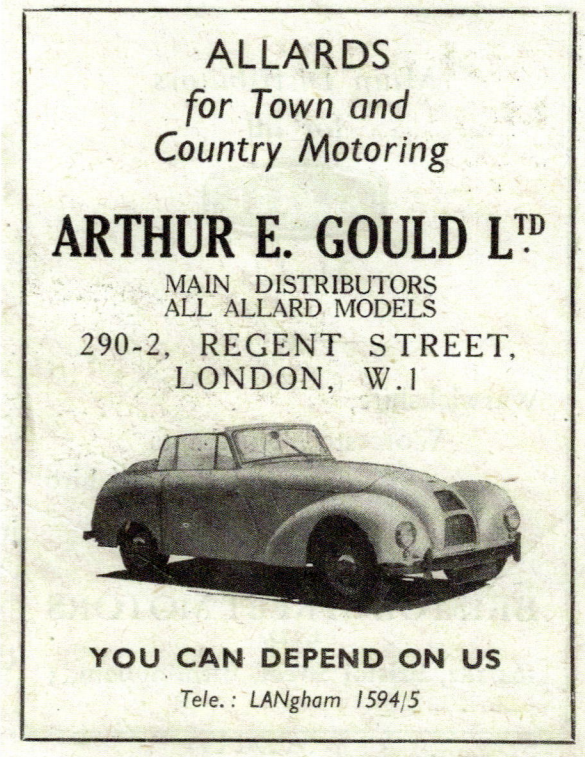

ALLARDS
*for Town and
Country Motoring*

ARTHUR E. GOULD L™

MAIN DISTRIBUTORS
ALL ALLARD MODELS

290-2, REGENT STREET,
LONDON, W.1

YOU CAN DEPEND ON US

Tele.: LANgham 1594/5

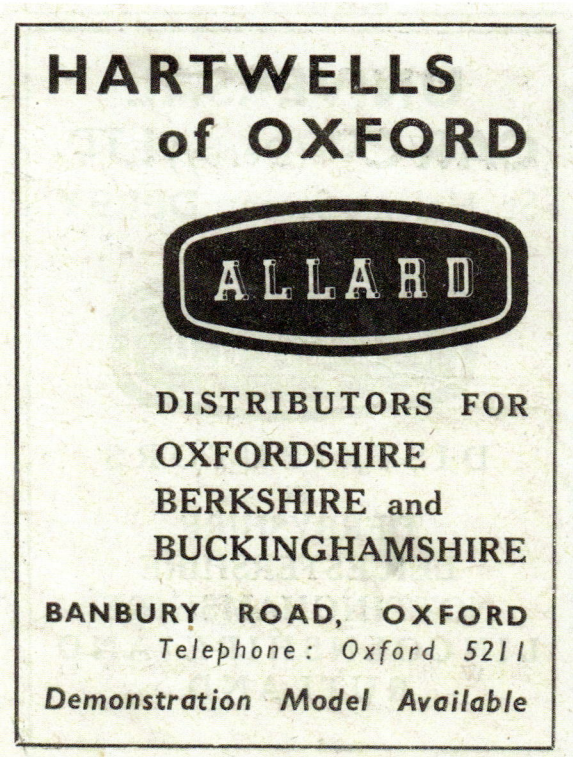

HARTWELLS
of OXFORD

ALLARD

DISTRIBUTORS FOR

OXFORDSHIRE
BERKSHIRE and
BUCKINGHAMSHIRE

BANBURY ROAD, OXFORD
Telephone : Oxford 5211

Demonstration Model Available

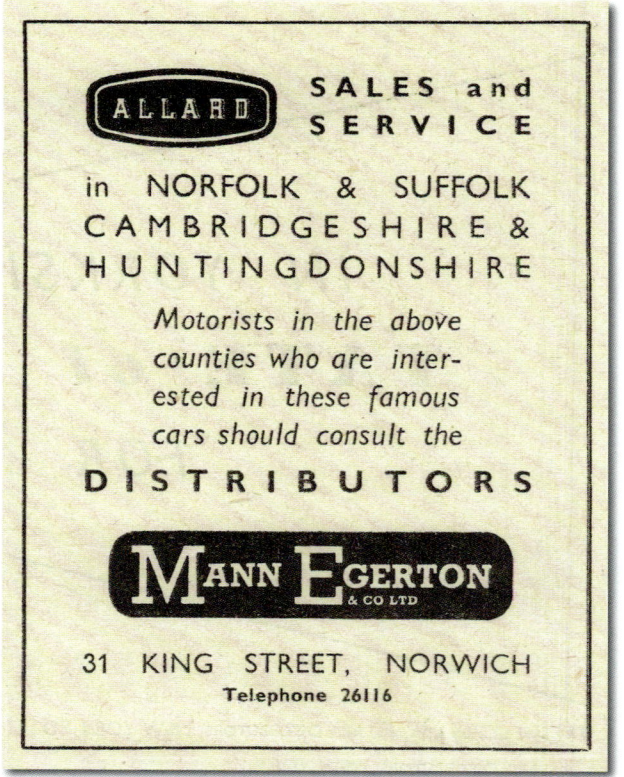

ALLARD SALES and SERVICE

in NORFOLK & SUFFOLK
CAMBRIDGESHIRE &
HUNTINGDONSHIRE

*Motorists in the above
counties who are inter-
ested in these famous
cars should consult the*

DISTRIBUTORS

Mann Egerton & CO LTD

31 KING STREET, NORWICH
Telephone 26116

F. ENGLISH LTD.

MAIN *Ford* DEALERS
BRANKSOME, BOURNEMOUTH
—— Phone : 5850 ——

Sole **ALLARD**
DISTRIBUTORS FOR
DORSET, HAMPSHIRE,
WILTSHIRE & ISLE OF WIGHT

TAYLORS
(GLOUCESTER)
LTD.

WORCESTER STREET
GLOUCESTER
Phone : Gloucester 22228

ALLARD

MAIN
DEALERS
FOR

GLOUCESTERSHIRE
& HEREFORDSHIRE

A wonderful selection of the
UK dealerships, all sold Allards
of multiple models.

Bristol Street Motors of Birmingham were one of Allard's biggest clients, and are a huge franchise today, including Ford.

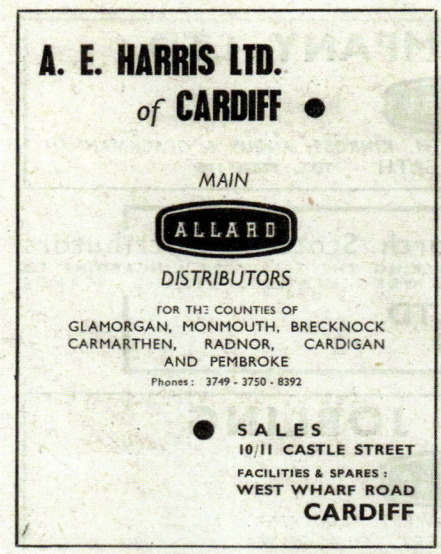

A. E. HARRIS LTD. of CARDIFF •

MAIN

ALLARD

DISTRIBUTORS

FOR THE COUNTIES OF
GLAMORGAN, MONMOUTH, BRECKNOCK
CARMARTHEN, RADNOR, CARDIGAN
AND PEMBROKE

Phones: 3749 - 3750 - 8392

• SALES
10/11 CASTLE STREET

FACILITIES & SPARES:
WEST WHARF ROAD
CARDIFF

MAIN ALLARD DEALERS

A. E. HARRIS LTD.

Sales 10/11, CASTLE STREET

Repairs / Spares WEST WHARF ROAD

CARDIFF

Telephone :- 3749 — 3750 — 8392 ; (Spares) 2312

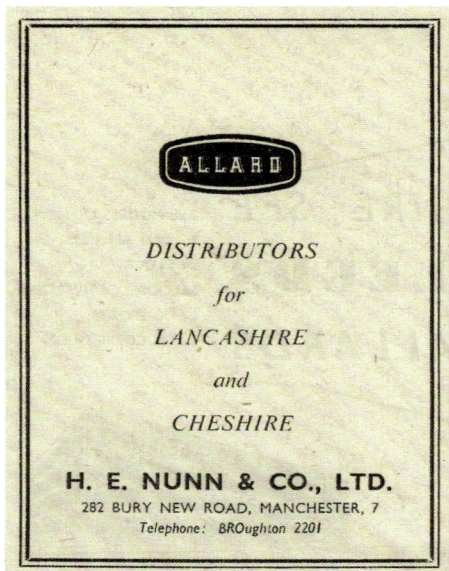

ALLARD

DISTRIBUTORS
for
LANCASHIRE
and
CHESHIRE

H. E. NUNN & CO., LTD.
282 BURY NEW ROAD, MANCHESTER, 7
Telephone: BROughton 2201

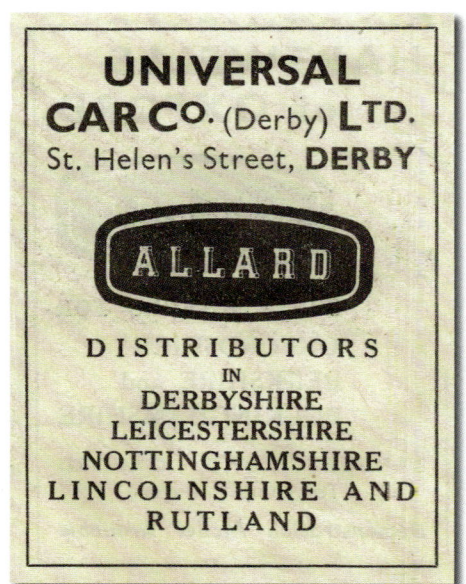

UNIVERSAL CAR CO. (Derby) LTD.
St. Helen's Street, DERBY

ALLARD

DISTRIBUTORS
IN
DERBYSHIRE
LEICESTERSHIRE
NOTTINGHAMSHIRE
LINCOLNSHIRE AND
RUTLAND

Allard Distributors for

DEVONSHIRE and CORNWALL

ALLARD

NEW CENTRAL GARAGE LTD.
Liskeard, Cornwall

★ GEORGE & JOBLING

ALLARD

DISTRIBUTORS FOR SOUTH-WEST SCOTLAND
140-160 BOTHWELL STREET, GLASGOW

TELEPHONE:
GLASGOW CENTRAL 6251/2/3

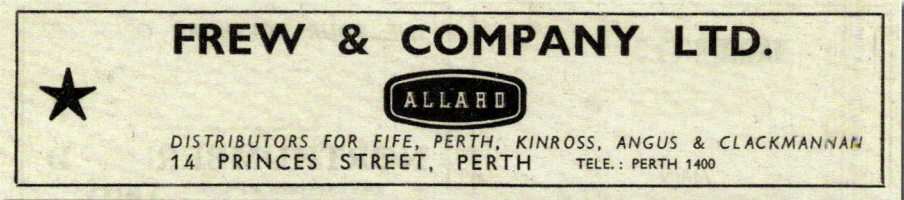

FREW & COMPANY LTD.

★ ALLARD

DISTRIBUTORS FOR FIFE, PERTH, KINROSS, ANGUS & CLACKMANNAN
14 PRINCES STREET, PERTH   TELE.: PERTH 1400

All of these were regular customers of Allard.

For ALLARDS in —

YORKSHIRE

- Quick and Efficient Repair Service
- Finest Car Valeting Station in the North
- Garage for over 2,000 cars

(Guaranteed Used Cars in Stock)

DISTRIBUTORS FOR YORKSHIRE

TATE of LEEDS LTD.

New York Road, Leeds   Tel. 31281

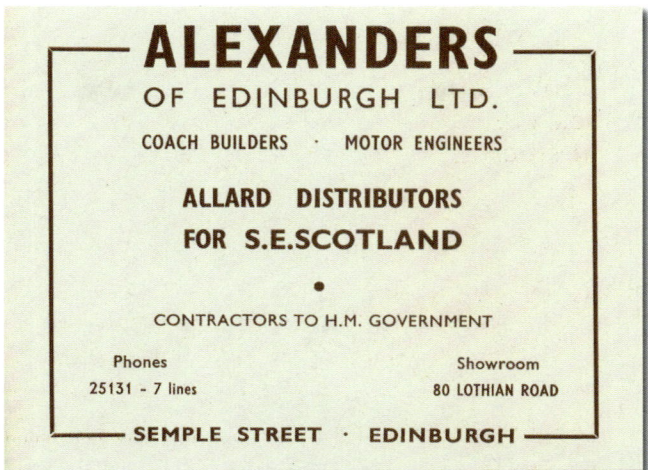

ALEXANDERS
OF EDINBURGH LTD.

COACH BUILDERS · MOTOR ENGINEERS

ALLARD DISTRIBUTORS
FOR S.E. SCOTLAND

•

CONTRACTORS TO H.M. GOVERNMENT

Phones   Showroom
25131 - 7 lines   80 LOTHIAN ROAD

SEMPLE STREET · EDINBURGH

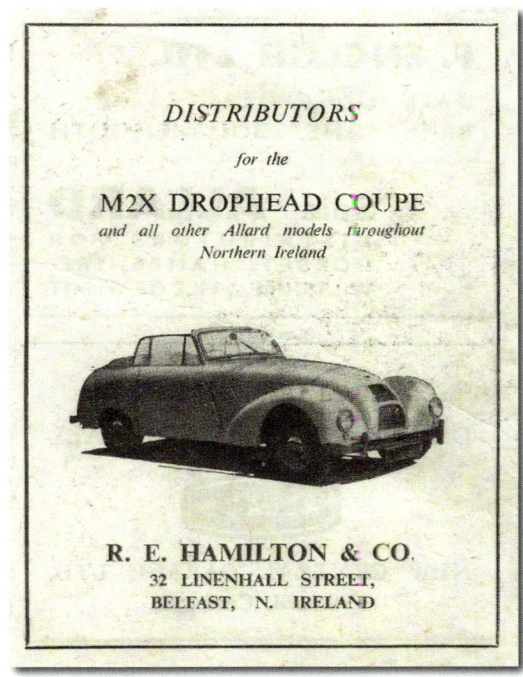

DISTRIBUTORS
for the

M2X DROPHEAD COUPE
and all other Allard models throughout Northern Ireland

R. E. HAMILTON & CO.
32 LINENHALL STREET,
BELFAST, N. IRELAND

IN YORKSHIRE SEE
TATE of LEEDS
FOR ALLARDS

ALL MODELS OF NEW & USED ALLARDS IN STOCK.
SALOON, CONVERTIBLE
2-STR. SPORTS
2-STR. COMPETITION

TATE of LEEDS Ltd., ALLARD DISTRIBUTORS, NEW YORK RD., LEEDS. Tel. 31281

Tates were the dominant dealership in the North of England, their showrooms and offices of enough architectural merit to be recorded within the RIBA's (Royal Institute of British Architects) records.

THE FOUR NORTHERN COUNTIES

CUMBERLAND
DURHAM
NORTHUMBERLAND
WESTMORLAND

MAIN **ALLARD** DEALERS

We specialize in
"SERVICE"

R.H. Patterson AND CO. LTD.

Forth Street,
NEWCASTLE UPON TYNE, I

ALLARD

Allard's Palm Beach
Sure is a "peach"

New stocks now here

Allard prices are $2995 and up
NOEL KIRK MOTORS
7176 SUNSET BLVD., HOLLYWOOD
ALLARD DISTRIBUTORS
for the Southwest U.S.A.

The new Noel Kirk Motors business were Allard fans and that was reflected in the orders. Being located on Sunset Boulevard with full length windows and a J2X in the window one would be mad not to walk in and if you could not stretch to a J2 you could have a Palm Beach or if not a Hillman Minx. (COURTESY OF KERRY HORAN)

The two J2Xs are tremendous eye candy and the advertising card notes 190hp plus! These are most possibly red J2X, chassis 3148, and Ivory J2X, chassis 3146, and places the photograph as early 1953. (COURTESY OF KERRY HORAN)

The exterior of Noel Kirk Motors, with floor space for five cars, and neon signs to be installed shortly. Two windows facing Sunset Boulevard. Apparently next door was a beauty parlour of good calibre. (COURTESY OF KERRY HORAN)

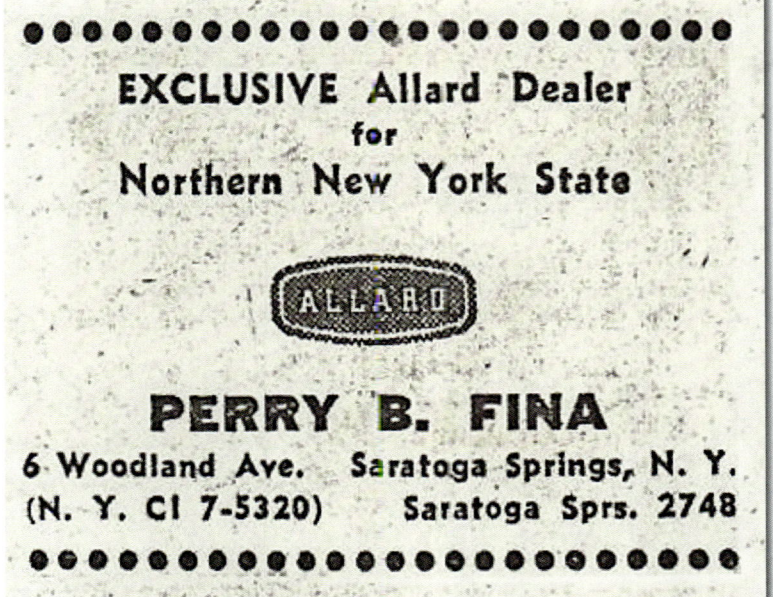

EXCLUSIVE Allard Dealer
for
Northern New York State

PERRY B. FINA

6 Woodland Ave.   Saratoga Springs, N.Y.
(N. Y. CI 7-5320)   Saratoga Sprs. 2748

ALLARD
Attention Dealers!

Eliminate your engine installation headaches. We are the leading Allard Distributors in the U.S.A. We will supply you with Allard Sports Cars complete with Cadillac, Chrysler, or other V-8 engines and other required equipment, ready for delivery to your clients.
Liberal discounts
R/P Imported Motor Car Co.
147 West 54th Street, New York 19, N. Y.
JUdson 6-5150
Major R. D. Seddon   Perry B. Fina

EXCLUSIVE Allard Dealer
for
Pennsylvania and Maryland

MAJOR RICHARD D. SEDDON
290 Park Ave., New York, N. Y.
JUdson 6-5150   MUrray Hill 8-5062 (eves.)

New K.3
Touring 3-Seater
on display

THE ALLARD MOTOR COMPANY LTD.
of London, England
Announces the Opening of
ALLARD MOTOR COMPANY, Inc.

. . . as sole and exclusive distributors of the world famous ALLARD Motor Cars for continental United States and Mexico. Current orders accepted for Spring delivery.

ALLARD MOTOR COMPANY, Inc.
141 West 53 St.
New York 19   Circle 6-9091

Congratulations to Auto magazine
Congratulations to the Allard
Winner of the Nevada State Cup at the Reno Sports Car Races

We can provide immediate delivery of these superb sports cars

The Allard J2	The Allard K2
$3450 PLUS ENGINE	$3420 PLUS ENGINE

Full-race Cadillac and V-8 Chrysler engines available

British Motor Car Co.

SAN FRANCISCO SHOWROOMS	SAN FRANCISCO SERVICE BUILDING
214 Van Ness Avenue on Automobile Row Pine and Sansome Streets in the Financial District	Complete Parts and Service 1460 Pine Street

WEST'S LARGEST DEALERS IN FOREIGN CARS
REPRESENTING MG, RILEY, JAGUAR, ROLLS ROYCE, HILLMAN MINX, DAIMLER, SUNBEAM-TALBOT, ASTON-MARTIN, HUMBER HAWK, MORRIS, SINGER, ROVER, SIMCA.

The J2 and J2X were strong sellers in the USA, occasionally multiple cars would be shipped in a group to some of these outlets, no mean feat for a small company.

GRANCOR
AUTOMOTIVE SPECIALISTS

Distributors

5150 N. WESTERN AVENUE
CHICAGO 25, ILLINOIS
Phone Longbeach 1-8088

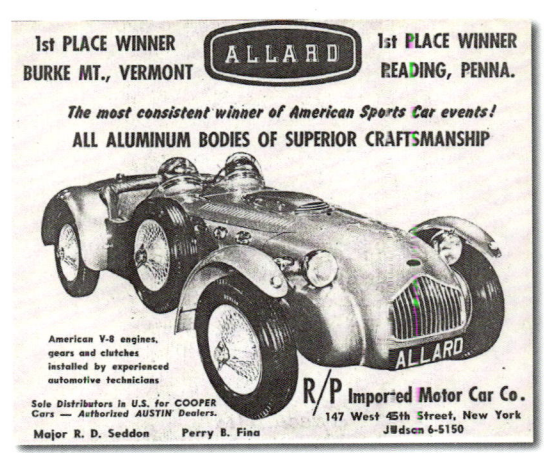

1st PLACE WINNER   1st PLACE WINNER
BURKE MT., VERMONT   READING, PENNA.

The most consistent winner of American Sports Car events!
ALL ALUMINUM BODIES OF SUPERIOR CRAFTSMANSHIP

American V-8 engines, gears and clutches installed by experienced automotive technicians

Sole Distributors in U.S. for COOPER Cars — Authorized AUSTIN Dealers.

R/P Imported Motor Car Co.
147 West 45th Street, New York
JUdson 6-5150
Major R. D. Seddon   Perry B. Fina

This unmarked photograph is clearly from a South American location but neither the J2 nor names on the building have allowed themselves to be identified. What is certain is that Allard's J2 and K2 were sold in low numbers to nations in this region of the world.

ABOVE: Peru was one of the South American countries where a J2 went.

RIGHT: In direct competition with Noel Kirk Motors their rival Moss wanted to offer all the models, however I have never before seen the description 'Sports Pheaton'.

Bell majored on the fierce competition car and even offered the ARDUN overhead valve conversion of the flathead 'flatty' engine with a significant uplift on the standard unit.

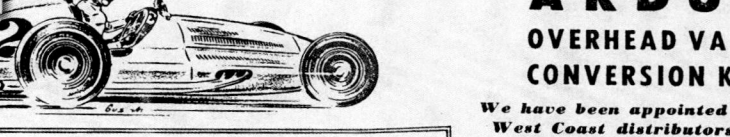

A J2 directly outside Bell's speedshop, identity unknown. The bar assembly on the front does the car no favours until the nose is bumped.

A COLOUR SLICE OF 1948

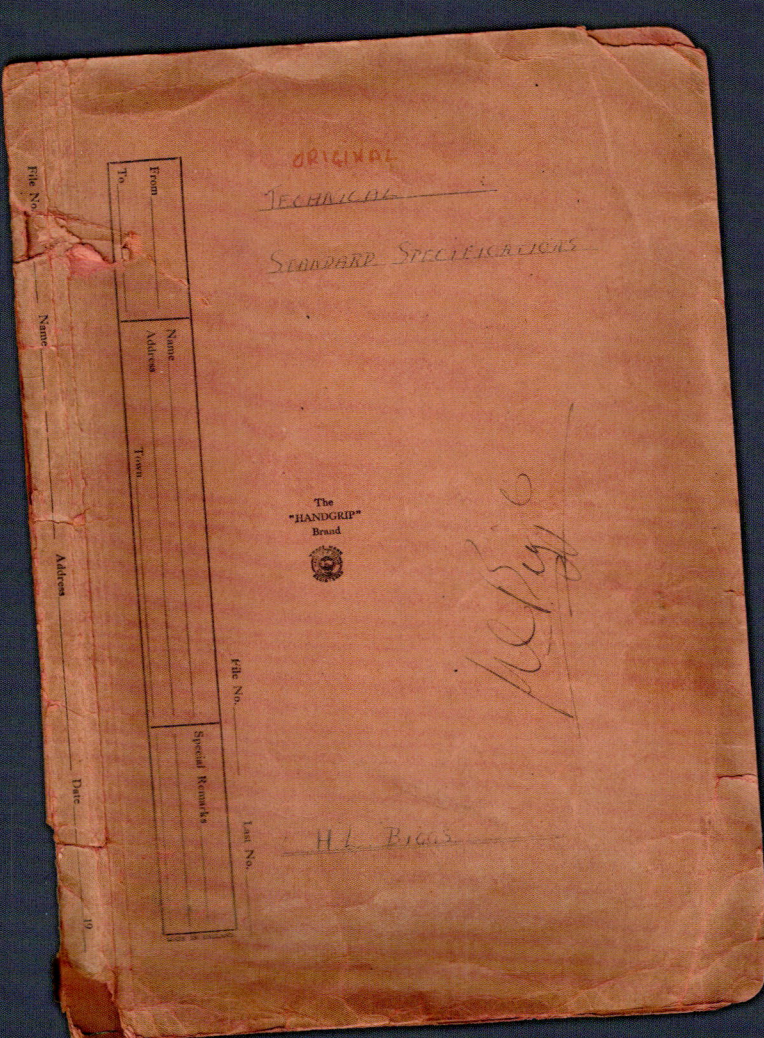

The discovery of a file with the name H. L. Biggs and contents all pertaining to the year 1948, raised my interest and joy.

Interest in who H. L. Biggs was and what he did, and joy at discovering a list of Allard colours which had never been seen before or known to exist.

I learned Harold Biggs was another friend of the family back in the Streatham and District Motorcycle Club, according to my father's memory and we know he was employed in the Parts department at the old Hugon Road site until 1946 when it moved. Perhaps he remained in that role and had these documents with him at Acre Lane, Brixton.

There were three documents in the folder, all shown on the opposite page.

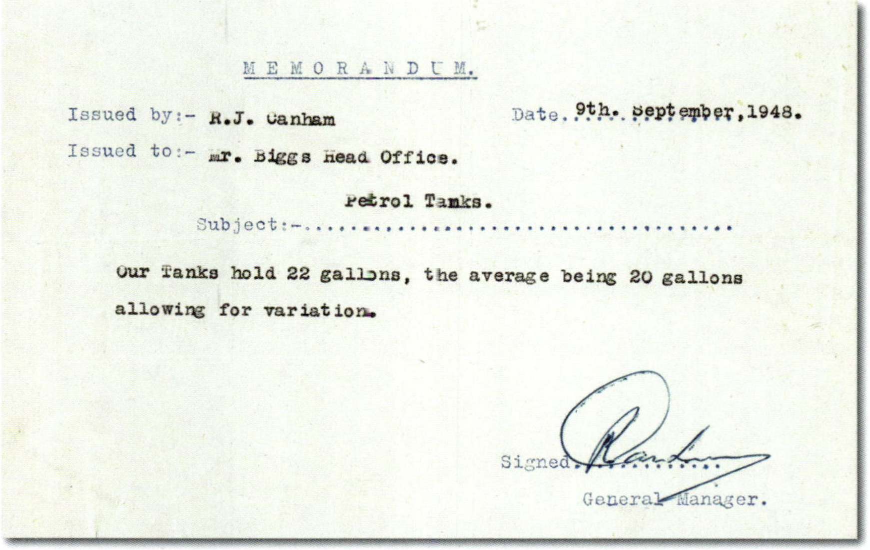

MEMORANDUM.

Issued by:- R.J. Canham   Date. 9th. September,1948.

Issued to:- Mr. Biggs Head Office.

Petrol Tanks.

Subject:-.......................................

Our Tanks hold 22 gallons, the average being 20 gallons
allowing for variation.

Signed
General Manager.

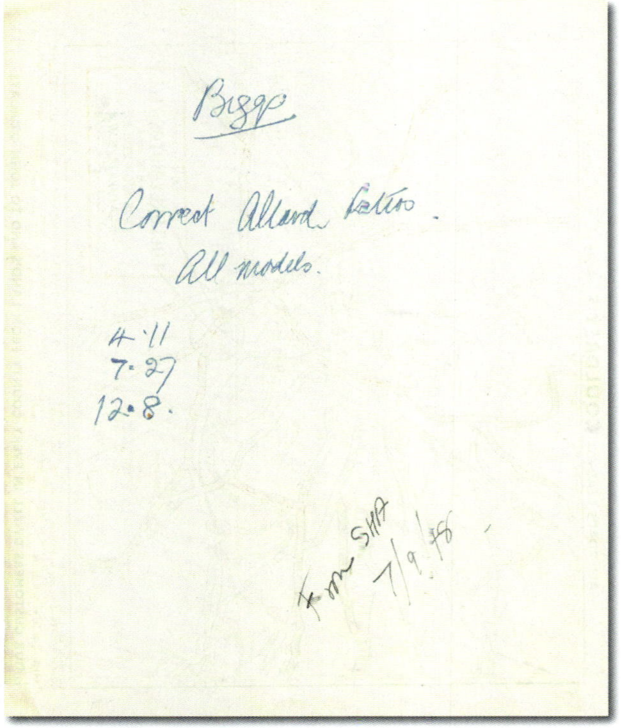

Biggs

Correct Allard Letter.
All models.

4.11
7.27
12.8.

From SWA
7/9/76

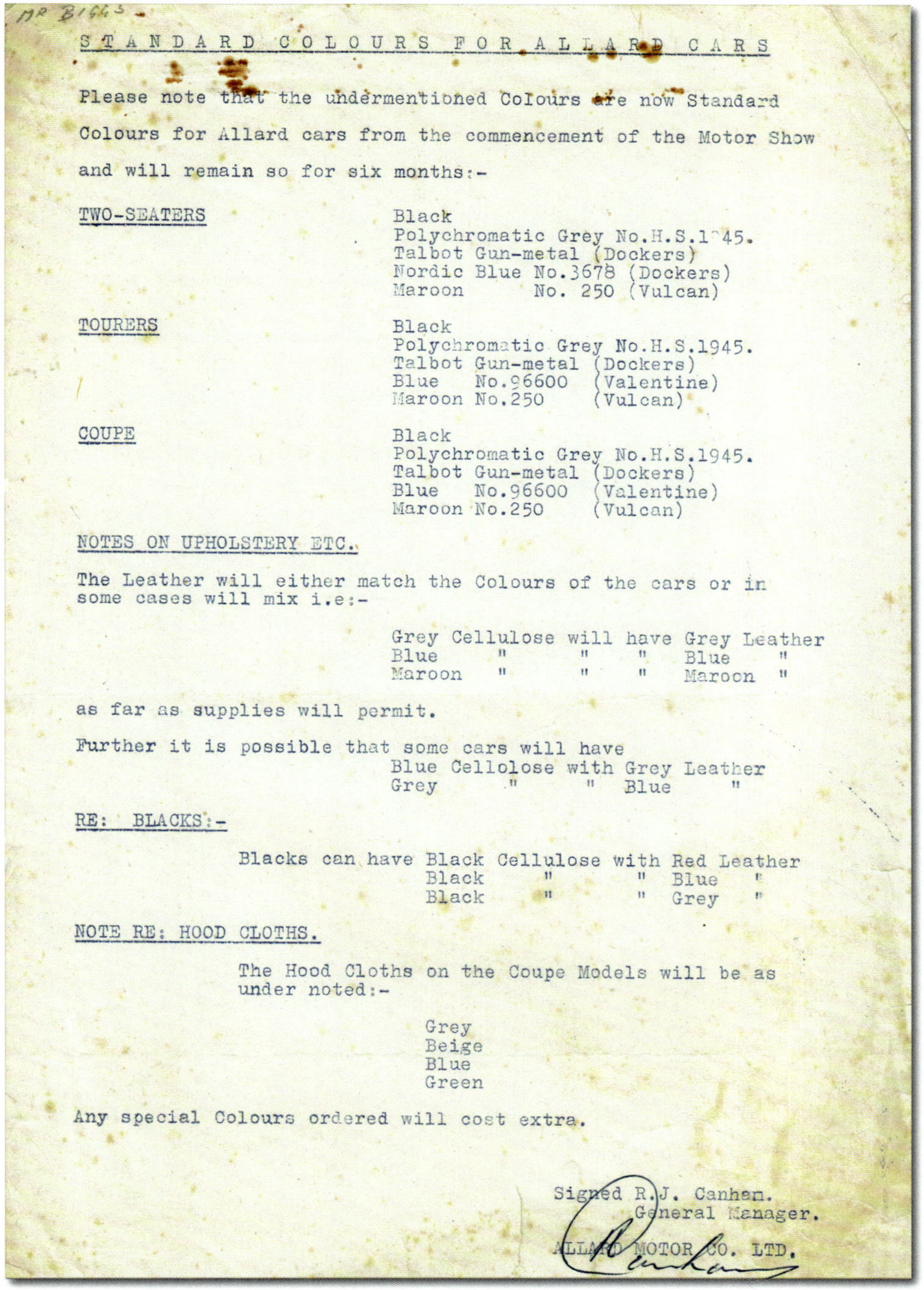

Until now, no known
statement of Allard
colours existed.

STANDARD COLOURS FOR ALLARD CARS

Please note that the undermentioned Colours are now Standard
Colours for Allard cars from the commencement of the Motor Show
and will remain so for six months:-

TWO-SEATERS   Black
                            Polychromatic Grey No.H.S.1945.
                            Talbot Gun-metal (Dockers)
                            Nordic Blue No.3678 (Dockers)
                            Maroon   No. 250 (Vulcan)

TOURERS   Black
                            Polychromatic Grey No.H.S.1945.
                            Talbot Gun-metal (Dockers)
                            Blue   No.96600   (Valentine)
                            Maroon No.250   (Vulcan)

COUPE   Black
                            Polychromatic Grey No.H.S.1945.
                            Talbot Gun-metal (Dockers)
                            Blue   No.96600   (Valentine)
                            Maroon No.250   (Vulcan)

NOTES ON UPHOLSTERY ETC.

The Leather will either match the Colours of the cars or in
some cases will mix i.e:-

                Grey Cellulose will have Grey Leather
                Blue   "   "   "   Blue   "
                Maroon "   "   "   Maroon "

as far as supplies will permit.

Further it is possible that some cars will have
                Blue Cellulose with Grey Leather
                Grey   "   " Blue   "

RE: BLACKS:-

                Blacks can have Black Cellulose with Red Leather
                Black   "   " Blue   "
                Black   "   " Grey   "

NOTE RE: HOOD CLOTHS.

                The Hood Cloths on the Coupe Models will be as
                under noted:-

                Grey
                Beige
                Blue
                Green

Any special Colours ordered will cost extra.

                            Signed R.J. Canham.
                            General Manager.
                            ALLARD MOTOR CO. LTD.

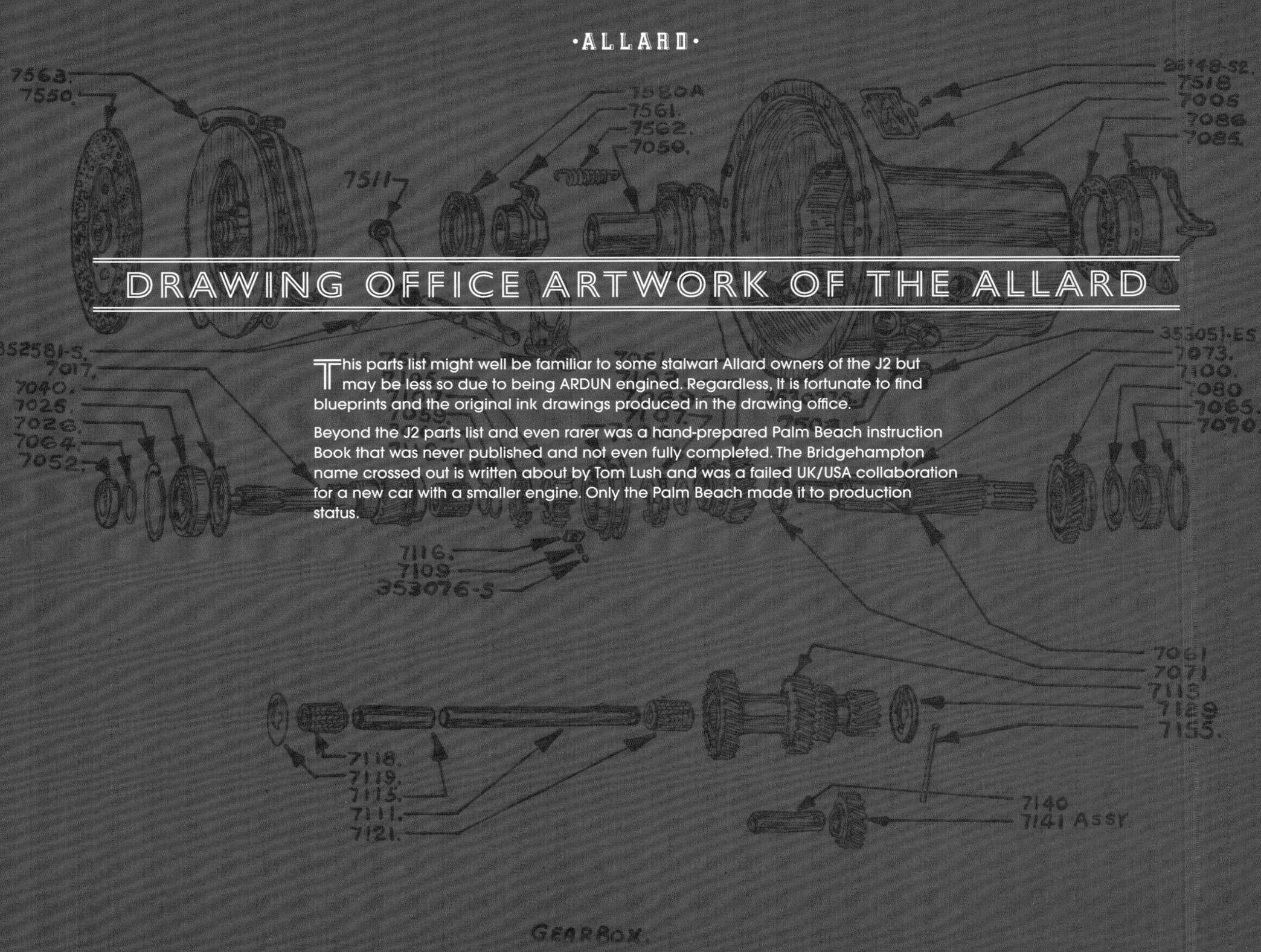

DRAWING OFFICE ARTWORK OF THE ALLARD

This parts list might well be familiar to some stalwart Allard owners of the J2 but may be less so due to being ARDUN engined. Regardless, It is fortunate to find blueprints and the original ink drawings produced in the drawing office.

Beyond the J2 parts list and even rarer was a hand-prepared Palm Beach instruction Book that was never published and not even fully completed. The Bridgehampton name crossed out is written about by Tom Lush and was a failed UK/USA collaboration for a new car with a smaller engine. Only the Palm Beach made it to production status.

GEARBOX.

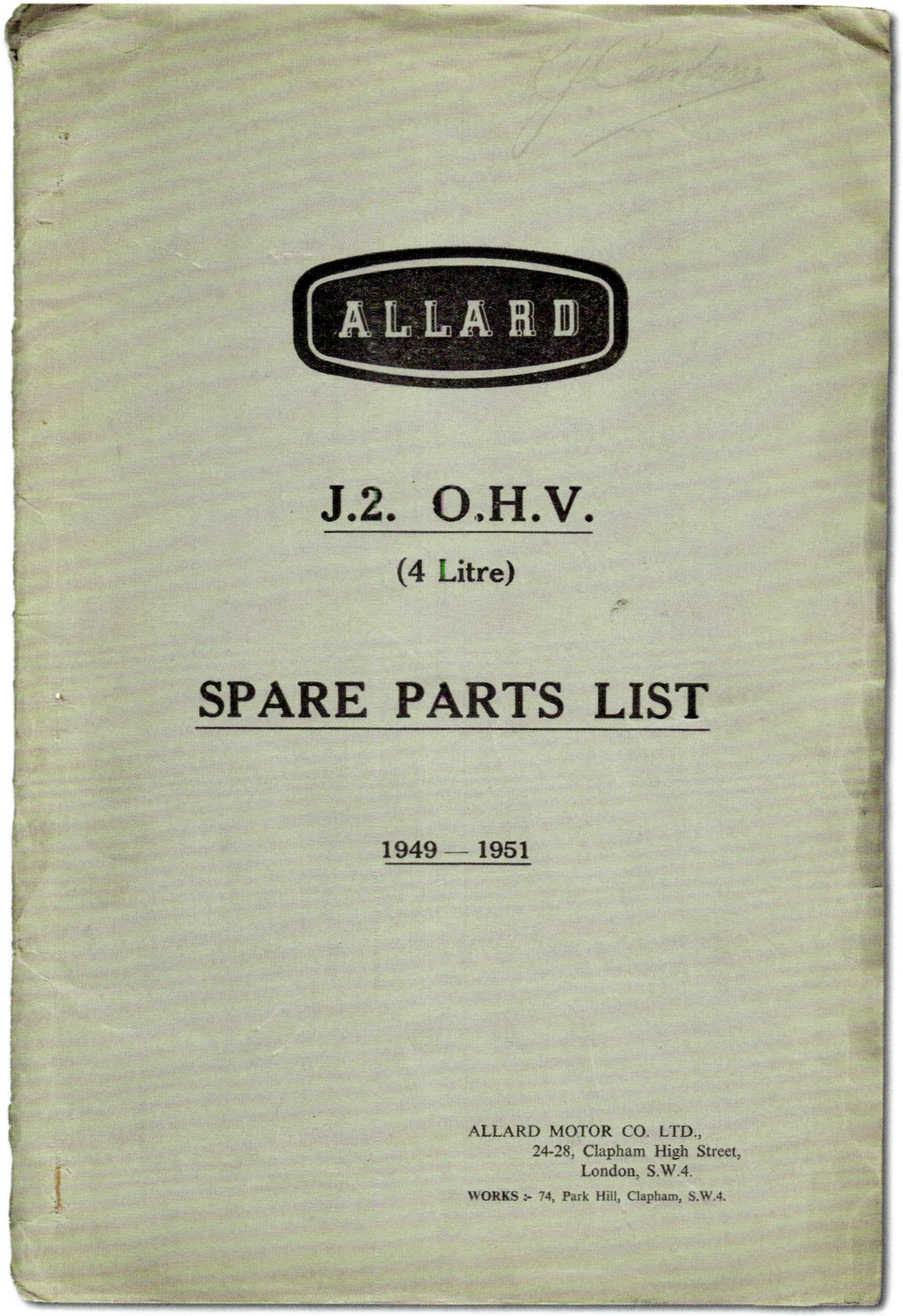

ALLARD

J.2. O.H.V.

(4 Litre)

SPARE PARTS LIST

1949 — 1951

ALLARD MOTOR CO. LTD.,
24-28, Clapham High Street,
London, S.W.4.

WORKS :- 74, Park Hill, Clapham, S.W.4.

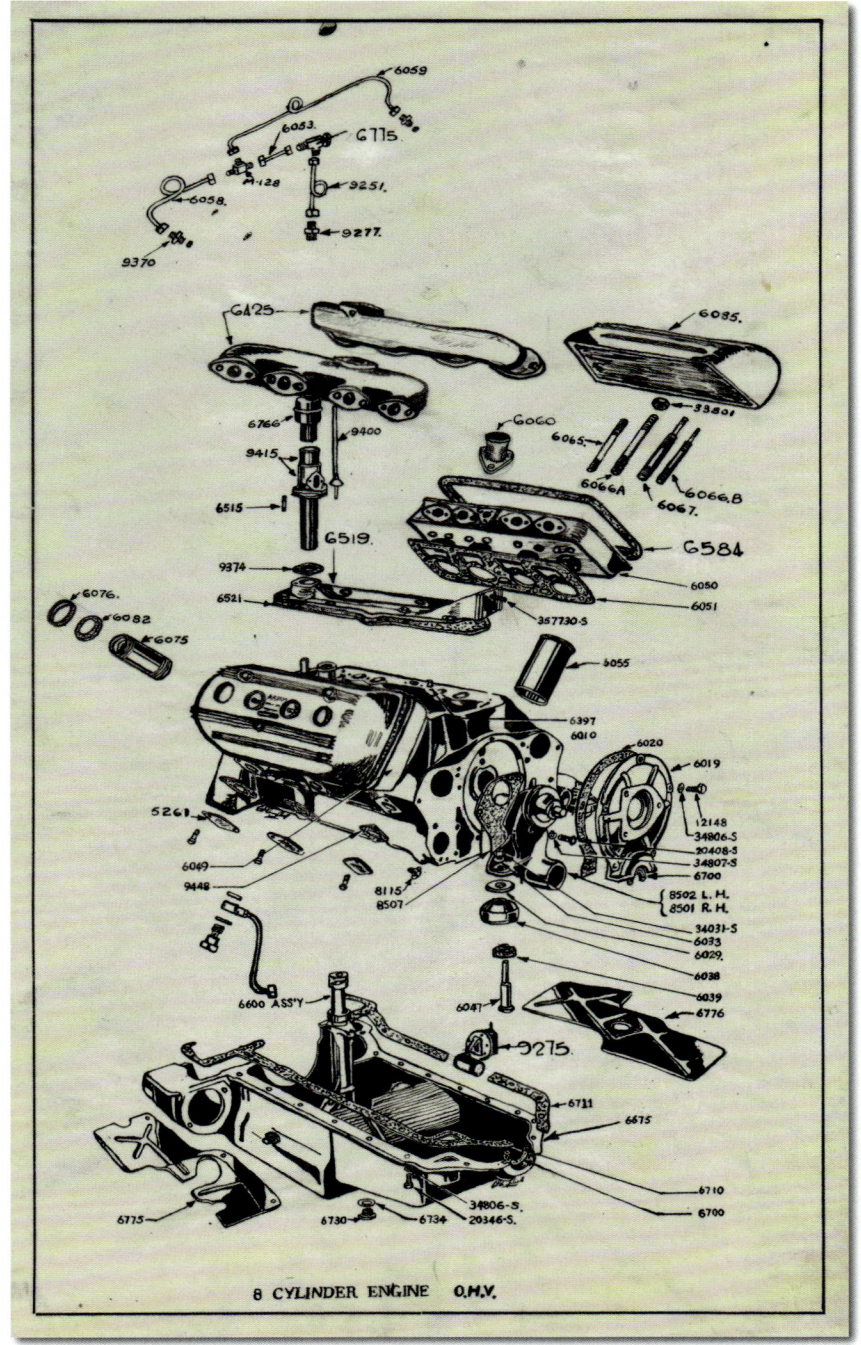

8 CYLINDER ENGINE O.H.V.

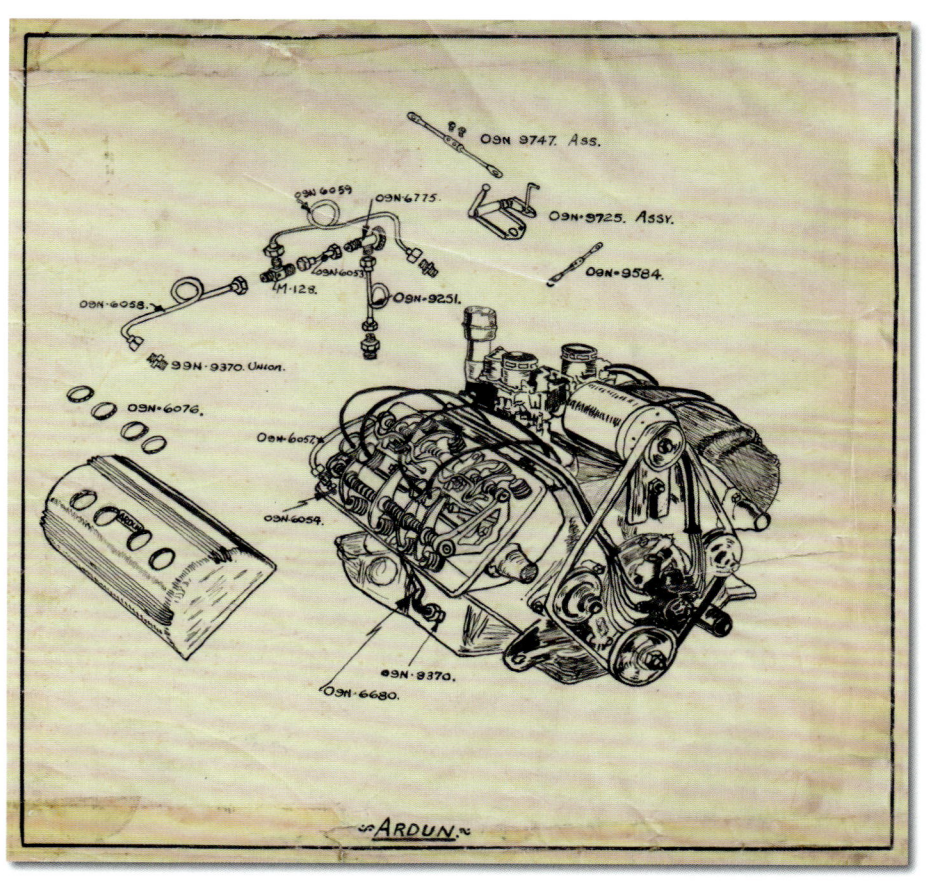

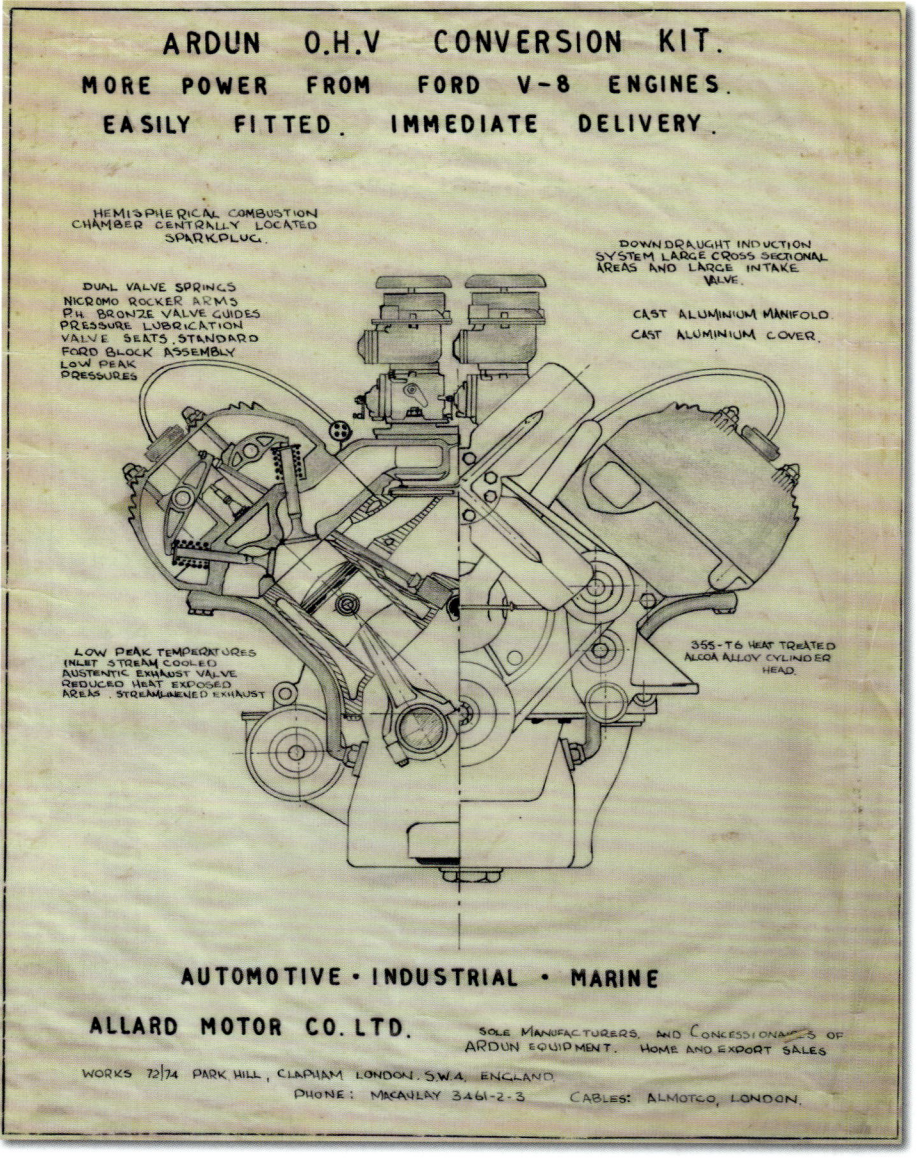

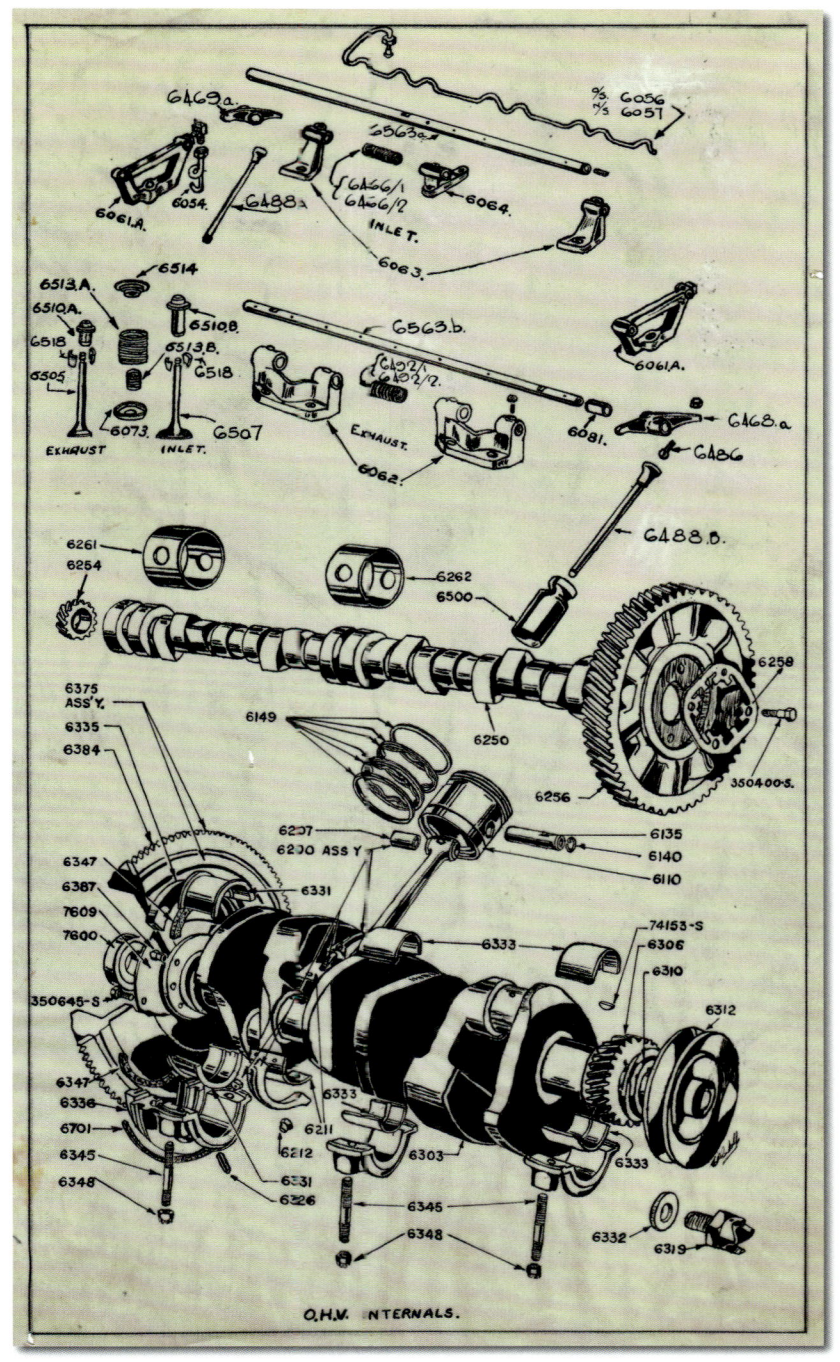

O.H.V. INTERNALS.

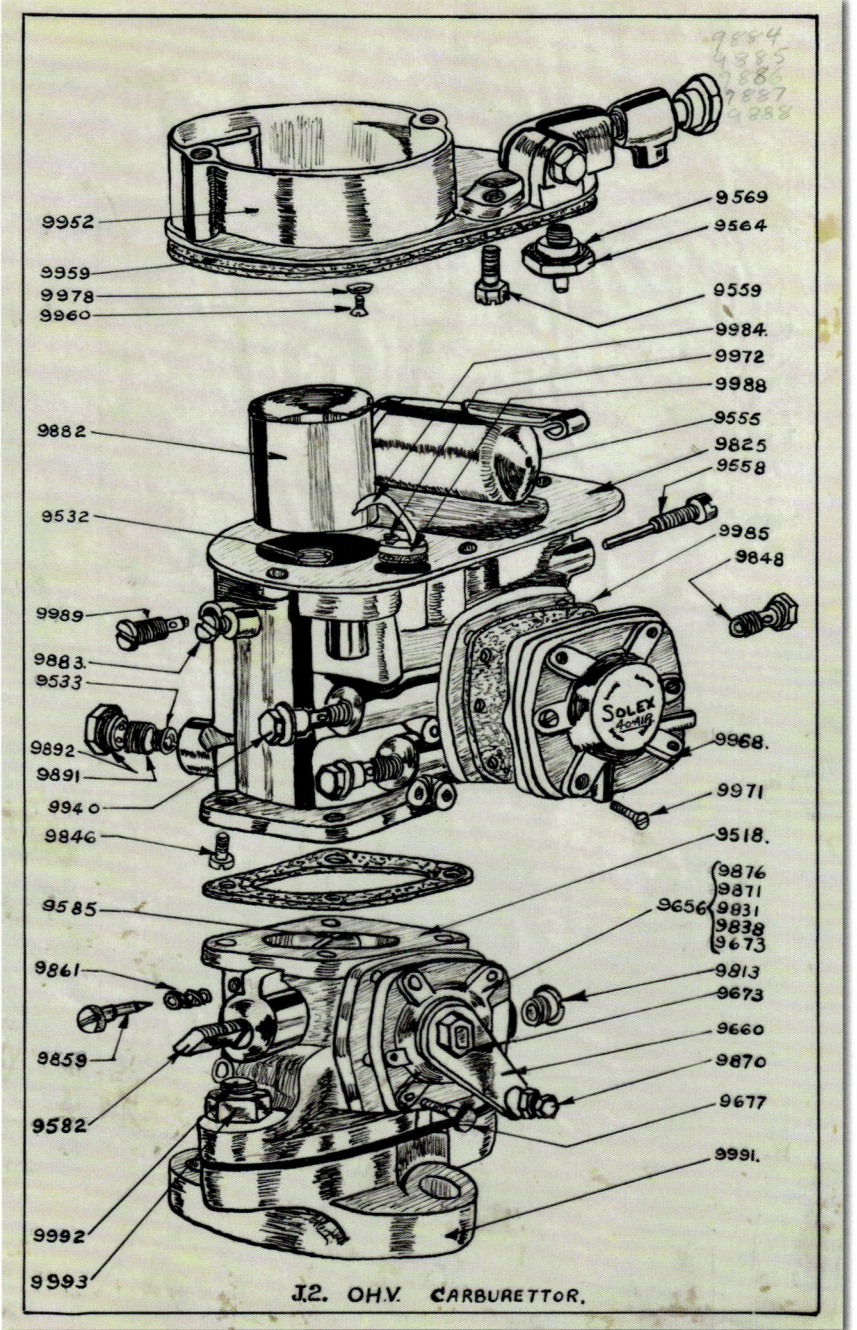

J.2. OH.V. CARBURETTOR.

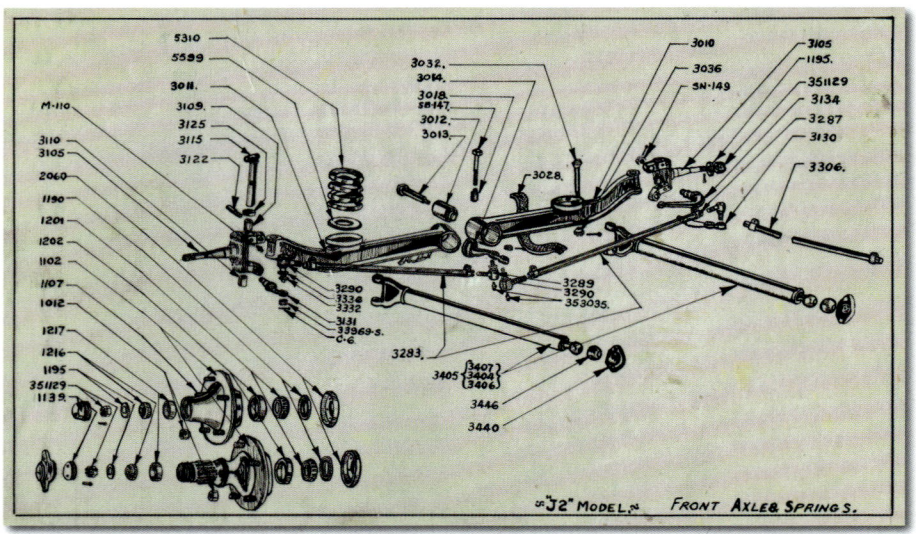

"J2" MODEL. FRONT AXLE & SPRINGS.

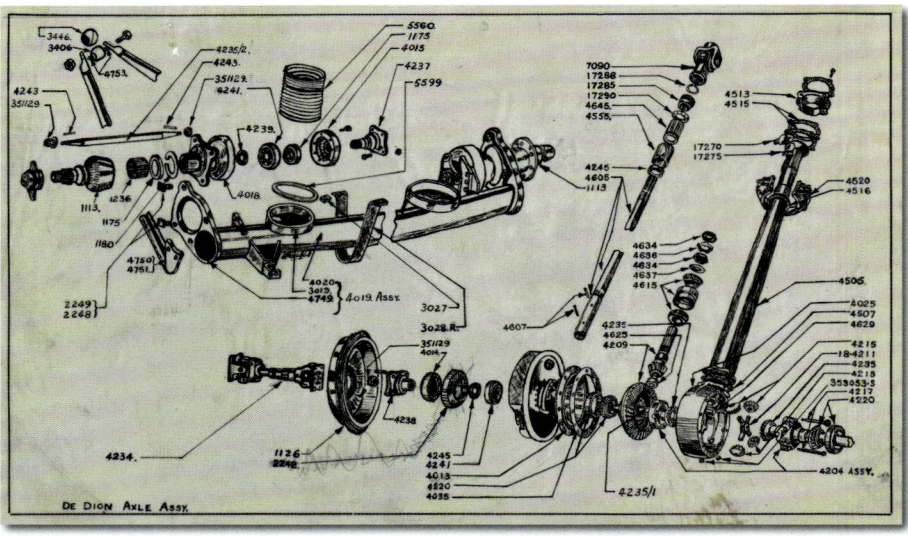

DE DION AXLE ASSY.

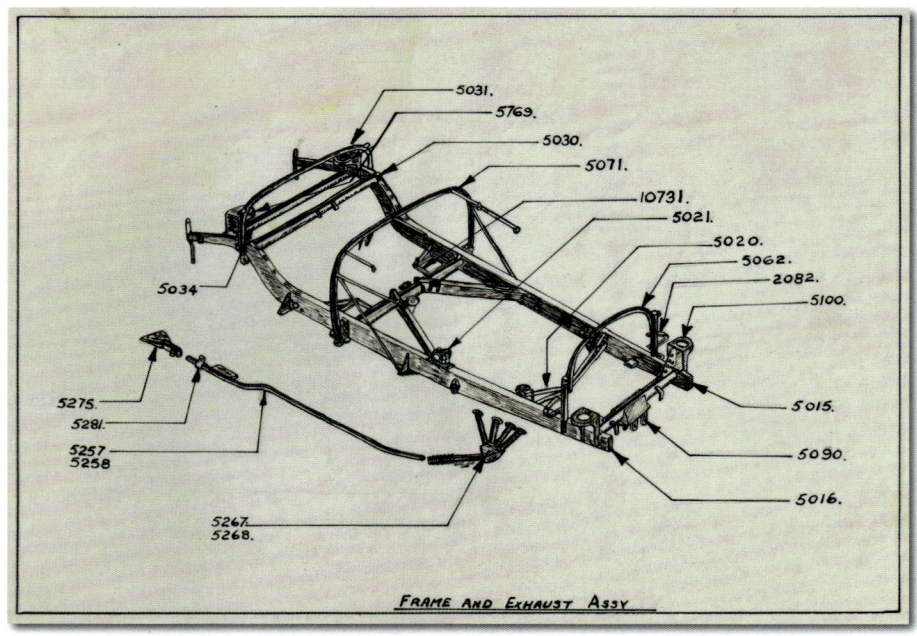

FRAME AND EXHAUST ASSY.

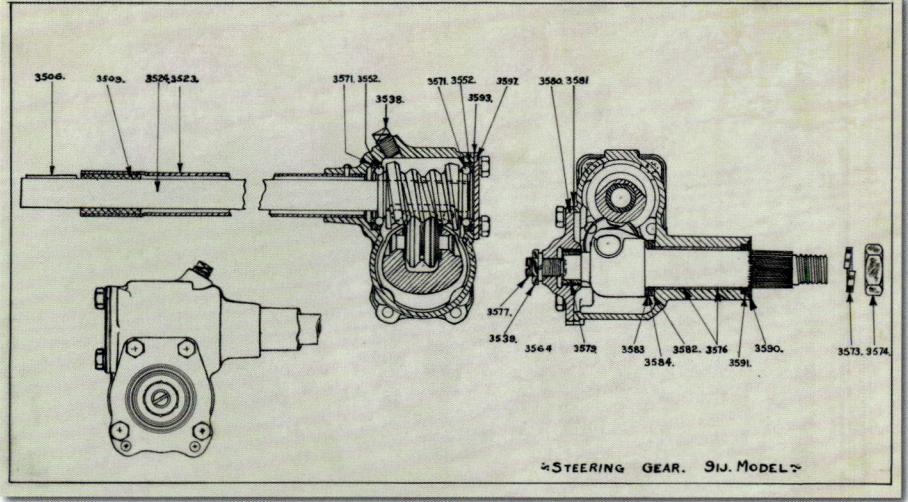

STEERING GEAR. 9IJ. MODEL.

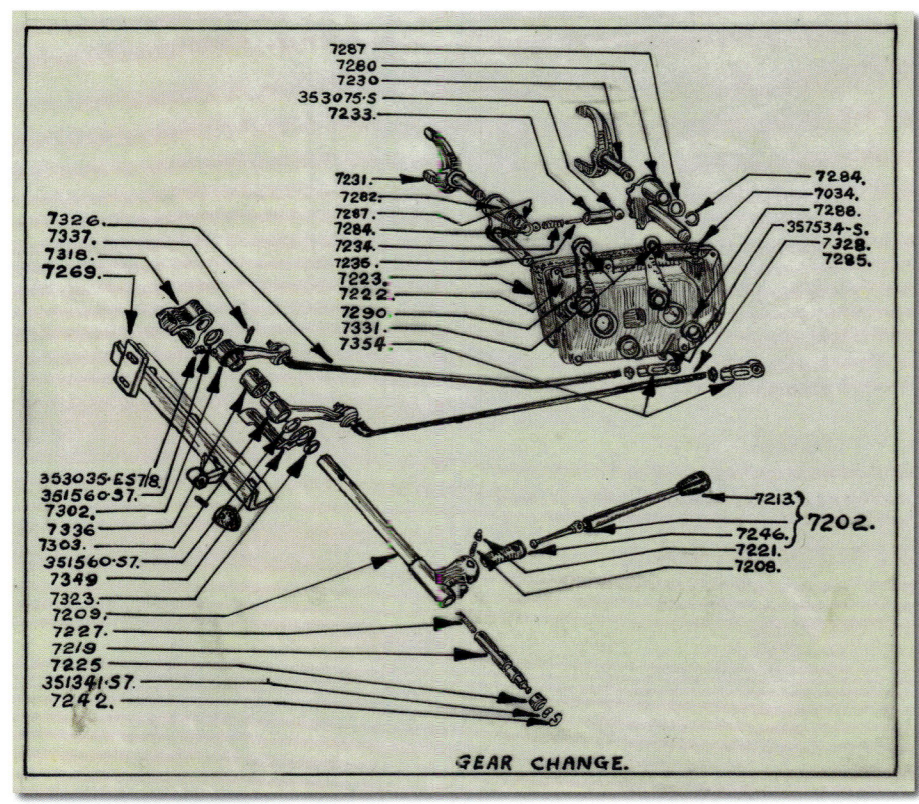

GEAR CHANGE.

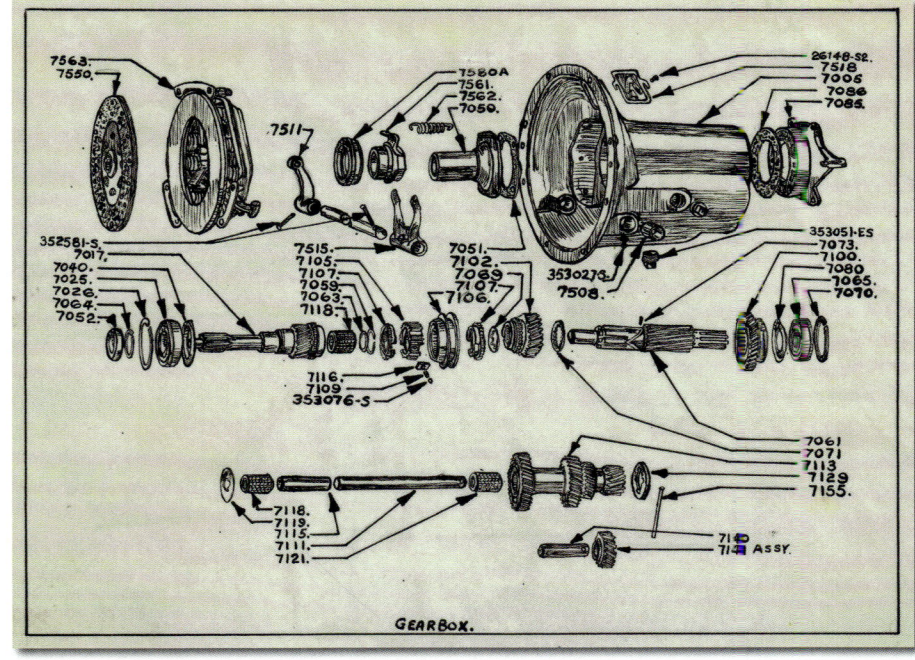

GEARBOX.

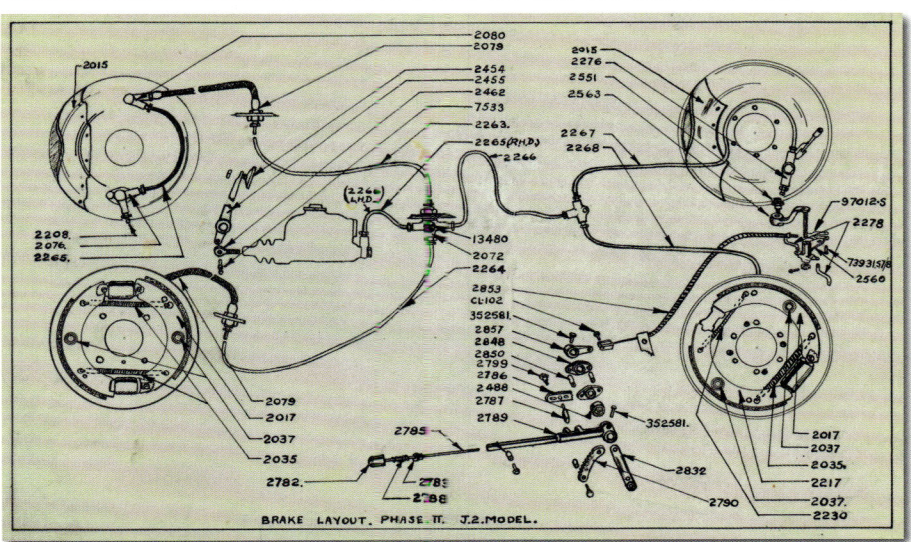

BRAKE LAYOUT. PHASE Ⅱ. J.2. MODEL.

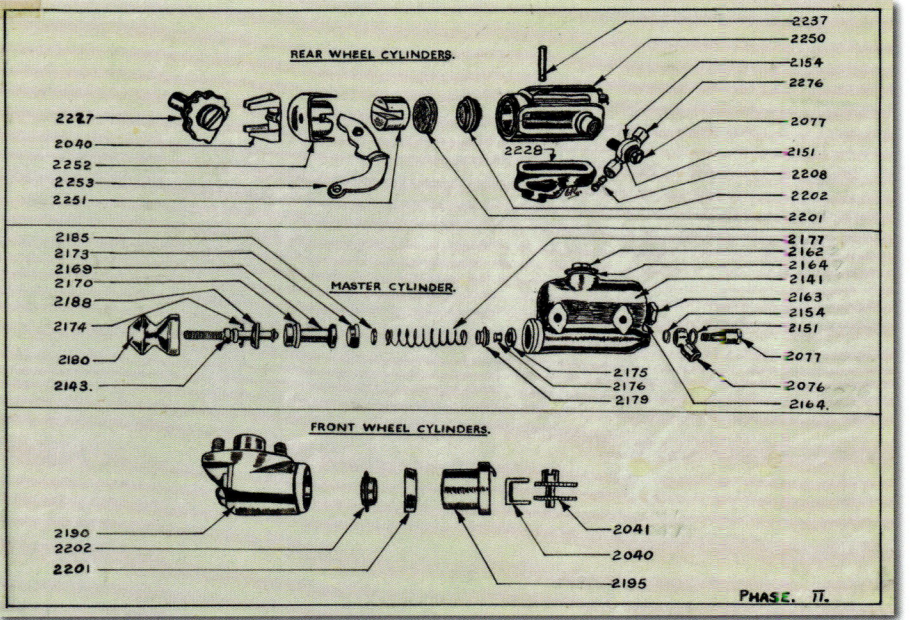

PHASE. Ⅱ.

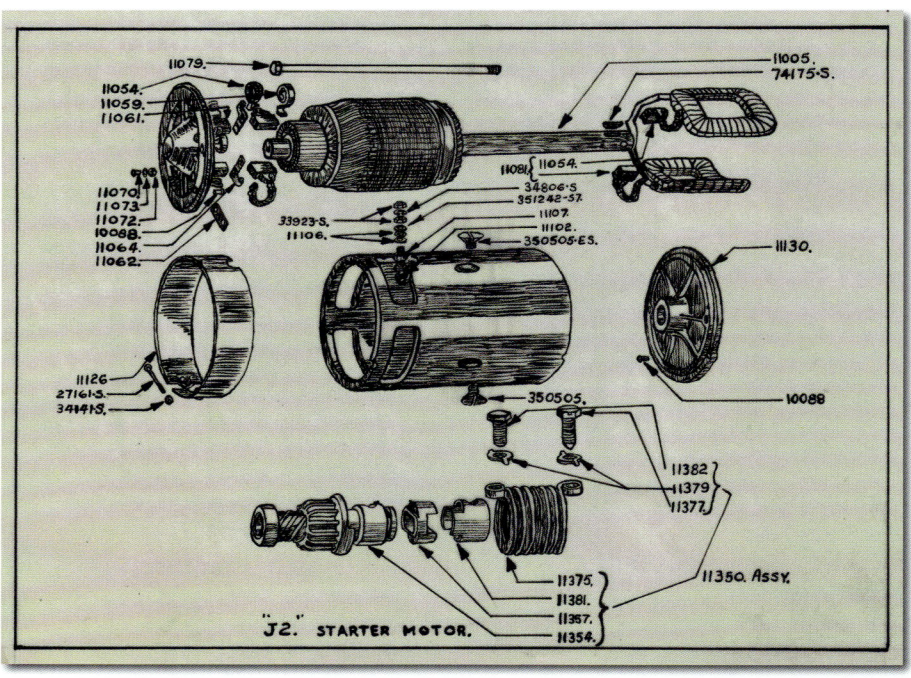

"J2." STARTER MOTOR.

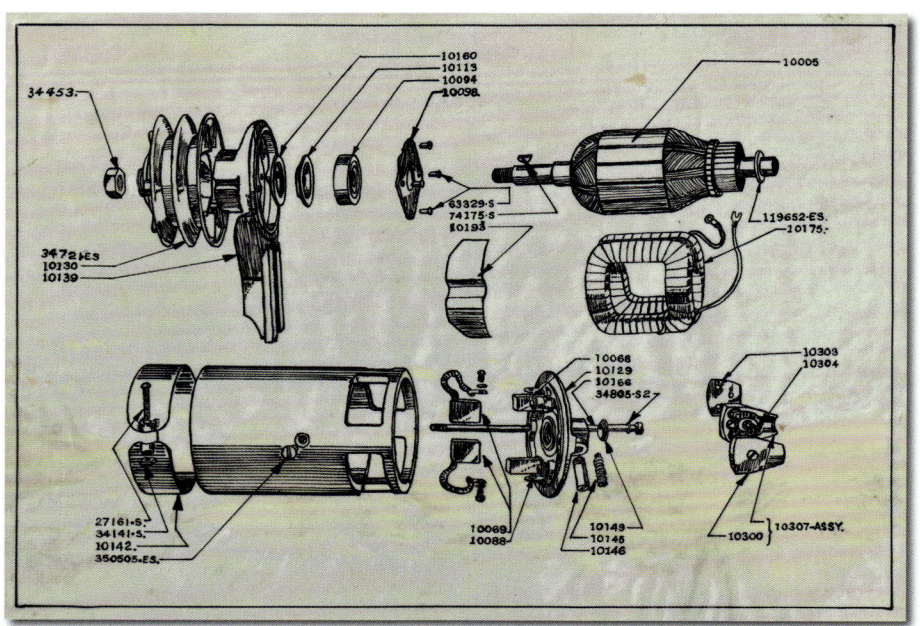

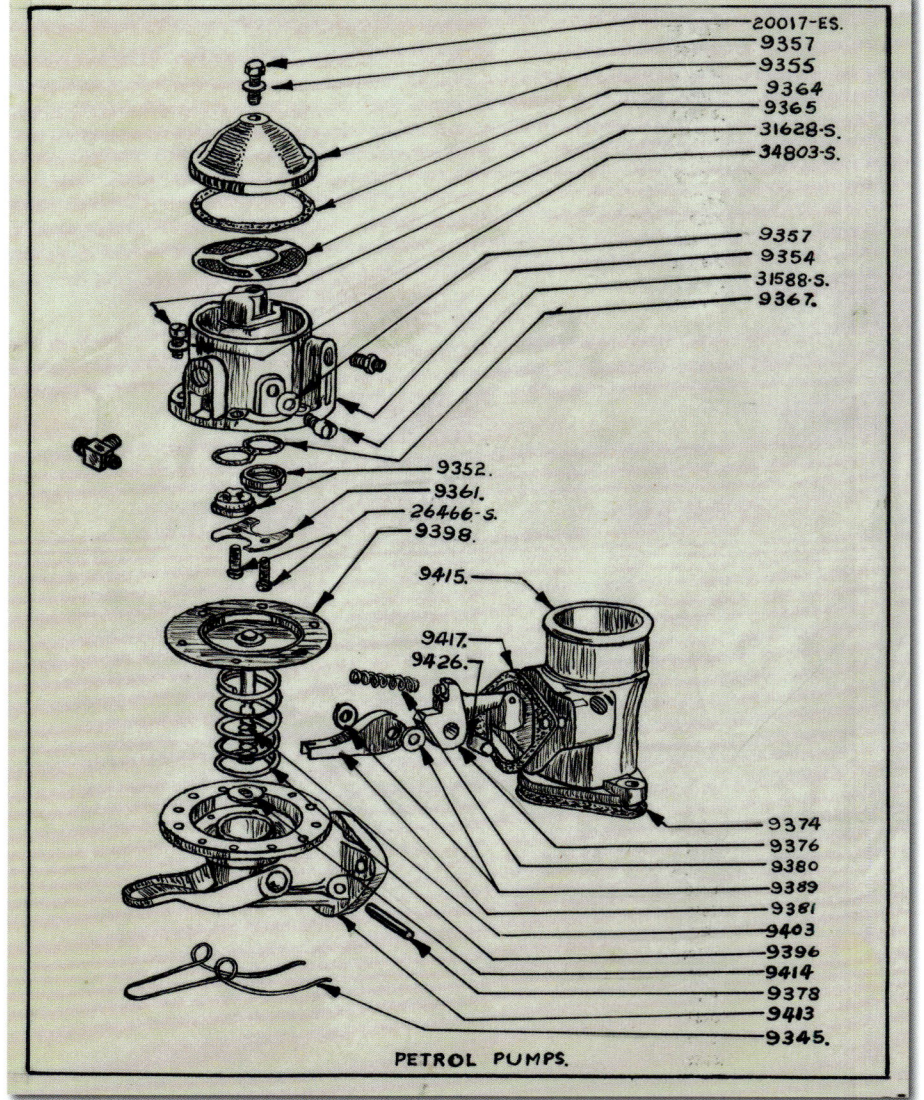

PETROL PUMPS.

Allard
1952
INSTRUCTION BOOK
FOR THE
"PALM BEACH"
AND
"~~BRIDGEHAMPTON~~"
ALLARD MOTOR COMPANY.
CLAPHAM. LONDON.

REAR UNIVERSAL JOINT LUBRICATOR
FILLER AND LEVEL PLUG
DRAIN PLUG.

DIPSTICK
DANGER
SAFE RANGE

LUBRICATOR

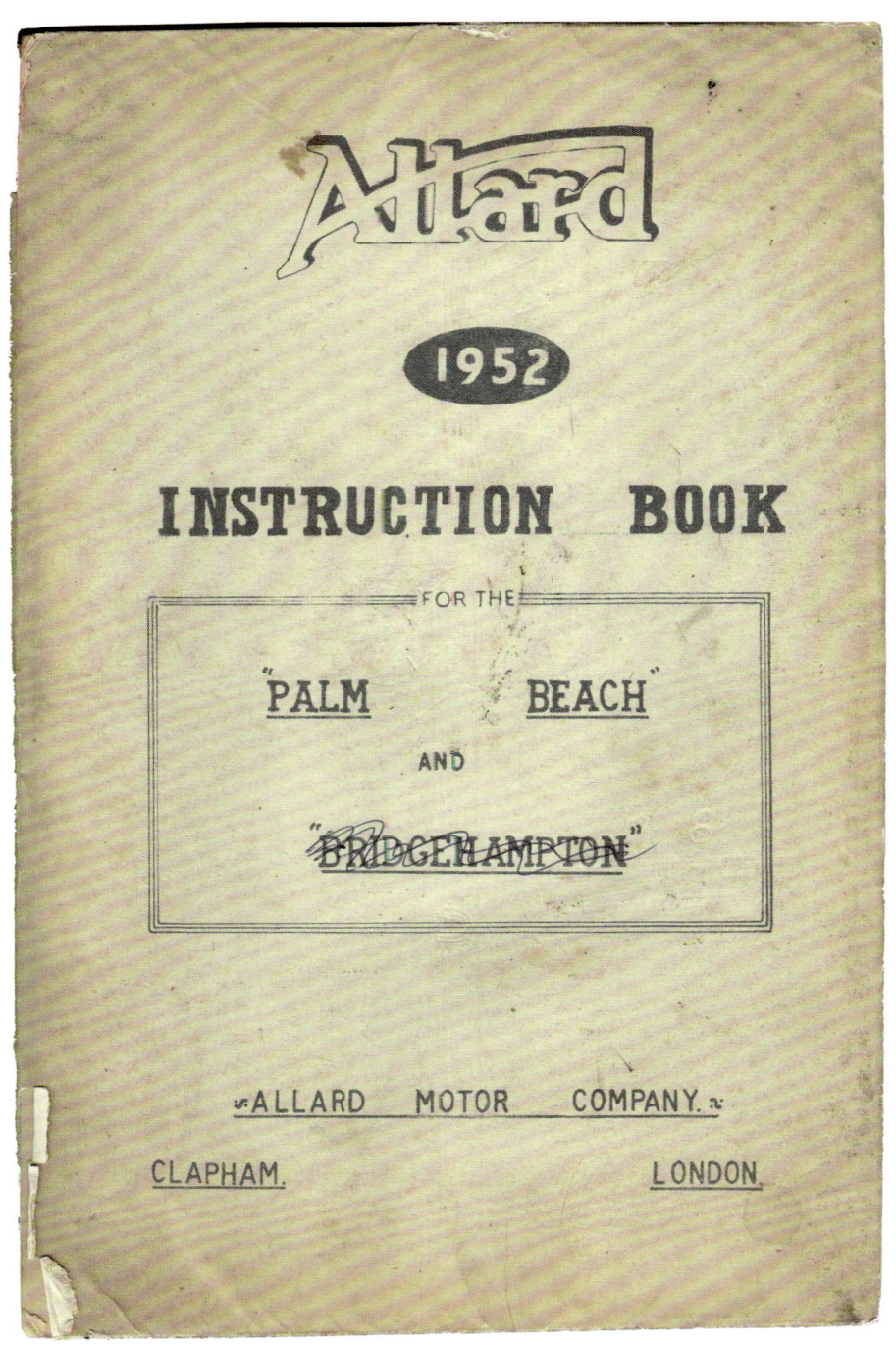

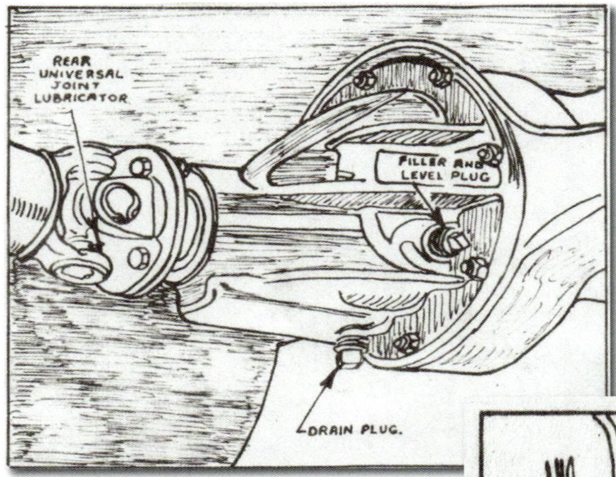

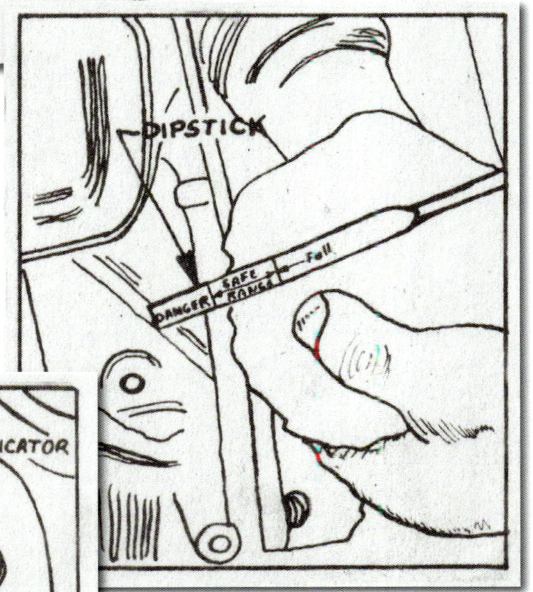

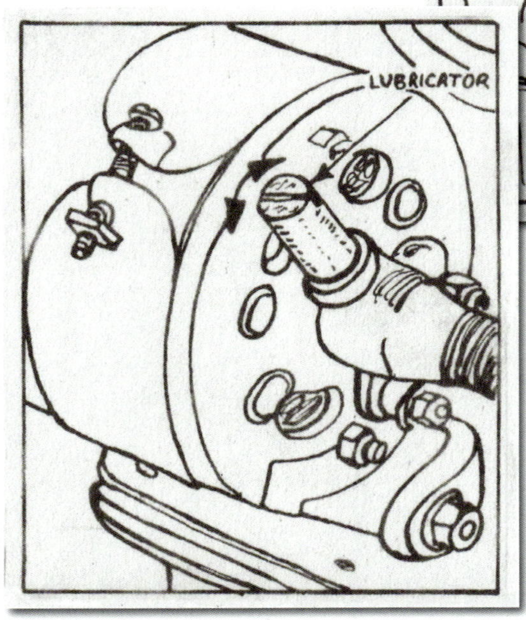

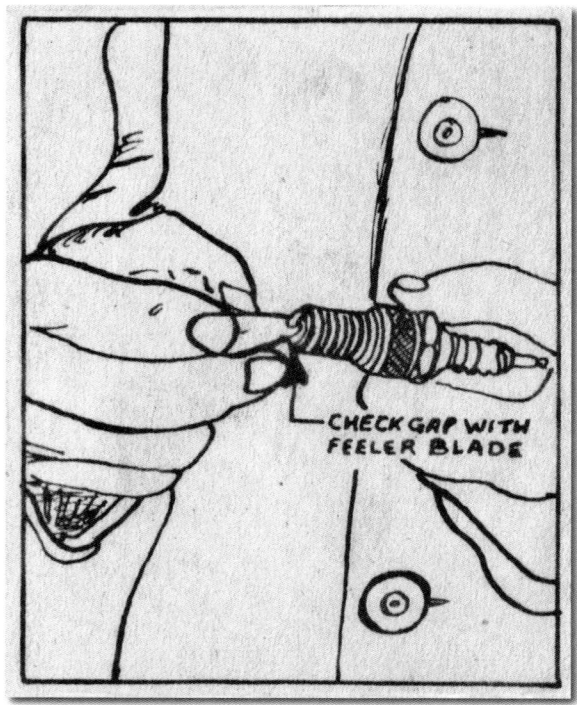

CHECK GAP WITH FEELER BLADE

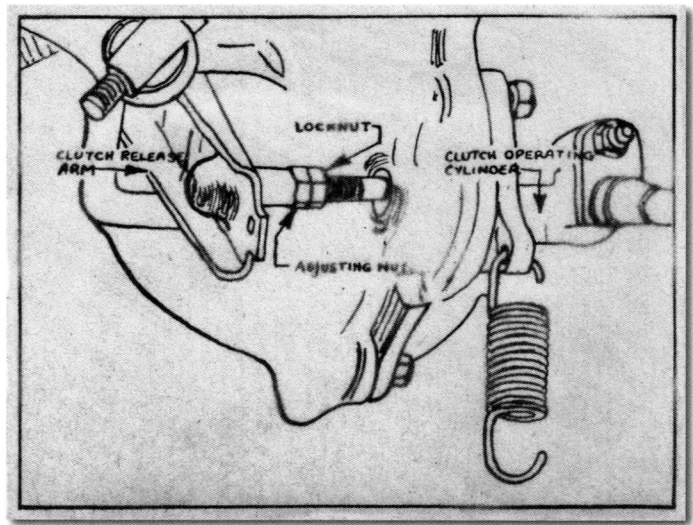

CLUTCH RELEASE ARM

LOCKNUT

CLUTCH OPERATING CYLINDER

ADJUSTING NUT

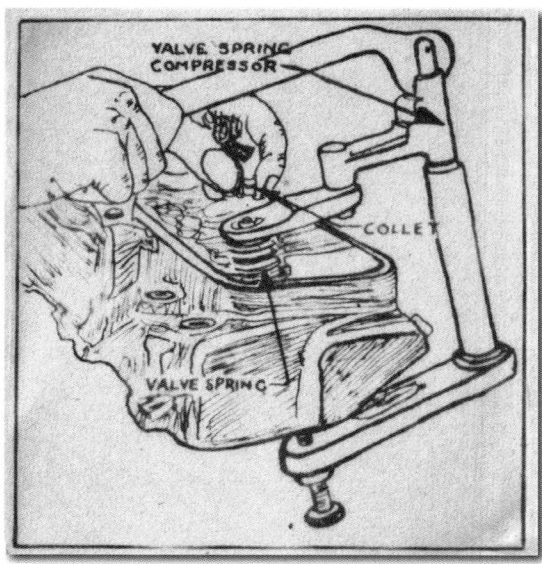

VALVE SPRING COMPRESSOR

COLLET

VALVE SPRING

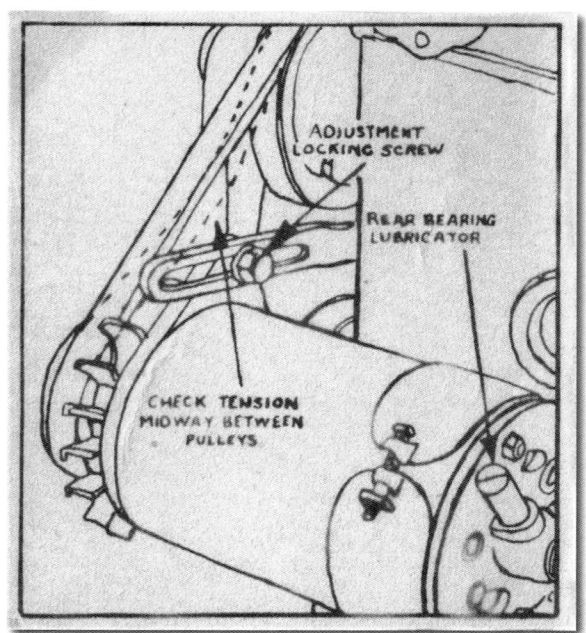

ADJUSTMENT LOCKING SCREW

REAR BEARING LUBRICATOR

CHECK TENSION MIDWAY BETWEEN PULLEYS

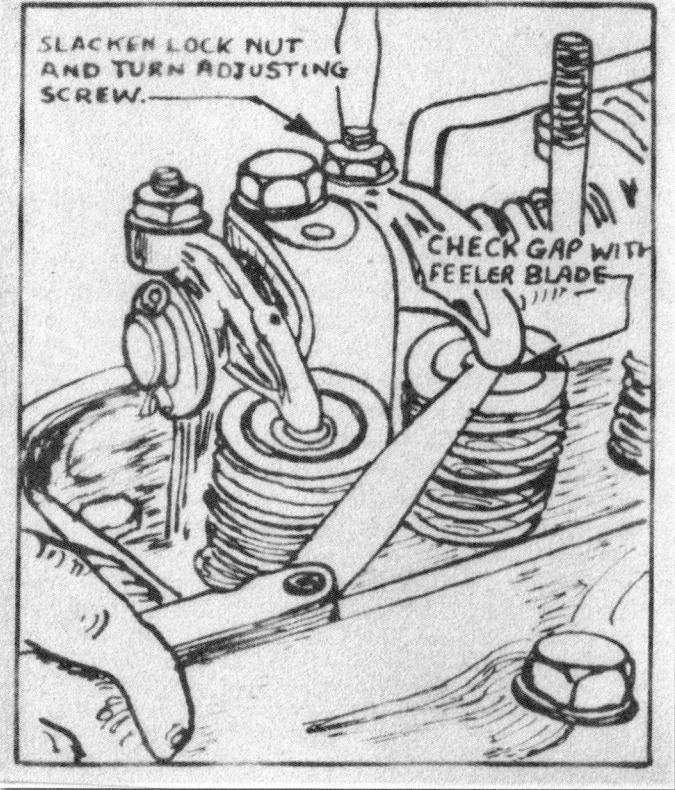

SLACKEN LOCK NUT AND TURN ADJUSTING SCREW.

CHECK GAP WITH FEELER BLADE

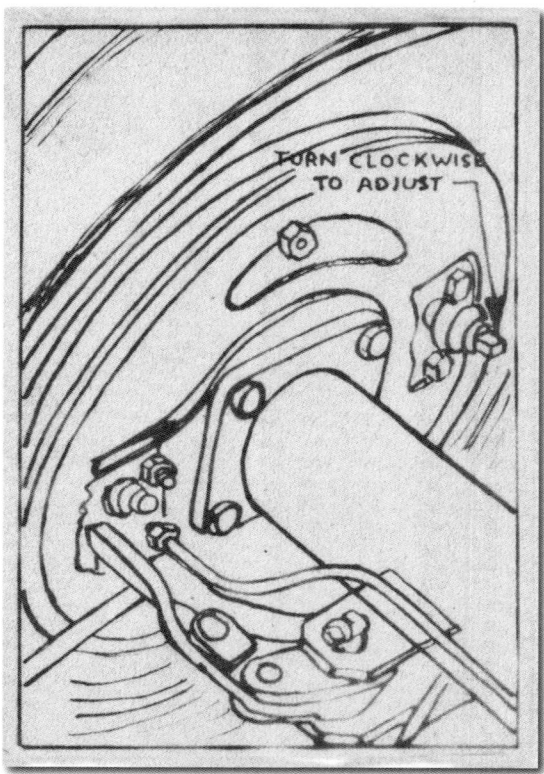

TURN CLOCKWISE TO ADJUST

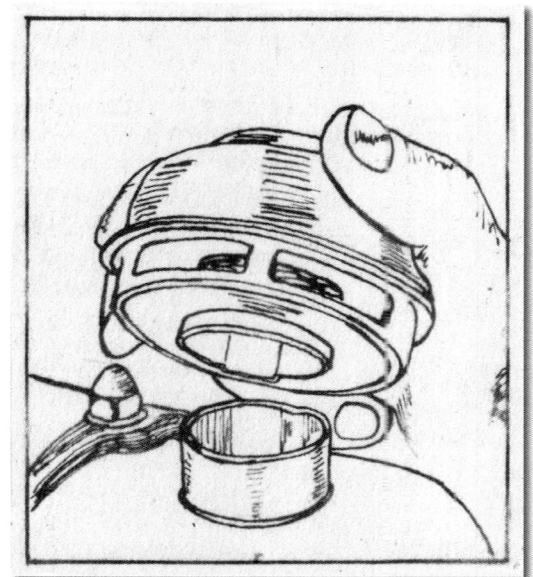

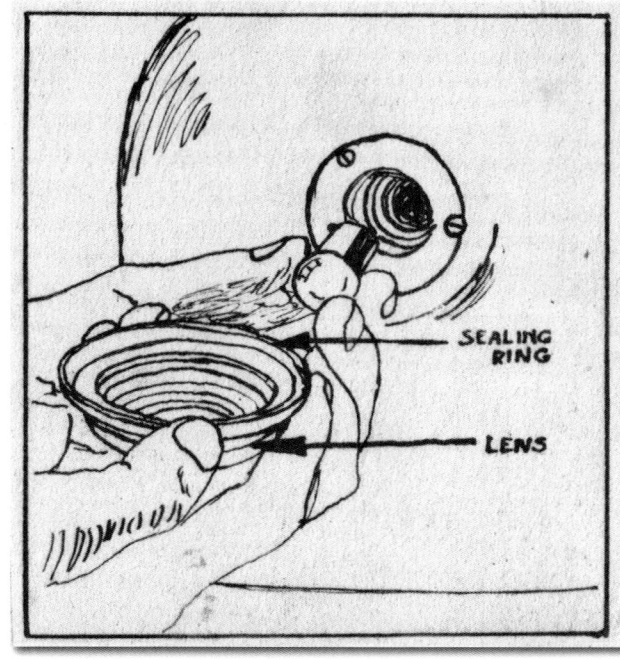

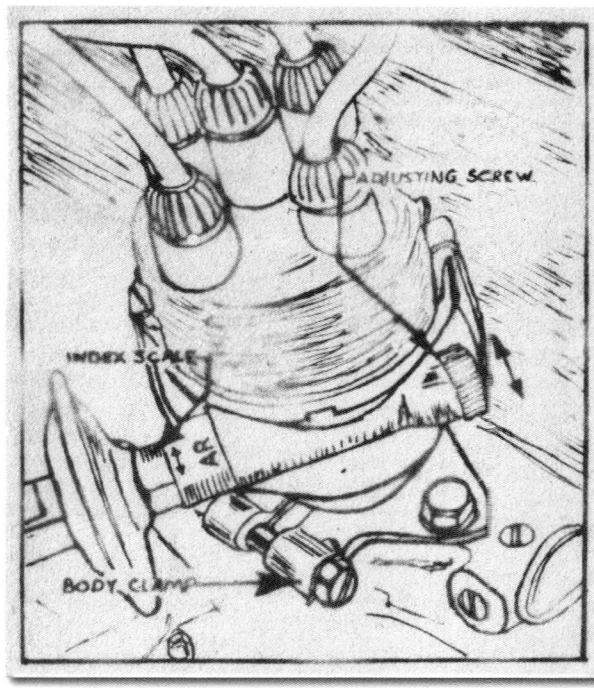

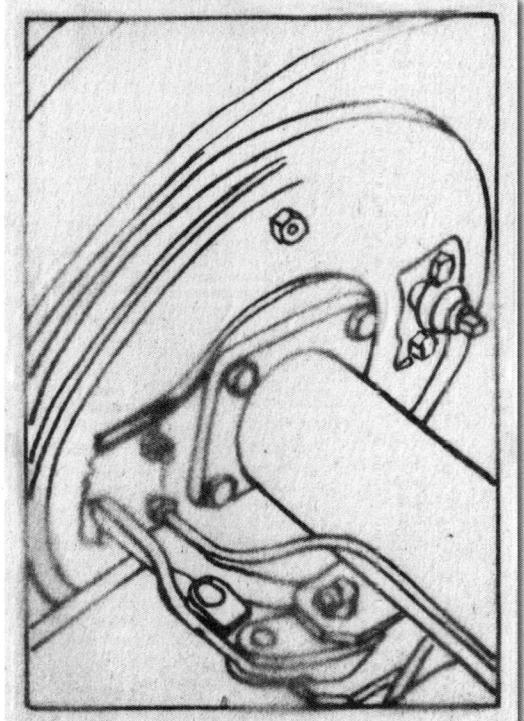

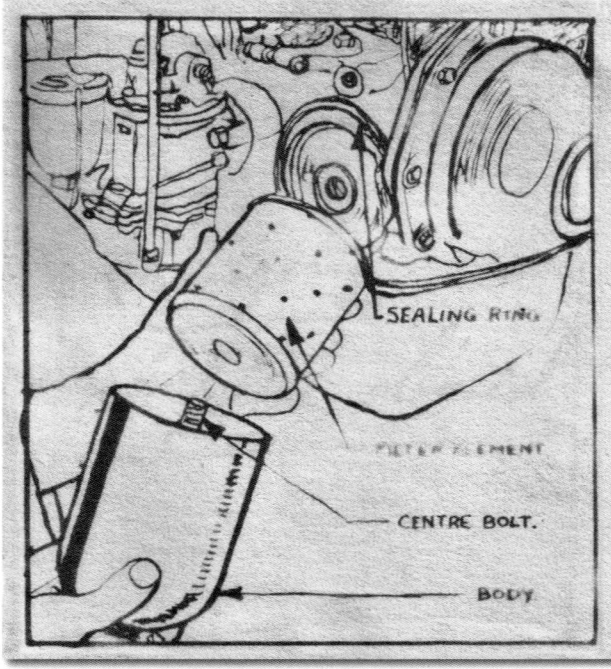

PROOF ARTWORK OF THE ALLARD

THE NEW "MONTE CARLO" SALOON

Specification

Brakes: Lockheed 12" 2 L.S. Front

Suspension:
Front: Divided Axle, Coil Springs
Rear: De-Dion Type, " "

Tyres: 625 x 16
Shock Absorbers: Hydraulic Telescopic
12 Volt Lighting Equipment
Fuel Capacity: 18 Imp. Gall.

Wheelbase: 9ft. 4ins.
Width: 5ft. 11ins.
Height: 5ft.
Weight: 28½ cwt.
Ground Clearance: 8ins.
Turning Circle: 40ft.
Floor Height: 15ins.
Front Track: 4ft. 8½ins.
Rear " 4ft. 10½ins.
Overall Length: 16ft.

TRANSMISSION

Clutch: Single Dry Plate   3 Speed Gearbox. (Outside Gear Change)
Overall Gear ratios: Top: 3·78; 1 — 2nd. 6·68: 1 — 1st. 11·75: 1

Strikingly modern in design, the ALLARD "MONTE CARLO" is the perfect combination of a comfortable saloon car with the sleek lines and general roadworthiness of the sports car.

The ALLARD has all the features to make the ideal car for any conditions — comfortable driving, plenty of power, speed when you want it, and unequalled servicing facilities throughout the world.

The New Tubular Chassis Frame is designed to accommodate the CADILLAC and CHRYSLER V.8. Motors with 3 speed manually operated gear box, or the CADILLAC with hydramatic transmission.

The archive collection holds hundreds of advertising proofs likely checked once and never looked at again. Normally these items would be discarded, but someone chose to retain them when they had no further purpose.

A selection of proofs are presented in loosely chronological order from wartime until 1953. Often there are remarks handwritten on them by Sydney.

Allard were resourceful by reusing graphics from other sources when budgets were limited – an example of this can be found on page 667.

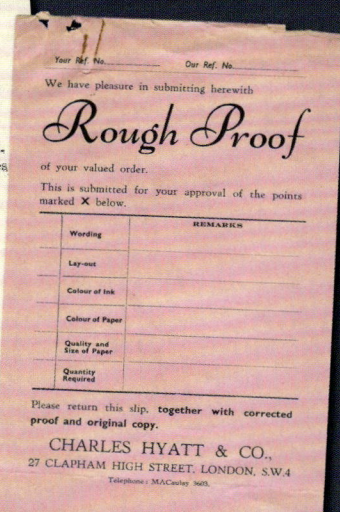

Rough Proof of your valued order.
This is submitted for your approval of the points marked X below.
CHARLES HYATT & CO., 27 CLAPHAM HIGH STREET, LONDON, S.W.4

Copy for Feb '45

EVEN whilst we are concentrating on what we hope to be the great penultimate effort, we are not neglecting the development of our post-war plans.

ADLARDS MOTORS LTD.

*Manufacturers
of
Allard Cars*

New Block to be made from photo h/w

Branches at
**PUTNEY, BRIXTON
and FULHAM**

NOW as victory takes shape before our eyes, so does the design of our post-war **ALLARD** car.

ADLARDS MOTORS LTD.

*Manufacturers
of
Allard Cars*

Branches at
**PUTNEY, BRIXTON
and FULHAM**

Proof Artwork of the Allard

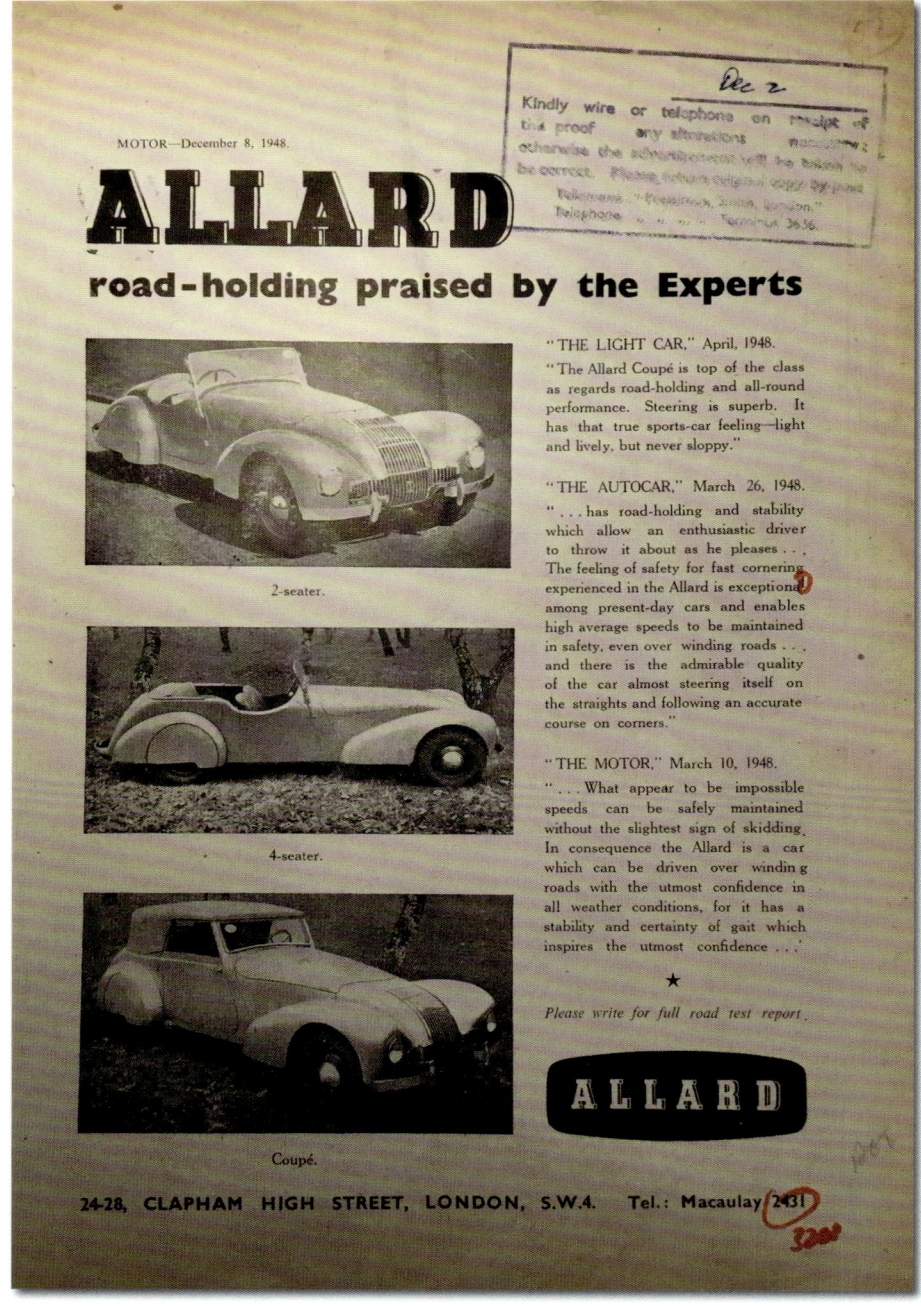

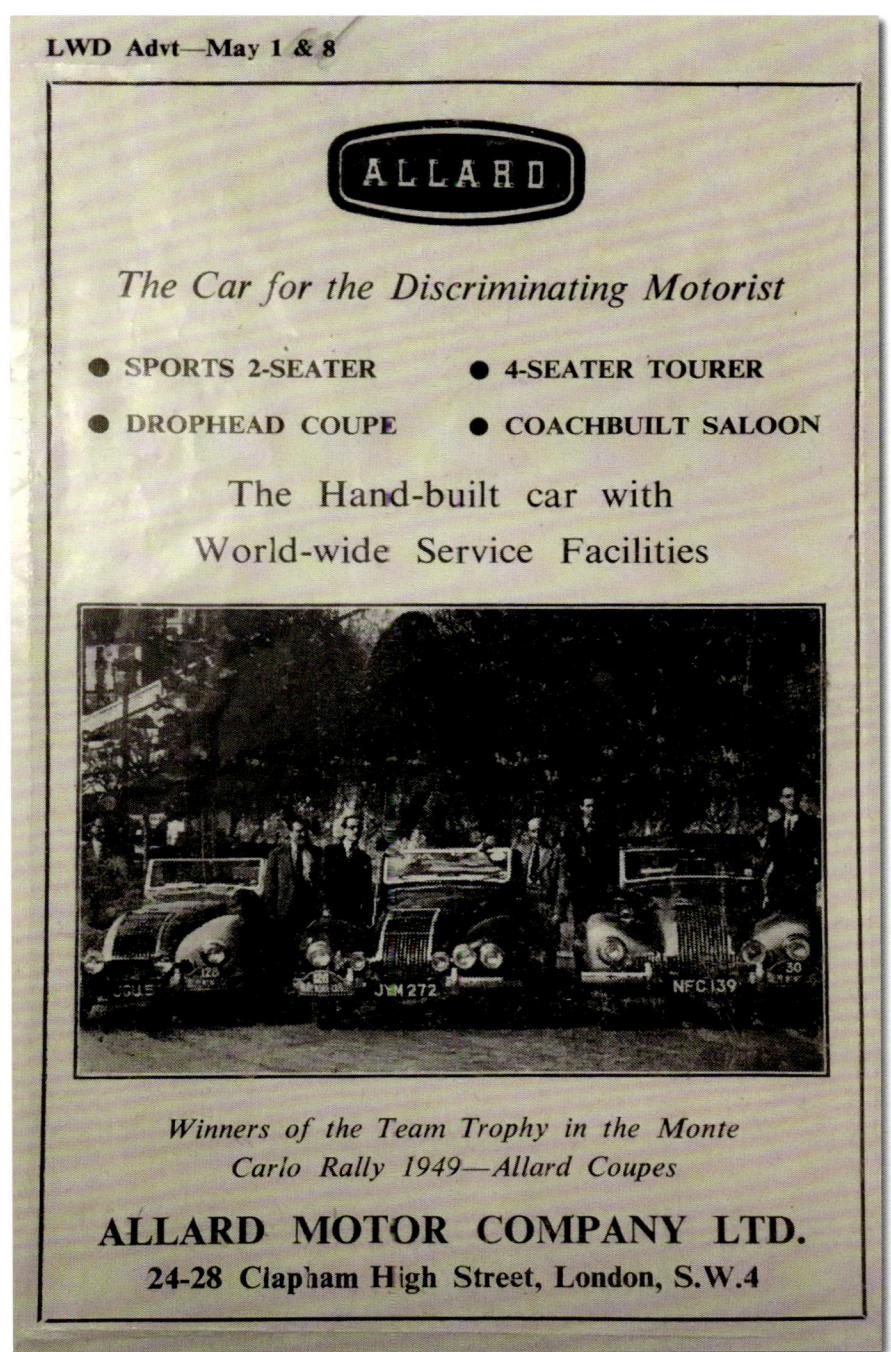

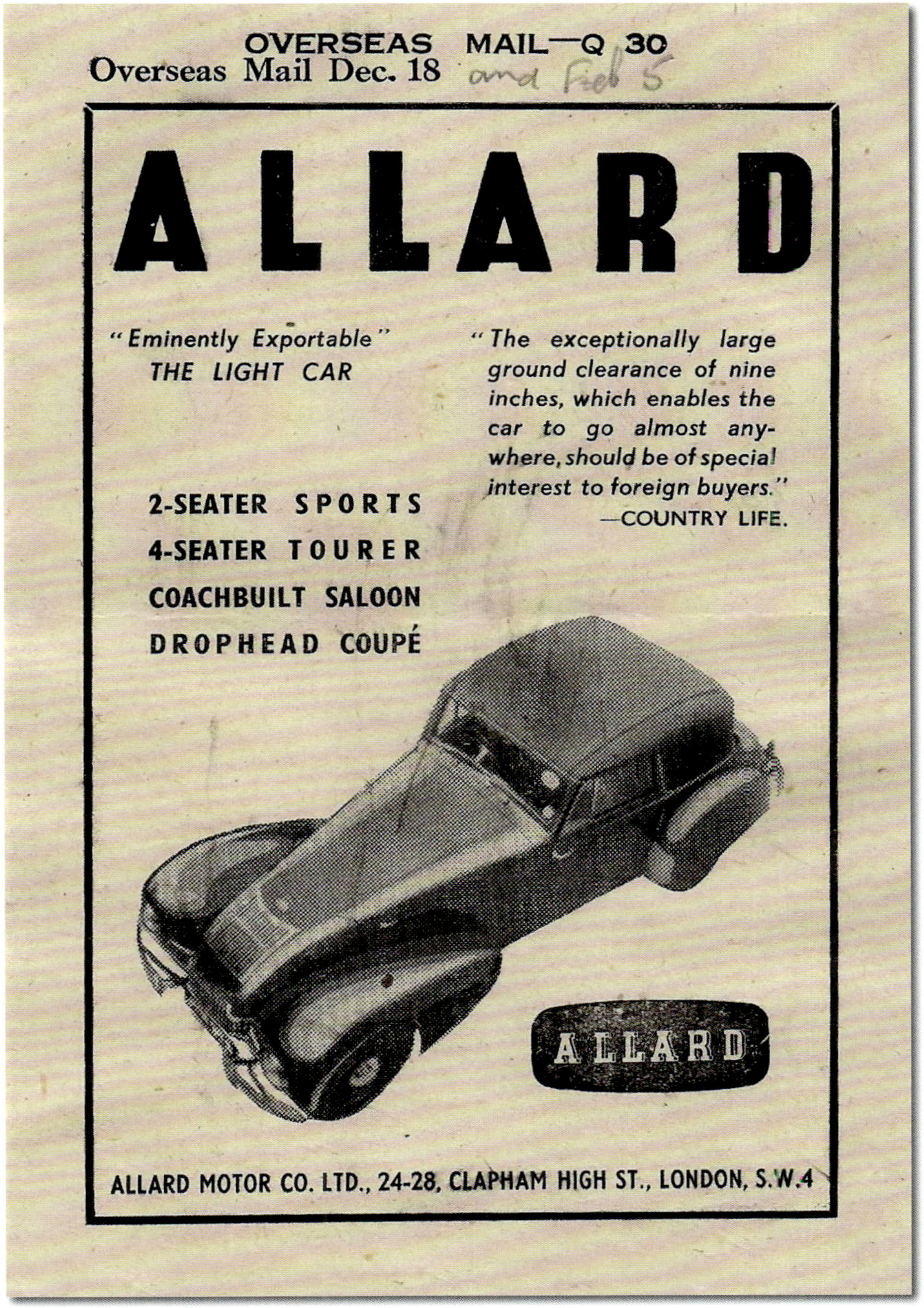

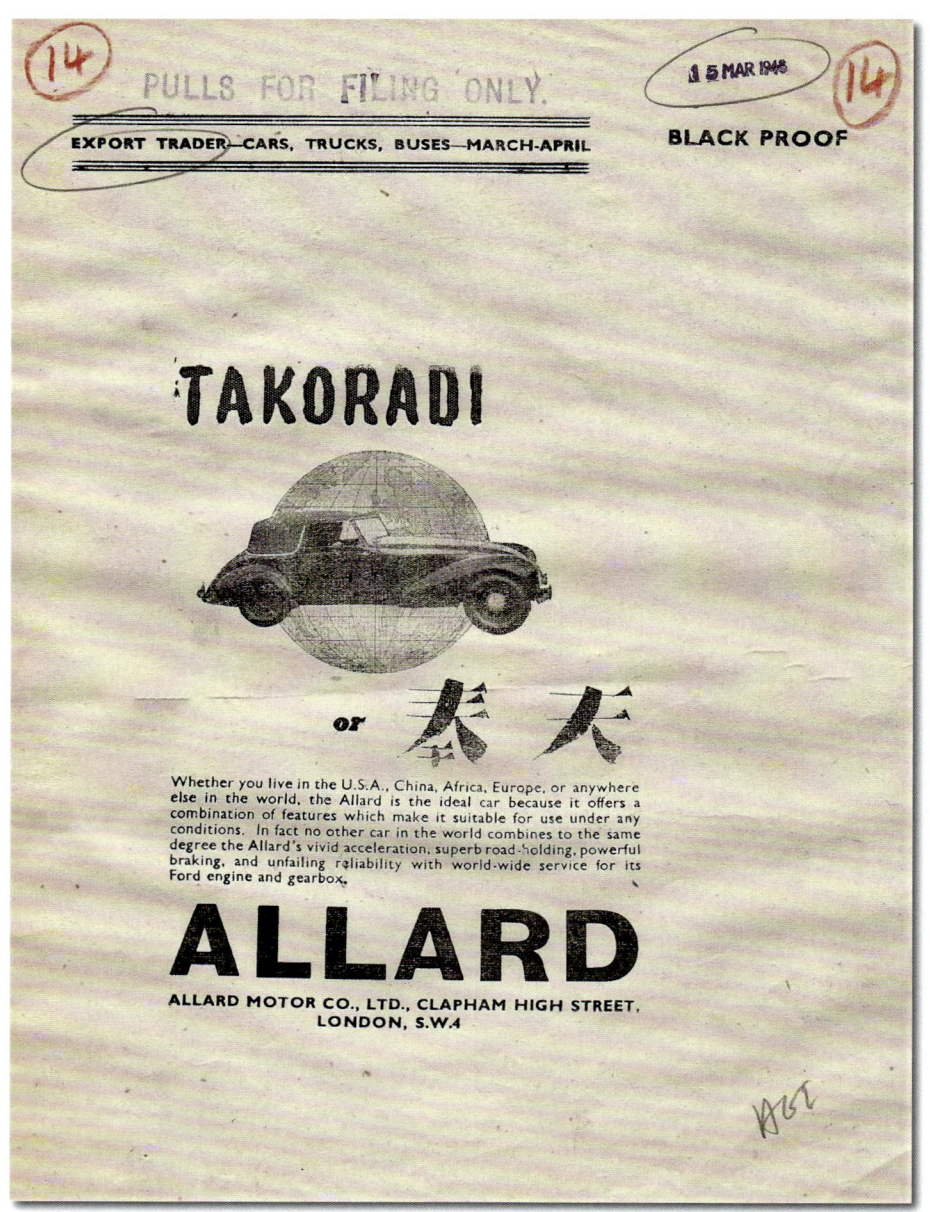

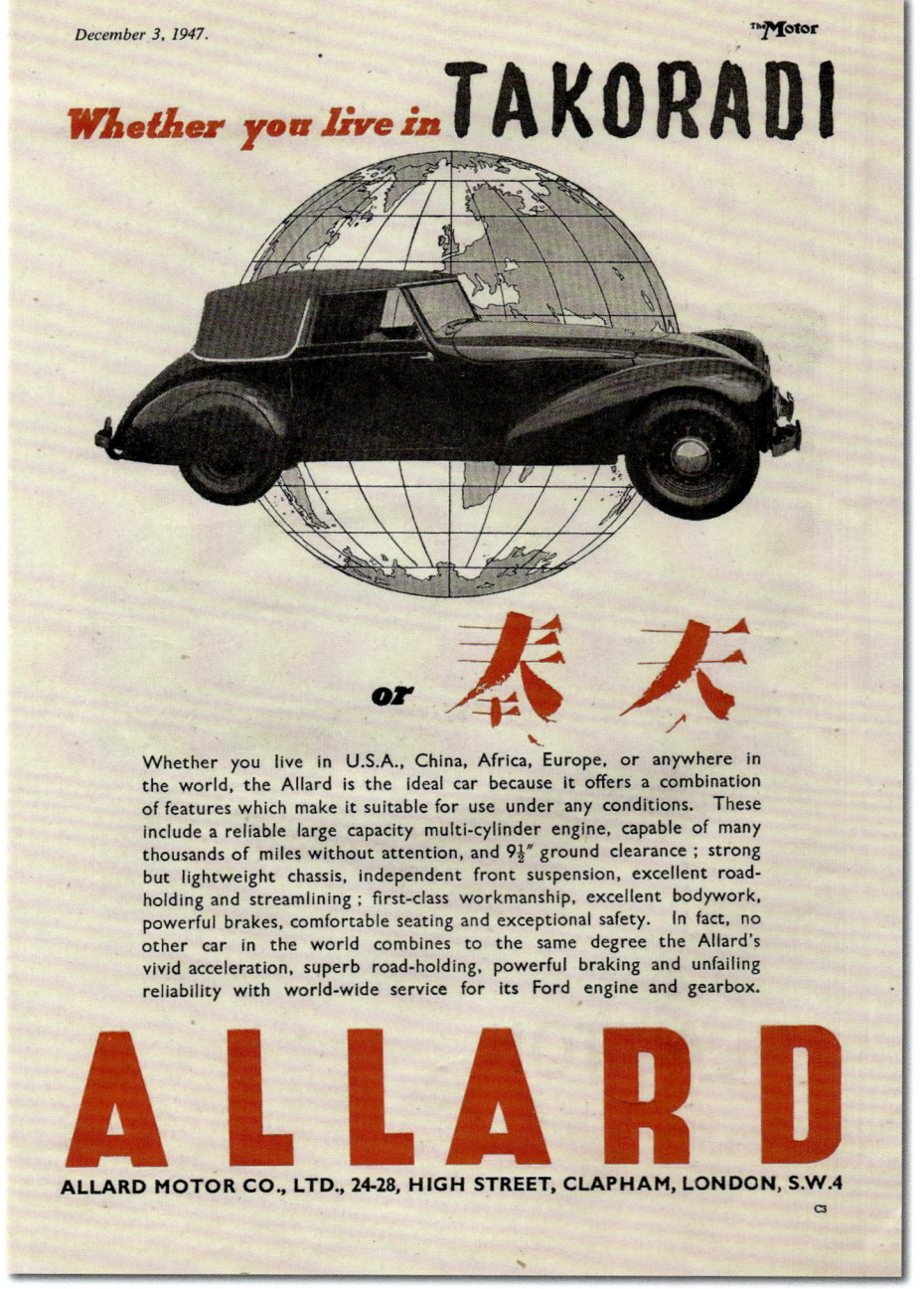

August 27, 1947.   The Motor 7

The cockpit with all controls ideally positioned shows some of the practical advantages gained by Allard competition experience.

Three post-war models are in production—a sports two-seater, sports four-seater and a drop-head coupe. Each of these is outstanding in its class. No other car in the world combines to the same degree the Allard's vivid acceleration, superb road holding, powerful braking, streamlined appearance, unfailing reliability with world-wide service for its Ford engine and gear box.

The post-war Allard has proved its worth in International Competitions. In each of the four events in which a post-war Allard has been entered on the Continent it has won a Trophy—1st Lisbon Rally, 1st Maloja Hill Climb, 1st driving and manoeuvrability test, Rally des Alpes 1st over 3,000 c.c. Devilier-des-Rangier Hill Climb. In each case the Allard was driven and entered by A. Gofrey Imhof.

ALLARD

ALLARD MOTOR COMPANY LTD., 24-28, High Street, Clapham, London, S.W.4.   Macaulay 2431.

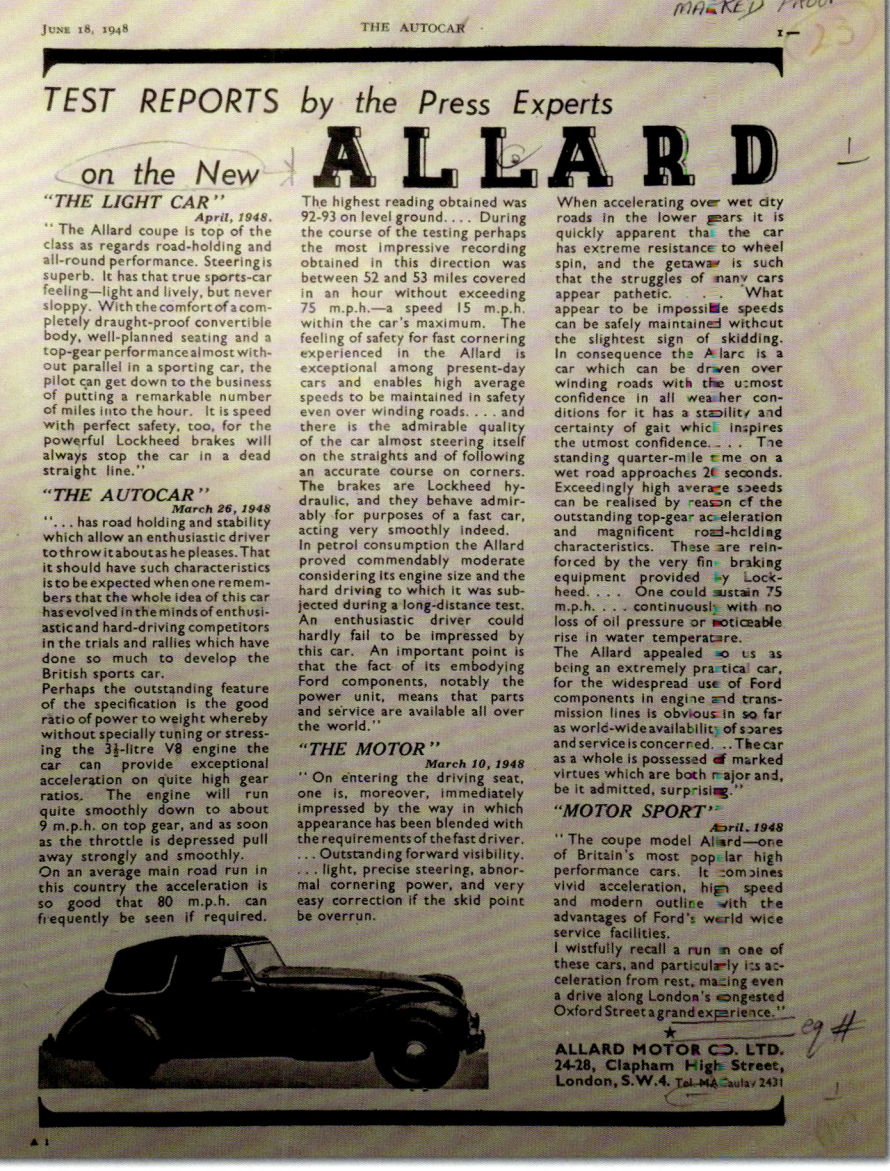

JUNE 18, 1948   THE AUTOCAR

MARKED PROOF

TEST REPORTS by the Press Experts

on the New ALLARD

"THE LIGHT CAR"
April, 1948.
"The Allard coupe is top of the class as regards road-holding and all-round performance. Steering is superb. It has that true sports-car feeling—light and lively, but never sloppy. With the comfort of a completely draught-proof convertible body, well-planned seating and a top-gear performance almost without parallel in a sporting car, the pilot can get down to the business of putting a remarkable number of miles into the hour. It is speed with perfect safety, too, for the powerful Lockheed brakes will always stop the car in a dead straight line."

"THE AUTOCAR"
March 26, 1948
". . . has road holding and stability which allow an enthusiastic driver to throw it about as he pleases. That it should have such characteristics is to be expected when one remembers that the whole idea of this car has evolved in the minds of enthusiastic and hard-driving competitors in the trials and rallies which have done so much to develop the British sports car.
Perhaps the outstanding feature of the specification is the good ratio of power to weight whereby without specially tuning or stressing the 3½-litre V8 engine the car can provide exceptional acceleration on quite high gear ratios. The engine will run quite smoothly down to about 9 m.p.h. on top gear, and as soon as the throttle is depressed pull away strongly and smoothly.
On an average main road run in this country the acceleration is so good that 80 m.p.h. can frequently be seen if required.

The highest reading obtained was 92-93 on level ground. . . . During the course of the testing perhaps the most impressive recording obtained in this direction was between 52 and 53 miles covered in an hour without exceeding 75 m.p.h.—a speed 15 m.p.h. within the car's maximum. The feeling of safety for fast cornering experienced in the Allard is exceptional among present-day cars and enables high average speeds to be maintained in safety even over winding roads. . . . and there is the admirable quality of the car almost steering itself on the straights and of following an accurate course on corners. The brakes are Lockheed hydraulic, and they behave admirably for purposes of a fast car, acting very smoothly indeed.
In petrol consumption the Allard proved commendably moderate considering its engine size and the hard driving to which it was subjected during a long-distance test. An enthusiastic driver could hardly fail to be impressed by this car. An important point is that the fact of its embodying Ford components, notably the power unit, means that parts and service are available all over the world.

"THE MOTOR"
March 10, 1948
"On entering the driving seat, one is, moreover, immediately impressed by the way in which appearance has been blended with the requirements of the fast driver. . . . Outstanding forward visibility. . . . light, precise steering, abnormal cornering power, and very easy correction if the skid point be overrun."

When accelerating over wet city roads in the lower gears it is quickly apparent that the car has extreme resistance to wheel spin, and the getaway is such that the struggles of many cars appear pathetic. . . . What appear to be impossible speeds can be safely maintained without the slightest sign of skidding. In consequence the Allard is a car which can be driven over winding roads with the utmost confidence in all weather conditions for it has a stability and certainty of gait which inspires the utmost confidence. . . . The standing quarter-mile time on a wet road approaches 20 seconds. Exceedingly high average speeds can be realised by reason of the outstanding top-gear acceleration and magnificent road-holding characteristics. These are reinforced by the very fine braking equipment provided by Lockheed. . . . One could sustain 75 m.p.h. . . . continuously with no loss of oil pressure or noticeable rise in water temperature.
The Allard appealed to us as being an extremely practical car, for the widespread use of Ford components in engine and transmission lines is obvious in so far as world-wide availability of spares and service is concerned. . . . The car as a whole is possessed of marked virtues which are both major and, be it admitted, surprising."

"MOTOR SPORT"
April, 1948
"The coupe model Allard—one of Britain's most popular high performance cars. It combines vivid acceleration, high speed and modern outline with the advantages of Ford's world wide service facilities.
I wistfully recall a run in one of these cars, and particularly its acceleration from rest, making even a drive along London's congested Oxford Street a grand experience."

ALLARD MOTOR CO. LTD.
24-28, Clapham High Street,
London, S.W.4. Tel. Macaulay 2431.

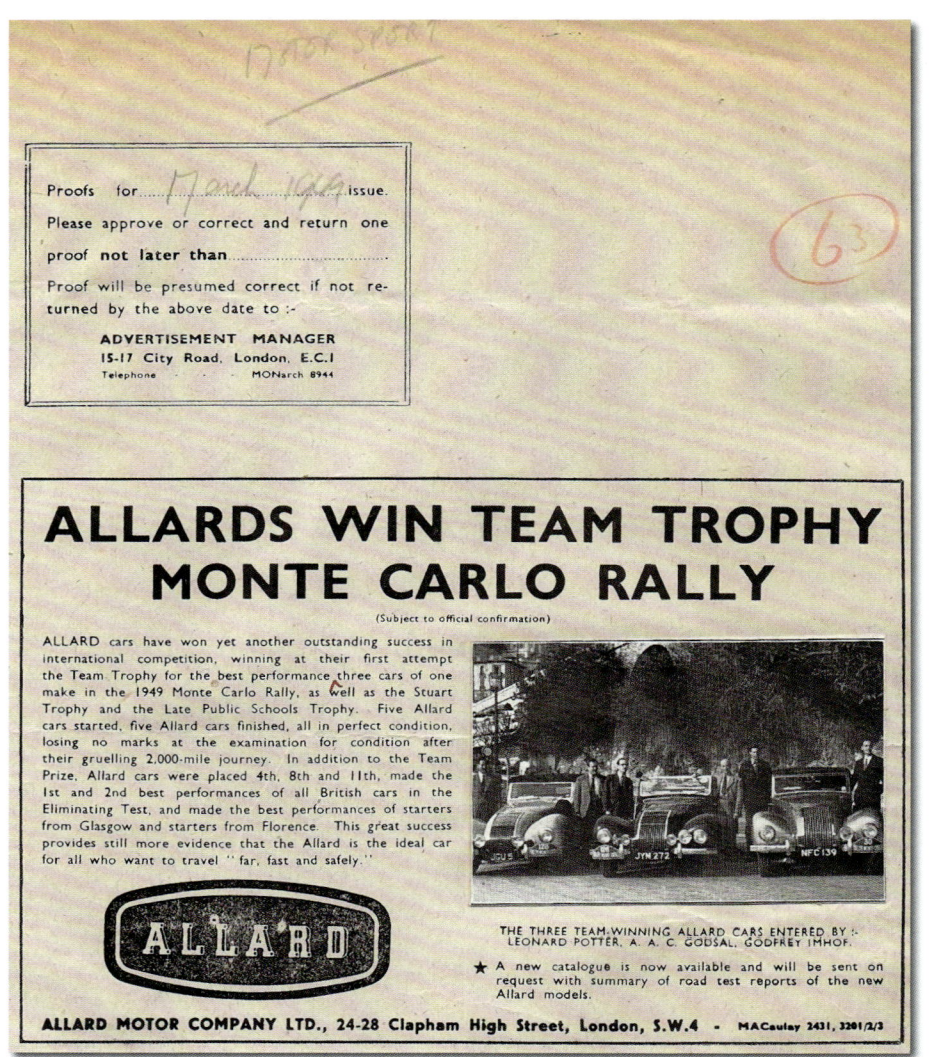

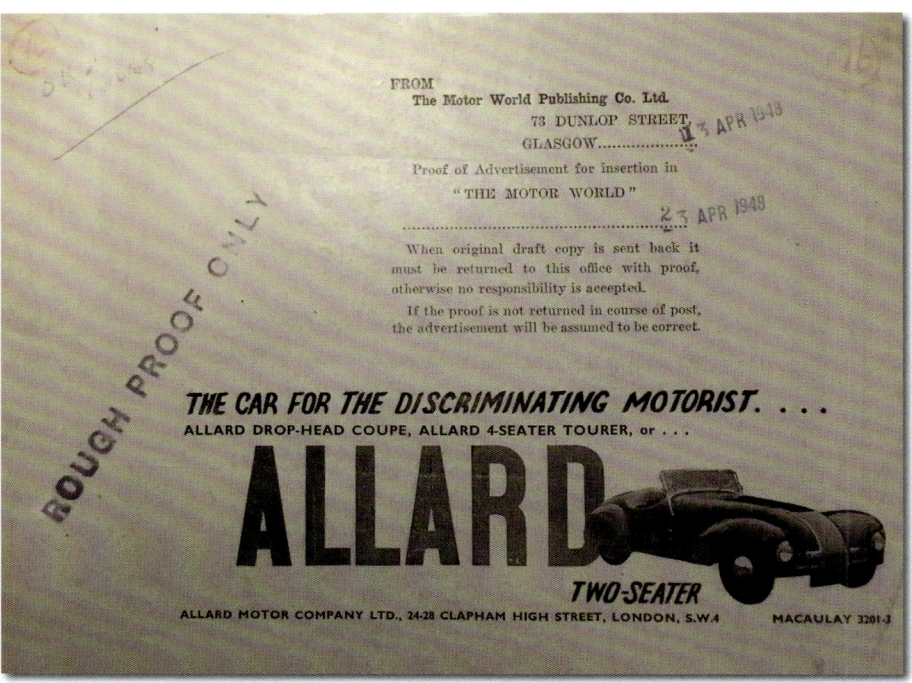

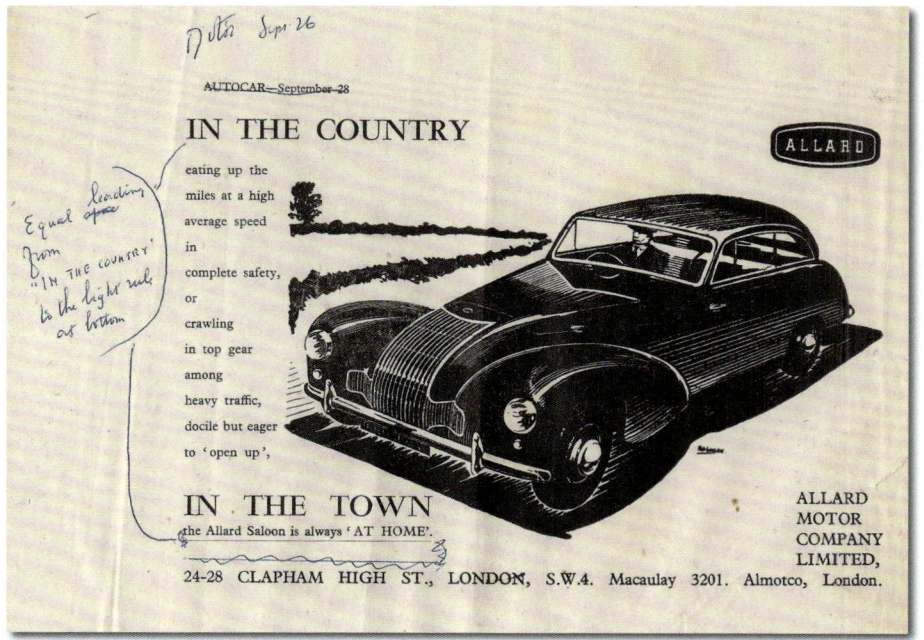

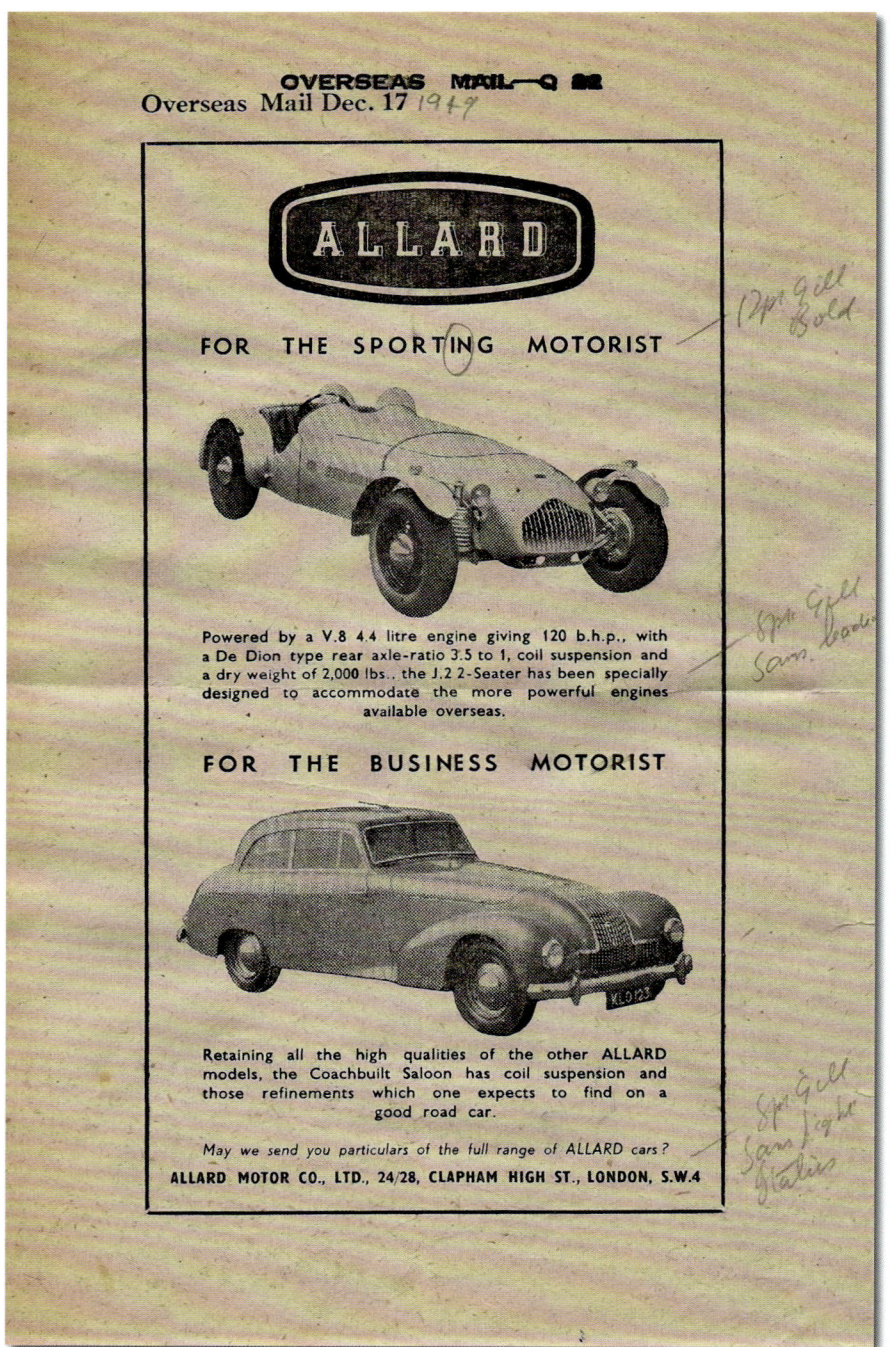

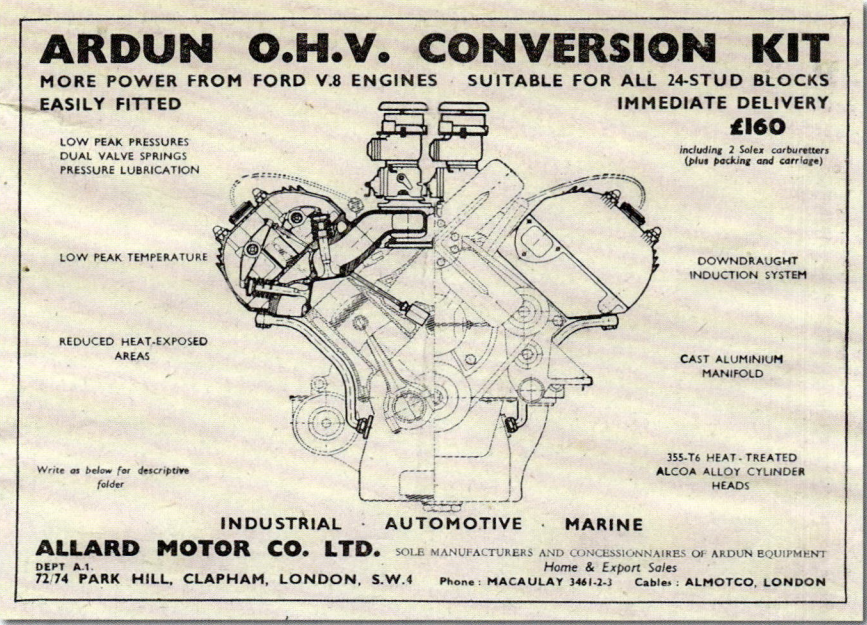

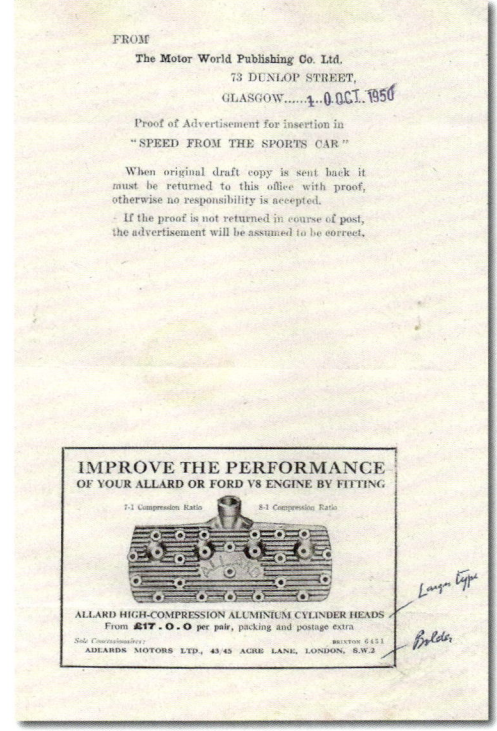

The Motor 3

DIFFERENT FACE BUT SAME FEATURES

Although the frontal aspect of the Allard Saloon has been changed by reducing the size of the radiator grille, this very popular model retains all those features so appreciated by discerning motorists.

● Extra large Luggage Boot with enclosed tool lockers.

● Controlled Air Conditioning and Heating.

● Opening Windscreen.

STAND No. 147
EARLS COURT—OCT. 17-27

● Cigar Lighter and ample Ashtrays.

● Automatic Reversing and Interior Lights.

ALLARD

MOTOR COMPANY LIMITED

24-28 CLAPHAM HIGH STREET, LONDON, S.W.4

Phone : Macaulay 3201-2-3   Cables : Almotco, London

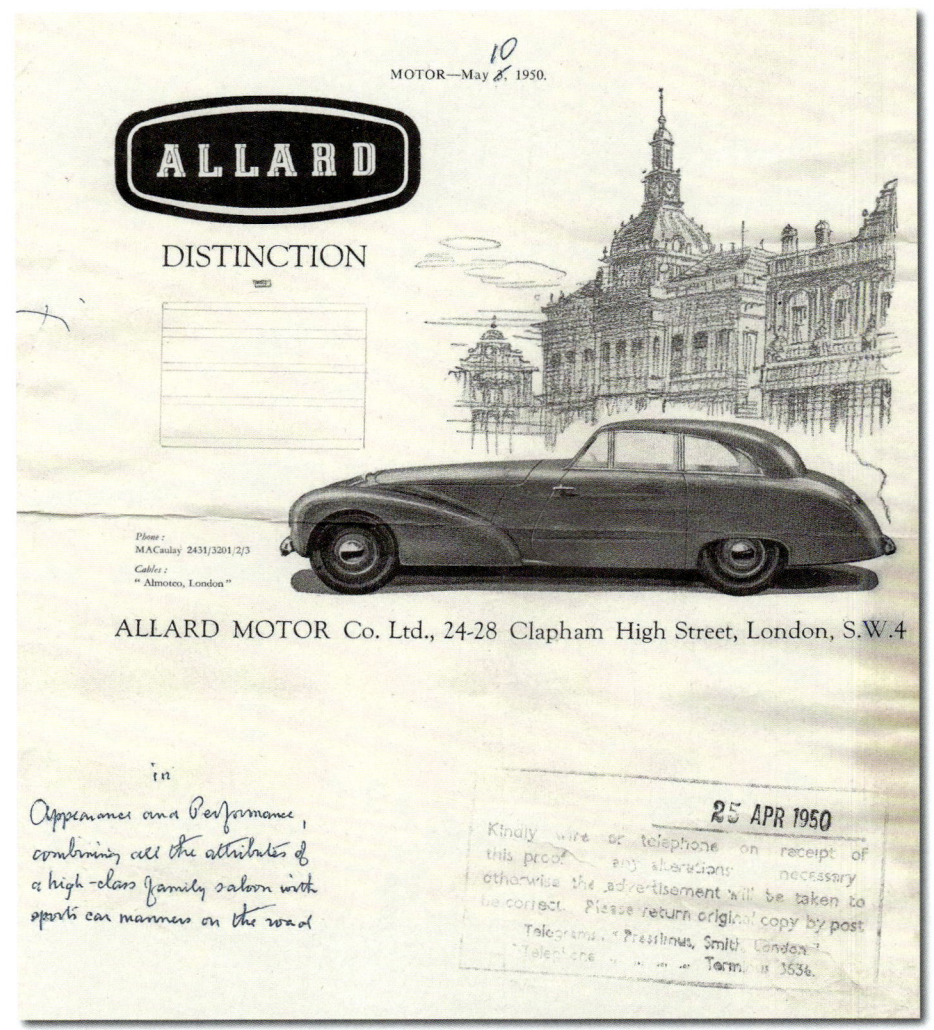

MOTOR—May 8, 1950.

ALLARD

DISTINCTION

Phone :
MACaulay 2431/3201/2/3
Cables :
" Almotco, London "

ALLARD MOTOR Co. Ltd., 24-28 Clapham High Street, London, S.W.4

Appearance and Performance, combining all the attributes of a high-class family saloon with sports car manners on the road

25 APR 1950

Kindly wire or telephone on receipt of this proof any alterations necessary otherwise the advertisement will be taken to be correct. Please return original copy by post

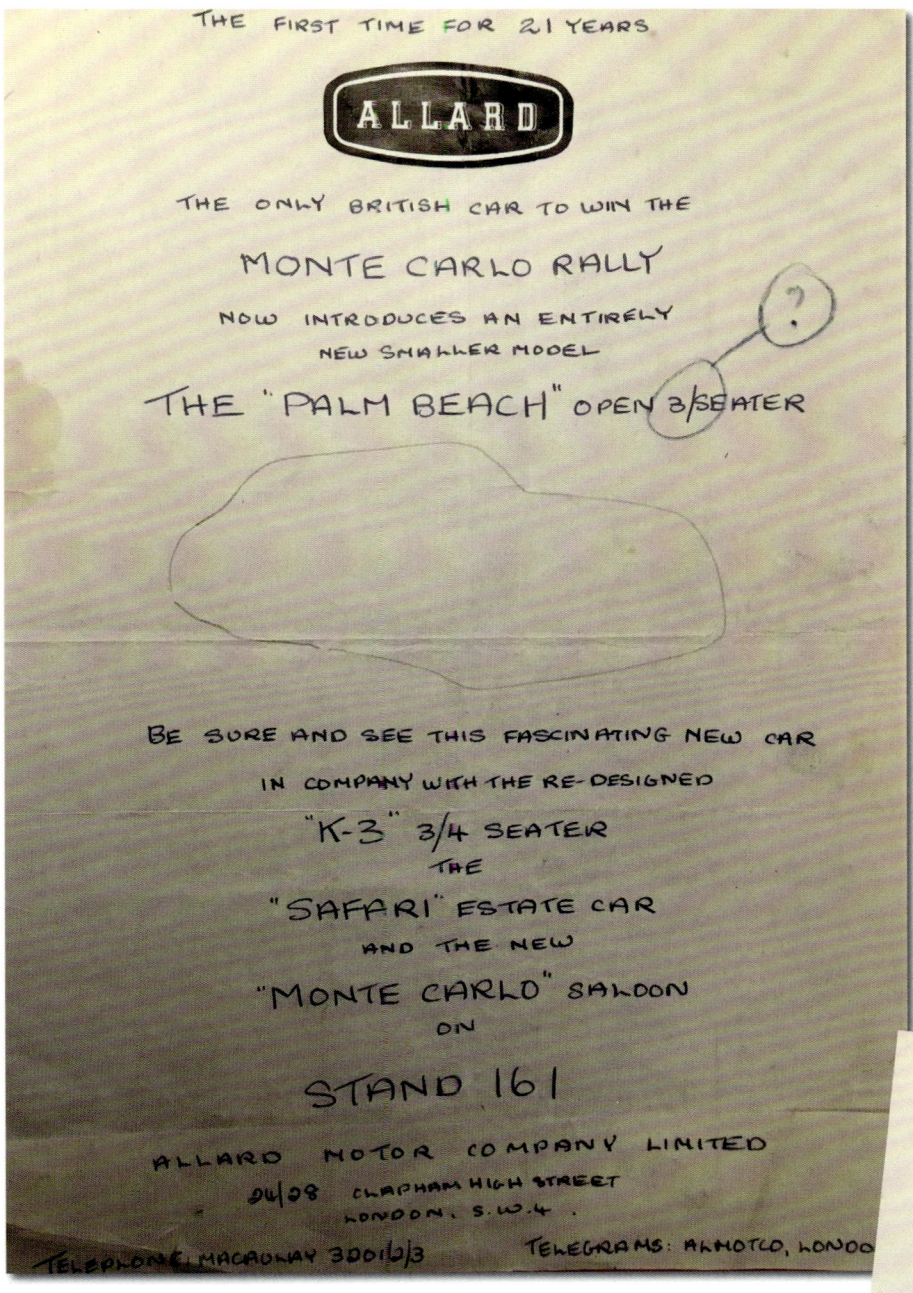

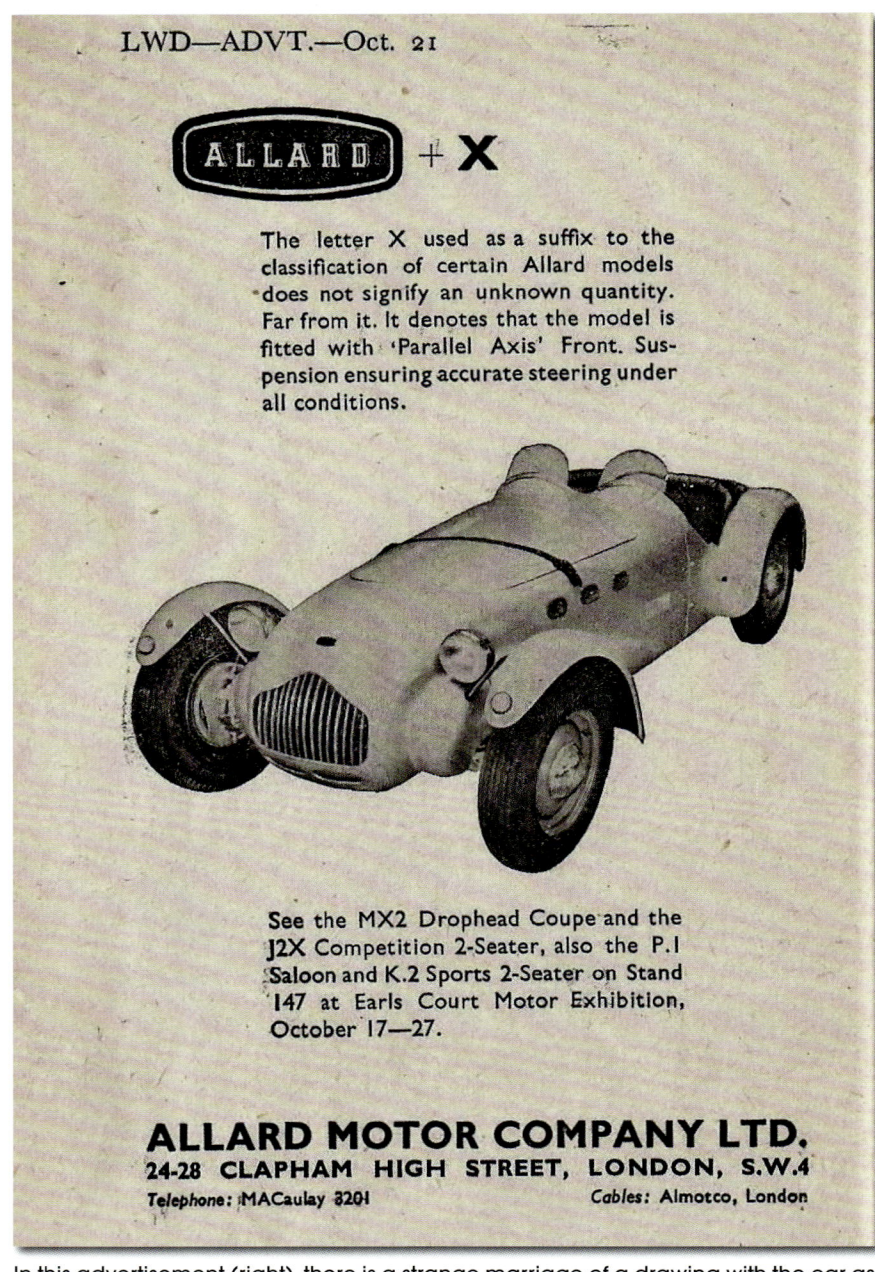

LWD—ADVT.—Oct. 21

ALLARD + **X**

The letter X used as a suffix to the classification of certain Allard models does not signify an unknown quantity. Far from it. It denotes that the model is fitted with 'Parallel Axis' Front. Suspension ensuring accurate steering under all conditions.

See the MX2 Drophead Coupe and the J2X Competition 2-Seater, also the P.1 Saloon and K.2 Sports 2-Seater on Stand 147 at Earls Court Motor Exhibition, October 17—27.

ALLARD MOTOR COMPANY LTD.
24-28 CLAPHAM HIGH STREET, LONDON, S.W.4
Telephone: MACaulay 3201   Cables: Almotco, London

In this advertisement (right), there is a strange marriage of a drawing with the car as the boys seem right out of an Enid Blyton story. Maybe the onlooking boy could be said to be dreaming of a drive.

OCTOBER 20, 1950 — *Autocar* — 107

FOR FILING ONLY.

ALLARD

This latest addition to the Allard range will be on view, for the first time in this country, at the INTERNATIONAL MOTOR EXHIBITION, EARLS COURT, LONDON (Stand No. 136), OCTOBER 18-28, together with other models designed for the competition or business motorist.

K.2 SPORTS 2-SEATER

ALLARD MOTOR COMPANY LTD., 24-28 CLAPHAM HIGH STREET, LONDON, S.W.4
Telephones : Macaulay 3201-2-3   Telegrams : Almotco, Clapcom, London
N7

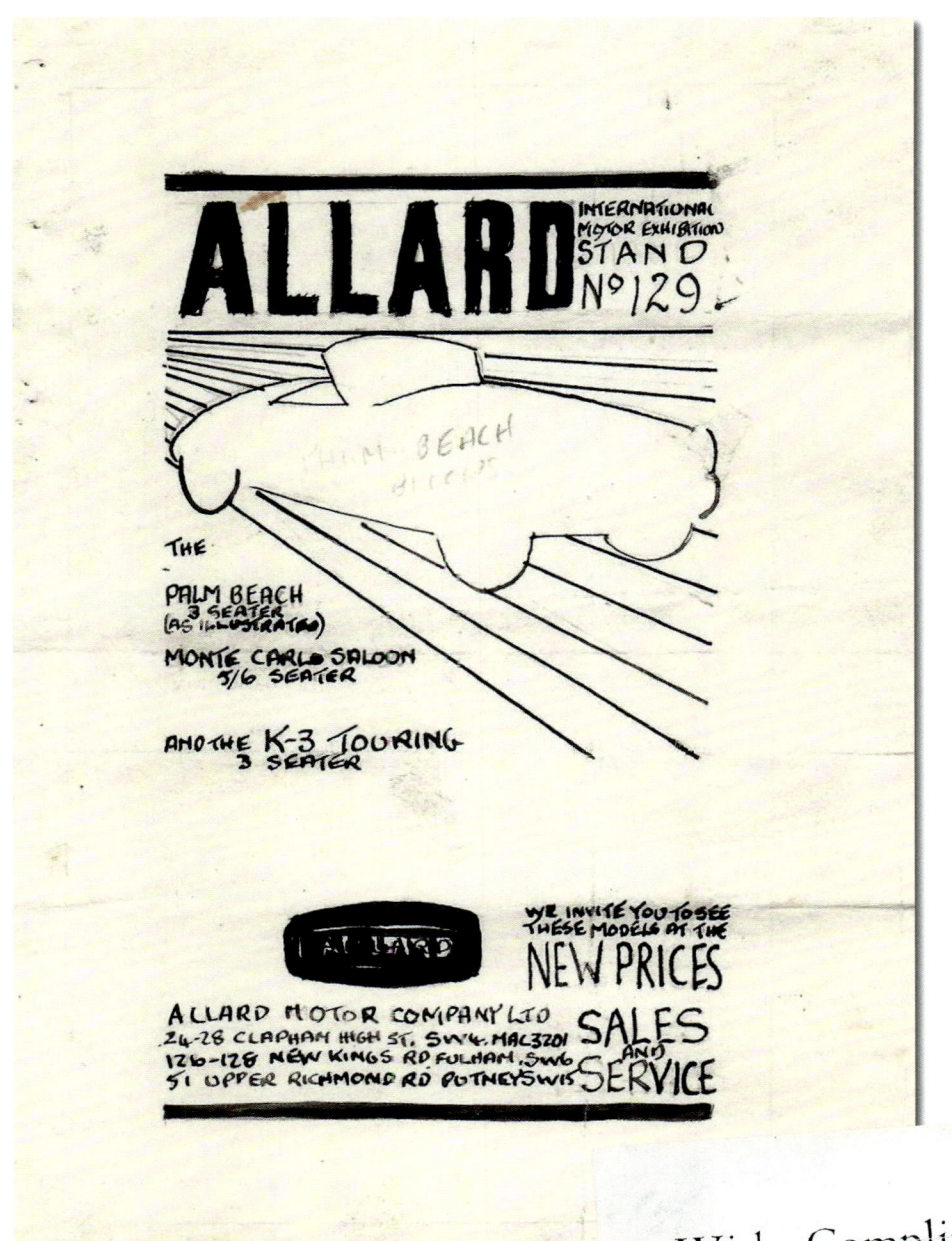

Proof Artwork of the Allard

THE MOTOR YEAR BOOK

ALLARD

The Most Consistently Successful Car in Recent Years

WINNER OF THE

1952 MONTE-CARLO RALLY

The first British Car to do so for Twenty-One Years

Illustrated is the **"PALM BEACH"** open three seater

ALLARD MOTOR COMPANY LIMITED
24-28 CLAPHAM HIGH STREET, LONDON, S.W.4

Phone : MACAULAY 3201   Cables : ALMOTCO, LONDON

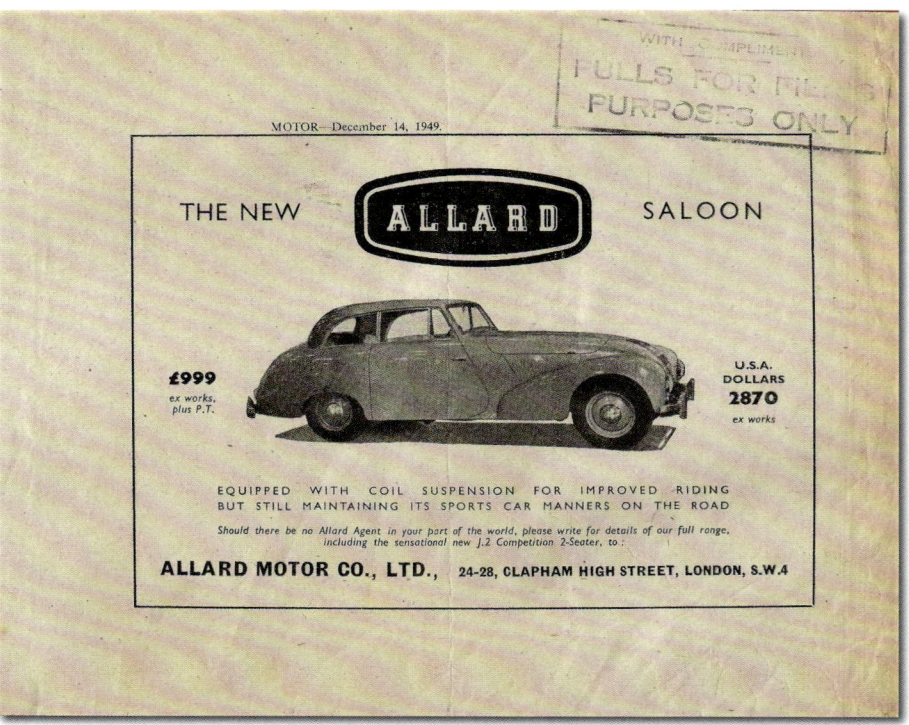

MOTOR—December 14, 1949.

THE NEW **ALLARD** SALOON

£999 ex works, plus P.T.   **U.S.A. DOLLARS 2870** ex works

EQUIPPED WITH COIL SUSPENSION FOR IMPROVED RIDING BUT STILL MAINTAINING ITS SPORTS CAR MANNERS ON THE ROAD

Should there be no Allard Agent in your part of the world, please write for details of our full range, including the sensational new J.2 Competition 2-Seater, to :

ALLARD MOTOR CO., LTD., 24-28, CLAPHAM HIGH STREET, LONDON, S.W.4

Proof Artwork of the Allard

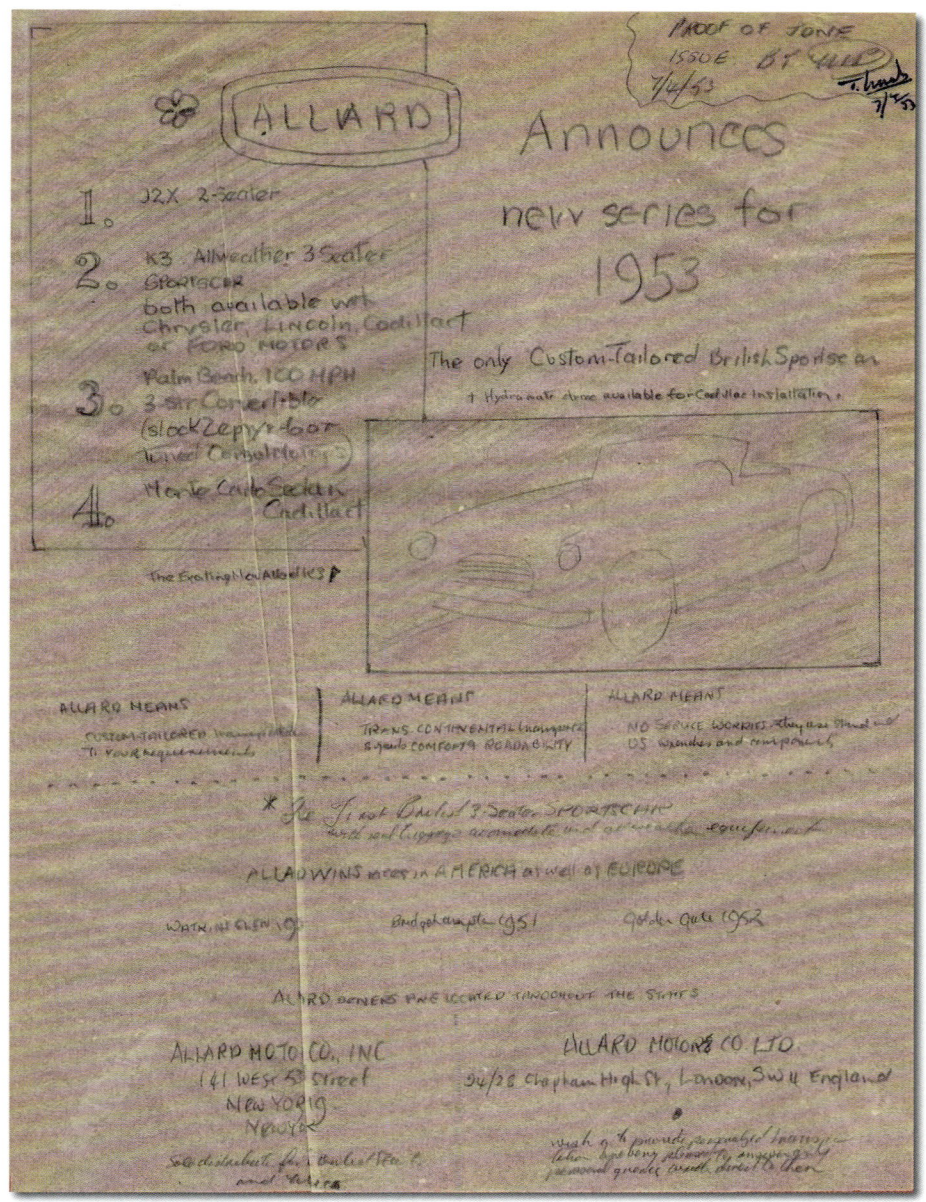

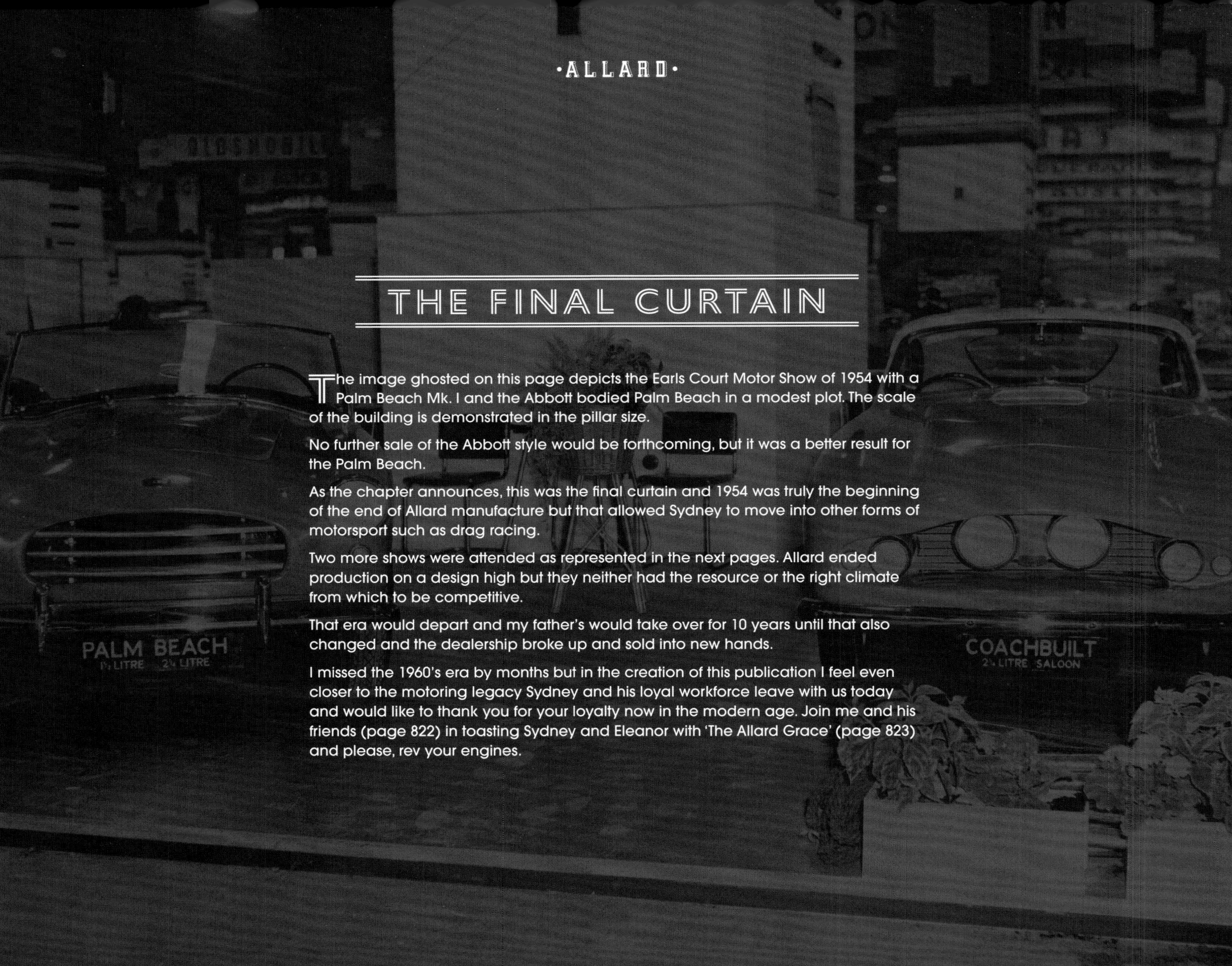

THE FINAL CURTAIN

The image ghosted on this page depicts the Earls Court Motor Show of 1954 with a Palm Beach Mk. I and the Abbott bodied Palm Beach in a modest plot. The scale of the building is demonstrated in the pillar size.

No further sale of the Abbott style would be forthcoming, but it was a better result for the Palm Beach.

As the chapter announces, this was the final curtain and 1954 was truly the beginning of the end of Allard manufacture but that allowed Sydney to move into other forms of motorsport such as drag racing.

Two more shows were attended as represented in the next pages. Allard ended production on a design high but they neither had the resource or the right climate from which to be competitive.

That era would depart and my father's would take over for 10 years until that also changed and the dealership broke up and sold into new hands.

I missed the 1960's era by months but in the creation of this publication I feel even closer to the motoring legacy Sydney and his loyal workforce leave with us today and would like to thank you for your loyalty now in the modern age. Join me and his friends (page 822) in toasting Sydney and Eleanor with 'The Allard Grace' (page 823) and please, rev your engines.

The 1956 Earls Court Motor Show.

The 1957 Earls Court Motor Show and the last time Allard cars were shown.

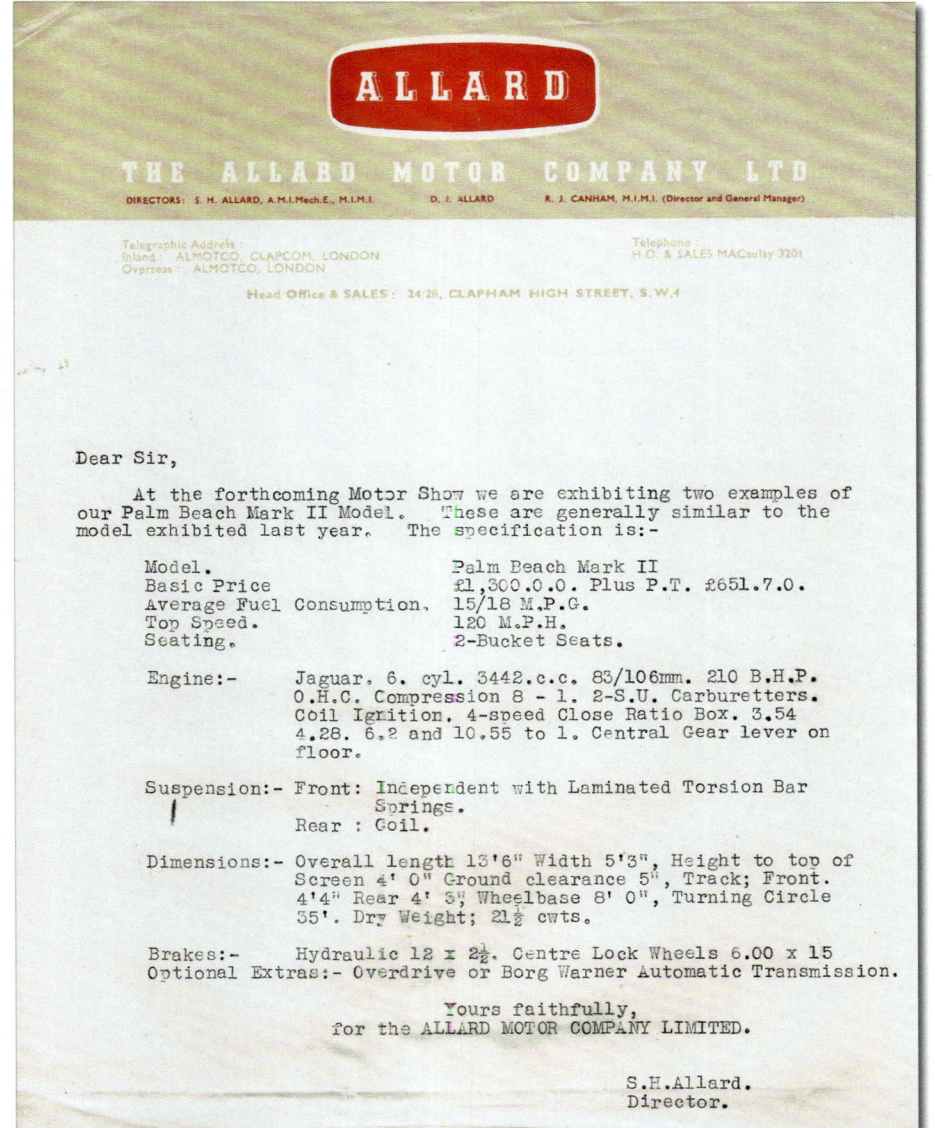

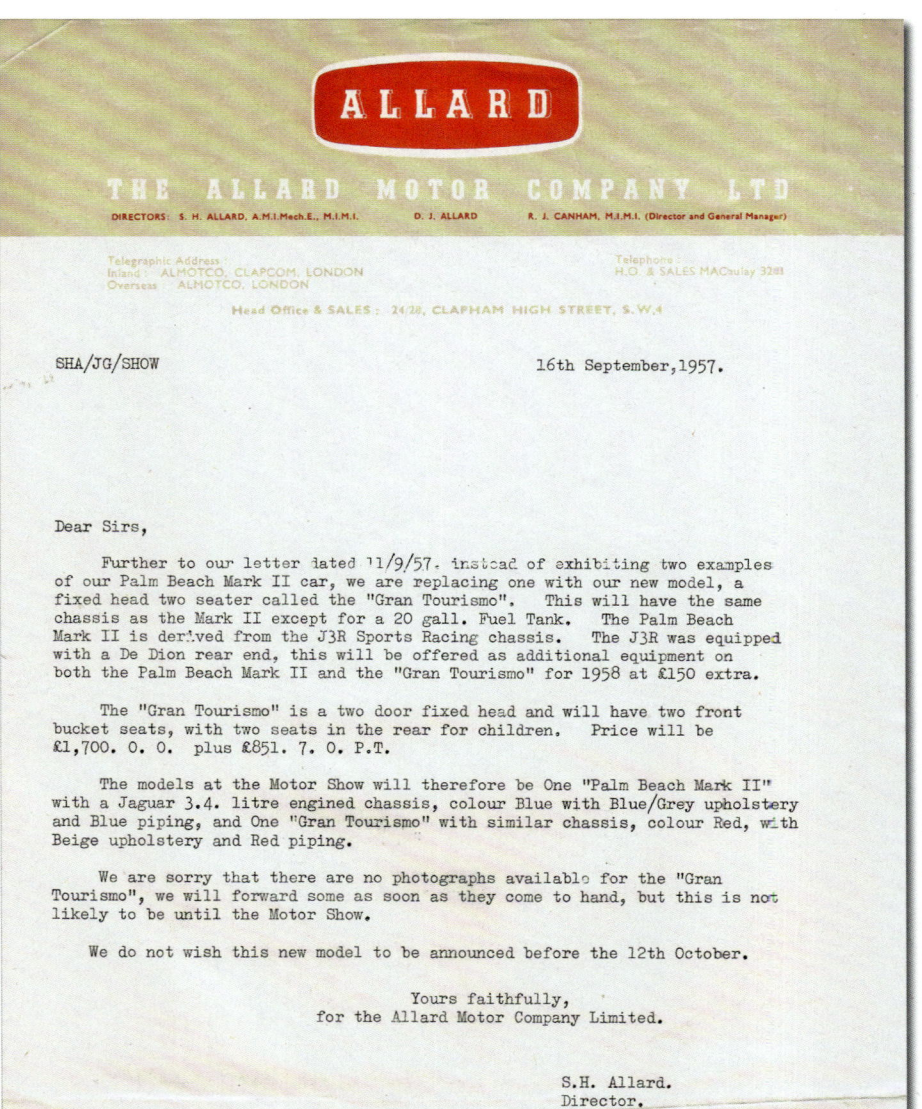

·ALLARD·

THE ALLARD MOTOR COMPANY LTD

DIRECTORS: S. H. ALLARD, A.M.I.Mech.E., M.I.M.I.   D. J. ALLARD   R. J. CANHAM, M.I.M.I. (Director and General Manager)

Telegraphic Address:
Inland: ALMOTCO, CLAPCOM, LONDON
Overseas: ALMOTCO, LONDON

Telephone:
H.O. & SALES MACaulay 3201

Head Office & SALES: 24/28, CLAPHAM HIGH STREET, S.W.4

Dear Sir,

At the forthcoming Motor Show we are exhibiting two examples of our Palm Beach Mark II Model. These are generally similar to the model exhibited last year. The specification is:-

Model.	Palm Beach Mark II
Basic Price	£1,300.0.0. Plus P.T. £651.7.0.
Average Fuel Consumption.	15/18 M.P.G.
Top Speed.	120 M.P.H.
Seating.	2-Bucket Seats.

Engine:- Jaguar. 6. cyl. 3442.c.c. 83/106mm. 210 B.H.P. O.H.C. Compression 8 - 1. 2-S.U. Carburetters. Coil Ignition. 4-speed Close Ratio Box. 3.54 4.28. 6.2 and 10.55 to 1. Central Gear lever on floor.

Suspension:- Front: Independent with Laminated Torsion Bar Springs.
Rear : Coil.

Dimensions:- Overall length 13'6" Width 5'3", Height to top of Screen 4' 0" Ground clearance 5", Track; Front. 4'4" Rear 4' 5" Wheelbase 8' 0", Turning Circle 35'. Dry Weight; 21½ cwts.

Brakes:- Hydraulic 12 x 2½. Centre Lock Wheels 6.00 x 15
Optional Extras:- Overdrive or Borg Warner Automatic Transmission.

Yours faithfully,
for the ALLARD MOTOR COMPANY LIMITED.

S.H.Allard.
Director.

·ALLARD·

THE ALLARD MOTOR COMPANY LTD

DIRECTORS: S. H. ALLARD, A.M.I.Mech.E., M.I.M.I.   D. J. ALLARD   R. J. CANHAM, M.I.M.I. (Director and General Manager)

Telegraphic Address:
Inland: ALMOTCO, CLAPCOM, LONDON
Overseas: ALMOTCO, LONDON

Telephone:
H.O. & SALES MACaulay 3201

Head Office & SALES: 24/28, CLAPHAM HIGH STREET, S.W.4

SHA/JG/SHOW   16th September, 1957.

Dear Sirs,

Further to our letter dated 11/9/57. instead of exhibiting two examples of our Palm Beach Mark II car, we are replacing one with our new model, a fixed head two seater called the "Gran Tourismo". This will have the same chassis as the Mark II except for a 20 gall. Fuel Tank. The Palm Beach Mark II is derived from the J3R Sports Racing chassis. The J3R was equipped with a De Dion rear end, this will be offered as additional equipment on both the Palm Beach Mark II and the "Gran Tourismo" for 1958 at £150 extra.

The "Gran Tourismo" is a two door fixed head and will have two front bucket seats, with two seats in the rear for children. Price will be £1,700. 0. 0. plus £851. 7. 0. P.T.

The models at the Motor Show will therefore be One "Palm Beach Mark II" with a Jaguar 3.4. litre engined chassis, colour Blue with Blue/Grey upholstery and Blue piping, and One "Gran Tourismo" with similar chassis, colour Red, with Beige upholstery and Red piping.

We are sorry that there are no photographs available for the "Gran Tourismo", we will forward some as soon as they come to hand, but this is not likely to be until the Motor Show.

We do not wish this new model to be announced before the 12th October.

Yours faithfully,
for the Allard Motor Company Limited.

S.H. Allard.
Director.

Sydney's letters did not drum up much more trade, however the Palm Beach GT was completed in time for the show.

· APPENDIX 1 ·

THE 'DOMESDAY' BOOK

Some readers might know that the real Domesday Book is the earliest British public record dated from 1086 which was created for William the Conqueror as a stocktaking list of the assets of Britain. The Allard Domesday Book is a stocktake of known Allard cars by one of the prior Allard Owners Club archivists, possibly from the 1980s.

The quality is rough but this document will supplement your records and it is particularly useful in adding previously unknown UK registration numbers.

Owners through the years are noted with only the current/most recent owner omitted for privacy.

·ALLARD·

PREWAR (left page)

Chassis	Reg Nº	Reg Date	Orig Description	Latest Description
842 (Ford Chassis)	CLK 5	Mar '36	2 Seats V8 Pointed tail	then War button?

S.H. Allard. Last seen in Middx area in 1961, May '71. Last registered owner Mr Upton, sold car in 1956, Dec '71. (Tony Booth's friend?) Euan Nelson Apr '62

| AM1 | AUK 795 | Apr '37 | 2/4 Seats V8 Slab Tank Yellow/Black | Bought from Mr Holmes in 1986, Chorley 1990. |

David Gilson. reg. OHA 695. Very little left (non orig chassis)

| | ELL 300 | Nov '37 | 4 Seater V8 black Tailwagger | |

H. Allard. to J.F. Guest.

| | ELX 50 | Dec '37 | 2/4 Seats V12 White | Converted to Rav engine by L. Parke. 1950 Scrapped. |

Hutchinson sold to C. Ian Craig

| AM8 | EXH 455 | Mar '38 | 4 Seater V8 | Cream 1990 |

J.H. Bowles, Liversedge (for sale) OCT '62, Bought by Robin Sadler (article) Aug '67. Clad Senior, Peter G. Valentine Jan '69, Ken E. Nelson, Hutton, Essex, restoring Sep '71, Feb '82.

| AM5 | EYO 750 | Jul '38 | 2/4 Seats V8 | Green Mercury V8, shortened chassis simple body, Mercato. 5/86 |

reg GGE 523 in 1953.

| | FGF 290 | Aug '38 | 2 Seats V8 then V12 Pointed tail | Scrapped. |

reg. HPX 57. C. Hutchinson, re-registered by Victor Biggs in 1948, owned & raced by Frank Vardell (1950s), R. Threlfall 1950, Tom Norton (early 50s).

| AM11 | FGP 750 | Sep '38 | 2 Seats V8 Pointed tail | In Allard Catalogue Blue, Mercury. In Allard Catalogue 1950 (Special Nº2) J? |

Sold to Clarke in 1939, bought by Hutchinson Jan '69. S.H. Allard. North of England Jan '69, Article Dec '71. Des Sowes by Sep '77.

| | FLX 650 | Mar '39 | 3 Seats V12 Newlook | (Special Nº 10?) |

Whittingham & Mitchell body work. Dr Silcock, Ken McAlpine, Written off 866 in 1950 Alpine Rally by Len Potter.

| AM12 | FXP 469 | May '39 | 2/4 Seats V8 | |

Gates Jan '69.

| | FXP 470 | May '39 | 4 Seats V8 "Newlook" | In Allard Catalogue 1950 |

Whittingham & Mitchell body work. V.S.A. Biggs (Special Nº5?)

| | LMG 192 | Sep '41 | 4 Seats V8 "Newlook" | Stillaround, needing restoration Jan '69. Apr '61, for sale in Jul '63 £125 (restoration nearly complete) |

S.H. Allard - Completed 1946. 1st post war event at Bristol, then owned by Wick brothers.

left in a field under the snow? the sale this at PDC speed+ diner 2000.

Wrexham had prewar Allard Feb '59.

Sawbridgeworth, Herts has prewar Allard Special, Royal blue with Alloy bonnet, Merc Engine Jul '71. Seen at Shelsley Walsh '63 re-registered JY....? (+161 = K1)

KUW 239 - Re-registered car.

J1 (right page)

G. Allard check 18.10.13   16 chassis in build register!!

| 103 | HLB 430 | 22.3.47 | LONDON | S.H. Allard. (delivered) | Original Demo Car. |
| 106 | HLP 5 / KLD 5 | 28.7.46 | LONDON | G. Imhoff | Per Fred Damodar — Dave Kinsella has HLP 5 body & chassis but no log book. Green. |

Brian Croot Apr '63, Article May '72, Apr '72

| 109 | JHW 100 / LHW 100 | 5.9.46 | LONDON | Ken Burgess | |

S.C. Gray. Supercharged flat head, 5 Sep '59 Brighton Speed trials, stillowned Aug '63 (with flat head). G.P. Dobbins, Salisbury Apr '64, Selling. Burgess J1 fitted Jag Engine & gearbox, Irvine Mar '65. Ardun heads sold separately Apr '65. A.A. Mortimer Jun '65. Adrian Mortimer selling (Jag engined) Mar '66. Tim Peters, Brighton, Mistrale body, Jag Engine, selling Feb '88. Bill Brooks mid 70s on — knockabout — used since 73? green with red stripe, body burnt & chassis repaired scrapped.

| 110* | HXC 578 | 3.9.46 | LONDON | Jim Appleton | (Original Reg Nº transferred to Appleton) is this J4? ✗ |

Bill George, Cornwall. Peter Valentine (Bought '62 & Re-restored) Jan '65, Previously owned by Les Davies. Had more engine Jul '65, Had Chevrolet engine Aug '66. Seen by Peter Mear at Poole Power Stn. 1974/75. Prior to going to Australia.
* Tom... CKG TXH613 !! N/O.

111	GOM 2	31.10.46	BIRMINGHAM	Geoffrey Mansell	✓
112		19.12.46	JERSEY	✓	Note. Allocher book says #869 J but reg empty!
117	HYW 331	3.4.47	LONDON	Maurice Wide ✓	Also # 396 J!

Tom notes this number

| 148 | HRR 472 | 4.3.47 | DERBY | → CHASSIS ONLY ✓ | Also # 415 J! This was built as front car. |

Tom notes this number

152	S2		28.3.47	LONDON	Len Potter. → CHASSIS ONLY. —	Also # 386 J
273	73 or NRC 640 MPC 640	29.9.47	LONDON	Len Potter. → CHASSIS ONLY	Build Record says this is K1 'Competition' Allocher says J1 ✓
274	74 GAB 779	5.9.47	GLOUCESTER	Harac Robert. ✓ J1 CHASSIS ONLY.	→ Allocher book says J1
275	75 KPB 242	22.1.48	LONDON	Len Potter. Mead	was 386, then (within 1 year) Incandescent blue. → Record says Special chassis K1 Red.

F.W. Lock, Kensal Rise Aug '63, Woburn Park Hillclimb Nov '63, Duxford Jun '66, for sale Jul '64, Robin Sadler Jun '65, A.K. Naber, Tolworth, Nov '65, Robin Sadler at Blackbushe 9 Oct '66, Nov '66, Robin Sadler Selling Oct '67, Peter Bosworth, Southampton Feb '68, Brunton Hillclimb Jun '68, P. Bosworth selling Jan '69, Don Batchelor .83

| 415 | H15 | MPG 250 | | Ted Frost | "Reconstructed Vehicle" | Black .9/86 |

Ralph Venables, H. Gledhill Oct '61, Selling Sep '62 £250, Don E. Batchelor Aug '63. Noted by Tom with notes — but this is a "GAB" entry — only J1 notes. → Service recs — 14.10.48 — Fast J1. JGP 473   S.H. Allard   2nd Post War Special based on J1 chassis

J2

Chassis	Reg	Date	Notes	Owner key	Date
888	888 KXC 170	23.3.51	Prototype. Mercury, then Ardun, then Cadillac.		
	(Built June '49) S.H. Allard, Annable, John Humphries, Nayler (N° England)				1991
1512	512	30.1.50	Uruguay. LHD.		
1513	513	2.3.50	USA. LHD.		
	Bell.				
1514	514	13.10.49	USA. Cadillac 331ci (5425cc) Red grill, wires & interior.	Silver (Monterey 1990)	USA 1986, 1990
	Cole				
1515	515 KUC 31	24.8.49	USA. 2nd Prototype J2 3917cc	(Monterey 1990)	
	Zora Atkins Ardun - Duntov.			Tom Turner 1990	
1555	555	7.1.50	USA. LHD		
1556	556	20.3.50	USA. LHD	Chrome Wires (Monterey 1990)	Red
	Goldschmidt. (New York Show Car - frame only)			USA	1990
1557	557 CWG 12	28.2.50	Halstead Motor Co. London. Cadillac		Red
	Roy Clarkeson. R Grebe 1980, USA, Mark Allard 1989				1989
1558	558 KOF 999	14.4.50	Bristol St. Birmingham		Red
	Clark. (S.C. Clark - Autosport 1950)			USA 1990	
1559	559 OS 7525	15.4.50	George & Jobling, Glasgow Mercury Ardun, then Olds. was all enveloping body		
	Mort, Simpson, Peter S. Lee, Chorley Lancs Jun 65, Chris Lyons Aug 66, Sep 70				1989 91
1570	570 MWE 254	26.1.50	Tate, Leeds. Jag engine Sep 70.		Green
	(Curtis) T.C. Hattison. G.H. Dungworth Sheffield Oct 64 Selling Mai 65, P.A. Hope, Eccles Apr 67, Sep 70, Apr 72, for Sale				1981
1571	571 VGN 681	24.4.50	USA. LHD		
	Moss. D.B. Clark, Calif, USA, Dec 67			USA 1982	
1572	572	4.5.50	Universal, Derby.		
	Sleight				
1573	573 NUB 863	11.5.50	Tate, Leeds. Ford Flathead		Red
	YSU 722 Hewitt	Chris Drake Feb 1989		Coys NEC May 1990.	
1574	574 OBB 377	25.5.50	Patterson, Newcastle. Cadillac		White.
	Curtis, Ex J. Davidson (2nd to Fred Wacker at 1950 Sebring) Leslie Newell Sep '78				1988
1575	575 BJV 365	15.6.50	Nunns, Manchester. Ford Flathead. (was Green)	(Monterey 1990)	Red
	Hyde, Dell, Peter Moor, Jul-Jul '57 to 58 John Tinsley, Fred Damodaran Jun '61 Selling American at Mildenhall at Layton Scott			Tom Turner USA 1986, 1990	
1576	576 KLJ 2	26.5.50	English, Bournemouth.		
	Wan-Hope.				

J2 PAGE 2

Chassis	Reg	Date	Notes	Owner key	Date
1577	577	8.6.50	USA.		
	Tom Cole - F. Wacker				
1578	578 (Not registered in UK)	30.8.50	USA. 1950 Le Mans Car (N° 4)		
	S.H. Allard. Recently found in poor condition.			USA 1990	
1579	579	21.4.50	Spain. LHD		
1690	690	5.7.50	Sweden LHD Cadillac 390ci		
	Bought, Ramen, Stockholm, Sweden Jun '64			Sweden May '78 still '78	
1691	691	22.6.50	Peru LHD		
1692	692	23.5.50	Portugal LHD		Red
				Portugal 1987-199	
1693	693 LLP 797	7.10.50	Adlards, London Ardun 4545cc Pea Green, Silver, Dark Green, cream, dk green, red, white, dk green then Red!	(Monterey 1990)	
	Col Rupert de Cartinaga, J. Peskett, Leics Aug 67 (selling £325 Aug 67)			Sep 72 Dec 74 Nov 71 199	
1694	694	7.6.50	Portugal. LHD Ardun (rolling chassis 1990) 1693 - 2011 rebuilt up to		
				Lisbon, Portugal 1992	
1695	695 MTA 635	22.8.50	Exeter Australia NCC Ladies Hol Trial Easter 1952		
	Watkins, E.D. Scobeig, Peter J. Jackson, Houghton, Hunts Jan 70 (at Worcester Manor) (Concours 1972)			1990	
1696	696 BJS 369	25.7.50	USA. LHD Cadillac		Red
	Frederick Gibbs, USA Paul Pappalardo 1979, 1984				
1697	697	25.7.50	USA LHD		
	Siddon,				
1698	698	26.1.51	Australia		
1699	699 BTB 402 (Aust Reg 19)	18.1.51	Australia. Ardun (In need of restoration after 15 years (under a tarpaulin) - 1990)		Blue
	Gardiners. J.E. Jackson, Sydney Australia Apr 64 (Being restored Nov 73)			Australia 1990	
1730	730		Adlards Chassis only - Demo.		
	Duntov				
1731	731	8.8.50	Australia		
1732	732	2.8.50	USA. LHD Ardun Disc Wheels, tan hide Bare Ally (Monterey 1990)		
				USA 1990	
1733	733	11.9.50	USA LHD Full Winged.		
	Claude May			Illinois 1989	

J2 PAGE 3

1734	734		15.8.50	USA	LHD			
			Finn, USA, May '69					
1735	735 LLP 798	No Record	London	Mercury Ardun (Sydney's TT car)			Dark Blue
		Brian Golder Jun '61.					
1736	736 (unpainted)		13.9.50	USA	LHD	Cadillac 331ci (5424cc)	Disc Wheels, Red Chassis, Black Interior, Bare Alloy
	Ken Moss	Michael	R. via J.C. en fred. +				British Columbia 1990
1737	737		14.8.50	Canada	LHD		
1738	738		25.8.50	USA	Chrysler (1951)		Red.
			Mass USA Jun '64, Apr '66				Still owned 1986
1739	739		19.9.50	USA	LHD	Buick	
			Wilbur F. Saunders, Dearborn, Michigan Jun '65, Nov '69.				
1780	780		4.9.50	USA			
1781	781		6.10.50	Australia			
		Driven by Reggie Hunt '53-'54.	Laurence H. Jackson Sydney, Australia Jan '70, for Sale, Monterey Auction 1990				
1782	82		13.11.50	Australia			Black interior Red
		owned by same family 35 years.	for Sale at The Five Car Store, USA.				1991
1783	783 NCV 942		6.2.51	New Central, Liskeard	Ardun Mercury		Green
		Ken Watkins, Potter, John Patterson (4-5 yrs)				Derbyshire 1989.
1784	784 LXD 517		9.1.51	Adlards, London		Chevrolet	Orange
			feb '60.				1990
1785	785		22.1.51	Turkey	(Show car)		
1786	786		22.9.50	Portugal	LHD		
1787	787		21.11.50	USA	LHD		
1788	788		21.11.50	USA	LHD		
1789	789		7.11.50	USA	LHD		
1850	850		25.1.51	USA	LHD	5899cc Red wires, Red hide, Black
		Fred Workers (Car # '46')				(Monterey 1990) USA 1990

J2 Page 4

1851	851	No Record	USA. LHD Mag Wheels, 603cc, Outside Exhaust, Red Wheels			Black
	David Fogg (Car #15)					(Monterey 1990) USA 1990
1852	852 QD 4890		5.3.51	USA	LHD	Chrysler	White
	John Perona		Mike Bradbrook 1988, Several Dealers, for sale 1990				
1853	853	No Record		LHD	Chrysler		
			...num, Mass USA, wanting most Article by Still awaiting restoration 1990. White May '69, Jun T, Jul '69				
1854	854		17.5.51	USA	LHD		
1855	855		17.5.51	Geo Wales Garage, Geneva	LHD		
			...Switzerland Jan '78.				
1856	856	No Record					
1857	857	No Record (New York Show) LHD Cadillac (original)					Red.
	Preston Grey.					Mass USA May '69 Still 1986
1858	858		21.2.51	USA	LHD		
1859	859		5.3.51	USA	LHD		
1910	1910 OVT 983		1.4.51	Nunns, Manchester	Hitchins & Reece No2 (1951 LeMans Car)		
	Hitchins, car bought by Larrinaga. Reg. N° Transferred to J2X then JR. Car exported to Rhodesia without any papers or...						
1911	1911 JWP 800 NMD 2 (later) MTE 857 (by Stanley)		29.3.51	[chassis discarded after Healey first crash of 4 X for Allac - chassis to John Lowery 1990] Pete Collins 1951, then to Midland Bus in area, then Dunford 1957 (Cadillac cc) Mrs Collins 1951, later Collins 1957 + Fairthac MK2 in 1960. Sold to Laurie/Bruno Ferrati in mid 60's. Ferrari selling Sep '68, Aug '70. John Hooper owned it in late Seventies +			Green then Gold.
							1986, ?
1912	1912 LXY 15		10.4.51	Allards, London			# 1412 USA
	Cyril Wick	W. Cook, Ringwood Nov '63		H.G. Eckert USA (licence 14/03/18)			
1971	1971 LXR 949		7.9.51	London. Mille Miglia Car & Girode Sicily			Red
	S.H. Allard					Kansas City USA 1990
1972	1972 LXT 5		17.3.51	London	Cadillac.		
	Imhof, Harry Weston May '63, Thurston, ...						1988
1973	1973 MGC 530		7.6.51	Argentina	LHD		
1974	1974		30.3.51	USA	LHD		
1975	1975		13.7.51	USA			

J2 PAGE 5

2010 — 2010 LYV 366 No Record London. Dural Hubs, Some boxing cut out of frame 'Lightweight car.' Blue.
S.H.Allard? — H.W.Whyte (killed at Bonars) Sold to Jersey, 2 brothers who did Sand racing - man killed, buried in Sand?

2011 — 2011 LXN 5 London Lengthened Chassis - Coupé
Imhof, George Fisher Oct'62 Selling Oct'68, C. Macadam, Nottingham for Sale Jan68, Feb69 1988

2012 — 2012 NKT 17 20.6.51 Adlards London (was Ardun) (23.6.52) Ford Flathead Red
Tatham Dr Roger Bagshaw, Buxton 1972 Mass USA 1986

2013 — 2013 No Record.

2014 — 2014 No Record (Le Mans Car) 1951 (Backup car.)
S.H.Allard.

2015 — 2015 GJB 1 2.4.51 London Lengthened J2 chassis All enveloping body.
JFM 780 Saloon body, then open sports 'Le Monstre', chassis Roan Godsal
Godsal John Williams 1956 car purchased by D Swansea, Dunstable from
built to body - all fell through & unfinished car was sold on

2016 — 2016 20.4.51 Finland LHD

2017 — 2017 25.4.51 Finland LHD Cadillac 390ci Red
Finland 1986

2018 — 2018 12.7.51 USA LHD

2019 — 2019 18.9.51 USA LHD

2020 — 2020 13.7.51 USA LHD

2059 — 2059 LYV 364 No Date Australia. Ford Flathead NZ event 15/3/06 Red
W.J.Glasson, N.Zealand 1986, ; N.Zealand 1986

2086 — 2086 20.4.51 USA LHD Cadillac Red.
Paul R. Brownall, Milwaukee USA Aug'69, Oct'69 still 1986.

2087 — 2087 No Record.

2088 — 2088 24.5.51 New Zealand.
Donovan,

2089 — 2089 31.7.51 Cuba Chrome Wires Red
(Monterey 1990) 1990

2090 — 2090 OUG 601 13.7.51 Tate, Leeds Corvette + Speed 5420cc Black interior Wires Green
Richard Petty, ; Washington Dec 73 (Monterey 1990) still 1990

J2 PAGE 6

2120 — 2120 OZ 4444 1.9.51 Hamilton, Belfast (Festival Car)
J. Desmond Titterington 1951, sold to A.R.P.Ramsey 1954, Ramsey in Calcutta Jun'63, in Calcutta May'80. Found in breaker yard

2121 — 2121 FBA 685 27.8.51 Nunns, Manchester. Mercury then Cobra Engine
Gerry Belton Robert Judd Jun'66 Jacksonville Feb'70

2122 — 2122 ONK 21 1.5.52 Dagenham Motors, London Mercury.
Selling Mercury J2 Feb'60, N. Mowl, Droitwich Sep'61, still got Jul'66.

2123 — 2123 31.8.51 USA LHD

2124 — 2124 11.9.51 Finland LHD

2125 — 2125 10.1.52 No Record. LHD

2136 — 2136 6.7.51 Australia (Show Chassis)

2137 — 2137 25.7.51 Peru LHD (Le Mans Car) 1951 No 1
Driven by Allard & Tom Cole 1951 Le Mans.

2138 — 2138 MGT 850 7.9.51 Adlards London (Prototype J2X) (Nash Healey body) Silver
Simmonds (driven by Peter Fargurson 1959? or was it MGF?) 1988

2155 — 2155 WMX 814 30.4.52 Dagenham Motors, London Performance Cars body 1968.
J.A.R. Grice, Buxton Salmon, Yorks 1968-1971, Brian Golder 1992

2156 — 2156 No Date USA LHD

2157 — 2157 11.10.51 Venezuela

2179 — 2179 17.10.51 USA 5500cc Black disc Wheels, Red Interior Black
Michigan USA May69 (Monterey 1990) 1978 & 1990

2180 — 2180 21.11.51 USA (1st J2X chassis)

J2X

2191	2191	29.11.51 USA LHD		
	Fry.		Bussières, Poitevine France May '78	
2192	2192	22.1.52 USA LHD		
	Wood			
2193	2193	14.12.51 USA LHD		
	Moss		J. R (Roger) Morrello, Montgomery Ohio, rebuilding May '74,	1981
2219	2219	9.1.52 USA LHD		
	Erwin Goldsmith			
2221	2221	23.1.52 USA LHD		
	Seddon			
2222	2222	23.1.52 USA LHD		
	Seddon			
2223	2223	29.12.51 PERU LHD 5424cc	(Monterey 1990)	
			, USA 1990	
2224	2224 PKJ 412 14.1.52 Aero Essex			1999 (not use body)
	R. J. Cross (Aero Essex)	See Separate Sheet		1989
3037	3037	29.1.52 USA LHD		
	Seddon		, California USA 1990	
3038	3038	12.2.52 USA LHD		
	Seddon			
3039	3039	14.2.52 USA LHD		
	Denver			
3040	3040	25.2.52 USA HD Cadillac		
	California Tom Cole,	R.W. Kilpey m 1978, Jack Boretom USA (selling) Feb 1989		
3041	3041	6.3.52 USA LHD Chevrolet		Metallic blue
			Frank Busingey California, Apr '69 and 1990	
3042	3042	29.2.52 USA LHD 5420cc	(1990 Monterey)	
	Reimported.		Robert Dunn, USA 1990	
3043	3043 7274 HJ 29.2.52 USA HD Cadillac (BVM 506N)			Black
	Seddon, Erwin Goldsmith, Major Dawe, W.E, Bridgeforth, Virginia Jan '69			T. Dutton 1989
3044	3044	26.3.52 USA LHD.		
	Denver			
3045	3045	27.3.52 USA LHD.		
	Moss			

3046	3046	27.3.52 USA LHD Cadillac 330ci	(Monterey 1990)	Red
	---	---	---	---
	California	John Queen (selling) Dec 88	1990 for Sale Monterey Auction	1990
3047	3047	2.4.52 No Record LHD		
3048	3048	2.4.52 No Record LHD.		
3049	3049 MXF 974	(Chrysler Engined Le Mans Car) Le Mans Body. Cad 4 speed box		Maroon
	Curtis	Butch-Hinton Special - See Separate sheet.		France 19.
3050	3050	1.5.52 USA LHD		
	Barry Steele			
3051	3051	17.4.52 USA LHD 5400cc	(Monterey 1990)	
	California			1990
3052	3052	18.4.52 USA LHD Cad. 4 speed box.		
	California.			
3053	3053 ORL 320 9.5.52 Liskeard, Cornwall Chrysler ('53) Caddi ('60)			Maroon → Green (1990) (Monterey 1990)
	Watkins, T. J (John) Williams Nov '59, Jul '60, May '61, Jun '61 Dec '61 Sold Sep '62, Fred Damadoran, rebuilt Aug '71		Resale Nov '65,	198.
3054	3054	26.5.52 Nairobi		
	Craigu			
3055	3055 MXF 969 13.8.52 USA 1952 Le Mans Car Le Mans Body.		— FOR SALE USA OCT '07	Green
	S. H Allard (R.P. Imported Mtr Co) Allard & Ray Merrick at Le Mans, Paul Pfohl (1952)			1990
3056	3056	6.9.52 USA LHD White wires		Blue
	Seddon		, New York Jul '69, article Mar '70, still Oct '199.	
3057	3057	27.5.52 USA LHD		
	Seddon			
3058	3058	27.5.52 USA LHD		
	Seddon			
3059	3059	26.6.52 USA LHD 6651cc	(Monterey 1990)	
	Imported Motor Co.		, Austin, Texas Jun '64 still 1990	
3060	3060	27.5.52 USA LHD		
	Seddon	See Separate sheet.	Sep '61	
3061	3061	17.6.52 USA LHD		
	Seddon			
3062	3062	25.6.52 USA LHD		
	el Kirk			

J2X PAGE 3

3063	5063	10.6.52 SINGAPORE		Red
	SN 2960 (2013)	(at Northampton 1988 from Hong Kong/Tokyo)	Apr 2013 — enquiry for Hong Kong owner	
3064	5064	2.7.52 USA LHD		
	Seddon			
3065	5065	2.7.52 USA Chrysler		Red
			(selling) Feb 1989	
3066	5066	2.12.52 USA Chrysler. Le Mans Body		
	Captain Leslie USAF		, California 1978	
3067	5067	18.8.52 USA Raced in US in '50s Supercharged.		
	P Imported Motor Co. Harry Payne Whitney,	Wilmer Belgium Jul 74 and St Helens New Zealand (letter May)		
3068	5068	15.7.52 USA Cadillac		White
	California Sports Car	(at Northampton 1989 — used in Mille Miglia)		
3069	5069	15.7.52 USA		
	California Sports Car			
3070	5070	27.6.52 NAIROBI		
3071	5071	6.1.53 USA Le Mans Body		
	el Kirk Motors			
3072	5072	22.7.52 USA 5424cc	(Monterey 1990)	
	tor Sport Inc.		, USA, 1983 & 1990	
3073	5073	9.9.52 USA.	(Monterey 1990)	
	peedcraft Enterprises		Mountville USA May '78 and 1990	
3074	5074	25.9.52 USA		
	California Sports Car			
3075	5075	1.9.52 USA.		
	el Kirk Motors			
3076	5076	30.9.52 USA		
	Crawnes Motor Co			
3077	5077	7.10.52 USA Cadillac Fawn Interior		Red
	el Kirk Motors	C.A.R. Howard Feb '89 (Morris?)	, Penn USA 1991	
3140	5140	24.12.52 USA Le Mans Body		
	peedcraft Enterprises		, Milwaukee USA Aug '69 Oct '69.	
3141	5141	7.1.53 USA Le Mans Body		
	lard Motors Co Inc			

J2X PAGE 4

3142	5142	27.3.53 USA 5735cc	(Monterey 1990)	Red.
	ports Car Inc.			1990, 199
3143	5143	10.10.52 USA.		
	el Kirk Motors	J.J. Huenholz, Washington USA Apr '69		
3144	5144	19.11.52 USA		
	el Kirk Motors		, California 1978	
3145	5145	19.11.52 USA.		
	el Kirk Motors			
3146	5146	20.11.52 USA Chrysler 5500cc	(Monterey 1990)	Red
	el Kirk Motors Shelby ,	Mrs McKee, USA, selling Nov 1988,	USA 1990	
3147	5147	13.3.53 USA		
	ports Car Inc			
3148	5148	29.11.52 USA 5200cc	(Monterey 1990)	
	el Kirk Motors	D.J.W. McCarthy 1978,	NJ. USA 1990	
3149	5149	7.1.53 USA. Le Mans Body		
	el Kirk Motors			
3150	5150	27.10.52 USA Cadillac		
	Juan Riu Pan American			
3151	5151	6.1.53 USA		
	el Kirk Motors			
3152	5152	24.2.53 USA Le Mans Body.		
	ports Car Inc			
3153	5153	15.5.53 USA Le Mans Body Chrysler. 331cc		
	Norman K. Patton, Chicago		, USA 1990	
3154	5154	9.1.53 USA.		
	lard Motors Co			
3155	5155	8.4.53 USA. Le Mans Body	5780cc Metallic Red Monterey 1990	1990
	ports Cars Inc.	Written off in fatal accident at Bridgehampton (Bob Wylde).		
3156	5156	5.3.53 USA		
	Jaguar Bergengren			
3157	5157	10.12.52. USA		
	S. Robinson (Firestone Tires)		, Miami 1980	
3158	5158 M24352	22.4.53 USA. Ardun OHV Black interior		Red
	ports Car Inc	Brosse Ljungfelt, Sweden, Scandinavian Museum, Sotheby Monaco May 1990		
	5158	NYC July 2013 correspondence (on nobili?!)		

J2X PAGES

3161	3161	2.5.53 USA	(Needing restoration 1992)			
	Shawnee Motors Co					1992
3162	3162	3.2.53 USA	Buick 5966cc	(Monterey 1990)		
	...oto Cars Inc	Wilbur F. Sanders, Dearborn, Michigan Nov 69				1990
3163	3163	2.5.53 USA				
	...ustom Automotive					
3164	3164	24.9.53 USA	Chrysler			
	...asil K Evans (Allard Motor Co)					
3200	3200	16.7.53 USA				
	...ports Cars Inc					
3201	3201	15.10.53 USA	Le Mans Body			
	...Merrimack St Garages					
3202	3202	22.7.53 USA	Le Mans Body 5424cc	White Wire	Green	
	Shawnee Motors Co		(Monterey 1990)			1990
3205	3205	16.5.54 USA				
	...llard Motors Co					
3208	3208	24.8.53 USA				
	...ritish Motor Car Dist					
3209	3209 XPA 076	16.5.53 CANADA				
	...udd + Dyer bros.	Fred Hayes, Dave Pidgeon Sep 58,		Ontario Canada Apr 62 Apr '65 letter Nov '77		
3211	...211	26.8.53 GUATEMALA	Chromewires, Oldsmobile		Red	
	...trimany + Co. Ltd. T.M Wallace 1979, J.E. Harden 1985, Beaulieu Auction 1988, John Gasline USA Mar 89,			(Monterey 1990)		1990
3213	...213	24.8.54 COLOMBIA	Le Mans Body. Cadillac			
	...ntonio 12 Quierdo, Bogota.					
3214	...214	29.11.54 USA				
	...Whitestine					
1910	...10 OVT 983	(No Record)	Le Mans Body		Blue.	
	...77 JM 7942					
	Rupert de Larrinaga	See Separate Sheet				1989.

J2R

3401	3401	28.3.53 USA. 5.4 Caddy. Bill Dick Motors.		Red, Red Trim		
	Irwin Goldschmidt, New York. sold in Aug 54 by			-, New Hampshire restoring 1977		
3402	3402 NLN 652	(Sydney Allards)	5.4 Caddy Le Mans Car. '53	25.7.53 USA.	Blue, Blue Trim	
	Col. Schilling, Omaha Air Base, Nebraska, Paul Emery, Dr Pierre de Haverland, Belgium Liège May report					
	P. de Haverland selling Jan 78. (Jag Engined Jan 78), P. Reilly, M.Y. Johnson, Belfast, C. Wick					
3403	3403 NLN 650	(Zora Duntov) York Krymenick	Le Mans Car. '53	5.8.53 USA.	5400cc Blue, Blue Trim (Monterey 1990)	
	Col. K. Tilley, Omaha		returned to UK 1975			1990
3404	3404	19.6.53 USA Built as spare for Le Mans.	Caddy & quick change diff.		Blue, Blue Trim	
	Gen Curtis le May, W.M. Vance, USA Dick, rebuilt by Shawnee Motors, Topeka USA ('77)					
3405	3405 OLT 101		The Sphynx.			
	Tommy Sopwith		Brian Croot Dorset Apr '63 (until ~73?)			
	-, Shaftesbury, Jan '80.					
3407	3407 OVT 983	registration transferred from his Le Mans car.	Now with 427ci Ford.		Green	
	Rupert de Larrinaga	Mr St. Clair, USA.	T.M. Rundle, Canada Nov 62.			
	David Dubrul, Burlington Vermont USA Jan 80.				(1982)	
3406	3406		Cadillac			
	Norman Moffat,	shipped to Ontario, Canada Mar '56.			(selling) Feb '98	
3408	#3408	Lloyd + Alan Allard ground up construction of new JR. 1953 Cadillac engine. to FIA standard. Sold at Auction UK. & Tech advice by original engineer. Dudley Hume.				2021
	Q. are 3406 and 3407 the other way round? ✓					

K TYPES

CHASSIS	REG No	LAST KNOWN	CHASSIS	REG No	LAST KNOWN
143	HEL 306	1990	577	FMR 11/346 JGX	1990
156	JGP 467	1990	586	?	1968
158	?	1990	595	JYK 438	1949
161	HDV 288/JYG 462T	1990	617	JOE 884	1990
162	SMC 665	1963 *Exists 2007 SA*	621	AKS 747	1990
165	?	1969	633	JDH 167	1990
222	GZ 8959	1990	644	HRU 815	1990
237	?	1969	647	VMG 579	1990
240	?	1967	653	UMC 561	1990
242	SH 8025	1990	681	KOJ 888	1990
250	HOL 846	1969	717	SH 8990	1987
372	ENT 295	1988	770	?	1990
374	SMV 519	1962	775	?	1990
404	LUB 906/PNW 503	1988	796	?	1990
419	?	1989	?	SMT 268	1971
436	FUS 365	1988	?	B 46511	1971
457	LUM 89	1963	?	JKD 874	1978
458	KWJ 770	1990	?	MBB 802	1988
467	GRK 384	1990	?	JGP 474	?
476	PRF 35	1990	(?)145	CHM 316	?
487	HRU 2	1990	? 510	JUC 310	?
511	DHS 760	SCRAPPED	? 290	JOC 63	1963
544	FVJ 257	1990	~~435~~	JND 955	1990 / 2007
553	KTA 309 ?	1990	?	FFH 211	?
			?	HOL 848	?

K 1

143 43 HEL 306 25.8.47 Bournemouth *Motor Dealer in Devon, had had body, was chassis, at Dulac chassis from John Pegretts 1975* Red
R.G. Craske Sep'61, Joe F. Clegg Aug'66, H J Sibley 1976, < Stewart, R Lye, Greece 1990 M Bradbrook 1988

161 61 HDV 288 20.8.47 Exeter Red Tan Interior 1990 3-9 Litr. was Black, Then Copper, Red 1990
(?JYG 462T) Regd Oct'87 Johannesburg Eamon O'Higgins ex South Africa 1988, (To South Africa 1990) for sale (S.V. Restorations) 1990.

162 62 SMC 665 26.7.47 London
J.F. Harris, Kingsbridge Nov'63 Approx 1997 onwards East Horsley, From USA Fort Worth, Texas.

165 65 8.8.47 USA Cadillac Engine
, Tulsa, Oklahoma USA Apr'69

240 40 1.10.47 Birmingham
, London Apr'67.

242 42 SH 8025 13.10.47 Edinburgh (was Purple) Black. '73 to '88
Blackburn Selling Dec'66 G Weston Mace, George Werns Weldwin Motors Dalblair Motors Bobbie McIntyre 7/88

250 50 HOL 846 10.10.47 Birmingham
G.B. Home Oct'62, George Home, Woodgym Selling Feb'65. Leighton Buzzard Jan

372 72 ENT 295 5.4.48 Shrewsbury (was Red). Cream/Black 65,000 miles
Gordon Rose (up to 1985+) (156 road since 2.5.61) 1988

374 74 SMV 519 9.4.48 London

416 416A HDV 256 J. Chapman Sep'62 11/20 Metallic Red.

404 04 LUB 906 20.4.48 Leeds
PNW 503 (Registry Hill) T.W. Burgess, London Apr'67, G.H. Gardner, Wittersham, Kent, Aug'69 1988

436 36a FUS 365 5.5.48 Glasgow Engine 7197339 Blue/Black
J.C. Green, Newbury Barrie Gillies 1986.

457 57 LUM 89 8.6.48 Leeds
W.J. Hughes, Londonderry N.I. Jun'63 (Noted as 71K 4570 ?)

458 58a KWJ 770 29.6.48 Leeds Blue.
Aug 18.8.48. A.G Foster, Walsall Nov63, Ch. Richardson, Aldridge, Staffs Oct69, B. L. Senter,

467 67 GRK 384 5.7.48 London now chassis is only 1983 1989.
J.M. Wheadon, Loughborough, Leics Oct'64 (Since 1975)

476 76 PRF 35 5.7.48 Birmingham Nigel Wallace Smith, Nov90 Red
D.A. Buckley, Stockport Jul'69, Aug'71 (Mrs Tate) Selling Aug'91 Clash, 1989

487 87 HRU 2 9.7.48 Birmingham Arden (May90) Red
Regd France 1990 A.R. Hope Birth Apr'69, Chagford, Devon, Nov'73. Govs NEC May91 for sale in France Jun'91+

K1 — PAGE 2

511	511 DHS 760	13.2.48 Glasgow		
		D. Tudor-Hughes, Riseley, Beds Jun '65 — Scrapped.		
544	544 FVJ 257	30.7.48 Gloucester	was White	Red.
		B.J. Bennett, Hereford, Aug '67	ex Hamilton Estate.	, 1989.
577	577 FMR 11 / 346 JGX	28.7.48 Bournemouth.	(1990 Monterey)	Red. 1991.
		Nick Jubert		USA 1992
586	586	29.7.48 Oxford.	24.04.09 - Orange Chy. N.J. For Sale on Ebay. (white, tan and drive) $50k bid ($25k) $75 buy it now	
		V. F. Medina, New Jersey USA Aug '68		
617	617 JOE 884	16.9.48 Birmingham	White	
		Peter McGee, London Jun '65 Selling Oct '65, M.E. Lunghi, Leatherhead Apr '67	D.R.M Cawson, Guildford Dec '69.	1989
644	644 HRU 815	23.12.48 Bournemouth		Green
				198
647	647 VMG 579	14.11.47 London.		Gunmetal Grey. For sale
			Phillips Auction 9 Oct '89,	Car Feb 90.
653	653 UMC 561	6.5.49 London		Red
			since 1968	198
717	717 SH 8990	5.11.49 Leeds (Eng No & block do not match)	assume correct but— 3622cc	Red
		Bryan B.D. Jones Northampton Aug '63 selling Feb '65	, Beds, 1987	
775	775	15.7.49 Leeds	chassis only 1989 (since 1975)	1989.
	? SMT 268	Used in 1967 Kodak advert Jun 71, later on history Oct 71.	Blue.	
		Nov '66 Robert Judd 1968,	Gloucester Virginia USA Jan '69.	
	? B 46511			
		Stockholm Sweden Apr 71		
156	156 JGP 467	12.12.47 London		Blue.
		1946 to 1949 Allard Motors Co (Demonstrator and Rally Car). 1949 → complete 2 years Capt. A. Everard (a Leicestershire brewer). Then sold Former Leicester and in Barn 1960 to 70. Being restored by J. Peskett, Leicester May 77	→ Sparkford Motor Museum 1988	
485	485A JKD 874	9.7.48 Rupert de Larrinaga.	Jaguar Engined.	was Grey Green.
		Clive Richardson, Aldridge, Staffs, owned since 1971, selling Jan '78, Rupert de Larrinaga 1990		
621	621 AKS 747	29.9.48 Edinburgh.		Blue
		Dave Richland		1989
251	? MBB 802		was White	
		Laurie Juniper		1988.

K1 — PAGE 3.

154	? JGP 474		White
		G. Imhoff — Alpine Trial Car	
145	145 CHM 316	6.2.47 London	Red
		M. Wick — Alpine Trial Car	
510	510 JUC 310 Not recorded.	used in Dick Barton strikes back. Ex Demo Car.	
595	595 JYK 438	0.7.48 London	Light Blue
		Works Car - Potter in Alpine Trial 1948 & 1949.	
237	K 237	17.12.47 Australia.	
		, Victoria, Australia Feb '69	
770	770	26.1.50 USA	5424cc (Races with Cycle Wings) Maroon (1990 Monterey)
		Alan Moss, USA 1950, R. Grebe 1980	, Seattle 1990
419	419 DFR 259 Rowse	7.5.48 Manchester	21 stud Ford
			P. Chichester ~ 1978. For Sale USA Mar '89.
681	681 KOJ 888	28.11.49 Derby	
		(since 1980).	, Edinburgh 1990
796	796	31.3.50 Birmingham	Flathead	Blue
		(US living in London)	1990
633	633 JDH 167	26.11.48 Birmingham	
			1990
290	290 JOC 63	1.10.47 Birmingham, L'Escargot, 1949 K1 chassis with 1951 French 2 Seater F.H. Coupe Body. (chassis)	A. C. Pritchard selling Feb '63.
158	158	8.8.47 USA.	4588cc	Red. (1990 Monterey) , Memphis 1990
435	435 JND 955	Eural David Maley 15 Oct 2007	was Silver. Red 1990
	FFH 211	(Grace Roberts photos) — early flat headlamp rims & multibar grill	
222	K 222 GZ 8959	7.8.47 Belfast.	
			, Banbury 1990
553	K 553 KTA 309	16.8.47 Exeter	Blue.
		Edward Wynne Jones 1961, Christopher Patterson 1963 then owned since 1970.	, Blaenau Ffestiniog 1990
	HOL 848		

K1 PAGE 4

? EBA 505 ?

(Monterey 1990) USA 1990

41 9.2.50 Uruguay Coil springs

(Has Montevideo Nº plate) , Sweden 1991

? LUG 408 ? Early Car, Short Grill ⊕, in Classic Cars A-Z.

K1 — # 262 Reg UMX 82 - Yorkshire
(was supplied Chassis only).

K1 = # 416A. - Yorkshire
(ref. 14.07.13)

Reg. HDV 56.
(too though it was a K2)

K2

1700	700	USU 339	9.5.50 CANADA		Silver Grey
			ADT Auction Bellevue T		~198?
1703	03	MGG 917	14.5.50 USA		
			L. John Harthan, California Jan'70, -	1983	
1743	43		12.3.51 SWEDEN	LHD.	
			Jan Bellander, Sweden Feb'63,	, Marstrand, Sweden Sep'68	
1804	04		1.12.50 USA		
			, California, Jan'69		
1978	78		12.3.51 USA		
			, Vancouver, Canada Sep'77		
2029	29		7.6.51 HOLLAND		
			, the Hague Feb'70 (+address)		
2032	032		12.5.51 USA.	Black Interior, Black Wings, Light Blue Body	
			L. John Harthan, California Jan'70	(Monterey 1990) USA 1990	
2033	033	JGD 294	9.4.51 GLASGOW.		
			, Co. Tyrone. Aug'68		
2035	035	153 AFK	7.6.51 BIRMINGHAM	Ardun Mercury	Green
		LOJ 211	J.R. Rice-Evans, Abergavenny Apr'64 selling Nov Dec'67		198?
2080	080	BCW 14	29.8.51 MANCHESTER		Cream
			(see separate note.)		198?
2090	092	HAW 717	27.6.51 SHREWSBURY		
			J. May, Cheltenham Apr'67, for sale Apr'67, P.V. Bond, Solihul Sep'68 selling Sep'68.		
2107	107	OUM 59	23.6.51 LEEDS		
			C. Robinson, Bletsoe, Beds Oct'67, D.H.L. Nugent, Newbury Jan'70.		
2108	108	BUG 200 (Aussy reg Nº)	20.8.51 AUSTRALIA		
			J.E. Jackson, Sydney, Australia Apr'64.	-(selling) 1990	
2109	109	XMC 365	26.7.51 LONDON		
			E.F. Everard, Sep'62, E.W. Forbes, Los Angeles Jul'69.	-, Calif 1976	
2154	154		11-12.51 USA		
			, Toluca Lake, California Sep'77.		
3026	026		9.5.52 USA		
			, Michigan USA Sep'68		
3028	028		9.7.52 USA.	5424cc	Red
			G.R. Myers, California Jul'69	(Monterey 1990) , Calif 1990	

K2 PAGE 2

3029	3029	17.6.52 USA.		
		S.W. Spring, New York, USA Mar 78		
	LOH 921	Jaguar Engine		Maroon
		M. Raiment Osterley Aug 63 for sale Mar 64		198_
2203	2203 MLP 117 21.3.52 London Autocar Road Test Car 1952 Mercury Engine {Piston Lush – K2 × chassis / driven by Darton in Belgium}			
	OKM 728 (Aug 21.3.52?)			
	Martin Thompson D. Mayston, Leigh on Sea for sale Apr 64 and Jul 64		Junior Freddy Lobnitz, Glasgow ~ 1980?	
1924	1924 WHX 777 21.2.51 London			
	1922/52? sold 18 months later			
	Don Farrell, Bill Moss, Croston N^r Preston,			, 1985
	LOL 773			Green
				– 198_
2196	2196 LON 909 29.9.51 Birmingham	WIRE WHEELS		GREEN
				198_
	MMG 861	In Dave Kinsella's book		
1705	1705	27.7.50 USA.		
			USA 1976	
1742	1742	6.9.50 USA		
			, USA 1987	
1841	1841	12.2.50 USA.		
			J, Texas 1979.	
1843	1843	17.1.51 USA.		White
		(Monterey 1990)	, California 1979. and 1990	
2031	2031	12.5.51 USA.		
			, USA ~ 1978.	
2085	2085	30.8.51 USA	Joint owners with (car in USA)	_ , USA.
2150	2150	C.B. Altenus, Conn, USA ~ 1978,		o, Church Stretton 199_
	2150 ULK 996 8.8.51 MANCHESTER.			
			, Scotland 1976	
2197	2197	10.1.52 USA		
			Arizona, USA ~ 1978	
3126	3126	22.9.52 USA.		
		Major Seaton ?	For sale, Monterey Auction 1990	
			, LA. USA 1990?	
2082	2082 LGW 999 4.6.51 USA.			
	(for rate info – but)			New York 1990

K2 PAGE 3

1846	846	16.1.51 USA.	Cadillac		Red
				USA (selling) Mar 1989	
1972	977	12.3.51 USA.	5835cc		(1990 Monterey) Red
				, USA, Dewey Dellinger, Calif. 1990	
2202	202 YMC 693 20.11.51 London				
	A.L. Sinclair			Maryland USA 1991	
1986	986	21.4.51 USA.	Cadillac 8M 597, Auto Transmission		Blue
		1953		New Jersey 1990.	
841	74	9.2.50 URUGUAY	5426cc		
				~ (1990 Monterey) , USA 1990	
3035	035	3.9.52 USA	5424cc		Red
			N'88 –	(1990 Monterey) , USA 1990	
3017	017	12.2.52 USA.	4785cc		Black
				(1990 Monterey) , USA 1990	
3020	020	2.4.52 USA			White
			(Monterey 1990)	USA 199_	
2093	093	28.5.51 Malaya			Red
		G. Lee.	(Monterey 1990) !	USA 19_	
2083	083	28.7.51 USA	Primrose Yellow, black Wings		
		C.S. Warner (bought new from dealer) Penn' USA 1991 (for sale)			
1985	985	21.6.51 USA.			
				, Iowa, USA, 1991	
1807	1807	12.12.50 USA	Mercury 4.4hr	(again 2013)	Red.
			(NY) called GLA 13/12/08.		
			Bought car for full restoration.		
			Allard Head. ( ).		
3036	3036	- USA	LINCOLN V8 (original claimed)		White Red/white leather
			21.09.09 car restored for sale		34 ?
			with dealer – Eugene Oregon USA – end at		

K3

| 3166 | 66 | 22.2.53 USA |
| H.H. Barnes, N. Carolina Sep'77 | , Ohio 1980 |

| 3191 | 91 | 24.4.53 USA | '55 Chrysler 331ci |
| , California 1986 |

| 3194 | 94 | 8.4.53 USA | Ford Flathead |
| J.E. Harden 1985 | , Wisconsin 1986 |

| 3195 | 95 | 20.8.53 USA. |
| D. Baron, Lansing, Michigan Jan'78 |

| 3250 | 50 | 29.4.53 USA | '58 Lincoln | Black Wires (Monterey 1990) | Silver |
| , Florida 1986 |

| 3253 | 53 | 24.9.53 USA. |
| Pete Bland, New Hampshire Aug'69, May'78 |

| 3266 | 66 | 20.7.53 USA | '53 Cadillac | White |
| J.S. Blaine, Detroit Sep'68 | still 1986 |

| 3283 | 83 | 5.4.54 USA | '59 Cadillac 395ci, B×M. Hydramatic | Red |
| , California 1986 |

| 3286 | 86 PLE 888 | 8.10.54 LONDON. | RHD Ford Flathead | Blue |
| J.L (Len) Ball, Car damaged in Hillclimb in 1959, No.66, Oct'70 | , Broadway 1986 |

| 3179 | 79 | 14.5.53 USA. |
| Wayne F. Pottes, Chicago, Fred Woods, Chicago | For Sale, Monterey Auction 1990. |

| 3170 | 170 | 14.3.53 USA. |
| N.York USA 1981 |

| 3175 | 175 | 5.2.53 USA. |
| M. Spector USA 1976 | - , MICHIGAN 199 |

| 3176 | 176 (NGP 970) Wrong No | 4.2.53 USA | LHD. | Red |
| W. Marquess 1980, B. Sharp | 1989 |

| 3183 | 183 | 24.2.53 USA. |
| A.W. Edmister, Calif 1977, | Calif 1979. |

| 3192 | 192 | 10.7.53 USA. |
| Calif 1983. |

| 3185 | 85 | 22.4.53 USA |
| For Sale in USA Jan'89 |

| 3186 | 86 | 7.5.53 USA. |
| J.F Dallas, Los Angeles | Beverley Hills 1990 |

| 3190 | 90 | 17.3.53 USA |

K3 PAGE 2

| 3261 | 261 | 16.9.53 USA. | Chrome Wires (Monterey 1990) i | Light Blue | USA 1990 |

| 3184 | 184 | 5.5.53 USA. | (Racing Tour !) (Monterey 1990) i | Red | USA 1990 |

| 3030 | 30 NGP 970 | 3.11.52 USA. |
| General Griswold |

| 3256 | 256 CSK 413 | 29.5.53 India | Black |
| Mrs | , India | (In the family since new). | N43 1978 |

L TYPES

CHASSIS	REG No	LAST KNOWN	CHASSIS	REG No	LAST KNOWN
102	HLB 424	1947	460	GGG 831	1990
116	?	1964	508	?	1990
127	JGY 708	1988	516	GUY 831	1988
134	?	1990	521	UMC 363	1964
141	JGX 651	~~SCRAPPED~~ Robinson-Collins Aug 05 Exists	525	BFR 82	1990
164	?	1973	538	?	1973
201	SMH 107 ?	1986	548	NFC 577	1963
203	MWL 380	1990	632	XS 6484	1990
212	LUA 882	~~1967~~ 1990	642	EVJ 594	1986
243	JLK 958	1990	757	?	1986
253	LUB 652	1979	837	VHX 555	1978
278	MPD 28	1969	852	KLO 128	1989
284	MJO 380	1990	867	LKR 963	1976
311	LKJ 47	1990	?	THX 875	1984
344	?	1969	?	GOU 25	1967
345	JNC 400	1990	?	ETH 88	1987
387	582 LUG	1990	?	CES 360 Restored	? ARU – Devonshire
390	JLY 163	1990	?	JLM 3	?
393	JLT 913	1990	?	JGY 719	?
407	JNF 39	1990	?	KLD 758	1963
411	?	1977	?	DVD 567	1963
442	LBH 691	1965	?	FFH 373	1965
			478	LHU 407	2013

August 2012

L: LHW 107.

L. 478

L (handwritten register, right page)

102 — 02 HLB 424 18.3.47 LONDON   The first Post War Production Allard!   Red.

116 — 6   15.4.47 LONDON
, Otorohange, New Zealand Oct '64

127 — 27 JGY 708 28.6.47 LONDON   Maroon
J.W. Jenkins, Essex 1979 J. Johnson, Suffolk 198

134 — 34   17.1.47 BELGIUM   Supplied as Chassis (Non Std Body) 3-9 Lite Fed
Bought Nov 66. New Jersey USA Oct '67.   still 1986, for Sale 1990

141 — H JGX 651 25.6.47 LONDON
Fred Damodaen (Little Abner) Pater (carottes), NFC Mason Nov'61, Bert Ansell converted & scrapped mid 60s - 26.8.05 not scrapped but in pieces.

164 — 64   9.7.47 LONDON
J.R. Allard, Washington USA Nov 73 (register)

203 — 03 MWL 380 15.8.47 OXFORD   Trials Body.   Oct'92 → Blue Green
Mike Bradbrook,

212 — 12 LUA 882 13.11.47 LEEDS   1990
C.E. Hughes, Timperley Cheshire Apr '67.

243 — 43 JLK 958 4.2.48 LONDON   Black
R.F. Inskip, Whitchurch Apr'67, G.S. Mitchell, Heston, Roger Murray Evans   1989

253 — 53 LUB 652 17.10.47 LEEDS   called Hortense Oct 65.   Merc Engine '69
L.H. Singleton, Sheffield May 63 R.C.A. Chambers, Sheffield Jun 65, A. Thompson, Leeds Nov 65, P.J. Davies, Aug 67. J.S.G. Taylor Leicester, Aug 68, Sep '68 rally Jut Saughalls Spigotren seen in Watkin stove! in 1979

278 — 78 MPD 28 21.4.48 LONDON
K. Sutton Denham, Aug 68,   L. Kenton Feb 69.

284 — 84 MJO 380 20.10.47 OXFORD   3622 Flat Head.   Maroon Interior.   White
R. Seas R. Lumb   1989

311 — 11 LKJ 47 4.11.47 LONDON   Had M Special body. Special Body, Tom Hutchinson Merc Engine.   Cream
C. Skeaping Feb'63 P.L. Marriage, Notts, J. Norfolk, Essex 1980,   Blackheath, Essex.   1989

344 — 44   12.12.47 LEEDS
Oregon USA Apr '69

345 — 345 JNC 400 18.12.47 MANCHESTER   Red Interior.   Black
M.W. Munday, Lancs 1976.   ? 1989

411 — 11   22.4.48 LONDON
, Cheltenham Sep 77

442 — 42 LBH 691 29.5.48 DERBY.
, Harrow Jun 65

·ALLARD·

L PAGE 2

460 — 460 GGG 831 5.5.48 GLASGOW   Special Body.   Green
R. Bromwich Oct'65, Robin Sadler Nov'65, at Blackenhithe 17 Oct 65, selling by Sadler Feb'66
T.P.C. Doe, Norwich May'66. Moto described Feb'69.   1983

508 — 508 BWG 181 No Record GLASGOW   Taken to bits 1962/63.   Red
Wreck recovered in Wrexham Cheshire Roger Hayes 1988   199

516 — 516 Guy 440 2.3.48 BIRMINGHAM   Red
J.E. Finch, Leics. Oct'67   N. Bolton.   1988

521 — 521 UMC 363 4.3.48 LONDON
Welwyn G.C. Aug'63, selling Feb'64

525 — 525 BFR 82 23.3.48 MANCHESTER   (Dismantled 1990)
(Reg May 48)   H.D. Kennedy, Keighly, Aug'67 selling Jan'68   1990

538 — 538   14.6.48 LONDON
, Washington USA Apr'69. Nov'73 (again)

548 — CES 110
548 NFC 577 12.7.48 PERTH
(presum. reg.)   £ , London May'63.

632 — 632 XS 6484 1.9.48 GLASGOW   Black
J. Wooliscroft, Wem, Salop Feb'68 (still 1980)   o'198

852 — 852 KLO 128 17.3.49 LONDON.   1989

411 — ? THX 875 for sale in MotoSport May 83 to Jan'84   White

393 — 393 JLT 913 11.2.48 London   Mercury.   Blue
Alan Brinton 1985 James Smith   1989

? Gou 25   Triple Carb Mercury Edelbrook inlet, Allard Heads   Yellow
C.M. Craven, Cheadle Apr'67 Charles Wells Oct'73 gone to USA

843 — L343 ETH 88 – for sale ... USA 12.02.06 (petrol send)   Red   1987

679 — 679   30.8.48 USA   Wires, Metallic Blue.
Mr Hoffman   (at Monterey 1990)   i.   ,USA 1990

718 — ? CES 360
Distributors Car Perth, Scotland.

314 — 314 JLM 3 20.11.47 London   Flying Gherkin

446 — JGY 719
Used in "Dick Barton Special Agent".

L PAGE 3

688 — 688G KLD 758   a 48 Motor Show Car.
H.L. Vickery.   D.C. Bawden selling Apr'60
W.F. James selling Aug 63

DVD 567   ,Banstead Nov'63

FFH 373   ,New Malden Nov'65

867 — 867 LKR 963 24.8.49 London   In V8 Book
,Weybridge Jun 71 (x WILTS 1976)

201 — 201 SMH 107 16.9.1947 LONDON   42 Mercury Engine.   Red
Mr Craddock   ,New Zealand 1986.

390 — 390 JLY 163 13.2.48 LONDON   L–Special (like stock racer)   Black
(visiting Monterey 1990) Jan'72   II Calif USA 1986 199

642 — 642 EUJ 594 7.9.48 SHREWSBURY   Green
D.A. Thompson, Shrewsbury 1978.   Switzerland 1986

757 — 757   26.11.49 BOURNEMOUTH   Maroon
USA 1986

JGX 365   Dubious entry — confused with JGX 651 and BJV 365!
Fred Damazala ten to Brooklxx   dismantled mid 60s

387 — 387 582 LUG 27.1.48 Leeds   Red.
I.J. McLeod, York 1981, R. White, Leeds 1984.   1989

837 — 837 VHX 555 16.12.49 London
C.J. Titterton, Stockport.   ,Notthants 1978. still in 1992

407 — 407 JNF 39 18.2.48 Manchester   1990
(Registered July 48)

772 — 772 LGY 397 22.12.49 London.   Red
(Monterey 1990),   USA 1990

856 — 856   8.12.49 Uruguay
,Uruguay 1991.

822 — 822 UMC 486 20.5.49 London
Taken with ...   09/12/06 Mr...   contacted peter
re turn car for classic N2.   ,Bury 1992
(Cheshire)

692

Appendix 1: The 'Domesday' Book

_ L Z X - K _

740   40 JRA 727 27.9.50 SWEDEN.   L chassis, K2 bodywork, De Dion, Cadillac.

discovered in breakers yard in late 60's.

S. Tellander, Boros, Sweden Feb '68.

d, Sweden 1986.

destroyed in Museum fire
1990's? → pic supplied shows
wrecks piled on each other — Allard
is at bottom — TOTAL LOSS

L TYPE

Pics emailed to Club. Hereford.   Swiss 1957 to 68
Phone call 07/02/09
771   771 ✳ MPK 36   must marked spares, cycle wings   01568 750553
Previously owned by   (Phil).

M TYPES   JONK 04.05.17

CHASSIS	REG NO	LAST KNOWN	CHASSIS	REG NO	LAST KNOWN
231	JLM 245 ✳	1962	884	HUE 574	~~1970~~ 1989
270	JLW 490	1963	885	MUA 837	1967
321	GGB 331	1990	887	(EXPORT)	~~1980~~ 1990
324	UMV 5	1990	892	MUA 631 (NOW J614)	1990
401	?	1990	894	GGD 857	1984
434	MND 490 ✳	1963	901	GKY 832	1966
451	?	1962	1015	KLP 812	1967
453	GFS 555	1968	1019	DFX 826	1990
536	JYR 671	1962	1021	KLO 196	1962
537	JFJ 293	1966	1023	JOL 626	1963
547	OMN 514	1988	1029	KLP 820	~~1975~~ 1990
561	JYO 534	1963	1030	LKT 645	1963
587	?	1962	1034	HWD 248	1962
593	TML 164	1967	1039	JRU 772	1982
594	JYM 272	1989	1041	HUY 140	1990
620	(EXPORT)	~~1986~~ 1990	1046	KNN 919	1962
682	VOE 820	~~1963~~ 71	1054	LTV 218	1967
705	JOF 189 ✳	1990 2013	1059	JON 971	1977.
719	KLO 130	1950	1069	YTL 940	1989
751	UMV 207	1964	1072	KUW 567	1967
761	JNG 878	1986	1075	NPB 977	1968
806	(EXPORT)	1990	?	KGC 224	1961
813	HRU 994	1965	?	NZ 7515	1963
816	SY 9088	~~1964~~ 2007 (44)	?	LUG 269	1968
820	KFJ 549	1963	?	JYF 14	1988
823	JC 9688	1990	?	JLK 957	1948
834	?	1986	?	HXV 210	1947
851	?	1980	?	JYT 950	1949
859	DJT 876	1970	?	NFC 139	1949
862	HAA 106	1989	745 or ✳ 107 ? MRB 441	1949	
871	TMX 5	1990	?	JGU 5	1949
872	JAO 308	1990	?	GSC 660 P Type	1964 1990
876	?	1961	?	JYT 944	? 1988
877	JVF 14	~~1974~~ 1988	?	LTV 218	?
			?	GFH 70	?
697	KAL 143	1990			
733	JHN 674	1990	1056	KPK 11	1983
873	Scrapped	—	1066	UMC 538	1974
835	HZ 2552	1990	627	KLO 123	1949
1004	FOW 732	1990	290	JOC 63	1990 1990
309	?	1973	1081	MPD 482	1990
873	?	1973			

updated ~~Sep 90~~ Dec '90

M

231　31 JLM 245　19.12.47 LONDON　Mr M.Millward　Sep'62

270　70 JLW 490　25.4.48 LONDON　(P101 Tom Lush's book) In Allard Catalogue of 1950.
P.M. Ball Apr'63

321　21 GGB 331　6.11.47 GLASGOW　Registered 15 Apr 48　engine replaced 1957. Was 1157630, now 21388631　Special Body, Special Chassis, was Maroon.　White
(seven newcastles)　Randall Mahone Horley 1956, selling Apr'64, Donald Foster & Gordon Foster 1966 (brothers)　1987 + 1989

401　01 MZ 1201　24.3.48 BELFAST
D.P. Johnson.　1989

434　34 NNO 490　20.5.48 LONDON
& Wisconsin USA Aug'63

451　51　13.5.48 BOURNEMOUTH.
Oct'62

453　53 GFS 555　26.6.48 EDINBURGH
Eindhoven, Holland Nov'68

536　36 JYR 671　28.6.48 LONDON
Oct'62 - scrapped in 1962.

537　37 JFJ 293　24.6.48 EXETER　selling Oct'64 E+S.
CFH 70　H. Jenkins Sep'61, D.Tudor-Hughes, Riseley Jun'65,　n May'66.

561　61 JYO 534　19.7.48 LONDON
Cranshaw　Feb'63

587　87'　8.6.48 ISLE OF MAN
Apr'62 selling Jun'62 x Sep'62.

593　93 TML 164　16.6.48 LONDON
, Bucks Dec'67 (Selling M Type Saloon Oct'67)

620　20　26.8.48 SOUTHERN RHODESIA　White
Mr I.Douglas.　(visiting Monterey 1990)　1990
; USA 1986

682　82 JOE 820　17.9.48 BIRMINGHAM
Burke-Collis May'62.　R.W. Darke London May'63 for Sale Jun'63,　, Woodford Essex 1971 (Green)

751　51 UMV 207　No Record LONDON
London Jun'63 selling Feb'64, Jul'64

761　61 JNG 878　17.11.48 NORWICH　Black
, Middlesbrough Apr'67. Jan'75　selling Oct'92
; Sweden 1986

813　13 HRU 994　4.1.49 BOURNEMOUTH
Huddersfield Nov'63, stolen Dec'64, for sale Sep'65.

816　16 SY 9088　17.3.49 EDINBURGH
Fl.Lt. R.E Pride, Norfolk Jul'61, G.O Fleming Sep'62, R.H. Savage, Wooton Bassett, Wilts Apr'64,　Mar 07　Billing Markham USA

820　20 KFJ 549　17.1.49 EXETER

M PAGE 2

823　23 JC 9688　21.12.48 SHREWSBURY.　Beige
Melvyn A. Herman, Prestatyn, Wales Jan'70, Nov'71　r 1989

834　34 GSF 756　27.1.49 EDINBURGH　Grey
In USA since 1971, Larry Johansen owned since 1984　'f USA 1990

859　59 DJT 876　23.2.49 BOURNEMOUTH　Needs restoration Oct'92　(was grey) Maroon
D.Kirk, Wattisham Feb'68, A.J. Lindley, Wattisham, Suffolk Feb'70.　Tony Eaton selling Oct'92　; selling 199

862　62 HAA 106　21.1.49 BOURNEMOUTH　(65) DK Blue
E.C. Gardiner, Wolverhampton selling Nov'65　" "　W.Midlands 1979 (In Birmingham 1989)

871　71 TMX 5　19.1.49 LONDON　NOW M2X　Maroon
M.Valentine, Shrewsbury Apr'67 (selling M2X Maroon Apr'67), Peter Whitley, Blackburn selling Jun'68　1982

872　72 JAO 308　12.2.49 NEWCASTLE ON TYNE.　Mercury　Blue
-1987　Newport 1989

876　76　28.1.49 LONDON
D.M M. Harris, Sep'61

884　84 HUE 574　2.2.49 LONDON　Black
M. Hill, Reigate Aug'67　1989

885　85 MUA 837　10.2.49 LEEDS
A.E. Batt, Bristol Apr'67

892　92 MUA 631　10.2.49 LEEDS　White
J 614　B. McKenzie, Sheffield Aug'69　Jersey 1989

894　94 GGD 857　14.2.49 GLASGOW
D.B. Keating, Portland, Dorset Apr'67　; Bristol 1984.

901　01 GKY 832　7.3.49 LEEDS　4.4 Engine. Body reskinned (1990)　Maroon
P.Mikhailoff, London, May'66 + sold 1966　New body bought 1971　1990
; Chelmsford

1015　15 B KLP 812　23.3.49 BOURNEMOUTH　Purple
G. Helmes, Southampton Oct'64, R.G. Morley, Southampton Nov'65 selling Jan'66, Jan'67

1019　19 DFX 826　21.3.49 BOURNEMOUTH　Mercury.　Blue
, Orpington, May'66.　1989.

1021　21 KLO 196　18.3.49 LONDON
L. Perrins Sep'62

1023　23 JOL 626　21.3.49 BIRMINGHAM
W.R German Feb'63,　; Southampton 1974

1030　30 LKT 645　29.3.49 LONDON
Feb'63

M PAGE 3

1034	034 HWD 248 2.4.49 BIRMINGHAM		
	~ ~ , Nov '62		
1039	039 JRU 772 13.4.49 BOURNEMOUTH (Beaulieu Picture? 1988?) J. Amiel, Cambridge Red		
	C.L. Waddoups, Dover Feb '68 later Mar '70 selling Jun '71 V.P. ... Dorset 198		
1046	046 KNN 919 13.4.49 DERBY		
	G. Cooper Oct '61 ~ Oct '62		
1054	054 B LTV 218 19.5.49 DERBY		
	Mumbridge ~ ., Coventry, Aug '67 ... Maroon, then Dark Green in '63		
1059	059 JON 971 4.5.49 BIRMINGHAM cars ... and short grill fitted. ✗ 1977		
	Robin Richards of Richards & Cox, Rugby 1958, Ron Grantham, Rugby '58 to 1965, Rugby April		
1069	069 YTL 940 16.5.49 LONDON Red		
	~ ., Glasgow 1989		
1072	072 KUW 567 No record LONDON Lawne (L.M Knight, Kent Breaking M. Dec '67)		
	A. Meredith, Brighton, Jan '64, L.M. Knight, Edenbridge Kent Nov '65, Hagham Dec		
1075	075 NPB 977 18.5.49 LONDON		
	T.P. Beren, Toronto, Canada Aug '68		
1625	625 24.8.50 SWEDEN [P CHASSIS, M. BODY] Silver		
	move to P ., Koblenz 1989		
698	98 KGC 224 27.9.48 London		
	Mrs Gee Apr '61		
?	NZ 7515		
	~ ~ ., May '63.		
?	CUG 269		
	A.J. Willis, London, Jun '63 . Sonninghill, Berks Nov '68.		
719	19 KLO 130 No record LONDON. Mercury. Blue Leather Blue		
	Sydney Allard 1950 Monte Carlo Car.		
331	331 JLK 957 20.7.48 London Motor Test Car Howards 1948 Demo. Blue Leather Silver		
	Dimbleby, ., 1954,		
1511	HXV 210 (early Type grille ~ Mar '47) – could be chassis .107		
	Davis 1947		

M PAGE 4

326	326 JYT 950 10.11.47 London		
	K. Hole. Driven by Wick, Appleton, Haesendonck in 1949 Monte Carlo.		
527	527 NFC 139 12.4.48 Oxford. A. Godsal		
	Driven by Godsal & Money-Coutts in 1949 Monte Carlo.		
745	57 or 745 MRB 441 (no date) – Works Demo. after 22.10.48		
	Driven by Sydney Allard, Lush, May in 1949 Monte Carlo.		
594	594 JYM 272 No record, London 1949 Monte Carlo - Richards, Roberts & Potter. (bought ~ 1989)		
	Ted Liseaves imported to USA ~ 1975/76 USA - 2 other - 17		
217	217 JGU 5 2.7.47 London		
	Driven by Imhoff in 1949 Monte Carlo.		
	JYT 944 Maroon Maidstone		
	(History of the Motor Car book) Marden, Kent 1975 1988		
	GSC 660 [IS THIS A P TYPE?]		
	P. Rawlings, Ilford Mar '64 – John Pitney's Special (x2) 1990.		
	GER 966 1991		
547	547 then OMN 517 12.7.48 Norwich.		
	(long reg in Cambridge, then Isle of Man). (clock-wise Par !! →) IOM 1988		
697	697 KAL 143 17.9.48 Derby (dismantled 1990)		
	1990		
851	851 2.3.49 Derby		
	USA. 1980		
877	877 JVF 14 27.1.49 Norwich Red.		
	KSU 755 (new reg 1991) Nov 72 < J. Knight 1974 Brighton 1991		
887	887 KLY 15 4.5.49 USA LHD. 3-9 2 stud. Body of chassis – basket case 1990.		
	(Reg for temporary use in England) (called "John"!) sold, damaged, stolen, old Aclcopfrom (bought after 1976)		
	Ordered Nov 1948, Shipped 14.6.49. William Harold Leathers, up to ~ 1962, Tom Vance, to frenð 1990		
1029	029 KLP 820 29.3.49 Edinburgh		
	(Colin Daniels?) M.R. Harwood 1979 1990		
324	324 UMV 5 10.11.47 London. 2 door FHC body		
	(since 1970) 1990		
705	705 JOF 189 29.9.48 BIRMINGHAM.		
	., Calif, USA 1990		
806	806 18.3.49 MALAYA. Needs restoration '91 92 (UK 2013)		
	, Atlanta, USA selling oct '92 1990		
1041	M 1041 B HUY 140 9.4.49 BIRMINGHAM. Basket Case!		
	In a Quarry, Wadebridge, Cornwall. , Wales 1990 1990		

M - PAGE 5

1025	(025?) Jo. 616	D.H. Foursome, full flowing wings (into body) probably M chassis	

Built by Riverlee Motor Bodies of Birmingham for

| 733 | 733 JHW 674 15.10.48 Newcastle. (at Monterey 1990) | Red Interior purchased 15 Apr'90 | White Canada |

Imported to Canada 1950 ... 18yrs Retored 1989 ... 19...

| 873 | 873 JUF 470 27.1.49 London. |
Reg 3 Feb... Supplied to Hartley, Midgeley, Jeanne Burrows Snelling, Derek Rogers, Jim Tilles. Scrapped.

GFH 10   Black - used to be serviced by Hartwells.

| 835 | 835 HZ ...52 7. 49 Belfast |
Reg 15 Feb ...   Lawrie Juniper 1990

| 1004 | 1004 FOW '32 7.3.47 Bournemouth, Mercury 3.9 Engine N2 332124   Blue |
Reg 24.8.47   1984 David Hance, Hastings;   ..., Woking 1990

| 309 | 309 UMV 5... 27.10.47 London |
Balfour   f...., Luton 1973

| 879 | 879 UMK 735 27.1.49 London |
(K.J. Allen 150!)   ..., London N20, 1972

| 1056 | 1056 KPX ... 14.5.49 London |
I (aute...   — , Poole 1983

| 1066 | 1066 UMr ...38 23.1.49 London |
                         '' — , Halesowen, Warcs, 1974

| 627 | 627 KLO ...3 8.12.48 London   SALOON |
Works demonstrator for about 1 year following 1949 Motor Show (Apr'72)

| 290 | 290 Jo. 63 1.10.47 Birmingham   Steel body 2+2 coupe, Oldsmobile Rocket |
Peter Thurston   Suffolk 19...

| 1081 | 1081 MP... 82 14...49 Guildford, Torsion front suspension, Brami Wires, Alfins, Messes'   Broad |
+ Col G ... Campbell Dec'62   — 1991   Selling 1990

| 353 | 353 NPC ... 27.1.48 London   Chopped - Trials Special.   Red |
Reg 26/6/48   '49 C... Onley, '88 John Leek, '69 Guy Greenwell, '86 Graham Pierce, '88'... — selling Dec 1990.

| 208 | 208 LBH 856 29.1.47 London |
S... ...t G...

| 214 | 214 JGU 4 14.7.47 London |
Mr. ...hof senior.

| 430 | 430 LUN 596 19.3.48 Leeds. Special Body by Lea Francis — Illustrated in complete |
list or cat of British Cars

| 528 | 528 JLW 89. 30.3.48 USA (Ex demo car) |

M - PAGE 6

| 529 | 529 KLO 122 17.2.50 Ex Demo - Experimental Model. |

NPG 827

| 511 | 511 (MRB 449(?)). No date. Experimental Coupe |

KXF 820 (Service Records 13/10/50)

| 525 | 525 KXP 830 13.12.49 Cornwall,   Demo, Coil Springs |

GWF 654

— , J. Tonbridge (sold).

| 828 | 828 NNU 8 13.1.49 Derby   Metallic Green/Grey. |
Porteous,   ..., Wales, 1961 to '64.

MBB 312   Silver

                         Robin Stellfox (1950s?)

| 809 | 809 KKA 222 16.12.48 Manchester   (fairly rough! 1991)   Blue Green |
E.W. Taylor, Liverpool   J. Phillips (20yrs to 1991)   1991

| 563 | 563 FWM 453 22.7.48 Manchester   (was LHD now RHD) |
Jan'60 Claude Arbuthnot Brighton, Jul'60 Colin Bird Lewes, Aug'62 James Peters Brighton, Aug'64 Thomas Birnie Abingdon, Oct'64 to 1992 Simon Burke Brighton, — , 1992

| 1000 | 1000 MUA 735 7.3.49 Leeds. |
P.M.G. Thorpe, Leeds,   F.W. P de Winton, Simon Burke, —   1992

| 812 | 812 22055 28.12.48 Malta   Red. |
J.M. Pirotta,   (was 14061)   See separate note. ...6   — , Jan 1979 to 1992

P

				Now restored	2014
1516	16 CCF 768	10.11.49 LONDON		Alan Allard 1998.	
		T. Every, Bletchley Aug'68.			1990
1517	17 KKF 752	26.11.49 SHREWSBURY		Ford Flathead.	Grey
					i. Penn 1986
1567	67 KYL 949	19.1.50 LONDON			
		M. Wheeler, Farnham May'66			
1601	01	3.2.50 USA			
		J.R. Allard, Washington Nov'73.			
1602	02	13.3.50 SWEDEN		4 4litre Mercury.	Grey
					i. Sweden 1986
1622	22 KSM 704	11.4.50 GLASGOW			
		J.M. Watson, Renfrewshire (History Feb'67) Apr'67 May'69			
1625	25	24 8 50 SWEDEN	Custom Built Coupe, Colombia Axle		
					i. Sweden 1994
1627	27 EBA 666	14.4.50 MANCHESTER	3622cc Flathead.	Dark Blue	
		G.W. Selles, Benfleet May'78. Keith Stewart 1984		1986	1988
1645	45 HGE 895	13.5.50 GLASGOW	Jaguar engined in Sep'71		1990
		Derek M. Jeffery, Ilfracombe, Jan'70. selling Sep'71. (			Devon 1981
1646	46 TRF 696	23.5.50 DERBY			
		R.J. Hammond, London, Jan'63. Nov'63.			
1678	78 LGX 679	1.7.50 LONDON			
		R. Lippingale, Norwich Mar'78			i. SPA into 1991
1680	80 JAA 500	4.7.50 BOURNEMOUTH		Ford Flathead.	Green
		Milwaukee, USA Aug'69 oct'69.			Still owned 1986
1682	82	10.7.50 NEWCASTLE ON TYNE.			
		. Darlington Jan'64.			
1710	710 CCH 111	18.7.50 DERBY		Scrapped (used to rebuild AEN 392)	
		i. Sale, Chesh Apr'67, J.D. Slates		Nov'77.	1990
1712	712 WME 816	20.7.50 LONDON			
		. Frimley Green, Aug'66. Selling Feb'67.			
1721	721 GJU 514	1.8.50 BIRMINGHAM			Red.
		i. Lorn Allerton 1950 Merryhill Classics, restored Feb'90. for Sale Jun 90 £29500!			
1722	722 LPX 552	3.8.50 LONDON			

P - PAGE 2

1751	51 OPH 518	30.8.50 LONDON			
		. West Parley, Dorset Oct'64			
1795	95 AEN 392	2. 10.50 MANCHESTER			Gunmetal.
		J.D. Slates, Cheadle Hulme Nov'77. Andrew Gilling N. Yorks.			1976
1814	14 JCE 911	7.10.50 NORWICH			
		5, Upminster Nov'63			
1870	70	22.11.50 BOURNEMOUTH			
		1 Apr'62			
1893	93 KRU 602	18.12.50 BOURNEMOUTH		Ford Flathead.	White
		Phillip Morton, Stockport Mar'78			i. 1986
1904	04 WOD 350	8.1.51 LONDON			
		R.J. Graham Feb'63. (Breaking up PI, May'64)			
1907	7 JGA 595	10.1.51 GLASGOW			Maroon
		(since 1985) i. . 3, Crewe			1989
1909	9 LXM 903	12.1.51 DERBY		Ford Flathead.	Black
		'21, 3, Aberdeen 1986			
1915	5 LXU 597	18.1.51 LONDON		was Ford Flathead.	
	A.L. Gooda	D. Halsey, London Aug'63 Scrapped by Brian Sharp 1986.			
		22.1.51 BIRMINGHAM Chassis only.			
		(Tom Lush, Tech College rebuild car)			1990
1932	32 WHX 123	15.2.51 LONDON	Ford Flathead.		1990
		M.K. Forkin, Middlesborough Apr'67. Keith Stewart 1983			California
1935	35 LVM 682	10.2.51 MANCHESTER.			
		C.W. Stone, Sale, Chesh. Apr'67 selling Mar'70.			
1936	36 NRL 466	14.2.51 EXETER			
		Dawlish Sep'68			
1937	37 BAZ 500	28.2.51 AUSTRALIA			
	(Aus) Reg. N°?	J.E. Jackson, Sydney Australia Apr'64. i. (selling) 1990			
1950	50	26.2.51 MANCHESTER			
1951	51 WMF 910	26.2.51 LONDON		Mercury.	(Had it in Nov'77)
	Reg. 2.3.51	Jack George, Coyton, H. Wallwork, Gt. Shelfad, Cambs Mar'64.			Surrey 1986
1956	56 AF 3705	22.3.51 NEW ZEALAND			
		Dunedin, New Zealand Oct'64.			

P — PAGE 3

1957	57 FPN 300	5.3.51 LONDON	('Special' by R. Hayes)	was Blue.	
		Dr Rex Bennet, Overseas Visitors Club SW5, Oct'64			1986
1996	96 ERJ 701	30.3.51 MANCHESTER.			Red
		GPD Wright, Oldham Apr64 Selling Jul'65.		Arizona USA 1986	
1998	98	6.4.51 LEEDS	Ford Flathead.		Blue
				(1978) o' Avon 1986	
		now owned by Son.			
2021	21 JWP 700	9.4.51 GLOUCESTER.			
		Effingham in Nov 62 selling Apr'65.			
2050	50 NRL 837	30.4.51 EXETER.			
		, Eindhoven, Holland Nov'68.			
2051	051 PBB 589	1.5.51 NEWCASTLE ON TYNE.			
		, Ewell Feb'68.			
2118	118 FBA 50	19.7.51 MANCHESTER			
		, Tunbridge Wells Nov'77.			
2126	26 GAP 269	2.2.52 LONDON			
		, Abingdon, Berks May'63.			
2127	127 MGK 470	17.7.51 LONDON			
		, Stansted Aug'68.			
2132	132 MRR 68	31.7.51 DERBY			
	(Reg. Aug 51)	, Eccles, Lancs Jul'69.			1990
2168	168 DRH 895	18.9.51 AUSTRALIA.			
	(Aus. Reg No?)	J.E. Jackson, Sydney, Australia Apr'64.		(selling) 1990	
2186	186 BCW 276	1.10.51 MANCHESTER.			
		, Sale, Chesh Apr'67.			
2207	07 MLO 312	17.10.51 LONDON.	floorchange.		Black
	Reg 31 Oct 51	James Whittle, Market Drayton 1-7.84 + Bill Gallimore Nov87, D.J. True, bought in March 1970 (lies 2nd PT in a bad state) Jan 71. selling Dec 73			1990
2208	08	23.10.51 BOURNEMOUTH.			
		Sep'61			
2232	232 XMX 989	6.11.51 LONDON.			
		W.C.S. Walker Nov'61, , Southampton Nov'65.			
2250	250 MLW 873	1.12.51 MANCHESTER.			
		Basildon Oct'64, selling Oct'65			
2267	267 GJO 224	18.12.51 OXFORD.			
		Coventry May'64			
2269	2269 MUC 189	(info from M. Kacprowski 15.10.14) ?			

P — PAGE 4

2284	284 HUJ 487	5.2.52 SHREWSBURY.		East Peckham, Kent, Apr'72	
		D.B Crowther, Shipley, Yorks Nov'65, selling May'66 Jul'67,		, Sheffield Aug'68,	
2289	289 XMY 590	19.2.52 LONDON.			
		, Norwich Apr'67.			
2291	91 MOB 962	28.2.52 BIRMINGHAM.			
		, Welling, Kent May'69.			
2292	92 ORL 87	15.2.52 EXETER	Ford Flathead		Green.
		B.C. English		1986, , Southport 128	
3079	079 MON 381	5.3.52 BIRMINGHAM.	(see separate sheet)	Henfield, Sussex	
		Ludmilla Rado, Nottingham Aug'67 (selling Jul'67)		Apr'72 , Sussex 19?	
3080	080 MXN 420	3.4.52 LONDON.			
		, Kingston Aug'66, letter Jan'68.			
3081	081 OTT 992	13.3.52 EXETER.		Red Hide	Red
		Jim Peters, Brighton Oct'64, selling Feb68 Aug'71.			
3084	084 HUJ 760	4.4.52 SHREWSBURY	362cu Offenhauser engine.	was White.	
	Viscount Boyne.	Ian H Grant Oct'62, H.B Digby Nov'62, Cross Keys Motor Service, Lydford on Fosse, Somset Nov'68, selling Sep62		1986, , Lincs 198?	
3103	103	23.7.52 SWEDEN.		Scrapped in 1959.	
3107	107	2.10.52 SWEDEN.	Lincoln	Scrapped in 1962.	
2165	NTA 582				
3270	270 KGA 165	2.1.52 GLASGOW			
	(KJA?)	, Feb'63, , 1982			
		AG 2575			
		, New Zealand Jul'66.			
1672	672 LGX 678	1.7.50 London.			
		Mrs Wymes , Croydon Jul'66			
1632	632 KYP 640	22.4.50 London Demo Car –	Auto Car test 1950		
2275	275 MLX 381	(No Date) 1952 Monte Carlo Winner. (Cars N° 146)			Metallic Blue.
		Sydney Allard Curtis , Sep'62.			

P – Page 5

1548	...48 KYM 669 23.12.49 London.
1816	...16 LXD 515 2.2.51 London. In Tom Lush's Book.
2185	...85 GMO 999 26.9.51 Oxford. In V8 Book.
2005	...98 LLP 797 } This is the J2!
	HGE 149 Special Body & running gear. ... 1989
2237?	GEA 334 pulled from scrap yard in Leics (Thought to be M2X) Leics 1990
1643	...43 GKW 155 9.5.50 Leeds. (re reg KYV 642?) ⟶ Simon Richards – Scrapped.
1615	...15 KEL 821 30.3.50 Bournmouth (Gutted Chassis 1990) M.L Taylor, Sheffield 1985 Brian Handy of Sheffield looked after it but Richard O'Dell b/c Milton Keynes. 1990 Leics
1885	...85 13.12.50 Birmingham. Light Blue. Imported to USA by Ted Liseares '75/76, Tom Vance 1980, 1990
1914	...14 JGA 661 16.1.51 Glasgow. Scotland 1973
2160	...60 OUM 51 8.7.51 Leeds. 1983
2173	...73 MJJ 459 16.10.51 London USA 1980
2246	...246 13.11.51 New Zealand. Norway 1987
2252	...52 MLW 872 1.12.51 London. Mercury Red leather, Silver Grey/Maroon top. Appears to be 2 cars re: call 19.5.09 also blue car (no chassis plates on either!) H.D Williams, Gwent 1988, selling 1991 (claims to have this car 1990)
2253	...53 AG 2575 14.12.51 New Zealand N. Zealand 1980
2280	...280 PUM 797 6.3.52 Leeds This reg no. used on several cars by Les Brooks. Scrapped.
2288	...288 9.2.52 London now Chassis Only. Jim Watson, Ayrshire (bought from friend of farming relative – chopped special) Nov'74. 1990

P – Page 6

594C	? JYM 272 Trials special on P9 chassis. (was M type reg. No). Blue 1989
	? ERG 303 J.E. Jackson, Sydney, Australia, (selling) 1990
1933	...933 MBC 476 9.2.51 Birmingham (reg MAS 51) 1990
2056	...056 EFV 778 9.5.51 Manchester. 1990
1823	...823 NKJ 631 16.10.50 London (1956 Monte Carlo Car No 152) Blade Mrs Weaver (Driven by Allard in Rally).
1725	...725 FBA 90 21.8.50 Manchester (in garden) 1990
	FBW 123 Silver – used to be serviced by Hartwells.
	GSC 660 Now "K2" special (tree fell on the Saloon!) Eric Patterson 1989, 1990
	ERJ 775 .51 Mercury 3-9. 1990
	PMW 503 3 yrs in Scrap Yard then Sunbury (Restoring) Jan'72
	LOB 872 J.S. Thurston, East Peckham, Kent Apr'72.
2095	...095 ERJ 966 8.6.51 Manchester. Used by Silver City Airways, Southend Airport for advertising during the '50s Sep'72
	JUS 781 (Chassis Only) 1990
2293	...293 PVK 718 22.2.52 Newcastle. (being restored 1990) 1990
2285	...285 MLX 400 13.3.52 London (1952 Monte Carlo Car No 131) Blue Driven by Edna & Hilda Allard.
1964	...964 LXR 946 10.3.51 London. (1953 Monte Carlo Car No 184) Black S.H Allard, McDowell.

3079 | P 3079 MON 381 Engine 7269838 Metallic Grey Blue Interior.
Bristol Street Motors, Birmingham 5/3/52.
Registered 16/9/52.
Floor Gear Change. Present engine 1124078

original owner 17/9/52 J.H. Hill, 238 Soho Rd, Handsworth, Birmingham.
19/6/54 G.W. Dethick, The Cottage, Biggin by Holland, Derby.
1/8/57 D. Pike, 165 Ross Rd, South Norwood SE25
2/5/60 A.N. Johnstone, 12 Bury Close, Upwood, Hunts.
16/6/66 D.F. Cox, Elizabeth Cottage, Castlecamps, Cambridge.
? Tony Batt
17/4/67 Ludmilla Rado, 8, Hadon Rd, West Bridgeford, Nottingham.
Leslie Allard.
? Rodney Fuller, Rushmeas Nursery, Sandy Lane, Hinfield, Sussex.
10/11/88 ████████, 10 Dawn Close, Beeding, Steyning, W. Sussex.

3096 | 3096 SVG 894 1.5.52 Norwich (chassis plate might have shown 3096?) originally 5·4 litre. CREAM (Dorset?)
Brian Rance recovered from breakers ~1962, √ 1988, now in South west England 19

3091 | 3091 9.2.52 BIRMINGHAM
..., Washington USA, Nov 73

3119 | 3119 YMD 692 12.9.52 LONDON. (bought 1977) 1990
Ad Lavels Sold car 1956 to Dave Fuller (Allard apparted) → Ted Liscate imported to USA ~75/76, ↑
1957 too J.D. Bardolph, Ascot, Jun 65, Robert Judd, London Nov 65, Jan 66, selling Aug 66.
was in Kent.
TMX 5 (this was M chassis 871) — — Maroon
√ 1988

2006 | 2006 MLP 116 27.9.51 London. Motor to ºcar 1952
used by Eddie MacDowell (an Allard Director).

3124 | 3124 6.8.52 SWEDEN — WRITTEN OFF IN 1954 — SCRAPPED

2001 | 2001 4.6.51 USA. M2

1709 | 1709 LXR 942 18.6.51 London. M2 Geneva Show Coupé.

3098 | 3098 MYL 773 4.6.52 London. Scrapped(?)
Lt. Col. Patrick Sullivan - Tailyur Jul 57, Lt. Col. Francis Johnson Apr 58, John Smulders Aug 59, 1 Jan 68

P2.

4000 — 000 MXA 555 1-12.51 LONDON SAFARI
Dennis Allard (Syds broker) De Dion diff being sold by Patterson Nov'67 – Car broken?

4001 — 001 MXA 554 No Record LONDON SAFARI
(as 3000)

4003 — 003 NLD 412 15.11.52 WORCESTER SAFARI was Chrysler in Oct'67. Cadillac BRONZE
R.E. Wright, Wolverhampton Oct'67. 1989

4501 — 501 OLC 655 23.12.53 LONDON MONTE CARLO Ford Flathead Black.
1989

4502 — 502 24.9.53 SWEDEN MONTE CARLO. Lincoln Silver
, Sweden 1986

4505 — 505 TZ300 24.8.54 BELFAST MONTE CARLO Chrysler. Red
Australia 1986

4509 — 509 794 BMY 30.6.54 LONDON MONTE CARLO Daimler 4.5 litre Cream
P.B. Robbins, Brierley Hills, Staffs, Jun'65, Andrew Sep'71. 1990

4513 — 513 No Record (1955) SAFARI, old Wood, Lincoln Small Bonnet, Cream
original Dr? Gene Wells, Canada 1986, 1990

4512 — 512 TGT 703 MONTE CARLO
Eric Alexander, selling Mar'62, John Williams May'63 , Swansea 1989

4009 — 009 OUE 79 28.1.54 Birmingham SAFARI Plymouth
Reg. 1 Rd54 sold aid 88 to 1991
Mary Gee, Sutton Coldfield (MOG?) Lawrence Koenig, Manchester for sale May 1987.

4504 — 504 MDG 160 16.6.53 London. (The Uxbridge Car?!) (Something same as PUM 797)
Les Brooks. Stanmore Jan'72

? GBJ 1
Ex Godsal lengthened J2 body, put on P2 chassis. 1989

N.B. Pat has TGT 702 listed as chassis No. 4505 wrong per Tom Lush, check with P.J. Mabbett

Palm Beach MkI

5000 — Z 5000 29.3.52 USA. first MkI chassis built, fibreglass body by Anchorage Plastic Corp (now), Rhode Island USA. Nov77

5017 — C 5017 12.5.53 SWEDEN
current owner since 1964, in Sweden 1986

5080 — Z 5080 4655 H 14.7.53 LONDON Jaguar 3781cc, Alloy FHC body. Yellow
John Paddy Carstairs current owner since 1958, London 1986

5102 — Z 5102 KDK 56 11.4.53 MANCHESTER Owned by ... wrote 1976 Red, KDK 56 is a MkII body Red 1990
Mr Scott 1953, D.H. Gardner, Basing, Hants Oct'64.

5104 — 5104 NYO 66 No Record LONDON
M.P. Black, Nottingham Dec'67 , Australia 1984

5105 — 5105 TUA 900 No Record LEEDS. Dk Blue.
L.W. Baker, Oct'61, London selling Feb'66 . Enfield Feb'68. (still?)

5108 — 5108 NYO 6 8.1.54 LONDON Blue
F 1986.

5144 — 5144 9.5.53 SWEDEN
, Sweden 1986

5145 — 5145 24.9.53 SWEDEN.
, Sweden 1986

5151 — 5151 OGY 456 2.4.54 ARGENTINA Red Ram
Allard Motor Co, for sale Jul'66, C.J. Girling, Ilford Oct'67, G.A.G. Mayne, Essex Feb'68. Malcolm Elder, Oxford owned it for a short time.

5158 — 5158 No Record No Record
PB1 chassis used for new body PBII – see PBII 72/7000 2

5164 — 5164 FPM 806 No Record No Record. Red
, Sweden 1986

5009 — 5009 NGN 567 15.11.52 London. Palm Beach prototype, Zephyr Engine.
Allard Co Demo Car W.A. Reynolds May'61, Feb'63, Apr'64, Jun'64, Oct'64.
2 BML , Pontefract Jan'69.

5111 — 5111 700 BME 1.4.54 London
Mr Knight (1954) A.G. Portes, Gutes Jun'71. J.S. Thurston, East Peckham Apr'72. 1990

5028 — Z 5028 23.2.53 USA.
, USA 1980

5107 — Z 5107 FES 888 2.11.53 Perth.
1976

Palm Beach MK I   Page 2

5149   IZ 5149   6.5.54   USA.   2450cc   Wire wheels.   White
                                 (Monterey 1990)
                                 California 1977 × 1990

5155   IZ 5155   16.4.55   USA

                          R. Allard, California 1980.

5081   IC 5081   20.4.53   USA.   1500cc   (Monterey 1990)   Red
       Mr Scott, Fulla Export.   Calif 1990

5148   IZ 5148   20.10.53   USA   2267cc   (Monterey 1990)
                                      1990

5110   Z 5110   6.1.54   Abbotts of Farnham Coupé.
               (director of Abbotts)

5200   C 5200   NYF 595   17.7.53   R.A.C. Panels   Saloon

5201   C 5201   NXY 451   10.7.53   RAC. Panels   Saloon.

5140   C 5140   JFY 600   31.7.53   Manchester

                                    Somerton, 1991

Palm Beach Mk II

                                  Lloyd Allard 2012   Researched.

7000   Z/7000 Z   545 EXR   MK II body on MK I chassis (see 2 IZ 5158) Zephyr. '56 Motor Show Car   Maroon
                    A.R.W Skirving Jul'60, Jun'61 Selling Jul'61.   Allard Motors Selling Dec'66.
     (but J McLhad   John McLellan, New Zealand, Dec'62, Apr'63, Jun'63, Jul'64, Apr'65, Feb'69 M
     2 IZ 5158, did   Ward '69
     one or a other been
     chass 22/70002 ?   Prof A.T. Simmonds, Sunbury, Jan'64, W.W. Hemsworth, Enfield, Jul'69. Oct'70 Nov'71

7101   Z/7101 XK   TYu 414   XK140 Engine. '56 Motor Show Chassis.   Engine No 7013 HS   Red
     Log book No 'y   3442cc   Vought 1988   Germany
     72- 7001 XK)   Reg 6.6.57   £25,000   1990
     Edward Neilson Short, Stafford 12 Feb 58, 2nd owner, London 23/1/60, 3rd A.R.W. Skirving, Oxfordshire

7102   Z/7102 XK   UXB 793   GT. Coupe. Jaguar Engine. de Dion rear. '57 Motor Show car
               Sydney Allard, Alan Allard   R.H. Givvin 1984   1988
                                                   2010
                                                  USA 2013

7103   Z/7103 XK   Jaguar Engine. '57 Motor Show Car to Houston Aug'58.   Blue
                 2020 Brought back to U.K by

7104   Z/7104 Z   Shipped to USA.
                         Dedham, Mass. Jan'70.

7105   Z/7105 CHR   GT. Coupe   Tuned Chrysler engine 6426cc   Red
                   Dupont family.   (Monterey 1990)
                                               1990

7106   Z/7106 XK   Jaguar Engine (C type).
           Ray May Oct'67   Then sold to USA.

7107   Z/7107 XK.   Jaguar Engine. Shipped to USA.   White

                   ?   Abbot Coupe.   It's a MK I
     Commissioned by R.G. Sutherland (director? of Abbotts).
7106   174 BLP (is this 7106??) ✓   Black

Clipper!

Ray May has '55 Clipper Sep '61.
. Richland selling '55 clipper Nov '68.
— wreck in woods Illinois. now for restoration 2022
USA. G. Allard to provide info assist.

Reallocate   Oddities — What Car?

400	..o M	JUC 302		J, London, Apr 61	Red XL ...
				To M	'63
206	..06 K	JLK 618	K1 or M?	T.H. Deans Sep 62, ... "	Apr '63
1087	..87 M	SRE 801	Fr.. — .. ..i..de, Wotten, Norfolk Jul '61		M 1087
		VXA 234		London Aug '63.	
	..4 x M	K KMV 713		1 BFPO 53 Jun '64.	
		888 CXb		, Croydon Aug '68	
		OZ 3652	Sold to Mr Scott, Northern Ireland May 1951	Oct '70.
			(— Chrysler Engined Saloon?)	
		PKJ 412	Allard Special on test by Tony Batt May '69.	Essex Aw..
114	..4	HLF 601	1st Post War Special. — Used Ford chassis side rails	
		S.H. Allard, Guy Warburton	Next owner had garage broken into — car was	
			then allowed to deteriorate away.	
		KRW 239.	Pre war?	M 1051	
		VUL 534	2nd Steyr car (built on Clarke car bits) — Scrapped.	
		JUC 5	1949 special — forerunner of the J2.	
		G Imhof.	(see J2 pages)	
	..203 X	OKM 728	G — .er.	
2280	..280 i	PUM 797	Les Brooks P2, J1 etc etc etc. (used on all his cars!)	
		PGH 613	Manta Jag. (built by Gordon Viola with De Dion rear/s..	
			.. ..s (since ~ 1980)	1990
		JGP 473	2nd Post War Special (on J chassis)	

Sold to man in Plymouth — fire at works & insurance claim — car
destroyed (This was while Tom Lush was still at Allards).

·APPENDIX 2·

ALLARD CHASSIS NUMBER SPREADSHEETS

The spreadsheet summarizes Allard Motor Company records for their cars. It has been created to show the information extracted from the original Allard Allocation Books and the page references to all entries on a car whether in the Allard Record Cards, Allard Warranty Book or Allard Service Records.

During this lengthy manual process I have endeavoured to accurately record the details. Sometimes handwriting varies significantly and I have made my educated verdict on the text.

Example record one (see right) is typical of what is in the records. Some vehicles only have a single entry which indicates that Allard had no further involvement with the car.

I must offer my belated apologies to Decca Records who owned an Allard M-type, chassis 400; this car has more records than any other, mostly in the servicing file. The Allard service personnel must have been very familiar with this car!

If you see S.O.R. written, this means the car has been taken by the dealer on a sale or return basis from Allard. The dealer was not under a contractual agreement to purchase the car from Allard unless that dealer could find a buyer. This appears quite often in the records and I suspect this would have been a vehicle put on display in the showroom.

Page References	Chassis	Original Engine Number	UK Registration	Type	LHD?	Body Style	Original Colour	Original Interior	Original Hood	Original Delivery	Allocation	First Customer	Remarks
CHASSIS NUMBER PAGE REFERENCE KEY: Allocation Books (pages 1-77), Record Cards (pages 78-167), Warranty Book (pages 168-201), Service Records (pages 202-393)													
10, 244, 249, 259, 265, 271, 277, 343, 345, 347	391	7193621	LVK 765	L	RHD	Tourer	Maroon	Brown	Beige	16/3/48	Patterson		
10, 212	392	7193107	AFB 798	L	RHD	Tourer	Grey	Grey	Grey	3/10/48	Hughes (Simons)		
10, 245, 265, 271, 282, 293, 692	393	7193620	JLT 913	L	RHD	Tourer	Chassis and body	Not noted	Not noted	2/11/48	Dagenhams (Bentley)		Untrimmed, materials supplied
10	394	7195199	Not noted	L	RHD	Tourer	Chassis and body	Brown	Beige	13/2/48	Tate		
10	395	7195131	Not noted	L	RHD	Tourer	Chassis	Chassis	Chassis	30/1/48	Taylors (Whiteladies Garage)		
10	396	Not used	Not used	J*	Not used	Not used	Not used	Not used	Not used	Not used	Not used		* Noted as J but not used
10, 216, 219, 230, 233, 245, 253, 257, 263, 267, 283, 284, 290, 296, 303, 304, 307, 310, 314, 316, 331, 333, 334, 341	397A	7193812	NEV 26	M	RHD	Coupe	Maroon	Grey	Maroon	3/3/48	Gould (Richard Bros)		One record says regn. NEV 27
10	398A	7193624	Not noted	P	RHD	Coupe	Black	Red	Beige	3/12/48	Bristol Street Motors (Erskins)		
10	399	7193087	Not noted	M	RHD	Coupe	Black	Red	Beige	3/8/48	Alexanders (Dr. Patterson)		
10, 214, 217, 219, 221, 227, 228, 230, 232, 234, 236, 237, 241, 249, 254, 257, 262, 267, 269, 281, 284, 286, 290, 293, 294, 297, 300, 309, 312, 316, 321, 330, 333, 334, 337, 341, 345, 703, 704	400	7195655	JUC 302	M	RHD	Coupe	Grey	Grey	Grey	4/5/48	Adlards	Decca Records	The most recorded Allard of all
10, 262, 694	401	7194902	MZ 1201	PI	RHD	Coupe	Maroon	Red	Maroon	24/3/48	Hamilton		
10	402	7193817	Not noted	K	RHD	2-Seater	Chassis	Chassis	Chassis	2/2/48	Tate (Harrison)		
10	403	7193837	Not noted	K	RHD	2-Seater	Grey	Not noted	Not noted	30/4/48	Adlards (Freeilright)		
10, 232, 686	404	7195796	LUB 906	K	RHD	2-Seater	Grey	Not noted	Not noted	20/4/48	Tate		Domesday Book has reference to PNW 503
10, 248, 294, 340, 352	405	7195784	JYM 271	M	RHD	Coupe	Chassis	Chassis	Chassis	25/3/48	Adlards (Johnson)		Experimental

Example record one.

Example record two (see right) has sections noting 'Not used'. These are where the Allard Motor Company never used the available chassis number and I would be concerned if a vehicle has any of these numbers, if it does it will require further investigation for validation.

The only known areas where this might not apply is to the later Palm Beach Mk.I model where it does appear that some cars exist that were not recorded and particularly those that went to Scandinavian nations, the other is to the Allard JR, chassis 3408, which is a 2018 continuation car of the original seven JR's and currently is the only valid Allard not constructed between 1946 – 1959, this car being created by Alan and Lloyd Allard.

It should be noted that in some instances, the model field will reflect the model as stated in the Allocation Book records, and not necessarily the usual, current terminology. For instance, some cars are shown as a J model, but are now considered as a J2.

Page References	Chassis	Original Engine Number	UK Registration	Type	LHD?	Body Style	Original Colour	Original Interior	Original Hood	Original Delivery	Allocation	First Customer	Remarks
CHASSIS NUMBER PAGE REFERENCE KEY: Allocation Books (pages 1-77), Record Cards (pages 78-167), Warranty Book (pages 168-201), Service Records (pages 202-393)													
28	991	Not used	Not used	Not used	Not used	Not used	Not used	Not used	Not used	Not used	Not used		
28	992	Not used	Not used	Not used	Not used	Not used	Not used	Not used	Not used	Not used	Not used		
28	993	Not used	Not used	Not used	Not used	Not used	Not used	Not used	Not used	Not used	Not used		
29	994	Not used	Not used	Not used	Not used	Not used	Not used	Not used	Not used	Not used	Not used		
29	995	Not used	Not used	Not used	Not used	Not used	Not used	Not used	Not used	Not used	Not used		
29	996	Not used	Not used	Not used	Not used	Not used	Not used	Not used	Not used	Not used	Not used		
29	997	Not used	Not used	Not used	Not used	Not used	Not used	Not used	Not used	Not used	Not used		
29	998	Not used	Not used	Not used	Not used	Not used	Not used	Not used	Not used	Not used	Not used		
29	999	Not used	Not used	Not used	Not used	Not used	Not used	Not used	Not used	Not used	Not used		
29, 194, 696	1000	7207230	Not noted	M	RHD	Coupe	Blue	Blue	Blue	3/7/49	Tate	P. M. G. Thorpe	
29, 173, 229, 234, 237, 241, 244, 249, 257, 259, 262, 264, 268, 269, 270	1001	7207231	KLL 999	M	RHD	Coupe	Blue	Blue	Blue	3/5/49	Dagenham Motors (H. C. Paul)	J. Greenhalgh	
29, 178, 281	1002	7207111	HHA 478	M	RHD	Coupe	Grey	Blue	Grey	3/11/49	English (E. W. Cox & Co.)	Dr. H. D. White	
29, 169, 233, 283, 286, 323, 344	1003	7207144	KLO 127	M	RHD	Coupe	Grey	Blue	Blue	3/9/49	Adlards (W. Shaker)		Possible KLO 127 on page 344
29, 178, 696	1004	7207582	FOW 732	M	RHD	Coupe	Blue	Grey	Blue	3/7/49	English (South Hants Motor Co.)	D. J. Philipson	
29, 169, 226, 229, 233, 238, 242, 248, 258, 274, 279, 288, 291, 294, 315, 329, 333, 375	1005	7207734	KLL 736	M	RHD	Coupe	Black	Grey	Black	3/2/49	Adlards (L. A. Mitchell)	D. E. Godfery	Page 375 shows 974 CPL
29, 169	1006	7207750	Not noted	M	RHD	Coupe	Blue	Blue	Blue	3/7/49	Adlards (Hartley & Midgley)	Not noted	
29, 169, 231, 243, 261, 266, 275, 276, 277, 285, 298, 313, 314, 326, 331, 341	1007	7207733	EPM 96	M	RHD	Coupe	Grey	Grey	Blue	3/5/49	Adlards	Not noted	
29, 200	1008	7207021	Not noted	M	RHD	Coupe	Grey	Grey	Black	3/11/49	Frew (D. McIntosh)	W. Lindsay Gillies	

Example record two.

· A L L A R D ·

Page References	Chassis	Original Engine Number	UK Registration	Type	LHD?	Body Style	Original Colour	Original Interior	Original Hood	Original Delivery	Allocation	First Customer	Remarks
CHASSIS NUMBER PAGE REFERENCE KEY: Allocation Books (pages 1-77), Record Cards (pages 78-167), Warranty Book (pages 168-201), Service Records (pages 202-393)													
1	101	Not noted	Not noted	L	RHD	Tourer	Not noted	Not noted	Not noted	Not noted	Experimental		Subsequently dismantled
1, 266, 268, 270, 275, 289, 291, 295, 308, 452, 628, 691	102	S/27733/E	HLB 424	L	RHD	Tourer	Red	Red Leather	Not noted	18/3/47	Demonstrator		Show car at 1946 SMMT Jubilee Cavalcade, London – First Allard post-war car
1, 679	103	BOB 32/103	HLB 430	J1	RHD	2-Seater	Blue	Blue Leather	Not noted	22/3/47	Demonstrator		
1, 233, 448	104	S/27726 E	Not noted	K	RHD	2-Seater	Red	Red Leather	Not noted	22/10/46	Belgium		First K-type
1	105	S/27732 E	Not noted	L	RHD	Tourer	Grey	Not noted	Not noted	29/11/46	Argentina		
1, 215, 272, 443, 452, 628, 679	106	K 12311	HLP 5	J1	RHD	2-Seater	White	Not noted	Not noted	28/7/46	A. G. Imhof	A. G. Imhof	Show car at 1946 SMMT Jubilee Cavalcade, London
1, 455	107	S/27726 E 7175879	Not noted	M	RHD	D.H. Coupe	Maroon	Red Leather	Not noted	Not noted	Demonstrator		First M-type Drophead Coupe – prototype
1	108	7079928	Not noted	K	RHD	2-Seater	White	Red Leather	Not noted	31/3/47	U.S.A.		T. Lush notes he drove this personally to Southampton for shipment Monday 31st March
1, 208, 679	109	K 12312	KHW 100	J1	RHD	2-Seater	White	Not noted	Not noted	7/5/46	K. E. O. Burgess (Allard Motor Co.)	K. E. O. Burgess	
1, 281, 282, 446, 447, 679	110	K 12313	JYH 613	J1	RHD	2-Seater	White	Not noted	Not noted	9/3/46	J. H. Appleton (Allard Motor Co.)	J. H. Appleton	Also noted as HXC 578 (pages 446, 447 and 706)
1, 679	111	S/27194 E	GOM 2	J1	RHD	2-Seater	Black	Not noted	Not noted	31/10/46	G. N. Mansell (Allard Motor Co.)	G. N. Mansell	
1, 679	112	S/270035	Not noted	J1	RHD	2-Seater	Black	Not noted	Not noted	19/12/46	Jersey		
1	113	Not used	Not used		Not used	Not used	Not used	Not used	Not used	Not used	Not used	Not used	Not used
1, 521, 703	114	Not noted	HLF 601		RHD	Special	Not noted	Not noted	Not noted	Not noted	S. H. Allard (Allard Motor Co.)	S. H. Allard	Special built at S1 workshop (special development space run by Sydney Allard behind Clapham showrooms) – some welding and other work at Park Hill under this number – SHA first post-war competition car
1	115	7079927	Not noted	L	RHD	Tourer	Red	Red Leather	Not noted	1/10/47	Belgium		
1, 203, 205, 691	116	7079932	NHX 498	L	RHD	Tourer	Blue	Blue Leather	Not noted	15/4/47	Dagenham Motors (Richards)		Also shown in Service Record on page 205 as NHX 798
1, 245, 246, 679, 781	117	EOM 32/1028/AM	HYW 331	J1	RHD	2-Seater	Metallic	Blue Leather	Not noted	4/3/47	Maurice Wick (Allard Motor Co.)	Maurice Wick	
1	118	Not used	Not used		Not used	Not used	Not used	Not used	Not used	Not used	Not used	Not used	Not used
1	119	Not used	Not used		Not used	Not used	Not used	Not used	Not used	Not used	Not used	Not used	Not used
1	120	Not used	Not used		Not used	Not used	Not used	Not used	Not used	Not used	Not used	Not used	Not used
1, 206, 207, 287, 315, 334	121	7079931	JLF 575	M	RHD	D.H. Coupe	Frame	body	Not noted	6/2/47	Adlards (Lucas)		
1, 218, 331	122	7079929	JLY 51	L	RHD	Tourer	Red	Red Leather	Not noted	3/10/47	Switzerland		T. Lush notes he drove this personally to Newhaven for shipment Monday 10th March
1, 246, 265, 268	123	7079953	CRJ 218	L	RHD	Tourer	Grey	Grey Leather	Not noted	13/5/47	Nunn		Page 268 shows GRJ 218
1, 368, 370	124	7079926	Not noted	L	RHD	Tourer	Blue	Blue Leather	Black	3/12/47	Palestine		
1, 307, 311	125	7079954	BES 495	L	RHD	Tourer	Black	Brown Leather	Fawn	29/4/47	Frew (Lomas)		

Page References	Chassis	Original Engine Number	UK Registration	Type	LHD?	Body Style	Original Colour	Original Interior	Original Hood	Original Delivery	Allocation	First Customer	Remarks
CHASSIS NUMBER PAGE REFERENCE KEY: Allocation Books (pages 1-77), Record Cards (pages 78-167), Warranty Book (pages 168-201), Service Records (pages 202-393)													
1, 330	126	7079941	Not noted	L	RHD	Tourer	Green	Blue Leather	Grey	18/6/47	South Africa (Hotchkiss)		
1, 206, 281, 296, 307, 319, 322, 325, 337, 344, 352, 356, 364, 375, 380, 386, 691	127	7079952	JGY 708	L	RHD	Tourer	Red	Red Leather	Not noted	28/6/47	Adlards		Page 364 appears to show IGY 708. Pages 380 and 386 shows JGN 708
1, 204, 205, 230	128	7079924	SMC 649	L	RHD	Tourer	Blue	Blue Leather	Not noted	19/6/47	Dagenham Motors		
2	129	7079930	Not noted	L	RHD	Tourer	Skeleton body	Skeleton body	Skeleton body	21/4/47	Dagenham Motors		
2	130	7079923	Not noted	L	RHD	Tourer	Maroon	Red Leather	Not noted	15/5/47	U.S.A.		
2	131	Not used	Not used		Not used	Not used	Not used	Not used	Not used	Not used	Not used	Not used	Not used
2	132	7079947	Not noted	L	RHD	Tourer	Skeleton body	Skeleton body	Skeleton body	1/10/47	Belgium		
2, 203	133	7079563	Not noted	L	RHD	Tourer	Maroon	Red Leather	Not noted	7/1/47	Jersey		
2, 691	134	7125295	Not noted	L	RHD	Tourer	Skeleton body	Skeleton body	Skeleton body	17/1/47	Belgium		
2	135	7125299	Not noted	L	RHD	Tourer	Skeleton body	Skeleton body	Skeleton body	17/1/47	Belgium		
2	136	7125302	Not noted	L	RHD	Tourer	Maroon	Maroon Leather	Not noted	10/9/47	Taylors		
2	137	7125293	Not noted	L	RHD	Tourer	Skeleton body	Skeleton body	Skeleton body	5/8/47	Universal (Premier Garage)		
2, 206	138	7125297	JAL 465	L	RHD	Tourer	Skeleton body	Skeleton body	Skeleton body	22/3/47	Universal (Premier Garage)		
2, 214	139	7125301	Not noted	L	RHD	Tourer	Skeleton body	Skeleton body	Skeleton body	24/4/47	Universal (Premier Garage)		
2, 204, 225, 235, 246, 248, 262	140	7125300	JGY 720	L	RHD	Tourer	Red	Red Leather	Maroon	31/7/47	Adlards		Red wheels
2, 204, 691	141	7125291	JGX 651	L	RHD	Tourer	Maroon	Red Leather	Maroon	25/6/47	Gould		Red wheels
2	142	7079950	Not noted	K	RHD	2-Seater	Blue	Blue Leather	Not noted	23/4/47	Hughes (L. Watkins)		
2, 205, 686	143	7079939	HEL 306	K	RHD	2-Seater	Red	Red Leather	Not noted	25/8/47	English		Tatham
2, 204	144	7124860	Not noted	K	RHD	2-Seater	Black	Red Leather	Not noted	16/5/47	Gould (Currie)		
2, 240, 253, 256, 264, 272, 310, 687	145	K-145	CHM 316	K	RHD	2-Seater	Skeleton body	Skeleton body	Skeleton body	2/6/47	Adlards (MacPhee)		
2, 213, 237, 317, 364, 378, 382	146	7116827	HUB 331	K	RHD	2-Seater	Blue	Blue Leather	Not noted	15/5/47	Switzerland		Page 378 notes HUD 481. Page 237 refers to car as unregistered
2, 204, 207, 208, 209	147	7125292	FFH 211	K	RHD	2-Seater	Green	Blue Leather	Not noted	18/7/47	Taylors (Horace Roberts)	Horace Roberts	

Page References	Chassis	Original Engine Number	UK Registration	Type	LHD?	Body Style	Original Colour	Original Interior	Original Hood	Original Delivery	Allocation	First Customer	Remarks
CHASSIS NUMBER PAGE REFERENCE KEY: Allocation Books (pages 1-77), Record Cards (pages 78-167), Warranty Book (pages 168-201), Service Records (pages 202-393)													
2, 204, 219, 278, 279, 281, 285, 286, 289, 292, 679	148	S2-773138	HRR 472	J1	RHD	Chassis	Chassis	Chassis	Chassis	3/4/47	Universal (Premier Garage)		
2, 389	149	7179622	Not noted	K	RHD	2-Seater	Red	Grey Leather	Not noted	6/9/47	Argentina		
2, 203	150	7479628	Not noted	K	RHD	2-Seater	Maroon	Red Leather	Maroon	25/6/47	Bristol Street Motors		Red wheels
2, 205	151	7179623	Not noted	K	RHD	2-Seater	Black	Brown Leather	Crossed out	30/7/47	Taylors		Red wheels
2, 679	152	J152	Not noted	J1	RHD	Chassis	Chassis	Chassis	Chassis	28/3/47	Allard Motor Co. (L. Potter)		J152 later quoted when FGP 290 was re-registered as HPX 57 with solid front axle
2, 191	153	7125303	Not noted	M	LHD	D.H. Coupe	Light Blue	Red Leather	Grey	3/4/47	Brazil		
2, 204, 239, 245, 250, 255, 383, 687	154	7179627	JGP 474	K	RHD	2-Seater	White	Blue Leather	Blue	28/6/47	Belgium (Bunn)		Blue wheels
2	155	7179564	Not noted	K	RHD	2-Seater	Chassis	Chassis	Chassis	3/10/47	R. E. Hamilton (R. Baird)		
2, 687	156	7179617	JGP 467	K	RHD	2-Seater	Blue	Blue Leather	Crossed out	12/12/47	Allard Motor Co.		Maroon wheels
2	157	7179626	Not noted	K	RHD	2-Seater	White	Dark Green Leather	Crossed out	12/5/47	Gibraltar		Green wheels. Local registration 11472, Maltese car possibly re-imported
2, 204, 687	158	7179625	Not noted	K	RHD	2-Seater	Blue	Blue Leather	Blue	8/8/47	U.S.A.		Blue wheels
2, 206	159	7179562	Not noted	K	RHD	2-Seater	Skeleton body	Skeleton body	Skeleton body	28/4/47	Gould (Bonallack)		
2, 204	160	7179565	Not noted	K	RHD	2-Seater	Red	Red Leather	Not noted	7/9/47	Hartwells		
3, 205, 686	161	7179604	HDV 288	K	RHD	2-Seater	Black	Blue Leather	Not noted	20/8/47	Hughes (Central Garage)		
3, 205, 211, 214, 233, 243, 280, 686	162	7179546	SMC 665	K	RHD	2-Seater	Maroon	Grey Leather	Not noted	26/7/47	Dagenham Motors		Page 214 refers records regn. as SMC 655 but this is incorrect
3, 205	163	7179084	Not noted	K	RHD	2-Seater	Red	Red Leather	Beige	15/9/47	Patterson		
3, 204, 205, 228, 691	164	7179877	DPM 159	L	RHD	Tourer	Black	Brown Leather	Not noted	7/9/47	Adlards (Capt. Richards)		
3, 204, 686	165	7177876	Not noted	K	RHD	2-Seater	Red	Brown	Not noted	8/8/47	U.S.A.		
3	166	Not used	Not used		Not used	Not used	Not used	Not used	Not used	Not used	Not used	Not used	Not used
3	167	Not used	Not used		Not used	Not used	Not used	Not used	Not used	Not used	Not used	Not used	Not used
3	168	Not used	Not used		Not used	Not used	Not used	Not used	Not used	Not used	Not used	Not used	Not used
3	169	Not used	Not used		Not used	Not used	Not used	Not used	Not used	Not used	Not used	Not used	Not used
3	170	Not used	Not used		Not used	Not used	Not used	Not used	Not used	Not used	Not used	Not used	Not used
3	171	Not used	Not used		Not used	Not used	Not used	Not used	Not used	Not used	Not used	Not used	Not used
3	172	Not used	Not used		Not used	Not used	Not used	Not used	Not used	Not used	Not used	Not used	Not used
3	173	Not used	Not used		Not used	Not used	Not used	Not used	Not used	Not used	Not used	Not used	Not used

Page References	Chassis	Original Engine Number	UK Registration	Type	LHD?	Body Style	Original Colour	Original Interior	Original Hood	Original Delivery	Allocation	First Customer	Remarks
							CHASSIS NUMBER PAGE REFERENCE KEY: Allocation Books (pages 1-77), Record Cards (pages 78-167), Warranty Book (pages 168-201), Service Records (pages 202-393)						
3	174	Not used	Not used		Not used	Not used	Not used	Not used	Not used	Not used	Not used	Not used	Not used
3	175	Not used	Not used		Not used	Not used	Not used	Not used	Not used	Not used	Not used	Not used	Not used
3	176	Not used	Not used		Not used	Not used	Not used	Not used	Not used	Not used	Not used	Not used	Not used
3	177	Not used	Not used		Not used	Not used	Not used	Not used	Not used	Not used	Not used	Not used	Not used
3	178	Not used	Not used		Not used	Not used	Not used	Not used	Not used	Not used	Not used	Not used	Not used
3	179	Not used	Not used		Not used	Not used	Not used	Not used	Not used	Not used	Not used	Not used	Not used
3	180	Not used	Not used		Not used	Not used	Not used	Not used	Not used	Not used	Not used	Not used	Not used
3	181	Not used	Not used		Not used	Not used	Not used	Not used	Not used	Not used	Not used	Not used	Not used
3	182	Not used	Not used		Not used	Not used	Not used	Not used	Not used	Not used	Not used	Not used	Not used
3	183	Not used	Not used		Not used	Not used	Not used	Not used	Not used	Not used	Not used	Not used	Not used
3	184	Not used	Not used		Not used	Not used	Not used	Not used	Not used	Not used	Not used	Not used	Not used
3	185	Not used	Not used		Not used	Not used	Not used	Not used	Not used	Not used	Not used	Not used	Not used
3	186	Not used	Not used		Not used	Not used	Not used	Not used	Not used	Not used	Not used	Not used	Not used
3	187	Not used	Not used		Not used	Not used	Not used	Not used	Not used	Not used	Not used	Not used	Not used
3	188	Not used	Not used		Not used	Not used	Not used	Not used	Not used	Not used	Not used	Not used	Not used
3	189	Not used	Not used		Not used	Not used	Not used	Not used	Not used	Not used	Not used	Not used	Not used
3	190	Not used	Not used		Not used	Not used	Not used	Not used	Not used	Not used	Not used	Not used	Not used
3	191	Not used	Not used		Not used	Not used	Not used	Not used	Not used	Not used	Not used	Not used	Not used
3	192	Not used	Not used		Not used	Not used	Not used	Not used	Not used	Not used	Not used	Not used	Not used
4	193	Not used	Not used		Not used	Not used	Not used	Not used	Not used	Not used	Not used	Not used	Not used
4	194	Not used	Not used		Not used	Not used	Not used	Not used	Not used	Not used	Not used	Not used	Not used
4	195	Not used	Not used		Not used	Not used	Not used	Not used	Not used	Not used	Not used	Not used	Not used
4	196	Not used	Not used		Not used	Not used	Not used	Not used	Not used	Not used	Not used	Not used	Not used
4	197	Not used	Not used		Not used	Not used	Not used	Not used	Not used	Not used	Not used	Not used	Not used
4	198	Not used	Not used		Not used	Not used	Not used	Not used	Not used	Not used	Not used	Not used	Not used
4	199	Not used	Not used		Not used	Not used	Not used	Not used	Not used	Not used	Not used	Not used	Not used
4, 205, 207	200	7179554	DEX 939	L	RHD	Tourer	Cordoba Grey	Red Leather	Not noted	28/7/47	Harris (Edwards)		
4, 171, 228, 248, 264, 273, 283, 306, 313, 327, 334, 692	201	7179891	SMH 107	L	RHD	Tourer	Maroon	Brown Leather	Not noted	16/9/47	Dagenham Motors (Craddock)		
4	202	7179618	Not noted	L	RHD	Tourer	Red	Red Leather	Not noted	9/12/47	English (Morton)		

Page References	Chassis	Original Engine Number	UK Registration	Type	LHD?	Body Style	Original Colour	Original Interior	Original Hood	Original Delivery	Allocation	First Customer	Remarks
4, 205, 215, 238, 275, 281, 300, 333, 338, 355, 691, 713	203	7179889	MWL 380	L	RHD	Tourer	Green	Blue Leather	Beige.	15/8/47	Hartwells (Frey)		
4, 325	204	7179887	Not noted	K	RHD	2-Seater	White	Blue Leather	Not noted	29/10/47	Brazil		
4, 204	205	7180314	Not noted	K	LHD	2-Seater	Black	Red Leather	Grey	10/6/47	Argentina		Blue wheels
4, 243, 300, 703	206	7179890	JLK 618	K	RHD	2-Seater	Black	Red Leather	Not noted	9/12/47	Gould		
4, 358, 710	207	7179881	Not noted	K	RHD	2-Seater	Skeleton body	Skeleton body	Skeleton body	16/5/47	Adlards (Wayne)		Page 358 refers to 207 but should be 2071
4, 207, 208, 209, 212, 330, 455, 696, 713	208	7179886	LBH 856	M	RHD	Coupe	Chassis	Chassis	Chassis	29/4/47	Adlards (Stormont Eng)		Dolphin Special Body – electric folding hard roof/ LBH 856 is listed for both chassis 283 and 208
4, 204	209	7180025	Not noted	L	RHD	Tourer	Maroon	Red Leather	Grey	8/8/47	U.S.A.		
4	210	7180045	Not noted	L	RHD	Tourer	Not noted	Blue	Beige	11/6/47	Nunn		Noted as untrimmed
4, 328	211	7180041	Not noted	L	RHD	Tourer	Chassis	Chassis	Chassis	30/4/47	Tate		
4, 691	212	7179884	LUA 882	L	RHD	Tourer	Not noted	Grey	Grey	15/10/47	Tate		Noted as untrimmed
4, 205, 209, 710, 711	213	7180043	Not noted	K	LHD	2-Seater	Maroon	Maroon	Grey	11/5/47	Brazil		Page 207 refers to 213 but this should be 231
4, 203, 206, 218, 222, 225, 243, 258, 287, 316, 696	214	7180027	JGU 4	M	RHD	Coupe	Skeleton chassis	Skeleton chassis	Skeleton chassis	14/7/47	Adlards (Mrs Imhof)		
4	215	7180038	KHW 100	M	RHD	Coupe	Skeleton chassis	Skeleton chassis	Skeleton chassis	30/6/47	Adlards (Burgess)		
4, 208, 217, 219, 222, 226, 243, 711	216	7180050	JLU 676	M	RHD	Coupe	Chassis	Chassis	Chassis	6/3/47	Gould		
4, 203, 206, 208, 215, 219, 223, 231, 234, 243, 257, 265, 280, 283, 290, 322, 334, 348, 695	217	7180033	JGU 5	M	RHD	Coupe	Skeleton chassis	Skeleton chassis	Skeleton chassis	2/7/47	Adlards (Imhof)		
4	218	7180036	Not noted	L	LHD	Tourer	Maroon	Maroon	Maroon	12/5/47	Gibraltar		
4, 295	219	7180044	Not noted	K	RHD	2-Seater	Chassis	Chassis	Chassis	6/4/47	Tate		
4	220	7180125	Not noted	K	RHD	2-Seater	Chassis	Chassis	Chassis	5/7/47	Hamilton		
4, 205	221	7180126	Not noted	K	RHD	2-Seater	Red	Grey Leather	Grey	25/8/47	George & Jobling		
4, 205, 687	222	7180121	GZ 8959	K	RHD	2-Seater	Maroon	Red Leather	Not noted	8/7/47	Hamilton		
4	223	7180128	Not noted	L	RHD	Tourer	Chassis	Chassis	Chassis	19/5/47	Hamilton		

CHASSIS NUMBER PAGE REFERENCE KEY: Allocation Books (pages 1-77), Record Cards (pages 78-167), Warranty Book (pages 168-201), Service Records (pages 202-393)

Page References	Chassis	Original Engine Number	UK Registration	Type	LHD?	Body Style	Original Colour	Original Interior	Original Hood	Original Delivery	Allocation	First Customer	Remarks
						CHASSIS NUMBER PAGE REFERENCE KEY: Allocation Books (pages 1-77), Record Cards (pages 78-167), Warranty Book (pages 168-201), Service Records (pages 202-393)							
4, 205, 243, 258, 270, 274, 280, 289, 299, 304	224	7180127	SMT 946	L	RHD	Tourer	Blue	Blue Leather	Grey	26/7/47	Dagenham Motors		
5	225	7180140	Not noted	L	RHD	Tourer	Chassis	Chassis	Chassis	6/3/47	Dagenham Motors		
5, 207, 210	226	7180195	EAW 163	L	RHD	Tourer	Blue	Grey	Grey	21/11/47	Furrows		
5	227	7180139	Not noted	L	RHD	Tourer	Blue	Blue	Grey	28/11/47	George & Jobling		
5, 204, 254, 261, 283	228	7180201	JLT 6	M	RHD	Coupe	Chassis	Chassis	Chassis	26/6/47	Dagenham Motors (Adlards)		
5	229	7180194	Not noted	M	RHD	Coupe	Chassis	Chassis	Chassis	25/7/47	Adlards (Stormont)		One sub-bonnet (perhaps a temporary one) supplied.
5, 206	230	7180200	Not noted	M	RHD	Coupe	Maroon	Crossed out	Crossed out	17/12/47	Australia (Clement Shaw)		
5, 207, 208, 209, 214, 227, 230, 240, 248, 256, 266, 271, 280, 282, 336, 694, 710, 711	231	7180191	JLM 245	M	RHD	Coupe	White	Red	Maroon	19/12/47	Dagenham		Maroon wheels. Page 207 refers to 213 but should be 231. Page 271 shows 231
5	232	7180138 (crossed out)	Not noted	M	?	Coupe	Not noted	Not noted	Not noted	24/3/48	Demonstrator		Engine 7180138 crossed out
5	233	7180190	Not noted	K	RHD	2-Seater	Skeleton body	Skeleton body	Skeleton body	14/6/47	Dagenham Motors (Hume)		
5, 204	234	7180198	Not noted	K	RHD	2-Seater	Skeleton body	Skeleton body	Skeleton body	17/7/47	Universal (Bemier)		
5	235	7180193	Not noted	K	RHD	2-Seater	Blue	Red Leather	Black	9/12/47	Nunn		
5, 203, 214, 241, 249, 251, 292	236	7180259	BGS 825	K	RHD	2-Seater	Skeleton body	Skeleton body	Skeleton body	26/6/47	Frew		Page 243 suggests 216 is chassis number
5, 328, 687	237	7180196	Not noted	K	RHD	2-Seater	Maroon	Maroon Leather	Beige	17/12/47	Australia (Clement Shaw)		
5	238	7180197	Not noted	K	RHD	2-Seater	Blue	Grey Leather	Grey	26/9/47	Brazil		Evans Shiwan, possibly a dealership
5, 207, 244, 330	239	7180224	CUD 818	K	RHD	2-Seater	Black	Maroon	Beige	17/11/47	Hartwells		
5, 205, 221, 686	240	7180225	EBW 525	K	RHD	2-Seater	Chassis	Chassis	Chassis	10/1/47	Bristol Street Motors		
5, 206, 219, 223, 226, 711, 719	241	7180262	MPJ 219	K	RHD	2-Seater	Black	Red Leather	Black	29/10/47	Brazil		MPJ 219 appears with both chassis number 421 and 241
5, 686	242	7180261	SH 8C25	K	RHD	2-Seater	Black	Blue Leather	Black	13/10/47	Alexanders		
5, 206, 691	243	7180260	JLK 958	L	RHD	Tourer	Red	Grey	Grey	2/4/48	Demonstrator		
5	244	7180258	Not noted	L	RHD	Tourer	Blue	Grey Leather	Grey	11/7/47	Mann Egerton		
5	245	7180257	Not noted	L	RHD	Tourer	Red	Red	Beige	12/5/47	Tate		
5, 203	246	7180263	Not noted	L	RHD	Tourer	Chassis	Chassis	Chassis	30/7/47	Dagenham Motors (Sandos)		
5	247	7180266	Not noted	L	RHD	Tourer	Not noted	Red	Grey	15/10/47	George & Jobling		Brass windscreen deficient

Page References	Chassis	Original Engine Number	UK Registration	Type	LHD?	Body Style	Original Colour	Original Interior	Original Hood	Original Delivery	Allocation	First Customer	Remarks
5, 204, 220, 231, 248, 258, 263, 321, 343	248	7180291	KKX 672	K	RHD	2-Seater	Chassis	Chassis	Chassis	7/8/47	Hartwells (R. J. Heming)		
5, 203	249	7180298	Not noted	K	RHD	2-Seater	Chassis	Chassis	Chassis	27/6/47	Dagenham Motors (Sandos)		
5, 206, 289, 686	250	7180297	HOL 846	K	RHD	2-Seater	Blue	Blue Leather	Grey	10/10/47	Bristol Street Motors		
5, 204, 213, 687	251	7180296	MBB 802	K	RHD	2-Seater	Chassis	Chassis	Chassis	18/7/47	Tate		
5, 204, 217, 218, 222	252	7180293	MPH 429	K	RHD	2-Seater	Chassis	Chassis	Chassis	7/8/47	Hartwells		
5, 206, 691	253	7180295	LUB 650	L	RHD	Tourer	Crossed out	Brown	Beige	17/10/47	Tate		Noted as untrimmed
5	254	7180294	Not noted	L	RHD	Tourer	Chassis	Chassis	Chassis	10/1/47	Furrows (Oakleys)		
5	255	7180292	Not noted	L	RHD	Tourer	Red	Grey	Grey	17/12/47	Australia (Clement Shaw)		
5, 204, 217	256	7180268	NHK 461	L	RHD	Tourer	Chassis	Chassis	Chassis	15/7/47	Dagenham Motors (Featherstone)		
6, 204, 213, 330, 332, 342, 345	257	7180301	MPG 118	L	RHD	Tourer	Chassis	Chassis	Chassis	13/8/47	Dagenham Motors (Dr. Du Fame)		
6, 204	258	7180310	Not noted	K	RHD	2-Seater	Chassis	Chassis	Chassis	8/6/47	Adlards		
6, 204	259	7180303	Not noted	K	RHD	2-Seater	Chassis	Chassis	Chassis	10/1/47	Patterson		
6, 204, 297	260	7180270	MPH 823	K	RHD	2-Seater	Chassis	Chassis	Chassis	10/3/47	Adlards (Salford)		
6, 205	261	7180302	Not noted	K	RHD	2-Seater	Chassis	Chassis	Chassis	10/1/47	Bristol Street Motors		
6, 205	262	7180308	Not noted	K	RHD	2-Seater	Chassis	Chassis	Chassis	10/3/47	Dagenham Motors		
6, 207	263	7180299	BGS 1	M	RHD	Coupe	Black	Blue	Black	28/11/47	Frew		
6, 211, 230, 247, 254	264	7180305	JYT 949	M	RHD	Coupe	Chassis	Chassis	Chassis	24/8/47	Gould (Wick)		Delivered as chassis on 11/10/1947
6, 273, 274, 285, 314, 316, 326, 342	265	7180304	QB 7315	M	RHD	Coupe	Black	Blue	Beige	1/9/48	West Africa (Thomson)		Later regn. noted as LXK 44
6	266	7180306	Not noted	M	RHD	Coupe	Chassis	Chassis	Chassis	11/11/47	Tate (Emerson)		
6, 221, 231, 243, 249, 352, 369	267	7180300	EDR 121	M	RHD	Coupe	Chassis	Chassis	Chassis	7/4/47	Hughes		
6, 219, 224	268	7180312	MPD 27	M	LHD	Coupe	Maroon	Brown	Maroon	14/4/48	Adlards		
6	269	7180313	Not noted	N	LHD	Coupe	Grey	Red	Grey	22/4/48	Nunn		
6, 215, 317, 318, 321, 324, 328, 330, 333, 335, 694	270	7180317	JLW 490	M	LHD	Coupe	Maroon	Not noted	Maroon		Demonstrator		

CHASSIS NUMBER PAGE REFERENCE KEY: Allocation Books (pages 1-77), Record Cards (pages 78-167), Warranty Book (pages 168-201), Service Records (pages 202-393)

Page References	Chassis	Original Engine Number	UK Registration	Type	LHD?	Body Style	Original Colour	Original Interior	Original Hood	Original Delivery	Allocation	First Customer	Remarks
CHASSIS NUMBER PAGE REFERENCE KEY: Allocation Books (pages 1-77), Record Cards (pages 78-167), Warranty Book (pages 168-201), Service Records (pages 202-393)														
6, 303, 307, 318, 322, 326, 331, 337, 340, 344, 345, 346, 354, 376	271	7195529	DBA 772	M	LHD	Coupe	Grey	Grey	Grey	27/4/48	Nunn		Old style windows
6, 261, 274	272	7180315	JYV 272	M	LHD	Coupe	Red	Maroon	Not noted	22/6/48	Nunn		
6, 679	273	J-273	NPC 640	J1	RHD	2-Seater	Chassis	Chassis	Chassis	9127/47	L. Potter (Allard)		Domesday Book also refers to MPC 640
6, 679	274	J-274	GAB 779	J1	RHD	2-Seater	Chassis	Chassis	Chassis	9/5/47	Taylors (Horace Roberts)		
6, 679	275	J-275	KPB 242	J1	RHD	2-Seater	Not noted	Not noted	Not noted	22/1/48	L. Potter (Allard Motor Co.)		
6	276	7191968 erased	Not noted	K	RHD	2-Seater	Not noted	Not noted	Not noted	Not noted	Demonstrator		
6	277	7188842	Not noted	K	RHD	2-Seater	Chassis	Chassis	Chassis	21/10/47	Bristol Street Motors		
6, 691	278	7180309	Not noted	L	LHD	Tourer	Blue	Grey	Grey	21/4/48	Adlards		
6, 213	279	7186425	LUG 265	L	LHD	Tourer	Blue	Grey	Grey	21/4/48	Tate		
6, 213	280	7126444	Not noted	L	LHD	Tourer	Maroon	Brown	Beige	23/4/48	Nunn		
6, 220	281	7180316	DFR 118	L	LHD	Tourer	Blue	Grey	Grey	22/4/48	Nunn		
6	282	7186641	Not noted	L	LHD	Tourer	Black	Maroon	Maroon	28/4/48	Nunn		
6, 710	283	7187082	LBH 856	L	RHD	Tourer	Chassis	Chassis	Chassis	10/1/47	Bristol Street Motors		LBH 856 is listed for both chassis 283 and 208
6, 691	284	7186688	Not noted	L	RHD	Tourer	Untrimmed	Blue	Grey	20/10/47	Hartwells		2 battery lids and without brass windscreen
6	285	7187006	Not noted	L	RHD	Tourer	Chassis	Chassis	Chassis	10/1/47	Bristol Street Motors		
6, 209	286	7186959	LVK 160	L	RHD	Tourer	Blue	Grey	Grey	24/11/47	Patterson		
6	287	7186448	Not noted	L	RHD	Tourer	Blue	Blue	Beige	15/12/47	South Africa (Butters)		
6, 353	288	7186833	CVG 428	L	RHD	Tourer	Chassis	Chassis	Chassis	10/2/47	Hughes		Later record notes regn. LUO 468
7	289	7186644	Not noted	M	RHD	Coupe	Chassis	Chassis	Chassis	9/5/47	A. E. Gould		
7, 242, 368, 687, 696	290	7180811	JOC 63	M	RHD	Coupe	Chassis	Chassis	Chassis	10/1/47	Bristol Street Motors		
7	291	7180307	Not noted	N	RHD	Coupe	Chassis	Chassis	Chassis	10/1/47	Bristol Street Motors		
7	292	7187003	Not noted	M	RHD	Coupe	Chassis	Chassis	Chassis	9/3/47	George & Jobling		
7, 243	293	7186888	Not noted	M	LHD	Coupe	Maroon	Brown	Maroon	5/1/48	Tate		
7	294	7188097	Not noted	M	LHD	Coupe	Chassis	Chassis	Chassis	12/8/48	Gibraltar		
7, 226, 377	295	7188894	HPD 142	M	LHD	Coupe	Blue	Blue	Grey	26/4/48	Not noted		Previously recorded as HPD 149 but on further review appears to be HPD 142, eg page 377
7	296	7188004	Not noted	M	LHD	Coupe	Chassis	Chassis	Chassis	5/3/48	Taylors (Horace Roberts)		
7, 209, 220, 226, 230, 235, 236	297	7188856	GRK 222	M	LHD	Coupe	Grey	Brown	Grey	13/4/48	Adlards (Moss & Lawson)		

Page References	Chassis	Original Engine Number	UK Registration	Type	LHD?	Body Style	Original Colour	Original Interior	Original Hood	Original Delivery	Allocation	First Customer	Remarks
						CHASSIS NUMBER PAGE REFERENCE KEY: Allocation Books (pages 1-77), Record Cards (pages 78-167), Warranty Book (pages 168-201), Service Records (pages 202-393)							
7, 222, 225, 262, 287	298	7188839	CYG 428	L	RHD	Tourer	Chassis	Chassis	Chassis	15/10/47	Mann Egerton (Layton)		Page 262 shows CVG 428
7	299	7188846	Not noted	L	RHD	Tourer	Chassis	Chassis	Chassis	15/10/47	Gatterson (Crabtree)		
7, 228, 344, 348, 360, 371, 716	300	7188052	GGD 594	L	RHD	Tourer	Chassis	Chassis	Chassis	20/10/47	George & Jobling		Supplied without proper battery lid
7	301	7188035	Not noted	L	RHD	Tourer	Chassis	Chassis	Chassis	29/10/47	Alexanders		
7	302	7188044	Not noted	L	RHD	Tourer	Chassis	Chassis	Chassis	11/11/47	Adlards (Linnery)		
7	303	7186493	Not noted	M	RHD	Coupe	Chassis	Chassis	Chassis	20/10/47	Furrows		Supplied without proper battery lid
7	304	7188841	Not noted	M	RHD	Coupe	Chassis	Chassis	Chassis	20/10/47	Furrows		Supplied without proper battery lid
7	305	M-305	Not noted	M	RHD	Coupe	Chassis and body	Untrimmed	Untrimmed	12/9/47	Universal (Tongue)		
7	306	7188847	Not noted	M	RHD	Coupe	Chassis	Chassis	Chassis	20/10/47	Gould		Supplied without proper battery lid
7, 254, 299, 714	307	7188840	JLY 858	M	RHD	Coupe	Chassis	Chassis	Chassis	27/10/47	Dagenham Motors		Page 254 notes UMV 59 as 307
7	308	7188845	Not noted	M	RHD	Coupe	Chassis	Chassis	Chassis	24/10/47	Harris		
7, 207, 250, 289, 295, 696	309	7188843	UMV 59	M	RHD	Coupe	Chassis	Chassis	Chassis	21/10/47	Gould		
7, 259, 295	310	7188055	CWP 777	L	RHD	Tourer	Chassis	Chassis	Chassis	29/10/47	Bristol Street Motors		Page 259 notes regn. GWP 777 or QWP 777, character indistinct
7, 691	311	7188034	LKJ 47	L	RHD	Tourer	Chassis	Chassis	Chassis	11/4/47	Adlards (Rootes)		
7, 276, 296	312	7187074	JYO 634	L	RHD	Tourer	Chassis	Chassis	Chassis	11/4/47	Dagenham Motors (Bentley)		
7, 228	313	7187967	NFC 965	L	RHD	Tourer	Chassis and body	Blue	Grey	21/11/47	Hartwells		Untrimmed
7, 161, 217, 240, 249, 259, 265, 311, 377, 386, 692	314	7190989	JLM 3	L	RHD	Tourer	Chassis and body	Grey	Beige	20/11/47	Allard Motor Co. (Dent)		Untrimmed
7	315	7188054	Not noted	L	RHD	Tourer	Black	Brown	Beige	1/5/48	Hamilton		
7	316	7886646	Not noted	M	RHD	Coupe	Chassis	Chassis	Chassis	11/7/47	English (Dibben & Sons)		
7, 214, 221, 255, 337, 338, 342, 347, 351, 353, 361, 362, 366	317	7188049	JYO 585	M	RHD	Coupe	Chassis	Chassis	Chassis	11/5/47	Gould (Wick)		JYB 685 or JYB 685 on page 342
7	318	7188078	Not noted	M	RHD	Coupe	Chassis	Chassis	Chassis	11/6/47	George & Jobling (Hill)		
7, 229, 242, 258	319	7187949	JYO 365	M	RHD	Coupe	Chassis	Chassis	Chassis	11/6/47	Dagenham Motors (McMillan)		
7	320	7188001	Not noted	M	RHD	Coupe	Chassis	Chassis	Chassis	11/6/47	Dagenham Motors (Firbank)		
8, 292, 694, 714	321	7187960	Not noted	M	RHD	Coupe	Chassis	Chassis	Chassis	11/7/47	George & Jobling		Domesday Book has reference to GGB 331 for 321

Page References	Chassis	Original Engine Number	UK Registration	Type	LHD?	Body Style	Original Colour	Original Interior	Original Hood	Original Delivery	Allocation	First Customer	Remarks
				CHASSIS NUMBER PAGE REFERENCE KEY: Allocation Books (pages 1-77), Record Cards (pages 78-167), Warranty Book (pages 168-201), Service Records (pages 202-393)									
8, 217, 222, 237, 251, 274, 278, 284, 301, 314	322	7187943	IYO 134	M	RHD	Coupe	Chassis	Chassis	Chassis	11/7/47	Dagenham Motors (Regent Park)		
8	323	7187952	Not noted	M	RHD	Coupe	Chassis	Chassis	Chassis	11/7/47	Hughes		
8, 241, 695	324	7191972	JMV 5	M	RHD	Coupe	Chassis	Chassis	Chassis	11/10/47	Gould (Leigh)		
8, 209, 210, 213, 224	325	7191969	JLY 637	M	RHD	Coupe	Chassis	Chassis	Chassis	11/10/47	Gould (K. Hole)		
8, 218, 223, 226, 236, 239, 244, 268, 281, 294, 298, 332, 695	326	7191961	LYT 950	M	RHD	Coupe	Chassis	Chassis	Chassis	11/10/47	Gould (K. Hole)		
8, 224, 275, 306, 321	327	7191838 was 7188002	KLF 633	M	RHD	Coupe	Chassis	Chassis	Chassis	12/12/47	Dagenham Motors (Bentley)		Two records note regn. KLF 639
8, 266, 272, 273	328	7187945 was 7191839	LYO 646	M	RHD	Coupe	Chassis	Chassis	Chassis	25/11/47	Dagenham Motors (Bentley)		
8, 241, 257, 277, 302, 328, 336, 360, 455	329	7191967	HWE 28	M	RHD	Coupe	Chassis	Chassis	Chassis	20/11/47	Tate		Engine loaned from 340. Pages 257 and 336 indicates possibly KWE 28
8, 269	330	7191965	SYH 446	M	RHD	Coupe	Chassis	Chassis	Chassis	11/11/47	Dagenham Motors (Kroyer)		
8, 219, 221, 224, 227, 230, 237, 244, 258, 262, 263, 456, 695	331	578476	LLK 957	M	RHD	Coupe	Chassis	Chassis	Chassis	20/7/48	Demonstrator		Engine numbers changed three times
8	332	7191966	Not noted	L	RHD	Tourer	Chassis and body	Blue	Not noted	28/11/47	Tate		Untrimmed
8	333	7190966	Not noted	L	RHD	Tourer	Chassis	Chassis	Chassis	24/11/47	Adlards (Turner)		
8	334	7188898	Not noted	L	RHD	Tourer	Chassis	Chassis	Chassis	28/11/47	Taylors (Whiteladies Garage)		
8	335	7191971	LUB 501	L	RHD	Tourer	Chassis and body	Grey	Grey	12/11/47	Tate		Untrimmed
8, 246	336	7171904	HLJ 292	L	RHD	Tourer	Chassis and body	Blue	Grey	31/12/47	English		Untrimmed
8	337	7191840	Not noted	L	RHD	Tourer	Chassis and body	Grey	Grey	12/11/47	Tate		Untrimmed
8, 360	338	7179880	Not noted	L	RHD	Tourer	Chassis and body	Brown	Beige	12/11/47	Tate		Untrimmed
8	339	7188003	Not noted	K	LHD	2-Seater	Black	Not noted	Not noted	20/4/48	Hoffman		
8, 715	340	7191839 was 7191846	Not noted	M	RHD	Coupe	Maroon	Red	Beige	2/2/48	Nunn		
8, 217	341	7191850	HLJ 161	M	RHD	Coupe	Jade	Blue	Beige	23/2/48	English		
8, 292	342	7187938	A 8055	M	RHD	Coupe	Blue	Grey	Blue	2/12/48	Nigeria		
8, 311, 330, 336	343	7190964	KWE 27	M	RHD	Coupe	Chassis	Chassis	Chassis	12/12/47	Tate		

Page References	Chassis	Original Engine Number	UK Registration	Type	LHD?	Body Style	Original Colour	Original Interior	Original Hood	Original Delivery	Allocation	First Customer	Remarks
						CHASSIS NUMBER PAGE REFERENCE KEY: Allocation Books (pages 1-77), Record Cards (pages 78-167), Warranty Book (pages 168-201), Service Records (pages 202-393)							
8, 691	344	7191970	Not noted	L	RHD	Tourer	Chassis and body	Blue	Grey	12/11/47	Tate		Untrimmed
8, 691	345	7186856	JNC 400	L	RHD	Tourer	Chassis and body	Grey	Grey	18/12/47	Nunn		Untrimmed
8	346	7188849	Not noted	L	RHD	Tourer	Chassis and body	Brown	Beige	17/12/47	Bristol Street Motors		Untrimmed
8, 336, 348	347	7188848	Not noted	L	RHD	Tourer	Maroon	Brown	Maroon	30/1/48	Bristol Street Motors		
8	348	7188850	Not noted	L	RHD	Tourer	Chassis and body	Brown	Beige	1/12/48	Bristol Street Motors		Untrimmed
8	349	7188892	Not noted	L	RHD	Tourer	Chassis and body	Grey	Black	1/5/48	Frew		Untrimmed
8	350	7186919	Not noted	L	RHD	Tourer	Maroon	Brown	Beige	15/1/48	Alexanders		
8, 248, 270, 273, 343	351	7186994	JLT 522	L	RHD	Tourer	Chassis and body	Not noted	Not noted	31/12/48	Dagenham Motors		Untrimmed
8, 249	352	7188169	HNF 842	M	RHD	Coupe	Chassis	Chassis	Chassis	15/12/47	Taylors		
9, 224, 696	353	7188124	Not noted	M	RHD	Coupe	Chassis	Chassis	Chassis	27/1/48	Adlards		Page 224 refers to car as unregistered
9, 211, 215, 224, 288, 294	354	7188043	JYK 439	M	RHD	Coupe	Chassis	Chassis	Chassis	25/3/48	Adlards (Mears Bros)		
9, 252	355	7187965	PD 1606	M	LHD	Coupe	Black	Blue	Grey	14/2/48	Italy		Italian export car appears to be on trade plate QD 1606 or PD 1606
9	356	7186870	Not noted	L	RHD	Tourer	Blue	Grey	Black	30/1/48	Universal		
9	357	7193179	Not noted	L	RHD	Tourer	Black	Brown	Beige		Mann Egerton		
9	358	7186647	Not noted	L	RHD	Tourer	Chassis	Chassis	Chassis	29/12/47	Universal (Hall)		
9	359	7186892	Not noted	L	RHD	Tourer	Chassis	Chassis	Chassis	23/1/48	Taylors (Whiteladies Garage)		
9, 270, 360, 365, 380, 382, 389	360	7193638	LHT 839	L	RHD	Tourer	Chassis	Chassis	Chassis	22/12/47	Taylors (Whiteladies Garage)		Incorrectly recorded as chassis 300 on page 371 of the Service Record
9, 223, 312, 338	361	7186640	LHU 836	L	RHD	Tourer	Chassis	Chassis	Chassis	1/5/48	Taylors (Whiteladies Garage)		
9, 240, 373	362	7193586	MAO 717	L	RHD	Tourer	Chassis	Chassis	Chassis	1/2/48	Patterson		
9	363	7193629	Not noted	L	RHD	Tourer	Chassis	Chassis	Chassis	1/9/48	Taylors (Whiteladies Garage)		
9, 311	364	Not used	Not used	J*	Not used	Not used	Not used	Not used	Not used	Not used	Not used		* Noted as J but not used
9, 216	365	7193319	KKM 777	K	RHD	2-Seater	Black	Red	Not noted	24/3/48	Adlards (Bligh)		
9	366	7188053	Not noted	K	LHD	2-Seater	Gunmetal	Grey	Black	19/3/48	Brazil		
9, 213, 216, 232, 233, 237, 244, 253, 263, 272, 278, 317, 450	367	7193623	THX 323	K	RHD	2-Seater	Chassis	Chassis	Chassis	13/1/48	Dagenham Motors (Abbott)		

Page References	Chassis	Original Engine Number	UK Registration	Type	LHD?	Body Style	Original Colour	Original Interior	Original Hood	Original Delivery	Allocation	First Customer	Remarks
CHASSIS NUMBER PAGE REFERENCE KEY: Allocation Books (pages 1-77), Record Cards (pages 78-167), Warranty Book (pages 168-201), Service Records (pages 202-393)													
9, 79	368	7193088	Not noted	K	LHD	2-Seater	Black	Maroon	Beige	9/9/49	U.S.A. (Ardun Engineering Co.)	Richard B. Parker	
9	369	7193630	Not noted	K	RHD	2-Seater	Chassis	Chassis	Chassis	2/2/48	Tate		
9	370	7188850	Not noted	K	RHD	2-Seater	Not noted	Not noted	Not noted	Not noted	Not noted	No delivery date	
9	371	7193111	Not noted	K	RHD	2-Seater	Maroon	Maroon	Not noted	4/6/48	Hamilton		
9, 211, 686	372	7193092	ENT 295	K	RHD	2-Seater	Red	Red	Beige	4/5/48	Furrows (S & C)		
9, 209, 212	373	7193803	ECF 206	K	RHD	2-Seater	Chassis	Chassis	Chassis	15/1/48	Mann Egerton (Lee)		
9, 214, 294, 302, 342, 686	374	7193633	SMV 519	K	RHD	2-Seater	Red	Red	Not noted	4/9/48	Dagenham Motors		
9	375	7193370	Not noted	K	RHD	2-Seater	Blue	Grey	Not noted	4/6/48	Tate		
9	376	7191836	Not noted	M	RHD	Coupe	Chassis	Chassis	Chassis	20/1/48	Nunn (Wynroe)		
9	377	7186648	Not noted	M	RHD	Coupe	Chassis	Chassis	Chassis	30/1/48	Alexanders (Aiken)		
9	378	7193829	Not noted	M	RHD	Coupe	Chassis	Chassis	Chassis	27/1/48	Adlards (Allen)		
9	379	7190967	Not noted	M	RHD	Coupe	Chassis	Chassis	Chassis	30/1/48	Tate (Bancroft)		
9	380	7195147	Not noted	M	RHD	Coupe	Chassis	Chassis	Chassis	2/2/48	Hughes (Windgely)		
9	381	7193261	Not noted	M	RHD	Coupe	Chassis	Chassis	Chassis	30/1/48	Tate (Harrison)		
9	382	7193179	Not noted	M	RHD	Coupe	Blue	Grey	Blue	16/2/48	Tate (Price)		
9	383	7193089	Not noted	M	RHD	Coupe	Maroon	Red	Maroon	23/2/48	Taylors		
9	384	7193110	Not noted	M	RHD	Coupe	Grey	Grey	Grey	3/2/48	Universal (Southhall)		
10	385A	7193816	Not noted	M	RHD	Coupe	Grey	Blue	Blue	2/7/48	C. Edwards		Ace discs, ash tray, lights, visor
10	386	Not used	Not used	J*	Not used	Not used	Not used	Not used	Not used	Not used	Not used		* Noted as J but not used
10, 236, 273, 295, 308, 692	387	7193852	LUM 1	L	RHD	Tourer	Chassis and body	Brown	Beige	27/1/48	Tate	J. Reiss	
10, 233, 238, 239, 246, 250, 256, 258, 272, 274, 277, 282, 284, 285, 288, 290, 292, 296, 298, 301, 305, 309, 312, 318, 334, 336, 339, 344	388	7195170	SMX 278	L	RHD	Tourer	Blue	Grey	Grey	23/2/48	Gould		
10	389	7187951	Not noted	L	RHD	Tourer	Chassis and body	Grey	Grey	2/3/48	Tate		Untrimmed
10, 346, 692	390	7195114	JLY 153	L	RHD	Tourer	Chassis and body	Not noted	Not noted	13/2/48	Dagenham Motors (Bentley)		Untrimmed, materials supplied

Page References	Chassis	Original Engine Number	UK Registration	Type	LHD?	Body Style	Original Colour	Original Interior	Original Hood	Original Delivery	Allocation	First Customer	Remarks
10, 244, 249, 259, 265, 271, 277, 343, 345, 347	391	7193621	LVK 765	L	RHD	Tourer	Maroon	Brown	Beige	16/3/48	Patterson		
10, 212	392	7193107	AFB 798	L	RHD	Tourer	Grey	Grey	Grey	3/10/48	Hughes (Simons)		
10, 245, 265, 271, 282, 293, 692	393	7193620	JLT 913	L	RHD	Tourer	Chassis and body	Not noted	Not noted	2/11/48	Dagenhams (Bentley)		Untrimmed, materials supplied
10	394	7195199	Not noted	L	RHD	Tourer	Chassis and body	Brown	Beige	13/2/48	Tate		
10	395	7195131	Not noted	L	RHD	Tourer	Chassis	Chassis	Chassis	30/1/48	Taylors (Whiteladies Garage)		
10	396	Not used	Not used	J*	Not used	Not used	Not used	Not used	Not used	Not used	Not used		* Noted as J but not used
10, 216, 219, 230, 233, 245, 253, 257, 263, 267, 283, 284, 290, 296, 303, 304, 307, 310, 314, 316, 331, 333, 334, 341	397A	7193812	NEV 26	M	RHD	Coupe	Maroon	Grey	Maroon	3/3/48	Gould (Richard Bros)		One record says regn. NEV 27
10	398A	7193624	Not noted	P	RHD	Coupe	Black	Red	Beige	3/12/48	Bristol Street Motors (Erskins)		
10	399	7193087	Not noted	M	RHD	Coupe	Black	Red	Beige	3/8/48	Alexanders (Dr. Patterson)		
10, 214, 217, 219, 221, 227, 228, 230, 232, 234, 236, 237, 241, 249, 254, 257, 262, 267, 269, 281, 284, 286, 290, 293, 294, 297, 300, 309, 312, 316, 321, 330, 333, 334, 337, 341, 345, 703, 704	400	7195655	JUC 302	M	RHD	Coupe	Grey	Grey	Grey	4/5/48	Adlards	Decca Records	The most recorded Allard of all
10, 262, 694	401	7194902	MZ 1201	PI	RHD	Coupe	Maroon	Red	Maroon	24/3/48	Hamilton		
10	402	7193817	Not noted	K	RHD	2-Seater	Chassis	Chassis	Chassis	2/2/48	Tate (Harrison)		
10	403	7193837	Not noted	K	RHD	2-Seater	Grey	Not noted	Not noted	30/4/48	Adlards (Freeilright)		
10, 232, 686	404	7195796	LUB 906	K	RHD	2-Seater	Grey	Not noted	Not noted	20/4/48	Tate		Domesday Book has reference to PNW 503
10, 248, 294, 340, 352	405	7195784	JYM 271	M	RHD	Coupe	Chassis	Chassis	Chassis	25/3/48	Adlards (Johnson)		Experimental

CHASSIS NUMBER PAGE REFERENCE KEY: Allocation Books (pages 1-77), Record Cards (pages 78-167), Warranty Book (pages 168-201), Service Records (pages 202-393)

Page References	Chassis	Original Engine Number	UK Registration	Type	LHD?	Body Style	Original Colour	Original Interior	Original Hood	Original Delivery	Allocation	First Customer	Remarks
12, 271	450	7196743	Not noted	M	RHD	Coupe	Maroon	Maroon	Maroon	5/11/48	Tate		
12, 224, 694	451	7196783	HLJ 636	M	RHD	Coupe	Black	Red	Black	13/5/48	English		
12	452	7197469	Not noted	M	RHD	Coupe	Grey	Grey	Grey	16/6/48	Patterson		
12, 694	453	7197486	GFS 555	M	RHD	Coupe	Maroon	Maroon	Maroon	26/5/48	Alexanders		
12, 211	454	7197659	JYM 273	M	RHD	Coupe	Grey	Grey	Green	7/5/48	Adlards (Mills)		
12, 229, 232, 235, 237, 239, 242, 252, 261, 263, 265, 299, 348	455	7197658	LKX 146	L	RHD	Tourer	Chassis and body	Red	Maroon	5/3/48	Dagenham Motors		Untrimmed
12	456	7197713	Not noted	L	RHD	Tourer	Chassis and body	Brown	Beige	23/4/48	Tate		Untrimmed
12, 213, 393, 686	457	7197711	LUM 89	K	RHD	2-Seater	Maroon	Maroon	Maroon	6/8/48	Tate		
12, 315, 686	458	7197712	KWJ 770	K	RHD	2-Seater	Blue	Blue	Blue	29/6/48	Tate		
12, 234	459	7197716	KPO 564	M	RHD	Coupe	Chassis	Chassis	Chassis	4/5/48	Gould (Linfield)		
12, 692	460	7197714	GGG 831	L	RHD	Tourer	Chassis and body	Grey	Grey	5/5/48	George & Jobling (Callinder)		
12	461	7197662	Not noted	K	RHD	2-Seater	Black	Brown	Beige	7/1/48	Nunn		
12	462	7197850	Not noted	K	LHD	2-Seater	Chassis	Chassis	Chassis	21/4/48	Portugal		
12, 234, 269, 281	463	7197611	QB 2119	M	RHD	Coupe	Grey	Grey	Grey	22/6/48	Hong Kong		This car appears to return from Hong Kong for a service, perhaps temporarily reimported
12, 213, 232, 314	464	7197815	MBF 343	M	RHD	Coupe	Grey	Grey	Grey	19/7/48	Adlards (Armitage)		
12	465	7194769	Not noted	M	LHD	Coupe	Maroon	Maroon	Beige	21/6/48	Egypt		
12	466	7197467	Not noted	M	RHD	Coupe	Maroon	Maroon	Beige	23/7/48	Taylors		New gear
12, 211, 228, 686	467	7197808	GRK 384	K	RHD	2-Seater	Grey	Grey	Grey	7/5/48	Adlards (Ratcliffes Garage)		
12	468	7197847	Not noted	M	RHD	Coupe	Maroon	Maroon	Not noted	15/6/48	Bristol Street Motors		
12, 393	469	7198245	JOL 616	M	RHD	Coupe	Chassis	Chassis	Chassis	28/4/48	Bristol Street Motors		
12, 220, 256, 267, 291, 320	470	7197773	JYE 359	M	RHD	Coupe	Grey	Grey	Grey	6/2/48	Adlards (McDowell)		
12, 319, 331	471	7197807	ARC 419	M	RHD	Coupe	Maroon	Maroon	Maroon	15/6/48	Universal		
12, 161, 213, 221, 383	472	7197829	DFR 376	M	LHD	Coupe	Blue	Grey	Blue	22/1/48	Nunn		
12	473	7197848	Not noted	L	RHD	Tourer	Chassis and body	Maroon	Maroon	28/4/48	Bristol Street Motors		Untrimmed
12	474	7198130	Not noted	L	RHD	Tourer	Chassis	Chassis	Chassis	19/4/48	Nunn (Thomas Motors)		
12	475	7198113	Not noted	L	RHD	Tourer	Chassis	Chassis	Chassis	26/4/48	Shummin (Isle of Man)		

CHASSIS NUMBER PAGE REFERENCE KEY: Allocation Books (pages 1-77), Record Cards (pages 78-167), Warranty Book (pages 168-201), Service Records (pages 202-393)

Page References	Chassis	Original Engine Number	UK Registration	Type	LHD?	Body Style	Original Colour	Original Interior	Original Hood	Original Delivery	Allocation	First Customer	Remarks

CHASSIS NUMBER PAGE REFERENCE KEY: Allocation Books (pages 1-77), Record Cards (pages 78-167), Warranty Book (pages 168-201), Service Records (pages 202-393)

Page References	Chassis	Original Engine Number	UK Registration	Type	LHD?	Body Style	Original Colour	Original Interior	Original Hood	Original Delivery	Allocation	First Customer	Remarks
12, 686	476	7197816	PRF 35	K	RHD	2-Seater	Black	Red	Beige	7/5/48	Bristol Street Motors		
12	477	7198131	Not noted	K	RHD	2-Seater	Grey	Grey	Grey	23/6/48	Patterson		
12, 227, 271, 344	478	7198117	LHW 107	L	RHD	Tourer	Chassis	Chassis	Chassis	26/4/48	Taylors (Whiteladies Garage)		
12	479	7198232	Not noted	L	RHD	Tourer	Chassis	Chassis	Chassis	27/4/48	Taylors (Whiteladies Garage)		
12, 285	480	7198283	DFK 62	K	RHD	2-Seater	Chassis	Chassis	Chassis	26/4/48	Taylors (Fisher)		First letter of registration number is hard to discern
13	481	7198292	Not noted	K	RHD	2-Seater	Grey	Grey	Grey	29/6/48	Bristol Street Motors		
13, 79, 243, 245	482	7197861	KUW 556	K	LHD	2-Seater	Grey	Grey	Grey	9/4/49	Egypt	A. Crookston	Conversion to left hand drive
13	483	7198317	Not noted	L	RHD	Tourer	Chassis and body	Brown	Beige	18/5/48	George & Jobling		Untrimmed
13, 223, 272, 273, 274, 276	484	7198351	TMX 560	L	RHD	Tourer	Blue	Blue	Grey	24/6/48	Dagenham Motors (Mr Davis)		Also noted as THX 560 on pages 273 and 274
13, 161, 245, 265, 267, 386, 391, 687	485	7198210	JKD 874	K	RHD	2-Seater	Grey	Grey	Grey	7/9/48	Nunn		Page 267 notes regn. JKD 877
13	486	7198390	Not noted	L	RHD	Tourer	Chassis and body	Maroon	Maroon	25/5/48	Nunn		
13, 686, 724	487	7178347	HRU 2	K	RHD	2-Seater	Grey	Grey	Grey	7/9/48	Bristol Street Motors		
13, 169, 236, 298	488	7198187	MPF 647	K	RHD	2-Seater	Black	Maroon	Black	8/6/48	Adlards (E. D. Abbott)	J. A. Birrmeir	Maroon wheels
13, 294	489	7191968	HDG 105	K	RHD	2-Seater	Chassis	Chassis	Chassis	19/7/48	Whiteladies Garage		Altered from K-276 (demo) prototype
13	490	Not used	Not used	Not used	Not used	Not used	Not used	Not used	Not used	Not used	Not used		
13	491	Not used	Not used	Not used	Not used	Not used	Not used	Not used	Not used	Not used	Not used		
13	492	Not used	Not used	Not used	Not used	Not used	Not used	Not used	Not used	Not used	Not used		
13, 369	493	Not used	Not used	Not used	Not used	Not used	Not used	Not used	Not used	Not used	Not used		
13	494	Not used	Not used	Not used	Not used	Not used	Not used	Not used	Not used	Not used	Not used		
13	495	Not used	Not used	Not used	Not used	Not used	Not used	Not used	Not used	Not used	Not used		
13	496	Not used	Not used	Not used	Not used	Not used	Not used	Not used	Not used	Not used	Not used		
13	497	Not used	Not used	Not used	Not used	Not used	Not used	Not used	Not used	Not used	Not used		
13	498	Not used	Not used	Not used	Not used	Not used	Not used	Not used	Not used	Not used	Not used		
13	499	Not used	Not used	Not used	Not used	Not used	Not used	Not used	Not used	Not used	Not used		
13	500	7188022	Not noted	L	RHD	Tourer	Blue	Grey	Beige	2/10/48	George & Jobling		

Page References	Chassis	Original Engine Number	UK Registration	Type	LHD?	Body Style	Original Colour	Original Interior	Original Hood	Original Delivery	Allocation	First Customer	Remarks
						CHASSIS NUMBER PAGE REFERENCE KEY: Allocation Books (pages 1-77), Record Cards (pages 78-167), Warranty Book (pages 168-201), Service Records (pages 202-393)							
13	501	7196141	Not noted	M	RHD	Coupe	Chassis	Chassis	Chassis	2/6/48	Dagenham Motors (Archway)		
13	502	7196143	Not noted	M	RHD	Coupe	Blue	Blue	Blue	3/12/48	Hartwells (Mr Woolfe)		
13, 270, 274	503	7196230	JFJ 60	M	RHD	Coupe	Red	Maroon	Maroon	25/3/48	Hughes		
13	504	Not noted	Not noted	M	RHD	Coupe	Chassis	Chassis	Chassis	2/4/48	Adlards (Michael)		Less engine and gearbox
13	505	7195953	Not noted	M	RHD	Coupe	Chassis	Chassis	Chassis	22/3/48	Adlards (Hall)		
13, 267, 269, 273, 287, 310, 352, 359	506	7196140	DBA 631	M	RHD	Coupe	Light Blue	Blue	Dark Blue	5/12/48	Nunn		Seven records note regn. DBA 631
13, 250, 263, 307	507	7196121	ENT 184	M	RHD	Coupe	Blue	Blue	Grey	23/3/48	Furrows (Barker)		
13, 692	508	7195693	Not noted	L	RHD	Tourer & body	Not noted	Maroon	Maroon	Not noted	George & Jobling		Untrimmed. Domesday Book has reference to BWG 181
13, 211, 267	509	7175952	JUC 301	L	RHD	Tourer	Black	Brown	Beige	2/4/48	Adlards (Thompson)		
13, 209, 214, 217, 227, 233, 234, 295, 320, 354, 357, 363, 376, 687	510	7195768	JUC 310	K	RHD	2-Seater	Black	Not noted	Not noted	Not noted	Demonstrator sold	Stannard (Dick Barton)	
13, 687, 696	511	7195960	FVJ 257	K	RHD	2-Seater	Chassis	Chassis	Chassis	13/2/48	George & Jobling		
13	512	7195835	Not noted	L	RHD	Tourer	Chassis	Chassis	Chassis	Not noted	Universal (Brooks Motor Co.)		
14	513	7196123	Not noted	L	RHD	Tourer	Maroon	Maroon	Maroon	5/5/48	Nunn		Untrimmed
14, 239, 241	514	7195529	JYE 351	M	RHD	Coupe	Light Blue	Blue	Dark Blue	16/7/48	Demonstrator		
14, 228	515	7195539	EUJ 4	M	RHD	Coupe	Maroon	Brown	Beige	22/6/48	Furrows		
14, 692	516	7195546	GUY 831	L	RHD	Tourer and body	Not noted	Maroon	Maroon	3/2/48	Bristol Street Motors		Domesday Book has reference to GUY 440
14, 211, 216, 225, 240, 242, 262, 311, 327, 343	517	7195836	SMX 835	M	RHD	Coupe	Grey	Grey	Grey	4/7/48	Dagenham Motors		
14	518	7195659	Not noted	K	RHD	2-Seater	Chassis	Chassis	Chassis	3/1/48	Taylors (Horace Roberts)		
14, 306, 328, 334, 346, 358, 362, 376	519	7195653	HLJ 575	K	RHD	2-Seater	Black	Maroon	Beige	29/4/48	English		
14, 354	520	7195654	DYD 567	L	RHD	Tourer	Blue	Blue	Grey	31/3/48	Taylors		
14, 328, 379, 692	521	7196602	UMC 363	L	RHD	Tourer	Chassis	Chassis	Chassis	3/4/48	Dagenham Motors (Austins Garage)		
14	522	7195837	Not noted	M	RHD	Coupe	Chassis	Chassis	Chassis	3/12/48	Bristol Street Motors		
14	523	7195656	Not noted	M	RHD	Coupe	Chassis	Chassis	Chassis	15/3/48	Adlards (Harrison)		
14	524	7196231	Not noted	L	RHD	Tourer/Chassis and body	Maroon	Maroon	Maroon	4/7/48	Dagenham Motors		Untrimmed

Page References	Chassis	Original Engine Number	UK Registration	Type	LHD?	Body Style	Original Colour	Original Interior	Original Hood	Original Delivery	Allocation	First Customer	Remarks
14, 692, 696	525	7196745	BFR 82	L	RHD	Tourer/Chassis & body	Not noted	Not noted	Not noted	23/3/48	Nunn		Untrimmed, no material
14, 277, 284	526	7196598	HDF 396	M	RHD	Coupe	Black	Brown	Beige	19/5/48	Taylors		
14, 219, 223, 262, 268, 277, 289, 295, 299, 303, 305, 306, 323, 330, 695	527	7196599	NFC 139	M	RHD	Coupe	Grey	Grey	Blue	4/12/48	Hartwells		Alan Godsal 1949 Monte Carlo Rally car
14, 696	528	7196910	JLW 489	M	LHD	Coupe	White	Green	Not noted	30/3/48	U.S.A.		This car used with Berkeley Caravan in ex-demo regn. JLW 489
14, 170, 253, 257, 696	529	7198916	KLO 122	M	RHD	Coupe	Maroon	Maroon	Beige	17/2/50	S. H. Allard Motor Co. (Demonstrator)	Not noted	Experimental model, demo, KLO 122, S. H. Allard
14, 161, 299, 317, 340, 348, 371, 385	530	7198189	IL 4287	M	RHD	Coupe	Black	Brown	Beige	23/6/48	Hamilton		Page 385 shows IL 4278
14	531	7198300	Not noted	M	RHD	Coupe	Blue	Not noted	Not noted	23/6/48	Hamilton		
14, 250, 253, 258, 263, 265, 271, 274, 277	532	7198192	JPX 507	M	RHD	Coupe	Chassis	Chassis	Chassis	24/4/48	Gould		
14, 357, 524	533	7198363	GYG 609	M	RHD	Coupe	Chassis	Chassis	Chassis	14/5/48	Tate (Harrison)		Service Records incorrectly record as CYG 509
14, 236, 239, 247	534	7198346	JYR 71	M	RHD	Coupe	Chassis	Chassis	Chassis	5/7/48	Tate (Harrison)		Page 247 shows regn. LWA 19
14	535	7198532	Not noted	M	RHD	Coupe	Chassis	Chassis	Chassis	30/4/48	Frew		
14, 214, 216, 229, 234, 235, 277, 311, 313, 317, 318, 340, 694	536	7198355	JYR 671	M	RHD	Coupe	Blue	Grey	Grey	28/6/48	Gould		
14, 220, 694	537	7198364	JFJ 293	M	RHD	Coupe	Blue	Blue	Blue	24/6/48	Hughes		Stolen, London August 1967
14, 161, 361, 692	538	7198354	JYK 120	L	RHD	Tourer	Navy Blue	Grey	Grey	14/6/48	Gould		Late record notes JYK 120 as a K-type
14	539	7198350	Not noted	K	RHD	2-Seater	Maroon	Maroon	Not noted	Not noted	Hartwells		
14	540	7198362	Not noted	K	RHD	2-Seater	body and chassis	Not noted	Not noted	8/3/48	Eire		
14	541	7198392	Not noted	M	RHD	Coupe	Maroon	Red	Beige	20/7/48	English		
14, 229, 237, 255, 265, 270	542	7198393	GOR 827	M	RHD	Coupe	Blue	Blue	Blue	7/2/48	English		Page 255 shows HRU 2 (487)
14	543	7198394	Not noted	L	RHD	Tourer	Maroon	Maroon	Maroon	18/6/48	Canada (Howard)		
14, 687	544	7198395	FVJ 257	K	RHD	2-Seater	Maroon	Maroon	Maroon	30/7/48	Taylors		UK regn. noted FUG 257 but known as FVJ 257
15, 216, 333	545	7198523	JFJ 356	K	RHD	2-Seater	Red	Red	Not noted	26/7/48	Hughes		
15, 298, 299, 302, 312, 378	546	7198515	FFH 927	M	RHD	Coupe	Maroon	Maroon	Maroon	30/6/48	Taylors		
15, 310, 695	547	7198538	OMN 517	M	RHD	Coupe	Black	Red	Beige	7/12/48	Mann Egerton		Service record states regn. GER 966. Domesday Book refers to OMN 514

CHASSIS NUMBER PAGE REFERENCE KEY: Allocation Books (pages 1-77), Record Cards (pages 78-167), Warranty Book (pages 168-201), Service Records (pages 202-393)

Page References	Chassis	Original Engine Number	UK Registration	Type	LHD?	Body Style	Original Colour	Original Interior	Original Hood	Original Delivery	Allocation	First Customer	Remarks
CHASSIS NUMBER PAGE REFERENCE KEY: Allocation Books (pages 1-77), Record Cards (pages 78-167), Warranty Book (pages 168-201), Service Records (pages 202-393)													
15, 295, 379, 692	548	7198834	NFC 577	L	RHD	Tourer	Black	Brown	Beige	7/12/48	Frew (Aitken)		Domesday Book refers to CES 110 as well
15	549	7198897	Not noted	L	RHD	Tourer	Maroon	Red	Beige	7/8/48	Hartwells (Cookson)		
15, 220, 238, 243, 247, 261, 270, 287, 295, 297, 301, 303, 317, 326, 336, 337	550	7198389	TMH 812	M	RHD	Coupe	Maroon	Maroon	Maroon	7/1/48	Dagenham Motors		
15	551	7198902	Not noted	M	RHD	Coupe	Maroon	Maroon	Maroon	16/7/48	Nunn		
15	552	7178904	Not noted	M	RHD	Coupe	Black	Grey	Grey	7/6/48	Tate		
15, 180, 239, 264, 323, 687	553	7198514	KTA 309	K	RHD	2-Seater	Red	Red	Not noted	16/8/48	Hughes	J. J. Lockyer	
15, 184, 215, 279, 339	554	7198835	JFM 730	K	RHD	2-Seater	Red	Red	Beige	23/8/48	Furrows (Braid Bros)	K. F. Wild	
15	555	7198903	Not noted	M	RHD	Coupe	Black	Blue	Beige	7/5/48	Frew		
15, 217	556	7198900	GFS 971	M	RHD	Coupe	Black	Brown	Beige	7/9/48	New Zealand	Ian Brown	
15	557	7198898	Not noted	L	RHD	Tourer	Maroon	Brown	Beige	19/7/48	Patterson		
15, 174, 256	558	7198905	Not noted	K	RHD	2-Seater	Red	Red	Beige	16/12/49	Dagenham Motors	W. G. Gunter	Page 256 records the car as new
15, 79, 219	559	7198906	Not noted	K	LHD	2-Seater	Grey	Red	Grey	21/4/49	Uruguay (M. Salem & Cia)	M. Salem	
15, 161	560	7198233	UML 128	L	RHD	Tourer	Red	Brown	Beige	23/7/48	Dagenham Motors		
15, 216, 316, 694	561	7198824	JYO 534	M	RHD	Coupe	Grey	Grey	Grey	19/7/48	Dagenham Motors		
15	562	7199067	Not noted	M	RHD	Coupe	Blue	Blue	Blue	19/7/48	Pakistan (Rowley)		
15, 162, 216, 373, 696	563	7198907	FMW 453	M	LHD	Coupe	Maroon	Red	Beige	22/7/48	Nunn		Page 373 shows indistinct FMW. Could be FWM, FWH. Domesday Book shows FWM 453
15, 253, 297	564	7198901	MPF 342	M	LHD	Coupe	Grey	Blue	Blue	22/7/48	Adlards (Armitage)		
15, 200, 231	565	7199064	Not noted	M	RHD	Coupe	Chassis	Chassis	Chassis	22/5/48	Frew	J. L. Fraser	Sold as chassis May 1948. Page 231 refers to car as unregistered
15, 252, 256, 262, 264, 266, 272, 281, 313, 316, 322, 336, 338, 364, 386	566	7199276	MNW 474	M	RHD	Coupe	Chassis	Chassis	Chassis	6/8/48	Tate		Page 272 may say MMW 474
15	567	7197272	Not noted	M	RHD	Coupe	Chassis	Chassis	Chassis	26/5/48	Nunn (Thomas Motors)		
15, 214, 730	568	7199071	NWL 138	M	RHD	Coupe	Grey	Blue	Blue	19/7/48	Hartwells		NWL 138 is also shown for 653
15	569	7199181	Not noted	M	RHD	Coupe	Maroon	Maroon	Beige	7/7/48	Australia		
15	570	Not noted	Not noted	L	RHD	Tourer	Chassis	Chassis	Chassis	18/6/48	Nunn (Thomas Motors)		Less engine

Page References	Chassis	Original Engine Number	UK Registration	Type	LHD?	Body Style	Original Colour	Original Interior	Original Hood	Original Delivery	Allocation	First Customer	Remarks

CHASSIS NUMBER PAGE REFERENCE KEY: Allocation Books (pages 1-77), Record Cards (pages 78-167), Warranty Book (pages 168-201), Service Records (pages 202-393)

Page References	Chassis	Original Engine Number	UK Registration	Type	LHD?	Body Style	Original Colour	Original Interior	Original Hood	Original Delivery	Allocation	First Customer	Remarks
15	571	7199187	Not noted	K	RHD	2-Seater	Chassis	Chassis	Chassis	29/5/48	Gould (Gray)		
15, 79, 218	572	7199206	Not noted	K	LHD	2-Seater	Red	Red	Grey	20/4/49	Uruguay (Emelas & Cia Limitada)	M. Salem	Page 218 shows car in final works before delivery
15	573	7199160	Not noted	M	RHD	Coupe	Chassis	Chassis	Chassis	6/3/48	Adlards (Stormont)		
15	574	7199197	Not noted	M	LHD	Coupe	Blue	Blue	Blue	17/8/48	Denmark		
15	575	Not noted	Not noted	M	RHD	Coupe	Chassis	Chassis	Chassis	6/10/48	Nunn (Thomas Motors)		Less engine
15	576	7199435	Not noted	M	RHD	Coupe	Chassis	Chassis	Chassis	Not noted	Tate		
16, 687	577	7199277	346 JGX	K	RHD	2-Seater	Black	Maroon	Beige	28/7/48	English		Maroon wheels
16	578	7199439	Not noted	M	RHD	Coupe	Chassis	Chassis	Chassis	25/6/48	Tate		
16, 242, 344	579	7199371	GGA 282	M	RHD	Coupe	Maroon	Maroon	Beige	23/7/48	George & Jobling		
16	580	7199436	Not noted	M	RHD	Coupe	Chassis	Chassis	Chassis	6/9/48	Universal		
16, 173	581	7199448	Not noted	K	RHD	2-Seater	Grey	Brown	Grey	8/11/48	Dagenham Motors	Not noted	
16, 182, 211, 225	582	7199374	GFH 27	M	RHD	Coupe	Blue	Blue	Blue	8/12/48	Taylors	J. P. Round	
16, 186	583	7199387	Not noted	M	RHD	Coupe	Blue	Blue	Blue	8/10/48	Bristol Street Motors	Wilmott Taylor	
16, 216	584	7199372	JJF 339	M	RHD	Coupe	Blue	Blue	Blue	19/7/48	Nunn		
16, 213, 214	585	7199449	JYU 271	K	RHD	2-Seater	Grey	Grey	Grey	9/3/48	Creswick		Export to Mombassa
16, 247, 256, 687	586	7199370	EBL 14	K	RHD	2-Seater	Grey	Brown	Grey	29/7/48	Hartwells		Grey wheels. Page 256 refers to car as FBL 14
16, 694	587	7199452	Not noted	M	RHD	Coupe	Chassis	Chassis	Chassis	6/8/48	Central Motors		
16	588	7199471	Not noted	M	RHD	Coupe	Chassis	Chassis	Chassis	16/6/48	Tate		
16	589	7199673	Not noted	M	LHD	Coupe	Grey	Grey	Grey	19/8/48	Hoffman		Old type
16	590	7199065	Not noted	L	RHD	Tourer	Chassis	Chassis	Chassis	15/6/48	Tate (Clarke)		
16, 178	591	7199664	Not noted	K	RHD	2-Seater	Blue	Blue	Blue	9/8/48	English (Westover Garage)	E. Martin	
16, 178	592	7199720	Not noted	K	RHD	2-Seater	Grey	Red	Not noted	17/8/48	English (Waring)	Boiface	
16, 227, 229, 230, 235, 239, 241, 299, 301, 694	593	7199712	TML 164	M	RHD	Coupe	Chassis	Chassis	Chassis	16/6/48	Adlards		Converted to 1949 chassis by Putney
16, 215, 221, 224, 226, 257, 264, 266, 269, 271, 458, 695, 699	594C	7199499	JYM 272	M	RHD	Coupe	Blue	Blue	Blue	Not noted	Demonstrator		L. Potter for the 1949 Monte Carlo. Page 269 shows registration number JYM 271

CHASSIS NUMBER PAGE REFERENCE KEY: Allocation Books (pages 1-77), Record Cards (pages 78-167), Warranty Book (pages 168-201), Service Records (pages 202-393)

Page References	Chassis	Original Engine Number	UK Registration	Type	LHD?	Body Style	Original Colour	Original Interior	Original Hood	Original Delivery	Allocation	First Customer	Remarks
16, 79, 235, 242, 246, 252, 255, 265, 268, 273, 283, 291, 310, 312, 314, 317, 322, 324, 326, 327, 329, 333, 344, 687	595	7199438	JYK 438	K	RHD	2-Seater	Light Blue	Blue	Not noted	24/7/48	Allard Motor Co.	L. Potter	1948 Alpine Rally
16	596	7199676	Not noted	L	RHD	Tourer	Chassis	Chassis	Chassis	16/6/48	Bristol Street Motors		
16, 224, 225, 228, 234, 236, 321, 326	597	7199718	MPF 570	M	RHD	Coupe	Chassis	Chassis	Chassis	21/6/48	Dagenham Motors (Knox)		
16	598	7199699	Not noted	M	RHD	Coupe	Grey	Grey	Green	16/8/48	Australia (Everett)		
16, 178	599	7199688	Not noted	K	RHD	2-Seater	Grey	Grey	Black	Not noted	English (G. Hartwell)	C. F. S. Brooks	
16, 173, 222, 262	600	7199671	JYW 64	K	RHD	2-Seater	Blue	Blue	Blue	31/8/48	Dagenham Motors (Difford & Sons)	D. J. Pieise	
16, 363	601	7199663	KKP 816	L	RHD	Tourer	Blue	Blue	Grey	8/11/48	English		
16	602	7199788	Not noted	L	RHD	Tourer	Chassis	Chassis	Chassis	29/6/48	George & Jobling		
16, 178, 216, 217, 226, 283, 306, 314	603	7199755	HRU 201	M	RHD	Coupe	Black	Red	Black	19/8/48	English (Westover Garage)	B. W. Parks	
16, 194, 268	604	7199762	Not noted	M	RHD	Coupe	Grey	Grey	Blue	8/12/48	Tate	D. C. Hall	
16	605	7199273	Not noted	K	RHD	2-Seater	Grey	Brown	Grey	20/12/48	Rhodesia (Hindley)		
16, 226, 227, 232, 240, 248, 261, 267, 279, 281, 288, 297	606	7199993	KLM 9	M	RHD	Coupe	Chassis	Chassis	Chassis	24/10/48	Dagenham Motors (Ferraris)		
16, 173, 213, 224, 324	607	7200060	JYT 881	K	RHD	2-Seater	Grey	Brown	Grey	Not noted	Dagenham Motors (Blue Star Gr)	E. F. Richardson	
16, 194	608	7200052	Not noted	K	RHD	2-Seater	Maroon	Maroon	Maroon	17/10/48	Tate	Unreadable	
17, 184	609	7199780	Not noted	M	RHD	Coupe	Grey	Grey	Grey	16/8/48	Furrows	E. M. Houghton	
17, 183, 211, 225, 245, 262	610	7199789	EBX 761	M	RHD	Coupe	Black	Red	Black	18/8/48	Harris (George Rees & Sons)	Dr. L. C. Edwards	
17, 314	611	7199996	GBL 844	L	RHD	Tourer	Chassis	Chassis	Chassis	7/7/48	Taylors (Whiteladies Garage)		
17, 186, 247	612	7179989	JOE 972	K	RHD	2-Seater	Maroon	Maroon	Maroon	22/9/48	Bristol Street Motors	J. Manfield	
17, 217, 223, 224, 228, 229, 230, 234, 236, 244, 254, 264, 275, 279	613	7199985	EBK 338	M	RHD	Coupe	Chassis	Chassis	Chassis	7/8/48	Adlards (Stevens)		

Page References	Chassis	Original Engine Number	UK Registration	Type	LHD?	Body Style	Original Colour	Original Interior	Original Hood	Original Delivery	Allocation	First Customer	Remarks
CHASSIS NUMBER PAGE REFERENCE KEY: Allocation Books (pages 1-77), Record Cards (pages 78-167), Warranty Book (pages 168-201), Service Records (pages 202-393)														
17, 169, 230, 236, 239, 240, 244, 245, 252, 253, 254, 266, 288, 319, 325, 353, 380	614	7200014	JYL 272	M	RHD	Coupe	Black	Red	Black	9/9/48	Adlards (Okill)	G. O. Field	Page 380 appears to show the registration as JYV 272
17, 169, 230, 245, 282, 284, 286, 293	615	7200061	JYR 13	M	RHD	Coupe	Black	Brown	Beige	19/8/48	Adlards (Turner)	F. A. Turner	
17, 194	616	7200000	Not noted	L	RHD	Tourer	Blue	Blue	Grey	13/9/48	Tate (J. R. Graham Co. Ltd.)	J. W. France	New gears
17, 186, 217, 687	617	7200184	JOE 884	K	RHD	2-Seater	Grey	Brown	Grey	16/9/48	Bristol Street Motors	P. Mould	New gears
17, 169, 212, 214, 215, 216, 217, 218, 220, 222, 226, 234, 235, 239, 240, 246, 247, 248, 259, 266, 272, 274, 276, 283, 291, 297, 310, 313, 335, 737	618	7200071	JYT 943	M	RHD	Coupe	Black	Red	Beige	9/1/48	Adlards	Dr. S. Compton	Per pages 274 and 276, registration may be JYT 443
17, 177, 262, 330	619	7200161	KLD 5	M	RHD	Coupe	Black	Brown	Beige	24/9/48	Gould	Major G. Whitehead	
17, 694	620	7200187	Not noted	M	RHD	Coupe	Maroon	Red	Beige	23/8/48	South Rhodesia	Ian Douglas	
17, 199, 687	621	7200192	AKS 747	K	RHD	2-Seater	Grey	Blue	Blue	29/9/48	Alexanders (Milligan & Bell)	C. Bell	
17, 179, 238, 253, 263, 268, 273, 274, 275, 277, 365, 382	622	7210193	KUW 565	K	RHD	2-Seater	Maroon	Maroon	Maroon	7/6/50	English	Not noted	Demo
17, 189	623	7200158	Not noted	M	RHD	Coupe	Maroon	Maroon	Beige	27/8/48	Universal (Bartholomew)	P. P. Ayre	
17, 197	624	7200148	Not noted	M	RHD	Coupe	Grey	Grey	Grey	27/8/48	George & Jobling (J. M. Miller Ltd.)	A. J. J. Ross	
17, 169	625	7200168	Not noted	M	RHD	Coupe	Maroon	Maroon	Beige	9/6/48	Adlards (Stuart)	F. O. Wacher	
17	626	7200203	Not noted	L	LHD	Tourer	Silver Grey	Light Blue	Maroon	Crossed out	U.S.A. (Moss Motors)		
17, 170, 218, 232, 255, 257, 258, 259, 261, 264, 265, 269, 271, 275, 291, 352, 370, 390, 468, 696	627	7200186	KLO 123	P	RHD	Saloon	Green	Orange	Not noted	12/8/48	Adlards	G. O. Kill	Prototype and Demo. Shown at 1948 Earl's Court Motor Show. Page 218 notes car as unregistered, and as an M-type (as does page 255), but it was the new P-type
17, 324, 325, 328	628	7200216	GOU 758	M	RHD	Coupe	Chassis	Chassis	Chassis	7/10/48	Adlards (Potter)		
17, 357	629	7200204	Not noted	K	RHD	2-Seater	Grey	Blue	Blue	14/12/48	Kenya (Carnege)		

Page References	Chassis	Original Engine Number	UK Registration	Type	LHD?	Body Style	Original Colour	Original Interior	Original Hood	Original Delivery	Allocation	First Customer	Remarks
17, 180	630	7200147	Not noted	M	RHD	Coupe	Black	Red	Black	9/9/48	Hughes (Midsomer Norton Motor Co.)	G. B. Beauchamp	
17, 173, 211	631	7200208	Not noted	M	RHD	Coupe	Grey	Grey	Grey	27/8/48	Dagenham Motors (Car Mart)	C. E. Marshall	
17, 197, 692	632	7200470	XS 6484	L	RHD	Tourer	Black	Red	Beige	9/1/48	George & Jobling (Paisby Motor Co.)	Dr. R. Allan	
17, 186, 687	633	7200466	JDH 167	K	RHD	2-Seater	Maroon	Maroon	Maroon	26/11/48	Bristol Street Motors (Frank Guest Ltd.)	R. Palechamp	
17, 338	634	7200345	HAB 313	M	RHD	Coupe	Chassis	Chassis	Chassis	16/7/48	Taylors (Blades)		
17, 186	635	7200149	Not noted	M	RHD	Coupe	Grey	Grey	Green	31/8/48	Bristol Street Motors (Mists Garage)	H. Tipper	
17, 180	636	7200409	Not noted	M	RHD	Coupe	Grey	Grey	Green	9/3/48	Hughes	F. Grevif	
17, 287	637	7200473	Not noted	L	RHD	Tourer	Chassis	Chassis	Chassis	22/7/48	Taylors (Whiteladies Garage)		
17, 194, 234	638	7200767	MNW 624	K	RHD	2-Seater	Grey	Brown	Grey	2/9/49	Tate	E. N. Riddiough	
17, 169, 233, 236, 240, 250, 263, 274, 275, 288, 290, 292, 304, 312, 326, 342	639	7200952	KLX 473	K	RHD	2-Seater	Grey	Brown	Grey	20/5/49	Adlards (Keswick)		
17, 196, 390	640	7200374	NBB 836	M	RHD	Coupe	Grey	Light Blue	Blue	30/8/48	Patterson	A. J. Hogg	
18, 191	641	7200665	Not noted	M	RHD	Coupe	Chassis	Chassis	Chassis	8/10/48	Nunn (A. E. Chatfield)	F. Lea	
18, 184, 692	642	7200563	EUJ 594	L	RHD	Tourer	Grey	Grey	Grey	9/7/48	Furrows	J. E. Stevens	
18, 178	643	7200816	Not noted	K	RHD	2-Seater	Grey	Brown	Grey	26/11/48	English	J. Schmeidler	
18, 178, 384, 687	644	7200970	HRU 815	K	RHD	2-Seater	Grey	Brown	Grey	23/12/48	English (Knott Bros Ltd.)	E. E. Longmead	
18, 200, 242	645	7189886	CES 146	M	RHD	Coupe	Black	Light Blue	Black	9/6/48	Frew (Grassicks Garage)	J. R. Scott	
18, 178	646	7200672	Not noted	M	RHD	Coupe	Maroon	Red	Beige	Not noted	English (Westover Garage)	J. Ward	
18, 174, 237, 249, 687	647	7200763	VMG 579	K	RHD	2-Seater	Grey	Brown	Grey	14/11/47	Dagenham Motors S. O. R. Tate	C. E. Devereux	
18, 186	648	7200817	Not noted	K	RHD	2-Seater	Grey	Brown	Grey	22/2/49	Bristol Street Motors (Central Motors)	Fosse Knitwear Ltd.	
18	649	7200390	Not noted	M	RHD	Coupe	Chassis	Chassis	Chassis	21/7/48	Frew		
18, 199, 218, 232, 242	650	7200941	GSC 374	M	RHD	Coupe	Black	Blue	Beige	9/3/48	Alexanders	Lt. P. G. Guest	
18, 182	651	7200951	Not noted	M	RHD	Coupe	Black	Maroon	Black	9/8/48	Taylors	H. J. Bunton	
18, 178, 381	652	7200762	GOO 25	L	RHD	Tourer	Grey	Grey	Grey	18/10/48	English (G. W. Cox)	A. J. F. A. Haimswaich	
18, 173, 308, 687	653	7200754	UMC 561	K	RHD	2-Seater	Grey	Brown	Grey	5/6/49	Dagenham Motors (Chaserside Motors)	U. J. Painter	

CHASSIS NUMBER PAGE REFERENCE KEY: Allocation Books (pages 1-77), Record Cards (pages 78-167), Warranty Book (pages 168-201), Service Records (pages 202-393)

Page References	Chassis	Original Engine Number	UK Registration	Type	LHD?	Body Style	Original Colour	Original Interior	Original Hood	Original Delivery	Allocation	First Customer	Remarks
18, 191, 257, 295, 307	654	7200757	KVM 713	K	RHD	2-Seater	Maroon	Maroon	Maroon	28/12/49	Nunn (Central Motors)	T. Hope & Sankey Hudson Ltd.	
18, 186	655	7200783	Not noted	K	RHD	2-Seater	Maroon	Maroon	Maroon	12/3/48	Bristol Street Motors	S. F. Smith	
18, 173, 220, 225, 233, 253, 329	656	7200774	TMH 616	M	RHD	Coupe	Maroon	Red	Maroon	16/9/48	Dagenham Motors	R. E. Fowler	Later exported to Uruguay – refer to record card
18, 183	657	7200946	Not noted	M	RHD	Coupe	Black	Red	Beige	9/9/48	Harris (Gibbs Bros)	D. Spector	
18, 180, 216, 264, 269, 274, 279, 284, 288, 305, 317, 326, 333, 335, 339, 342, 343, 725	658	7200939	NWL 138	M	RHD	Coupe	Maroon	Maroon	Beige	16/9/48	Hughes (Brown's Garages)	L. Sawyer	Later records states regn. AGL 377. NWL 138 is also shown for 568
18, 355, 368	659	7200478	KMB 674	M	RHD	Coupe	Chassis	Chassis	Chassis	21/7/48	Nunn		KMB 874 is shown on page 368
18	660	7200661	Not noted	M	RHD	Coupe	Chassis	Chassis	Chassis	21/7/48	Bristol Street Motors		
18	661	7200745	Not noted	M	RHD	Coupe	Chassis	Chassis	Chassis	21/7/48	Bristol Street Motors		
18	662	7200742	Not noted	M	RHD	Coupe	Chassis	Chassis	Chassis	20/7/48	Nunn		
18	663	7200694	Not noted	M	RHD	Coupe	Chassis	Chassis	Chassis	30/7/48	Tate		New Gear
18, 323, 325, 343, 345, 352, 359, 364, 365, 366, 368	664	7200660	LWB 773	M	RHD	Coupe	Chassis	Chassis	Chassis	29/7/48	Tate		New Gear
18, 374	665	E7/47/89887	LWB 664	M	RHD	Coupe	Chassis	Chassis	Chassis	29/7/48	Tate		New Gear
18, 182, 320	666	7200748	JDD 702	M	RHD	Coupe	Chassis	Chassis	Chassis	24/8/48	Taylors (Edwards Marshall Ltd.)	E. G. P. Martin	New Gear
18, 182	667	7200722	Not noted	M	RHD	Coupe	Chassis	Chassis	Chassis	8/12/48	Taylors	E. N. Dickins	New Gear
18	668	7200692	Not noted	M	RHD	Coupe	Chassis	Chassis	Chassis	20/8/48	Kenya		New Gear
18	669	Not noted	Not noted	Not noted	Not noted	Not noted	Not noted	Not noted	Not noted	Not noted	Not noted	Not noted	Not noted
18, 189, 226, 229, 231, 233, 236	670	7200768	KGC 895	L	RHD	Tourer	Grey	Grey	Grey	21/6/49	Universal (Standhill Garage)	Mr Simpkin	Demo
18, 178, 213	671	7200778	Not noted	L	RHD	Tourer	Red	Maroon	Beige	10/7/48	English	G. Morton	
18, 182, 221	672	7250765	Not noted	L	RHD	Tourer	Chassis	Chassis	Chassis	9/1/48	Taylors	Not noted	Page 221 refers to car as unregistered
19, 182	673	7200943	Not noted	M	RHD	Coupe	Maroon	Maroon	Beige	16/9/48	Taylors (E. Williams Ltd.)	T. P. Baineby	
19, 173, 223, 311, 341	674	7200770	JML 3	M	RHD	Coupe	Black	Grey	Grey	9/9/48	Dagenham Motors	H. Hodgson	One later record notes TML 209 but confused writing
19	675	7200973	Not noted	L	LHD	Tourer	Maroon	Maroon	Beige	23/8/48	U.S.A. (Illinois Hamill)		
19	676	7202305	Not noted	M	LHD	Coupe	Chassis	Chassis	Chassis	17/8/48	Denmark		Returned and taken apart

Page References	Chassis	Original Engine Number	UK Registration	Type	LHD?	Body Style	Original Colour	Original Interior	Original Hood	Original Delivery	Allocation	First Customer	Remarks
								CHASSIS NUMBER PAGE REFERENCE KEY: Allocation Books (pages 1-77), Record Cards (pages 78-167), Warranty Book (pages 168-201), Service Records (pages 202-393)					
19, 189, 221	677	7202507	Not noted	M	RHD	Coupe	Blue	Blue	Blue	2/4/49	Universal (Bennetts Ltd.)	J. R. W. Jackson	Page 223 refers to car as unregistered
19, 194, 332	678	7200982	FKU 916	M	RHD	Coupe	Blue	Blue	Blue	21/9/48	Tate (B. Waterhouse)	L. Moseley	
19, 692	679	7200978	Not noted	L	LHD	Tourer	Black	Red	Beige	30/8/48	U.S.A. (Hoffman)		
19, 191	680	7200776	Not noted	K	RHD	2-Seater	Chassis	Chassis	Chassis	27/8/48	Nunn	Not noted	
19, 187, 189, 313, 687	681	7260676	KOJ 888	K	RHD	2-Seater	Maroon	Maroon	Maroon	28/11/49	Bristol Street Motors (Universal)	Dr. C. E. Bigger	
19, 186, 283, 694	682	7200766	JOE 820	M	RHD	Coupe	Maroon	Red	Beige	17/9/48	Bristol Street Motors	L. K. Greene	
19, 178, 230, 301	683	7200769	HRU 404	M	RHD	Coupe	Maroon	Red	Maroon	13/9/48	English (Lee Motors)	P. L. Fargaharol	
19, 194, 238, 731, 732	684	7200771	MNW 149	M	RHD	Coupe	Maroon	Red	Beige	17/9/48	Tate	F. Broadbent	MNW 149 is mentioned in service records as both chassis 684 and 702 but not been possible to resolve
19, 185, 217, 221, 223, 228, 231, 238, 245, 246, 249, 352, 356, 367	685G	7200746	KLF 147	K	RHD	2-Seater	Blue	Blue	Blue	15/11/48	Mann Egerton (Wm. H. King)	Munns Transport	Show car
19	686G	7202521	Not noted	K	RHD	2-Seater	Bronze	Red	Beige	14/12/48	Kenya		Show car
19, 184, 385	687G	7200743	EUX 371	M	RHD	Coupe	Grey	Grey	Grey	25/11/48	Furrows	S. Coates Parker	Show car
19, 169, 218, 220, 332, 692	688G	7200691	KLD 758	L	RHD	Tourer	Maroon	Maroon	Maroon	24/11/48	Adlards	Hubert L. Vickery	Show car
19, 173, 381	689	7200755	KAR 612	L	RHD	Tourer	Black	Blue	Grey	30/9/48	Dagenham Motors (Chimneys Gr)	W. A. Alderton	
19, 177	690	7202223	Not noted	L	RHD	Tourer	Grey	Grey	Grey	15/10/48	Gould	D. P. Preewick	
19, 184, 254	691	7202186	Not noted	K	RHD	2-Seater	Maroon	Maroon	Maroon	12/1/49	Furrows	J. B. Carr	Page 254 records new car which was delivered next day
19, 181, 344	692	7200736	NFC 819	M	RHD	Coupe	Blue	Blue	Blue	22/9/48	Hartwells (A. A. Clark)	H. K. Marsden	
19, 184	693	7200698	Not noted	M	RHD	Coupe	Blue	Blue	Slue	24/9/48	Furrows (Braid Bros)	Dr. J. B. Hargreaves	
19, 191	694	7200490	Not noted	L	RHD	Tourer	Grey	Red	Grey	25/10/48	Nunn (Puckingtons)	Managing Dir. W. Haynes	
19, 173, 248, 250, 251, 261, 263, 306, 325	695	7202236	TMH 383	L	RHD	Tourer	Blue	Blue	Grey	11/8/48	Dagenham Motors (Showrooom)	J. McNally	
19, 170, 248, 258, 264, 266, 269, 290, 297, 302, 315, 327, 367, 386	696	7200475	KXC 162	K	RHD	2-Seater	Maroon	Maroon	Maroon	Not noted	Adlards	H. E. Quimmell	
19, 189, 695	697	7200697	KAL 143	M	RHD	Coupe	Blue	Blue	Blue	17/9/48	Universal (Brooks Motor Co.)	W. Sanders	
19, 177, 244, 303, 308, 329, 695	698	7200082	KGC 224	M	RHD	Coupe	Black	Grey	Grey	27/9/48	Gould	N. J. Miles	

CHASSIS NUMBER PAGE REFERENCE KEY: Allocation Books (pages 1-77), Record Cards (pages 78-167), Warranty Book (pages 168-201), Service Records (pages 202-393)

Page References	Chassis	Original Engine Number	UK Registration	Type	LHD?	Body Style	Original Colour	Original Interior	Original Hood	Original Delivery	Allocation	First Customer	Remarks
19, 80, 244, 250, 252	699	7203238	QB 2705	K	RHD	2-Seater	Grey	Blue	Blue Grey	22/8/49	Germany (R/M Overseas Motor Sales Ltd.)	J. R. Miles	Cancelled export to Japan, page 244 refers to car as unregistered
19	700	7206393	Not noted	L	RHD	Tourer	Grey	Grey	Grey	15/12/48	Kenya		
19, 191	701	7200671	Not noted	M	RHD	Coupe	Blue	Blue	Blue	30/9/48	Nunn	J. Brown	
19, 194, 227, 731, 732	702	7202468	MNW 149	M	RHD	Coupe	Maroon	Red	Maroon	27/9/48	Tate	L. Chappell	MNW 149 is mentioned in service records as both chassis 684 and 702 but not been possible to resolve
19, 191	703	7189889	Not noted	M	RHD	Coupe	Maroon	Red	Maroon	10/9/48	Nunn (F. Ellison)	J. Tennant	
19, 194, 222, 223, 224, 243, 334	704	7200772	DRD 505	M	RHD	Coupe	Chassis	Chassis	Chassis	13/9/48	Tate	L. H. Hobday	
20, 186, 231, 344, 348, 695	705	7200726	JOF 189	M	RHD	Coupe	Maroon	Brown	Maroon	29/9/48	Bristol Street Motors	J. E. Keightley	
20, 200, 278	706	7200728	CES 375	M	RHD	Coupe	Black	Grey	Grey	10/1/48	Frew	W. H. Lomas	
20, 199	707	7200727	Not noted	M	RHD	Coupe	Black	Grey	Grey	30/9/48	Alexanders	J. H. Stionery	
20, 177	708	7200402	Not noted	K	RHD	2-Seater	Chassis	Chassis	Chassis	14/9/48	Gould	J. H. Gotch	
20, 169, 231, 239, 240, 244, 247, 253, 258, 261, 264, 268, 269, 284, 291, 298	709	7202469	KGC 893	M	RHD	Coupe	Black	Grey	Grey	10/2/48	Adlards	B. D. Napper	
20, 191, 229	710	7202462	DRJ 120	M	RHD	Coupe	Green	Brown	Green	15/10/48	Nunn	J. B. Shaw	
20, 181, 306, 335	711	7202488	NML 355	M	RHD	Coupe	Black	Brown	Grey	10/1/48	Hartwells	Philippe M. Lamb	
20, 197	712	7202514	Not noted	M	RHD	Coupe	Grey	Blue	Blue	10/11/48	George & Jobling	J. L. Stevenson	
20, 189, 240, 244, 268, 278	713	7200761	GUK 660	K	RHD	2-Seater	Grey	Brown	Grey	Not noted	Universal	Not noted	Page 240 refers to car as unregistered
20, 184, 377	714	7202450	EY 8941	M	RHD	Coupe	Green	Grey	Grey	15/11/48	Furrows (H. R. Williams)	Dr. E. R. Hughes	
20, 184, 246	715	7202486	EUJ 999	M	RHD	Coupe	Grey	Grey	Blue	10/12/48	Furrows	C. L. Dennis	
20, 194, 224, 252	716	7202454	Not noted	M	RHD	Coupe	Maroon	Red	Beige	28/2/49	Tate	H. L. Mosley	Page 224 refers to car as unregistered
20, 194, 199, 687	717	7200764	SH 8990	K	RHD	2-Seater	Grey	Brown	Grey	11/5/49	Tate (W. B. Turnbull)	R. W. D. Boswell	Transferred to Alexanders
20, 200, 391, 692	718	7200471	CES 360	L	RHD	Tourer	Grey	Grey	Black	11/1/48	Frew	J. L. Fraser	
20, 214, 215, 220, 227, 230, 233, 254, 293, 322, 324, 346, 695	719	7200691	KLO 130	M	RHD	Coupe	N. Blue	Blue	Black	Not noted	Demonstrator		Sydney H. Allard Special coupe 2-Seater

Page References	Chassis	Original Engine Number	UK Registration	Type	LHD?	Body Style	Original Colour	Original Interior	Original Hood	Original Delivery	Allocation	First Customer	Remarks
						CHASSIS NUMBER PAGE REFERENCE KEY: Allocation Books (pages 1-77), Record Cards (pages 78-167), Warranty Book (pages 168-201), Service Records (pages 202-393)							
20, 169, 227, 240, 248, 267, 289, 341	720	7202506	MPJ 200	M	LHD	Coupe	Black	Grey	Grey	24/11/48	Adlards	C. S. Bell	
20, 169, 258, 338, 345, 347	721	7202491	LKG 780	M	RHD	Coupe	Blue	Beige	Blue	12/2/48	Adlards	Dr. Pearlman	Records on pages 338, 345 and 347 show LKE 780, but page 258 could be LKG 780, as E is indistinct
20, 178, 222, 249, 278, 281, 293, 328	722	7202949	CTK 830	M	RHD	Coupe	Grey	Grey	Grey	10/12/48	English (E. C. Childs & Sons)	K. S. D. Digby	Page 249 and 278 refer to the car as CTK 930
20, 182	723	7202946	Not noted	M	RHD	Coupe	Grey	Maroon	Grey	11/12/48	Taylors	P. L. J. Parkes	
20, 191	724	7200557	Not noted	K	RHD	2-Seater	Maroon	Maroon	Not noted	17/1/49	Nunn	A. F. Simon	Tonneau cover
20, 169, 219, 224, 239, 251, 305, 733	725	7202444	MPH 147	M	RHD	Coupe	Chassis	Chassis	Chassis	10/6/48	Adlards	Not noted	MPH 147 is shown in records as both 725 and 726. Page 305 refers to NPD 82
20, 169, 251, 252, 385, 733	726	7202971	MPH 147	M	RHD	Coupe	Black	Grey	Grey	14/10/48	Adlards	Not noted	MPH 147 is shown in records as both 725 and 726.
20, 197	727	7202988	Not noted	M	RHD	Coupe	Chassis	Chassis	Chassis	10/4/48	George and Jobling	Dr. T. Scott Glover	Less headlamps, bumpers, cowl, grille, bulkhead, petrol tank
20, 80	728	7202526	Not noted	K	RHD	2-Seater	Light Blue	Blue	Blue	23/1/50	Venezuela	L. Bockh & Cia	
20, 200, 384	729	7202315	CES 615	L	RHD	Tourer	Cream	Brown	Black	13/12/48	Frew	Dr. W. E. Robinson	Petrol tank lock, alteration to seat and pedals, ignition switch.
20, 169, 238, 245, 264, 268, 270, 273, 275, 280, 284, 299, 305, 311, 316, 329, 332, 338, 341	730	7202464	KBP 466	M	RHD	Coupe	Black	Maroon	Beige	14/10/48	Adlards (Barkers)	G. S. Mundell	Page 264 shows KDP 466
20, 189	731	7202466	Not noted	M	RHD	Coupe	Chassis	Chassis	Chassis	24/9/48	Universal (Lindley)	Not noted	
20, 186	732	7202447	Not noted	M	RHD	Coupe	Chassis	Chassis	Chassis	23/9/48	Bristol Street Motors	Not noted	
20, 196, 228, 696	733	7202998	JHW 674	M	RHD	Coupe	Grey	Blue	Blue	15/10/48	Patterson (Z. Gabtree & Co.)	S. W. Wood	
20, 181	734	7202999	Not noted	M	RHD	Coupe	Grey	Grey	Blue	16/10/48	Hartwells	J. B. Powell	Was crossed of Patterson warranty list
20, 173, 216, 221, 226, 230, 241, 249, 251, 258, 261, 263, 265, 271, 280, 287, 295, 733	735	7203950	JYW 749	M	RHD	Coupe	Grey	Grey	Blue	15/10/48	Dagenham Motors (H. C. Nelson)	L. E. De Rouit	Page 258 says chassis 735 for this registration and page 216 records regn. as JWW 749
20, 186	736	7202944	Not noted	M	RHD	Coupe	Chassis	Chassis	Chassis	22/9/48	Bristol Street Motors	Hughes Motor Fitments	
21, 191, 298	737	7202953	GBU 78	M	RHD	Coupe	Chassis	Chassis	Chassis	24/9/48	Nunn	Not noted	
21, 182, 351, 355, 361	738	7202979	CFK 765	M	RHD	Coupe	Maroon	Brown	Beige	20/10/48	Taylors (T. J. Daniel Ltd.)	F. Probert	
21, 178	739	7202951	Not noted	M	RHD	Coupe	Blue	Grey	Blue	11/1/48	English (G. W. Cox)	A. J. F. A. Haimswaich	

Page References	Chassis	Original Engine Number	UK Registration	Type	LHD?	Body Style	Original Colour	Original Interior	Original Hood	Original Delivery	Allocation	First Customer	Remarks
							CHASSIS NUMBER PAGE REFERENCE KEY: Allocation Books (pages 1-77), Record Cards (pages 78-167), Warranty Book (pages 168-201), Service Records (pages 202-393)						
21, 219, 223, 259, 693	740	7202960	KGC 896	M	RHD	Coupe	Maroon	Maroon	Beige	5/6/49	Demonstrator		
21, 184	741	7203195	Not noted	M	RHD	Coupe	Chassis	Chassis	Chassis	30/9/48	Furrows (Wrexham Motor Co.)	Mr Brown	
21, 180	742	7202408	Not noted	K	RHD	2-Seater	N. Blue	Blue	Blue	21/1/49	Hughes (Elliot & Sons)	J. Foden	
21, 183	743	7202527	Not noted	L	RHD	Tourer	Maroon	Brown	Beige	12/2/48	Harris (Central Garage)	W. S. Gordow Rees	Tonneau cover
21, 191	744	7202987	Not noted	M	RHD	Coupe	Maroon	Maroon	Beige	28/10/48	Nunn (F. Ellison)	H. L. Gee	
21, 189, 216, 220, 223, 253, 264, 289, 292, 695	745	7202936	MRB 441	M	RHD	Coupe	Maroon	Maroon	Beige	22/10/48	Universal	Butterfly Co. Ltd.	
21, 194	746	7203157	Not noted	M	RHD	Coupe	Maroon	Brown	Beige	29/10/48	Tate	S. Emmott	
21, 169	747	7202978	Not noted	M	RHD	Coupe	Maroon	Brown	Beige	26/10/48	Adlards (Seddon)	Birmand Seddon	
21, 197	748	7203194	Not noted	M	RHD	Coupe	Chassis	Chassis	Chassis	22/10/48	George & Jobling	Not noted	Bonnet fitted
21, 194, 227, 255, 262, 287, 294, 303	749	7203591	DRD 723	M	RHD	Coupe	Chassis	Chassis	Chassis	15/10/48	Tate	K. N. Hole	
21, 178	750	7202562	Not noted	M	RHD	Coupe	Black	Brown	Beige	16/11/48	English (Andrew Sloane)	Dr. J. L. D. Lewis	
21, 173, 276, 293, 303, 346, 375, 379, 382, 388, 694	751	7202168	UMV 207	M	RHD	Coupe	Blue	Blue	Blue	Not noted	Dagenham Motors (University Motors)	Unreadable	One record notes regn. KDK 799
21, 200	752	7203450	Not noted	M	RHD	Coupe	Blue	Blue	Blue	Not noted	Frew (Harper Motor Co.)	Major G. B. Mardew	
21, 177	753	7242593	Not noted	M	RHD	Coupe	Grey	Grey	Grey	19/11/48	Gould	Geddes Hyslop	
21, 173, 231, 235, 249, 280, 284, 290, 298, 321, 322, 330	754	7203627	KLO 300	M	RHD	Coupe	Chassis	Chassis	Chassis	17/11/48	Dagenham Motors	Not noted	
21, 80, 186, 271, 275, 378, 734	755	7202176	JON 710	K	RHD	2-Seater	Red	Red	Beige	21/4/49	Bristol Street Motors	R. A. Langley	Later exported to Australia – refer to record card
21, 162, 183, 220, 232, 235, 239, 366	756	7203506	FDW 92	M	RHD	Coupe	Blue	Blue	Blue	11/8/48	Harris (Gibbs Bros)	H. Shepherd	
21, 178, 692	757	7202218	LKX 145*	L	RHD	Tourer	Maroon	Maroon	Beige	11/1/49	English (G. W. Cox)	Unreadable	* Regn. record for chassis 755 on page 378, but assumed as error as this is nearest L-type
21, 200, 261, 362	758	7203465	VAL 317	M	RHD	Coupe	Grey	Grey	Grey	12/8/48	Frew	W. F. Barber	
21, 191, 244, 279	759	7203491	LMB 595	M	RHD	Coupe	Black	Grey	Beige	11/10/48	Nunn (Wisteston Garage)	V. M. White	
21, 169, 274, 279, 306, 321, 340, 343	760	7203768	OPE 237	M	RHD	Coupe	Chassis	Chassis	Chassis	18/11/48	Adlards (Young)	Warranty void	Car has been resold

·ALLARD·

CHASSIS NUMBER PAGE REFERENCE KEY: Allocation Books (pages 1-77), Record Cards (pages 78-167), Warranty Book (pages 168-201), Service Records (pages 202-393)

Page References	Chassis	Original Engine Number	UK Registration	Type	LHD?	Body Style	Original Colour	Original Interior	Original Hood	Original Delivery	Allocation	First Customer	Remarks
21, 185, 235, 694	761	7203589	JNG 878	M	RHD	Coupe	Black	Brown	Black	17/11/48	Mann Egerton (Wm. H. King)	Mr Rex Carter	
21, 173, 222, 281	762	7203590	KJH 505	M	RHD	Coupe	Black	Brown	Black	17/11/48	Dagenham Motors (Car Mart)	A. L. Pollard	
21	763	7202313	Not noted	K	RHD	2-Seater	Chassis	Chassis	Chassis	Not noted	Not noted		
21, 182, 225, 229, 235, 251, 266, 271, 312, 340	764	7203614	LHW 523	M	RHD	Coupe	Black	Grey	Beige	12/3/48	Taylors (Whiteladies Garage)	Dr. K. W. Vandy	
21, 182	765	7203605	Not noted	M	RHD	Coupe	Blue	Blue	Blue	11/5/48	Taylors (Apex Motors Ltd.)	H. S. Bayley	
21, 186	766	7203774	Not noted	M	RHD	Coupe	Chassis	Chassis	Chassis	21/10/48	Bristol Street Motors		Warranty Book shows sent to body builders 13th Nov
21, 250, 270	767	7203610	KLD 473	M	RHD	Coupe	Blue	Blue	Blue	11/9/48	Adlards (Skrine)		One record, page 270, notes regn. KLD 423 or KLP 423
21, 178	768	7203625	Not noted	M	RHD	Coupe	Maroon	Maroon	Beige	25/1/49	English	Not noted	
22, 183, 232	769	7203789	OMC 938	M	RHD	Coupe	Chassis	Chassis	Chassis	23/11/48	Harris (Madigans Garage)	S. Southhall	Bonnet fitted
22, 80, 687	770	7202511	Not noted	K	RHD	2-Seater	Maroon	Maroon	Maroon	26/1/50	U.S.A.	Moss Motors Ltd.	
22, 304, 693	771	7202538	MPK 36	L	RHD	Tourer	Maroon	Maroon	Beige	12/6/48	Italy		Mr Jarrat, proprietor of H.W. Motors of Italy, imported it
22, 174, 255, 387, 391, 393, 692	772	7202171	LGY 397	L	RHD	Tourer	Maroon	Brown	Beige	22/12/49	Dagenham Motors (Red Ric)	W. A. Watson	51 Upper Richmond Rd 1/12/57 "Prepare for Docks" LGY397
22, 186	773	7200408	Not noted	L	RHD	Tourer	Maroon	Brown	Beige	12/1/48	Bristol Street Motors (Frank Guest Ltd.)	G. L. Bedwaich	
22, 80	774	7221938	Not noted	K2	LHD	2-Seater	Red	Red	Maroon	2/9/50	Uruguay (Emelas & Cia Limitada)	Salem	Coil springs
22, 194, 687	775	7200477	Not noted	K	RHD	2-Seater	Nordic blue	Blue	Blue	15/7/49	Tate	Unreadable	
22, 191	776	7203621	Not noted	M	RHD	Coupe	Grey	Grey	Blue	12/8/48	Nunn (Seaview Motors)	R. Parker Davies	
22, 196, 303, 318, 346, 348	777	7203623	JM 7942	M	RHD	Coupe	Maroon	Maroon	Beige	28/11/48	Patterson (Stoutes Garage)	Harry Ingram	Larrinaga
22, 191	778	7203643	Not noted	M	RHD	Coupe	Grey	Grey	Blue	12/7/48	Nunn (A. W. Webb Ltd.)	S. H. Lomax	
22, 181	779	7203784	Not noted	M	RHD	Coupe	Chassis	Chassis	Chassis	18/11/48	Furrows	Not noted	
22, 197	780	7203766	Not noted	M	RHD	Coupe	Black	Maroon	Beige	17/11/48	George & Jobling (J. R. Alexander)	Unreadable	
22, 183, 233, 269, 277	781	7203884	KDE 794	M	RHD	Coupe	Blue	Blue	Blue	12/11/48	Harris (Edwards)	F. Rhys Davies	
22, 197, 286	782	7203893	GGD 769	M	RHD	Coupe	Chassis	Chassis	Chassis	15/11/48	George & Jobling	Stoberou	Bonnet fitted
22, 178, 218, 247, 287, 299	783	7203734	HRU 739	M	RHD	Coupe	Grey	Grey	Grey	17/11/48	English (Tice & Sons)	T. H. Haydon	
22, 186, 263, 314	784	7203863	FPY 521	M	RHD	Coupe	Grey	Grey	Grey	17/11/48	Bristol Street Motors (Central Motors)	L. R. Curtis	
22, 180, 242	785	7203735	JFJ 621	M	RHD	Coupe	Maroon	Maroon	Beige	25/11/48	Hughes	Dr. Scarborough	

Page References	Chassis	Original Engine Number	UK Registration	Type	LHD?	Body Style	Original Colour	Original Interior	Original Hood	Original Delivery	Allocation	First Customer	Remarks
						CHASSIS NUMBER PAGE REFERENCE KEY: Allocation Books (pages 1-77), Record Cards (pages 78-167), Warranty Book (pages 168-201), Service Records (pages 202-393)							
22, 181, 236, 241, 243	786	7203733	NJO 335	M	RHD	Coupe	Chassis	Chassis	Chassis	30/11/48	Hartwells	J. Hywood Jones	Engine invoiced as 7203733
22, 194	787	7203885	Not noted	M	RHD	Coupe	Chassis	Chassis	Chassis	23/11/48	Tate (T. C. Harrison)	J. F. Eadon	Bonnet fitted
22, 197, 240	788	7203948	GGD 210	M	RHD	Coupe	Maroon	Maroon	Beige	12/3/48	George & Jobling (Cameron & Campbell)	T. Johnston	
22, 178, 254	789	7203953	HRU 800	M	RHD	Coupe	Blue	Blue	Blue	17/12/48	English	Not noted	
22, 194, 385	790	7203954	MNW 622	M	RHD	Coupe	Maroon	Maroon	Beige	12/2/48	Tate	F. Tate	
22, 184	791	7203882	Not noted	M	RHD	Coupe	Chassis	Chassis	Chassis	17/11/48	Furrows	A. L. Stevens	
22, 180	792	7204185	Not noted	L	RHD	Tourer	Black	Blue	Beige	18/8/49	Hughes	G. S. W. Chapple	
22, 173, 218, 220, 234, 271, 285, 294, 297	793	7204088	TME 3	M	RHD	Coupe	Maroon	Maroon	Beige	12/7/48	Dagenham Motors (H. M. Bartley)	I. F. Stamp	Page 218 shows car in final works before delivery
22, 196	794	7204089	Not noted	M	RHD	Coupe	Maroon	Maroon	Beige	1/7/49	Patterson (Country Garage)	N. Gillig	
22, 178, 279, 337, 339	795	7203944	HOR 595	M	RHD	Coupe	Chassis	Chassis	Chassis	11/8/48	English (Erskine Motors)	R. N. Everett	One record on page 337 notes regn. HLR 595
22, 187, 687	796	7204739	Not noted	K	RHD	2-Seater	Nordic Blue	Blue	Blue	31/3/50	Bristol Street Motors	D. St. Clair	
22, 191	797	7204034	Not noted	M	RHD	Coupe	Blue	Blue	Blue	12/3/48	Nunn (Burrows & Seed Ltd.)	J. R. Sunderland	
22, 199	798	7204087	Not noted	M	RHD	Coupe	Maroon	Maroon	Beige	13/12/48	Alexanders	L. Jackson	
22, 181, 225, 275	799	7203959	Not noted	M	RHD	Coupe	Chassis	Chassis	Chassis	11/9/48	Hartwells	Not noted	Page 225 refers to car as unregistered
22, 169, 222, 321	800	7204759	KLD 759	L	RHD	Tourer	Nordic Blue	Brown	Beige	17/12/48	Italy	P. Q. Greene	
23, 186	801	7204070	Not noted	M	RHD	Coupe	Grey	Grey	Blue	23/2/49	Bristol Street Motors (Central Motors)	C. Binns	
23, 173, 186, 266, 298, 313, 348, 369, 384, 390, 392	802	7204091	KNK 28	M	RHD	Coupe	Grey	Grey	Grey	2/4/49	Dagenham Motors (J. W. Whalley)	E. N. Griffith	Bristol Street Motors warranty list notes cancelled 24/11/48
23	803	7204094	Not noted	M	RHD	Coupe	Maroon	Maroon	Beige	21/12/48	Hartwells		
23, 177, 222, 238, 256, 353, 355, 363, 367, 373, 386	804	7204233	TMX 198	M	RHD	Coupe	Black	Red	Black	23/12/48	Gould	Paul Zetter	Page 386 may say THX 198
23, 189	805	7204248	Not noted	M	RHD	Coupe	Blue	Blue	Blue	12/8/48	Universal (Standhill Garage)	Bradbury & Sons	
23, 82, 227, 228, 232, 234, 235, 695	806	7203958	KLP 818	M	RHD	Coupe	Grey	Red	Grey	18/3/49	Malaya	W. R. Plunkett	Export
23, 194	807	7204738	Not noted	L	RHD	Tourer	Blue	Blue	Beige	11/5/49	Tate		
23, 186	808	7204186	Not noted	M	RHD	Coupe	Blue	Blue	Blue	12/4/48	Bristol Street Motors	Dr. G. Shepherd	
23, 191, 696	809	7204312	Not noted	M	RHD	Coupe	Blue	Blue	Blue	16/12/48	Nunn (A. W. Webb Ltd.)	E. W. Taylor	

Page References	Chassis	Original Engine Number	UK Registration	Type	LHD?	Body Style	Original Colour	Original Interior	Original Hood	Original Delivery	Allocation	First Customer	Remarks
CHASSIS NUMBER PAGE REFERENCE KEY: Allocation Books (pages 1-77), Record Cards (pages 78-167), Warranty Book (pages 168-201), Service Records (pages 202-393)													
23	810	7204251	Not noted	M	RHD	Coupe	Chassis	Chassis	Chassis	15/12/48	Not noted		
23, 173	811	7204491	Not noted	K	RHD	2-Seater	Black	Maroon	Maroon	5/3/49	Dagenham Motors	Richards	Solex Ltd. noted in Warranty Book
23, 696	812	7204304	Not noted	M	RHD	Coupe	Red	Red	Beige	28/12/48	Malta		Domesday Book showing registration 22055, previously 14061
23, 178, 365, 386, 694	813	7204368	HRU 994	M	RHD	Coupe	Grey	Blue	Blue	1/4/49	English (Knott Bros Ltd.)	E. Gaytor	Regn. also noted as KRU 994 on page 365
23, 184	814	7203464	Not noted	M	RHD	Coupe	Grey	Maroon	Grey	23/2/49	Furrows (A. J. Hemmings Ltd.)	W. B. Clegg	
23, 174	815	7203384	Not noted	L	RHD	Tourer	Maroon	Maroon	Maroon	11/11/49	Dagenham Motors	Beltcherton	
23, 199, 270, 694	816	7204414	SY 9088	M	RHD	Coupe	Black	Brown	Beige	3/7/49	Alexanders (J. Brown & Co.)	D. G. Clark	
23, 194	817	7204415	Not noted	M	RHD	Coupe	Maroon	Maroon	Beige	3/7/49	Tate (Ripleys Ltd.)	J. A. Shaw	
23, 82, 169, 221, 239, 263, 737	818	7204333	KLM 561	M	RHD	Coupe	Black	Red	Black	2/9/49	Germany	Capt. H. R. Sykes	A service record notes regn. JYT 443, but this could be a confusion over 618 and 818. Page 239 records regn. QB 1446 which is likely a trade plate'
23, 328	819	7204313	Not noted	M	RHD	Coupe	Black	Blue	Black	17/12/48	Kenya		
23, 180, 280, 287, 297, 306, 694	820	7204413	KFJ 549	M	RHD	Coupe	Maroon	Maroon	Beige	17/1/49	Hughes		Noted as 'not sold yet'
23, 189, 314	821	7204461	NNU 519	M	RHD	Coupe	Black	Brown	Beige	18/2/49	Universal	E. Hammond	
23, 173, 692	822	7204734	UMC 486	L	RHD	Tourer	Grey	Blue	Black	20/5/49	Dagenham Motors (Wembley Court Motors)	E. T. Gane	
23, 184, 694	823	7204436	JC 9688	M	RHD	Coupe	Black	Red	Black	21/12/48	Furrows	Not noted	
23, 196, 227, 357	824	7204450	MTN 575	M	RHD	Coupe	Blue	Blue	Blue	16/12/48	Patterson	E. Dugdale	
23, 191	825	7204525	Not noted	M	RHD	Coupe	Black	Brown	Beige	17/2/49	Nunn (S. Lever)	L. Greenwood	
23, 169, 223, 244, 245, 318	826	7204737	KLN 45	K	RHD	2-Seater	Blue	Blue	Blue	2/2/49	Adlards	R. Peacock	
23, 191, 229	827	7204466	KKA 32	M	RHD	Coupe	Blue	Blue	Blue	23/12/48	Nunn (F. B. Anderson & Co.)	Dr. D. Barton	
23, 189, 241, 271, 696	828	7204674	MNU 8	M	RHD	Coupe	Grey	Blue	Blue	13/1/49	Universal (Standhill Garage)	E. M. Panteenis	
23, 194	829	7204526	Not noted	M	RHD	Coupe	Grey	Blue	Blue	1/11/49	Tate	H. G. Johnson	
23, 196	830	7204740	Not noted	L	RHD	Tourer	Grey	Grey	Grey	6/7/49	Patterson (County Garage)	A. G. Abraham	
23, 184, 247, 280, 314, 322, 369	831	7206817	FJN 649	M	RHD	Coupe	Chassis	Chassis	Chassis	3/10/49	Furrows (Braid Bros)	Lady O'Carey Edwards	No bonnet
23, 178, 209	832	7204556	Not noted	M	RHD	Coupe	Black	Brown	Beige	22/2/49	English (G. W. Cox)	A. H. Saunders	
24, 191	833	7204527	Not noted	M	RHD	Coupe	Blue	Blue	Blue	31/1/49	Nunn (S. Lever)	J. D. Greenwood	

Page References	Chassis	Original Engine Number	UK Registration	Type	LHD?	Body Style	Original Colour	Original Interior	Original Hood	Original Delivery	Allocation	First Customer	Remarks
						CHASSIS NUMBER PAGE REFERENCE KEY: Allocation Books (pages 1-77), Record Cards (pages 78-167), Warranty Book (pages 168-201), Service Records (pages 202-393)							
24, 199, 609, 694	834	7204486	GSF 756	M	RHD	Coupe	Black	Maroon	Black	27/1/49	Alexanders	R. Manson	
24, 201, 696	835	7204573	HZ 2552	M	RHD	Coupe	Grey	Grey	Blue	1/7/49	Hamilton (Dugleys Garage)	Dr. H. Watson	
24, 169	836	7204587	Not noted	M	RHD	Coupe	Chassis	Chassis	Chassis	12/7/48	Adlards (Wilberts)	J. Pearce	Bonnet fitted, heavy type rear spring
24, 174, 255, 692, 738	837	7204735	VHX 555	L	RHD	Tourer	Blue	Blue	Beige	16/12/49	Dagenham Motors	E. G. Fiteterton	Page 255 records 837 as a new car
24, 197	838	7204597	Not noted	M	RHD	Coupe	Black	Blue	Black	23/12/48	George & Jobling (J. R. Alexander)	J. C. Blair	
24, 186, 253	839	7204586	JOK 114	M	RHD	Coupe	Maroon	Red	Beige	18/1/49	Bristol Street Motors	J. L. Collis	
24, 194	840	7204658	Not noted	M	RHD	Coupe	Chassis	Chassis	Chassis	19/1/49	Tate (Central Motors)	Robert Clark	Bonnet taken off
24, 80, 689	841	7223840	Not noted	K2	LHD	2-Seater	Grey	Grey	Grey	2/9/50	Uruguay (Emelas & Cia Limitada)	Salem	Coil springs
24, 185	842	7204598	Not noted	M	RHD	Coupe	Grey	Blue	Blue	1/3/49	Mann Egerton (Wm. H. King)	Bramley F. Bussell	
24, 186, 692	843	7204589	Not noted	M	RHD	Coupe	Grey	Blue	Blue	1/10/49	Bristol Street Motors	T. W. Tomkinson Ltd.	
24, 184	844	7204848	Not noted	M	RHD	Coupe	Chassis	Chassis	Chassis	23/3/49	Furrows	N. W. A. Socheby	Bonnet taken off
24, 181, 231, 248	845	7204736	ERX 946	L	RHD	Tourer	Grey	Grey	Grey	25/2/49	Hartwells	Not noted	
24, 186, 218, 311	846	7206530	FJF 84	M	RHD	Coupe	Blue	Blue	Blue	16/2/49	Bristol Street Motors (Bradshaw Cars)	W. Rowan Co.	Page 218 refers to car as chassis only
24, 186	847	7206593	Not noted	M	RHD	Coupe	Blue	Blue	Blue	16/2/49	Bristol Street Motors (Central Motors)	Dr. B. C. Jennings	
24, 200	848	7204668	Not noted	M	RHD	Coupe	Black	Grey	Black	23/12/48	Frew (Elgin Garage)	Geo. N. Gray	
24, 194, 242	849	7204665	HWT 814	M	RHD	Coupe	Black	Red	Beige	23/12/48	Tate (Fred Binns)	Sam Wells	
24, 199	850	7204756	Not noted	M	RHD	Coupe	Black	Grey	Black	30/12/48	Alexanders	E. B. Murray	
24, 189, 266, 695	851	7206589	Not noted	M	RHD	Coupe	Grey	Grey	Grey	3/2/49	Universal (Standhill Garage)	R. J. Glainster	
24, 169, 225, 232, 239, 252, 299, 692	852	7206928	KLO 128	L	RHD	Tourer	Maroon	Maroon	Beige	17/3/49	Adlards	Mrs Pamela May	
24, 162, 173, 225, 241, 248, 252, 270, 275, 283, 285, 293, 297, 352, 370, 371, 375	853	7204657	KLL 138	M	RHD	Coupe	Grey	Grey	Blue	22/1/49	Dagenham Motors (Russell Motors)	F. H. W. Clarke	
24, 191	854	7204769	Not noted	M	RHD	Coupe	Grey	Red	Grey	21/1/49	Nunn	Not noted	
24, 197, 237	855	7206586	GSG 196	M	RHD	Coupe	Black	Maroon	Black	18/2/49	George & Jobling	R. L. Larnie	
24, 81, 692	856	7207042	Not noted	L	RHD	Tourer	Blue	Blue	Black	12/8/49	Uruguay	Salero	Appears repaint and resale, refer to record card, page 81
24, 162, 169, 375	857	7204742	KPO 65	M	RHD	Coupe	Grey	Grey	Blue	1/11/49	Adlards	R. Clifford-Brown	

Page References	Chassis	Original Engine Number	UK Registration	Type	LHD?	Body Style	Original Colour	Original Interior	Original Hood	Original Delivery	Allocation	First Customer	Remarks
						CHASSIS NUMBER PAGE REFERENCE KEY: Allocation Books (pages 1-77), Record Cards (pages 78-167), Warranty Book (pages 168-201), Service Records (pages 202-393)							
24, 189, 252, 262, 277, 300, 311, 314, 347	858	7204635	NNU 326	M	RHD	Coupe	Maroon	Maroon	Beige	28/1/49	Universal (Butterfly Co.)	Fletcher	
24, 178, 694	859	7207238	DJT 876	M	RHD	Coupe	Grey	Grey	Maroon	23/2/49	English (Lee Motors)	H. R. Paul	
24, 194, 277	860	7206932	KPR 118	L	RHD	Tourer	Blue	Blue	Grey	5/6/49	Tate (Bawtry Motors)	E. J. Taylor	
24, 182	861	7204641	Not noted	M	RHD	Coupe	Maroon	Red	Beige	18/1/49	Taylors (Apex Motors Ltd.)	Not noted	
24, 178, 369, 372, 694	862	7204819	HAA 106	M	RHD	Coupe	Blue	Grey	Grey	21/1/49	English (G. W. Cox)	Dr. W. L. Milligan	
24, 191	863	7204650	Not noted	M	RHD	Coupe	Maroon	Maroon	Beige	21/1/49	Nunn	Not noted	
24, 194	864	7204615	Not noted	M	RHD	Coupe	Blue	Blue	Blue	25/1/49	Tate	J. Dixon	
25, 197, 321	865	7204624	Not noted	M	RHD	Coupe	Maroon	Red	Beige	19/1/49	George & Jobling (J. Martin Ltd.)	J. D. C. Mackay	
25, 173, 246, 247, 267, 342	866	7206963	KXH 502	L	RHD	Tourer	Grey	Grey	Black	30/9/49	Dagenham Motors (Car Mart)	R. J. McDougal	Page 246 refers to car as unregistered
25, 170, 323, 346, 692	867	7207204	LKR 963	L	RHD	Tourer	Maroon	Red	Beige	24/8/49	Adlards (Soams and Dunn)	A. B de Hoxar	
25, 191	868	7207804	Not noted	L	RHD	Tourer	Grey	Grey	Black	17/10/49	Nunn	Leadbeaters Ltd.	Steering column gear change
25, 194, 379, 387	869	7204812	KAT 226	M	RHD	Coupe	Maroon	Red	Beige	21/1/49	Tate (Lawson Motor Co.)	Bowes Booch	
25, 186, 224, 238, 266, 298, 312, 331, 348	870	7204841	FRY 449	M	RHD	Coupe	Black	Maroon	Beige	28/1/49	Bristol Street Motors (Central Motors)	W. C. Smith	
25, 173, 222, 298, 387, 694	871	7204805	TMX 5	M	RHD	Coupe	Blue	Blue	Blue	19/1/49	Dagenham Motors	G. E. R. Osbourne	
25, 196, 381, 694	872	7206520	JAO 308	M	RHD	Coupe	Blue	Blue	Grey	2/12/49	Patterson (S. M. T. Saler & Services)	Margaret E. Jaffer	
25, 169, 303, 307, 309, 310, 318, 389, 696	873	7206587	JUF 470	M	RHD	Coupe	Blue	Grey	Grey	27/1/49	Adlards (Hartley and Mudgley)	E. G. Midgley	
25, 163, 173, 222, 229, 267, 282, 285, 299, 304, 317, 331, 352, 357, 359, 380, 388	874	7206612	KLK 657	M	RHD	Coupe	Black	Maroon	Black	28/1/49	Dagenham Motors (Mann Egerton)	F. S. L. Compton	Reg later changed to foreign plate?
25, 169	875	7204934	Not noted	M	RHD	Coupe	Blue	Blue	Blue	25/1/49	Adlards (Peacocks)	K. C. Delingpole	
25, 173, 236, 694	876	7204973	KLK 535	M	RHD	Coupe	Black	Blue	Black	28/1/49	Dagenham Motors	Not noted	
25, 163, 185, 226, 232, 234, 246, 377, 695	877	7206613	JVF 14	M	RHD	Coupe	Blue	Blue	Blue	27/1/49	Mann Egerton (W. H. Chitty)	O. C. Bisset Pearce	
25, 189	878	7206526	Not noted	M	RHD	Coupe	Black	Blue	Grey	2/2/49	Universal (Lincs Motor Co.)	J. W. Ellmore	

Page References	Chassis	Original Engine Number	UK Registration	Type	LHD?	Body Style	Original Colour	Original Interior	Original Hood	Original Delivery	Allocation	First Customer	Remarks
								CHASSIS NUMBER PAGE REFERENCE KEY: Allocation Books (pages 1-77), Record Cards (pages 78-167), Warranty Book (pages 168-201), Service Records (pages 202-393)					
25, 177, 251, 279, 299, 302, 306, 343, 344, 352, 354, 358, 360, 377, 380, 392, 696	879	7206667	UMC 735	M	RHD	Coupe	Black	Maroon	Beige	27/1/49	Gould (W. Perry Ltd.)	Belty Box Film Services Ltd.	Reg UMK 735 also noted several times, including pages 343, 344 and 380
25, 178, 339, 348	880	7206627	HAA 325	M	RHD	Coupe	Grey	Blue	Blue	2/7/49	English (G. W. Cox)	Charles St. John	
25, 173, 243, 250, 279, 343	881	7206811	TMX 744	M	RHD	Coupe	Grey	Blue	Blue	2/2/49	Dagenham Motors	E. G. Valve	
25, 184, 226	882	7206591	EUX 808	M	RHD	Coupe	Grey	Grey	Grey	2/2/49	Furrows	L. Hemmingway	
25, 178, 245, 265, 267	883	7206521	FMW 416	M	RHD	Coupe	Black	Brown	Beige	2/2/49	English (Andrew Sloane)	G. P. Shea Simmonds	
25, 186, 694	884	7206591	HUE 574	M	RHD	Coupe	Black	Brown	Beige	2/2/49	Bristol Street Motors (Overdale Motors)	M. Stone	M. Hill A. O. C. Reigate 08/09/67
25, 194, 694	885	7206686	MUA 837	M	RHD	Coupe	Grey	Grey	Grey	2/10/49	Tate	H. Kinneau	
25	886	7186429	Not noted	K	RHD	2-Seater	Chassis	Chassis	Chassis	16/12/48	Portugal		
25, 82, 233, 235, 695	887	7206871	KLY 15	M	LHD	Coupe	Silver Grey	Grey	Grey	5/4/49	U.S.A.	John W. Forbes	
25, 116, 171, 298, 301, 304, 310, 462, 463, 464, 680	888	20074	KXC 170	J2	RHD	2-Seater	Red	Red	Not noted	23/3/51	Allard Motor Co.	D. F. Annable	S. H. A. Prototype J2. Record on page 25 shows engine number 7202936 crossed out, as car had experimental Cadillac engine installed
25, 169, 252, 268	889	7206771	KLO 126	M	RHD	Coupe	Blue	Grey	Grey	21/2/49	Adlards	A. C. Wild	
25, 163, 173, 247, 308, 339, 348	890	7200864	KLL 577	M	RHD	Coupe	Maroon	Maroon	Beige	2/11/49	Dagenham Motors (Gollys Garage)	Dr. P. W. Nathan	
25, 194, 310, 319, 335	891	7206796	MUA 241	M	RHD	Coupe	Maroon	Maroon	Beige	15/2/49	Tate (Brown & White)	T. H. White	
25, 194, 694	892	7207010	MUA 631	M	RHD	Coupe	Maroon	Maroon	Beige	2/10/49	Tate	H. Walker	
25, 200	893	7206838	Not noted	M	RHD	Coupe	Grey	Grey	Black	14/2/49	Frew	Edith May Davidson	
25, 197, 694	894	7207143	GGD 857	M	RHD	Coupe	Maroon	Red	Beige	14/2/49	George & Jobling (J. R. Alexander)	I. G. Craig	
25, 186, 256	895	7207122	JOL 85	M	RHD	Coupe	Maroon	Maroon	Beige	25/2/49	Bristol Street Motors	Lilian Clark	
25, 185	896	7207274	Not noted	M	RHD	Coupe	Blue	Blue	Blue	14/2/49	Mann Egerton (Wm. H. King)	D. R. Grey	
26, 194, 241	897	7207123	HWW 222	M	RHD	Coupe	Maroon	Red	Beige	25/2/49	Tate (Ernest Dews Ltd.)	H. W. H. Price	
26, 200, 313, 315, 332, 335, 342, 347, 359, 364	898	7207288	LGS 99	M	RHD	Coupe	Maroon	Red	Beige	28/2/49	Frew	Dr. Jessie Robinson	One record notes regn. GGS 99 on page 364 and CGS 99 on page 342
26, 173	899	7202148	Not noted	M	RHD	Coupe	Grey	Blue	Blue	22/2/49	Dagenham Motors (University Motors)	J. W. Glegg	

Page References	Chassis	Original Engine Number	UK Registration	Type	LHD?	Body Style	Original Colour	Original Interior	Original Hood	Original Delivery	Allocation	First Customer	Remarks

CHASSIS NUMBER PAGE REFERENCE KEY: Allocation Books (pages 1-77), Record Cards (pages 78-167), Warranty Book (pages 168-201), Service Records (pages 202-393)

Page References	Chassis	Original Engine Number	UK Registration	Type	LHD?	Body Style	Original Colour	Original Interior	Original Hood	Original Delivery	Allocation	First Customer	Remarks
26, 194	900	7207110	Not noted	M	RHD	Coupe	Blue	Blue	Blue	3/8/49	Tate	Not noted	
26, 194, 329, 694	901	7207207	GKY 832	M	RHD	Coupe	Maroon	Maroon	Beige	3/9/49	Tate (Brown & White)	G. Ramsden	
26, 81	902	7207805	Not noted	L	RHD	Tourer	Red	Red	Beige	21/4/49	Kenya (Engineering & Industrial Exports Ltd.)	C. G. Fane	
26, 174, 275, 346	903	7207826	LGT 175	L	RHD	Tourer	Blue	Grey	Beige	14/11/49	Dagenham Motors (Kevill Davies)	E. D. Graham	Black hood also noted
26, 81	904	7207818	Not noted	L	LHD	Tourer	Maroon	Red	Beige	12/8/49	Venezuela	L. Bockh & Cia	Colour and delivery differ on record card refer page 81
26, 170, 263, 265, 268, 271, 272, 280, 281, 285, 288, 291, 292, 294, 302	905	7207822	KYP 636	L	RHD	Tourer	Maroon	Red	Beige	24/2/50	Adlards	T. D. Adkin	
26	906	Not used	Not used	Not used	Not used	Not used	Not used	Not used	Not used	Not used	Not used		
26	907	Not used	Not used	Not used	Not used	Not used	Not used	Not used	Not used	Not used	Not used		
26	908	Not used	Not used	Not used	Not used	Not used	Not used	Not used	Not used	Not used	Not used		
26	909	Not used	Not used	Not used	Not used	Not used	Not used	Not used	Not used	Not used	Not used		
26	910	Not used	Not used	Not used	Not used	Not used	Not used	Not used	Not used	Not used	Not used		
26	911	Not used	Not used	Not used	Not used	Not used	Not used	Not used	Not used	Not used	Not used		
26	912	Not used	Not used	Not used	Not used	Not used	Not used	Not used	Not used	Not used	Not used		
26	913	Not used	Not used	Not used	Not used	Not used	Not used	Not used	Not used	Not used	Not used		
26	914	Not used	Not used	Not used	Not used	Not used	Not used	Not used	Not used	Not used	Not used		
26	915	Not used	Not used	Not used	Not used	Not used	Not used	Not used	Not used	Not used	Not used		
26	916	Not used	Not used	Not used	Not used	Not used	Not used	Not used	Not used	Not used	Not used		
26	917	Not used	Not used	Not used	Not used	Not used	Not used	Not used	Not used	Not used	Not used		
26	918	Not used	Not used	Not used	Not used	Not used	Not used	Not used	Not used	Not used	Not used		
26, 223, 226	919	Not used	Not used	Not used	Not used	Not used	Not used	Not used	Not used	Not used	Not used		
26	920	Not used	Not used	Not used	Not used	Not used	Not used	Not used	Not used	Not used	Not used		
26	921	Not used	Not used	Not used	Not used	Not used	Not used	Not used	Not used	Not used	Not used		

Page References	Chassis	Original Engine Number	UK Registration	Type	LHD?	Body Style	Original Colour	Original Interior	Original Hood	Original Delivery	Allocation	First Customer	Remarks
								CHASSIS NUMBER PAGE REFERENCE KEY: Allocation Books (pages 1-77), Record Cards (pages 78-167), Warranty Book (pages 168-201), Service Records (pages 202-393)					
26	922	Not used	Not used	Not used	Not used	Not used	Not used	Not used	Not used	Not used	Not used		
26	923	Not used	Not used	Not used	Not used	Not used	Not used	Not used	Not used	Not used	Not used		
26	924	Not used	Not used	Not used	Not used	Not used	Not used	Not used	Not used	Not used	Not used		
26	925	Not used	Not used	Not used	Not used	Not used	Not used	Not used	Not used	Not used	Not used		
26	926	Not used	Not used	Not used	Not used	Not used	Not used	Not used	Not used	Not used	Not used		
26	927	Not used	Not used	Not used	Not used	Not used	Not used	Not used	Not used	Not used	Not used		
26	928	Not used	Not used	Not used	Not used	Not used	Not used	Not used	Not used	Not used	Not used		
27	929	Not used	Not used	Not used	Not used	Not used	Not used	Not used	Not used	Not used	Not used		
27	930	Not used	Not used	Not used	Not used	Not used	Not used	Not used	Not used	Not used	Not used		
27	931	Not used	Not used	Not used	Not used	Not used	Not used	Not used	Not used	Not used	Not used		
27	932	Not used	Not used	Not used	Not used	Not used	Not used	Not used	Not used	Not used	Not used		
27	933	Not used	Not used	Not used	Not used	Not used	Not used	Not used	Not used	Not used	Not used		
27	934	Not used	Not used	Not used	Not used	Not used	Not used	Not used	Not used	Not used	Not used		
27	935	Not used	Not used	Not used	Not used	Not used	Not used	Not used	Not used	Not used	Not used		
27	936	Not used	Not used	Not used	Not used	Not used	Not used	Not used	Not used	Not used	Not used		
27	937	Not used	Not used	Not used	Not used	Not used	Not used	Not used	Not used	Not used	Not used		
27	938	Not used	Not used	Not used	Not used	Not used	Not used	Not used	Not used	Not used	Not used		
27	939	Not used	Not used	Not used	Not used	Not used	Not used	Not used	Not used	Not used	Not used		
27	940	Not used	Not used	Not used	Not used	Not used	Not used	Not used	Not used	Not used	Not used		
27	941	Not used	Not used	Not used	Not used	Not used	Not used	Not used	Not used	Not used	Not used		
27	942	Not used	Not used	Not used	Not used	Not used	Not used	Not used	Not used	Not used	Not used		
27	943	Not used	Not used	Not used	Not used	Not used	Not used	Not used	Not used	Not used	Not used		
27	944	Not used	Not used	Not used	Not used	Not used	Not used	Not used	Not used	Not used	Not used		

Page References	Chassis	Original Engine Number	UK Registration	Type	LHD?	Body Style	Original Colour	Original Interior	Original Hood	Original Delivery	Allocation	First Customer	Remarks

CHASSIS NUMBER PAGE REFERENCE KEY: Allocation Books (pages 1-77), Record Cards (pages 78-167), Warranty Book (pages 168-201), Service Records (pages 202-393)

Page References	Chassis	Original Engine Number	UK Registration	Type	LHD?	Body Style	Original Colour	Original Interior	Original Hood	Original Delivery	Allocation	First Customer	Remarks
27	945	Not used	Not used	Not used	Not used	Not used	Not used	Not used	Not used	Not used	Not used		
27	946	Not used	Not used	Not used	Not used	Not used	Not used	Not used	Not used	Not used	Not used		
27	947	Not used	Not used	Not used	Not used	Not used	Not used	Not used	Not used	Not used	Not used		
27	948	Not used	Not used	Not used	Not used	Not used	Not used	Not used	Not used	Not used	Not used		
27, 213	949	Not used	Not used	Not used	Not used	Not used	Not used	Not used	Not used	Not used	Not used		
27	950	Not used	Not used	Not used	Not used	Not used	Not used	Not used	Not used	Not used	Not used		
27	951	Not used	Not used	Not used	Not used	Not used	Not used	Not used	Not used	Not used	Not used		
27	952	Not used	Not used	Not used	Not used	Not used	Not used	Not used	Not used	Not used	Not used		
27	953	Not used	Not used	Not used	Not used	Not used	Not used	Not used	Not used	Not used	Not used		
27	954	Not used	Not used	Not used	Not used	Not used	Not used	Not used	Not used	Not used	Not used		
27	955	Not used	Not used	Not used	Not used	Not used	Not used	Not used	Not used	Not used	Not used		
27	956	Not used	Not used	Not used	Not used	Not used	Not used	Not used	Not used	Not used	Not used		
27	957	Not used	Not used	Not used	Not used	Not used	Not used	Not used	Not used	Not used	Not used		
27	958	Not used	Not used	Not used	Not used	Not used	Not used	Not used	Not used	Not used	Not used		
27	959	Not used	Not used	Not used	Not used	Not used	Not used	Not used	Not used	Not used	Not used		
27	960	Not used	Not used	Not used	Not used	Not used	Not used	Not used	Not used	Not used	Not used		
28	961	Not used	Not used	Not used	Not used	Not used	Not used	Not used	Not used	Not used	Not used		
28	962	Not used	Not used	Not used	Not used	Not used	Not used	Not used	Not used	Not used	Not used		
28	963	Not used	Not used	Not used	Not used	Not used	Not used	Not used	Not used	Not used	Not used		
28	964	Not used	Not used	Not used	Not used	Not used	Not used	Not used	Not used	Not used	Not used		
28	965	Not used	Not used	Not used	Not used	Not used	Not used	Not used	Not used	Not used	Not used		
28	966	Not used	Not used	Not used	Not used	Not used	Not used	Not used	Not used	Not used	Not used		
28	967	Not used	Not used	Not used	Not used	Not used	Not used	Not used	Not used	Not used	Not used		

•ALLARD•

Page References	Chassis	Original Engine Number	UK Registration	Type	LHD?	Body Style	Original Colour	Original Interior	Original Hood	Original Delivery	Allocation	First Customer	Remarks
		CHASSIS NUMBER PAGE REFERENCE KEY: Allocation Books (pages 1-77), Record Cards (pages 78-167), Warranty Book (pages 168-201), Service Records (pages 202-393)											
28	968	Not used	Not used	Not used	Not used	Not used	Not used	Not used	Not used	Not used	Not used		
28	969	Not used	Not used	Not used	Not used	Not used	Not used	Not used	Not used	Not used	Not used		
28	970	Not used	Not used	Not used	Not used	Not used	Not used	Not used	Not used	Not used	Not used		
28	971	Not used	Not used	Not used	Not used	Not used	Not used	Not used	Not used	Not used	Not used		
28	972	Not used	Not used	Not used	Not used	Not used	Not used	Not used	Not used	Not used	Not used		
28	973	Not used	Not used	Not used	Not used	Not used	Not used	Not used	Not used	Not used	Not used		
28, 745	974	Not used	Not used	Not used	Not used	Not used	Not used	Not used	Not used	Not used	Not used		
28	975	Not used	Not used	Not used	Not used	Not used	Not used	Not used	Not used	Not used	Not used		
28	976	Not used	Not used	Not used	Not used	Not used	Not used	Not used	Not used	Not used	Not used		
28	977	Not used	Not used	Not used	Not used	Not used	Not used	Not used	Not used	Not used	Not used		
28	978	Not used	Not used	Not used	Not used	Not used	Not used	Not used	Not used	Not used	Not used		
28	979	Not used	Not used	Not used	Not used	Not used	Not used	Not used	Not used	Not used	Not used		
28	980	Not used	Not used	Not used	Not used	Not used	Not used	Not used	Not used	Not used	Not used		
28	981	Not used	Not used	Not used	Not used	Not used	Not used	Not used	Not used	Not used	Not used		
28	982	Not used	Not used	Not used	Not used	Not used	Not used	Not used	Not used	Not used	Not used		
28	983	Not used	Not used	Not used	Not used	Not used	Not used	Not used	Not used	Not used	Not used		
28	984	Not used	Not used	Not used	Not used	Not used	Not used	Not used	Not used	Not used	Not used		
28	985	Not used	Not used	Not used	Not used	Not used	Not used	Not used	Not used	Not used	Not used		
28	986	Not used	Not used	Not used	Not used	Not used	Not used	Not used	Not used	Not used	Not used		
28	987	Not used	Not used	Not used	Not used	Not used	Not used	Not used	Not used	Not used	Not used		
28	988	Not used	Not used	Not used	Not used	Not used	Not used	Not used	Not used	Not used	Not used		
28	989	Not used	Not used	Not used	Not used	Not used	Not used	Not used	Not used	Not used	Not used		
28	990	Not used	Not used	Not used	Not used	Not used	Not used	Not used	Not used	Not used	Not used		

Page References	Chassis	Original Engine Number	UK Registration	Type	LHD?	Body Style	Original Colour	Original Interior	Original Hood	Original Delivery	Allocation	First Customer	Remarks
						CHASSIS NUMBER PAGE REFERENCE KEY: Allocation Books (pages 1-77), Record Cards (pages 78-167), Warranty Book (pages 168-201), Service Records (pages 202-393)							
28	991	Not used	Not used	Not used	Not used	Not used	Not used	Not used	Not used	Not used	Not used		
28	992	Not used	Not used	Not used	Not used	Not used	Not used	Not used	Not used	Not used	Not used		
28	993	Not used	Not used	Not used	Not used	Not used	Not used	Not used	Not used	Not used	Not used		
29	994	Not used	Not used	Not used	Not used	Not used	Not used	Not used	Not used	Not used	Not used		
29	995	Not used	Not used	Not used	Not used	Not used	Not used	Not used	Not used	Not used	Not used		
29	996	Not used	Not used	Not used	Not used	Not used	Not used	Not used	Not used	Not used	Not used		
29	997	Not used	Not used	Not used	Not used	Not used	Not used	Not used	Not used	Not used	Not used		
29	998	Not used	Not used	Not used	Not used	Not used	Not used	Not used	Not used	Not used	Not used		
29	999	Not used	Not used	Not used	Not used	Not used	Not used	Not used	Not used	Not used	Not used		
29, 194, 696	1000	7207230	Not noted	M	RHD	Coupe	Blue	Blue	Blue	3/7/49	Tate	P. M. G. Thorpe	
29, 173, 229, 234, 237, 241, 244, 249, 257, 259, 262, 264, 268, 269, 270	1001	7207231	KLL 999	M	RHD	Coupe	Blue	Blue	Blue	3/5/49	Dagenham Motors (H. C. Paul)	J. Greenhalgh	
29, 178, 281	1002	7207111	HHA 478	M	RHD	Coupe	Grey	Blue	Grey	3/11/49	English (E. W. Cox & Co.)	Dr. H. D. White	
29, 169, 233, 283, 286, 323, 344	1003	7207144	KLO 127	M	RHD	Coupe	Grey	Blue	Blue	3/9/49	Adlards (W. Shaker)		Possible KLO 127 on page 344
29, 178, 696	1004	7207582	FOW 732	M	RHD	Coupe	Blue	Grey	Blue	3/7/49	English (South Hants Motor Co.)	D. J. Philipson	
29, 169, 226, 229, 233, 238, 242, 248, 258, 274, 279, 288, 291, 294, 315, 329, 333, 375	1005	7207734	KLL 736	M	RHD	Coupe	Black	Grey	Black	3/2/49	Adlards (L. A. Mitchell)	D. E. Godfery	Page 375 shows 974 CPL
29, 169	1006	7207750	Not noted	M	RHD	Coupe	Blue	Blue	Blue	3/7/49	Adlards (Hartley & Midgley)	Not noted	
29, 169, 231, 243, 261, 266, 275, 276, 277, 285, 298, 313, 314, 326, 331, 341	1007	7207733	EPM 96	M	RHD	Coupe	Grey	Grey	Blue	3/5/49	Adlards	Not noted	
29, 200	1008	7207021	Not noted	M	RHD	Coupe	Grey	Grey	Black	3/11/49	Frew (D. McIntosh)	W. Lindsay Gillies	

Page References	Chassis	Original Engine Number	UK Registration	Type	LHD?	Body Style	Original Colour	Original Interior	Original Hood	Original Delivery	Allocation	First Customer	Remarks
29, 194, 258	1009	7207938	GDT 523	M	RHD	Coupe	Grey	Grey	Grey	3/11/49	Tate (E. Claybourn)	J. H. Gousley	
29, 82, 227, 746	1010	7207779	KLP 819	M	RHD	Coupe	Grey	Blue	Blue	31/3/49	Kenya (Engineering & Industrial Exports Ltd.)	Capt. McBean	Delivery dates vary, record card says 29/03/49 for #1010
29, 184	1011	7207362	Not noted	M	RHD	Coupe	Grey	Grey	Blue	17/3/49	Furrows (Wrexham Motor Co.)	A. F. McIntyre	
29, 178	1012	7207297	Not noted	M	RHD	Coupe	Black	Grey	Black	21/3/49	English		
29, 173, 231, 233, 237, 243, 250, 254, 266, 267, 269, 278, 282, 285, 286, 290, 291, 294, 301, 311, 313, 315, 320, 329, 335, 342, 343, 747	1013	7207757	UMC 924 *	M	RHD	Coupe	Black	Maroon	Golden Brown	23/3/49	Dagenham Motors	J. P. Janurin	* Or regn. UMC 24. Refer to #1013 for apparent misallocation to #1030
29, 199, 301	1014	7207258	SY 9099	M	RHD	Coupe	Black	Red	Black	17/3/49	Alexanders	H. E. Gould	
29, 178, 694	1015	7206832	KLP 812	M	RHD	Coupe	Grey	Grey	Blue	23/3/49	English (Lee Motors)	S. A. Saver	
29, 169	1016	7209290	Not noted	M	RHD	Coupe	Grey	Maroon	Grey	29/3/49	Adlards	B. G. Clark	
29, 173	1017	7209271	Not noted	M	RHD	Coupe	Black	Brown	Brown	18/3/49	Dagenham Motors	Stanley Baker	
29, 82, 228, 746	1018	7209273	KLP 821	M	RHD	Coupe	Black	Maroon	Beige	26/3/49	Germany (British & Overseas Merchants)	Cole	Delivery dates vary, record card says 19/03/49 for #1018
29, 178, 333, 357, 363, 366, 694	1019	7209286	DFX 826	M	RHD	Coupe	Maroon	Red	Beige	21/3/49	English		
29, 169, 235, 247, 259, 319, 324, 333, 358, 381	1020	7207291	KLR 294	M	RHD	Coupe	Maroon	Maroon	Beige	18/3/49	Adlards (Phillips)	Not noted	
29, 173, 252, 272, 276, 284, 286, 306, 316, 324, 333, 342, 694	1021	7209281	KLO 196	M	RHD	Coupe	Maroon	Maroon	Beige	18/3/49	Dagenham Motors (Afford)	P. Smith	One record on page 252 says KLO 96
29, 169, 233, 339	1022	7209287	JUF 620	M	RHD	Coupe	Maroon	Maroon	Beige	23/3/49	Adlards (Hartley & Midgley)	R. A. Jenner	
29, 186, 694	1023	7209393	JOL 626	M	RHD	Coupe	Maroon	Maroon	Beige	21/3/49	Bristol Street Motors	M. J. Deeley	
29, 185	1024	7209269	Not noted	M	RHD	Coupe	Blue	Blue	Blue	23/3/49	Mann Egerton	A. R. Mann	
29, 186, 696	1025	7209387	Not noted	M	RHD	Coupe	Blue	Blue	Blue	22/3/49	Bristol Street Motors	J. W. Bond	
30, 191	1026	7209399	Not noted	M	RHD	Coupe	Blue	Red	Blue	22/3/49	Nunn (S. Lever)	J. Bardsley	
30, 189, 289, 362, 368, 746	1027	7209272	KNN 879	M	RHD	Coupe	Blue	Blue	Blue	28/3/49	Universal (Standhill Garage)	Midland Model Dairy	Page 368 shows the registration as KNN 897. Page 376 could be 1097 or 1027
30, 82	1028	7209388	Not noted	M	RHD	Coupe	Cream	Red	Beige	29/3/49	Kenya	Engineering & Industrial Exports Ltd.	

CHASSIS NUMBER PAGE REFERENCE KEY: Allocation Books (pages 1-77), Record Cards (pages 78-167), Warranty Book (pages 168-201), Service Records (pages 202-393)

Page References	Chassis	Original Engine Number	UK Registration	Type	LHD?	Body Style	Original Colour	Original Interior	Original Hood	Original Delivery	Allocation	First Customer	Remarks
						CHASSIS NUMBER PAGE REFERENCE KEY: Allocation Books (pages 1-77), Record Cards (pages 78-167), Warranty Book (pages 168-201), Service Records (pages 202-393)							
30, 199, 228, 229, 281, 695	1029	7209396	KLP 820	M	RHD	Coupe	Grey	Red	Grey	29/3/49	Alexanders (H. C. Hutchison)	W. B. Black	Page 228 refers to car as unregistered
30, 169, 250, 313, 329, 694	1030	7207815	LKT 645	M	RHD	Coupe	Grey	Blue	Grey	29/3/49	Adlards (Peacocks)	Not noted	
30, 191, 229	1031	7206840	Not noted	M	RHD	Coupe	Blue	Blue	Blue	4/9/49	Nunn	R. Halt	Page 229 refers to car as unregistered
30, 169, 231, 232, 238, 242, 244, 249, 259, 301, 337, 340, 380	1032	7207281	NPA 871	M	RHD	Coupe	Grey	Grey	Blue	4/1/49	Adlards (Mears Bros)	W. G. Broomfield	
30, 181	1033	7209682	Not noted	M	RHD	Coupe	Grey	Grey	Grey	31/3/49	Hartwells	F. C. Hancock	
30, 186, 695	1034	7209609	HWD 248	M	RHD	Coupe	Grey	Grey	Blue	4/2/49	Bristol Street Motors (Chambers of Sutton)	J. Wickes	
30, 189, 247	1035	7207616	CJL 795	M	RHD	Coupe	Black	Maroon	Beige	30/3/49	Universal (Audin Munks)	Noel Jaques	
30, 186	1036	7209611	Not noted	M	RHD	Coupe	Black	Maroon	Beige	4/11/49	Bristol Street Motors (Central Motors)	Lord Allerton	
30, 200, 318, 356, 359, 361	1037	7209615	SE 6997	M	RHD	Coupe	Black	Blue	Black	4/5/49	Frew (Elgin Garage)	R. D. Christie	
30, 178	1038	7209747	Not noted	M	RHD	Coupe	Black	Blue	Black	4/4/49	English (G. Hartwells)	R. Cole	
30, 178, 695	1039	7209762	JRU 772	M	RHD	Coupe	Black	Maroon	Beige	13/4/49	English	F. Woolford	
30, 197, 365	1040	7209403	Not noted	M	RHD	Coupe	Maroon	Red	Maroon	4/8/49	George & Jobling	C. D. Moodie	
30, 186, 245, 252, 695	1041	7209743	HUY 140	M	RHD	Coupe	Maroon	Maroon	Beige	4/9/49	Bristol Street Motors	Miss B. N. Pullen	Page 252 says HDY 141 or HUY 141
30, 178	1042	7209744	Not noted	M	RHD	Coupe	Maroon	Red	Beige	4/5/49	English	Not noted	
30, 257, 258, 263	1043*	Not used	Not used	Not used	Not used	Not used	Not used	Not used	Not used	Not used	Not used		* Refer to 1013
30	1044	Not used	Not used	Not used	Not used	Not used	Not used	Not used	Not used	Not used	Not used		
30	1045	Not used	Not used	Not used	Not used	Not used	Not used	Not used	Not used	Not used	Not used		
30, 189, 286, 695	1046	7209760	KNN 919	M	RHD	Coupe	Maroon	Brown	Brown	13/4/49	Universal (Standhill Garage)	Midland Model Dairy	
30, 169, 249, 257, 291	1047	7209749	KLR 872	M	RHD	Coupe	Blue	Blue	Blue	14/4/49	Adlards (Hungerford Motors)		
30, 194, 253	1048	7207933	Not noted	M	RHD	. Coupe	Maroon	Red	Beige	20/4/49	Tate (E. Dews Ltd.)	J. F. Marriott Co. Ltd.	
30, 194	1049	7207882	Not noted	M	RHD	Coupe	Blue	Grey	Blue	19/7/49	Tate	W. Ward	
30, 173, 231, 234, 237, 239, 246, 262, 264, 284	1050	7209894	TML 804	M	RHD	Coupe	Blue	Grey	Blue	13/4/49	Dagenham Motors (Wembley Court Motors)	H. S. Lindsay	
30, 170, 240, 250, 298	1051	7209892	KUW 239	M	RHD	Coupe	Blue	Grey	Grey	7/7/49	Adlards (Peacocks)	B. S. Gordon	Page 240 refers to car as unregistered'

Page References	Chassis	Original Engine Number	UK Registration	Type	LHD?	Body Style	Original Colour	Original Interior	Original Hood	Original Delivery	Allocation	First Customer	Remarks
30, 181, 261, 265, 266, 270, 273, 286	1052	7209991	NJO 504	M	RHD	Coupe	Grey	Grey	Grey	21/4/49	Hartwells	D. Emmet	
30, 173, 264, 289, 371, 373	1053	7209941	QB 7202	M	RHD	Coupe	Blue	Blue	Blue	25/4/49	Dagenham Motors (Car Mart)	Major A. Graham	One later record notes regn. KLY 854 on pages 371 and 373
30, 189, 249, 305, 695	1054	7209897	LTV 218	M	RHD	Coupe	Grey	Blue	Blue	19/5/49	Universal (Standhill Garage)	J. W. Batt	
30, 200	1055	7209955	Not noted	M	RHD	Coupe	Grey	Grey	Blue	5/6/49	Frew (P. S. Nicholson (Forres) Ltd.)	W. Scott	
30, 169, 238, 295, 301, 696	1056	7210550	KPX 11	M	RHD	Coupe	Maroon	Red	Beige	14/5/49	Adlards (D. Rowe)	P. J. Sainsbury	
30, 178	1057	7210568	Not noted	M	RHD	Coupe	Grey	Grey	Grey	5/6/49	English (Pennington Cross Garage)	Dr. B. M. Thorton	
31, 163, 173, 232, 236, 244, 246, 256, 261, 277, 289, 294, 327, 340, 348, 372, 386	1058	7210579	UMC 938	M	RHD	Coupe	Black	Grey	Black	28/4/49	Dagenham Motors	W. Toung Craig	Page 386 may say UHC 938
31, 186, 266, 274, 285, 301, 695	1059	7210551	JON 971	M	RHD	Coupe	Maroon	Red	Beige	5/4/49	Bristol Street Motors	J. C. McWhirter	
31, 197	1060	7210523	Not noted	M	RHD	Coupe	Black	Brown	Brown	27/4/49	George & Jobling (Cameron & Campbell)	I. D. K. Stuart	
31, 197	1061	7210555	Not noted	M	RHD	Coupe	Black	Brown	Brown	5/9/49	George & Jobling (J. Martin Ltd.)	South British Locomotive Ltd.	
31, 169, 240, 241, 259, 283	1062	7210565	KLY 14	M	RHD	Coupe	Grey	Grey	Grey	5/4/49	Adlards	Capt. C. Freen	
31, 200	1063	7210570	Not noted	M	RHD	Coupe	Black	Red	Black	29/4/49	Frew	Mrs G. H. Cook	
31, 181, 241, 272, 288	1064	7210700	FBL 687	M	RHD	Coupe	Maroon	Red	Beige	26/5/49	Hartwells (Stevensons Auto Sales)	J. S. Pewy	
31, 186, 748	1065	7210747	Not noted	M	RHD	Coupe	Black	Red	Beige	29/4/49	Bristol Street Motors	P. B. Hudsons & Son	Might be 1068
31, 173, 251, 267, 276, 282, 287, 294, 298, 304, 306, 316, 320, 328, 329, 330, 337, 338, 343, 696	1066	7210708	UMC 538	M	RHD	Coupe	Maroon	Red	Beige	23/5/49	Dagenham Motors	Eric Coates	
31, 186, 238	1067	7210710	KPX 1	M	RHD	Coupe	Blue	Blue	Beige	5/9/49	Bristol Street Motors	C. Mould	Entry on page 369 is showing KPX 1 as 1069
31, 173, 237, 242, 272, 346, 348, 359, 363, 748	1068	7210744	UMD 798	M	RHD	Coupe	Blue	Blue	Blue	6/1/49	Dagenham Motors	H. F. Robinson	Might be 1065
31, 169, 369, 695, 748	1069	7210821	YTL 940	M	RHD	Coupe	Maroon	Maroon	Beige	16/5/49	Adlards (D. Rowe)	W. G. Lewis	Page 369 shows 1069 as regn. KPX 1

CHASSIS NUMBER PAGE REFERENCE KEY: Allocation Books (pages 1-77), Record Cards (pages 78-167), Warranty Book (pages 168-201), Service Records (pages 202-393)

Page References	Chassis	Original Engine Number	UK Registration	Type	LHD?	Body Style	Original Colour	Original Interior	Original Hood	Original Delivery	Allocation	First Customer	Remarks
							CHASSIS NUMBER PAGE REFERENCE KEY: Allocation Books (pages 1-77), Record Cards (pages 78-167), Warranty Book (pages 168-201), Service Records (pages 202-393)						
31, 163, 186, 358, 375, 378, 384	1070	7210933	JOP 851	M	RHD	Coupe	Blue	Grey	Grey	22/6/49	Bristol Street Motors	Dr. C. Edgar Biggers	One record notes regn. JPO 851 and another JOP 857 (page 384)
31, 169, 252, 254, 265, 290, 309, 316	1071	7210988	KLY 24	M	RHD	Coupe	Blue	Blue	Grey	19/5/49	Adlards	Mr Jack Walker	
31, 170, 282, 318, 324, 341, 382, 695	1072	7210925	KUW 567	M	RHD	Coupe	Blue	Blue	Blue	Not noted	Adlards		Mr Holland. Used by Adlards
31, 181, 279	1073	7210931	FMO 333	M	RHD	Coupe	Grey	Grey	Grey	6/11/49	Hartwells (Wheelers Ltd.)	F. J. Reynolds Ltd.	
31, 170, 268, 300, 311, 316, 321, 327, 331, 335, 345	1074	7210937	EPM 890	M	RHD	Coupe	Grey	Grey	Grey	16/6/49	Adlards (Phillips)	P. C. Chorley	Registration is EPM 90 on page 345
31, 169, 695	1075	7210934	NPB 977	M	RHD	Coupe	Grey	Red	Grey	18/5/49	Adlards (Coombs)		
31, 83, 749	1076	7210698	Not noted	M	LHD	Coupe	Light Blue	Blue	Blue	29/4/49	Uruguay	M. Salem & Cia	Delivery dates vary, record card says 30/03/49 for #1076
31, 83	1077	7210709	Not noted	M	RHD	Coupe	Light Blue	Blue	Blue	29/4/49	Uruguay	M. Salem & Cia	Colours differ
31, 173, 246, 254, 282	1078	7210935	UMD 681	M	RHD	Coupe	Grey	Blue	Grey	21/6/49	Dagenham Motors	D. L. Perena	Page 282 shows UMD 680
31, 199	1079	7210811	Not noted	M	RHD	Coupe	Grey	Red	Grey	26/5/49	Alexanders (D. Harrison)	P. Laing	
31, 183, 253, 341, 344	1080	7210823	FWN 689	M	RHD	Coupe	Black	Red	Black	27/5/49	Harris	Ivor L Roberts	
31, 169, 247, 696	1081	7210810	NPD 482	M	RHD	Coupe	Black	Brown	Black	14/6/49	Adlards (Coombs)	C. Jenkinson	
31, 197	1082	7212057	Not noted	M	RHD	Coupe	Black	Brown	Brown	6/11/49	George & Jobling (Park Auto Co.)	W. Burns (Glasg	
31, 197, 344	1083	7212029	LXD 525	M	RHD	Coupe	Black	Red	Black	6/1/49	George & Jobling (Cameron & Campbell)	J. R. Anderson	
31, 173, 238, 255, 261	1084	7212070	KLU 7	M	RHD	Coupe	Grey	Grey	Blue	30/5/49	Dagenham Motors (Afford & Sons)	D. J. Pierce	
31, 189, 256	1085	7212103	BEE 277	M	RHD	Coupe	Grey	Blue	Black	30/5/49	Universal (Lincs Motor Co.)	Mr Phillips	(Lincolnshire Motor Co.)
31, 83, 252	1086	7212059	SV 1655	M	RHD	Coupe	Black	Grey	Grey	21/6/49	Malaya (Kyle Palmer & Co.)	James L. Ross	
31, 189, 284, 288, 342, 353, 383, 385, 703	1087	7212145	SRE 861	M	RHD	Coupe	Black	Grey	Black	15/7/49	Universal	Not noted	
31, 173, 250, 296	1088	7210924	UMD 460	M	RHD	Coupe	Maroon	Red	Beige	16/6/49	Dagenham Motors	K. A. Pearce	
31, 173, 247, 256, 356, 357, 749	1089	7212094	UMD 816	M	RHD	Coupe	Maroon	Red	Beige	6/10/49	Dagenham Motors	R. B. Walpole	Two records, pages 356 and 357, note regn. SRE 801 (1089)
32, 186	1090	7210930	Not noted	M	RHD	Coupe	Maroon	Maroon	Beige	7/8/49	Bristol Street Motors	J. Godrich	
32, 177, 300, 311, 314	1091	7212013	OVW 750	M	RHD	Coupe	Grey	Grey	Grey	7/11/49	Gould (Wag Bennett & Sons)	B. Wyers	

Page References	Chassis	Original Engine Number	UK Registration	Type	LHD?	Body Style	Original Colour	Original Interior	Original Hood	Original Delivery	Allocation	First Customer	Remarks
							CHASSIS NUMBER PAGE REFERENCE KEY: Allocation Books (pages 1-77), Record Cards (pages 78-167), Warranty Book (pages 168-201), Service Records (pages 202-393)							
32, 177, 248	1092	7212020	OVW 625	M	RHD	Coupe	Grey	Red	Grey	7/7/49	Gould (Wag Bennett & Sons)	Deil Stephans	
32, 173, 241, 243, 305, 324	1093	7212113	UMD 465	M	RHD	Coupe	Grey	Blue	Blue	22/7/49	Dagenham Motors	Mjr W. H. P. Buryeat	Page 241 refers to car as unregistered
32, 191	1094	7212331	Not noted	M	RHD	Coupe	Black	Red	Black	7/5/49	Nunn (Cliff Holden Motors)	Ashworths Ltd.	
32, 194	1095	7212354	Not noted	M	RHD	Coupe	Black	Brown	Black	8/4/49	Tate	P. Warrington	
32, 173, 241, 277	1096	7212352	LTA 300	M	RHD	Coupe	Black	Red	Black	19/7/49	Dagenham Motors	Rev. Sir A. P. Ferguson	Page 241 refers to car as unregistered
32, 265, 376, 746	1097	25539 132	KUC 40	M	RHD	Coupe	Grey	Grey	Grey	25/6/49	Allard		
32, 191	1098	7212297	Not noted	M	RHD	Coupe	Maroon	Red	Beige	3/2/49	Nunn (Seymore Motors Ltd.)	Not noted	
32, 194	1099	7212353	Not noted	M	RHD	Coupe	Maroon	Maroon	Beige	8/9/49	Tate (through Furrows)	C. S. Walley & Co. Ltd.	
32, 170, 251, 257, 261, 271, 274, 286, 302, 314, 320, 334, 337	1100	7212112	KXF 819	M	RHD	Coupe	Grey	Grey	Blue	28/9/49	Adlards	Oscar King Hardy	
32, 184	1101	18F-7209282	Not noted	M	RHD	Coupe	Chassis only	Chassis only	Chassis only	25/6/49	Furrows	Not noted	Warranty Book notes body not yet completed
32, 163, 164, 197, 321, 361, 362	1102	7212148	GYS 513	M	RHD	Coupe	Grey	Blue	Blue	19/8/49	George & Jobling (Queens Garage)	A. S. Gardiner	
32, 197	1500	7207588	Not noted	P	RHD	Saloon	Green	Orange	Not applicable	24/10/49	George & Jobling	James Anderson	
32, 196, 276	1501	7212295	DHH 556	P	RHD	Saloon	Green	Grange	Not applicable	21/10/49	Patterson	Not noted	
32, 178, 264, 468	1502	7212115	Not noted	P	RHD	Saloon	Green	Orange	Not applicable	16/9/49	English (Lee Motors)	Mrs K. M. Copley	
32, 184	1503	7212114	Not noted	P	RHD	Saloon	Black	Brown	Not applicable	21/9/49	Furrows	Dr. G. Jerome	(Dr. Jerome)
32, 191, 352, 355, 358, 363, 369, 373, 380, 392	1504	7212336	KNF 599	P	RHD	Saloon	Green	Orange	Not applicable	23/9/49	Nunn (Didsbury Garages Ltd.)	M. Salen & Sons	
32, 186	1505	7200691	Not noted	P	RHD	Saloon	Green	Orange	Not applicable	10/11/49	Bristol Street Motors	W. H. Smartale	
32, 174, 259, 289, 294, 308, 354, 367, 369, 378	1506	7212146	UMX 875	P	RHD	Saloon	Green	Orange	Not applicable	10/4/49	Dagenham Motors	Mrs C. M. Gleadow	Struck off Adlards Warranty record
32, 197, 292	1507	7212107	HGA 833	P	RHD	Saloon	Ming Blue	Red	Not applicable	12/8/49	George & Jobling (Cameron & Campbell)	J. Findlary	
32, 194, 288	1508	7212076	CHE 940	P	RHD	Saloon	Green	Orange	Not applicable	10/11/49	Tate (Reynolds Ltd.)	G. B. Creighton	
32, 186	1509	7200761	Not noted	P	RHD	Saloon	Green	Orange	Not applicable	26/10/49	Bristol Street Motors	F. H. Pagett	

Page References	Chassis	Original Engine Number	UK Registration	Type	LHD?	Body Style	Original Colour	Original Interior	Original Hood	Original Delivery	Allocation	First Customer	Remarks
		CHASSIS NUMBER PAGE REFERENCE KEY: Allocation Books (pages 1-77), Record Cards (pages 78-167), Warranty Book (pages 168-201), Service Records (pages 202-393)											
32, 81	1510	5345/33	Not noted	L	LHD	Tourer	Red	Red	Beige	26/5/50	U.S.A. (George Joseph Mercantile Co.)	E. V. Shugart	Colour differs on record card refer page 81
32, 227, 325, 695	1511	R571372P	HXV 210	M	RHD	Coupe	Maroon	Not noted	Not noted	Not noted	Not noted		
32, 124, 680	1512	D198	Not noted	J	LHD	2-Seater	Bug. Blue	Blue	Not noted	30/1/50	Uruguay (Emelas & Cia Limitada)	Oscar Mario Gonzalez	Mercury engine
32, 110, 680	1513	3953/52	Not noted	J	LHD	2-Seater	Silver	Red	Not noted	3/2/50	U.S.A.	Bell Auto Parts	
32, 110, 680	1514	Less engine	Not noted	J	LHD	2-Seater	Silver	Red	Not noted	13/10/49	U.S.A. (Tom Cole)	Jon Perona	Perona-Night Club Proprietor
32, 110, 462, 463, 680	1515	Less engine	KUC 31	J	LHD	2-Seater	Silver	Red	Not noted	24/8/49	U.S.A. (Ardun Engineering Co.)	Robert J. Wilder	Ex-Demonstrator for Zora Arkus-Duntov
32, 177, 697	1516	7193088	CCF 768	P	RHD	Saloon	Grey	Blue	Not applicable	11/10/49	Gould (Cleats Ltd.)	J. G. Craig	
32, 184, 255, 281, 312, 383, 385, 697	1517	7217525	KKF 752	P	RHD	Saloon	Grey	Grey	Not applicable	26/11/49	Furrows (Betws-y-coed Motor Service)	B. Smith	Looks like KNF both on pages 383 and 385
32, 170	1518	7215392	Not noted	P	RHD	Saloon	Black	Maroon	Not applicable	25/11/49	Adlards (Gardiners)	Gardiners	
32, 170	1519	7217522	Not noted	P	RHD	Saloon	Black	Maroon	Not applicable	11/9/49	Adlards (Buttening)	The Bullerley Co. Ltd.	
32, 183, 259, 273, 346	1520	7217520	GUH 726	P	RHD	Saloon	Black	Brown	Not applicable	26/11/49	Harris	E. Robinson	Page 273 may say EUH 726
32, 173	1521	7209742	Not noted	M	RHD	Coupe	BLue	BLue	Blue	30/8/49	Dagenham Motors (Dunham & Haines)	M. Guissin	
33, 170, 251, 254, 256, 267, 268, 272, 273, 280, 284, 287, 291, 296, 302, 310, 317, 332, 334, 336, 338	1522	7210822	KXK 865	M	RHD	Coupe	Maroon	Maroon	Beige	10/1/49	Adlards (Coopers)	Harry Wm. Maxwell Felling	
33, 170, 288, 295, 299, 300, 307, 315, 319, 320, 321, 324, 330, 332, 343, 347	1523	7215400	KXK 714	M	RHD	Coupe	Grey	Grey	Blue	28/9/49	Adlards Coopers)	Not legible	
33, 170, 246, 251, 255, 297	1524	7215392	KXF 815	M	RHD	Coupe	Grey	Blue	Blue	20/9/49	Adlards (Gardiners)	Not noted	Once noted as regn. KXF 814 and page 246 refers to car as unregistered
33, 180, 253, 284	1525	7215388	KXF 820	M	RHD	Coupe	Maroon	Maroon	Beige	13/12/49	Hughes	New Central Garage	(L. G. Johnson)
33, 197	1526	7215399	Not noted	M	RHD	Coupe	Pale Beige	Off White	Not noted	12/8/49	George & Jobling (J. Martin Ltd.)	Mr N. K. Gordon	(Show model)
33, 191	1527	7215393	Not noted	M	RHD	Coupe	Black	Red	Maroon	9/8/49	Nunn (Union Garage Co. Ltd.)	E. J. Gaskill	
33, 174, 269	1528	7215512	UMV 360	M	RHD	Coupe	Grey	Grey	Grey	9/12/49	Dagenham Motors	B. E. Birdsall	

Page References	Chassis	Original Engine Number	UK Registration	Type	LHD?	Body Style	Original Colour	Original Interior	Original Hood	Original Delivery	Allocation	First Customer	Remarks
							CHASSIS NUMBER PAGE REFERENCE KEY: Allocation Books (pages 1-77), Record Cards (pages 78-167), Warranty Book (pages 168-201), Service Records (pages 202-393)							
33, 189	1529	7215524	Not noted	M	RHD	Coupe	Grey	Grey	Grey	20/9/49	Universal	J. Derner	
33, 191, 255, 259, 264, 276, 278, 282, 291, 297, 300	1530	7215521	KXM 943	M	RHD	Coupe	Blue	Blue	Black	10/7/49	Nunn	Dr. Hobson	
33, 174, 339	1531	7215523	UMX 874	M	RHD	Coupe	Blue	Blue	Blue	17/10/49	Dagenham Motors	D. P. F. Embleton	
33, 170, 249, 366	1532	7212357	EPN 603	M	RHD	Coupe	Grey	Blue	Blue	23/9/49	Adlards (Phillips)	F. I. Moore	Page 249 refers to the car as unregistered
33, 196	1533	7202305	Not noted	M	RHD	Coupe	Maroon	Maroon	Beige	13/10/49	Patterson	Not noted	(S. W. Wood)
33, 174, 261, 263, 274, 286, 339, 345, 347	1534	7217523	UMX 720	M	RHD	Coupe	Blue	Blue	Blue	29/10/49	Dagenham Motors	D. M. Campbell	Page 347 shows UMX 726
33	1535	7217529	Not noted	P	RHD	Saloon	Black	Brown	Not applicable	16/11/49	Nunn		
33, 196	1536	7217643	Not noted	P	RHD	Saloon	Grey	Grey	Not applicable	22/11/49	Patterson	W. G. A. Swan	
33, 178, 336	1537	7217637	DPR 650	P	RHD	Saloon	Black	Red	Not applicable	11/7/49	English (Dibben & Sons)	Mrs A. Foomer	
33, 174, 255, 257, 262, 265, 268, 269, 271, 274, 278, 281, 288, 291, 295, 305, 308, 313, 320, 324, 325, 326, 327, 334, 343, 347	1538	7217638	UMX 450	P	RHD	Saloon	Grey	Blue	Not applicable	12/2/49	Dagenham Motors	W. G. Broomfield	
33, 185	1539	7212149	Not noted	P	RHD	Saloon	Grey	Maroon	Not applicable	12/2/49	Mann Egerton	S. W. Burroughes	
33, 183, 284, 315, 320	1540	7202519	JAX 234	P	RHD	Saloon	Show Blue	Red	Not applicable	12/8/49	Harris	Gibbs Bros Garages	
33, 177	1541	7206959	Not noted	P	RHD	Saloon	Black	Red	Not applicable	12/10/49	Gould	Greaves & Thomas Ltd.	
33, 186	1542	7217705	GBC 845	P	RHD	Saloon	Maroon	Maroon	Not applicable	13/12/49	Bristol Street Motors (Central Motors)	C. E. Rudkin	
33, 201, 256, 366	1543	7217634	MZ 7880	P	RHD	Saloon	Black	Red	Not applicable	19/12/49	Hamilton	J. F. McCandless & Sons	Page 256 refers to the car as unregistered
33, 197	1544	7219356	Not noted	P	RHD	Saloon	Maroon	Red	Not applicable	1/5/50	George & Jobling	Mrs M. K. Wilson	
33, 83, 455	1545	E429845P	Not noted	M	LHD	Coupe	Red	Natural	Beige	1/7/50	U.S.A. (Grancor Automotive Specialists)	Lt. L. W. Leslie M. D	Offutt Air Base Nebraska
33, 85	1546	7228019	Not noted	K2	LHD	2-Seater	Blue	Blue	Not noted	20/3/50	U.S.A.	Moss	
33, 189, 271	1547	7219362	LHL 437	P	RHD	Saloon	Maroon	Maroon	Not applicable	30/12/49	Universal (Standhill Garage)	E. Hobson	

Page References	Chassis	Original Engine Number	UK Registration	Type	LHD?	Body Style	Original Colour	Original Interior	Original Hood	Original Delivery	Allocation	First Customer	Remarks

CHASSIS NUMBER PAGE REFERENCE KEY: Allocation Books (pages 1-77), Record Cards (pages 78-167), Warranty Book (pages 168-201), Service Records (pages 202-393)

Page References	Chassis	Original Engine Number	UK Registration	Type	LHD?	Body Style	Original Colour	Original Interior	Original Hood	Original Delivery	Allocation	First Customer	Remarks
33, 170, 257, 258, 261, 266, 270, 274, 275, 283, 288, 293, 297, 299, 308, 311, 313, 322, 324, 325, 327, 335, 357, 368, 380, 386, 389, 699	1548	7219361	KYM 6E9	P	RHD	Saloon	Black	Brown	Not applicable	23/12/49	Adlards (A. Mitchell)	Godfrey (Balham) Ltd.	
33, 178	1549	7219357	Not noted	P	RHD	Saloon	Black	Red	Not applicable	30/12/49	English	H. F. Adeney	
33, 98	1550	7222478	Not noted	P	LHD	Saloon	Black	Grey	Not applicable	1/6/50	Uruguay (Emelas & Cia Limitada)	Mr Irasi Delleon	On record card number is 7202313 (car 1584) and delivery was 19th Dec 1949
33, 174, 257, 268, 276, 291, 373	1551	7219363	KYM 774	P	RHD	Saloon	Maroon	Red	Not applicable	19/12/49	Dagenham Motors (Nash)	P. A. Gibb	
33, 174, 261, 269, 279, 296, 327, 368	1552	7219818	DVG 440	P	RHD	Saloon	Green	Brown	Not applicable	1/10/50	Dagenham Motors (Car Mart)	H. R. Chapman	
33, 180, 284	1553	7219819	KFJ 5E9	P	RHD	Saloon	Green	Orange	Not applicable	1/10/50	Hughes	A. J. Perry	
34, 186	1554	7221926	Not noted	P	RHD	Saloon	Green	Orange	Not applicable	16/1/50	Bristol Street Motors (Central Motors)	C. R. Curtis	
34, 110, 680	1555	LAK0107	Not noted	J	LHD	2-Seater	Silver	Red	Not noted	1/7/50	U.S.A.	Grancor Automotive Specialists	Delivery date differs to record card
34, 110, 680	1556	Less engine	Not noted	J	LHD	2-Seater	Red	Red	Not noted	21/3/50	U.S.A. (Havell Motors)	A. E. Goldschmidt	New York Show, Caddy mods, wire wheels, won Watkins Glen 9/23/1950
34, 116, 291, 680	1557	29411	CWG 12	J	RHD	2-Seater	Silver	Not noted	Not noted	28/2/50	Halstead Motor Co.	R. Clarkson	Mercury engine
34, 117, 187, 680	1558	3956/90/E283	KOF 999	J	RHD	2-Seater	Not noted	Not noted	Not noted	14/4/50	Bristol Street Motors	Mr S. C. Clark	
34, 117, 197, 318, 319, 320, 324, 326, 680	1559	3958/60	OS 7525	J	RHD	2-Seater	Red	Not noted	Not noted	15/4/50	George & Jobling (J. McHarnie Ltd.)	Mr J. S. Mort	Engine changed to ARDUN 2034
34, 98	1560	7219817	Not noted	P	LHD	Saloon	Grey	Maroon	Not applicable	23/1/50	Venezuela	L. Bockh & Cia	Export
34, 98	1561	7219823	Not noted	P	LHD	Saloon	Black	Red	Not applicable	17/1/50	Uruguay (Emelas & Cia Limitada)	Atilio Calo	Export
34, 98	1562	7219814	Not noted	P	LHD	Saloon	Black	Brown	Not applicable	17/1/50	Uruguay (Salem)	Emelas & Cia Limitada	
34, 184	1563	7221934	Not noted	P	RHD	Saloon	Green	Orange	Not applicable	26/1/50	Furrows	Francis Garages Ltd.	
34, 189	1564	7221924	Not noted	P	RHD	Saloon	Green	Orange	Not applicable	19/1/50	Universal (Standhill Garage)	W. Greg	
34, 191	1565	7221923	Not noted	P	RHD	Saloon	Grey	Grey	Not applicable	23/1/50	Nunn (A. W. Webb Ltd.)	E. C. Smallwood	
34, 196, 273	1566	7222123	KUP 904	P	RHD	Saloon	Grey	Grey	Not applicable	1/5/50	Patterson (H. Young (Motors) Ltd.)	J. G. Thompson	

Page References	Chassis	Original Engine Number	UK Registration	Type	LHD?	Body Style	Original Colour	Original Interior	Original Hood	Original Delivery	Allocation	First Customer	Remarks

CHASSIS NUMBER PAGE REFERENCE KEY: Allocation Books (pages 1-77), Record Cards (pages 78-167), Warranty Book (pages 168-201), Service Records (pages 202-393)

Page References	Chassis	Original Engine Number	UK Registration	Type	LHD?	Body Style	Original Colour	Original Interior	Original Hood	Original Delivery	Allocation	First Customer	Remarks
34, 177, 267, 697	1567	7222084	KYL 949	P	RHD	Saloon	Grey	Blue	Not applicable	19/1/50	Gould	G. L. Millington	
34, 194	1568	7222086	Not noted	P	RHD	Saloon	Grey	Blue	Not applicable	26/1/50	Tate		
34, 186, 300	1569	7222083	BJG 490	P	RHD	Saloon	Grey	Blue	Not applicable	26/1/50	Bristol Street Motors (Central Motors)	Dr. Freer	
34, 117, 195, 680	1570	3930/108	MWE 254	J	RHD	2-Seater	Black	Red	Not noted	26/1/50	Tate (T. C. Harrison)	M. Wilde	
34, 110, 680	1571	Less engine	VGN 681	J	LHD	2-Seater	Black	Green	Not noted	24/4/50	U.S.A.	Moss Motors Ltd.	Rev counter
34, 117, 189, 680	1572	5341/29	Not noted	J	RHD	2-Seater	Green	Green	Not noted	5/4/50	Universal (Lincs Motor Co.)	Mr G. F. Sleight	Red wheels
34, 118, 164, 195, 680	1573	5355/40	NUB 862	J	RHD	2-Seater	Grey	Maroon	Not noted	5/11/50	Tate	Mr E. N. R. Hewitt	Mercury engine
34, 118, 196, 680	1574	3933/114	OBB 377	J	RHD	2-Seater	Blue	Not noted	Not noted	25/5/50	Patterson	F. G. Curtis & Co.	Mercury engine
34, 118, 191, 343, 680	1575	5343/31	BJV 365	J	RHD	2-Seater	Poly. Steel Grey	Grey	Not noted	15/6/50	Nunn (Wm. Arnold Ltd.)	Mr E. Hyde	
34, 118, 178, 680	1576	5335/23	KLT 2	J	RHD	2-Seater	Green	Green	Not noted	26/5/50	English	Mr J. G. A. Way Hope	
34, 111, 680	1577	Less engine	Not noted	J	RHD	2-Seater	Black	Not noted	Not noted	6/8/50	U.S.A. (Tom Cole)	Fred G. Wacker Jr	Mr F. Wacker car, called '8-Ball'
34, 111, 680	1578	Less engine	Not noted	J	RHD	2-Seater	Green	Green	Not noted	30/8/50	U.S.A. (R/P Imported Motor Co.)	S. H. Allard	Ex-Sydney Allard 1950 Le Mans then shipped to Seddon
34, 124, 680	1579	Less engine	Not noted	J	LHD	2-Seater	Chassis	Chassis	Chassis	21/4/50	Spain (Alfredo Deu)	Salvador Fabregas Bas	ARDUN engine supplied later date
34, 183, 263	1580	7222111	HTH 50	P	RHD	Saloon	Grey	Grey	Not applicable	27/1/50	Harris (W. Edwards & Sons)	D. Evans	(Edwards)
34, 196	1581	7222487	Not noted	P	RHD	Saloon	Chassis	Chassis	Chassis	1/11/50	Patterson	Not noted	Warranty Book states not yet completed 4/3/50
34, 164, 191, 378, 386	1582	7222493	KLV 880	P	RHD	Saloon	Black	Brown	Not applicable	2/2/50	Nunn (A. W. Webb Ltd.)	H. G. Goldrich	
34, 200, 334, 346, 375	1583	7222477	HGP 757	P	RHD	Saloon	Dark Blue	Maroon	Not applicable	2/1/50	Frew (Robbs Garage)	T. K. Lockhart	Page 334 and 346 shows HSP 757 rather than HGP 757
34, 183, 753	1584	7202313	Not noted	P	LHD	Saloon	Black	Brown	Not applicable	2/3/50	Harris	Not noted	
34, 98	1585	7223833	Not noted	P	LHD	Saloon	Show (Light) Blue	Blue	Not applicable	22/2/50	Peru (Somerin)	Sociedad Mercantil	Export
35, 174, 297, 316, 338, 340	1586	7222488	VMG 577	P	RHD	Saloon	Black	Blue	Not applicable	2/3/50	Dagenham Motors	P. Barrett	
35, 170, 388	1587	7223852	KYP 622	P	RHD	Saloon	Black	Red	Not applicable	2/9/50	Adlards	A. W. H Eastwood	
35, 178, 354, 370, 382	1588	7223857	HOT 631	P	RHD	Saloon	Grey	Red	Not applicable	13/2/50	English (G. W. Cox)	P. M. Coombes	
35, 189, 312, 336, 340	1589	7223823	GTL 231	P	RHD	Saloon	Show Blue	Red	Not applicable	13/2/50	Universal (Grantham Garage)	G. Johnston	Page 336 shows ETL 231
35, 174, 281, 286, 292, 335	1590	7223880	VHX 883	P	RHD	Saloon	Green	Brown	Not applicable	13/2/50	Dagenham Motors	K. J. Tovey	Also listed customer as H. A. Clayman Ltd.

Page References	Chassis	Original Engine Number	UK Registration	Type	LHD?	Body Style	Original Colour	Original Interior	Original Hood	Original Delivery	Allocation	First Customer	Remarks

CHASSIS NUMBER PAGE REFERENCE KEY: Allocation Books (pages 1-77), Record Cards (pages 78-167), Warranty Book (pages 168-201), Service Records (pages 202-393)

Page References	Chassis	Original Engine Number	UK Registration	Type	LHD?	Body Style	Original Colour	Original Interior	Original Hood	Original Delivery	Allocation	First Customer	Remarks
35, 170, 279	1591	7223879	MKM 109	P	RHD	Saloon	Green	Orange	Not applicable	16/2/50	Adlards (Haynes)	D. H. Dobrah	
35, 98, 304, 389	1592	7223878	MGJ 99	P	RHD	Saloon	Cream	Maroon	Not applicable	22/2/50	Chile	McDermott	Export
35, 177, 262, 263, 266, 273, 281, 356, 363, 375, 390	1593	7223889	KYO 680*	P	RHD	Saloon	Green	Orange	Not applicable	17/2/50	Gould	Dr. E. Keighley	* Some records note regn. KYO 689 (pages 266, 363 and 375) and one KLO 689 (page 390)
35, 187	1594	7223836	KOH 43	P	RHD	Saloon	Green	Orange	Not applicable	20/2/50	Bristol Street Motors	M. E. Meles	
35, 170, 266, 268, 282, 292, 297, 302, 319	1595	7188852	KYP 630	P	RHD	Saloon	Black	Brown	Not applicable	21/3/50	Adlards	S. G. Pirelli	Demonstrator. Page 268 shows JYP 630
35, 197	1596	7224160	Not noted	P	RHD	Saloon	Dark Blue	Blue	Not applicable	23/2/50	George & Jobling (Cameron & Campbell)	J. Park	This owner and driver took part in the 1952 Rally of Great Britain
35, 170, 270, 327, 341, 344, 347	1597	7224156	LPO 257	P	RHD	Saloon	Grey	Grey	Not applicable	21/2/50	Adlards (Rowe)	R. Clifford-Brown	Two service records note regn. LPO 251
35, 185	1598	7224198	Not noted	P	RHD	Saloon	Grey	Maroon	Not applicable	24/2/50	Mann Egerton	E. O. Benton	
35, 189	1599	7224197	Not noted	P	RHD	Saloon	Grey	Blue	Not applicable	25/2/50	Universal (Standhill Garage)	J. Burnside	
35, 174, 271, 296	1600	7224155	LGO 133	P	RHD	Saloon	Grey	Grey	Not applicable	3/8/50	Dagenham Motors (H. C. Nelson)	Sir Theo	
35, 99, 697	1601	7224205	Not noted	P	LHD	Saloon	Green	Red	Not applicable	2/3/50	U.S.A.	Moss Motors Ltd.	Export
35, 99, 697	1602	7225864	Not noted	P	RHD	Saloon	Dove Grey	Green	Not applicable	13/3/50	Sweden (Motortillbehor)	Douglas Dickson	Export
35, 174, 292, 305, 328	1603	7225837	KYX 642	P	RHD	Saloon	Grey	Blue	Not applicable	3/9/50	Dagenham Motors (Car Mart)	J. W. Arthur	
35, 184, 263	1604	7225843	Not noted	P	RHD	Saloon	Show Blue	Blue	Not applicable	3/10/50	Furrows	R. L. Sanderson	
35, 191	1605	7225839	Not noted	P	RHD	Saloon	Black	Brown	Not applicable	3/9/50	Nunn (Messrs Didsbury)	J. G. Hope	
35, 174, 359, 716	1606	7225896	VHX 885	P	RHD	Saloon	Black	Red	Not applicable	13/3/50	Dagenham Motors	O. Owen	
35, 191, 332	1607	7225886	LKA 491	P	RHD	Saloon	Black	Brown	Not applicable	14/3/50	Nunn (A. W. Webb Ltd.)	J. Hemmings Ltd.	
35, 194, 264	1608	7226137	Not noted	P	RHD	Saloon	Grey	Blue	Not applicable	17/3/50	Tate	Waller Drink & Sons	
35, 187, 289	1609	7226083	KOH 253	P	RHD	Saloon	Blue	Blue	Not applicable	16/3/50	Bristol Street Motors	Lt. Col. H. J. Tedder	
35, 189	1610	7226141	Not noted	P	RHD	Saloon	Black	Brown	Not applicable	16/3/50	Universal (Standhill Garage)	D. J. Whitaker	
35, 184, 265, 277, 296	1611	7226136	GAW 564	P	RHD	Saloon	Black	Brown	Not applicable	21/3/50	Furrows (Bromfields Motors Ltd.)	W. H. Cable	

CHASSIS NUMBER PAGE REFERENCE KEY: Allocation Books (pages 1-77), Record Cards (pages 78-167), Warranty Book (pages 168-201), Service Records (pages 202-393)

Page References	Chassis	Original Engine Number	UK Registration	Type	LHD?	Body Style	Original Colour	Original Interior	Original Hood	Original Delivery	Allocation	First Customer	Remarks
35, 191, 333	1612	7226082	LXA 492	P	RHD	Saloon	Black	Maroon	Not applicable	21/3/50	Nunn (A. W. Webb Ltd.)	J. Hemmings Ltd.	
35, 178, 288, 308	1613	7226135	LYD 165	P	RHD	Saloon	Grey	Red	Not applicable	20/3/50	English	South Somerset Glove Co.	
35, 177	1614	7226077	Not noted	P	RHD	Saloon	Black	Brown	Not applicable	25/3/50	Gould	Dr. R. J. Talbot	
35, 178, 273, 699	1615	7226085	KEL 821	P	RHD	Saloon	Blue	Blue	Not applicable	30/3/50	English (G. Hartwell)	R. J. Cole	
35, 194	1616	7226076	Not noted	P	RHD	Saloon	Blue	Blue	Not applicable	28/3/50	Tate	N. Ward	
35, 194	1617	7228009	Not noted	P	RHD	Saloon	Grey	Blue	Not applicable	31/3/50	Tate	Brown Ogden & Co. Ltd.	
36, 185, 268, 272, 352, 358	1618	7228018	CCF 915	P	RHD	Saloon	Black	Brown	Not applicable	4/3/50	Mann Egerton (Creswell Garage)	Dr. Barber	Page 272 suggests CLF 915
36, 194, 278	1619	7228015	DHE 34	P	RHD	Saloon	Green	Green	Not applicable	4/5/50	Tate (Reynolds Ltd.)	Mr G. Royston	
36, 99	1620	5540-28	Not noted	P	LHD	Saloon	Maroon	Maroon	Not applicable	26/4/50	Portugal	Cond de Monte Real	Mercury engine
36, 189, 282, 305, 325	1621	7228247	LNN 415	P	RHD	Saloon	Blue	Blue	Not applicable	4/12/50	Universal (Standhill Garage)	Midland Model Dairy	
36, 197, 697	1622	7224205	KSM 704	P	RHD	Saloon	Black	Brown	Not applicable	4/11/50	George & Jobling (Mc. Kight Motors Ltd.)	Dr. J. Watson	
36, 185, 271, 298, 384	1623	7233881	DVG 779	P	RHD	Saloon	Black	Maroon	Not applicable	13/4/50	Mann Egerton	D. E. Layton	
36, 183	1624	7228241	Not noted	P	RHD	Saloon	Grey	Blue	Not applicable	14/4/50	Harris	E. D. Jones	
36, 99, 695, 697	1625	799T-1423980	Not noted	P	RHD	Coupe	Grey	Red	Not applicable	24/8/50	Sweden (Motortillbehor)	Ewald Hagstrom	ARDUN engine 7228240 swapped
36, 187, 278, 279, 280	1626	7228238	KOH 761	P	RHD	Saloon	Black	Red	Not applicable	4/12/50	Bristol Street Motors	B. Thornton	
36, 191, 697	1627	7228017	EBA 666	P	RHD	Saloon	Blue	Maroon	Not applicable	14/4/50	Nunn	H. Callerall Ltd.	
36, 187, 274	1628	7228520	KOJ 343	P	RHD	Saloon	Blue	Blue	Not applicable	19/4/50	Bristol Street Motors	The Repetition Wood Turning Co.	
36, 195, 292, 353, 359, 361, 364, 367, 374, 378, 379, 383, 388, 391	1629	7228525	NUB 861	P	RHD	Saloon	Grey	Blue	Not applicable	21/4/50	Tate	W. A. Hogg Ltd.	
36, 170, 272, 276, 285, 373	1630	7228510	LGK 100	P	RHD	Saloon	Grey	Blue	Not applicable	19/4/50	Adlards (Naylor and Root)	L. G. Drew	
36, 184, 279	1631	7228518	GCA 866	P	RHD	Saloon	Grey	Grey	Not applicable	21/4/50	Furrows (Hutchison & Wilde)	Unreadable	
36, 170, 268, 269, 278, 280, 698, 756	1632	7228907	KYP 640	P	RHD	Saloon	Black	Brown	Not applicable	22/4/50	Adlards	Not noted	Demonstrator. Page 268 shows 1362, which should be 1632 as there is no such number

Page References	Chassis	Original Engine Number	UK Registration	Type	LHD?	Body Style	Original Colour	Original Interior	Original Hood	Original Delivery	Allocation	First Customer	Remarks
CHASSIS NUMBER PAGE REFERENCE KEY: Allocation Books (pages 1-77), Record Cards (pages 78-167), Warranty Book (pages 168-201), Service Records (pages 202-393)													
36, 187, 276	1633	7228924	KYP 690	P	RHD	Saloon	Grey	Blue	Not applicable	25/4/50	Bristol Street Motors (Reeve & Stedeford Ltd.)	N. Hartell	
36, 187	1634	7228904	Not noted	P	RHD	Saloon	Black	Brown	Not applicable	28/4/50	Bristol Street Motors (Central Motors)	E. N. Groocock	
36, 170, 275, 280, 287, 319, 347, 355, 367, 379, 382	1635	7228918	LGK 36	P	RHD	Saloon	Grey	Blue	Not applicable	25/4/50	Adlards (Owen)	Portenery & Co. Ltd.	
36, 191	1636	7228517	Not noted	P	RHD	Saloon	Black	Brown	Not applicable	5/4/50	Nunn (A. W. Webb Ltd.)	T. J. Milbourne	
36, 174, 309	1637	7228905	LGP 36	P	RHD	Saloon	Blue	Blue	Not applicable	5/1/50	Dagenham Motors (Car Mart)	Lt. Col. J. B. S. Lewin	
36, 189, 288	1638	7228239	LRR 537	P	LHD	Saloon	Grey	Grey	Not applicable	21/8/50	Universal (Standhill Garage)	Unreadable	
36, 200	1639	7228917	Not noted	P	RHD	Saloon	Black	Brown	Not applicable	5/4/50	Frew	Capt. L. Jackson	
36, 170, 272, 296	1640	7228509	EDY 177	P	RHD	Saloon	Black	Brown	Not applicable	5/4/50	Adlards	Holingsworth	Page 272 may show CDY 177
36, 196	1641	7229717	Not noted	P	RHD	Saloon	Grey	Grey	Not applicable	5/4/50	Patterson	F. H. Tawrick	
36, 189, 283, 366, 371, 374	1642	7229762	TRF 692	P	RHD	Saloon	Grey	Blue	Not applicable	5/11/50	Universal (Standhill Garage)	J. Smee	
36, 195, 276, 298, 370, 699	1643	7229764	GKW 155	P	RHD	Saloon	Grey	Grey	Not applicable	5/9/50	Tate (W. Parkinson & Son)	L. Sutcliffes Ltd.	
36, 191	1644	7229765	Not noted	P	RHD	Saloon	Black	Brown	Not applicable	19/5/50	Nunn (A. W. Webb Ltd.)	B. Rotheram	
36, 197, 320, 335, 697	1645	7229693	HGE 895	P	RHD	Saloon	Black	Brown	Not applicable	13/5/50	George & Jobling (Stobeross Co. Ltd.)	Not noted	
36, 189, 296, 361, 697	1646	7229718	TRF 696	P	RHD	Saloon	Black	Brown	Not applicable	23/5/50	Universal	Lt. Col. Sir Brocklehurst	
36, 164, 174, 270, 272, 351	1647	7229759	LGP 1	P	RHD	Saloon	Grey	Red	Not applicable	16/5/50	Dagenham Motors (Warwick Wright)	Standard Range & Foundry Co.	
36, 187	1648	7229713	Not noted	P	RHD	Saloon	Black	Brown	Not applicable	16/5/50	Bristol Street Motors	H. E. Whitehouse	
36, 174, 273, 282, 304, 339, 360	1649	7229739	VHX 560	P	RHD	Saloon	Black	Brown	Not applicable	18/5/50	Dagenham Motors	C. L. Mardall	VXH 560 also noted
37, 170, 270, 272, 284, 293	1650	7229903	KYP 638	P	RHD	Saloon	Black	Maroon	Not applicable	19/5/50	Adlards	R. Langstone-Jones Co. Ltd.	Mr Grundy
37, 178, 275	1651	7229920	KLJ 90	P	RHD	Saloon	Grey	Blue	Not applicable	19/5/50	English	P. W. Moore	
37, 170, 287, 292, 293, 355, 380	1652	7229726	KYP 637	P	RHD	Saloon	Black	Brown	Not applicable	25/5/50	Adlards	N. L. Cowling	
37, 195	1653	7229916	Not noted	P	RHD	Saloon	Black	Maroon	Not applicable	25/5/50	Tate	W. D. Lane	

Page References	Chassis	Original Engine Number	UK Registration	Type	LHD?	Body Style	Original Colour	Original Interior	Original Hood	Original Delivery	Allocation	First Customer	Remarks

CHASSIS NUMBER PAGE REFERENCE KEY: Allocation Books (pages 1-77), Record Cards (pages 78-167), Warranty Book (pages 168-201), Service Records (pages 202-393)

Page References	Chassis	Original Engine Number	UK Registration	Type	LHD?	Body Style	Original Colour	Original Interior	Original Hood	Original Delivery	Allocation	First Customer	Remarks
37, 196, 305	1654	7229904	OBB 604	P	RHD	Saloon	Grey	Grey	Not applicable	22/5/50	Patterson	Wm. Duns	
37, 187, 285	1655	7231831	GJF 110	P	RHD	Saloon	Black	Brown	Not applicable	31/5/50	Bristol Street Motors (Central Motors)	T. L. White	
37, 189	1656	7231834	Not noted	P	RHD	Saloon	Grey	Blue	Not applicable	26/5/50	Universal	Not noted	
37, 170, 273, 276, 284, 344	1657	7231838	KYP 635	P	RHD	Saloon	Black	Blue	Not applicable	6/2/50	Adlards	L. W. Salmond	
37, 170, 374	1658	7231852	LGX 671	P	RHD	Saloon	Black	Brown	Not applicable	6/2/50	Adlards	F. A. Norton	
37, 200	1659	7231829	Not noted	P	RHD	Saloon	Grey	Red	Not applicable	6/7/50	Frew (Grassicks Garage)	Dr. W. Shaw	
37, 191	1660	5342/30	Not noted	P	RHD	Saloon	Black	Brown	Not applicable	6/8/50	Nunn	A. W. Webb Ltd.	
37, 191	1661	7229853	Not noted	P	RHD	Saloon	Blue	Blue	Not applicable	6/6/50	Nunn	Pooles Central Warehouse	
37, 164, 177, 330, 339, 390	1662	7229911	LGP 258	P	RHD	Saloon	Black	Red	Not applicable	6/7/50	Gould	A. H. Hunter	
37, 183	1663	7229772	Not noted	P	RHD	Saloon	Grey	Blue	Not applicable	13/6/50	Harris (George Rees & Sons)	A. P. Davies	
37, 179	1664	7232476	Not noted	P	RHD	Saloon	Black	Brown	Not applicable	6/10/50	English (G. W. Cox)	H. P. While	
37, 201	1665	7232436	Not noted	P	RHD	Saloon	Black	Brown	Not applicable	13/6/50	Hamilton (L. Porter Ltd.)	R. W. Lightbody	
37, 197	1666	7232462	Not noted	P	RHD	Saloon	Black	Brown	Not applicable	17/6/50	George and Jobling (Grovesnor Motor Works)	Mr W. Blyth	
37, 189	1667	7232479	Not noted	P	RHD	Saloon	Black	Brown	Not applicable	16/6/50	Universal	L. N. Bakewell	
37, 197	1668	7233186	Not noted	P	RHD	Saloon	Black	Brown	Not applicable	16/6/50	George & Jobling (A. E. Penmam)	F. M. Donald	
37, 185, 272, 276, 290, 291, 295, 313, 315, 319, 322	1669	7233207	BJE 490	P	RHD	Saloon	Grey	Maroon	Not applicable	22/6/50	Mann Egerton (Wm. H. King)	Downs & Co. Ltd.	
37, 183	1670	7233210	Not noted	P	RHD	Saloon	Black	Brown	Not applicable	17/6/50	Harris (W. H. Baker)	S. Williams	
37, 187	1671	7228240	Not noted	P	RHD	Saloon	Black	Brown	Not applicable	21/6/50	Bristol Street Motors (Frank Guest Ltd.)	N. F. Vaughan	
37, 170, 278, 285, 289, 291, 296, 301, 307, 321, 326, 331, 337, 353, 698	1672	7232488	LGX 678	P	RHD	Saloon	Black	Brown	Not applicable	7/1/50	Adlards	F. J. Wymer	Same regn. as 1673 in service records
37, 195, 758	1673	7233173	HUG 722	P	RHD	Saloon	Grey	Blue	Not applicable	27/6/50	Tate	B. D. S. Porter	Partially stripped, under restoration in London in August 1967. Stolen

Page References	Chassis	Original Engine Number	UK Registration	Type	LHD?	Body Style	Original Colour	Original Interior	Original Hood	Original Delivery	Allocation	First Customer	Remarks

CHASSIS NUMBER PAGE REFERENCE KEY: Allocation Books (pages 1-77), Record Cards (pages 78-167), Warranty Book (pages 168-201), Service Records (pages 202-393)

Page References	Chassis	Original Engine Number	UK Registration	Type	LHD?	Body Style	Original Colour	Original Interior	Original Hood	Original Delivery	Allocation	First Customer	Remarks
37, 195	1674	7233157	Not noted	P	RHD	Saloon	Blue	Blue	Not applicable	29/6/50	Tate	M. P. Clark	
37, 187, 290	1675	7233183	KOP 392	P	LHD	Saloon	Ming Blue	Blue	Not applicable	25/8/50	Bristol Street Motors	D. W. Rees	
37, 187	1676	7233217	Not noted	P	LHD	Saloon	Black	Red	Not applicable	25/8/50	Bristol Street Motors	J. H. Beard	
37, 183	1677	7242409	Not noted	P	RHD	Saloon	Black	Red	Not applicable	2/3/51	Harris	E. Light & Sons	
37, 170, 278, 311, 697	1678	7232560	LGX 679	P	RHD	Saloon	Black	Brown	Not applicable	7/1/50	Adlards	H. D. Greenwood	
37, 184	1679	7233167	Not noted	P	RHD	Saloon	Black	Brown	Not applicable	7/4/50	Furrows	Mr N. of Kirk	
37, 179, 697	1680	7231846	JAA 500	P	RHD	Saloon	Black	Maroon	Not applicable	7/4/50	English (Stevens Bros)	Sir Paul Pechell	
37, 197, 278, 387	1681	7232480	HUS 202	P	RHD	Saloon	Black	Brown	Not applicable	19/7/50	George & Jobling	Prof. L. J. Davies	
38, 196, 697	1682	7233192	Not noted	P	RHD	Saloon	Grey	Grey		7/10/50	Patterson (H. Young (Motors) Ltd.)	Dr. A. Charlton	
38, 189, 309	1683	7229913	MTV 287	P	RHD	Saloon	Grey	Grey		7/11/50	Universal	Not noted	
38, 192, 286, 296, 759	1684	7235353	GWM 309	P	RHD	Saloon	Ming Blue	Blue		7/11/50	Nunn (Holland Motors)	M. J. Wright	
38, 187, 309	1685	7233193	KON 359	P	RHD	Saloon	Blue	Blue		7/10/50	Bristol Street Motors	G. N. Appleton	
38, 174, 276	1686	7233689	LFM 1	P	RHD	Saloon	Grey	Grey		7/11/50	Dagenham Motors (Brooklands of Bond St)	D. H. Leicester	
38, 192, 310	1687	7233680	GWM 309*	P	RHD	Saloon	Black	Brown		13/7/50	Nunn (Paramount Garage Ltd.)	R. J. Willan Ltd.	* Reg notes in one service record same as 1684
38, 170, 276, 280, 327	1688	7233678	LLC 40	P	RHD	Saloon	Grey	Maroon		19/7/50	Adlards	R. G. Swiss	
38, 179, 303, 304	1689	7235793	JCG 99	P	RHD	Saloon	Grey	Red		8/1/50	English (G. W. Cox)	PR. Stephens	
38, 124, 680	1690	5336/24	Not noted	J	LHD	2-Seater	Blue	Red		7/5/50	Sweden	Motortillbehor	Export
38, 124, 680	1691	5354/39	Not noted	J	LHD	2-Seater	Silver	Red		22/6/50	Peru (Sociedad Mercantil Int)	Eduado 'Chachi' Dibos	ARDUN modification
38, 124, 680	1692	5356/41	Not noted	J	LHD	2-Seater	Red	Red		23/5/50	Portugal (Palacio Ford de Manoel Alves)	Mr Jose Cabral	Full windscreen and top
38, 119, 171, 285, 313, 680	1693	2005	LLP 797	J	RHD	2-Seater	Green	Green		10/7/50	Adlards	R de Larrinaga	ARDUN engine
38, 124, 680	1694	5350/38	LGX 672	J	LHD	2-Seater	Silver	Red		6/7/50	Portugal (Palacio Ford de Manoel Alves)	Casimero Oliveira	Mercury engine
38, 119, 680	1695	7219817	MTA 635	J	RHD	2-Seater	Green	Not noted		22/8/50	Watkins	Ken Watkins	
38, 111, 680	1696	8M-216	BJS 369	J	LHD	2-Seater	Red	Red		25/7/50	U.S.A.	Frederic H. Gibbs	Export
38, 125, 270, 680	1697	5348/36	Not noted	J	LHD	2-Seater	Red	Red		25/7/50	Denmark (Nellemann)	Robert Nellemann	ARDUN engine

Page References	Chassis	Original Engine Number	UK Registration	Type	LHD?	Body Style	Original Colour	Original Interior	Original Hood	Original Delivery	Allocation	First Customer	Remarks
								CHASSIS NUMBER PAGE REFERENCE KEY: Allocation Books (pages 1-77), Record Cards (pages 78-167), Warranty Book (pages 168-201), Service Records (pages 202-393)					
38, 125, 680	1698	8M-931	Not noted	J	RHD	2-Seater	Red	Red		26/1/51	Australia (Gardiners Motor Services)	Jack E. Murray	Cadillac engine
38, 125, 680	1699	2008X	Not noted	J	RHD	2-Seater	Blue	Not noted		18/1/51	Australia (Gardiners Motor Services)	Hastings Dearing	ARDUN engine
38, 85, 472, 688	1700	7228029	USU 339	K2	LHD	2-Seater	Light Blue	Tan	Beige	5/9/50	Canada (Charmbury)	Revd. John K. Moffatt	Interior colour differs refer record card
38, 81, 452	1701	Less engine	Not noted	L	LHD	Tourer	Silver Grey	Light Blue	Maroon	27/4/50	U.S.A. (Moss Motors)	Howard A. Bosken	Export
38, 85	1702	Not noted	Not noted	K2	LHD	2-Seater	Black	Red		31/5/50	U.S.A.	J. C. Woodhull	Export
38, 85, 688, 760	1703	7228922	MGG 917	K2	LHD	2-Seater	Dark Blue	Blue	Blue	14/5/50	U.S.A. (Forbes)	Paul D. Broderick	Delivery dates vary, record card says 04/04/50 for #1703
38, 85	1704	Not noted	Not noted	K2	LHD	2-Seater	Blue	Blue		7/5/50	U.S.A. (R/P Imported Motor Co.)	Seddon	Export
38, 85, 689	1705	Not noted	Not noted	K2	LHD	2-Seater	Blue	Blue		27/7/50	U.S.A. (R/P Imported Motor Co.)	Seddon	Export
38, 86	1706	Not noted	Not noted	K2	LHD	2-Seater	Silver Grey	Blue		21/8/50	U.S.A. (Moss Motors)	Dr. Henry M. Ure	Export
38, 86	1707	Not noted	Not noted	K2	LHD	2-Seater	Grey	Red		11/9/50	U.S.A. (R/P Imported Motor Co.)	Seddon	Export
38, 86	1708	Not noted	Not noted	K2	LHD	2-Seater	Black	Red		19/9/50	U.S.A. (R/P Imported Motor Co.)	Seddon (Donald Dyne)	Export
38, 331, 700	1709	B18F7200203	LXR 942	M2	RHD	Coupe	Black	Not noted	Black	18/6/51	Adlards		Geneva Show
38, 189, 697	1710	7235800	CCH 111	P	RHD	Saloon	Blue	Blue		18/7/50	Universal	A. E. F. Thrupp	
38, 183, 289	1711	7235798	FBO 945	P	RHD	Saloon	Black	Brown		21/7/50	Harris	G. Davies	
38, 174, 314, 333, 345, 354, 697	1712	7235796	WME 816	P	RHD	Saloon	Black	Brown		20/7/50	Dagenham Motors	A. L. Sinclair	Page 345 shows WME 810
38, 187, 316	1713	7235794	HOP 52	P	RHD	Saloon	Grey	Blue		25/7/50	Bristol Street Motors (Old Hill Motor Co.)	D. Dunn	
39, 192	1714	7233679	Not noted	P	RHD	Saloon	Black	Brown		27/7/50	Nunn (A. W. Webb Ltd.)	F. Lunn & Co. Ltd.	
39, 164, 174, 277, 280, 285, 288, 305	1715	7233880	WME 227	P	RHD	Saloon	Grey	Grey		27/7/50	Dagenham Motors (Proctor Motors)	T. Parkers & Sons	
39, 197	1716	7233677	Not noted	P	RHD	Saloon	Black	Brown		31/7/50	George & Jobling (Cameron & Campbell)	W. R. Ralley	
39, 195	1717	7233681	Not noted	P	RHD	Saloon	Grey	Blue		29/7/50	Tate	John Hartley & Sons Ltd.	
39, 189	1718	7235801	Not noted	P	RHD	Saloon	Black	Brown		31/7/50	Universal	F. W. Hampshire & Co. Ltd.	
39, 185	1719	7235354	Not noted	P	RHD	Saloon	Grey	Maroon		31/7/50	Mann Egerton	J. F. Andrews	
39, 170, 335, 343, 345	1720	7240741	NKJ 73	P	RHD	Saloon	Black	Maroon		28/9/50	Adlards (J. F. Pritchard)	H. F. Pout	Later entry could be MKJ 73
39, 187, 282, 697	1721	7228242	GJU 514	P	RHD	Saloon	Grey	Grey		8/1/50	Bristol Street Motors (Central Motors)	Lord Allerton	
39, 170, 697	1722	7235795	LPX 552	P	RHD	Saloon	Black	Bright Red		8/3/50	Adlards (Masons)	Mr R. Hamilton	

CHASSIS NUMBER PAGE REFERENCE KEY: Allocation Books (pages 1-77), Record Cards (pages 78-167), Warranty Book (pages 168-201), Service Records (pages 202-393)

Page References	Chassis	Original Engine Number	UK Registration	Type	LHD?	Body Style	Original Colour	Original Interior	Original Hood	Original Delivery	Allocation	First Customer	Remarks
39, 177, 354, 384, 386	1723	7235359	DJD 345	P	RHD	Saloon	Black	Brown		8/2/50	Gould (Bonattacks & Sons)	J. L. Kaufman	
39, 174, 283, 289	1724	7235799	LLH 951	P	RHD	Saloon	Black	Brown		8/1/50	Dagenham Motors (Kevill Davies)	GASL Whilelaw	
39, 192, 699	1725	7235797	FBA 9C	P	RHD	Saloon	Maroon	Maroon		21/8/50	Nunn (A. W. Webb Ltd.)	F. Shepherd	
39, 192, 305, 313	1726	7233903	LKD 39	P	RHD	Saloon	Grey	Red		21/8/50	Nunn (A. W. Webb Ltd.)	R. W. Dickson Ltd.	
39, 170, 292, 373	1727	7233878	LPX 719	P	RHD	Saloon	Black	Brown		17/8/50	Adlards (Hare & Sons)	J. W. D. L. Godfrey	
39, 179, 279, 282, 288, 312, 341	1728	7233902	KLJ 374	P	RHD	Saloon	Grey	Red		21/8/50	English	V. G. Boyle	
39, 187	1729	7233156	Not noted	P	RHD	Saloon	Blue	Blue		18/8/50	Bristol Street Motors	Sm. Appleton Ltd.	
39, 119, 680	1730	2006X	Not noted	J	RHD	2-Seater	Blue	Not noted		Not noted	Allard Motor Co.	Not noted	Chassis only, Zora Arkus-Duntov Demonstrator
39, 125, 680	1731	5338/26	Not noted	J	RHD	2-Seater	Red	Red		8/8/50	Australia	Gardiners Motor Services	Delivered date differs on record card
39, 111, 680	1732	Less engine	Not noted	J	LHD	2-Seater	Black	Red		8/2/50	U.S.A. (R/P Imported Motor Co.)	Seddon (Steinmetz)	Export
39, 111, 680	1733	Less engine	Not noted	J	LHD	2-Seater	Blue	Red		9/11/50	U.S.A. (Jack Fry)	Perry Boswell	Record card interior colour differs
39, 111, 681	1734	Less engine	Not noted	J	LHD	2-Seater	Red	Blue		15/8/50	U.S.A.	Jean Davidson	Cadillac engine modification
39, 119, 165, 356, 466, 681, 761, 762	1735	2029Z	LLP 798	J	RHD	2-Seater	Green	Green		Not noted	Allard Motor Co.	Brian Golder	ARDUN engine. Page 360 shows 1753 but should be 1735
39, 112, 681	1736	Less engine	Not noted	J	LHD	2-Seater	Vermillion Red	Red		13/9/50	U.S.A.	Moss Motors Ltd.	Cadillac engine modifications
39, 125, 681	1737	5347/35	Not noted	J	LHD	2-Seater	Red	Red		14/8/50	Canada (Trident Motors)	Judge John P Madden	Mercury engine
39, 112, 681	1738	Less engine	Not noted	J	LHD	2-Seater	Vermillion Red	Red		25/8/50	U.S.A. (Moss Motors)	Col. Steinmetz	ARDUN engine modification
39, 112, 681	1739	Less engine	Not noted	J	LHD	2-Seater	Red	Red		19/9/50	U.S.A. (R/P Imported Motor Co.)	Seddon	Cadillac engine modification
39, 86, 536	1740	L2X Caddy	JRA 727	K	LHD	2-Seater	Grey	Red		29/9/50	Sweden	Gunnar Bengston	Tourer body on P chassis, K2 front grill, L-type rear, De Dion
39, 86	1741	Not noted	Not noted	K2	LHD	2-Seater	Green	Red		13/10/50	U.S.A. (R/P Imported Motor Co.)	Seddon	Cadillac Modification
39, 86, 689	1742	Not noted	Not noted	K2	LHD	2-Seater	Grey	Red		9/6/50	U.S.A. (R/P Imported Motor Co.)	Seddon	Less engine
39, 87, 688	1743	7250830	Not noted	K2	LHD	2-Seater	Blue	Red		3/12/51	Sweden	Motortillbehor	Export
39, 87	1744	Not noted	Not noted	K2	LHD	2-Seater	Grey	Not noted		10/9/50	U.S.A. (R/P Imported Motor Co.)	Seddon	Ford engine to be fitted in USA
39, 87	1745	8607/154	Not noted	K2	RHD	2-Seater	Black	Red		12/6/50	Australia	Wangaratta	Overbored Mercury engine
40, 184	1746	7237910	Not noted	P	RHD	Saloon	Black	Brown		24/8/50	Furrows	S. R. B. Greensmith	

Page References	Chassis	Original Engine Number	UK Registration	Type	LHD?	Body Style	Original Colour	Original Interior	Original Hood	Original Delivery	Allocation	First Customer	Remarks
						CHASSIS NUMBER PAGE REFERENCE KEY: Allocation Books (pages 1-77), Record Cards (pages 78-167), Warranty Book (pages 168-201), Service Records (pages 202-393)							
40, 182, 316	1747	7237911	HFH 544	P	RHD	Saloon	Grey	Maroon		24/8/50	Taylors	A. F. Jommi	
40	1748	7237908	Not noted	P	RHD	Saloon	Grey	Grey		25/8/50	New Central		
40, 170	1749	7237913	Not noted	P	RHD	Saloon	Black	Brown		29/8/50	Adlards (Eastbourne Motor Co.)	D. A. Oades	
40, 196, 279	1750	7237914	Not noted	P	RHD	Saloon	Grey	Grey		31/8/50	Patterson	C. E. Shafts	
40, 170, 329, 330, 334, 697	1751	7226140	OPH 518	P	RHD	Saloon	Grey	Blue		30/8/50	Adlards (Drift Bridge)	W. D. Frome	
40, 174, 289, 297	1752	7238774	JDM 636	P	RHD	Saloon	Blue	Blue		9/4/50	Dagenham Motors (Arthur Gell)	Laxton Bros.	
40, 183, 360, 761, 762	1753	7238767	Not noted	P	RHD	Saloon	Grey	Blue		9/2/50	Harris	Dr. W. Hughes	Page 360 shows 1753 but should be 1735
40, 170, 351, 353, 374	1754	7238756	LLC 445	P	RHD	Saloon	Black	Brown		9/2/50	Adlards	D. Gordon	Two records note regn. LLC 45
40, 189	1755	7238765	Not noted	P	RHD	Saloon	Grey	Blue		9/4/50	Universal	F. Hibbert	
40, 174	1756	7238759	Not noted	P	RHD	Saloon	Black	Brown		9/4/50	Dagenham Motors (W. H. Arthur & Co.)	M. N. Foster	
40, 174, 309, 347	1757	7238770	LLK 801	P	RHD	Saloon	Black	Brown		9/6/50	Dagenham Motors (Brooklands of Bond St)	G. D. Peters & Co.	
40, 179	1758	7238777	Not noted	P	RHD	Saloon	Blue	Blue		9/6/50	English (Ward Motors)	P. D. Anstie	
40, 187	1759	7238763	Not noted	P	RHD	Saloon	Blue	Blue		7/7/50	Bristol Street Motors (Central Motors)	Mr N. Taylor	
40, 192, 281	1760	7238764	NLG 38	P	RHD	Saloon	Blue	Blue		9/11/50	Nunn (Fustrams Ltd.)	E. B. F. Jakeson	
40, 170, 280, 284, 285, 293, 295, 299, 304, 308, 312, 317, 322, 323, 328, 335, 337, 342, 348, 361, 373, 384	1761	7238761	LLM 565	P	RHD	Saloon	Black	Maroon		9/8/50	Adlards	A. F. Winstone	
40, 174	1762	7238779	Not noted	P	RHD	Saloon	Black	Brown		14/9/50	Dagenham Motors (W. H. Arthur & Co.)	Miss M. C. Watson	
40, 187, 341	1763	7238800	KOV 223	P	RHD	Saloon	Grey	Blue		13/9/50	Bristol Street Motors		
40, 195	1764	7238768	Not noted	P	RHD	Saloon	Blue	Blue		15/9/50	Tate	D. Thorton	
40, 179, 287	1765	7238783	Not noted	P	RHD	Saloon	Grey	Maroon		22/9/50	English	F. H. Joyce	
40, 182	1766	7238782	Not noted	P	RHD	Saloon	Blue	Blue		20/9/50	Taylors (Stow Valley Motor Co.)	The Birmingham Sound Reproducers Ltd.	
40, 195	1767	7240049	Not noted	P	RHD	Saloon	Black	Maroon		19/9/50	Tate (E. B. Myers)	E. Vere Way	
40, 189, 306	1768	7240041	AFA 166	P	RHD	Saloon	Black	Maroon		20/9/50	Universal (Craners Garage)	M. Gersh	

Page References	Chassis	Original Engine Number	UK Registration	Type	LHD?	Body Style	Original Colour	Original Interior	Original Hood	Original Delivery	Allocation	First Customer	Remarks
40, 187	1769	7240030	Not noted	P	RHD	Saloon	Black	Maroon		20/7/50	Universal		
40	1770	Not used	Not used	Not used		Not used	Not used	Not used	Not used	Not used	Not used		
40	1771	Not used	Not used	Not used		Not used	Not used	Not used	Not used	Not used	Not used		
40	1772	Not used	Not used	Not used		Not used	Not used	Not used	Not used	Not used	Not used		
40	1773	Not used	Not used	Not used		Not used	Not used	Not used	Not used	Not used	Not used		
40	1774	Not used	Not used	Not used		Not used	Not used	Not used	Not used	Not used	Not used		
40	1775	Not used	Not used	Not used		Not used	Not used	Not used	Not used	Not used	Not used		
40	1776	Not used	Not used	Not used		Not used	Not used	Not used	Not used	Not used	Not used		
40	1777	Not used	Not used	Not used		Not used	Not used	Not used	Not used	Not used	Not used		
41	1778	Not used	Not used	Not used		Not used	Not used	Not used	Not used	Not used	Not used		
41	1779	Not used	Not used	Not used		Not used	Not used	Not used	Not used	Not used	Not used		
41, 112, 681	1780	Less engine	Not noted	J	RHD	2-Seater	Maroon	Blue		9/4/50	U.S.A. (R/P Imported Motor Co.)	Senator Woods	Cadillac modification
41, 125, 681	1781	5339/27	Not noted	J	RHD	2-Seater	Bugatti Blue	Blue		10/6/50	Australia	Gardiners Motor Services	Export
41, 126, 282, 681	1782	5307/61	CPT 804	J	RHD	2-Seater	Bugatti Blue	Blue		13/11/50	Australia	Gardiners Motor Services	Mercury engine
41, 120, 681	1783	2009Y	NCV 942	J2	RHD	2-Seater	Blue	Blue		2/6/51	New Central	Ken Watkins	ARDUN engine
41, 120, 171, 681	1784	2004X	LXD 517	J2	RHD	2-Seater	Red	Red		1/9/51	Adlards	Dr. Manton	ARDUN engine. Ex Demonstrator
41, 126, 681, 767	1785	Not noted	LXD 516	J	LHD	2-Seater	Red	Red		22/1/51	Turkey	Halim Celaloglu	Cadillac engine. LXD 516 is listed for both 1785 and 1881
41, 126, 681	1786	5357/42	Not noted	J	LHD	2-Seater	Bugatti Blue	Blue		22/9/50	Portugal	Palacic Ford	Delivery dates differ from record card
41, 112, 681	1787	Less engine	Not noted	J	LHD	2-Seater	Silver	Natural		21/11/50	U.S.A. (Bell Auto Parts)	J. Chapman	Cadillac modification
41, 112, 681	1788	Less engine	Not noted	J	LHD	2-Seater	Black	Red		21/11/50	U.S.A. (Bell Auto Parts)	J. G. Armstrong (Test pilot)	Cadillac modification
41, 113, 681	1789	Less engine	Not noted	J	LHD	2-Seater	Bronze	Red		11/7/50	U.S.A.	Wood Motors	Cadillac modification
41, 177, 286, 290, 314, 354	1790	7240048	LXB 561	P	RHD	Saloon	Black	Maroon		20/9/50	Gould	D. Stone	
41, 195	1791	7238824	Not noted	P	RHD	Saloon	Black	Brown		27/9/50	Tate (Station Garages Ltd.)	W. Broady & Son	
41, 170, 296, 300, 314, 332, 334, 352, 385, 389	1792	7240023	LLC 44	P	RHD	Saloon	Grey	Maroon		10/7/50	Adlards	G. D. Carter	

CHASSIS NUMBER PAGE REFERENCE KEY: Allocation Books (pages 1-77), Record Cards (pages 78-167), Warranty Book (pages 168-201), Service Records (pages 202-393)

Page References	Chassis	Original Engine Number	UK Registration	Type	LHD?	Body Style	Original Colour	Original Interior	Original Hood	Original Delivery	Allocation	First Customer	Remarks

CHASSIS NUMBER PAGE REFERENCE KEY: Allocation Books (pages 1-77), Record Cards (pages 78-167), Warranty Book (pages 168-201), Service Records (pages 202-393)

Page References	Chassis	Original Engine Number	UK Registration	Type	LHD?	Body Style	Original Colour	Original Interior	Original Hood	Original Delivery	Allocation	First Customer	Remarks
41, 192, 300	1793	7240038	LND 503	P	RHD	Saloon	Black	Maroon		21/9/50	Nunn (Paramount Garage Ltd.)	Mr Hardy	
41, 174, 286, 317, 342	1794	7238766	WMC 39	P	RHD	Saloon	Grey	Grey		27/9/50	Dagenham Motors (Proctor Motors)	Not readable	
41, 192, 697	1795	5369/44	AEN 392	P	RHD	Saloon	Black	Maroon		10/2/50	Nunn (Carrs Ltd.)	Messrs J. Hunt Ltd.	Large engine
41, 197	1796	7238822	Not noted	P	RHD	Saloon	Grey	Grey		28/9/50	George and Jobling (Callanders Garage)	Dr. D. L. Armstrong	
41, 200	1797	7238786	Not noted	P	RHD	Saloon	Black	Maroon		29/9/50	Frew (W. H. Harris)	H. Paterson	
41, 192	1798	7238801	Not noted	P	RHD	Saloon	Blue	Blue		10/4/50	Nunn (F. Timms & Sons Ltd.)	Laxton Metals Ltd.	
41, 165, 187, 388	1799	7240739	KNX 847	P	RHD	Saloon	Grey	Blue		27/9/50	Bristol Street Motors (Abbey Garage)	L. Goode	
41, 87	1800	Less engine	Not noted	K2	LHD	2-Seater	Ivory	Tan		28/11/50	U.S.A. (R/P Imported Motor Co.)	Seddon (Robert Ellis)	Cadillac modification
41, 87	1801	Less engine	Not noted	K2	LHD	2-Seater	Green	Green		28/11/50	U.S.A. (R/P Imported Motor Co.)	Seddon	Cadillac modification
41, 87	1802	Less engine	Not noted	K2	LHD	2-Seater	Bug. Blue	Red		12/11/50	U.S.A. (R/P Imported Motor Co.)	Seddon (Arthur J. Ferguson)	Cadillac modification
41, 187	1803	7240932	Not noted	K2	RHD	2-Seater	Blue	Blue		11/10/50	Bristol Street Motors	LH. Newton & Co. Ltd.	Show car
41, 88, 380, 688	1804	Less engine	Not noted	K2	LHD	2-Seater	Danube Blue	Blue		12/1/50	U.S.A. (R/P Imported Motor Co.)	Moss	Ford engine to be fitted in USA
41, 88	1805	5344/32	Not noted	K2	LHD	2-Seater	Silver Grey	Red		21/12/50	Peru	Sociedad Mercantil	Export
41, 88	1806	5346/34	Not noted	K2	LHD	2-Seater	Cream	Red		12/12/50	U.S.A. (Motor City)	Clifton A. Priest	Export
41, 88, 689	1807	8606/151	Not noted	K2	LHD	2-Seater	Red	Natural leather		12/12/50	U.S.A. (Motor City)	John Wallace Graham	Mercury engine
41, 88	1808	Less engine	Not noted	K2	LHD	2-Seater	Gunmetal Grey	Red		1/5/51	U.S.A.	Wood Motors	Oldsmobile modification
41, 88	1809	Less engine	Not noted	K2	LHD	2-Seater	Black	Red		1/3/51	U.S.A. (R/P Imported Motor Co.)	Seddon	Cadillac modification
42, 179, 290	1810	7240732	KRU 38	P	RHD	Saloon	Black	Maroon		10/3/50	English (The Carberry Garage)	C. Lord Ltd.	
42, 189, 286, 295	1811	7240727	MTV 953	P	RHD	Saloon	Black	Brown		10/3/50	Universal (Standhill Garage)	O. J. Bradbury & Sons	
42, 195	1812	7240730	Not noted	P	RHD	Saloon	Grey	Blue		10/5/50	Tate	C. Miles	
42, 171	1813	7240933	Not noted	P	RHD	Saloon	Grey	Blue		14/10/50	Adlards	H. K. Mercer	
42, 185, 307, 317, 322, 697	1814	7240935	JCE 911	P	RHD	Saloon	Black	Maroon		10/7/50	Mann Egerton (Marshalls)	J. Yord Ltd.	
42, 174, 328, 360, 379	1815	7240943	WMC 515	P	RHD	Saloon	Black	Brown		10/10/50	Dagenham Motors	R. Day	
42, 171, 296, 304, 316, 336, 699	1816	7240726	LXD 515	P	RHD	Saloon	Light gun Grey	Blue		2/2/51	Allard Motor Co.	Not noted	Show car
42, 199	1817	7240930	Not noted	P	RHD	Saloon	Grey	Grey		14/10/50	Alexanders	V. C. E. Harrington	

Page References	Chassis	Original Engine Number	UK Registration	Type	LHD?	Body Style	Original Colour	Original Interior	Original Hood	Original Delivery	Allocation	First Customer	Remarks
CHASSIS NUMBER PAGE REFERENCE KEY: Allocation Books (pages 1-77), Record Cards (pages 78-167), Warranty Book (pages 168-201), Service Records (pages 202-393)														
42, 187, 293	1818	7240936	KOX 272	P	RHD	Saloon	Black	Maroon		13/10/50	Bristol Street Motors	H. H. Morris	
42, 313	1819	7240931	WCV 79	P	RHD	Saloon	Grey	Grey		18/10/50	New Central		
42, 171	1820	7242158	Not noted	P	RHD	Saloon	Black	Brown		10/11/50	Adlards (Caffyns)	Alderman A. Johnson	
42, 192	1821	7242134	Not noted	P	RHD	Saloon	Grey	Grey		18/10/50	Nunn (Parkers Ltd.)	N. J. Sherwood & Co. Ltd.	
42, 182, 321	1822	7242159	JUY 89	P	RHD	Saloon	Black	Brown		19/10/50	Taylors	Not noted	Crossed off A. E. Harris dealer list
42, 171, 292, 294, 355, 361, 369, 370, 373, 699	1823	7242408	NKJ 631	P	RHD	Saloon	Black	Maroon		16/10/50	Adlards (Pritchards)	J. R. Weaver	
42, 171, 287, 301	1824	7242135	MPB 216	P	RHD	Saloon	Black	Red		19/10/50	Adlards (Caffyns)	A. E. Jacques	
42, 195	1825	7242436	Not noted	P	RHD	Saloon	Blue	Blue		20/10/50	Tate	Mark Day Ltd.	
42, 192, 285, 290, 293, 316, 348	1826	7242427	ERJ 220	P	RHD	Saloon	Black	Maroon		20/10/50	Nunn	M. Donigir Ltd.	
42, 192	1827	7242415	Not noted	P	RHD	Saloon	Blue	Blue		27/10/50	Nunn (F. Timms & Sons Ltd.)	J. W. Wilde Ltd.	
42, 189	1828	7242419	Not noted	P	RHD	Saloon	Grey	Blue		11/2/50	Universal	J. Ward	
42, 174, 331	1829	7242414	RVX 333	P	RHD	Saloon	Black	Red		27/10/50	Dagenham Motors (Cleals Ltd.)	R. D. Haplock	
42, 192, 345	1830	7242449	AWG 454	P	RHD	Saloon	Grey	Maroon		31/10/50	Nunn (The Bank Top Motor House Ltd.)	W. Brown	
42, 171	1831	7242157	Not noted	P	RHD	Saloon	Black	Brown		31/10/50	Adlards	John Lees	Isle of Man
42, 192	1832	7242160	Not noted	P	RHD	Saloon	Maroon	Maroon		31/10/50	Nunn (A. W. Webb Ltd.)	Mr P. Williams	
42, 174	1833	7240728	Not noted	P	RHD	Saloon	Black	Brown		11/3/50	Dagenham Motors (Brooklands of Bond St)	C. V. A. Dick	
42, 190, 286, 351, 371	1834	7242146	CCH 527	P	RHD	Saloon	Blue	Blue		13/11/50	Universal	V. M. O. Withington	
42, 182, 294	1835	7242421	NHU 930	P	RHD	Saloon	Grey	Red		11/6/50	Taylors	Cecil Collin Evans	
42, 179, 331, 365	1836	7242413	KRU 344	P	RHD	Saloon	Grey	Grey		11/6/50	English (Lee Motors)	J. C. Bugg	
42, 183, 296	1837	7242988	KTG 652	P	RHD	Saloon	Black	Brown		11/6/50	Harris	D. A. Low	
42, 174	1838	7242992	Not noted	P	RHD	Saloon	Green	Green		13/11/50	Dagenham Motors (W. H. Arthur & Co.)	B. Carnshaw	
42, 184, 290, 292, 315, 339, 345, 357, 360	1839	7242985	GUN 606	P	RHD	Saloon	Grey	Blue		11/8/50	Furrows (Francis Garages Ltd.)	G. C. Gibbs	
42, 89, 768	1840	Less engine	WMC 579	K2	LHD	2-Seater	Bronze	Beige		17/1/51	U.S.A. (R/P Imported Motor Co.)	Seddon	Cadillac modification
42, 89, 689	1841	9089/80	Not noted	K2	LHD	2-Seater	Black	Natural leather		12/12/50	U.S.A. (Motor City)	F. D. Mayer	Mercury engine

Page References	Chassis	Original Engine Number	UK Registration	Type	LHD?	Body Style	Original Colour	Original Interior	Original Hood	Original Delivery	Allocation	First Customer	Remarks
										CHASSIS NUMBER PAGE REFERENCE KEY: Allocation Books (pages 1-77), Record Cards (pages 78-167), Warranty Book (pages 168-201), Service Records (pages 202-393)			
43, 89	1842	Less Engine	Not noted	K2	LHD	2-Seater	Green	Red		16/1/51	U.S.A. (R/P Imported Motor Co.)	Seddon	Cadillac modification
43, 89, 689	1843	Less Engine	Not noted	K2	LHD	2-Seater	Black	Red		17/1/51	U.S.A. (R/P Imported Motor Co.)	Seddon	Cadillac modification
43, 89	1844	Less Engine	Not noted	K2	LHD	2-Seater	Silver	Red		3/5/51	U.S.A. (R/P Imported Motor Co.)	Seddon	Cadillac modification
43, 89	1845	Less Engine	Not noted	K2	LHD	2-Seater	Black	Red		4/3/51	U.S.A. (R/P Imported Motor Co.)	Seddon	Cadillac modification
43, 90, 689	1846	Less Engine	Not noted	K2	LHD	2-Seater	Red	Red		16/1/51	U.S.A. (R/P Imported Motor Co.)	Seddon	Cadillac modification
43, 90	1847	Less Engine	Not noted	K2	LHD	2-Seater	Dark Green	Red		18/1/51	U.S.A. (R/P Imported Motor Co.)	Seddon (Carl B. Schmidt)	Cadillac modification
43, 90	1848	Less Engine	Not noted	K2	LHD	2-Seater	Ivory	Blue		18/1/51	U.S.A. (R/P Imported Motor Co.)	Seddon	Cadillac modification
43, 90	1849	Less Engine	Not noted	K2	LHD	2-Seater	Grey	Red		31/1/51	U.S.A. (R/P Imported Motor Co.)	Seddon (F. D. Heastand)	Cadillac modification
43, 113, 681	1850	Less Engine	Not noted	J	LHD	2-Seater	Primer	Red		25/1/51	U.S.A. (British Car Sales)	Tom Carstens	Cadillac modification, wire wheels
43, 113, 681	1851	Less Engine	Not noted	J	LHD	2-Seater	Blue	Blue		30/1/51	U.S.A. (British Car Sales)	Dave Fogg	Cadillac modification, wire wheels
43, 113, 275, 681	1852	Less Engine	Not noted	J	LHD	2-Seater	Green	Red		3/5/51	U.S.A. (R/P Imported Motor Co.)	Seddon	Cadillac modification, wire wheels
43, 113, 681	1853	Less Engine	Not noted	J	LHD	2-Seater	Red	Red		31/1/51	U.S.A.	Bill Co.	Cadillac modification
43, 113, 681	1854	Less Engine	Not noted	J	LHD	2-Seater	Green	Red		17/5/51	U.S.A. (Custom Automotive)	Mr Charles Adams	Cadillac modification
43, 126, 681	1855	2015/Z	Not noted	J	LHD	2-Seater	B. R. Green	Red		17/5/51	Switzerland (George Wales)	Otterino Volonterio	ARDUN engine
43, 681	1856	Not used	Not used	Not used	Not used	Not used	Not used	Not used	Not used	Not used	Not used	Not used	Not used
43, 114, 681	1857	Less Engine	Not noted	J	LHD	2-Seater	Bronze	Brown		21/2/51	U.S.A. (R/P Imported Motor Co.)	Seddon	Cadillac modification
43, 114, 681	1858	Less Engine	Not noted	J	LHD	2-Seater	Red	Red		21/2/51	U.S.A.	California Sports Car Co.	Cadillac modification
43, 114, 681	1859	Less Engine	Not noted	J	LHD	2-Seater	Green	Brown/Biscuit		3/5/51	U.S.A. (R/P Imported Motor Co.)	Seddon (M. E. Abentroth)	Cadillac modification
43, 99	1860	Not noted	Not noted	P	LHD	Saloon	Silver	Red		18/1/51	U.S.A. (R/P Imported Motor Co.)	Seddon	
43, 187	1861	7242991	Not noted	P	RHD	Saloon	Grey	Grey		11/10/50	Bristol Street Motors (Central Motors)	J. B. Greencock & Sons	
43, 371, 377, 385	1862	7242986	HCX 430	P	RHD	Saloon	Grey	Grey		14/11/50	New Central		Pages 377 and 385 notes regn. NCV 430
43, 187, 286, 288, 308	1863	7242987	KOX 744	P	RHD	Saloon	Blue	Blue		14/11/50	Bristol Street Motors (Meteor Car Ltd.)	Messr Ewert Ltd.	
43, 195	1864	7242990	Not noted	P	RHD	Saloon	Black	Maroon		14/11/50	Tate	Hurst Mills	
43, 183	1865	7244325	Not noted	P	RHD	Saloon	Green	Orange		17/11/50	Harris (W. H. Baker)	Mrs L. Davies	

Page References	Chassis	Original Engine Number	UK Registration	Type	LHD?	Body Style	Original Colour	Original Interior	Original Hood	Original Delivery	Allocation	First Customer	Remarks
								CHASSIS NUMBER PAGE REFERENCE KEY: Allocation Books (pages 1-77), Record Cards (pages 78-167), Warranty Book (pages 168-201), Service Records (pages 202-393)					
43, 197	1866	7244327	Not noted	P	RHD	Saloon	Blue	Blue		17/11/50	Geoge and Jobling (Cameron & Campbell)	Elginton Star Hosiery Co.	
43, 179	1867	7244328	Not noted	P	RHD	Saloon	Grey	Grey		16/11/50	English (Carr's Cars)	F. Holdoway & Sons	
43, 192	1868	7244326	Not noted	P	RHD	Saloon	Blue	Blue		22/11/50	Nunn (Paramount Garage Ltd.)	A. Wilkinson	
43, 181, 358	1869	7244333	EUD 740	P	RHD	Saloon	Grey	Grey		20/11/50	Hartwells	E. Worth	
43, 179, 697	1870	7244323	Not noted	P	RHD	Saloon	Grey	Blue		22/11/50	English (G. W. Cox)	A. A. Thompson	
43, 177	1871	7244329	Not noted	P	RHD	Saloon	Black	Red		20/11/50	Gould	Mrs E. Hunter	
43, 185, 348, 354, 355, 362, 373, 376, 381, 384	1872	7244485	LVP 363	P	RHD	Saloon	Grey	Maroon		24/11/50	Mann Egerton	W. C. Saunders	Registration also noted as LVF 363 (pages 373, 376 and 384) and LVJ 363 (page 362)
43, 171	1873	7244484	Not noted	P	RHD	Saloon	Black	Maroon		27/11/50	Adlards (Caffyns)	A. J. Farie	
44, 174, 290, 298, 301, 317, 318, 326, 330, 333, 337, 341	1874	7244501	WMF 831	P	RHD	Saloon	Grey	Grey		24/11/50	Dagenham Motors	The Motor Rag Co.	
44, 187	1875	7244481	Not noted	P	RHD	Saloon	Black	Grey		28/11/50	Bristol Street Motors (Abbey Garage)	W. Bennett	
44, 179	1876	7244482	Not noted	P	RHD	Saloon	Blue	Blue		29/11/50	English	P. G. Bankhart	
44, 199	1877	7244506	Not noted	P	RHD	Saloon	Black	Maroon		30/11/50	Alexanders (G. MacAndrews & Co.)	R. L. Scott	
44, 177, 289, 294, 296, 300, 304, 307, 309, 312, 315, 319, 323, 341, 345, 348	1878	7244504	LXF 445	P	RHD	Saloon	Grey	Red		12/1/50	Gould	E. D. Freadman	
44, 192, 329, 332	1879	7244958	LXF 645	P	RHD	Saloon	Grey	Red		30/11/50	Nunn (The Bank Top Motor House Ltd.)	H. Walton & Sons Ltd.	
44, 171, 326, 379, 381, 391	1880	7244929	PPA 830	P	RHD	Saloon	Black	Maroon		12/1/50	Adlards	Kenwood Timber Co.	
44, 171, 289, 329, 763	1881	7244920	LXD 516	P	RHD	Saloon	Black	Maroon		12/1/50	Adlards	C. C. Tyson	LXD 516 is listed for both 1785 and 1881
44, 197	1882	7244981	Not noted	P	RHD	Saloon	Show Grey	Blue		12/7/50	George and Jobling (J. Martin)	Dr. A. E. Blair	
44, 174, 303, 384	1883	7244972	LXF 746	P	RHD	Saloon	Grey	Grey		12/11/50	Dagenham Motors (Henlys Ltd.)	H. F. Cooper	
44, 171	1884	7244934	Not noted	P	RHD	Saloon	Green	Orange		12/7/50	Adlards (Pritchards)	Unreadable	
44, 187, 699	1885	7244956	Not noted	P	RHD	Saloon	Grey	Maroon		13/12/50	Bristol Street Motors	Mr W. E. Grey	
44, 190, 334	1886	7233877	LVO 895	P	RHD	Saloon	Grey	Grey		12/11/50	Universal (Standhill Garage)	J. T. Topping	
44, 171	1887	7244998	Not noted	P	RHD	Saloon	Show Grey	Blue		1/12/51	Adlards	Llewellyn & Son	

CHASSIS NUMBER PAGE REFERENCE KEY: Allocation Books (pages 1-77), Record Cards (pages 78-167), Warranty Book (pages 168-201), Service Records (pages 202-393)

Page References	Chassis	Original Engine Number	UK Registration	Type	LHD?	Body Style	Original Colour	Original Interior	Original Hood	Original Delivery	Allocation	First Customer	Remarks
44, 192, 298	1888	7246360	LLV 559	P	RHD	Saloon	Show Grey	Blue		1/1/51	Nunn (A. W. Webb Ltd.)	A. R. Wilson	
44, 187	1889	7246359	Not noted	P	RHD	Saloon	Black	Maroon		13/12/50	Bristol Street Motors (Central Motors)	Lt. W. L. Glazebrook	
44, 174, 333, 374, 376	1890	7244999	WMC 579*	P	RHD	Saloon	Met Grey	Red		14/12/50	Dagenham Motors (Roundabout Garages)	English Metal Power Co. Ltd.	* Appears to be mixed up with 1840 over numerous records
44, 200, 297	1891	7246358	GSA 99	P	RHD	Saloon	Black	Brown		14/12/50	Frew (Mutch Motors)	H. R. Spence	
44, 99	1892	7246427	Not noted	P	RHD	Saloon	Cream	Red		25/1/51	Kenya (Engineering & Industrial Exports Ltd.)	J. H. Carvill	Export
44, 179, 697	1893	7246430	KRU 602	P	RHD	Saloon	Black	Brown		18/12/50	English	G. R. Read	
44, 192	1894	7246428	Not noted	P	RHD	Saloon	Black	Maroon		21/12/50	Nunn (The Bank Top Motor House Ltd.)	J. E. Metcalf Ltd.	
44, 195	1895	7246470	Not noted	P	RHD	Saloon	Blue	Blue		22/12/50	Tate	Simpsons of Kirkgate Ltd.	
44, 174, 292	1896	7246469	WMF 906	P	RHD	Saloon	Grey	Blue		21/12/50	Dagenham Motors (Roundabout Garages)	English Metal Power Co. Ltd.	
44, 190	1897	7246479	Not noted	P	RHD	Saloon	Blue	Blue		28/12/50	Universal (Standhill Garage)	R. Harwood	
44, 183	1898	7246514	Not noted	P	RHD	Saloon	Black	Maroon		29/12/50	Harris (Glanfield Lawrence Ltd.)	Lionette Specialists	
44, 197	1899	7246503	Not noted	P	RHD	Saloon	Show Grey	Blue		27/12/50	George and Jobling (Callanders Garage)	R. J. Carswell	
44	1900	7246502	Not noted	P	RHD	Saloon	Grey	Grey		1/1/51	New Central		
44, 171, 300, 327, 344	1901	7246494	FFN 539	P	RHD	Saloon	Black	Brown		1/1/51	Adlards (Central)	R. Warren	
44, 100	1902	7246506	Not noted	P	RHD	Saloon	Grey	Grey		25/1/51	Kenya (Engineering & Industrial Exports Ltd.)	Capt. W. F. O. Trench	Export
44, 192, 293, 312	1903	7246519	ERJ 521	P	RHD	Saloon	Blue	Blue		13/1/51	Nunn	Davies	
44, 174, 318, 325, 337, 375, 378, 697	1904	7246817	WMD 350	P	RHD	Saloon	Grey	Blue		1/8/51	Dagenham Motors (G. Davis Ltd.)	Lilley & Skinner	
44, 187	1905	7246895	Not noted	P	RHD	Saloon	Blue	Blue		5/1/1951	Bristol Street Motors	J. H. Hill	
45, 196, 377	1906	7246816	OVK 395	P	RHD	Saloon	Show Grey	Blue		1/8/51	Patterson	G. N. Carrick	
45, 197, 697	1907	7246914	JGA 595	P	RHD	Saloon	Show Grey	Red		1/10/51	George and Jobling (Cameron & Campbell)	J. H. Capel	
45, 179	1908	7246896	Not noted	P	RHD	Saloon	Black	Red		15/1/51	English (Lee Motors)	M. A. Pitt-Rivers	
45, 190, 293, 297, 697	1909	7246880	LXM 903	P	RHD	Saloon	Black	Red		1/12/51	Universal (Standhill Garage)	W. R. Hart	
45, 120, 139, 192, 681, 685	1910	8M 861	OVT 983	J2	RHD	2-Seater	Green	Green		4/1/51	Nunn	A. P. Hitchings	Cadillac engine
45, 120, 681	1911	8M 580	JWP 100	J2	RHD	2-Seater	B. R Green	Green		29/3/51	Not noted	Peter Collins	Cadillac engine
45, 121, 171, 307, 338, 376, 681	1912	2019-Z	LXY 15	J2	RHD	2-Seater	Grey	Red		4/10/51	Adlards	Maurice Wick	ARDUN engine

Page References	Chassis	Original Engine Number	UK Registration	Type	LHD?	Body Style	Original Colour	Original Interior	Original Hood	Original Delivery	Allocation	First Customer	Remarks
								CHASSIS NUMBER PAGE REFERENCE KEY: Allocation Books (pages 1-77), Record Cards (pages 78-167), Warranty Book (pages 168-201), Service Records (pages 202-393)					
45, 200	1913	7246897	Not noted	P	RHD	Saloon	Show Grey	Blue		15/1/51	Frew (Robbs Garage)	T. Menzies	
45, 171, 197, 639	1914	7246826	JGA 661	P	RHD	Saloon	Blue	Blue		16/1/51	George and Jobling (David Inglis)	Morton	
45, 174, 296, 324, 697	1915	7246818	LXU 597	P	RHD	Saloon	Black	Brown		18/1/51	Dagenham Motors (Brooklands of Bond St)	R. Gooda	
45, 192	1916	7246930	Not noted	P	RHD	Saloon	Grey	Grey		18/1/51	Nunn (Loxhams Garages)	H. S. Davies	
45	1917	7246916	Not noted	P	RHD	Saloon	Black	Red		24/1/51	Adlards	E. Tyler	
45, 171, 295, 306, 311, 313, 319, 328, 336	1918	7246844	LXM 906	P	RHD	Saloon	Blue	Blue		26/1/51	Adlards	Mrs B. Frayling	Page 295 could show LTM 906
45, 183, 311	1919	7246894	HCY 1	P	RHD	Saloon	Blue	Blue		20/1/51	Harris (Handel Davies)	L. Thomas	
45, 171, 326, 347, 348	1920	7246931	LXM 908	P	RHD	Saloon	Black	Red		24/1/51	Adlards	Eastes & Loud	
45, 187	1921	7246915	Not noted	P	RHD	Saloon	Grey	Grey		22/1/51	Bristol Street Motors	M. J. Libbins	
45, 171	1922	7246917	Not noted	P	RHD	Saloon	Black	Red		4/4/51	Adlards	J. B. Guinness	
45, 188	1923	7244921	Not noted	K2	RHD	2-Seater	Green	Green		19/2/51	Bristol Street Motors	E. A. H. Lawrence	
45, 175, 299, 312, 333, 689	1924	7249344	WHX 777	K2	RHD	2-Seater	Show Blue	Blue		21/2/51	Dagenham Motors	Mr Acland Geddes	
45, 171, 295, 299, 304, 309, 338	1925	9088/144	LXT 335	K2	RHD	2-Seater	Dark Green	Green		19/2/51	Adlards	T. N. Blockley	
45, 171, 294, 310	1926	7246913	LXO 502	P	RHD	Saloon	Grey	Grey		27/1/51	Adlards	Barbara Agnew	
45, 183, 301	1927	7249402	FKG 873	P	RHD	Saloon	Black	Brown		20/1/51	Harris	Principality Furnishers	
45, 195, 335	1928	7249341	Not noted		RHD	Saloon	Black	Maroon		2/6/51	Tate	Dr. Crowe	
45, 165, 175, 292, 305, 325, 326, 329, 33 , 333, 354, 355	1929	7249342	WMF 837	P	RHD	Saloon	Black	Brown		29/1/51	Dagenham Motors	A. Fall	
45, 196	1930	7249401	Not noted	P	RHD	Saloon	Show Grey	Blue		2/7/51	Patterson (County Garage)	Allen W. Carrick	
45, 192, 293	1931	7249408	Not noted	P	RHD	Saloon	Black	Maroon		2/7/51	Nunn	A. K. Thorton	
45, 175, 293, 294, 297, 313, 697	1932	7249599	WHX 123	P	RHD	Saloon	Grey	Maroon		15/2/51	Dagenham Motors (Sanders Garage)	Mr Seear	
45, 187, 699	1933	7249375	MBC 478	P	RHD	Saloon	Blue	Blue		2/9/51	Bristol Street Motors (Central Motors)	H. Christian & Co. Ltd.	
45, 190, 339	1934	7249410	CEE 300	P	RHD	Saloon	Show Grey	Blue		2/12/51	Universal (Lincs Motor Co.)	John Robinson	
45, 192, 697	1935	7249351	Not noted	P	RHD	Saloon	Blue	Blue		2/10/51	Nunn (H. J. Quick Ltd.)	Ruth Barton	

Page References	Chassis	Original Engine Number	UK Registration	Type	LHD?	Body Style	Original Colour	Original Interior	Original Hood	Original Delivery	Allocation	First Customer	Remarks

CHASSIS NUMBER PAGE REFERENCE KEY: Allocation Books (pages 1-77), Record Cards (pages 78-167), Warranty Book (pages 168-201), Service Records (pages 202-393)

Page References	Chassis	Original Engine Number	UK Registration	Type	LHD?	Body Style	Original Colour	Original Interior	Original Hood	Original Delivery	Allocation	First Customer	Remarks
45, 697	1936	7249651	Not noted	P	RHD	Saloon	Grey	Grey		14/2/51	New Central		
45, 100, 697	1937	7249594	Not noted	P	RHD	Saloon	Dark green	Grey		28/2/51	Australia (L. H. Green Pty Ltd.)	M. J. Grille	Andre tele-controls, 600 x 16 tyres
46, 183, 306, 586	1938	7249652	KTX 393	P	RHD	Saloon	Metallic Grey	Maroon		3/1/51	Harris	W. R. Graves	
46, 197	1939	7249440	Not noted	P	RHD	Saloon	Black	Brown		22/2/51	George & Jobling (Grovesnor Motor Works)	Dr. D. W. Burke	
46, 175	1940	7249601	Not noted	P	RHD	Saloon	Black	Brown		19/2/51	Dagenham Motors (The Service Garage)	E. G. Nash	
46, 192, 332	1941	7249597	ERJ 600	P	RHD	Saloon	Metallic Grey	Maroon		20/2/51	Nunn	B. Forster & Co. Ltd.	
46, 195	1942	7250064	Not noted	P	RHD	Saloon	Show Grey	Blue		19/2/51	Tate	H. G. Graham & Sons Ltd.	
46, 165, 199, 303, 335, 336, 340, 343, 346, 354, 355, 358, 362, 373, 375, 383, 385, 388, 390, 393	1943	7250061	HWS 853	P	RHD	Saloon	Metallic Grey	Red		19/2/51	Alexanders (D. Harrison)	R. Gairn	
46	1944	7250067	Not noted	P	RHD	Saloon	Black	Brown		20/2/51	Bristol Street Motors (Central Motors)	E. M. Sowter	
46, 175, 382	1945	7250054	Not noted	P	RHD	Saloon	Black	Brown		21/2/51	Dagenham Motors	British Heat Resisting Glass Co.	
46	1946		Not noted	J	RHD	Not noted	Not noted	Not noted	Not noted	Not noted	Not noted		Single seater
46	1947		Not noted	J	RHD	Not noted	Not noted	Not noted	Not noted	Not noted	Not noted		Single seater
46, 183, 304, 312, 339, 371	1948	7250056	KTX 337	P	RHD	Saloon	Black	Maroon		22/2/51	Harris	Burlington Gloves Ltd.	Page 371 shows registration JYW 614
46, 196	1949	7249400	Not noted	P	RHD	Saloon	Black	Maroon		22/2/51	Patterson	Dr. W. H. Skinner	
46, 192, 697	1950	7250049	Not noted	P	RHD	Saloon	Metallic Grey	Blue		26/2/51	Nunn (Paramount Garage Ltd.)	Bradbury (Kingsway) Ltd.	
46, 165, 175, 697	1951	7250065	WMF 910	P	RHD	Saloon	Metallic Grey	Red		26/2/51	Dagenham Motors (Roundabout Garages)	Thompson & Norris	
46, 187, 303, 323, 355, 367	1952	7250062	LUG 822	P	RHD	Saloon	Metallic Grey	Blue		28/2/51	Bristol Street Motors	P. R. Authur	One service record notes regn. LOE 822 on page 367 and another shows LOF 822
46, 177, 296, 329	1953	7250059	LXV 301	P	RHD	Saloon	Black	Brown		28/2/51	Gould	G. Whitehead	
46, 200	1954	7249596	LLC 45	P	RHD	Saloon	Show Grey	Red		3/1/51	Frew (George McLean)	I. S. Smillie	
46, 192, 302	1955	7250060	LVR 314	P	RHD	Saloon	Buck Brown	Beige		3/7/51	Nunn (Paramount Garage Ltd.)	R. H. Harris	Leathercloth
46, 100, 697	1956	7250845	Not noted	P	RHD	Saloon	Black	Maroon		22/3/51	New Zealand	Singer Ltd.	Export

Page References	Chassis	Original Engine Number	UK Registration	Type	LHD?	Body Style	Original Colour	Original Interior	Original Hood	Original Delivery	Allocation	First Customer	Remarks
						CHASSIS NUMBER PAGE REFERENCE KEY: Allocation Books (pages 1-77), Record Cards (pages 78-167), Warranty Book (pages 168-201), Service Records (pages 202-393)							
46, 171, 306, 311, 343, 368, 392, 698	1957	7250837	FPN 300	P	RHD	Saloon	Metallic Grey	Red		3/5/51	Adlards (Phillips)	P. C. Chorley	
46, 100	1958	7251628	Not noted	P	RHD	Saloon	Metallic Grey	Blue		22/3/51	New Zealand	Singer Ltd.	Export
46, 192, 315, 357, 387	1959	7250851	NTB 268	P	RHD	Saloon	Black	Orange		13/3/51	Nunn (Autocars St Annes)	Photofinishers Ltd.	
46, 187, 333	1960	7250831	Not noted	P	RHD	Saloon	Blue	Blue		3/9/51	Bristol Street Motors	C. M. Armstrong	
46, 179	1961	7250980	Not noted	P	RHD	Saloon	Black	Maroon		3/12/51	English (G. W. Cox)	Boshers	
46, 195	1962	7250978	Not noted	P	RHD	Saloon	Black	Maroon		14/3/51	Tate	Catton & Co. Ltd.	
46, 171, 308	1963	7250977	EDY 615	P	RHD	Saloon	Grey	Maroon		3/12/51	Adlards	H. G. Powell	
46, 171, 321, 699	1964	7250979	LXR 946	P1	RHD	Saloon	Black	Maroon		3/10/51	Adlards	Mr McDowell	S. H. Allard used as 1953 Monte Carlo entry
46, 199	1965	7252602	Not noted	P	RHD	Saloon	Grey	Maroon		19/3/51	Alexanders	J. Graham	Derelict in garage in Dalmeny, Scotland 1981
46, 197	1966	7252809	Not noted	P	RHD	Saloon	Blue	Blue		21/3/51	George & Jobling (Callanders Garage)	G. C. Waddilove	
46, 177, 316, 758	1967	7252761	LXU 119	P	RHD	Saloon	Blue	Grey		3/9/51	Gould	Miss P. M. Read	
46, 90	1968	Less engine	Not noted	K2	LHD	2-Seater	Bug Blue	Red		3/3/51	U.S.A. (R/P Imported Motor Co.)	Seddon	Cadillac modification
46, 90	1969	Less engine	Not noted	K2	LHD	2-Seater	Sky Blue	Red		4/3/51	U.S.A. (R/P Imported Motor Co.)	Seddon	Cadillac modification
47, 91	1970	Less engine	Not noted	K2	LHD	2-Seater	Black	Ivory		3/3/51	U.S.A. (R/P Imported Motor Co.)	Seddon (David H. H. Felix)	Cadillac modification
47, 121, 171, 681	1971	1456291	LXR 949	J2	RHD	2-Seater	Green	Not noted		9/7/51	Adlards	Sydney H. Allard	Cadillac engine. Demonstrator car
47, 121, 171, 300, 315, 320, 324, 331, 337, 340, 681, 689	1972	Not noted	LXT 5	J2	RHD	2-Seater	Blue	Red		17/3/51	Adlards (Imhof)	A. G. Imhof	Cadillac, converted to J2X spec 11/12/55
47, 126, 303, 304, 681	1973	2010/Z	MGC 530	J2	LHD	2-Seater	Red	Red		17/6/51	Argentina (Bernardo Wolfenson)	J. Ibanez	ARDUN engine
47, 114, 681	1974	Less engine	Not noted	J	LHD	2-Seater	Bugatti Blue	Blue		30/3/51	U.S.A. (California Sports Car Co.)	George L. Dietz	Cadillac modification
47, 114, 681	1975	Less engine	Not noted	J	LHD	2-Seater	Dove Grey	Red	Black	13/7/51	U.S.A. (R/P Imported Motor Co.)	Seddon	Three cars on same boat 2018, 2030
47, 91, 763	1976	Less engine	Not noted	K2	LHD	2-Seater	Silver Grey	Red		3/12/51	U.S.A.	California Sports Car Co.	Cadillac modification
47, 91	1977	Less engine	Not noted	K2	LHD	2-Seater	Green	Green		3/12/51	U.S.A. (California Sports Car Co.)	Harry Mhoon Fair	Cadillac modification
47, 91, 688	1978	Less engine	Not noted	K2	LHD	2-Seater	Light Blue	Blue		3/12/51	U.S.A.	California Sports Car Co.	Cadillac modification
47, 91	1979	Less engine	Not noted	K2	LHD	2-Seater	Red	Red		30/3/51	U.S.A. (California Sports Car Co.)	C. Wallace, Walt Disney Studios	Cadillac modification

Page References	Chassis	Original Engine Number	UK Registration	Type	LHD?	Body Style	Original Colour	Original Interior	Original Hood	Original Delivery	Allocation	First Customer	Remarks

CHASSIS NUMBER PAGE REFERENCE KEY: Allocation Books (pages 1-77), Record Cards (pages 78-167), Warranty Book (pages 168-201), Service Records (pages 202-393)

Page References	Chassis	Original Engine Number	UK Registration	Type	LHD?	Body Style	Original Colour	Original Interior	Original Hood	Original Delivery	Allocation	First Customer	Remarks
47, 91	1980	Less engine	Not noted	K2	LHD	2-Seater	M. G. Red	Red		21/4/51	U.S.A. (R/P Imported Motor Co.)	Seddon	Cadillac modification
47, 92	1981	Less engine	Not noted	K2	LHD	2-Seater	Bronze	Brown	Black	28/7/51	U.S.A. (R/P Imported Motor Co.)	Seddon	Ford engine modification
47, 92	1982		Not noted	K2	LHD	2-Seater	Black	Red		20/4/51	U.S.A. (R/P Imported Motor Co.)	Seddon (Stanley L. Peterson)	Export
47, 92	1983	Less engine	Not noted	K2	LHD	2-Seater	Dove Grey	Red Hide		16/4/51	U.S.A. (R/P Imported Motor Co.)	Seddon	Cadillac modification
47, 92	1984	Less engine	Not noted	K2	LHD	2-Seater	Dark Blue	Blue		16/4/51	U.S.A. (R/P Imported Motor Co.)	Seddon	Export
47, 92, 689	1985	Less engine	Not noted	K2	LHD	2-Seater	Grey	Black		21/6/51	U.S.A. (Custom Automotive)	Major R. A. Duncan U.S.A. F	Cadillac modification
47, 92, 689	1986	Less Engine	Not noted	K	LHD	2-Seater	Dove Grey	Red Hide		21/4/51	U.S.A. (R/P Imported Motor Co.)	Seddon (Dr. E. J. Bien)	Cadillac modification
47, 100, 315	1987	40-69244F	MGC 529	P	LHD	Saloon	Cream	Red		18/6/51	Peru (Sociedad Mercantil Int)	Somerin (Crofton Atkins)	Mercury engine
47, 200	1988	7252736	Not noted	P	RHD	Saloon	Black	Brown		20/3/51	Frew (Mutch Motors)	J. Barron	
47, 171	1989		Not noted	P	RHD	Saloon	Chassis only			28/2/51	Adlards	Not noted	
47, 190, 312	1990	7252738	CEE 494	P	RHD	Saloon	Black	Brown		22/3/51	Universal (Whites Garage Ltd.)	Roland A. Smith	
47	1991	7252737	Not noted	P	RHD	Saloon	Blue	Blue		21/3/51	New Central		
47, 187	1992	7252760	Not noted	P	RHD	Saloon	Blue	Blue		28/3/51	Bristol Street Motors	G. W. Borley	
47, 179, 301	1993	7252759	LFL 317	P	RHD	Saloon	Metallic Grey	Red		29/3/51	English	H. Carruthers	
47, 175, 304, 310, 314, 315, 319, 322, 328, 330, 332, 334, 342	1994	7252765	WHX 935	P	RHD	Saloon	Black	Brown		29/3/51	Dagenham Motors	The Oilcakes & Oilseed Trading Co.	Also shown as WHX 535 (page 342)
47, 192	1995	7252773	Not noted	P	RHD	Saloon	Blue	Blue		4/2/51	Nunn (A. W. Webb Ltd.)	Mr T. Sanders	
47, 192, 316, 698	1996	7252739	ERJ 701	P	RHD	Saloon	Black	Maroon		30/3/51	Nunn	Mr T. S. Hartely	
47, 183, 298, 299, 300, 304, 309, 315, 316, 325, 591	1997	7252805	FUH 190	P	RHD	Saloon	Metallic Grey	Maroon		4/3/51	Harris	A. G. Textiles Ltd.	
47, 195, 698	1998	7252813	Not noted	P	RHD	Saloon	Blue	Blue		4/6/51	Tate	Stephen Emmott	
47, 182, 313, 318, 322, 324, 340, 341	1999	7252812	KDG 586	P	RHD	Saloon	Black	Brown		4/5/51	Taylors (Steels Cirencester Ltd.)	Hon. Mrs J. Paine	
47, 84, 307	2000	8-7483/2	LXY 20	M-2	RHD	Coupe	Grey	Red		5/2/51	Australia (Julian E. Hill)	E. Neely	Prototype M2 model of 'The Whale', not M2X
47, 84, 700	2001	7246933	Not noted	M-2	LHD	Coupe	Green	Natural	Tan	6/4/51	U.S.A.	Seddon	Prototype M2 model of 'The Whale', not M2X
48	2002		Not noted	M-2	Not noted	Not noted	Not noted	Not noted	Black	Not noted	Not noted	Not noted	

Page References	Chassis	Original Engine Number	UK Registration	Type	LHD?	Body Style	Original Colour	Original Interior	Original Hood	Original Delivery	Allocation	First Customer	Remarks
							CHASSIS NUMBER PAGE REFERENCE KEY: Allocation Books (pages 1-77), Record Cards (pages 78-167), Warranty Book (pages 168-201), Service Records (pages 202-393)						
48	2003	7268856	Not noted	M-2	LHD	Coupe	Green	Red	Beige	3/10/52	U.S.A.	Stewart	Prototype M2 model of 'The Whale', not M2X
48, 166	2004		Not noted	M-2?	Not noted	Not noted	Not noted	Not noted		25/12/50			Might have been J 2004, refer to index card (page 166)
48, 84, 699	2005	7260708	Not noted	M2X	LHD	Coupe	Cream	Red		30/8/51	Venezuela (L. Bockh & Cia)	Mr Geza Benedek	Colours differ to record card
48, 84, 700	2006	S 39953 E	MLP 116	M2X	RHD	Coupe	Show Grey	Grey	Tan	27/9/51	U.S.A. (R/P Imported Motor Co.)	Seddon	
48	2007		Not noted	M-2	LHD	Coupe	Sunshine	Orange		Not noted	Not noted		
48	2008		Not noted	M-2	Not noted	Not noted	Not noted	Not noted	Not noted	Not noted	Not noted		
48	2009		Not noted	M-2	Not noted	Not noted	Not noted	Not noted	Not noted	Not noted	Not noted		
48, 121, 342, 682	2010	8M-988	LYV 366	J	RHD	2-Seater	Blue	Blue	Not noted	Not noted	Allard Motor Co.	Sydney H. Allard	Lightweight Sydney H. Allard special with magnesium wheels
48, 122, 540, 682	2011	Not noted	LXN 5	J	RHD	2-Seater	Not noted	Not noted		17/3/51	Not noted	Mr Imhof	Lengthened chassis, Mercury engine
48, 122, 171, 339, 346, 682	2012	2020/Z	NKT 7	J	RHD	2-Seater	Bronze	Brown		20/6/51	Adlards (Rootes Ltd.)	A. J. Tatham	ARDUN engine. Page 346 shows NKT 17
48, 682	2013		Not noted	J	Not noted	Not noted	Not noted	Not noted	Not noted	Not noted	Not noted		
48, 478, 682	2014	2N 939	MGF 850	J2X	RHD	2-Seater	Green	Green			Allard Motor Co.	Sydney H. Allard	T. T. Car
48, 122, 166, 682	2015	2017/Z	GJB 1	J	RHD	2-Seater	Not noted	Not noted		4/2/51	Adlards	A. Godsal	Lengthened chassis, long wheel base saloon body
48, 126, 682	2016	2013/Z	Not noted	J	LHD	2-Seater	Cream/Ivory	Red		20/4/51	Finland (Suomen Autoteollisuus)	Mr Hamstadt	ARDUN engine
48, 127, 340, 682, 773, 776	2017	2014/Z	HCY 863	J	LHD	2-Seater	Cream	Red		25/4/51	Finland (Suomen Autoteollisuus)	Asser Wallenius	ARDUN engine. HCY 863 is listed as the registration number for both 2071 and 2017
48, 114, 682, 705, 771	2018	Less engine	Not noted	J	LHD	2-Seater	Red	Blue	Black	7/12/51	U.S.A. (R/P Imported Motor Co.)	Seddon	Cadillac modification
48, 115, 593, 682	2019	Less engine	Not noted	J	LHD	2-Seater	Dark Blue	Red	Black	18/8/51	U.S.A. (R/P Imported Motor Co.)	Seddon	Cadillac modification
48, 115, 682	2020	Less engine	Not noted	J	LHD	2-Seater	Red	Red		13/7/51	U.S.A. (Bill Co.)	John L. Negley	Ford modification
48, 182, 698	2021	7252811	JWP 700	P	RHD	Saloon	Black	Maroon		4/9/51	Taylors (Kidderminster Motors Ltd.)	Mrs E. Collins	
48, 175	2022	7252810	Not noted	P	RHD	Saloon	Metallic Grey	Maroon		4/9/51	Dagenham Motors (W. J. Brown Ltd.)	Lilley & Skinner	
48, 105, 306, 318	2023	7252814	LXY 14	P	RHD	Saloon	Metallic Grey	Grey		4/9/51	Australia	Mrs Cattien Thesingh	Temporary use in UK
48, 171, 192	2024	7252815	Not noted	P	RHD	Saloon	Chassis only			4/3/51	Nunn (Williams & Co. Ltd.)	R. O. Lace	
48, 175	2025	7252774	Not noted	P	RHD	Saloon	Black	Brown		4/9/51	Dagenham Motors (E. C. Stearns & Co.)	W. G. Gooda	
48, 171	2026	7252806	Not noted	P	RHD	Saloon	Black	Red		4/6/51	Adlards		

Page References	Chassis	Original Engine Number	UK Registration	Type	LHD?	Body Style	Original Colour	Original Interior	Original Hood	Original Delivery	Allocation	First Customer	Remarks

CHASSIS NUMBER PAGE REFERENCE KEY: Allocation Books (pages 1-77), Record Cards (pages 78-167), Warranty Book (pages 168-201), Service Records (pages 202-393)

Page References	Chassis	Original Engine Number	UK Registration	Type	LHD?	Body Style	Original Colour	Original Interior	Original Hood	Original Delivery	Allocation	First Customer	Remarks
48, 307	2027	7254519	JRK 321	P	RHD	Saloon	Show Grey	Maroon		4/9/51	Adlards (F. Watson)	L. F. F. Eldhar	
48, 93, 171, 366, 370, 374	2028	7249391	MLP 117	K2	RHD	2-Seater	Bronze	Brown		26/2/51	Switzerland (Salon De L'Auto)	Demonstrator	Geneva Show car. It took over the chassis number of the MLP 117 K2 (the first of that model) once that car's chassis number was changed to 2194, as that vehicle was a development car.
48, 93	2028	3958/60	Not noted	K2	RHD	2-Seater	Blue	Blue		4/10/51	Switzerland	Not noted	Former Geneva Show car
48, 93, 688	2029	7018/87	Not noted	K2	LHD	2-Seater	Blue	Red	Black	6/7/51	Holland (N. V. Haarlemsche Auto Centrale)	G. J. Th. A. Van Wuck	De Dion axle, 6 wire wheels, spare wheels in front wings
48, 93, 771	2030	Less engine	Not noted	K2	LHD	2-Seater	Red	Black	Black	7/12/51	U.S.A. (R/P Imported Motor Co.)	Seddon	Cadillac modification, De dion axle, 6 wire wheels, spare wheels in front wings
48, 93, 689, 774	2031	7252888	Not noted	K2	RHD	2-Seater	Red	Red Hide	Black	5/12/51	U.S.A. (All Sports Inc)	Don P. Schoenert	Delivery dates vary, record card says 09/04/51 for #2031
48, 93, 688, 774	2032	7256167	Not noted	K2	RHD	2-Seater	Green	Green	Black	5/12/51	U.S.A.	All Sports Inc.	Delivery dates vary, record card says 08/04/51 for #2032
49, 197, 688	2033	9615-86	JGD 294	K2	RHD	2-Seater	Show Grey	Blue		4/9/51	George & Jobling (Callanders Garage)	D. Watt	
49, 175, 347	2034	7249391	XMC 673	K2	RHD	2-Seater	Red	Red		6/7/51	Dagenham Motors	A. Goulandris	
49, 188, 303, 688	2035	7246933	LOJ 211	K2	RHD	2-Seater	Blue	Blue		6/7/51	Bristol Street Motors	A. Viall	Domesday Book shows LOJ 221 and 153 APK
49	2036		Not noted	K2	Not noted	Not noted	Not noted	Not noted	Not noted	Not noted	Not noted		
49, 93	2037	Less engine	Not noted	K2	RHD	2-Seater	Black	Red		24/5/51	U.S.A.	Moss	Cadillac modification, delivery date differs
49, 185	2038	7252989	Not noted	P	RHD	Saloon	Metallic Grey	Red		4/10/51	Mann Egerton	P. C. Gray	
49, 199	2039	7254520	Not noted	P	RHD	Saloon	Black	Blue		4/10/51	Alexanders (David Rose)	J. G. D. Clark	
49, 171	2040	7252985	LXY 16	P	RHD	Saloon	Metallic Grey	Maroon		4/10/51	Adlards	Rubbaglas Ltd.	Crossed out in Warranty Book then re-entered
49, 177, 300, 301, 305, 321, 342, 347, 357, 360, 363, 365, 368, 381, 389, 391	2041	7252956	LXY 399	P	RHD	Saloon	Metallic Grey	Blue		19/4/51	Gould	F. Fischel	
49, 192	2042	7252811	Not noted	P	RHD	Saloon	Metallic Grey	Maroon		20/4/51	Nunn	Leonard Fairclough	
49, 177, 192	2043	7254552	Not noted	P	RHD	Saloon	Blue	Blue		20/4/51	Nunn	B. J. Moon	
49, 195, 300, 301, 306, 309, 323, 328, 329, 334, 774, 776	2044	7254581	OUB 297	P	RHD	Saloon	Black	Maroon		25/4/51	Tate	H. S. Sharp	Page 370 indicates probably LYY 914 but not clear if chassis 2044 or 2074
49, 171, 342	2045	7254578	LYV 363	P	RHD	Saloon	Black	Blue		27/4/51	Adlards		
49, 181	2046	7254682	Not noted	P	RHD	Saloon	Metallic Grey	Maroon		30/4/51	Hartwells (North Oxford Garage)	J. W. Watts	
49, 106	2047	7254579	Not noted	P	RHD	Saloon	Black	Red		15/5/51	Australia (L. H. Green Pty Ltd.)	B. E. G. Admans	Export

Page References	Chassis	Original Engine Number	UK Registration	Type	LHD?	Body Style	Original Colour	Original Interior	Original Hood	Original Delivery	Allocation	First Customer	Remarks
								CHASSIS NUMBER PAGE REFERENCE KEY: Allocation Books (pages 1-77), Record Cards (pages 78-167), Warranty Book (pages 168-201), Service Records (pages 202-393)					
49, 192	2048	7254772	Not noted	P	RHD	Saloon	Black	Maroon		15/5/51	Nunn (The Davenport Garage)	G. G. Mellor	
49, 106	2049	7254684	Not noted	P	RHD	Saloon	Cream	Red		15/5/51	Australia	L. H. Green Pty Ltd.	Export
49, 302, 307, 333, 698	2050	7254761	NRL 837	P	RHD	Saloon	Blue	Blue		30/4/51	New Central		NRL 837 is listed for both 2050 and 2060
49, 196, 698	2051	7256025	PBB 589	P	RHD	Saloon	Show Grey	Blue		5/1/51	Patterson (Novomobiles Co. Ltd.)	Latimer & Co. Ltd.	
49, 107	2052	7256032	Not noted	P	RHD	Saloon	Metallic Grey	Red		15/5/51	Australia	L. H. Green Pty Ltd.	Export
49, 187	2053	7256036	Not noted	P	RHD	Saloon	Metallic Grey	Blue		5/4/51	Bristol Street Motors (Abbey Garage)	W. Hampton	
49, 192	2054	7254754	Not noted	P	RHD	Saloon	Metallic Grey	Blue		5/8/51	Nunn (A. W. Webb Ltd.)	E. H. Coates	
49, 179, 302, 323, 370, 376, 387, 392	2055	7256187	LEL 646	F	RHD	Saloon	Black	Grey		5/5/51	English	Lord Wardington	
49, 192, 699	2056	7256026	EVF 778	P	RHD	Saloon	Blue	Blue		5/9/51	Nunn (Loxhams Garages)	S. D. Karum & Sons	
49, 192	2057	7256176	Not noted		RHD	Saloon	Black	Red		5/11/51	Nunn (H. J. Quick Ltd.)	Vickles Electrical	
49, 366, 377, 494, 78', 801	2058	E1-U500	MXA 555	P2	RHD	Safari	Bronze	Brown/ natural wood		16/4/52	Allard Motor Co.	S. H. A.	Same registration as 2205 and 4000 in service records
49, 127, 682	2059	2017/X	LYV 364	J2	RHD	2-Seater	Red	Red		5/4/51	New Zealand	Dr. K. F. G. Mears	ARDUN engine, For home use before export registered UK
49, 187, 315, 344, 39'	2060	7256022	NRL 837	P	RHD	Saloon	Metallic Grey	Blue		5/9/51	Bristol Street Motors (Beacon Motors Ltd.)	H. S. Boon	NRL 837 is listed for both 2050 and 2060
49, 171	2061	7256225	Not noted	P	RHD	Saloon	Metallic Grey	Red		15/5/51	Adlards		
49, 197, 346	2062	7256177	JG 62062	P	RHD	Saloon	Metallic Grey	Blue		15/5/51	George & Jobling (Cameron & Campbell)	Dr. W. Young-Laidlaw	
49, 187	2063	7256161	Not noted	P	RHD	Saloon	Black	Red		16/5/51	Bristol Street Motors	Not noted	
49, 195	2064	7256029	Not noted	P	RHD	Saloon	Blue	Blue		18/5/51	Tate (Brown & White)	N. Shute	
50, 192, 310	2065	7252955	MKC 37	P	RHD	Saloon	Metallic Grey	Red		24/5/51	Nunn (A. W. Webb Ltd.)	Dr. Gould	
50, 201	2066	7254685	Not noted	P	RHD	Saloon	Black	Red		24/5/51	Hamilton	John Scott Ltd.	
50, 107	2067	7254553	Not noted	P	RHD	Saloon	Metallic Grey	Blue		21/5/51	Singapore (George Lee Motors)	A. J. Van der Loo	Export
50, 200, 316, 335	2068	7252890	SO 9724	P	RHD	Saloon	Black	Brown		24/5/51	Frew (P. S. Nicholson (Forres) Ltd.)	G. C. Shepherd	
50, 107	2069	7256164	Not noted	P	RHD	Saloon	Metallic Grey	Grey		21/5/51	Malaya	Kyle Palmer & Co. Ltd.	Export
50, 197, 304	2070	7256171	JCD 896	P	RHD	Saloon	Blue	Blue		28/5/51	George & Jobling	James C. Mitchell	

Page References	Chassis	Original Engine Number	UK Registration	Type	LHD?	Body Style	Original Colour	Original Interior	Original Hood	Original Delivery	Allocation	First Customer	Remarks
						CHASSIS NUMBER PAGE REFERENCE KEY: Allocation Books (pages 1-77), Record Cards (pages 78-167), Warranty Book (pages 168-201), Service Records (pages 202-393)							
50, 183, 323, 327, 389, 710, 773, 776	2071	7254760	HCY 863	P	RHD	Saloon	Metallic Grey	Blue		29/5/51	Harris (Handel Davies)	F. G. Barron	HCY 863 is listed as the registration number for both 2071 and 2017
50, 183	2072	7256764	Not noted	P	RHD	Saloon	Metallic Grey	Grey		29/5/51	Harris	P. Salawan	
50	2073	7256774	Not noted	P	RHD	Saloon	Green	Orange		6/4/51	Gould	Miss C. D. Scott	
50, 175, 370, 774, 776	2074	7256767	Not noted	P	RHD	Saloon	Metallic Grey	Red		6/4/51	Dagenham Motors (E. C. Stearns & Co.)	Barranovilla Securities Ltd.	Page 370 indicates probably LYY 914 but not clear if chassis 2044 or 2074
50, 188	2075	7256765	Not noted	P	RHD	Saloon	Black	Maroon		6/12/51	Bristol Street Motors (Abbey Garage)	J. F. Tipper	
50, 166, 171, 353	2076	7256766	LOH 800	P	RHD	Saloon	Black	Brown		6/1/51	Adlards		
50	2077	7256773	Not noted	P	RHD	Saloon	Blue	Blue		6/7/51	New Central		
50, 107, 318	2078	7256791	MGF 846	P	RHD	Saloon	Black	Brown		6/8/51	Ceylon	F. G. Werham	Record card shows Ceylonas Export location
50, 107	2079	12105/155	Not noted	P	LHD	Saloon	Grey	Red		25/6/51	Finland	Keskus Auto Cy	Mercury engine
50, 193, 314, 368, 688	2080	7260024	BCW 14	K2	RHD	2-Seater	Bronze	Brown		29/8/51	Nunn (The Bank Top Motor House Ltd.)	J. R. Brierley	
50, 94	2081	Less engine	Not noted	K2	LHD	2-Seater	Black	Beige		24/5/51	U.S.A.	Moss	Cadillac mods, delivery date and int colour differs
50, 94, 689	2082	9618/86	LGW 999	K2	LHD	2-Seater	Metallic (Pacific) Green	Green	Grey	6/4/51	U.S.A.	Import Motors	Mercury engine
50, 94, 689	2083	Less engine	Not noted	K2	LHD	2-Seater	Cream	Black		28/7/51	U.S.A. (R/P Imported Motor Co.)	Seddon	Ford engine modification, delivery date differs, black wings
50, 94	2084	Less engine	Not noted	K2	LHD	2-Seater	Metallic Blue	Brown		8/8/51	U.S.A. (Custom Automotive)	General Curtis LeMay	Commander US Air Force. Cadillac modifications
50, 94, 689	2085	Less engine	Not noted	K2	LHD	2-Seater	Pacific Green	Grey		30/8/51	U.S.A.	Col. Paul W. Tibbetts	First atom bomb pilot
50, 115, 682	2086	Less engine	Not noted	J	LHD	2-Seater	Red	Red		20/4/71	U.S.A.	Fred G. Wacker Jr	Cadillac modifications
50, 682	2087	Not used	Not used	Not used	Not used	Not used	Not used	Not used	Not used	Not used	Not used	Not used	Not used
50, 127, 682	2088	2018/Z	Not noted	J	RHD	2-Seater	Maroon	Maroon	Black	24/5/51	New Zealand (Andrew Donovan)	C. G. Smith	ARDUN engine
50, 127, 381, 682	2089	12104/154	MGT 846	J	LHD	2-Seater	Red	Red		31/7/51	Cuba	Julio C. Iglesias	Mercury engine. Page 381 shows registration number MUU 186. Page 127 has registration MGT 846
50, 122, 195, 682, 688	2090	12018. Z.	OUG 601	J2	RHD	2-Seater	Royal Blue	Blue		13/7/51	Tate	Richard Petty Ltd.	Close ratio gears
50, 166, 179, 327, 366	2091	7258575	HMR 162	K2	RHD	2-Seater	Grey	Grey		26/6/51	English (Carr's Cars)	G. Smith	Page 366 shows HMR 163
50, 184, 305, 320, 327	2092	7258571	HAW 717	K2	RHD	2-Seater	Blue	Red		27/6/51	Furrows	S. P. Dennis	
50, 94, 689	2093	7252887	Not noted	K2	RHD	2-Seater	Cream	Red	Grey	28/5/51	Malaya (George Lee Motors)	C. Haddon Cave	Export
50, 100	2094	7252807	Not noted	P	RHD	Saloon	Metallic Grey	Grey		14/6/51	New Zealand	Singer Ltd.	Delivery date and country on record card differs

Page References	Chassis	Original Engine Number	UK Registration	Type	LHD?	Body Style	Original Colour	Original Interior	Original Hood	Original Delivery	Allocation	First Customer	Remarks
						CHASSIS NUMBER PAGE REFERENCE KEY: Allocation Books (pages 1-77), Record Cards (pages 78-167), Warranty Book (pages 168-201), Service Records (pages 202-393)							
50, 192, 311, 699	2095	7258538	ERJ 966	P	RHD	Saloon	Black	Maroon		18/6/51	Nunn	G. V. H. Barrlin	
50, 199	2096	7258085	Not noted	P	RHD	Saloon	Black	Maroon		22/6/51	Alexanders	J. B. T. Loudon	
51, 185	2097	7258770	Not noted	P	RHD	Saloon	Black	Brown		7/9/51	Mann Egerton (Botwoods Ltd.)	F. R. Fisher	
51, 195	2098	7258540	Not noted	P	RHD	Saloon	Metallic Grey	Blue		21/6/51	Tate	Catton & Co.	
51, 200	2099	7257941	Not noted	P	RHD	Saloon	Metallic Grey	Blue		21/6/51	Frew (Robbs Garage)	Maxwell C. Dick	
51, 183	2100	7258039	Not noted	P	RHD	Saloon	Black	Blue		25/6/51	Harris (George Rees & Sons)	The Welsh Tinplate & Metal Stamping Ltd.	
51, 195, 322	2101	7258040	Not noted	P	RHD	Saloon	Black	Maroon		27/6/51	Tate (W. Parkinson & Son)	Allied Colloids Co. Ltd.	
51, 329, 338	2102	7258098	NTH 244	P	RHD	Saloon	Metallic Grey	Blue		27/6/51	New Central		
51, 175, 352	2103	7258087	SVX 165	P	RHD	Saloon	Black	Brown		29/6/51	Dagenham Motors (W. H. Arthur & Co.)	C. A. W. Harding	Radio
51, 95, 135	2104	9616/83	XMC 365	K	RHD	2-Seater	Black	Red		6/11/51	New Zealand (R. A. Gibbons & Co.)	Dr. V. B. Cook	Mercury engine
51, 95	2105	2023/Z	Not noted	K2	LHD	2-Seater	Black	Red		28/7/51	U.S.A. (Lambs Auto Supply Co.)	Jim Hoover	ARDUN engine
51, 95	2106	2024/Z	Not noted	K2	LHD	2-Seater	Red	Red		28/7/51	U.S.A.	Lambs Auto Supply Co.	ARDUN engine
51, 688	2107	7258746	OUM 59	K2	RHD	2-Seater	Metallic Green	Green		23/6/51	Tate	Mrs H. A. McCrum	
51, 95, 688	2108	Less engine	VIC GAN 582	K2	RHD	2-Seater	Red	Red		20/8/51	Australia (Gardiners Motor Services)	R. G. Cioccarelli	Mercury modification. Domesday Book shows Australian registration, BUG 200
51, 175, 308, 316, 319, 322, 325, 338, 340, 345, 688	2109	7259626	XMC 365	K2	RHD	2-Seater	Black	Red		26/7/51	Dagenham Motors	W. H. Gollings & Associates Ltd.	
51, 192	2110	7258084	Not noted	P	RHD	Saloon	Metallic Grey	Blue		7/2/51	Nunn	H. Hisbet	
51, 198	2111	7258765	Not noted	P	RHD	Saloon	Blue	Blue		7/4/51	George and Jobling (Wylies Ltd.)	H. M. Roemele & Co. Ltd.	
51, 192	2112	7259012	Not noted	P	RHD	Saloon	Blue	Blue		7/5/51	Nunn	J. Fletcher	
51, 198	2113	7258766	Not noted	P	RHD	Saloon	Black	Brown		7/11/51	George & Jobling (Dalblair Motors Ltd.)	G. Greenlees	600 x 16 tyres
51, 188, 366	2114	7259220	Not noted	P	RHD	Saloon	Black	Tan		7/11/51	Bristol Street Motors	W. H. Bedden	600 x 16 tyres
51, 193, 323	2115	7259227	BCW 10	P	RHD	Saloon	Black	Tan		17/7/51	Nunn (The Bank Top Motor House Ltd.)	W. Platt	600 x 16 tyres
51, 188	2116	7258771	Not noted	P	RHD	Saloon	Metallic Grey	Maroon		13/7/51	Bristol Street Motors	G. Bennett	600 x 16 tyres
51, 171, 308, 312, 348, 364, 371	2117	7258542	MGK 409	P	RHD	Saloon	Metallic Grey	Grey		18/7/51	Adlards	R. O. White	600 x 16 tyres

Page References	Chassis	Original Engine Number	UK Registration	Type	LHD?	Body Style	Original Colour	Original Interior	Original Hood	Original Delivery	Allocation	First Customer	Remarks
						CHASSIS NUMBER PAGE REFERENCE KEY: Allocation Books (pages 1-77), Record Cards (pages 78-167), Warranty Book (pages 168-201), Service Records (pages 202-393)							
51, 193, 363, 385, 698	2118	7258711	FBA 50	P	RHD	Saloon	Black	Maroon		19/7/51	Nunn	J. H. Milnes	600 x 16 tyres
51, 195	2119	7259636	Not noted	P	RHD	Saloon	Metallic Grey	Blue		20/7/51	Tate	J. G. Hailand	Remote gear change and heater
51, 123, 201, 682	2120	2022/Z	OZ 4444	J	RHD	2-Seater	Red	Red		9/1/51	Hamilton	J. D. Titterington	ARDUN engine. Also noted in Bristol Street Motors list
51, 123, 193, 682	2121	2026/Z	FBA 685	J	RHD	2-Seater	Metallic Grey	Blue		27/8/51	Nunn	Dr. A. W. Tilley	Hood, screen, luggage rack. Warranty says B. Scotwade owner
51, 123, 175, 188, 682	2122	2027/Z	ONK 21	J	RHD	2-Seater	Bronze	Brown		5/1/52	Dagenham Motors	Not noted	ARDUN engine
51, 115, 682	2123	Less engine	Not noted	J	LHD	2-Seater	Blue	Red		31/8/51	U.S.A.	Woods Motors	Cadillac modification
51, 127, 682	2124	2030/Z	Not noted	J	LHD	2-Seater	Cream	Red		9/11/51	Finland	Keskus	ARDUN engine
51, 115, 682	2125	2025/Z	Not noted	J	LHD	2-Seater	Riviera Blue	Blue		1/10/52	U.S.A.	Denver Imported Motors	ARDUN engine
51, 171, 698	2126	7258720	GAP 369	P	RHD	Saloon	Black	Red		5/2/57	Adlards (Phillips)	M. Crookshank	600 x 16 tyres
51, 177, 308, 309, 310, 321, 324, 326, 336, 341, 347, 356, 360, 362, 698	2127	7258764	MGK 470	P	RHD	Saloon	Blue	Blue		17/7/51	Gould	Reg Leather	600 x 16 tyres. Page 336 says MGK 670 and page 356 says MGH 470
51, 188	2128	7259272	Not noted	P	RHD	Saloon	Black	Maroon		20/7/51	Bristol Street Motors (Abbey Garage)	Col. W. J. O. Beach	
52, 193	2129	7259717	Not noted	P	RHD	Saloon	Black	Red		31/7/51	Nunn	D. Wastley	
52, 190	2130	7259721	Not noted	P	RHD	Saloon	Black	Brown		24/7/51	Universal	Hen. Sumner	600 x 16 tyres
52, 200	2131	7259634	Not noted	P	RHD	Saloon	Show Grey	Red		25/7/51	Frew (Mutch Motors)	E. C. Edwards	
52, 190, 698	2132	7259013	Not noted	P	RHD	Saloon	Black	Blue		31/7/51	Universal (Central Garage)	Gadley & Goulding	
52, 101	2133	7259275	Not noted	P	RHD	Saloon	Dark Blue	Blue		30/7/51	New Zealand (Tracspecs)	Singer Ltd. (J. H. Macdonald)	Delivery date on record card differs
52, 101	2134	7259286	Not noted	P	RHD	Saloon	Metallic Grey	Blue		30/7/51	New Zealand	Singer Ltd.	
52, 101	2135	7259281	Not noted	P	RHD	Saloon	Black	Maroon		31/7/51	New Zealand (Tracspecs)	Elizabeth Highet	Export
52, 127, 682	2136	2003	Not noted	J	RHD	Chassis	Chassis	Chassis		7/6/51	Australia	Gardiners Motor Services	ARDUN engine
52, 115, 682	2137	8M. 988	Not noted	J	RHD	2-Seater	Green	Not noted		25/7/51	Peru (Sociedad Mercantil Int)	Mr Santiago Pope	Cadillac engine, Sydney H. Allard Le Mans car
52, 171, 682	2138	2028/Z	MGT 850	J2X	RHD	2-Seater	Green	Black	Black	9/7/51	Adlards	Simmonds	Prototype J2X
52, 101	2139	7259285	Not noted	P	RHD	Saloon	Battleship Grey	Maroon		31/7/51	New Zealand	Singer Ltd.	Export
52, 101	2140	7259014	Not noted	P	RHD	Saloon	Metallic Grey	Grey		8/11/51	New Zealand	Singer Ltd.	Export

CHASSIS NUMBER PAGE REFERENCE KEY: Allocation Books (pages 1-77), Record Cards (pages 78-167), Warranty Book (pages 168-201), Service Records (pages 202-393)

Page References	Chassis	Original Engine Number	UK Registration	Type	LHD?	Body Style	Original Colour	Original Interior	Original Hood	Original Delivery	Allocation	First Customer	Remarks
52, 101	2141	7259287	Not noted	P	RHD	Saloon	Battleship Grey	Blue		13/8/51	New Zealand	Singer Ltd.	600 x 16 tyres
52, 188	2142	7259282	Not noted	P	RHD	Saloon	Black	Maroon		16/8/51	Bristol Street Motors (Rugby Autocar Co. Ltd.)	Geo. Roberts	600 x 16 tyres
52, 196	2143	7259221	Not noted	P	RHD	Saloon	Show Grey	Maroon		8/11/51	Patterson	A. L. Wallis	600 x 16 tyres
52, 195	2144	7259632	Not noted	P	RHD	Saloon	Blue	Blue		17/8/51	Tate	P. Nagele	600 x 16 tyres
52, 190	2145	7259628	Not noted	P	RHD	Saloon	Black	Maroon		9/1/51	Universal (Standhill Garage)	H. Goodman	
52, 188	2146	7259718	Not noted	P	RHD	Saloon	Metallic Grey	Grey		21/8/51	Bristol Street Motors	Not noted	
52, 175, 319, 325, 331, 335, 336, 341, 345, 347	2147	7259727	XMX 977	P	RHD	Saloon	Metallic Grey	Blue		9/11/51	Dagenham Motors	D. M. Leapman	
52, 79, 314, 320, 327, 342, 354, 357, 359, 380	2148	7260148	LLJ 488	P	RHD	Saloon	Metallic Grey	Grey		13/9/51	English	David W. D. R	
52, 88, 320, 321, 372	2149	7260352	LOL 773	K2	RHD	2-Seater	Pacific Green	Green	Black	8/2/51	Bristol Street Motors	R. H. Bailey	
52, 93, 689	2150	7260147	ULK 996	K2	RHD	2-Seater	Grey	Grey	Light Grey	8/5/51	Nunn	S. G. M. Forrester	
52, 193	2151	7260116	Not noted	K2	RHD	2-Seater	Bronze	Brown	Black	8/1/51	Nunn (The Bank Top Motor House Ltd.)	J. Cunliffe	
52, 95	2152	7260669	Not noted	K2	RHD	2-Seater	Pacific Green	Green		24/8/51	Australia (Gardiners Motor Services)	Haig Furst	Engine differ in record card
52, 95	2153	2103/153	Not noted	K2	LHD	2-Seater	Cream	Red		9/11/51	Finland	Keskus Auto	Mercury engine
52, 96, 688	2154	Less engine	Not noted	K2	LHD	2-Seater	Green	Red	Black	12/11/51	U.S.A.	Seddon	
52, 123, 175, 335, 682	2155	2131/Z	WMX 814	J	RHD	2-Seater	Red	Red		30/4/52	Dagenham Motors	Not noted	ARDUN engine
52, 116, 682	2156	Less engine	Not noted	J	LHD	2-Seater	Black	Red		Not noted	U.S.A.	Mr Reg Fudge Jr	Cadillac modification
52, 128, 682	2157	2033/Z	Not noted	J	LHD	2-Seater	Ivory	Red		10/11/51	Venezuela (Autoboc)	L. Bockh & Cia	ARDUN engine?
52, 112	2158	Less engine	Not noted	P	LHD	2-Seater	Green	Red		31/7/51	U.S.A. (R/P Imported Motor Co.)	Seddon	600 x 16 tyres
52, 193	2159	7260137	Not noted	P	RHD	Saloon	Metallic Grey	Blue		31/8/51	Nunn	G. H. Clegg	
52, 195, 689	2160	7260146	Not noted	P	RHD	Saloon	Metallic Grey	Blue		9/8/51	Tate	Mrs B. Todd	
53, 175, 320	2161	7260376	MLT 909	P	RHD	Saloon	Metallic Grey	Grey		30/8/51	Dagenham Motors	Rayner & Keeler Ltd.	
53, 184	2162	7261353	Not noted	P	RHD	Saloon	Black	Brown		13/9/51	Furrows	G. E. S. Pleavin	
53, 102	2163	7260356	Not noted	P	RHD	Saloon	Primer	Blue		9/6/51	Australia (Bricar)	Brisbane Motors Ltd.	600 x 16 tyres

Page References	Chassis	Original Engine Number	UK Registration	Type	LHD?	Body Style	Original Colour	Original Interior	Original Hood	Original Delivery	Allocation	First Customer	Remarks

CHASSIS NUMBER PAGE REFERENCE KEY: Allocation Books (pages 1-77), Record Cards (pages 78-167), Warranty Book (pages 168-201), Service Records (pages 202-393)

Page References	Chassis	Original Engine Number	UK Registration	Type	LHD?	Body Style	Original Colour	Original Interior	Original Hood	Original Delivery	Allocation	First Customer	Remarks
53, 102	2164	7260377	Not noted	P	RHD	Saloon	Primer	Maroon		9/6/51	Australia (Brisbane Motors Ltd.)	J. E. F. Abbiss	600 x 16 tyres
53, 356, 698	2165	7260026	NTA 582	P	RHD	Saloon	Blue	Blue		15/9/51	New Central		
53, 102	2166	7260707	Not noted	P	RHD	Saloon	Primer	Grey		9/7/51	Australia (Bricar)	Brisbane Motors Ltd.	600 x 16 tyres
53, 193, 337	2167	7261710	MNB 905	P	RHD	Saloon	Black	Green		18/9/51	Nunn (H. J. Quick Ltd.)	The Hon. Mark A. Rathbone	
53, 102, 698	2168	7260729	Not noted	P	RHD	Saloon	Primer	Maroon		9/8/51	Australia (Bricar)	Brisbane Motors Ltd.	600 x 16 tyres
53, 193, 374, 391	2169	7261750	NKA 727	P	RHD	Saloon	Metallic Grey	Blue		20/9/51	Nunn (Boyle & Co. Ltd.)	Thos. Jones	
53, 102	2170	7260025	Not noted	P	RHD	Saloon	Primer	Grey-blue		9/7/51	Australia (Bricar)	Brisbane Motors Ltd. (S. Y. Gresham)	600 x 16 tyres
53, 200	2171	7261748	Not noted	P	RHD	Saloon	Green	Orange		22/8/51	Frew (Mutch Motors)	R. M. Ledingham	
53, 103	2172	7260670	Not noted	P	RHD	Saloon	Primer	Blue		9/8/51	Australia (Bricar)	Brisbane Motors Ltd. (M. Roseblum)	600 x 16 tyres
53, 172, 318, 326, 333, 359, 362, 699	2173	7261749	MJJ 459	P	RHD	Saloon	Black	Maroon		16/10/51	Adlards	R. Simon & Co.	
53, 190	2174	7261367	Not noted	P	RHD	Saloon	Black	Brown		25/9/51	Universal	Herb E. Bowmer	
53, 172, 315, 327, 358, 362	2175	7261983	MJJ 460	P	RHD	Saloon	Blue	Blue		10/1/51	Adlards	Max Faulkner	
53, 103	2176	7261972	Not noted	P	LHD	Saloon	Green	Orange		10/4/51	Brazil	Planalto CommerCo. & Industrial	Export
53, 103	2177	7261966	Not noted	P	LHD	Saloon	Black	Red		10/4/51	Brazil (Planalto CommerCo. & Industrial)	Owswaldo Queiroz Guimaraes	Export
53	2178	Not used	Not used	Not used	Not used	Not used	Not used	Not used	Not used	Not used	Not used	Not used	Not used
53, 116, 462, 682	2179	Less engine	Not noted	J	LHD	2-Seater	Black	Red		17/10/51	U.S.A. (Custom Automotive)	Fred R. Cook	Last J2 Export
53, 128, 682	2180	Less engine	Not noted	J2X	LHD	2-Seater	Pacific Green	Red	Black	21/11/51	U.S.A. (Auto Imports)	John P. Elwood	Cadillac modification
53, 103	2181	4G-16377 F	Not noted	P	LHD	Saloon	Metallic Grey	Red		10/3/51	Finland	Keskus Auto	Mercury engine
53, 103	2182	3G-99168F	Not noted	P	LHD	Saloon	Maroon	Red		10/10/51	Finland	Keskus Auto	Mercury engine
53, 103	2183	14241/133	Not noted	P	LHD	Saloon	Metallic Blue	Blue		24/10/51	Finland	Keskus Auto	Mercury engine
53, 188	2184	7260369	Not noted	P	RHD	Saloon	Black	Brown		26/9/51	Bristol Street Motors (Ashmores Ltd.)	Braithwaite & Co.	
53, 181, 331, 339, 699, 780, 781	2185	7260728	GMO 999	P	RHD	Saloon	Metallic Grey	Red		26/9/51	Hartwells (Loddon Bridge Motors)	Betty Culpin	The seventh entry on page 322 should indicate 2185 and not 2188 as recorded at the time
53, 193, 330, 698	2186	7261360	BCW 276	P	RHD	Saloon	Black	Maroon		10/1/51	Nunn (The Bank Top Motor House Ltd.)	Don Burke	

Page References	Chassis	Original Engine Number	UK Registration	Type	LHD?	Body Style	Original Colour	Original Interior	Original Hood	Original Delivery	Allocation	First Customer	Remarks
						CHASSIS NUMBER PAGE REFERENCE KEY: Allocation Books (pages 1-77), Record Cards (pages 78-167), Warranty Book (pages 168-201), Service Records (pages 202-393)							
53, 175, 319, 323, 389	2187	7261359	XMF 656	P	RHD	Saloon	Black	Brown		10/4/51	Dagenham Motors	Major E. A. Ralle	
53, 322, 780, 781	2188	7261352	Not noted	P	RHD	Saloon	Blue	Blue		10/12/51	New Central		Page 322 has a reference to 2188 but this should have been 2185
53, 195, 380, 383	2189	7262013	NKH 727	P	RHD	Saloon	Metallic Grey	Blue		10/10/51	Tate (Brown & White)	The Farm Shops	
53, 193	2190	7261709	Not noted	P	RHD	Saloon	Grey	Red		11/4/51	Nunn (The Bank Top Motor House Ltd.)	H. D. Dole	Show
53, 128, 683	2191	Less engine	Not noted	J2X	LHD	2-Seater	Electric Blue	Blue	Black	29/11/51	U.S.A. (Jack Fry)	Jean Davidson	Cadillac modification
53, 128, 683	2192	Less engine	Not noted	J2X	LHD	2-Seater	Grey	Red		22/1/52	U.S.A. (Wood Motors)	Fred M. Warner	Cadillac modification, delivery date differs to record card
54, 129, 683	2193	Less engine	Not noted	J2X	LHD	2-Seater	Blue	Red	Black	14/12/51	U.S.A.	Motor Sport Inc.	Chrysler modification
54, 96, 774	2194	7259720	Not noted	K2	RHD	2-Seater	Red	Brown Hide		15/8/51	Switzerland		Export
54, 96	2195	Less engine	Not noted	K2	RHD	2-Seater	Red	Red		27/9/51	U.S.A.		Export
54, 188 689	2196	7261789	LON 909	K2	RHD	2-Seater	Green	Green		29/9/51	Bristol Street Motors	John Gurst	
54, 96, 689	2197	2036/Z	Not noted	K2	LHD	2-Seater	Electric Blue	Blue		1/10/52	U.S.A. (Denver Imported Motors)	James A. Sisler	ARDUN engine
54, 96	2198	Less engine	Not noted	K2	LHD	2-Seater	Electric Blue	Blue	Black	1/3/52	U.S.A. (R/P Imported Motor Co.)	Seddon	Cadillac modification
54, 96	2199	Less engine	Not noted	K2	LHD	2-Seater	Blue	Red	Black	2/7/52	U.S.A. (R/P Imported Motor Co.)	Seddon	Cadillac modification
54, 179	2200	7262943	Not noted	K2	RHD	2-Seater	Silver Grey	Grey		19/10/51	English	C. F. S. Street	
54	2201	7264458	Not noted	K2	RHD	2-Seater	Blue	Blue		20/10/51	Adlards		
54, 175, 345, 348, 689	2202	7264732	YMC 693	K2	RHD	2-Seater	Red	Red	Black	20/11/51	Dagenham Motors	A. L. Sinclair	
54, 172, 339, 689	2203	7269801	MPL 117	K2	RHD	2-Seater	Light Metallic Grey	Grey	Black	21/3/52	Adlards (A. B. Garages)	Martin Thompson	Believed to be driven by Zora Arkus-Duntov in Belgium. Page 339 shows registration as OKM 728, and page 689 notes MLP 117, rather than MPL 117.
54, 198	2204	7261753	Not noted	P	RHD	Saloon	Blue	Blue		10/11/51	George & Jobling (Cameron & Campbell)	Jonh. McKenna	
54, 193, 351, 352, 355, 361, 368, 369, 371, 775, 801	2205	7262460	MXA 555	P	RHD	Saloon	Black	Brown		23/10/51	Nunn	M. Lawrence	Same registration as 2058 and 4000 in service records
54, 188	2206	7262392	Not noted	P	RHD	Saloon	Blue	Blue		15/10/51	Bristol Street Motors (Flewitt Ltd.)	P. St. V. Tabberner	
54, 177, 318, 698	2207	7262343	MLO 312	P	RHD	Saloon	Metallic Grey	Blue		17/10/51	Gould	A. H. Carter	Radio
54, 179, 698	2208	7262561	Not noted	P	RHD	Saloon	Metallic Grey	Maroon		23/10/51	English	J. W. F. Coles	
54, 193	2209	7262957	Not noted	P	RHD	Saloon	Metallic Grey	Blue		24/10/51	Nunn (Paramount Garage Ltd.)	H. Hill	
54	2210	Not used	Not used		Not used	Not used	Not used	Not used	Not used	Not used	Not used	Not used	Not used

Page References	Chassis	Original Engine Number	UK Registration	Type	LHD?	Body Style	Original Colour	Original Interior	Original Hood	Original Delivery	Allocation	First Customer	Remarks
							CHASSIS NUMBER PAGE REFERENCE KEY: Allocation Books (pages 1-77), Record Cards (pages 78-167), Warranty Book (pages 168-201), Service Records (pages 202-393)						
54	2211	Not used	Not used		Not used	Not used	Not used	Not used	Not used	Not used	Not used	Not used	Not used
54	2212	Not used	Not used		Not used	Not used	Not used	Not used	Not used	Not used	Not used	Not used	Not used
54	2213	Not used	Not used		Not used	Not used	Not used	Not used	Not used	Not used	Not used	Not used	Not used
54	2214	Not used	Not used		Not used	Not used	Not used	Not used	Not used	Not used	Not used	Not used	Not used
54	2215	Not used	Not used		Not used	Not used	Not used	Not used	Not used	Not used	Not used	Not used	Not used
54	2216	Not used	Not used		Not used	Not used	Not used	Not used	Not used	Not used	Not used	Not used	Not used
54	2217	Not used	Not used		Not used	Not used	Not used	Not used	Not used	Not used	Not used	Not used	Not used
54	2218	Not used	Not used		Not used	Not used	Not used	Not used	Not used	Not used	Not used	Not used	Not used
54, 129, 683	2219	Less engine	Not noted	J2X	LHD	2-Seater	Red	Red		1/9/52	U.S.A.	A. E. Goldschmidt	Cadillac modification, appeared on cover 'LIFE' magazine
54	2220	Not used	Not used		Not used	Not used	Not used	Not used	Not used	Not used	Not used	Not used	Not used
54, 129, 683	2221	Less engine	Not noted	J2X	LHD	2-Seater	Red	Black	Black	23/1/52	U.S.A. (R/P Imported Motor Co.)	Seddon (Frank C. Adams)	Cadillac modification
54, 129, 683	2222	Less engine	Not noted	J2X	LHD	2-Seater	Royal Blue	Red		23/1/52	U.S.A. (R/P Imported Motor Co.)	P. W. Schwarts	Cadillac modification
54, 129, 683	2223	Less engine	Not noted	J2X	LHD	2-Seater	Silver Grey	Red		29/12/51	Peru (Somerin)	Eduardo 'Chachi' Dibos	Chrysler modification
54, 537, 683	2224	2017/Z	PKJ 412	J2X	RHD	Chassis only				14/1/52	Essex Aero Ltd.	P. J. Owen	Special chassis work, Cotal gearbox
55, 195, 337	2225	7262939	KWY 558	P	RHD	Saloon	Blue	Blue		29/10/51	Tate (Fred Binns)	John Wells Ltd.	New small grille and heater
55, 188	2226	7262937	Not noted	P	RHD	Saloon	Black	Brown		27/10/51	Bristol Street Motors (Ashmores Ltd.)	Braithwaite & Co.	New small grille and heater
55, 193	2227	7262952	Not noted	P	RHD	Saloon	Blue	Blue		11/1/51	Nunn (The Bank Top Motor House Ltd.)	H. H. Lane	New small grille and heater
55, 188, 317, 322, 330, 343, 360	2228	7261992	GEA 322	P	RHD	Saloon	Metallic Grey	Grey		29/10/51	Bristol Street Motors (Ashmores Ltd.)	Braithwaite & Co.	New small grille and heater
55, 193	2229	7262385	Not noted	P	RHD	Saloon	Metallic Grey	Maroon		27/11/51	Nunn	Mrs Hilary Higgins	New small grille and heater. Crossed out of Bristol Street Motors listing
55, 188	2230	7262468	Not noted	P	RHD	Saloon	Metallic Grey	Blue		11/1/51	Bristol Street Motors	G. M. Graham	New small grille and heater
55, 195	2231	7262389	Not noted	P	RHD	Saloon	Black	Blue		11/1/51	Tate	Chs. Lane & Sons Ltd.	
55, 175, 698	2232	7262934	XMX 989	P	RHD	Saloon	Black	Brown		11/6/51	Dagenham Motors	Pilcher Hersham & Partners	
55, 195, 341	2233	7262479	PUA 74	P	RHD	Saloon	Metallic Blue	Blue		11/8/51	Tate	W. H. Shaws & Sons Ltd.	
55, 195, 359	2234	7264457	Not noted	P	RHD	Saloon	Show Grey	Blue		11/8/51	Tate	Schofields	
55, 188, 334	2235	7262462	GEA 372	P	RHD	Saloon	Black	Maroon		11/7/51	Bristol Street Motors (Collals Defor ltd)	F. L. Firkin	
55, 195, 325	2236	7264506	OUM 876	P	RHD	Saloon	Metallic Grey	Maroon		11/8/51	Tate	Woods Bacon Factory Ltd.	

Page References	Chassis	Original Engine Number	UK Registration	Type	LHD?	Body Style	Original Colour	Original Interior	Original Hood	Original Delivery	Allocation	First Customer	Remarks

CHASSIS NUMBER PAGE REFERENCE KEY: Allocation Books (pages 1-77), Record Cards (pages 78-167), Warranty Book (pages 168-201), Service Records (pages 202-393)

Page References	Chassis	Original Engine Number	UK Registration	Type	LHD?	Body Style	Original Colour	Original Interior	Original Hood	Original Delivery	Allocation	First Customer	Remarks
55, 188, 353, 355, 375, 385, 699	2237	7262374	CEA 444	P	RHD	Saloon	Black	Tan		11/7/51	Bristol Street Motors (Ashmores Ltd.)	Braithwaite & Co.	One record notes regn. GEA 334 and pages 375 and 385 show GEA 337
55, 188, 372	2238	7263582	NOE 334		RHD	Saloon	Metallic Grey	Red		13/11/51	Bristol Street Motors	Not noted	
55, 104	2239	7264733	Not noted	P	RHD	Saloon	Metallic Grey	Blue		11/10/51	New Zealand	Singer Ltd.	Delivery date differs from record card
55, 104, 370	2240	7264494	Not noted	P	RHD	Saloon	Metallic Grey	Blue		13/11/51	New Zealand	Singer Ltd.	Delivery date differs from record card
55, 104, 371	2241	7264542	Not noted	P	RHD	Saloon	Blue	Blue		13/11/51	New Zealand	Singer Ltd.	Delivery date differs from record card
55, 188, 323	2242	7262014	LOU 600	K2	RHD	2-Seater	Bronze	Brown		10/3/51	Bristol Street Motors	W. H. Drew	
55	2243	Not noted	Not noted	K2	Not noted	2-Seater	Not noted	Not noted	Not noted	Not noted	Not noted	Not noted	Not noted
55	2244	Not used	Not used	Not used	Not used	Not used	Not used	Not used	Not used	Not used	Not used	Not used	Not used
55	2245	Not used	Not used	Not used	Not used	Not used	Not used	Not used	Not used	Not used	Not used	Not used	Not used
55, 104, 699	2246	7264696	Not noted	P	RHD	Saloon	Black	Tan		13/11/51	New Zealand	Singer Ltd.	Delivery date differs from record card
55, 104	2247	7264547	Not noted	P	RHD	Saloon	Metallic Grey	Blue		13/11/51	New Zealand	Singer Ltd.	Delivery date differs from record card
55, 104	2248	7262928	Not noted	P	RHD	Saloon	Black	Tan		13/11/51	New Zealand	Singer Ltd.	Delivery date differs from record card
55, 175, 200	2249	7262954	Not noted	P	RHD	Saloon	Blue	Blue		20/11/51	Frew	J. C. Smith	Transferred from Mutch Motors
55, 193, 318, 322, 327, 698	2250	7262969	MLW 873	P	RHD	Saloon	Metallic Grey	Red		12/1/51	Nunn (H. J. Quick Ltd.)	The Willey Key Co. Ltd.	
55, 177, 319, 351	2251	7262955	NAH 2	P	RHD	Saloon	Metallic Grey	Grey		21/11/51	Gould	R. D. Carter	
55, 172, 355, 356, 358, 360, 363, 366, 368, 370, 372, 377, 382, 699	2252	7263584	MLW 872	P	RHD	Saloon	Blue	Blue		12/1/51	Adlards	I. C. Trafford	Page 372 suggests HLU 872. Pages 366 and 382 appears to be MLU 872
55, 105, 699	2253	7265181	Not noted	P	RHD	Saloon	Black	Brown		14/12/51	New Zealand (Tracspecs)	W. R. Ashton	Export
55	2254	7265177	Not noted	P	RHD	Saloon	Black	Blue		29/11/51	New Central		
55, 188	2255	7265163	Not noted	P	RHD	Saloon	Black	Maroon		30/11/51	Bristol Street Motors (Ashmores Ltd.)	Birmingham Stopper and Cylde	
55, 172, 320, 336, 340	2256	7265164	MLO 469	P	RHD	Saloon	Blue	Blue		23/11/51	Adlards	Miss G. Garton	
56, 181	2257	7265763	Not noted	P	RHD	Saloon	Metallic Grey	Red		12/4/51	Hartwells (Loddon Bridge Motors)	H. M. Price	
56, 175	2258	7265700	Not noted	P	RHD	Saloon	Metallic Grey	Grey		12/3/51	Dagenham Motors	P. Clarke	
56, 175, 360, 363, 367, 384	2259	7265777	MRO 351	P	RHD	Saloon	Blue	Blue		12/5/51	Dagenham Motors (H. G. Greasey & Sons)	W. H. Davies & Sons	Page 384 notes regn. GRX 111

Page References	Chassis	Original Engine Number	UK Registration	Type	LHD?	Body Style	Original Colour	Original Interior	Original Hood	Original Delivery	Allocation	First Customer	Remarks
								CHASSIS NUMBER PAGE REFERENCE KEY: Allocation Books (pages 1-77), Record Cards (pages 78-167), Warranty Book (pages 168-201), Service Records (pages 202-393)					
56, 175, 322	2260	7265761	KNM 526	P	RHD	Saloon	Blue	Blue		12/5/51	Dagenham Motors (A. W. Watkins Ltd.)	Fords (Finsbury Ltd.)	
56, 201, 351, 354, 358, 359, 365, 367	2261	7265860	UI 4777	P	RHD	Saloon	Metallic Grey	Blue		12/10/51	Hamilton (John Patterson Ltd.)	A. T. Marshall	
56, 198	2262	7264737	Not noted	P	RHD	Saloon	Show Grey	Blue		12/6/51	George & Jobling (Callanders Garage)	Watt Bros. Ltd.	
56, 172	2263	7264876	Not noted	P	RHD	Saloon	Blue	Red		15/12/51	Adlards	L. W. Elliott	
56, 175, 383	2264	7263696	HXK 372	P	RHD	Saloon	Black	Brown		15/12/51	Dagenham Motors (Russell Motors)	Rt. Hon. Earl of Kimberley	
56, 105	2265	7264881	Not noted	P	RHD	Saloon	Black	Blue		14/12/51	New Zealand (Tracspecs)	Alexander Maccoll	Export
56, 198, 319	2266	7264738	Not noted	P	RHD	Saloon	Black	Maroon		13/12/51	George & Jobling	Paterson Scott Mackay Ltd.	
56, 181, 380, 698	2267	7266394	STO 224	P	RHD	Saloon	Metallic Grey	Red		18/12/51	Hartwells	W. J. Hopper	GJO 224 also noted as reg
56, 105	2268	7265169	Not noted	P	RHD	Saloon	Metallic Grey	Blue		18/12/51	New Zealand (Tracspecs)	Singer Ltd. (E. R. Moore)	Delivery date differs from record card
56, 172, 340, 353, 356, 698	2269	7265037	MUC 189	P	RHD	Saloon	Metallic Grey	Maroon		1/8/52	Adlards	C. J. M. Abbott	Radio
56, 166, 198, 357, 363, 372, 376, 379, 382, 386, 390, 393	2270	7266551	KGA 165	P	RHD	Saloon	Blue	Blue		1/2/52	George & Jobling (Callanders Garage)	Mrs M. Turner	
56, 105, 784	2271	7266542	Not noted	P	RHD	Saloon	Blue	Blue		20/12/51	New Zealand	Singer Ltd.	Mixed up record card with 2273
56, 167, 193, 381	2272	7266396	JFY 499	P	RHD	Saloon	Black	Brown		28/1/52	Nunn (Middleton Garage)	W. Fell	
56, 188, 784	2273	7265701	Not noted	P	RHD	Saloon	Black	Maroon		21/12/51	Bristol Street Motors	E. W. Stone	Mixed up record card with 2271
56, 175, 328	2274	7265854	XME 496	P	RHD	Saloon	Black	Brown		31/12/51	Dagenham Motors	C. B. E. Russell	
56, 352, 355, 698, 784	2275	E408	MLX 381	P1X	RHD	Saloon	Metallic Blue	Blue		9/1/52	Adlards	S. H. Allard	1952 Monte Carlo Rally winning car of S. H. Allard
56, 188, 358	2276	7265770	Not noted	P	RHD	Saloon	Black	Blue		1/3/52	Bristol Street Motors (Mists Garage)	W. Hill	One record notes regn. MLX 381 which is 2275
56, 105	2277	7266553	Not noted	P	RHD	Saloon	Metallic Grey	Maroon		1/4/52	New Zealand	Mr L. H. Kemp	Export
56, 105	2278	7265855	Not noted	P	RHD	Saloon	Metallic Grey	Red		1/4/52	New Zealand	Singer Ltd.	Export
56, 167, 190, 389	2279	7266539	KBC 148	P	RHD	Saloon	Metallic Grey	Maroon		28/1/52	Universal (Central Garage)	F. P. Faulkner	
56, 195, 699, 703	2280	7266441	PUM 797	P	RHD	Saloon	Blue	Blue		3/6/52	Tate	Not noted	Noted as warranty not necessary
56, 172, 324, 325, 332, 338, 340, 346	2281	7264458	MXA 546	P	RHD	Saloon	Blue	Blue		2/2/52	Adlards	Clarke Blanch & Co.	

Page References	Chassis	Original Engine Number	UK Registration	Type	LHD?	Body Style	Original Colour	Original Interior	Original Hood	Original Delivery	Allocation	First Customer	Remarks
CHASSIS NUMBER PAGE REFERENCE KEY: Allocation Books (pages 1-77), Record Cards (pages 78-167), Warranty Book (pages 168-201), Service Records (pages 202-393)														
56, 193, 374, 378, 382	2282	7266389	NNE 400	P	RHD	Saloon	Blue	Blue		13/3/52	Nunn	Not noted	
56, 195	2283	7268037	Not noted	P	RHD	Saloon	Black	Blue		2/2/52	Tate	W. A. Church	
56, 184, 698	2284	7268026	HUJ 487	P	RHD	Saloon	Black	Maroon		2/5/52	Furrows (The Station Garage)		
56, 172, 374, 699	2285	E409	MLX 400	P1X	RHD	Saloon	Metallic Grey	Maroon		13/3/52	Adlards	Mrs E. Allard	S. H. A. Mrs Allard's 1952 Monte Carlo car
56	2286	7268378	Not noted	P	RHD	Saloon	Black	Brown		2/1/52	New Central		
56, 106, 785, 790	2287	7268364	Not noted	P	RHD	Saloon	Black	Brown		13/3/53	Gold Coast	Mr S. Wilson	See 3100 and export card 2287
56, 177, 699	2288	7268379	Not noted	P	RHD	Saloon	Metallic Grey	Blue		2/9/52	Gould	Not noted	Bank et Arcas Ltd., Gold Coast
57, 175, 332, 336, 345, 698	2289	7268369	XMY 590	P	RHD	Saloon	Metallic Grey	Maroon		19/2/52	Dagenham Motors	P. Z. Henderson	
57	2290	7268860	Not noted	P	RHD	Saloon	Blue	Grey		15/2/52	New Central		
57, 138, 345, 698	2291	7268850	MOB 962	P	RHD	Saloon	Blue	Grey		28/2/52	Bristol Street Motors	Arthur Rowe and Sons	
57, 698	2292	7268851	ORL 87	P	RHD	Saloon	Black	Brown		15/2/52	New Central		
57, 136, 699	2293	7269443	PVK 718	P	RHD	Saloon	Black	Maroon		22/2/52	Patterson (Fewsters)	W. M. Humprey	
57, 175	2294	7269434	Not noted	P	RHD	Saloon	Black	Brown		26/2/52	Dagenham Motors	F. E. Griffiths	
57, 167, 172, 320, 324 331 334, 338, 347, 354, 363, 368, 476	2295	7265176	MLL 155	M2X	RHD	Coupe	Blue	Blue	Black	28/11/51	Adlards	Hable M. Escott	Some records, including page 368, note regn. MLX 155
57, 195	2296	7262377	Not noted	M2X	RHD	Coupe	Cream	Brown	Fawn	11/6/51	Tate	Not noted	
57, 188	2297	7265766	Not noted	M2X	RHD	Coupe	Grey	Blue	Black	12/11/51	Bristol Street Motors	Dr. John Leigh-Collis	
57, 84	2298	Less engine	Not noted	M2X	LHD	Coupe	Royal Blue	Red	Beige	24/1/52	U.S.A. (R/P Imported Motor Co.)	Seddon (D. W. Lockard)	Cadillac Modification
57, 175, 326	2299	7265691	XMX 237	M2X	RHD	Coupe	Metallic Grey	Red	Black	21/12/51	Dagenham Motors	F. G. B. Waddell	
57, 346	2300	Not used	Not used	Not used	Not used	Not used	Not used	Not used	Not used	Not used	Not used	Not used	Not used
57	2301	Not used	Not used	Not used	Not used	Not used	Not used	Not used	Not used	Not used	Not used	Not used	Not used
57	2302	Not used	Not used	Not used	Not used	Not used	Not used	Not used	Not used	Not used	Not used	Not used	Not used
57	2303	Not used	Not used	Not used	Not used	Not used	Not used	Not used	Not used	Not used	Not used	Not used	Not used
57	2304	Not used	Not used	Not used	Not used	Not used	Not used	Not used	Not used	Not used	Not used	Not used	Not used
57	2305	Not used	Not used	Not used	Not used	Not used	Not used	Not used	Not used	Not used	Not used	Not used	Not used

Page References	Chassis	Original Engine Number	UK Registration	Type	LHD?	Body Style	Original Colour	Original Interior	Original Hood	Original Delivery	Allocation	First Customer	Remarks

CHASSIS NUMBER PAGE REFERENCE KEY: Allocation Books (pages 1-77), Record Cards (pages 78-167), Warranty Book (pages 168-201), Service Records (pages 202-393)

Page References	Chassis	Original Engine Number	UK Registration	Type	LHD?	Body Style	Original Colour	Original Interior	Original Hood	Original Delivery	Allocation	First Customer	Remarks
57	2306	Not used	Not used	Not used	Not used	Not used	Not used	Not used	Not used	Not used	Not used	Not used	Not used
57	2307	Not used	Not used	Not used	Not used	Not used	Not used	Not used	Not used	Not used	Not used	Not used	Not used
57	2308	Not used	Not used	Not used	Not used	Not used	Not used	Not used	Not used	Not used	Not used	Not used	Not used
57	2309	Not used	Not used	Not used	Not used	Not used	Not used	Not used	Not used	Not used	Not used	Not used	Not used
57	2310	Not used	Not used	Not used	Not used	Not used	Not used	Not used	Not used	Not used	Not used	Not used	Not used
57	2311	Not used	Not used	Not used	Not used	Not used	Not used	Not used	Not used	Not used	Not used	Not used	Not used
57	2312	Not used	Not used	Not used	Not used	Not used	Not used	Not used	Not used	Not used	Not used	Not used	Not used
57	2313	Not used	Not used	Not used	Not used	Not used	Not used	Not used	Not used	Not used	Not used	Not used	Not used
57	2314	Not used	Not used	Not used	Not used	Not used	Not used	Not used	Not used	Not used	Not used	Not used	Not used
57	2315	Not used	Not used	Not used	Not used	Not used	Not used	Not used	Not used	Not used	Not used	Not used	Not used
57	2316	Not used	Not used	Not used	Not used	Not used	Not used	Not used	Not used	Not used	Not used	Not used	Not used
57	2317	Not used	Not used	Not used	Not used	Not used	Not used	Not used	Not used	Not used	Not used	Not used	Not used
57	2318	Not used	Not used	Not used	Not used	Not used	Not used	Not used	Not used	Not used	Not used	Not used	Not used
57	2319	Not used	Not used	Not used	Not used	Not used	Not used	Not used	Not used	Not used	Not used	Not used	Not used
57	2320	Not used	Not used	Not used	Not used	Not used	Not used	Not used	Not used	Not used	Not used	Not used	Not used
59, 801	3000	5337/25	MXA 554	P2	RHD	Safari	Not noted						Refer to chassis 4001. Prototype P2 Safari owned by Sydney's brother, Dennis
59	3001	Not used	Not used	Not used	Not used	Not used	Not used	Not used	Not used	Not used	Not used	Not used	Not used
59	3002	Not used	Not used	Not used	Not used	Not used	Not used	Not used	Not used	Not used	Not used	Not used	Not used
59	3003	Not used	Not used	Not used	Not used	Not used	Not used	Not used	Not used	Not used	Not used	Not used	Not used
59, 374, 786	3004	Not noted	16429	Not noted	Not noted	Not noted	Not noted	Not noted	Not noted	Not noted	Not noted	Not noted	Page 374 indicates PB 3004, suspect it may be 5004
59	3005	Not used	Not used	Not used	Not used	Not used	Not used	Not used	Not used	Not used	Not used	Not used	Not used
59	3006	Not used	Not used	Not used	Not used	Not used	Not used	Not used	Not used	Not used	Not used	Not used	Not used
59	3007	Not used	Not used	Not used	Not used	Not used	Not used	Not used	Not used	Not used	Not used	Not used	Not used

Page References	Chassis	Original Engine Number	UK Registration	Type	LHD?	Body Style	Original Colour	Original Interior	Original Hood	Original Delivery	Allocation	First Customer	Remarks

CHASSIS NUMBER PAGE REFERENCE KEY: Allocation Books (pages 1-77), Record Cards (pages 78-167), Warranty Book (pages 168-201), Service Records (pages 202-393)

Page References	Chassis	Original Engine Number	UK Registration	Type	LHD?	Body Style	Original Colour	Original Interior	Original Hood	Original Delivery	Allocation	First Customer	Remarks
59	3008	Not used	Not used	Not used	Not used	Not used	Not used	Not used	Not used	Not used	Not used	Not used	Not used
59	3009	Not used	Not used	Not used	Not used	Not used	Not used	Not used	Not used	Not used	Not used	Not used	Not used
59	3010	Not used	Not used	Not used	Not used	Not used	Not used	Not used	Not used	Not used	Not used	Not used	Not used
59	3011	Not used	Not used	Not used	Not used	Not used	Not used	Not used	Not used	Not used	Not used	Not used	Not used
59	3012	7266391	Not noted	M2X	RHD	Coupe	Metallic Grey	Red	Black	Not noted	English		S. O. R
59, 175, 351, 362, 364, 365, 367, 370, 372, 379, 382, 391	3013	7266552	YMD 688	M2X	RHD	Coupe	Black	Brown	Black	22/2/52	Dagenham Motors	Wimbldeon Speedway Ltd.	
59, 175	3014	7266545	Not noted	M2X	RHD	Coupe	Blue	Blue	Black	1/1/52	Dagenham Motors (Brooklands of Bond St)	H. M Palin	
59, 175, 323, 351, 378, 383, 388, 389, 391	3015	7268025	MLW 940	M2X	RHD	Coupe	Black	Brown	Black	25/1/52	Dagenham Motors (Tankard & Smith)	H. A. Gammride	K2?
59, 175, 325, 330, 356, 361, 367, 372, 374, 377, 787	3016	7268373	XME 222	M2X	RHD	Coupe	Metallic Light Blue	Blue	Black	25/1/52	Dagenham Motors (H. M. Bentley & Partners)	Ian Temerley Stamp	Page 361 refers to 3018 but is 3016
59, 639	3017	Less Engine	Not noted	K2	LHD	2-Seater	Ivory	Black	Black	2/12/52	U.S.A.	Jack Paw	De Dion axle
59, 787	3018	Less Engine	Not noted	K2	LHD	2-Seater	Grey	Red	Black	14/3/52	U.S.A.	Seddon	Page 361 refers to 3018 but is 3016
59	3019	Less Engine	Not noted	K2	LHD	2-Seater	Red	Black	Black	3/6/52	U.S.A.	Seddon	
59, 689	3020	Less Engine	Not noted	K2	LHD	2-Seater	French Grey	Black	Black	4/2/52	U.S.A.	Seddon	
59	3021	Less Engine	Not noted	K2	LHD	2-Seater	B. Grey	Red	Black	21/4/52	U.S.A.	Seddon	
59	3022	Less Engine	Not noted	K2	LHD	2-Seater	M. E. Red	Black	Black	5/6/52	U.S.A.	Seddon	
59	3023	Less Engine	Not noted	K2	LHD	2-Seater	Green	Green	Black	5/7/52	U.S.A.	Seddon	
59	3024	Less Engine	Not noted	K2	LHD	2-Seater	Cream/ Black	Black	Black	22/4/52	U.S.A.	Not noted	
59	3025	Less Engine	Not noted	K2	LHD	2-Seater	Red	Red	Beige	26/5/52	U.S.A.	Seddon	
59, 688	3026	2R-558	Not noted	K2	LHD	2-Seater	Metallic Blue	Orange	Beige	5/9/52	U.S.A.	Gen. Curtis LeMay	
59	3027	Less Engine	Not noted	K2	LHD	2-Seater	Green	Green	Black	31/5/52	Not noted	Not noted	
59, 683	3028	Less Engine	Not noted	K2	LHD	2-Seater	Red	Red	Black	7/9/52	U.S.A.	Kirk Motors	
59, 683	3029	Less Engine	LOH 921	K2	RHD	2-Seater	Green	Red	Black	17/6/52	U.S.A.	Seddon	
59, 690	3030	C52/8/45973	NGP 970	K3	LHD	3-Seater	Blue	Red	Not noted	11/3/52	U.S.A.	General Griswold	1952 Show Car
59	3031	Less Engine	Not noted	K2	RHD	2-Seater	Primer	Not noted	Not noted	12/8/52	U.S.A.	Distribuidora	

Page References	Chassis	Original Engine Number	UK Registration	Type	LHD?	Body Style	Original Colour	Original Interior	Original Hood	Original Delivery	Allocation	First Customer	Remarks

CHASSIS NUMBER PAGE REFERENCE KEY: Allocation Books (pages 1-77), Record Cards (pages 78-167), Warranty Book (pages 168-201), Service Records (pages 202-393)

Page References	Chassis	Original Engine Number	UK Registration	Type	LHD?	Body Style	Original Colour	Original Interior	Original Hood	Original Delivery	Allocation	First Customer	Remarks
59	3032	15870/146	Not noted	K2	RHD	2-Seater	Green	Green	Black	8/11/52	Panama	Dr. Auto's (Dr. Mahaff)	
60, 347, 501	3033	7275022	MXY 9	K2	RHD	2-Seater	Metallic Blue	Maroon	Black	30/7/52	U.S Embassy	John Charles Klaffenbach	
60	3034	Less Engine	Not noted	K2	RHD	2-Seater	Black	Red	Black	15/7/52	U.S.A.	Noel Kirk Motors	
60, 689	3035	7277942	Not noted	K2	RHD	2-Seater	Red	Red	Black	9/3/52	U.S.A.	A. Louis Straus	
60, 689	3036	7277954	Not noted	K2	RHD	2-Seater	Cream	Black	Black	9/3/52	U.S.A.	A. Louis Straus	
60, 129, 683	3037	Less Engine	Not noted	J2X	LHD	2-Seater	Red	Black	Black	29/1/52	U.S.A.	Seddon	Chrysler modification
60, 130, 683	3038	Less Engine	Not noted	J2X	LHD	2-Seater	Sky Blue	Red	Red	2/12/52	U.S.A.	Seddon	Chrysler modification
60, 130, 683	3039	Less Engine	Not noted	J2X	LHD	2-Seater	French racing Blue	Red	Black	14/2/52	U.S.A.	Denver Imported Motors	Cadillac mods, demonstrator car
60, 130, 683	3040	Less Engine	Not noted	J2X	LHD	2-Seater	Black	Red	Black	25/2/52	U.S.A.	California Sports Car Co.	Chrysler modification, 20 gallon fuel tank, quick change rear axle
60, 130, 683	3041	Less Engine	Not noted	J2X	LHD	2-Seater	Ivory	Red	Black	3/6/52	U.S.A.	Bill Co.	Chrysler modification
60, 130, 683	3042	Less Engine	Not noted	J2X	LHD	2-Seater	Red	Red	Black	29/2/52	U.S.A.	R/P Imported Motor Co.	Cadillac modification
60, 130, 683	3043	Less Engine	7274 HJ	J2X	LHD	2-Seater	B. R. Green	Green	Black	29/2/52	U.S.A.	Seddon	Cadillac modification
60, 131, 683	3044	Less Engine	Not noted	J2X	LHD	2-Seater	Red	Red	Not noted	26/3/52	U.S.A.	Denver Imported Motors	Oldsmobile modification
60, 131, 683	3045	Less Engine	Not noted	J2X	LHD	2-Seater	Royal Blue	Blue	Not noted	27/3/52	U.S.A.	Moss Motors	Cadillac modification
60, 131, 683	3046	Less Engine	Not noted	J2X	LHD	2-Seater	Red	Red	Not noted	27/3/52	U.S.A.	California Sports Car Co.	Cadillac modification
60, 131, 683	3047	Less Engine	Not noted	J2X	LHD	2-Seater	B. R. Green	Red	Black	4/2/52	U.S.A.	Seddon (Walter A. Grey)	Cadillac modification
60, 131, 683	3048	Less Engine	Not noted	J2X	LHD	2-Seater	White	Black	Black	4/2/52	U.S.A.	Seddon	Chrysler modification
60, 131, 188, 612, 613, 683	3049	CHR-151	MXF 974	J2X	RHD	2-seater Le Mans body	B. R. Green	Not noted	Not noted	6/1/52	Allard Motor Co.	Curtis	Chrysler engine, 4-speed box, quick change rear end/ Curtis rebuilt as Hinton special
60, 132, 683	3050	Less Engine	Not noted	J2X	LHD	2-Seater	Beige and Red	Red	Beige	5/1/52	U.S.A.	Harry Steele	Lincoln engine modification
60, 683	3051	Less Engine	Not noted	J2X	LHD	2-Seater	Red	Red	Not noted	17/4/52	U.S.A.	California	
60, 683	3052	Less Engine	Not noted	J2X	LHD	2-Seater	Blue	Blue	Not noted	18/4/52	U.S.A.	California	
60, 683	3053	C-I50	ORL 320	J2X	RHD	2-Seater	B. R. Green (Red)	Tan	Black	5/9/52	New Central	Watkins	Cadillac engine, 4-speed box
60, 683	3054	Less Engine	Not noted	J2X	RHD	2-Seater	Blue	Blue	Beige	26/5/52	Nairobi, Kenya	Craegin	
60, 491, 683	3055	CHR-100	MXF 969	J2X	RHD	2-seater Le Mans body	Green	Not noted	Not noted	8/3/52	U.S.A.	RIP Imported Motors	Chrysler engine retained, car shipped with Cadillac mountings
60, 683	3056	Less Engine	Not noted	J2X	LHD	2-Seater	Bugatti Blue	Red	Black	5/6/52	U.S.A.	Seddon	
60, 683	3057	Less Engine	Not noted	J2X	LHD	2-Seater	Black	Red	Not noted	27/5/52	U.S.A.	Seddon	
60, 683	3058	Less Engine	Not noted	J2X	LHD	2-Seater	Red	Red	Beige	27/5/52	U.S.A.	Seddon	

·ALLARD·

Page References	Chassis	Original Engine Number	UK Registration	Type	LHD?	Body Style	Original Colour	Original Interior	Original Hood	Original Delivery	Allocation	First Customer	Remarks
CHASSIS NUMBER PAGE REFERENCE KEY: Allocation Books (pages 1-77), Record Cards (pages 78-167), Warranty Book (pages 168-201), Service Records (pages 202-393)													
60, 683	3059	Less Engine	Not noted	J2X	LHD	2-Seater	Green	White	Black	26/6/52	U.S.A.	Imported Mot	
60, 683	3060	Less Engine	Not noted	J2X	LHD	2-Seater	Cream	Blue	Not noted	27/5/52	U.S.A.	Seddon	
60, 683	3061	Less Engine	Not noted	J2X	LHD	2-Seater	Green	Green	Black	17/6/52	U.S.A.	Seddon	
60, 683	3062	Less Engine 20412	Not noted	J2X	RHD	2-Seater	Ivory	Red	Black	25/6/52	U.S.A.	Noel Kirk Motors	
60, 684	3063	2041Z	Not noted	J2X	LHD	2-Seater	Bronze	Brown	Beige	6/10/52	Singapore	George Lee	
60, 684	3064	Less Engine	Not noted	J2X	LHD	2-Seater	Green	Red	Black	7/2/52	U.S.A.	Seddon	
60, 684	3065	Less Engine	Not noted	J2X	RHD	2-Seater	Royal Blue	Red	Black	7/2/52	U.S.A.		
61, 684	3066	C. 52-8-45975	Not noted	J2X	RHD	2-seater Le Mans body	Metallic Blue	Red	Black	2/12/52	U.S.A.	Captain Leslie U.S.A.F.	Chrysler engine
61, 684	3067	Less Engine	Not noted	J2X	RHD	2-Seater	White	Green	Green	18/8/52	U.S.A.	RIP Imported Motors	
61, 684	3068	Less Engine	Not noted	J2X	RHD	2-Seater	Black	Red	Black	15/7/52	U.S.A. (California Sports Car Co.)		
61, 684	3069	Less Engine	Not noted	J2X	RHD	2-Seater	Blue	Blue	Black	15/7/52	U.S.A. (California Sports Car Co.)		
61, 684	3070	2040 Z	Not noted	J2X	RHD	2-Seater	Red	Red	Black	27/6/52	Nairobi, Kenya		
61, 684	3071	Less Engine	Not noted	J2X	RHD	2-Seater	Red	Red	Black	1/6/53	U.S.A.	Noel Kirk Motors	Le Mans body?
61, 684	3072	Less Engine	Not noted	J2X	RHD	2-Seater	Light Blue	Red	Black	22/7/52	U.S.A.	Motorsport Inc.	
61, 684	3073	Less Engine	Not noted	J2X	RHD	2-Seater	Black	Brown	Not noted	9/9/52	Speedcraft Enterprises		
61, 684	3074	Less Engine	LYY 914	J2X	RHD	2-Seater	Primer	Red	Not noted	25/9/52	U.S.A. (California Sports Car Co.)		
61, 684	3075	Less engine	Not noted	J2X	RHD	2-Seater	Red	Red	Not noted	1/9/1952	U.S.A.	Noel Kirk Motors	
61, 684	3076	Less Engine	Not noted	J2X	RHD	2-Seater	Red	Red	Black	30/9/52	U.S.A.	Shawnee Motor Co.	
61, 684	3077	Less Engine	Not noted	J2X	RHD	2-Seater	Grey-red	Hide	Not noted	10/4/52	U.S.A.	Noel Kirk Motors	
61, 193	3078	7269845	Not noted	P	RHD	Saloon	Metallic Grey	Red		14/3/52	Nunn (The Bank Top Motor House Ltd.)	Alex Pilkles	
61, 698 700	3079	7269838	MON 381	P	RHD	Saloon	Metallic Grey	Blue		3/5/52	Bristol Street Motors	J. Howard Hill	Warranty Book crossed this off Furrows dealer list
61, 172, 332, 345, 698	3080	7269839	MXN 420	P	RHD	Saloon	Metallic Grey	Maroon		4/3/52	Adlards	Site Caterers Ltd.	Page 346 shows MXM 420
61, 698	3081	7269433	OTT 992	P	RHD	Saloon	Black	Brown		13/3/52	New Central		
61, 172	3082	7269840	Not noted	P	RHD	Saloon	Black	Brown		26/3/52	Adlards	C. E. Jenkins	
61, 183	3083	7270578	Not noted	P	RHD	Saloon	Black	Maroon		19/3/52	Harris (Norton Garage)	W. Bey Evans	
61, 184, 330, 337, 345, 357, 361, 362, 387, 390, 693	3084	7270583	HUJ 760	P	RHD	Saloon	Black	Brown		4/4/52	Furrows (Crown Motor Co.)	The Rt. Hon. W. Boyne	Two records on pages 357 and 361 state #3084 incorrectly and should be 3089. Page 362 shows QE9888
61, 198	3085	7270581	Not noted	P	RHD	Saloon	Metallic Bronze	Maroon		18/4/52	George & Jobling (H. Prossers & Sons)	Bartholomew Gross	

Page References	Chassis	Original Engine Number	UK Registration	Type	LHD?	Body Style	Original Colour	Original Interior	Original Hood	Original Delivery	Allocation	First Customer	Remarks
							CHASSIS NUMBER PAGE REFERENCE KEY: Allocation Books (pages 1-77), Record Cards (pages 78-167), Warranty Book (pages 168-201), Service Records (pages 202-393)						
61, 190	3086	7271485	Not noted	P	RHD	Saloon	Metallic Grey	Maroon		24/4/52	Universal	Not noted	
61, 196	3087	7271089	Not noted	P	RHD	Saloon	Black	Brown		5/9/52	Patterson	G. F. Clay	
61, 172	3088	7273164	Not noted	P	RHD	Saloon	Black	Brown		16/5/52	Adlards	Z. N. Gyerey	
61, 177, 353, 365, 369, 372, 377, 392, 393	3089	7268377	MUU 186	M2X	RHD	Coupe	Metallic Grey	Blue	Black	31/1/52	Gould	D. P. Prestwich	Two references may be mislabelled as 3084 on pages 357 and 361
61, 195	3090	7268859	Not noted	M2X	RHD	Coupe	Metallic Grey	Maroon	Black	2/7/52	Tate (Albert Farnell Ltd.)	F. A. Whitaker	Discovered in barn, AOC newsletter April '88
61, 188, 364, 700	3091	7268855	WRF 529	M2X	RHD	Coupe	Metallic Grey	Maroon	Black	2/9/52	Bristol Street Motors (Hewitts Garage)	A. Gourevitch	
61, 172, 325, 327, 329, 331, 341, 344	3092	7269430	MXA 551	M2X	RHD	Coupe	Black	Brown	Black	14/2/52	Adlards	Westinghouse Brake & Signal Co.	
61, 196	3093	7269429	Not noted	M2X	RHD	Coupe	Black	Brown	Black	29/3/52	Patterson	Corrugated Packing & Sheet Metal Ltd.	
61	3094	Less Engine	Not noted	M2X	LHD	Coupe	Blue	Red	Blue	17/3/52	U.S.A.	Seddon	
61	3095	7269344	Not noted	PX	LHD	Coupe	Metallic Blue	Blue	Blue	3/5/52	Norman Reeves		Export
61, 185, 700	3096	7270599	EVG 894	M2X	RHD	Coupe	Metallic Grey	Maroon	Black	1/5/52	Mann Egerton	F. S. Clayton	
61, 172	3097	7271488	Not noted	M2X	RHD	Coupe	Metallic Grey	Maroon	Black	26/4/52	Adlards	H. E. Tucor	
61, 172, 346, 700	3098	7274426	MYL 773	M2X	RHD	Coupe	Blue	Grey	Black	6/4/52	Adlards	D. Cussen	
62, 179	3099	7271156	Not noted	P	RHD	Saloon	Metallic Grey	Maroon	Not noted	5/9/52	English (G. W. Cox)	Camper & Nicholsons	Central remote gear change
62, 785	3100	18F 7268364	Not noted	P	RHD	Saloon	Black	Brown	Not noted	13/3/53	Tarkwa (Gold Coast)		Transferred and shipped under 2287
62, 188	3101	7280981	Not noted	P	RHD	Saloon	Metallic Grey	Maroon	Not noted	10/1/52	Bristol Street Motors	James Wesley	
62	3102	Not noted	Not noted	P	Not noted	Saloon	Black	Brown	Not noted	Not noted	Not noted	Not noted	Not noted
62, 106, 698	3103	EI-U-5101	MYM 593	P	LHD	Saloon	Blue	Red	Not noted	23/7/52	Sweden	Mme. Jocelyn Hjelme-Lundberg	
62	3104	7275028	Not noted	P	RHD	Saloon	Blue	Blue	Not noted	23/7/52	George & Jobling		S. O. R
62	3105	Not noted	Not noted	P	Not noted	Saloon	Not noted	Not noted	Not noted	Not noted	Not noted	Not noted	Not noted
62	3106	Not noted	Not noted	P	Not noted	Saloon	Not noted	Not noted	Not noted	Not noted	Not noted	Not noted	Not noted
62, 106, 468, 698	3107	9424 B	Not noted	P	LHD	Saloon	Black	Blue		10/2/52	Sweden	A. B Ingvar Bergengren	The client has separately arranged to import a Lincoln engine and gearbox from the USA
62	3108	Not used	Not used	Not used	Not used	Not used	Not used	Not used	Not used	Not used	Not used	Not used	Not used

Page References	Chassis	Original Engine Number	UK Registration	Type	LHD?	Body Style	Original Colour	Original Interior	Original Hood	Original Delivery	Allocation	First Customer	Remarks

CHASSIS NUMBER PAGE REFERENCE KEY: Allocation Books (pages 1-77), Record Cards (pages 78-167), Warranty Book (pages 168-201), Service Records (pages 202-393)

Page References	Chassis	Original Engine Number	UK Registration	Type	LHD?	Body Style	Original Colour	Original Interior	Original Hood	Original Delivery	Allocation	First Customer	Remarks
62	3109	Not used	Not used	Not used	Not used	Not used	Not used	Not used	Not used	Not used	Not used	Not used	Not used
62	3110	Not used	Not used	Not used	Not used	Not used	Not used	Not used	Not used	Not used	Not used	Not used	Not used
62	3111	Not used	Not used	Not used	Not used	Not used	Not used	Not used	Not used	Not used	Not used	Not used	Not used
62	3112	Not used	Not used	Not used	Not used	Not used	Not used	Not used	Not used	Not used	Not used	Not used	Not used
62	3113	Not used	Not used	Not used	Not used	Not used	Not used	Not used	Not used	Not used	Not used	Not used	Not used
62	3114	Not used	Not used	Not used	Not used	Not used	Not used	Not used	Not used	Not used	Not used	Not used	Not used
62	3115	Not used	Not used	Not used	Not used	Not used	Not used	Not used	Not used	Not used	Not used	Not used	Not used
62	3116	Not used	Not used	Not used	Not used	Not used	Not used	Not used	Not used	Not used	Not used	Not used	Not used
62	3117	Not used	Not used	Not used	Not used	Not used	Not used	Not used	Not used	Not used	Not used	Not used	Not used
62	3118	Not used	Not used	Not used	Not used	Not used	Not used	Not used	Not used	Not used	Not used	Not used	Not used
62, 167, 175, 353, 388, 393, 700	3119	7280348	YMD 692	M2X	RHD	Coupe	Black	Brown	Black	9/12/52	Dagenham Motors	Jackson & Curtiss (Builders) Ltd.	Refer to record cards, export to N. S. W., Australia
62, 193	3120	7271486	Not noted	M2X	RHD	Coupe	Black	Brown	Black	5/8/52	Nunn (A. W. Webb Ltd.)	Ian Douglas	
62	3121	Not noted	Not noted	M2X	Not noted	Coupe	Black	Brown	Not noted	Not noted	Not noted	Not noted	Not noted
62, 172, 346	3122	7274428	MXT 990	M2X	RHD	Coupe	Blue	Blue	Black	6/4/52	Adlards (Dominous)	C. E. Smith	Export
62	3123	Not noted	Not noted	M2X	Not noted	Coupe	Metallic Grey	Maroon	Black	Not noted	Stockholm		
62, 84 476 700	3124	15868/105	Not noted	M2X	LHD	Coupe	Cream	Red	Red	8/6/52	Stockholm	Ingvar Bergengren	Colours differ according to record card
62, 97	3125	Less Engine	Not noted	K2	LHD	2-Seater	Turquoise Blue	Fawn	Black	13/9/52	U.S.A.	Noel Kirk Motors	Cadillac modification
62, 97, 389	3126	Less Engine	Not noted	K2	LHD	2-Seater	Red	Red	Black	22/9/52	U.S.A.	Noel Kirk Motors	Cadillac modification
62, 97	3127	Less Engine	Not noted	K2	RHD	2-Seater	Pale Beige	Brown	Not noted	10/7/52	U.S.A.	Noel Kirk Motors	Cadillac modification
62, 97	3128	15869/108	Not noted	K2	RHD	2-Seater	Cream	Red	Black	27/10/52	Colombia (Panamerican Import)	Antonio Izguierdo	Mercury engine
62	3129	Not used	Not used	Not used	Not used	Not used	Not used	Not used	Not used	Not used	Not used	Not used	Not used
62, 97	3130	Less engine	Not noted	K2	LHD	2-Seater	Cream	Tan	Black	10/10/52	U.S.A. (Rivera Motors Inc.)	Thomas J. Stapleton	Cadillac modification
62	3131	Not used	Not used	Not used	Not used	Not used	Not used	Not used	Not used	Not used	Not used	Not used	Not used
63	3132	Not used	Not used	Not used	Not used	Not used	Not used	Not used	Not used	Not used	Not used	Not used	Not used

Page References	Chassis	Original Engine Number	UK Registration	Type	LHD?	Body Style	Original Colour	Original Interior	Original Hood	Original Delivery	Allocation	First Customer	Remarks
						CHASSIS NUMBER PAGE REFERENCE KEY: Allocation Books (pages 1-77), Record Cards (pages 78-167), Warranty Book (pages 168-20`), Service Records (pages 202-393)							
63, 97, 472	3133	Less Engine	Not noted	K2	LHD	2-Seater	Oxford Blue	Blue	Black	11/6/52	U.S.A.	Noel Kirk Motors	Cadillac modification
63	3134	Not used	Not used	Not used	Not used	Not used	Not used	Not used	Not used	Not used	Not used	Not used	Not used
63	3135	Not used	Not used	Not used	Not used	Not used	Not used	Not used	Not used	Not used	Not used	Not used	Not used
63	3136	Not used	Not used	Not used	Not used	Not used	Not used	Not used	Not used	Not used	Not used	Not used	Not used
63	3137	Not used	Not used	Not used	Not used	Not used	Not used	Not used	Not used	Not used	Not used	Not used	Not used
63	3138	Not used	Not used	Not used	Not used	Not used	Not used	Not used	Not used	Not used	Not used	Not used	Not used
63	3139	Not used	Not used	Not used	Not used	Not used	Not used	Not used	Not used	Not used	Not used	Not used	Not used
63, 132, 684	3140	Less Engine	Not noted	J2X	LHD	2-seater Le Mans body	White	Red		24/12/52	U.S.A.	Speedcraft Enterprises	Chrysler modification
63, 132, 684	3141	Less Engine	Not noted	J2X	LHD	2-seater Le Mans body	Primer	Brown pig skin		1/7/53	U.S.A. (Allard Motor Co. Inc.)	John Adler	Cadillac modification
63, 132, 684	3142	Less Engine	Not noted	J2X	LHD	2-Seater	Green	Pig-Skin Tan	Black	27/3/53	U.S.A. (Allard Motor Co. Inc.)	Sam Lortz	Cadillac modification
63, 132, 684	3143	Less Engine	Not noted	J2X	LHD	2-Seater	Red	Black	Black	10/10/52	U.S.A. (Noel Kirk Motors)	Dr. Fred Losee	Cadillac modification
63, 132, 684	3144	Less Engine	Not noted	J2X	LHD	2-Seater	Off White	Black	Black	19/11/52	U.S.A. (Noel Kirk Motors)	Albert T. Zugsmith	President American Pictures Corp. Cadillac modification
63, 133, 684	3145	Less Engine	Not noted	J2X	LHD	2-Seater	Bright Red	Black	Black	19/11/52	U.S.A. (Noel Kirk Motors)	Klaus F. J. Bythiner	Cadillac modification
63, 133, 639, 684	3146	Less Engine	Not noted	J2X	LHD	2-Seater	Cream/Ivory	Red	Black	20/11/52	U.S.A. (Noel Kirk Motors)	Roy Cherryhomes	Cadillac modification
63, 133, 684	3147	Less Engine	Not noted	J2X	LHD	2-Seater	Red	Tan pigskin	Not noted	13/3/53	U.S.A.	Allard Motor Co. Inc.	Cadillac modification
63, 133, 639, 684	3148	Less Engine	Not noted	J2X	LHD	2-Seater	Red	Black	Black	29/11/52	U.S.A. (Noel Kirk Motors)	Louis Yates	Cadillac modification
63, 133, 684	3149	Less Engine	Not noted	J2X	LHD	2-seater Le Mans body	Pale Biscuit	Red	Black	1/7/53	U.S.A.	Noel Kirk Motors	Cadillac modification
63, 133, 684	3150	8R. 177	Not noted	J2X	LHD	2-Seater	Red	Red	Red	27/10/52	Colombia (Panamerican Import)	Sr. Tomas Steuer	Cadillac engine
63, 134, 684	3151	Less Engine	Not noted	J2X	LHD	2-Seater	Black	Red	Not noted	1/6/53	U.S.A. (Noel Kirk Motors)	Fred M. Aley	Cadillac engine
63, 134, 684	3152	Less Engine	Not noted	J2X	LHD	2-seater Le Mans body	B. R. Green	Green	Black	24/2/53	U.S.A.	Allard Motor Co. Inc.	Chrysler modification
63, 134, 684	3153	S. 334	Not noted	J2X	LHD	2-seater Le Mans body	White	White	Black	14/5/53	U.S.A.	Norman K. Patton	Chrysler engine
63, 134, 684	3154	Less Engine	Not noted	J2X	LHD	2-Seater	Red	Red	Black	1/9/53	U.S.A.	Allard Motor Co. Inc.	Cadillac engine
63, 134, 684, 807	3155	Less Engine	Not noted	J2X	LHD	2-seater Le Mans body	White	White	Black	4/8/53	U.S.A. (Allard Motor Co. Inc.)	Edgar S. DeMayer	Chrysler modification

Page References	Chassis	Original Engine Number	UK Registration	Type	LHD?	Body Style	Original Colour	Original Interior	Original Hood	Original Delivery	Allocation	First Customer	Remarks
							CHASSIS NUMBER PAGE REFERENCE KEY: Allocation Books (pages 1-77), Record Cards (pages 78-167), Warranty Book (pages 168-201), Service Records (pages 202-393)						
63, 134, 684	3156	Less Engine	Not noted	J2X	LHD	2-Seater	Red	Red	Black	3/5/53	Sweden (Ingvar Bergengren)	Taure Martenson	Ford engine modification
63, 135, 684	3157	Less Engine	Not noted	J2X.	LHD	2-Seater	Red	Red	Black	12/10/52	U.S.A.	R. B. Robinson – Firestone tyre and Rubber Co.	Cadillac modification
63, 135, 684	3158	Less Engine	Not noted	J2X	LHD	2-Seater	Red	Red	Black	22/4/53	U.S.A.	Allard Motor Co. Inc.	Cadillac modification
63, 135	3159	Not used	Not used	Not used	Not used	Not used	Not used	Not used	Not used	Not used	Not used	Not used	Not used
63, 135	3160	Not used	Not used	Not used	Not used	Not used	Not used	Not used	Not used	Not used	Not used	Not used	Not used
63, 135, 685	3161	Less Engine	Not noted	J2X	LHD	2-Seater	Red	Red	Black	5/2/53	U.S.A. (Shawnee Motor Co.)	Warren B. Turner	Chrysler modification
63, 135, 685	3162	Less Engine	Not noted	J2X	LHD	2-Seater	Gunmetal	Red	Black	2/3/53	U.S.A. (Allard Motor Co. Inc.)	Fred B. Asche Jr	Cadillac modification
63, 135, 685	3163	Less Engine	Not noted	J2X	LHD	2-Seater	Blue	Red	Not noted	5/2/53	U.S.A. (Custom Automotive)	Gary B. Laughlin	Cadillac modification
63, 136, 172, 685	3164	55028	Not noted	J2X	RHD	2-Seater	Red	Red	Black	24/9/53	Brazil (Evans Shewan Importadora)	Basil K. Evans	Chrysler engine
64, 140	3165	Less Engine	Not noted	K3	LHD	3-Seater	Opalescent Blue	Blue	Black	1/7/53	U.S.A.	Allard Motor Co. Inc.	Cadillac modification
64, 140, 690	3166	Less Engine	Not noted	K3	LHD	3-Seater	Silver Grey	Red	Black	23/2/53	U.S.A. (Allard Motor Co. Inc.)	Frank Pohanka Jr	Chrysler modification
64, 140, 472	3167	Less Engine	Not noted	K3	LHD	3-Seater	Primer	Black	Black	1/12/53	U.S.A.	Overseas Equipment Corporation	Chrysler modification
64, 140, 503	3168	Less Engine	Not noted	K3	LHD	3-Seater	Cream	Black	Black	24/12/52	U.S.A. (Allard Motor Co. Inc.)	A. Ciano	Cadillac modification
64, 140	3169	Less Engine	Not noted	K3	LHD	3-Seater	Cream	Red	Black	3/2/53	U.S.A. (Noel Kirk Motors)	Wm. W. Valentine	Cadillac modification
64, 140, 690	3170	Less Engine	Not noted	K3	LHD	3-Seater	Black	Red	Black	14/3/53	U.S.A. (Allard Motor Co. Inc.)	Felippe Arno	Cadillac modification
64, 141	3171	1458614	Not noted	K3	LHD	3-Seater	Light (Cadillac) Grey	Red	Black	24/2/53	U.S.A. (Allard Motor Co. Inc.)	E. N. Cole	Cadillac engine. Chevrolet Chief Engineer
64, 141	3172	Less Engine	Not noted	K3	LHD	3-Seater	Met. Blue	Red	Black	1/7/53	U.S.A.	Allard Motor Co. Inc.	Cadillac modification
64, 141	3173	Less Engine	Not noted	K3	LHD	3-Seater	Met. Blue	Red	Black	27/3/53	Mexico (Jorge Barran Co. Cia)	Thomas B. Catron	Cadillac modification
64, 141	3174	Less Engine	Not noted	K3	LHD	3-Seater	Met. Grey	Red	Grey	18/3/53	U.S.A. (Allard Motor Co. Inc.)	Motorsports	Cadillac modification
64, 141, 690	3175	Less Engine	Not noted	K3	LHD	3-Seater	Royal Blue	Red	Black	2/5/53	U.S.A. (British Motor Car Distributors Ltd.)	W. E. Andrews	Chrysler modification
64, 141, 690	3176	Less Engine	Not noted	K3	LHD	3-Seater	Met. Blue	Blue	Black	2/4/53	U.S.A. (Noel Kirk Motors)	Bill Leyden	Cadillac modification
64, 142	3177	Less Engine	Not noted	K3	LHD	3-Seater	Maroon	Red	Black	2/4/53	U.S.A. (Noel Kirk Motors)	Frank Hathaway	Cadillac modification

Page References	Chassis	Original Engine Number	UK Registration	Type	LHD?	Body Style	Original Colour	Original Interior	Original Hood	Original Delivery	Allocation	First Customer	Remarks
							CHASSIS NUMBER PAGE REFERENCE KEY: Allocation Books (pages 1-77), Record Cards (pages 78-167), Warranty Book (pages 168-201), Service Records (pages 202-393)						
64, 142	3178	Less Engine	Not noted	K3	LHD	3-Seater	M. G. Red	Black	Black	1/8/53	U.S.A. (Allard Motor Co. Inc.)	L. B. Bartlett	Cadillac modification
64, 142, 690	3179	Less Engine	Not noted	K3	LHD	3-Seater	Red	Black	Black	14/5/53	U.S.A. (Allard Motor Co. Inc.)	Knaus Motor Sales (Wayne F. Potter)	Chrysler modification
64, 142	3180	Less Engine	Not noted	K3	LHD	3-Seater	Met. Blue	Red	Black	2/3/53	U.S.A. (Allard Motor Co. Inc.)	E. O. Hoe	Cadillac modification
64, 142	3181	Less Engine	Not noted	K3	LHD	3-Seater	(Gunmetal) M-Grey	Grey	Black	5/12/53	U.S.A.	Allard Motor Co. Inc.	Cadillac modification
64, 142	3182	Less Engine	Not noted	K3	LHD	3-Seater	Red	Black	Black	25/6/53	U.S.A. (Noel Kirk Motors)	E. Ritter	Cadillac modification
64, 143, 690	3183	Less Engine	Not noted	K3	LHD	3-Seater	(Cadet) Met. Grey	Red	Black	24/2/53	U.S.A. (Allard Motor Co. Inc.)	Dr. R. N. Sabourin	Cadillac modification
64, 143, 690	3184	Less Engine	Not noted	K3	LHD	3-Seater	Bronze	Tan	Black	5/5/53	U.S.A. (Allard Motor Co. Inc.)	Lt. Charles B. Gillett Jr	Cadillac modification
64, 143, 690	3185	Less Engine	Not noted	K3	LHD	3-Seater	Pacific Green	Tan	Black	22/4/53	U.S.A. (Allard Motor Co. Inc.)	H. T. Chickering	Cadillac modification
64, 143, 690	3186	Less Engine	Not noted	K3	LHD	3-Seater	Turquoise	Blue	Black	27/5/53	U.S.A. (Noel Kirk Motors)	J. P. Dallas	Cadillac modification
64, 143	3187	Less Engine	Not noted	K3	LHD	3-Seater	Cream	Black	Black	18/3/53	U.S.A. (Allard Motor Co. Inc.)	E. Kovacs	Chrysler modification
64, 143	3188	Less Engine	Not noted	K3	LHD	3-Seater	(Pacific) Met. Green	Tan	Black	15/3/53	Mexico	Jorge Barran Co. Cia	Chrysler modification
64, 144	3189	Less Engine	Not noted	K3	LHD	3-Seater	(Silver) Met. Grey	Green	Black	14/3/53	U.S.A. (Allard Motor Co. Inc.)	Leonard D. Henry	Chrysler modification
64, 144, 690	3190	Less Engine	Not noted	K3	LHD	3-Seater	Bronze	Tan	Black	19/3/53	U.S.A. (Allard Motor Co. Inc.)	S. Phillips	Chrysler modification
64, 144, 690	3191	Less Engine	Not noted	K3	LHD	3-Seater	Silver Grey	Red	Black	24/4/53	U.S.A. (British Motor Car Distributors Ltd.)	Henry Lofgren	Chrysler modification
64, 144, 690	3192	Less Engine	Not noted	K3	LHD	3-Seater	Green	Green	Black	7/10/53	U.S.A. (Noel Kirk Motors)	Dan Schacht	Cadillac modification
64, 144	3193	Less Engine	Not noted	K3	LHD	3-Seater	Crimson	Tan	Black	7/10/53	Costa Rica (Noel Kirk Motors)	Andre Challe	Cadillac modification
64, 144, 690, 807	3194	Less Engine	Not noted	K3	LHD	3-Seater	(Wine) Maroon	Black	Black	4/8/53	U.S.A. (Allard Motor Co. Inc.)	Lawrence W. Richards (George Saunders)	Cadillac modification
64, 145, 690	3195	Less Engine	Not noted	K3	LHD	3-Seater	Dark Blue	Red	Not noted	20/8/53	U.S.A. (Noel Kirk Motors)	Wm. A. Wallace	Cadillac modification
64, 145	3196	Less Engine	Not noted	K3	LHD	3-Seater	Met. Blue	Blue	Black	27/4/53	U.S.A. (Noel Kirk Motors)	Robert L. Downey	Cadillac modification
64, 145	3197	Less Engine	Not noted	K3	LHD	3-Seater	Met. Blue	Blue	Black	5/5/53	U.S.A.	Allard Motor Co. Inc.	Cadillac modification
65, 145	3198	Less Engine	Not noted	K3	LHD	3-Seater	Bronze	Tan	Black	6/4/53	U.S.A.	Allard Motor Co. Inc.	Cadillac modification
65, 145	3199	Less Engine	Not noted	K3	LHD	3-Seater	Bronze	Tan	Beige	25/6/53	U.S.A.	Allard Motor Co. Inc.	Chrysler modification
65, 136, 685	3200	Less Engine	Not noted	J2X	LHD	2-Seater	Red	Red	Black	16/7/53	U.S.A. (Allard Motor Co. Inc.)	Jack W. Symes. Jr	Cadillac modification

Page References	Chassis	Original Engine Number	UK Registration	Type	LHD?	Body Style	Original Colour	Original Interior	Original Hood	Original Delivery	Allocation	First Customer	Remarks

CHASSIS NUMBER PAGE REFERENCE KEY: Allocation Books (pages 1-77), Record Cards (pages 78-167), Warranty Book (pages 168-201), Service Records (pages 202-393)

Page References	Chassis	Original Engine Number	UK Registration	Type	LHD?	Body Style	Original Colour	Original Interior	Original Hood	Original Delivery	Allocation	First Customer	Remarks
65, 136, 685	3201	Less Engine	Not noted	J2X	LHD	2-seater Le Mans body	Red	Black	Not noted	15/10/53	U.S.A.	Merrimack St. Garages	Oldsmobile modification
65, 136, 685	3202	Less Engine	Not noted	J2X	RHD	2-seater Le Mans body	B. R. Green	Red	Black	22/7/53	U.S.A.	Shawnee Motor Co.	Many notes, see record card
65	3203	Not used	Not used	Not used	Not used	Not used	Not used	Not used	Not used	Not used	Not used	Not used	Number transferred to 3211
65	3204	Not used	Not used	Not used	Not used	Not used	Not used	Not used	Not used	Not used	Not used	Not used	Not used
65, 136, 685	3205	D. 1013/1554055	Not noted	J2X	LHD	2-Seater	Red	Red	Black	16/6/54	U.S.A.	Allard Motor Co. Inc.	Dodge Red Ram engine
65	3206	Not used	Not used	Not used	Not used	Not used	Not used	Not used	Not used	Not used	Not used	Not used	Not used
65	3207	Not used	Not used	Not used	Not used	Not used	Not used	Not used	Not used	Not used	Not used	Not used	Not used
65, 136, 685	3208	Less Engine	Not noted	J2X	LHD	2-Seater	Red	Black	Not noted	24/8/53	U.S.A. (British Motor Car Distributors Ltd.)	Don Barnesson	Cadillac modification
65, 137, 685	3209	Less Engine	Not noted	J2X	LHD	2-seater Sports	Beige	Red	Not noted	16/5/53	Canada (Budd & Dyer Ltd.)	David Gurd	Cadillac modification
65	3210	Not used	Not used	Not used	Not used	Not used	Not used	Not used	Not used	Not used	Not used	Not used	Not used
65, 137, 685, 795	3211	V8 3211	Not noted	J2X	LHD	2-seater Sports	Red	Red	Not noted	26/8/53	Guatemala	Gines Arimany	Ford sidevalve V8 engine
65	3212	Not used	Not used	Not used	Not used	Not used	Not used	Not used	Not used	Not used	Not used	Not used	Not used
65, 137, 685	3213	9T. 136	Not noted	J2X	LHD	2-seater Le Mans body	Red	Blue	Grey	24/8/54	Columbia	Antionio Izguierdo	Cadillac engine
65, 137, 478, 685	3214	Less Engine	Not noted	J2X	LHD	2-Seater	Red	Red	Not noted	29/11/54	Japan (Northwestern Export)	P. Whitestine	Chrysler modification
65	3215	Not used	Not used	Not used	Not used	Not used	Not used	Not used	Not used	Not used	Not used	Not used	Not used
65	3216	Not used	Not used	Not used	Not used	Not used	Not used	Not used	Not used	Not used	Not used	Not used	Not used
65	3217	Not used	Not used	Not used	Not used	Not used	Not used	Not used	Not used	Not used	Not used	Not used	
65	3218	Not used	Not used	Not used	Not used	Not used	Not used	Not used	Not used	Not used	Not used	Not used	
65	3219	Not used	Not used	Not used	Not used	Not used	Not used	Not used	Not used	Not used	Not used	Not used	
65	3220	Not used	Not used	Not used	Not used	Not used	Not used	Not used	Not used	Not used	Not used	Not used	
65	3221	Not used	Not used	Not used	Not used	Not used	Not used	Not used	Not used	Not used	Not used	Not used	
65	3222	Not used	Not used	Not used	Not used	Not used	Not used	Not used	Not used	Not used	Not used	Not used	
65	3223	Not used	Not used	Not used	Not used	Not used	Not used	Not used	Not used	Not used	Not used	Not used	

·ALLARD·

Page References	Chassis	Original Engine Number	UK Registration	Type	LHD?	Body Style	Original Colour	Original Interior	Original Hood	Original Delivery	Allocation	First Customer	Remarks
							CHASSIS NUMBER PAGE REFERENCE KEY: Allocation Books (pages 1-77), Record Cards (pages 78-167), Warranty Book (pages 168-201), Service Records (pages 202-393)						
65	3224	Not used	Not used	Not used	Not used	Not used	Not used	Not used	Not used	Not used	Not used	Not used	Not used
65	3225	Not used	Not used	Not used	Not used	Not used	Not used	Not used	Not used	Not used	Not used	Not used	Not used
65	3226	Not used	Not used	Not used	Not used	Not used	Not used	Not used	Not used	Not used	Not used	Not used	Not used
65	3227	Not used	Not used	Not used	Not used	Not used	Not used	Not used	Not used	Not used	Not used	Not used	Not used
65	3228	Not used	Not used	Not used	Not used	Not used	Not used	Not used	Not used	Not used	Not used	Not used	Not used
65	3229	Not used	Not used	Not used	Not used	Not used	Not used	Not used	Not used	Not used	Not used	Not used	Not used
65	3230	Not used	Not used	Not used	Not used	Not used	Not used	Not used	Not used	Not used	Not used	Not used	Not used
66	3231	Not used	Not used	Not used	Not used	Not used	Not used	Not used	Not used	Not used	Not used	Not used	Not used
66	3232	Not used	Not used	Not used	Not used	Not used	Not used	Not used	Not used	Not used	Not used	Not used	Not used
66	3233	Not used	Not used	Not used	Not used	Not used	Not used	Not used	Not used	Not used	Not used	Not used	Not used
66	3234	Not used	Not used	Not used	Not used	Not used	Not used	Not used	Not used	Not used	Not used	Not used	Not used
66	3235	Not used	Not used	Not used	Not used	Not used	Not used	Not used	Not used	Not used	Not used	Not used	Not used
66	3236	Not used	Not used	Not used	Not used	Not used	Not used	Not used	Not used	Not used	Not used	Not used	Not used
66	3237	Not used	Not used	Not used	Not used	Not used	Not used	Not used	Not used	Not used	Not used	Not used	Not used
66	3238	Not used	Not used	Not used	Not used	Not used	Not used	Not used	Not used	Not used	Not used	Not used	Not used
66	3239	Not used	Not used	Not used	Not used	Not used	Not used	Not used	Not used	Not used	Not used	Not used	Not used
66	3240	Not used	Not used	Not used	Not used	Not used	Not used	Not used	Not used	Not used	Not used	Not used	Not used
66	3241	Not used	Not used	Not used	Not used	Not used	Not used	Not used	Not used	Not used	Not used	Not used	Not used
66	3242	Not used	Not used	Not used	Not used	Not used	Not used	Not used	Not used	Not used	Not used	Not used	Not used
66	3243	Not used	Not used	Not used	Not used	Not used	Not used	Not used	Not used	Not used	Not used	Not used	Not used
66	3244	Not used	Not used	Not used	Not used	Not used	Not used	Not used	Not used	Not used	Not used	Not used	Not used
66	3245	Not used	Not used	Not used	Not used	Not used	Not used	Not used	Not used	Not used	Not used	Not used	Not used
66	3246	Not used	Not used	Not used	Not used	Not used	Not used	Not used	Not used	Not used	Not used	Not used	Not used

Appendix 2: Allard Chassis Number Spreadsheets

Page References	Chassis	Original Engine Number	UK Registration	Type	LHD?	Body Style	Original Colour	Original Interior	Original Hood	Original Delivery	Allocation	First Customer	Remarks

CHASSIS NUMBER PAGE REFERENCE KEY: Allocation Books (pages 1-77), Record Cards (pages 78-167), Warranty Book (pages 168-201), Service Records (pages 202-393)

Page References	Chassis	Original Engine Number	UK Registration	Type	LHD?	Body Style	Original Colour	Original Interior	Original Hood	Original Delivery	Allocation	First Customer	Remarks
66	3247	Not used	Not used	Not used	Not used	Not used	Not used	Not used	Not used	Not used	Not used	Not used	Not used
66	3248	Not used	Not used	Not used	Not used	Not used	Not used	Not used	Not used	Not used	Not used	Not used	Not used
66	3249	Not used	Not used	Not used	Not used	Not used	Not used	Not used	Not used	Not used	Not used	Not used	Not used
66, 145, 690	3250	Less Engine	Not noted	K3	LHD	3-Seater	Met. Blue	Red	Black	29/4/53	U.S.A. (Allard Motor Co. Inc.)	Earle A. Wiener	Cadillac engine
66, 146	3251	95-1509	Not noted	K3	LHD	3-Seater	Met. Blue	Red	Black	22/5/53	U.S.A.	Brig-Gen. Kern D. Metzger U.S.A.F.	Cadillac with Hydramatic
66, 146	3252	8. R. 394	NXC 617	K3	LHD	3-Seater	Biscuit	Red	Black	2/6/53	U.S.A.	Brig-Gen. J. P. McConnel	NLN 641 (Conflicts with export cards)
66, 146, 690	3253	Less Engine	Not noted	K3	LHD	3-Seater	(Pacific) Metallic Green	Green	Beige	24/9/53	U.S.A.	Allard Motor Co. Inc.	12v generator and coil
66, 146	3254	Less Engine	Not noted	K3	LHD	3-Seater	Red	Grey	Beige	26/6/53	U.S.A. (Motoresearch)	Raymond A. Wolff	Lincoln modification
66, 146	3255	Less Engine	Not noted	K3	LHD	3-Seater	Red	Black	Black	16/9/53	U.S.A.	Custom Automotive	5 wire wheels, 12v generator and coil
66, 146, 690	3256	7797600	CSK 413	K3	RHD	3-Seater	Black	Red	Grey	29/5/53	India	Mrs K. Sarabhai	Record card says NXC692
66, 147	3257	C. 53/8/1033	Not noted	K3	LHD	3-Seater	Biscuit	Tan	Beige	4/2/53	U.S.A. (Noel Kirk Motors)	Mr John E. Burrell Jr	Chrysler engine
66	3258	Not used	Not used	Not used	Not used	Not used	Not used	Not used	Not used	Not used	Not used	Not used	Not used
66, 147	3259	Less Engine	Not noted	K3	LHD	3-Seater	Primer	Tan	Fawn	8/6/53	U.S.A.	Mr Harry Steele	Lincoln planned by client
66, 147	3260	Less Engine	Not noted	K3	LHD	3-Seater	Red	Tan	Not noted	24/8/53	U.S.A. (Noel Kirk Motors)	A. T. Smith	Cadillac with Hydramatic modification
66, 147, 690	3261	Less Engine	Not noted	K3	LHD	3-Seater	Metallic Light Blue	Blue	Black	16/9/53	U.S.A. (Noel Kirk Motors)	David B. Sanderson	Cadillac with Hydramatic modification
66, 147	3262	Less Engine	Not noted	K3	LHD	3-Seater	(Pacific) Metallic Green	Green	Black	16/7/53	U.S.A. (Noel Kirk Motors)	Robert J. Wilson	Cadillac modification
66	3263	Not used	Not used	Not used	Not used	Not used	Not used	Not used	Not used	Not used	Not used	Not used	Not used
66	3264	Not used	Not used	Not used	Not used	Not used	Not used	Not used	Not used	Not used	Not used	Not used	Not used
67	3265	Not used	Not used	Not used	Not used	Not used	Not used	Not used	Not used	Not used	Not used	Not used	Not used
67, 147, 690	3266	Less Engine	Not noted	K3	LHD	3-Seater	White	Black	Black	20/7/53	U.S.A.	Allard Motor Co. Inc.	Cadillac modification
67, 148	3267	Less Engine	Not noted	K3	LHD	3-Seater	White	Black	Black	8/6/53	U.S.A. (Allard Motor Co. Inc.)	Clinton Lindberg	Cadillac modification
67, 148	3268	Less Engine	Not noted	K3	LHD	3-Seater	Metallic Blue	Red	Not noted	24/8/53	U.S.A.	Wm. R. Hervey	Cadillac modification
67, 148	3269	Less Engine	Not noted	K3	LHD	3-Seater	Primer	Black	Black	20/7/53	U.S.A. (Detroit Racing Equipment)	L. K. Wildberg	Cadillac with Hydramatic modification

·ALLARD·

CHASSIS NUMBER PAGE REFERENCE KEY: Allocation Books (pages 1-77), Record Cards (pages 78-167), Warranty Book (pages 168-201), Service Records (pages 202-393)

Page References	Chassis	Original Engine Number	UK Registration	Type	LHD?	Body Style	Original Colour	Original Interior	Original Hood	Original Delivery	Allocation	First Customer	Remarks
67, 148, 698	3270	2N-23/1460088	Not noted	K3	LHD	3-Seater	Metallic Blue	Red	Black	30/5/53	Belgium (Paul E. Cousin)	Baron Jean du Four	Cadillac engine
67	3271	Not used	Not used	Not used	Not used	Not used	Not used	Not used	Not used	Not used	Not used	Not used	Not used
67	3272	Not used	Not used	Not used	Not used	Not used	Not used	Not used	Not used	Not used	Not used	Not used	Not used
67	3273	Not used	Not used	Not used	Not used	Not used	Not used	Not used	Not used	Not used	Not used	Not used	Not used
67	3274	Not used	Not used	Not used	Not used	Not used	Not used	Not used	Not used	Not used	Not used	Not used	Not used
67, 148	3275	7284986	Not noted	K3	LHD	3-Seater	Larch Green	Tan	Black	24/7/53	Germany	Lt. Col. Alan C. Conway	Wire wheels, heater, aluminium heads
67	3276	Not used	Not used	Not used	Not used	Not used	Not used	Not used	Not used	Not used	Not used	Not used	Not used
67, 148	3277	Less Engine	Not noted	K3	LHD	3-Seater	Red	Black	Beige	21/9/53	U.S.A. (Sports Cars Inc)	J. W. Fisher	5 wire wheels
67, 149	3278	Less Engine	Not noted	K3	LHD	3-Seater	Red	Black	Not noted	13/11/53	U.S.A.	Noel Kirk Motors	Cadillac modification
67	3279	Not used	Not used	Not used	Not used	Not used	Not used	Not used	Not used	Not used	Not used	Not used	Not used
67, 149	3280	2 S 584	Not noted	K3	LHD	3-Seater	Cream	Red	Not noted	18/2/54	Venezuela (L. Bockh & Cia)	Mr Bernado R. Casanova	Cadillac engine
67, 149	3281	25-799	Not noted	K3	LHD	3-Seater	Blue	Red	Black	12/7/53	Canada (Westmount Garage)	Mr W. T. Leslie	Cadillac engine
67, 149	3282	Less Engine	Not noted	K3	LHD	3-Seater	Black	Red	Not noted	13/11/53	U.S.A.	Noel Kirk Motors	Cadillac with Hydramatic modification
67, 149, 690	3283	Less Engine	Not noted	K3	LHD	3-Seater	Pacific Green	Green	Not noted	4/5/54	U.S.A.	House of Allard	Cadillac with Hydramatic modification
67, 149	3284	Less Engine	Not noted	K3	LHD	3-Seater	Off White	Black	Black	6/11/54	Canada (Westmount Garage)	Duncan M. Hodson	Cadillac modification
67	3285	Not used	Not used	Not used	Not used	Not used	Not used	Not used	Not used	Not used	Not used	Not used	Not used
67, 172, 503, 690	3286	7290334	PLE 888	K3		3-Seater	Ming Blue	Grey	Black	10/8/54	Canada	Mr J. P. Carstairs	Film Director and Producer
67	3287	Not used	Not used	Not used	Not used	Not used	Not used	Not used	Not used	Not used	Not used	Not used	Not used
67	3288	Not used	Not used	Not used	Not used	Not used	Not used	Not used	Not used	Not used	Not used	Not used	Not used
67	3289	Not used	Not used	Not used	Not used	Not used	Not used	Not used	Not used	Not used	Not used	Not used	Not used
67	3290	Not used	Not used	Not used	Not used	Not used	Not used	Not used	Not used	Not used	Not used	Not used	Not used
67	3291	Not used	Not used	Not used	Not used	Not used	Not used	Not used	Not used	Not used	Not used	Not used	Not used
67	3292	Not used	Not used	Not used	Not used	Not used	Not used	Not used	Not used	Not used	Not used	Not used	Not used
67	3293	Not used	Not used	Not used	Not used	Not used	Not used	Not used	Not used	Not used	Not used	Not used	Not used

Page References	Chassis	Original Engine Number	UK Registration	Type	LHD?	Body Style	Original Colour	Original Interior	Original Hood	Original Delivery	Allocation	First Customer	Remarks
67	3294	Not used	Not used	Not used	Not used	Not used	Not used	Not used	Not used	Not used	Not used	Not used	Not used
67	3295	Not used	Not used	Not used	Not used	Not used	Not used	Not used	Not used	Not used	Not used	Not used	Not used
67	3296	Not used	Not used	Not used	Not used	Not used	Not used	Not used	Not used	Not used	Not used	Not used	Not used
67	3297	Not used	Not used	Not used	Not used	Not used	Not used	Not used	Not used	Not used	Not used	Not used	Not used
68	3397	Not used	Not used	Not used	Not used	Not used	Not used	Not used	Not used	Not used	Not used	Not used	Not used
68	3398	Not used	Not used	Not used	Not used	Not used	Not used	Not used	Not used	Not used	Not used	Not used	Not used
68	3339	Not used	Not used	Not used	Not used	Not used	Not used	Not used	Not used	Not used	Not used	Not used	Not used
68	3400	Not used	Not used	Not used	Not used	Not used	Not used	Not used	Not used	Not used	Not used	Not used	Not used
68, 138, 507, 685	3401	Less Engine	Not noted	JR	RHD	2-Seater	Red	Red	Red	28/3/53	U.S.A.	A. E. Goldschmidt	Cadillac modification
68, 138, 505, 508, 685	3402	25-316	NLN 652	JR	RHD	2-Seater	Blue	Blue	Not noted	25/7/53	U.S.A.	Col. Dave Schilling U.S.A.F.	Cadillac engine
68, 138, 506, 508, 685	3403	25-433	NLN 650	JR	RHD	2-Seater	AF Blue	Blue	Not noted	8/5/53	U.S.A.	Col. Reade Tilley	Cadillac engine
68, 138, 506, 685	3404	25439	Not noted	JR	RHD	2-Seater	Blue	Blue	Not noted	19/6/53	U.S.A.	Gen. Curtis E. LeMay	Cadillac engine
68, 138, 547, 685	3405	EXT-X2	OLT 101	JR	RHD	Chassis	Chassis	Chassis	Chassis	Not noted	Not noted	Tommy Sopwith	Sapphire Allard Sphinx
68, 138, 683	3406	91K 298	Not noted	JR	LHD	Not noted	Not noted	Not noted	Not noted	Not noted	Canada	Norman Moffat	
68, 139, 685	3407	OVT983	Not noted	JR	RHD	2-Seater	Green/Tan	Not noted	Not noted	Not noted	Allard Motor Co.	R. Larrinaga	Cadillac engine. See record card for extensive history
68, 593, 685, 705	3408	Not used	Not used	Not used	Not used	Not used	Not used	Not used	Not used	Not used	Not used	Not used	Not used
68	3409	Not used	Not used	Not used	Not used	Not used	Not used	Not used	Not used	Not used	Not used	Not used	Not used
68	3410	Not used	Not used	Not used	Not used	Not used	Not used	Not used	Not used	Not used	Not used	Not used	Not used
68	3411	Not used	Not used	Not used	Not used	Not used	Not used	Not used	Not used	Not used	Not used	Not used	Not used
68	3412	Not used	Not used	Not used	Not used	Not used	Not used	Not used	Not used	Not used	Not used	Not used	Not used
68	3413	Not used	Not used	Not used	Not used	Not used	Not used	Not used	Not used	Not used	Not used	Not used	Not used
68	3414	Not used	Not used	Not used	Not used	Not used	Not used	Not used	Not used	Not used	Not used	Not used	Not used
68	3415	Not used	Not used	Not used	Not used	Not used	Not used	Not used	Not used	Not used	Not used	Not used	Not used

CHASSIS NUMBER PAGE REFERENCE KEY: Allocation Books (pages 1-77), Record Cards (pages 78-167), Warranty Book (pages 168-201), Service Records (pages 202-393)

·ALLARD·

Page References	Chassis	Original Engine Number	UK Registration	Type	LHD?	Body Style	Original Colour	Original Interior	Original Hood	Original Delivery	Allocation	First Customer	Remarks

CHASSIS NUMBER PAGE REFERENCE KEY: Allocation Books (pages 1-77), Record Cards (pages 78-167), Warranty Book (pages 168-201), Service Records (pages 202-393)

Page References	Chassis	Original Engine Number	UK Registration	Type	LHD?	Body Style	Original Colour	Original Interior	Original Hood	Original Delivery	Allocation	First Customer	Remarks
68	3416	Not used	Not used	Not used	Not used	Not used	Not used	Not used	Not used	Not used	Not used	Not used	Not used
68	3417	Not used	Not used	Not used	Not used	Not used	Not used	Not used	Not used	Not used	Not used	Not used	Not used
68	3418	Not used	Not used	Not used	Not used	Not used	Not used	Not used	Not used	Not used	Not used	Not used	Not used
68	3419	Not used	Not used	Not used	Not used	Not used	Not used	Not used	Not used	Not used	Not used	Not used	Not used
68	3420	Not used	Not used	Not used	Not used	Not used	Not used	Not used	Not used	Not used	Not used	Not used	Not used
68	3421	Not used	Not used	Not used	Not used	Not used	Not used	Not used	Not used	Not used	Not used	Not used	Not used
68	3422	Not used	Not used	Not used	Not used	Not used	Not used	Not used	Not used	Not used	Not used	Not used	Not used
68	3423	Not used	Not used	Not used	Not used	Not used	Not used	Not used	Not used	Not used	Not used	Not used	Not used
68	3424	Not used	Not used	Not used	Not used	Not used	Not used	Not used	Not used	Not used	Not used	Not used	Not used
68	3425	Not used	Not used	Not used	Not used	Not used	Not used	Not used	Not used	Not used	Not used	Not used	Not used
68	3426	Not used	Not used	Not used	Not used	Not used	Not used	Not used	Not used	Not used	Not used	Not used	Not used
68	3427	Not used	Not used	Not used	Not used	Not used	Not used	Not used	Not used	Not used	Not used	Not used	Not used
68	3428	Not used	Not used	Not used	Not used	Not used	Not used	Not used	Not used	Not used	Not used	Not used	Not used
68	3429	Not used	Not used	Not used	Not used	Not used	Not used	Not used	Not used	Not used	Not used	Not used	Not used
69	3992	Not used	Not used	Not used	Not used	Not used	Not used	Not used	Not used	Not used	Not used	Not used	Not used
69	3993	Not used	Not used	Not used	Not used	Not used	Not used	Not used	Not used	Not used	Not used	Not used	Not used
69	3994	Not used	Not used	Not used	Not used	Not used	Not used	Not used	Not used	Not used	Not used	Not used	Not used
69	3995	Not used	Not used	Not used	Not used	Not used	Not used	Not used	Not used	Not used	Not used	Not used	Not used
69	3996	Not used	Not used	Not used	Not used	Not used	Not used	Not used	Not used	Not used	Not used	Not used	Not used
69	3997	Not used	Not used	Not used	Not used	Not used	Not used	Not used	Not used	Not used	Not used	Not used	Not used
69	3998	Not used	Not used	Not used	Not used	Not used	Not used	Not used	Not used	Not used	Not used	Not used	Not used
69	3999	Not used	Not used	Not used	Not used	Not used	Not used	Not used	Not used	Not used	Not used	Not used	Not used

Page References	Chassis	Original Engine Number	UK Registration	Type	LHD?	Body Style	Original Colour	Original Interior	Original Hood	Original Delivery	Allocation	First Customer	Remarks
						CHASSIS NUMBER PAGE REFERENCE KEY: Allocation Books (pages 1-77), Record Cards (pages 78-167), Warranty Book (pages 168-201), Service Records (pages 202-393)							
69, 491, 701, 775, 781	4000	EI/V500	MXA 555	P2		Safari	Bronze and natural wood	Not noted		Not noted	Allard Motor Co.	S. H. A.	This chassis built under 2058 and 2205. Prototype P2 Safari owned by Sydney Allard (SHA)
69, 701 786	4001	5337/25	MXA 554	P2		Safari	Bronze and natural wood	Not noted		Not noted	Allard Motor Co.	Dennis Allard	This chassis built as 3000, short doors and tailgate.
69, 193, 351, 357, 361 367, 371, 372 373, 380, 80	4002	7275054	NKE 461	P2		Safari	Bronze and natural wood	Not noted		14/7/52	Nunn	Mr M. W. Wilson	Pages 361, 371 and 372 show 4002 as being NKC 461 or HKC 461
69, 103, 172, 701	4003	8R-406	NLD 412	P2		Safari	Bronze and natural wood	Brown		15/11/52	Greece	D. A. Coutroubis	4375cc Aluminium heads. Noted as Worcester Windsheilds Ltd. as first customer in Warranty. Car not exported
69	4004	Not used	Not used	Not used	Not used	Not used	Not used	Not used	Not used	Not used	Not used	Not used	Not used
69, 108	4005	9L-21643	Not noted	P2		Monte Carlo Saloon	Maroon	Light Beige		15/1/53	Malaya	Dr. Reid Tweedie	Cadillac engine
69, 175	4006	7274425	Not noted	P2		Safari	Bronze and natural wood			8/6/52	Dagenham Motors (Brooklands of Bond St)	Iain A. Campbell	
69, 108	4007	7277928	Not noted	P2		Safari	Storm Grey and natural wood	Grey		28/3/52	Kenya (Carvill & Co.)	Col. F. R. C. Fosdick	Spare wheel, lifeguard inner tubes, 75.0 x 16 tyres
69, 108	4008	Less Engine	Not noted	P2	LHD	Safari	Bronze	Tan Leather		30/3/53	Mexico	Jorge Barran Co. Cia	Ford engine mod, Disc wheels
69, 188, 701	4009	7237341	OUE 79	P2		Safari	Bronze and natural wood	Brown		28/1/54	Bristol Street Motors (Central Motors)	Mary Nyce	Radio and aerial
69	4010	Not used	Not used	Not used	Not used	Not used	Not used	Not used	Not used	Not used	Not used	Not used	Not used
69	4011	Not used	Not used	Not used	Not used	Not used	Not used	Not used	Not used	Not used	Not used	Not used	Not used
69	4012	Not used	Not used	Not used	Not used	Not used	Not used	Not used	Not used	Not used	Not used	Not used	Not used
69	4013	Not used	Not used	Not used	Not used	Not used	Not used	Not used	Not used	Not used	Not used	Not used	Not used
69	4014	Not used	Not used	Not used	Not used	Not used	Not used	Not used	Not used	Not used	Not used	Not used	Not used
69	4015	Not used	Not used	Not used	Not used	Not used	Not used	Not used	Not used	Not used	Not used	Not used	Not used
69	4016	Not used	Not used	Not used	Not used	Not used	Not used	Not used	Not used	Not used	Not used	Not used	Not used
69	4017	Not used	Not used	Not used	Not used	Not used	Not used	Not used	Not used	Not used	Not used	Not used	Not used
69	4018	Not used	Not used	Not used	Not used	Not used	Not used	Not used	Not used	Not used	Not used	Not used	Not used

Page References	Chassis	Original Engine Number	UK Registration	Type	LHD?	Body Style	Original Colour	Original Interior	Original Hood	Original Delivery	Allocation	First Customer	Remarks

CHASSIS NUMBER PAGE REFERENCE KEY: Allocation Books (pages 1-77), Record Cards (pages 78-167), Warranty Book (pages 168-201), Service Records (pages 202-393)

Page References	Chassis	Original Engine Number	UK Registration	Type	LHD?	Body Style	Original Colour	Original Interior	Original Hood	Original Delivery	Allocation	First Customer	Remarks
69	4019	Not used	Not used	Not used	Not used	Not used	Not used	Not used	Not used	Not used	Not used	Not used	Not used
69	4020	Not used	Not used	Not used	Not used	Not used	Not used	Not used	Not used	Not used	Not used	Not used	Not used
69	4021	Not used	Not used	Not used	Not used	Not used	Not used	Not used	Not used	Not used	Not used	Not used	Not used
69	4022	Not used	Not used	Not used	Not used	Not used	Not used	Not used	Not used	Not used	Not used	Not used	Not used
69	4023	Not used	Not used	Not used	Not used	Not used	Not used	Not used	Not used	Not used	Not used	Not used	Not used
69	4024	Not used	Not used	Not used	Not used	Not used	Not used	Not used	Not used	Not used	Not used	Not used	Not used
70	4487	Not used	Not used	Not used	Not used	Not used	Not used	Not used	Not used	Not used	Not used	Not used	Not used
70	4488	Not used	Not used	Not used	Not used	Not used	Not used	Not used	Not used	Not used	Not used	Not used	Not used
70	4489	Not used	Not used	Not used	Not used	Not used	Not used	Not used	Not used	Not used	Not used	Not used	Not used
70	4490	Not used	Not used	Not used	Not used	Not used	Not used	Not used	Not used	Not used	Not used	Not used	Not used
70	4491	Not used	Not used	Not used	Not used	Not used	Not used	Not used	Not used	Not used	Not used	Not used	Not used
70	4492	Not used	Not used	Not used	Not used	Not used	Not used	Not used	Not used	Not used	Not used	Not used	Not used
70	4493	Not used	Not used	Not used	Not used	Not used	Not used	Not used	Not used	Not used	Not used	Not used	Not used
70, 361	4494	Not used	Not used	Not used	Not used	Not used	Not used	Not used	Not used	Not used	Not used	Not used	Not used
70	4495	Not used	Not used	Not used	Not used	Not used	Not used	Not used	Not used	Not used	Not used	Not used	Not used
70	4496	Not used	Not used	Not used	Not used	Not used	Not used	Not used	Not used	Not used	Not used	Not used	Not used
70	4497	Not used	Not used	Not used	Not used	Not used	Not used	Not used	Not used	Not used	Not used	Not used	Not used
70	4498	Not used	Not used	Not used	Not used	Not used	Not used	Not used	Not used	Not used	Not used	Not used	Not used
70	4499	Not used	Not used	Not used	Not used	Not used	Not used	Not used	Not used	Not used	Not used	Not used	Not used
70, 108	4500	Less Engine	Not noted	P2	LHD	Saloon	Black	Red		4/11/53	U.S.A. (Custom Auto)	Mr Lawrence A. Hart	Cadillac engine modifications, radio, fog/spot lamps
70, 172, 701	4501	7287263	OLC 655	P2		Saloon	Black	Red		23/12/53	Adlards (Mortlake of Putney)	Allied Collards	Bradford, Yorkshire
70, 701	4502	M-821-B	Not noted	P2	LHD	Saloon	Electric Blue	Blue		24/9/53	Sweden	Ingvar Bergengren	Lincoln engine
70, 109	4503	516245972	Not noted	P2		Saloon	Blue	Blue		11/11/53	Belgium (Paul E. Cousin)	Madame E. Wyckmans	Show car/sliding roof, 5 wire wheels with hubs and caps

Page References	Chassis	Original Engine Number	UK Registration	Type	LHD?	Body Style	Original Colour	Original Interior	Original Hood	Original Delivery	Allocation	First Customer	Remarks
						CHASSIS NUMBER PAGE REFERENCE KEY: Allocation Books (pages 1-77), Record Cards (pages 78-167), Warranty Book (pages 168-201), Service Records (pages 202-393)							
70, 167 182, 369, 7C1	4504	18/F7283424	MDG 160	P2	RHD	Saloon	Bentley Grey	Red		16/6/53	Taylors (Imperial Motor Mart)	Hon. Ms. Paine	
70, 108, 201, 378, 7C1	4505	9T 163	TZ 300	P2		Saloon	Oxford Blue	Maroon		24/8/54	Hamilton	Mr Scott	Blue wheels
70, 109	4506	Less Engine	Not noted	P2	RHD	Safari	Cream	Red		21/12/53	U.S.A. (Denver Imported Motors)	Mrs Caroline L. Paquin Madison	Tailgate rear door
70, 109	4507	72B76S1	Not noted	P2		Safari	Green	Green		14/4/54	Rhodesia (E. Whiteway & Co.)	Thomas Motors Ltd.	Metal panels, backboard and flooring
70, 109, 353, 494	4508	818-7293128	OXE 475	P2		Saloon	Light Blue	Blue		31/8/55	New Guinea (Morris Headstrom)	Mr William Edward Wyatt	Whitewall tyres, air pump
70, 176, 701	4509	7289179	794 BMY	P2		Saloon	Bristol Fawn	Red		30/6/54	Dagenham Motors	Barton's Radio	Black wheels
70, 109, 494	4510	A. V. 6644	Not noted	P2		Saloon	Black	Grey		2/2/55	Canada (Westmount Garage)	Dr. Paul Lariviere	Radio, Lucas fog and flamethrower lamps, 4 safety belts
70	4511	Not used	Not used	Not used	Not used	Not used	Not used	Not used	Not used	Not used	Not used	Not used	Not used
70, 392, 701	4512	Caddy	TGT 703	P2		Saloon	Blue	Blue		10/12/56	Not noted	Not noted	
70, 701	4513	Plymouth	Not noted	P2		Safari	Not noted	Not noted		Not noted	Not noted	Not noted	
70	4514	Not used	Not used	Not used	Not used	Not used	Not used	Not used	Not used	Not used	Not used	Not used	Not used
70	4515	Not used	Not used	Not used	Not used	Not used	Not used	Not used	Not used	Not used	Not used	Not used	Not used
70	4516	Not used	Not used	Not used	Not used	Not used	Not used	Not used	Not used	Not used	Not used	Not used	Not used
70	4517	Not used	Not used	Not used	Not used	Not used	Not used	Not used	Not used	Not used	Not used	Not used	Not used
70	4518	Not used	Not used	Not used	Not used	Not used	Not used	Not used	Not used	Not used	Not used	Not used	Not used
70	4519	Not used	Not used	Not used	Not used	Not used	Not used	Not used	Not used	Not used	Not used	Not used	Not used
71	4982	Not used	Not used	Not used	Not used	Not used	Not used	Not used	Not used	Not used	Not used	Not used	Not used
71	4983	Not used	Not used	Not used	Not used	Not used	Not used	Not used	Not used	Not used	Not used	Not used	Not used
71	4984	Not used	Not used	Not used	Not used	Not used	Not used	Not used	Not used	Not used	Not used	Not used	Not used
71	4985	Not used	Not used	Not used	Not used	Not used	Not used	Not used	Not used	Not used	Not used	Not used	Not used
71	4986	Not used	Not used	Not used	Not used	Not used	Not used	Not used	Not used	Not used	Not used	Not used	Not used
71	4987	Not used	Not used	Not used	Not used	Not used	Not used	Not used	Not used	Not used	Not used	Not used	Not used
71	4988	Not used	Not used	Not used	Not used	Not used	Not used	Not used	Not used	Not used	Not used	Not used	Not used

Page References	Chassis	Original Engine Number	UK Registration	Type	LHD?	Body Style	Original Colour	Original Interior	Original Hood	Original Delivery	Allocation	First Customer	Remarks
						CHASSIS NUMBER PAGE REFERENCE KEY: Allocation Books (pages 1-77), Record Cards (pages 78-167), Warranty Book (pages 168-201), Service Records (pages 202-393)							
71	4989	Not used	Not used	Not used	Not used	Not used	Not used	Not used	Not used	Not used	Not used	Not used	Not used
71	4990	Not used	Not used	Not used	Not used	Not used	Not used	Not used	Not used	Not used	Not used	Not used	Not used
71	4991	Not used	Not used	Not used	Not used	Not used	Not used	Not used	Not used	Not used	Not used	Not used	Not used
71	4992	Not used	Not used	Not used	Not used	Not used	Not used	Not used	Not used	Not used	Not used	Not used	Not used
71	4993	Not used	Not used	Not used	Not used	Not used	Not used	Not used	Not used	Not used	Not used	Not used	Not used
71	4994	Not used	Not used	Not used	Not used	Not used	Not used	Not used	Not used	Not used	Not used	Not used	Not used
71	4995	Not used	Not used	Not used	Not used	Not used	Not used	Not used	Not used	Not used	Not used	Not used	Not used
71	4996	Not used	Not used	Not used	Not used	Not used	Not used	Not used	Not used	Not used	Not used	Not used	Not used
71	4997	Not used	Not used	Not used	Not used	Not used	Not used	Not used	Not used	Not used	Not used	Not used	Not used
71	4998	Not used	Not used	Not used	Not used	Not used	Not used	Not used	Not used	Not used	Not used	Not used	Not used
71	4999	Not used	Not used	Not used	Not used	Not used	Not used	Not used	Not used	Not used	Not used	Not used	Not used
71, 150, 485, 542, 701	5000	A 4442	Not noted	21 Z	LHD	Sports	Cream	Black		24/3/52	U.S.A.	Graham Paige Organisation	Prototype with Bug-eyed body later dropped
71	5001	Not used	Not used	Not used	Not used	Not used	Not used	Not used	Not used	Not used	Not used	Not used	Not used
71	5002	Not used	Not used	Not used	Not used	Not used	Not used	Not used	Not used	Not used	Not used	Not used	Not used
71, 150	5003	EOTTA 48095	Not noted	21 C	RHD	Sports	Blue	Grey	Grey	3/9/52	U.S.A. (Overseas Equipment Co.)	Charles E. Gerard	Demo car for USA Allard concessionaires, interior colour varies
71, 150, 786	5004	EOTTA. 40646	Not noted	21 Z	LHD	Sports	Red	Blue	Black	19/5/53	Colombia (Panamerican Import)	Rafael Obregon	Radio, tonneau cover, curved windscreen.
71	5005	Not used	Not used	Not used	Not used	Not used	Not used	Not used	Not used	Not used	Not used	Not used	Not used
71, 151	5006	EOTA 70545	Not noted	21 C	LHD	Sports	Cream	Red	Black	20/7/53	U.S.A. (Allard Motor Co. Inc.)	Charles B. Wilson	Many notes, see record card
71	5007	Not used	Not used	Not used	Not used	Not used	Not used	Not used	Not used	Not used	Not used	Not used	Not used
71	5008	Not used	Not used	Not used	Not used	Not used	Not used	Not used	Not used	Not used	Not used	Not used	Not used
71, 701	5009	EOTTA 3823	NGN 567	21 Z	RHD	3-Seater	Bronze	Brown		Not noted	Allard Motor Co.	Demonstration car	
71	5010	Not used	Not used	Not used	Not used	Not used	Not used	Not used	Not used	Not used	Not used	Not used	Not used
71	5011	Not used	Not used	Not used	Not used	Not used	Not used	Not used	Not used	Not used	Not used	Not used	Not used

·ALLARD·

Page References	Chassis	Original Engine Number	UK Registration	Type	LHD?	Body Style	Original Colour	Original Interior	Original Hood	Original Delivery	Allocation	First Customer	Remarks
							CHASSIS NUMBER PAGE REFERENCE KEY: Allocation Books (pages 1-77), Record Cards (pages 78-167), Warranty Book (pages 168-201), Service Records (pages 202-393)						
71	5012	Not used	Not used	Not used	Not used	Not used	Not used	Not used	Not used	Not used	Not used	Not used	Not used
71	5013	Not used	Not used	Not used	Not used	Not used	Not used	Not used	Not used	Not used	Not used	Not used	Not used
71	5014	Not used	Not used	Not used	Not used	Not used	Not used	Not used	Not used	Not used	Not used	Not used	Not used
72	5015	Not used	Not used	Not used	Not used	Not used	Not used	Not used	Not used	Not used	Not used	Not used	Not used
72	5016	Not used	Not used	Not used	Not used	Not used	Not used	Not used	Not used	Not used	Not used	Not used	Not used
72, 151, 701	5017	EOTTA 54355	Not noted	21 C	LHD	3-Seater-Sports	Red	Red	Black	5/12/53	Sweden	Ingvar Bergengren	Curved windscreen, disc wheels
72	5018	Not used	Not used	Not used	Not used	Not used	Not used	Not used	Not used	Not used	Not used	Not used	Not used
72	5019	Not used	Not used	Not used	Not used	Not used	Not used	Not used	Not used	Not used	Not used	Not used	Not used
72	5020	Not used	Not used	Not used	Not used	Not used	Not used	Not used	Not used	Not used	Not used	Not used	Not used
72	5021	Not used	Not used	Not used	Not used	Not used	Not used	Not used	Not used	Not used	Not used	Not used	Not used
72	5022	Not used	Not used	Not used	Not used	Not used	Not used	Not used	Not used	Not used	Not used	Not used	Not used
72	5023	Not used	Not used	Not used	Not used	Not used	Not used	Not used	Not used	Not used	Not used	Not used	Not used
72	5024	Not used	Not used	Not used	Not used	Not used	Not used	Not used	Not used	Not used	Not used	Not used	Not used
72, 151	5025	EOTTA 15807	Not noted	21 Z	LHD	3-Seater-Sports	Blue	Red	Black	11/8/52	Germany	Major H. G. Fisher	Used in Danny Kaye film, special effects replica used in England filming, many notes refer to record card
72, 151	5026	EOTTA 37844	Not noted	21 Z	LHD	3-Seater-Sports	Green	Green	Black	17/4/53	Germany	Brig-Gen. S. F. Giffin	Curved windscreen
72, 151	5027	EOTTA 33285	Not noted	21 Z	LHD	3-Seater-Sports	Red	Grey	Black	3/4/53	Geneva, Switzerland	Autohall Servette S. A.	
72, 151, 701	5028	EOTTA 13954	Not noted	21 Z	LHD	3-Seater-Sports	Bronze	Brown	Black	23/2/53	U.S.A.	Allard Motor Co. Inc.	
72, 152	5029	EOTTA 28012	Not noted	21 Z	LHD	3-Seater-Sports	(Peacock) Light Blue	Blue	Black	2/5/53	U.S.A. (Allard Motor Co. Inc.)	Robert C. Edberg	Wire wheels, curved windscreen
72	5030	Not used	Not used	Not used	Not used	Not used	Not used	Not used	Not used	Not used	Not used	Not used	Not used
72	5031	Not used	Not used	Not used	Not used	Not used	Not used	Not used	Not used	Not used	Not used	Not used	Not used
72	5032	Not used	Not used	Not used	Not used	Not used	Not used	Not used	Not used	Not used	Not used	Not used	Not used
72	5033	Not used	Not used	Not used	Not used	Not used	Not used	Not used	Not used	Not used	Not used	Not used	Not used
72	5034	Not used	Not used	Not used	Not used	Not used	Not used	Not used	Not used	Not used	Not used	Not used	Not used

Page References	Chassis	Original Engine Number	UK Registration	Type	LHD?	Body Style	Original Colour	Original Interior	Original Hood	Original Delivery	Allocation	First Customer	Remarks

CHASSIS NUMBER PAGE REFERENCE KEY: Allocation Books (pages 1-77), Record Cards (pages 78-167), Warranty Book (pages 168-201), Service Records (pages 202-393)

Page References	Chassis	Original Engine Number	UK Registration	Type	LHD?	Body Style	Original Colour	Original Interior	Original Hood	Original Delivery	Allocation	First Customer	Remarks
72	5035	Not used	Not used	Not used	Not used	Not used	Not used	Not used	Not used	Not used	Not used	Not used	Not used
72	5036	Not used	Not used	Not used	Not used	Not used	Not used	Not used	Not used	Not used	Not used	Not used	Not used
72	5037	Not used	Not used	Not used	Not used	Not used	Not used	Not used	Not used	Not used	Not used	Not used	Not used
72, 152	5038	EOTTA 24657	Not noted	21 Z	LHD	3-Seater-Sports	Light Blue	Tan	Black	22/12/52	U.S.A. (Overseas Equipment Co.)	Allard Motor Co. Inc.	
72, 152	5039	EOTTA 36423	Not noted	21 Z	LHD	3-Seater-Sports	Red	Red	Black	22/4/53	U.S.A. (Allard Motor Co. Inc.)	Albert W. Martin	Curved windscreen
72	5040	Not used	Not used	Not used	Not used	Not used	Not used	Not used	Not used	Not used	Not used	Not used	Not used
72	5041	Not used	Not used	Not used	Not used	Not used	Not used	Not used	Not used	Not used	Not used	Not used	Not used
72	5042	Not used	Not used	Not used	Not used	Not used	Not used	Not used	Not used	Not used	Not used	Not used	Not used
72	5043	Not used	Not used	Not used	Not used	Not used	Not used	Not used	Not used	Not used	Not used	Not used	Not used
72	5044	Not used	Not used	Not used	Not used	Not used	Not used	Not used	Not used	Not used	Not used	Not used	Not used
72	5045	Not used	Not used	Not used	Not used	Not used	Not used	Not used	Not used	Not used	Not used	Not used	Not used
72	5046	Not used	Not used	Not used	Not used	Not used	Not used	Not used	Not used	Not used	Not used	Not used	Not used
72	5047	Not used	Not used	Not used	Not used	Not used	Not used	Not used	Not used	Not used	Not used	Not used	Not used
73	5048	Not used	Not used	Not used	Not used	Not used	Not used	Not used	Not used	Not used	Not used	Not used	Not used
73	5049	Not used	Not used	Not used	Not used	Not used	Not used	Not used	Not used	Not used	Not used	Not used	Not used
73	5050	Not used	Not used	Not used	Not used	Not used	Not used	Not used	Not used	Not used	Not used	Not used	Not used
73	5051	Not used	Not used	Not used	Not used	Not used	Not used	Not used	Not used	Not used	Not used	Not used	Not used
73	5052	Not used	Not used	Not used	Not used	Not used	Not used	Not used	Not used	Not used	Not used	Not used	Not used
73	5053	Not used	Not used	Not used	Not used	Not used	Not used	Not used	Not used	Not used	Not used	Not used	Not used
73, 152	5054	EOTTA 51009	Not noted	21 Z	LHD	3-Seater	Maroon	Tan	Black	8/6/53	U.S.A. (Noel Kirk Motors)	LT/Cmdr Patrick C. Doisey	5 wire wheels
73	5055	Not used	Not used	Not used	Not used	Not used	Not used	Not used	Not used	Not used	Not used	Not used	Not used
73	5056	Not used	Not used	Not used	Not used	Not used	Not used	Not used	Not used	Not used	Not used	Not used	Not used
73	5057	Not used	Not used	Not used	Not used	Not used	Not used	Not used	Not used	Not used	Not used	Not used	Not used

Page References	Chassis	Original Engine Number	UK Registration	Type	LHD?	Body Style	Original Colour	Original Interior	Original Hood	Original Delivery	Allocation	First Customer	Remarks
								CHASSIS NUMBER PAGE REFERENCE KEY: Allocation Books (pages 1-77), Record Cards (pages 78-167), Warranty Book (pages 168-201), Service Records (pages 202-393)					
73	5058	Not used	Not used	Not used	Not used	Not used	Not used	Not used	Not used	Not used	Not used	Not used	Not used
73	5059	Not used	Not used	Not used	Not used	Not used	Not used	Not used	Not used	Not used	Not used	Not used	Not used
73	5060	Not used	Not used	Not used	Not used	Not used	Not used	Not used	Not used	Not used	Not used	Not used	Not used
73, 152	5061	EOTTA 44766	Not noted	21 Z	LHD	3-Seater	Light Blue	Blue	Black	20/6/53	Mexico	Liberto Pujol Maynou	Curved windscreen, disc wheels
73	5062	Not used	Not used	Not used	Not used	Not used	Not used	Not used	Not used	Not used	Not used	Not used	Not used
73	5063	Not used	Not used	Not used	Not used	Not used	Not used	Not used	Not used	Not used	Not used	Not used	Not used
73, 152	5064	EOTTA 52035	Not noted	21 Z	LHD	3-Seater	Blue	Red	Black	8/7/53	Canada	Clark Simpkins Ltd.	
73	5065	Not used	Not used	Not used	Not used	Not used	Not used	Not used	Not used	Not used	Not used	Not used	Not used
73	5066	Not used	Not used	Not used	Not used	Not used	Not used	Not used	Not used	Not used	Not used	Not used	Not used
73	5067	Not used	Not used	Not used	Not used	Not used	Not used	Not used	Not used	Not used	Not used	Not used	Not used
73	5068	Not used	Not used	Not used	Not used	Not used	Not used	Not used	Not used	Not used	Not used	Not used	Not used
73	5069	Not used	Not used	Not used	Not used	Not used	Not used	Not used	Not used	Not used	Not used	Not used	Not used
73, 153	5070	EOTTA 44759	Not noted	21 Z	LHD	3-Seater	Blue	Red	Black	24/6/53	Columbia (Panamerican Import)	Sr. Jorge Saenz	Radio, tonneau cover, curved windscreen
73, 153	5071	EOTTA 61271	Not noted	21 Z	LHD	3-Seater	Light blue	Grey	Not noted	20/10/53	U.S.A.	Noel Kirk Motors	
73	5072	Not used	Not used	Not used	Not used	Not used	Not used	Not used	Not used	Not used	Not used	Not used	Not used
73	5073	Not used	Not used	Not used	Not used	Not used	Not used	Not used	Not used	Not used	Not used	Not used	Not used
73, 153	5074	EOTTA 36426	Not noted	21 Z	LHD	3-Seater	Grey	White	Black	4/9/53	U.S.A.	Allard Motor Co. Inc.	Shipped with J 3155 and K 3194
73, 153	5075	EOTTA 81337	Not noted	21 C	LHD	3-Seater	Dorchester Grey	Red	Black	17/3/53	Switzerland	Autohall Servette S. A.	
73	5076	Not used	Not used	Not used	Not used	Not used	Not used	Not used	Not used	Not used	Not used	Not used	Not used
73	5077	Not used	Not used	Not used	Not used	Not used	Not used	Not used	Not used	Not used	Not used	Not used	Not used
73	5078	Not used	Not used	Not used	Not used	Not used	Not used	Not used	Not used	Not used	Not used	Not used	Not used
73, 153	5079	EOTTA 47126	Not noted	21 Z	RHD	3-Seater	Red	Red	Black	7/1/53	Mexico	Augustin Legorreta	Many notes, see record card
73, 175, 721	5080	EOTTA 49589	4655 H	21 Z	RHD	3-Seater	Ming Blue	Grey	Black	14/7/53	Dagenham Motors	John Paddy Carstairs	Film director and producer
74, 153, 712	5081	EOTA 85180	NXD 322	21 C	LHD	3-Seater	Light Blue	Light Blue	Not noted	20/4/53	U.S.A.	Mr Scott Fuller	Curved windscreen, disc wheels
74	5082	Not used	Not used	Not used	Not used	Not used	Not used	Not used	Not used	Not used	Not used	Not used	Not used

Page References	Chassis	Original Engine Number	UK Registration	Type	LHD?	Body Style	Original Colour	Original Interior	Original Hood	Original Delivery	Allocation	First Customer	Remarks

CHASSIS NUMBER PAGE REFERENCE KEY: Allocation Books (pages 1-77), Record Cards (pages 78-167), Warranty Book (pages 168-201), Service Records (pages 202-393)

Page References	Chassis	Original Engine Number	UK Registration	Type	LHD?	Body Style	Original Colour	Original Interior	Original Hood	Original Delivery	Allocation	First Customer	Remarks
74	5083	Not used	Not used	Not used	Not used	Not used	Not used	Not used	Not used	Not used	Not used	Not used	Not used
74	5084	Not used	Not used	Not used	Not used	Not used	Not used	Not used	Not used	Not used	Not used	Not used	Not used
74	5085	Not used	Not used	Not used	Not used	Not used	Not used	Not used	Not used	Not used	Not used	Not used	Not used
74	5086	Not used	Not used	Not used	Not used	Not used	Not used	Not used	Not used	Not used	Not used	Not used	Not used
74	5087	Not used	Not used	Not used	Not used	Not used	Not used	Not used	Not used	Not used	Not used	Not used	Not used
74	5088	Not used	Not used	Not used	Not used	Not used	Not used	Not used	Not used	Not used	Not used	Not used	Not used
74	5089	Not used	Not used	Not used	Not used	Not used	Not used	Not used	Not used	Not used	Not used	Not used	Not used
74	5090	Not used	Not used	Not used	Not used	Not used	Not used	Not used	Not used	Not used	Not used	Not used	Not used
74	5091	Not used	Not used	Not used	Not used	Not used	Not used	Not used	Not used	Not used	Not used	Not used	Not used
74	5092	Not used	Not used	Not used	Not used	Not used	Not used	Not used	Not used	Not used	Not used	Not used	Not used
74	5093	Not used	Not used	Not used	Not used	Not used	Not used	Not used	Not used	Not used	Not used	Not used	Not used
74	5094	Not used	Not used	Not used	Not used	Not used	Not used	Not used	Not used	Not used	Not used	Not used	Not used
74	5095	Not used	Not used	Not used	Not used	Not used	Not used	Not used	Not used	Not used	Not used	Not used	Not used
74	5096	Not used	Not used	Not used	Not used	Not used	Not used	Not used	Not used	Not used	Not used	Not used	Not used
74	5097	Not used	Not used	Not used	Not used	Not used	Not used	Not used	Not used	Not used	Not used	Not used	Not used
74	5098	Not used	Not used	Not used	Not used	Not used	Not used	Not used	Not used	Not used	Not used	Not used	Not used
74	5099	Not used	Not used	Not used	Not used	Not used	Not used	Not used	Not used	Not used	Not used	Not used	Not used
74, 193, 374	5100	EOTTA 49587	OYM 949	21Z	RHD	3-Seater	Ming Blue	Blue	Black	16/7/53	Nunn	Sidwick Motors	
74	5101	Not used	Not used	Not used	Not used	Not used	Not used	Not used	Not used	Not used	Not used	Not used	Not used
74, 154, 193, 701	5102	EOTTA 37380	KDK 56	21Z	RHD	3-Seater	Black	Red	Black	4/11/53	Nunn (H. J. Quick Ltd.)	Mr D. G. Scott	Many notes, see record card. Differing owners information
74, 154	5103	EOTTA 226228	Not noted	21Z	LHD	3-Seater	Black	Red	Black	28/7/53	Austria (Brooklands of Bond)	William J. Hood	
74, 154, 355, 701	5104	EOTTA-5104E	NYO 66	21Z		3-Seater	Bronze	Brown	Not noted	Not noted	Adlards	N. F. Standfast	
74, 701	5105	EOTTA-61181	TUA 900	21Z		3-Seater	Ming Blue	Grey	Not noted	Not noted	Tate		
74, 154	5106	EOTTA-55382	Not noted	21Z	RHD	3-Seater	Ming Blue	Grey	Black	14/9/53	New Zealand (Tracspecs)	B. F. Francis	Colours vary, refer record card, page 154

Page References	Chassis	Original Engine Number	UK Registration	Type	LHD?	Body Style	Original Colour	Original Interior	Original Hood	Original Delivery	Allocation	First Customer	Remarks
							CHASSIS NUMBER PAGE REFERENCE KEY: Allocation Books (pages 1-77), Record Cards (pages 78-167), Warranty Book (pages 168-201), Service Records (pages 202-393)						
74, 701	5107	EOTTA-63603	FES 888	21Z		3-Seater	Black	Red	Black	11/1/53	Frew		Red wheels
74, 175, 701	5108	EOTTA-71017	NYO 6	21Z		3-Seater	Dark Green	Beige	Beige	1/8/54	Dagenham Motors (Petersham Garage)	Major A. Schweizer	Beige wheels
74, 201	5109	EOTTA-122656	Not noted	21C		3-Seater	Ming Blue	Grey	Black	2/6/54	Hamilton	Wrights Deliveries	
74, 172, 544, 702	5110	EOTT4-71016	Not noted	21Z		3-Seater	Chassis	Chassis	Chassis	1/6/54	Adlards	Abbotts of Farnham	Wire wheels
74, 176, 701	5111	EOTTA-81368	700 BME	21Z		3-Seater	Mug Blue	Black	Black	4/1/54	Dagenham Motors	Miss W. B. Knight	
74	5112	Not noted	Not noted	21		3-Seater	Not noted	Not noted	Not noted	Not noted	Not noted	Not noted	Not noted
74	5113	Not noted	Not noted	21		3-Seater	Not noted	Not noted	Not noted	Not noted	Not noted	Not noted	Not noted
75	5114	Not noted	Not noted	21		3-Seater	Not noted	Not noted	Not noted	Not noted	Not noted	Not noted	Not noted
75	5115	Not noted	Not noted	21		3-Seater	Not noted	Not noted	Not noted	Not noted	Not noted	Not noted	Not noted
75	5116	Not noted	Not noted	21		3-Seater	Not noted	Not noted	Not noted	Not noted	Not noted	Not noted	Not noted
75, 154	5117	EOTTA 47137	Not noted	21 Z	RHD	3-Seater	Cream/Oatmeal	Red	Black	7/3/53	Sweden	Ingvar Bergengren	Curved windscreen, whitewall tyres
75, 154	5118	EOTTA 84132	Not noted	21 Z	LHD	3-Seater	Dark Green	Green	Not noted	4/6/54	Canada	Westmount Garage	
75, 155	5119	EOTTA 68598	Not noted	21 Z	LHD	3-Seater	Pale Green	Green	Not noted	4/6/54	U.S.A. (House of Allard)	Mr Merwin Fischal	Disc wheels
75, 155	5120	EOTTA 68600	Not noted	21 Z	LHD	3-Seater	Metallic Grey	Red	Not noted	4/5/54	U.S.A. (House of Allard)	Scotte Gray	Disc wheels
75, 155	5121	EOTTA 65636	Not noted	21 Z	LHD	3-Seater	Black	Red	Not noted	25/11/53	Venezuela	Mr N. Willoughby	Disc wheels
75, 155	5122	EOTTA 86249	Not noted	21 Z	LHD	3-Seater	Bronze	Blue	Black	5/6/54	Colombia	Antonio Izguierdo	Many notes, see record card
75, 155	5123	EOTTA 87198	Not noted	21 7	LHD	3-Seater	Silver	Red	Black	5/6/54	Colombia	Antonio Izguierdo	Many notes, see record card
75, 155	5124	EOTTA 90976	Not noted	21 Z	RHD	3-Seater	Red	Grey	Black	21/5/54	New Zealand	Tractor Specialties Ltd.	Disc wheels
75, 156	5125	EOTTA 91995	Not noted	21 Z	RHD	3-Seater	Red	Grey	Black	21/5/54	New Zealand	Tractor Specialties Ltd.	Disc wheels
75, 156	5126	EOTTA 94306	Not noted	21 Z	RHD	3-Seater	Off White	Red	Black	17/6/54	Venezuela	Mr D. Sidnell	Many notes, see record card
75, 156	5127	EOTTA 98324	Not noted	21 Z	LHD	3-Seater	Green	Red	Black	8/5/54	Colombia	Antonio Izguierdo	Many notes, see record card
75, 156	5128	EOTTA 93835	Not noted	21 Z	RHD	3-Seater	Dark Green	Brown	Black	6/4/54	New Zealand	Tractor Specialties Ltd.	Disc wheels
75, 156	5129	EOTTA 96047	Not noted	21 Z	LHD	3-Seater	Beige	Tan	Black	22/7/54	Canada (Westmount Garage)	Mr Eugene Jousse	Fitted with overdrive
75, 156	5130	EOTTA 105816	Not noted	21 Z	RHD	3-Seater	Blue	Red	Black	10/11/54	Madagascar	Edwin Mayer & Co. Ltd.	Many notes, see record card
75, 157	5131	EOTTA 97184	Not noted	21 Z	LHD	3-Seater	Grey	Red	Black	8/10/54	U.S.A.	Herbert N. Berge	Many notes, see record card
75	5132	Not noted	Not noted	21 Z	LHD	3-Seater	Not noted	Not noted	Not noted	Not noted	Not noted	Not noted	Not noted
75	5133	Not noted	Not noted	Not noted	Not noted	Not noted	Not noted	Not noted	Not noted	Not noted	Not noted	Not noted	Not noted
75, 157	5134	EOTTA 103929	Not noted	21 Z	LHD	3-Seater	Ivory	Red	Black	23/11/54	Colombia	Antonio Izguierdo	Many notes, see record card
75, 157	5135	EOTTA 101665	Not noted	21 Z	LHD	3-Seater	Ivory	Maroon	Black	21/9/54	West Indies	L. H. Palacios N. V	Many notes, see record card
75, 157	5136	EOTTA 108970	Not noted	21 Z	LHD	3-Seater	Smoke Grey	Maroon	Black	23/11/54	West Indies	L. H. Palacios N. V	Many notes, see record card

Page References	Chassis	Original Engine Number	UK Registration	Type	LHD?	Body Style	Original Colour	Original Interior	Original Hood	Original Delivery	Allocation	First Customer	Remarks
CHASSIS NUMBER PAGE REFERENCE KEY: Allocation Books (pages 1-77), Record Cards (pages 78-167), Warranty Book (pages 168-201), Service Records (pages 202-393)													
75, 157	5137	EOTTA 52047	Not noted	21 Z	LHD	3-Seater	Ivory	Black	Not noted	20/8/53	U.S.A.	Noel Kirk Motors	Tonneau cover
75, 158	5138	EOTTA 42899	Not noted	21 Z	RHD	3-Seater	Metallic Grey	Red	Black	28/5/53	New Zealand (Tracspecs)	R. C. McDonald	Curved windscreen, disc wheels.
75, 158	5139	EOTTA 52046	Not noted	21 Z	LHD	3-Seater	White	Blue	Black	9/5/53	U.S.A. (Allard Motor Co. Inc.)	H. Parker Mason	
75, 193, 702	5140	EOTTA 100359	Not noted	21 C	RHD	3-Seater	Bronze	Brown	Black	31/7/53	Nunn	Not noted	
75, 175, 355, 362	5141	EOTTA 52036	2 BML	21 Z	RHD	3-Seater	Ming Blue	Blue	Black	8/6/53	Dagenham Motors	Not noted	
75, 158	5142	EOTTA 54624	Not noted	21 Z	RHD	3-Seater	Ming Blue	Blue	Black	14/9/53	New Zealand	Tractor Specialties Ltd.	
75, 158, 193, 810	5143	EOTTA 100347	Not noted	21 C		3-Seater	Red	Red	Black	7/1/54	Nunn	Not noted	Confusion with 5143/3 not rectified
75, 158	5143/3	EOTTA 53258	Not noted	21 Z	LHD	3-Seater	Dark Blue	Red	Black	28/8/53	Japan	Maj. Gen. Underhill	U.S.A.F. Joint Tactical Air Support Board
75, 158, 701	5144	EOTTA 55564	Not noted	21 Z	LHD	3-Seater	Red	Red	Black	9/9/53	Sweden	Ingvar Bergengren	
75, 158, 701	5145	EOTTA 58513	Not noted	21 Z	LHD	3-Seater	Red	Blue	Black	24/9/53	Sweden	Ingvar Bergengren	Wire wheels
75, 159	5146	EOTTA 62299	Not noted	21 Z	LHD	3-Seater	(Ming) Light Blue	Blue	Not noted	11/3/53	U.S.A.	Noel Kirk Motors	Wire wheels
76, 159	5147	EOTTA 53258	Not noted	21 Z	LHD	3-Seater	Black	Tan	Not noted	11/12/53	U.S.A. (Noel Kirk Motors)	. H. Richard Alexander	
76, 159, 702	5148	EOTTA 61179	Not noted	21 Z	LHD	3-Seater	Ivory	Red	Not noted	20/10/53	U.S.A.	British Motor Car Distributors Ltd.	Wire wheels
76, 159, 702	5149	EOTTA 80788	Not noted	21 Z	LHD	3-Seater	Cream	Green	Not noted	4/6/54	U.S.A.	House of Allard	Disc wheels
76, 159	5150	Less Engine	Not noted	21 H		Chassis	Chassis	Chassis	Chassis	Not noted	9/5/53	France	Facel	Flown to Paris for Hotchkiss engine with Facel
76, 159, 484, 701	5151	D-44/8387	OGY 456	21D	LHD	3-Seater	Red	Red	Not noted	2/4/54	Argentina	Bernardo Wolfenson S. A.	Red Ram Dodge V8 engine
76, 160	5152	EOTTA 65634	Not noted	21 Z	LHD	3-Seater	(Ming) Light Blue	Red	Not noted	20/11/53	U.S.A. (Noel Kirk Motors)	Charles Conn	Disc wheels
76, 188	5153	EOTTA 85213	Not noted	21 Z		3-Seater	Green	Green	Beige	4/7/54	Bristol Street Motors	John Bullock	
76, 160	5154	EOTTA 96029	Not noted	21 Z	RHD	3-Seater	Blue	Red	Black	27/8/54	New Zealand	Tractor Specialties Ltd.	Steel wheels
76, 160, 702	5155	EOTTA 137335	Not noted	21 Z	LHD	3-Seater	Red	Blue	Not noted	16/4/55	U.S.A. (Alexander Tarpinian)	Mr Albert Oettinger	Disc wheels, 3 carburettor manifold.
76, 160	5156	EOTTA 108596	Not noted	21 Z	LHD	3-Seater	Red	Red	Black	1/12/55	U.S.A. (Alexander Tarpinian)	John J. Woates Co.	Wire wheels, hubs and caps.
76, 160, 485	5157	EOTTA 146322	Not noted	21 Z		3-Seater	White	Red	Black	8/5/55	U.S.A.	Not noted	
76, 701, 813	5158	EOTTA 155308	Not noted	21 Z		3-Seater	Not noted	Not noted	Not noted	5/9/05	New Zealand	Not noted	AOC member in New Zealand claims ownership. PB1 chassis used for new body refer 7000
76	5159	Not noted	Not noted	Not noted	Not noted	3-Seater	Not noted	Not noted	Not noted	Not noted	Not noted	Not noted	Not used
76	5160	Not noted	Not noted	Not noted	Not noted	3-Seater	Not noted	Not noted	Not noted	Not noted	Not noted	Not noted	Not used
76	5161	Not used	Not used	Not used	Not used	Not used	Not used	Not used	Not used	Not used	Not used	Not used	Not used

Page References	Chassis	Original Engine Number	UK Registration	Type	LHD?	Body Style	Original Colour	Original Interior	Original Hood	Original Delivery	Allocation	First Customer	Remarks

CHASSIS NUMBER PAGE REFERENCE KEY: Allocation Books (pages 1-77), Record Cards (pages 78-167), Warranty Book (pages 168-201), Service Records (pages 202-393)

Page References	Chassis	Original Engine Number	UK Registration	Type	LHD?	Body Style	Original Colour	Original Interior	Original Hood	Original Delivery	Allocation	First Customer	Remarks
76	5162	Not used	Not used	Not used	Not used	Not used	Not used	Not used	Not used	Not used	Not used	Not used	Not used
76	5163	Not used	Not used	Not used	Not used	Not used	Not used	Not used	Not used	Not used	Not used	Not used	Not used
76, 701	5164	Not noted	FPM 806	21 Z	Not noted	Not noted	Not noted	Not noted	Not noted	5/9/05	Not noted	Not noted	Known to exist but not acknowledged in original factory records
76	5165	Not used	Not used	Not used	Not used	Not used	Not used	Not used	Not used	Not used	Not used	Not used	Not used
76	5166	Not used	Not used	Not used	Not used	Not used	Not used	Not used	Not used	Not used	Not used	Not used	Not used
76	5167	Not used	Not used	Not used	Not used	Not used	Not used	Not used	Not used	Not used	Not used	Not used	Not used
76	5168	Not used	Not used	Not used	Not used	Not used	Not used	Not used	Not used	Not used	Not used	Not used	Not used
76	5169	Not used	Not used	Not used	Not used	Not used	Not used	Not used	Not used	Not used	Not used	Not used	Not used
76	5170	Not used	Not used	Not used	Not used	Not used	Not used	Not used	Not used	Not used	Not used	Not used	Not used
76	5171	Not used	Not used	Not used	Not used	Not used	Not used	Not used	Not used	Not used	Not used	Not used	Not used
76	5172	Not used	Not used	Not used	Not used	Not used	Not used	Not used	Not used	Not used	Not used	Not used	Not used
76	5173	Not used	Not used	Not used	Not used	Not used	Not used	Not used	Not used	Not used	Not used	Not used	Not used
76	5174	Not used	Not used	Not used	Not used	Not used	Not used	Not used	Not used	Not used	Not used	Not used	Not used
76	5175	Not used	Not used	Not used	Not used	Not used	Not used	Not used	Not used	Not used	Not used	Not used	Not used
76	5176	Not used	Not used	Not used	Not used	Not used	Not used	Not used	Not used	Not used	Not used	Not used	Not used
76	5177	Not used	Not used	Not used	Not used	Not used	Not used	Not used	Not used	Not used	Not used	Not used	Not used
76	5178	Not used	Not used	Not used	Not used	Not used	Not used	Not used	Not used	Not used	Not used	Not used	Not used
76	5179	Not used	Not used	Not used	Not used	Not used	Not used	Not used	Not used	Not used	Not used	Not used	Not used
77	5180	Not used	Not used	Not used	Not used	Not used	Not used	Not used	Not used	Not used	Not used	Not used	Not used
77	5181	Not used	Not used	Not used	Not used	Not used	Not used	Not used	Not used	Not used	Not used	Not used	Not used
77	5182	Not used	Not used	Not used	Not used	Not used	Not used	Not used	Not used	Not used	Not used	Not used	Not used
77	5183	Not used	Not used	Not used	Not used	Not used	Not used	Not used	Not used	Not used	Not used	Not used	Not used
77	5184	Not used	Not used	Not used	Not used	Not used	Not used	Not used	Not used	Not used	Not used	Not used	Not used

Page References	Chassis	Original Engine Number	UK Registration	Type	LHD?	Body Style	Original Colour	Original Interior	Original Hood	Original Delivery	Allocation	First Customer	Remarks

CHASSIS NUMBER PAGE REFERENCE KEY: Allocation Books (pages 1-77), Record Cards (pages 78-167), Warranty Book (pages 168-201), Service Records (pages 202-393)

Page References	Chassis	Original Engine Number	UK Registration	Type	LHD?	Body Style	Original Colour	Original Interior	Original Hood	Original Delivery	Allocation	First Customer	Remarks
77	5185	Not used	Not used	Not used	Not used	Not used	Not used	Not used	Not used	Not used	Not used	Not used	Not used
77	5186	Not used	Not used	Not used	Not used	Not used	Not used	Not used	Not used	Not used	Not used	Not used	Not used
77	5187	Not used	Not used	Not used	Not used	Not used	Not used	Not used	Not used	Not used	Not used	Not used	Not used
77	5188	Not used	Not used	Not used	Not used	Not used	Not used	Not used	Not used	Not used	Not used	Not used	Not used
77	5189	Not used	Not used	Not used	Not used	Not used	Not used	Not used	Not used	Not used	Not used	Not used	Not used
77	5190	Not used	Not used	Not used	Not used	Not used	Not used	Not used	Not used	Not used	Not used	Not used	Not used
77	5191	Not used	Not used	Not used	Not used	Not used	Not used	Not used	Not used	Not used	Not used	Not used	Not used
77	5192	Not used	Not used	Not used	Not used	Not used	Not used	Not used	Not used	Not used	Not used	Not used	Not used
77	5193	Not used	Not used	Not used	Not used	Not used	Not used	Not used	Not used	Not used	Not used	Not used	Not used
77	5194	Not used	Not used	Not used	Not used	Not used	Not used	Not used	Not used	Not used	Not used	Not used	Not used
77	5195	Not used	Not used	Not used	Not used	Not used	Not used	Not used	Not used	Not used	Not used	Not used	Not used
77	5196	Not used	Not used	Not used	Not used	Not used	Not used	Not used	Not used	Not used	Not used	Not used	Not used
77	5197	Not used	Not used	Not used	Not used	Not used	Not used	Not used	Not used	Not used	Not used	Not used	Not used
77	5198	Not used	Not used	Not used	Not used	Not used	Not used	Not used	Not used	Not used	Not used	Not used	Not used
77	5199	Not used	Not used	Not used	Not used	Not used	Not used	Not used	Not used	Not used	Not used	Not used	Not used
77, 485, 702	5200	EOTTA 96671	NYF 595	21 C		Saloon	Maroon or Silver			17/7/53	R. A. C. Parnels		
77, 485, 702	5201	EOTTA 96670	NXY 451	21 C		Saloon	Maroon			7/10/53	R. A. C. Parnels		
77	5202	Not used	Not used	Not used	Not used	Not used	Not used	Not used	Not used	Not used	Not used	Not used	Not used
77	5203	Not used	Not used	Not used	Not used	Not used	Not used	Not used	Not used	Not used	Not used	Not used	Not used
77	5204	Not used	Not used	Not used	Not used	Not used	Not used	Not used	Not used	Not used	Not used	Not used	Not used
77	5205	Not used	Not used	Not used	Not used	Not used	Not used	Not used	Not used	Not used	Not used	Not used	Not used
77	5206	Not used	Not used	Not used	Not used	Not used	Not used	Not used	Not used	Not used	Not used	Not used	Not used
77	5207	Not used	Not used	Not used	Not used	Not used	Not used	Not used	Not used	Not used	Not used	Not used	Not used

Page References	Chassis	Original Engine Number	UK Registration	Type	LHD?	Body Style	Original Colour	Original Interior	Original Hood	Original Delivery	Allocation	First Customer	Remarks

CHASSIS NUMBER PAGE REFERENCE KEY: Allocation Books (pages 1-77), Record Cards (pages 78-167), Warranty Book (pages 168-201), Service Records (pages 202-393)

Page References	Chassis	Original Engine Number	UK Registration	Type	LHD?	Body Style	Original Colour	Original Interior	Original Hood	Original Delivery	Allocation	First Customer	Remarks
77	5208	Not used	Not used	Not used	Not used	Not used	Not used	Not used	Not used	Not used	Not used	Not used	Not used
77	5209	Not used	Not used	Not used	Not used	Not used	Not used	Not used	Not used	Not used	Not used	Not used	Not used
77	5210	Not used	Not used	Not used	Not used	Not used	Not used	Not used	Not used	Not used	Not used	Not used	Not used
77	5211	Not used	Not used	Not used	Not used	Not used	Not used	Not used	Not used	Not used	Not used	Not used	Not used
77	5212	Not used	Not used	Not used	Not used	Not used	Not used	Not used	Not used	Not used	Not used	Not used	Not used
	3408	556071969	Not registered	JR	LHD	2-Seater	Berkeley Green	Black	None	14/11/21	Allard Sports Cars	Switzerland	8th JR model constructed by Allard family 64 years after last JR
702, 810	7000	Zephyr	545 EXR	72/PB 2	RHD	2-Seater	Red	Maroon and Red	Tan	5/9/05	Demonstrator (Allard Motor Co.)	Not noted	PB 1 chassis refer 5158, 1956 Motor Show car No Allard Motor Co. factory record for this car
702	7101	Jaguar	TYU 414	72/PB 2	RHD	2-Seater	Red	Not noted	Not noted	5/9/05	Demonstrator (Allard Motor Co.)	Not noted	Displayed as chassis at 1956 Motor Show, bodied later No Allard Motor Co. factory record for this car
514, 702	7102	Jaguar	UXB 793	72/PB GT	RHD	2+2-Seater	Red	Red		5/10/05	S. H. Allard	S. H. Allard	Built for S. H. Allard, exhibited at 1957 Motor Show No Allard Motor Co. factory record for this car
702	7103	Jaguar	Not noted	72/PB 2		2-Seater	Blue	Not noted	Not noted	8/1/58	Demonstrator (Allard Motor Co.)	U.S.A.	Exhibited at 1957 Motor Show No Allard Motor Co. factory record for this car
702	7104	Zephyr	Not noted	72/PB 2		2-Seater	Not noted	Not noted	Not noted	Not noted	U.S.A.	Not noted	No Allard Motor Co. factory record for this car
514, 702	7105	Chrysler	Not noted	72/PB GT		2+2-Seater	Red	Red		5/11/05	U.S.A.	Du Pont	Chrysler 6426cc high tune engine No Allard Motor Co. factory record for this car
702	7106	Jaguar	174 BLP	72/PB 2	RHD	2-Seater	Black	Red	Not noted	Not noted	Not noted	Not noted	No Allard Motor Co. factory record for this car
702	7107	Jaguar	Not noted	72/PB 2	LHD	2-Seater	White	Red	Red	5/12/05	U.S.A.	Not noted	Disc brake conversion to front No Allard Motor Co. factory record for this car

· APPENDIX 3 ·

REGISTRATION NUMBER INDEX

Note that in some page references, the page number has an entry for the chassis number related to the registration number, and that the registration number may not directly appear on the page.

ALLARD FUTURE DISCOVERIES

It would be impossible to identify all the cars that might exist which nobody, beyond the owner, knows about, or abandoned cars yet to be discovered, therefore the following page is offered to make entries.

Perhaps the reader would also be gracious enough to inform me of their existence via the Allard Owners Club.

·ALLARD·

Date	Model	Chassis Number	Registration Number	Remarks

Allard Future Discoveries

The Allard Grace is a recent tradition created by Captain David Wixon, a notable AOC member and ex-Royal Navy submariner who served on the first British-made nuclear submarine, *HMS Valiant*. During his career, he was partial to writing the occasional grace for the Padre at the Royal Navy college in Plymouth, and it was with this background and his inspiring vocal tone that invoked AOC's Jim Tiller to ask him to speak at a few AOC dinners. The idea of a grace for the start of proceedings took root.

The former nuclear submarine engineer wrote what is on the adjoining page, perhaps reminding us that, for some, it is from God that existence and indeed special abilities, are derived. So in the late 1990s, with the AOC dinner aboard *HMS Belfast* in London, Captain Wixon delivered the grace for the first time with the starting line taken from a new hymn he remembered, giving myself and others present an evening never to be forgotten.

TOP: Sydney and Eleanor Allard stand at the start of the 1954 Allard Owners Club annual dinner and dance in London. Fourth person to Sydney's right is the guest speaker Raymond Baxter. What might he chose to speak about, you wonder? A WWII Spitfire fighter ace, leading BBC TV broadcaster, competitor in twelve Monte Carlo rallies where he met Sydney, he would have likely talked about all of these. INSET: Sydney stands to speak in response to the speaker (year thought to be 1952) as was and is the tradition of the Allard Owners Club.

The Allard Grace